T0211855

Lecture Notes in Computer Science 12784

More information about this subseries at http://www.springer.com/series/7409

Panayiotis Zaphiris · Andri Ioannou (Eds.)

Learning and Collaboration Technologies

New Challenges and Learning Experiences

8th International Conference, LCT 2021
Held as Part of the 23rd HCI International Conference, HCII 2021
Virtual Event, July 24–29, 2021
Proceedings, Part I

 Springer

Editors
Panayiotis Zaphiris ⓘ
Department of Multimedia and Graphic Arts
Cyprus University of Technology
Lemesos, Cyprus

Andri Ioannou ⓘ
Research Center on Interactive Media,
Smart Systems and Emerging
Technologies (CYENS)
Cyprus University of Technology
Limassol, Cyprus

ISSN 0302-9743   ISSN 1611-3349   (electronic)
Lecture Notes in Computer Science
ISBN 978-3-030-77888-0   ISBN 978-3-030-77889-7   (eBook)
https://doi.org/10.1007/978-3-030-77889-7

LNCS Sublibrary: SL3 – Information Systems and Applications, incl. Internet/Web, and HCI

This Springer imprint is published by the registered company Springer Nature Switzerland AG
The registered company address is: Gewerbestrasse 11, 6330 Cham, Switzerland

Foreword

Human-Computer Interaction (HCI) is acquiring an ever-increasing scientific and industrial importance, and having more impact on people's everyday life, as an ever-growing number of human activities are progressively moving from the physical to the digital world. This process, which has been ongoing for some time now, has been dramatically accelerated by the COVID-19 pandemic. The HCI International (HCII) conference series, held yearly, aims to respond to the compelling need to advance the exchange of knowledge and research and development efforts on the human aspects of design and use of computing systems.

The 23rd International Conference on Human-Computer Interaction, HCI International 2021 (HCII 2021), was planned to be held at the Washington Hilton Hotel, Washington DC, USA, during July 24–29, 2021. Due to the COVID-19 pandemic and with everyone's health and safety in mind, HCII 2021 was organized and run as a virtual conference. It incorporated the 21 thematic areas and affiliated conferences listed on the following page.

A total of 5222 individuals from academia, research institutes, industry, and governmental agencies from 81 countries submitted contributions, and 1276 papers and 241 posters were included in the proceedings to appear just before the start of the conference. The contributions thoroughly cover the entire field of HCI, addressing major advances in knowledge and effective use of computers in a variety of application areas. These papers provide academics, researchers, engineers, scientists, practitioners, and students with state-of-the-art information on the most recent advances in HCI. The volumes constituting the set of proceedings to appear before the start of the conference are listed in the following pages.

The HCI International (HCII) conference also offers the option of 'Late Breaking Work' which applies both for papers and posters, and the corresponding volume(s) of the proceedings will appear after the conference. Full papers will be included in the 'HCII 2021 - Late Breaking Papers' volumes of the proceedings to be published in the Springer LNCS series, while 'Poster Extended Abstracts' will be included as short research papers in the 'HCII 2021 - Late Breaking Posters' volumes to be published in the Springer CCIS series.

The present volume contains papers submitted and presented in the context of the 8th International Conference on Learning and Collaboration Technologies (LCT 2021), an affiliated conference to HCII 2021. I would like to thank the Co-chairs, Panayiotis Zaphiris and Andri Ioannou, for their invaluable contribution to its organization and the preparation of the proceedings, as well as the members of the Program Board for their contributions and support. This year, the LCT affiliated conference has focused on topics related to the design and development of learning technologies, the use of technologies such as games and gamification, chatbots, AR, VR, and robots in learning, and learning, teaching and collaboration experiences, with particular focus on the issue of online versus in class learning brought about by the pandemic.

I would also like to thank the Program Board Chairs and the members of the Program Boards of all thematic areas and affiliated conferences for their contribution towards the highest scientific quality and overall success of the HCI International 2021 conference.

This conference would not have been possible without the continuous and unwavering support and advice of Gavriel Salvendy, founder, General Chair Emeritus, and Scientific Advisor. For his outstanding efforts, I would like to express my appreciation to Abbas Moallem, Communications Chair and Editor of HCI International News.

July 2021   Constantine Stephanidis

HCI International 2021 Thematic Areas and Affiliated Conferences

Thematic Areas

- HCI: Human-Computer Interaction
- HIMI: Human Interface and the Management of Information

Affiliated Conferences

- EPCE: 18th International Conference on Engineering Psychology and Cognitive Ergonomics
- UAHCI: 15th International Conference on Universal Access in Human-Computer Interaction
- VAMR: 13th International Conference on Virtual, Augmented and Mixed Reality
- CCD: 13th International Conference on Cross-Cultural Design
- SCSM: 13th International Conference on Social Computing and Social Media
- AC: 15th International Conference on Augmented Cognition
- DHM: 12th International Conference on Digital Human Modeling and Applications in Health, Safety, Ergonomics and Risk Management
- DUXU: 10th International Conference on Design, User Experience, and Usability
- DAPI: 9th International Conference on Distributed, Ambient and Pervasive Interactions
- HCIBGO: 8th International Conference on HCI in Business, Government and Organizations
- LCT: 8th International Conference on Learning and Collaboration Technologies
- ITAP: 7th International Conference on Human Aspects of IT for the Aged Population
- HCI-CPT: 3rd International Conference on HCI for Cybersecurity, Privacy and Trust
- HCI-Games: 3rd International Conference on HCI in Games
- MobiTAS: 3rd International Conference on HCI in Mobility, Transport and Automotive Systems
- AIS: 3rd International Conference on Adaptive Instructional Systems
- C&C: 9th International Conference on Culture and Computing
- MOBILE: 2nd International Conference on Design, Operation and Evaluation of Mobile Communications
- AI-HCI: 2nd International Conference on Artificial Intelligence in HCI

List of Conference Proceedings Volumes Appearing Before the Conference

1. LNCS 12762, Human-Computer Interaction: Theory, Methods and Tools (Part I), edited by Masaaki Kurosu
2. LNCS 12763, Human-Computer Interaction: Interaction Techniques and Novel Applications (Part II), edited by Masaaki Kurosu
3. LNCS 12764, Human-Computer Interaction: Design and User Experience Case Studies (Part III), edited by Masaaki Kurosu
4. LNCS 12765, Human Interface and the Management of Information: Information Presentation and Visualization (Part I), edited by Sakae Yamamoto and Hirohiko Mori
5. LNCS 12766, Human Interface and the Management of Information: Information-rich and Intelligent Environments (Part II), edited by Sakae Yamamoto and Hirohiko Mori
6. LNAI 12767, Engineering Psychology and Cognitive Ergonomics, edited by Don Harris and Wen-Chin Li
7. LNCS 12768, Universal Access in Human-Computer Interaction: Design Methods and User Experience (Part I), edited by Margherita Antona and Constantine Stephanidis
8. LNCS 12769, Universal Access in Human-Computer Interaction: Access to Media, Learning and Assistive Environments (Part II), edited by Margherita Antona and Constantine Stephanidis
9. LNCS 12770, Virtual, Augmented and Mixed Reality, edited by Jessie Y. C. Chen and Gino Fragomeni
10. LNCS 12771, Cross-Cultural Design: Experience and Product Design Across Cultures (Part I), edited by P. L. Patrick Rau
11. LNCS 12772, Cross-Cultural Design: Applications in Arts, Learning, Well-being, and Social Development (Part II), edited by P. L. Patrick Rau
12. LNCS 12773, Cross-Cultural Design: Applications in Cultural Heritage, Tourism, Autonomous Vehicles, and Intelligent Agents (Part III), edited by P. L. Patrick Rau
13. LNCS 12774, Social Computing and Social Media: Experience Design and Social Network Analysis (Part I), edited by Gabriele Meiselwitz
14. LNCS 12775, Social Computing and Social Media: Applications in Marketing, Learning, and Health (Part II), edited by Gabriele Meiselwitz
15. LNAI 12776, Augmented Cognition, edited by Dylan D. Schmorrow and Cali M. Fidopiastis
16. LNCS 12777, Digital Human Modeling and Applications in Health, Safety, Ergonomics and Risk Management: Human Body, Motion and Behavior (Part I), edited by Vincent G. Duffy
17. LNCS 12778, Digital Human Modeling and Applications in Health, Safety, Ergonomics and Risk Management: AI, Product and Service (Part II), edited by Vincent G. Duffy

38. CCIS 1420, HCI International 2021 Posters - Part II, edited by Constantine Stephanidis, Margherita Antona, and Stavroula Ntoa
39. CCIS 1421, HCI International 2021 Posters - Part III, edited by Constantine Stephanidis, Margherita Antona, and Stavroula Ntoa

http://2021.hci.international/proceedings

8th International Conference on Learning and Collaboration Technologies (LCT 2021)

Program Board Chairs: **Panayiotis Zaphiris,** *Cyprus University of Technology, Cyprus,* **and Andri Ioannou,** *Cyprus University of Technology and CYENS, Cyprus*

- Ruthi Aladjem, Israel
- Kaushal Kumar Bhagat, India
- Fisnik Dalipi, Sweden
- Camille Dickson-Deane, Australia
- David Fonseca, Spain
- Francisco J. García-Peñalvo, Spain
- Yiannis Georgiou, Cyprus
- Tomaž Klobučar, Slovenia
- Birgy Lorenz, Estonia
- Alejandra Martínez-Monés, Spain
- Nicholas H. Müller, Germany
- Antigoni Parmaxi, Cyprus

The full list with the Program Board Chairs and the members of the Program Boards of all thematic areas and affiliated conferences is available online at:

http://www.hci.international/board-members-2021.php

HCI International 2022

The 24th International Conference on Human-Computer Interaction, HCI International 2022, will be held jointly with the affiliated conferences at the Gothia Towers Hotel and Swedish Exhibition & Congress Centre, Gothenburg, Sweden, June 26 – July 1, 2022. It will cover a broad spectrum of themes related to Human-Computer Interaction, including theoretical issues, methods, tools, processes, and case studies in HCI design, as well as novel interaction techniques, interfaces, and applications. The proceedings will be published by Springer. More information will be available on the conference website: http://2022.hci.international/:

General Chair
Prof. Constantine Stephanidis
University of Crete and ICS-FORTH
Heraklion, Crete, Greece
Email: general_chair@hcii2022.org

http://2022.hci.international/

Contents – Part I

Learning, Teaching and Collaboration Experiences

On-line vs. in Class Learning in Pandemic Times

Contents – Part II

xxii Contents – Part II

Chatbots in Learning

University Student Surveys Using Chatbots: Artificial Intelligence
Conversational Agents. 155
   Noorhan Abbas, Thomas Pickard, Eric Atwell, and Aisha Walker

An Overview of the Use of Chatbots in Medical
and Healthcare Education. 170
   Fotos Frangoudes, Marios Hadjiaros, Eirini C. Schiza,
   Maria Matsangidou, Olia Tsivitanidou, and Kleanthis Neokleous

Studying How to Apply Chatbots Technology in Higher-Education:
First Results and Future Strategies. 185
   Antonio M. Mora, Alberto Guillén, Francisco Barranco,
   Pedro A. Castillo, and Juan J. Merelo

'Are You OK?' Students' Trust in a Chatbot Providing
Support Opportunities 199
   Joonas A. Pesonen

Usability and User Experience of a Chat Application with Integrated
Educational Chatbot Functionalities. 216
   Dijana Plantak Vukovac, Ana Horvat, and Antonela Čižmešija

Envisioned Pedagogical Uses of Chatbots in Higher Education
and Perceived Benefits and Challenges 230
   Olia Tsivitanidou and Andri Ioannou

AR, VR and Robots in Learning

Towards a New Chemistry Learning Platform with Virtual Reality
and Haptics 253
   Doga Demirel, Abdelwahab Hamam, Caitlin Scott, Bayazit Karaman,
   Onur Toker, and Lyan Pena

Effect of Height in Telepresence Robots on the Users' Spatial Awareness . . . 268
   Oliver Gawron, Lisa Keller, Karsten Huffstadt, and Nicholas H. Müller

Driving Success: Virtual Team Building Through Telepresence Robots 278
   Lisa Keller, Oliver Gawron, Tamin Rahi, Philipp Ulsamer,
   and Nicholas H. Müller

Design of Children's Entertainment and Education Products Based
on AR Technology 292
   Yi Lu, Tao Huang, Jian Liu, and Jiangtao Gong

Designing and Developing Learning Technologies

A Blockchain-Based Collaboration Framework for Teaching Material Creation

Huichen Chou[1]($\boxtimes$) (ID), Donghui Lin[1] (ID), Takao Nakaguchi[2] (ID),
and Toru Ishida[3] (ID)

[1] Department of Social Informatics, Kyoto University, Kyoto 606-8501, Japan
chou.huichen.33e@st.kyoto-u.ac.jp
[2] The Kyoto College of Graduate Studies for Informatics, Kyoto, Japan
[3] School of Creative Science and Engineering, Waseda University,
Tokyo 169-8555, Japan

Abstract. Making use of existing resources to create teaching material can save effort and yield better quality. Although there are some resources that can be used freely for educational purposes, most come with significant IP protections. A technology is needed that can allow the usage of copyright restricted resources for collaboration in teaching material generation. We propose a system that provides a full record of multiple authorships and contribution shares when resources are used and such a record supports royalty sharing; its system framework is detailed in this paper. We also exploit the advantage of blockchain technology to bind participants when sharing resources and acknowledge other teachers when their teaching materials are used. In addition, the blockchain-based record can provide distributed management with security, transparency and immutability. Thus, teachers who create teaching materials have sufficient evidence to claim authorship. The smart contract on blockchain has two core functions: registering original material to allow sharing as well as recording multiple authorships of the materials used with contribution distribution. With blockchain as its core, it can be extended with addon functions, such as access management, external file storage and external version control system to support complicate editing activities. We use Remix-Ethereum IDE to implement a prototype. Our contributions are two-fold. First, we propose a blockchain-based framework to support the use of copyrighted resources when creating teaching materials. Second, we demonstrate its feasibility in a prototype implementation.

Keywords: Blockchain · Open collaboration · Educational resources

1 Introduction

Teaching materials are essential for education. They are used to transfer knowledge to students. Collaboration has a long history in education. In creating teaching materials (TMs), collaboration can reduce the effort need to create higher quality content [11]. One strand in collaboration is to make use of existing resources, TMs of other teachers, when creating one's own TM [10]. While many resources can be used freely based on copyright exemption for educational purpose or as open resources under collaborative commons license [1]. Many others are not. Authors who do not donate their works and

P. Zaphiris and A. Ioannou (Eds.): HCII 2021, LNCS 12784, pp. 3–14, 2021.
https://doi.org/10.1007/978-3-030-77889-7_1

want royalty sharing cannot collaborate. Wikipedia [20] is important as a dominant form of open collaboration but it is a platform for collaboration to reach a single goal and the royalty cannot be distributed among the contributors. Massive Open Online Courses (MOOCs) are free online courses that offer free enrollment to anyone [21], but they establish sharing with students not teachers.

Therefore, we propose a system that provides forensic records of multiple authorship and contribution share for the collaboration that makes use of other peoples' materials in creating TM. It allows the use of existing TMs with clear acknowledgement of the authors and the rates of contribution.

Blockchain has been suggested as a smart contract system among participants; it provides a public ledger with secured, transparent, immutable and distributed records without centralized control [2, 4, 14, 17]. It is suitable to provide a record of collaboration by facilitating the establishment of a smart contract among teachers when sharing material. However, existing blockchain-based academic publication systems mainly consider the collaboration of multiple authors in writing a single work [6, 8, 9, 16] and so do not support the usage of other people's material as in creating TM.

In the paper, we propose a blockchain-based framework with focus on the veracity of record keeping. The on-chain smart contract records the collaboration when teachers share their TMs to others as well as making use of them. The smart contract generates authorship transactions and contribution shares of the TM created from the collaboration and stores the data using a blockchain. We design two functions so that the smart contract can govern the interaction between participants. They are *createMaterial*, which gives each original TM a unique identity and a hash to represent its authorship in the system; *deriveMaterial* method which records transactions as the use of others' TMs in the new TM. The TM thus has a unique identity, a hash and array list contain identity information of TMs that exist in the new TM. In addition, the data of each material's contribution is derived by the *getProportion* function, which calculates the contribution share of each material incorporated in a new TM and the function is called when *deriveMaterial* runs.

With the core functions to store authorship and contribution distribution information on blockchain, the system can be easily extended with addon off-chain functions to facilitate its usage. For example, the TM file itself is proposed to be stored in the InterPlanetary File System (IPFS) [12, 18] to keep the data stored in the central system to a minimum with hashes being used to identify and locate files. Other functions can be added such as notifying an author when his/her TM is used, manage access to control the distribution of TM, calculate how many times a material is used etc. If the new TM is for sale, the payments can be shared between the authors according to their contribution record in the system.

Our research contributes to provide an alternative solution that solves the issue raised by using copyright-restricted resources. By having records of multiple authorships and contribution shares, the proposed system can simplify the usage of copyright restricted resources by giving full evidence for royalty sharing. The record can provide data for sharing the economic or other benefits of the TM created with other teachers' contributions. We also provide a system framework with blockchain technology to provide security, transparency and immutability with distributed management and demonstrate how multiple authorships and contribution distributions are recorded in the system.

The remainder of the paper is organized as follows. The following section reports related works on using blockchain technology to support collaboration in the academic context. The proposed framework of our blockchain-based system is introduced in the third section. In the fourth section, we detail our prototype implementation. Finally, the key contributions and implications are discussed in the fifth section. Conclusion and discussion of the study are raised in the sixth section.

2 Related Work

Education institutes and practitioners have a long history of collaboration. For collaboration in the creation of TMs, focus is traditionally placed on co-authorship and Open Educational Resources (OER) [1]. In this work, we aim to provide an alternative system to support collaboration beyond OER and exploit the advantages of blockchain technology. The following section explains blockchain technology and related work on applying blockchain technology to support collaboration in academic publications.

2.1 Blockchain Technology

Blockchain technology supports the distributed ledger and has attracted much attention and triggered multiple projects in different industries. In general, a blockchain consists of data sets that are packaged as a chain of data blocks. A block comprises multiple transactions. The blockchain is linked with another block to create a ledger of transaction history. To create the link, each block contains a timestamp and the hash value of the previous block. Transaction validity is based on network consensus achieved through cryptographic technology [14].

The blockchain system was first introduced as cryptocurrency – Bitcoin [2]. It uses linked block structure to store transaction history record of token changing hands and thus provide proof of the existence of the "money". It is a "permissionless" blockchain system which means anyone can join the network to do transactions or participate in verification of a transaction through network consensus. The usage of blockchain technology was extended with the "smart contract" concept. "Smart contract" is triggered by events or participant enquiries entered using a predefined computer protocol. Ethereum [15] is the most widely known system. It uses smart contact functionality to build decentralized applications that establish trust among participants. The blockchain can be "permissioned" which means the participants need to be approved before joining the network. Ethereum supports a broader scope of applications and it also introduces "Gas" to disrupt contact in a cost-effective manner if the run time of the smart contract exceeds preset "Gas" limits. After Ethereum, other blockchain systems were launched to support wider applications of this technology.

After considering the collaboration needed to create TMs by recording multiple authorships, we proposed the use of blockchain technology. Blockchain supports the sharing of a ledger of transactions among participants. It can provide highly secured, transparent, and immutable data records with decentralized management. Blockchain also supports teachers who will allow their materials to be used under the smart contract concept. Network consensus us used to ensure all blockchains in the network are legitimate and that all the copies in the network are the same.

2.2 Blockchain-Based Collaboration System for Academic Publication

There continues to be a lot of research effort on using blockchain systems in the context of education. As for supporting academic collaboration, research has focused on the collaboration for creating individual scientific papers or academic publications [6–8, 12, 16].

ScienceRoot [16] proposed a blockchain-enabled scientific ecosystem in 2017. It focuses on the research process and provide a science research marketplace with tokenization. Its "Science Token" supports grant funding, publishing and scientific collaboration. Orvium[8] was introduced in 2018; it is open source and acts as a decentralized platform to support blockchain-based collaboration for science publications. The system supports researchers and institutions in sharing their research with open access journals. The system provides a public and transparent trace of all activities on a research paper from first submission, revisions, peer reviews, copyright and user license changes. Paper files are stored in digital object identifier (doi) system with proof stamp to create a hash of the work.

Eureka [6] is a blockchain-based incentive publication model. It enables authors, referenced/linked authors, editors, data providers and reviewers to share the economic rewards (if any) via the digital token called 'EKA". Pozi et al. also considered collaboration in writing scientific publications. It proposed to use a blockchain system to preserve that editing history on a block together with calculated contribution rates. It uses the NEM smart asset platform to test its system design where each block can store up to 1024 characters [9].

Yet these works explored the collaboration conducted in creating one single output with blockchain technology. They ignore the collaboration involved in sharing ones work to allow others to use it. In creating TMs, making use of existing resources, other teacher's TM, is important and TMs can exist in different teachers' materials. In addition, TMs are likely to be updated from time to time, so authorship is dynamic. Previous works focused on use blockchain technology to record the collaboration of one academic paper and so cannot satisfy the needs inherent in TM collaboration.

3 Framework

3.1 Collaboration Model of Creating TM

When creating TM, the collaboration is largely making use of other's material in creating own TM [1, 10, 11]. We consider the main activities in collaboration are using other teacher's material and add it to one's own TM. We illustrate this simple collaboration mode of TM (TM) creation in Fig. 1.

There are four teachers in the figure. They are Teacher A, Teacher B, Teacher C, and Teacher D. We use colors to represent material from different teachers. Teacher A created TM_a and allows other teachers to use it. Teacher B used part of TM_a in his/her own TM, TM_b. So TM_b is a combination of TM_a (all or part) and Teacher Bs' material. The authorship of TM_b literately belongs to both Teacher A and Teacher B. Next, Teacher C uses TM_b in his/her TM, TM_c. So the authorship of TM_c belongs to Teacher A, Teacher B and Teacher C. Thus, we view TM creation as the collaboration of different teachers in that they share their materials. In addition, if a TM with multiple authorships is used to create a new material, the multiple authorship should be folded into the new material.

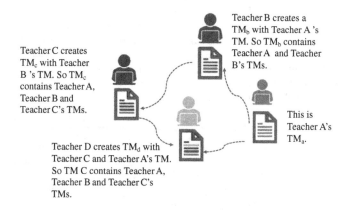

Teacher B creates a TM_b with Teacher A 's TM. So TM_b contains Teacher A and Teacher B's TMs.

Teacher C creates TM_c with Teacher B 's TM. So TM_c contains Teacher A, Teacher B and Teacher C's TMs.

Teacher D creates TM_d with Teacher C and Teacher A's TM. So TM C contains Teacher A, Teacher B and Teacher C's TMs.

This is Teacher A's TM_a.

Fig. 1. Example of collaboration in TM creation (TM)

3.2 System Framework

Based on the above collaboration model, we aim to design a blockchain system framework to support collaboration. For collaborative content creation, the collaboration system provides a platform allowing authors to co-write a document and record the version history that identifies authorship of different parts of a document [20]. The OER system, on the other hand, asks authors to donate their works to the platform and allows them to be used freely such as being used in new TMs or being redistributed to students. The OER platform acts as a library that stores educational resources but provides no records on how these resources are used.

The proposed system supports collaboration in the use of existing TMs and attributing authorship. That is to say, rather than recording the editing activities of different authors in the collaborative writing process, we record how different materials were used in creating a TM.

The features required for storing multiple authorships securely and transparently can be realized by blockchain. On the other hand, the features needed to compile various material files can be supported by existing word processing applications, such as MS word or GoogleDoc. After finish compiling or edit a TM, the information of authorship is extracted and turned into blockchain records.

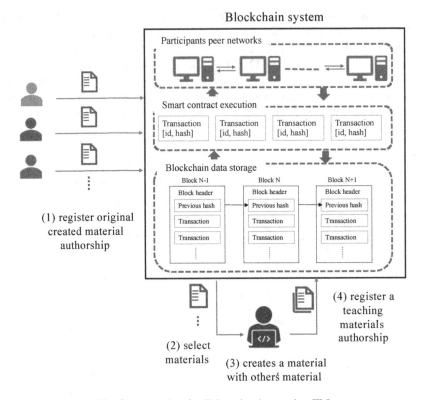

Fig. 2. Example of collaboration in creating TM

In Fig. 2, we outline the system framework, and a transaction example of creating a TM and the interaction with our proposed blockchain-based system. Blockchain consists of three elements, a P2P network whose nodes are the participants and a smart contract which governs the execution of transactions among the participants. The blockchain exists on a distributed database as stored transaction records.

The transaction example of creating TM starts with (1) Teachers register their original TM and authorship to the system to allow sharing. (2) Teacher selects materials that are going to be used in the new TM. These materials already registered in the blockchain system and the system also record which materials are selected. Next, (3) teacher compiles the TM using a word processing application. Upon completion, (4) the TM is registered with the blockchain. It extracts the authorship information of selected materials and creates a transaction that records the multiple authorship of the registered TM. When a TM is updated, it treats the process as creating a new TM and registers its multiple authorship with blockchain.

With blockchain as a core, many off-chain features can be added-on to provide all around support to TM usage. For example, the access management function can be supported by existing access control solutions, such as generating a crypto key to restricted blockchain access [13]. InterPlanetary File System (IPFS) has been suggested to support blockchain in handling large files [12, 18]. Access functions to control and count the number of accesses can also be added.

3.3 Blockchain Smart Contract

Blockchain uses smart contracts to govern the transactions among participants, in this paper's case, teachers. The contract is specified with functions. In order to create a record of multiple authorships and contribution shares in a collaboratively created material, the smart contact in the system must have records of authorships of each material involved as well as the authorships and contribution share information of a material which may contain other teachers' material. Thus the system must have two core functions: *createMaterial* and *deriveMaterial*. Details of these functions are listed in Table 2.

Table 2. Smart contract functions in the system

Function Name	Parameters	Return values	Description
createMaterial	name: string hash: string	ID of the created TM (number starting from 0)	Records the creation of material with blockchain. The creator is the account that executed this method
deriveMaterial	name: string hash: string ids: unit[] proportions: bytes[]	ID of the created TM (number starting from 0)	Records the created TMs that incorporate others materials with blockchain. The creator is the account that executed this method. The ids and proportions are an array of the IDs of the imported materials and an array of usage ratios. Percentage is a byte representation of a double-precision floating point number

createMaterial registers the authorship of a TM in the blockchain system. The creator is the account that executed this method. *deriveMaterial* records the authorship information of the materials involved in the TM. This function creates transactions to record the TM that incorporates the TMs of others with blockchain. The creator is the account that executed this method. The ids and proportions are stored in an array of the IDs of the imported materials and an array holding the usage ratios. Percentage is a byte representation of a double-precision floating point number. When *deriveMaterial* is invoked, the *getProportion* function is called to calculate the contribution share of materials present in the TM. It takes as input the contribution percentage of used material and calculates the remaining portion as the contribution from the teacher creating this new TM. This proportion share is then recorded.

4 Prototype Implementation

In this section, we give details of a prototype deployed on the Remix-Ethereum IDE platform [19]. We wrote the smart contract functions of the proposed system in Solidity language. We give scenarios that demonstrate our deployment and report the execution log results of the two functions and show the transactions stored in the blockchain.

In the new TM is created using another TM which already consists of multiple authorships, nesting calculation function can be added to derive the authorship. Calling the authorship and contribution share record of the used materials results in the calculation of authorship and contribution share of the new TM. The contribution share calculation also involves an additional function to account for file size, word counts, or pages etc. Currently we do not specify the contribution share evaluation method.

In scenario 1, a teacher registers an originally created TM which does not contain other people's works with the system. The system executes *createMaterial* method. The teacher with account{2} in the system registers her TM with name of "work3" and "work3hash" hash to the system. The system uses the smart contract (contract application binary interface) to execute the request and create a log record with timestamp as shown in Fig. 3.

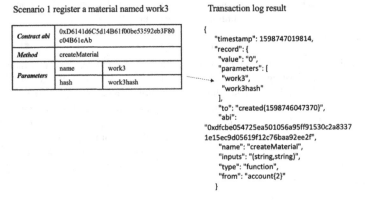

Fig. 3. Scenario1: Register an originally created TM with *createMaterial* function and transaction log result

Scenario 2 create teaching material named material1   Transaction log result

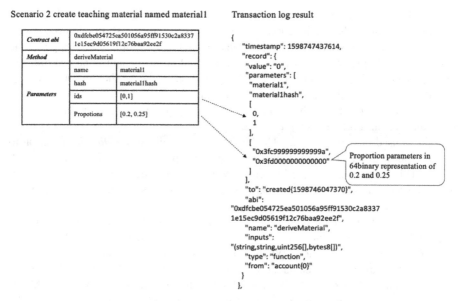

Contract abi	0xdfcbe054725ea501056a95ff91530c2a8337 1e15ec9d05619f12c76baa92ee2f	
Method	deriveMaterial	
Parameters	name	material1
	hash	material1hash
	ids	[0,1]
	Propotions	[0.2, 0.25]

```
{
    "timestamp": 1598747437614,
    "record": {
        "value": "0",
        "parameters": [
            "material1",
            "material1hash",
            [
                0,
                1
            ],
            [
                "0x3fc999999999999a",
                "0x3fd0000000000000"
            ]
        ],
        "to": "created{1598746047370}",
        "abi":
"0xdfcbe054725ea501056a95ff91530c2a8337
1e15ec9d05619f12c76baa92ee2f",
        "name": "deriveMaterial",
        "inputs":
"(string,string,uint256[],bytes8[])",
        "type": "function",
        "from": "account{0}"
    }
},
```

Proportion parameters in 64binary representation of 0.2 and 0.25

Fig. 4. Scenario 2: Register a collaboratively created TM with *deriveMaterial* function and transaction log result

In scenario2, we give an example of a teacher creating a TM that includes an existing TM. The multiple authorships and contribution shares of the material are recorded with the system. There is TM1 created by account{0} and TM2 created by account{1}. The teacher of account{2} used the TM of two previous teachers in creating "TM1". The contribution share of TM1 is 20% and contribution share of TM2 is 25%. So her own contribution share in "TM1" is 55%. In Fig. 4 we present the transaction details and log results. This execution creates a transaction in blockchain system and has the timestamp of "1598747437614" by calling the smart contract (contract hash is shown in abi) in the system. The transaction log shows that TM1 contains parts of two other TMs. They are work1 and work2.The list [0,1] represents the id of work1 and work2 which are used in the material1. The authorship proportions are represented in 64-bit binary format as ["0x3fc999999999999a", "0x3fd0000000000000"] for work1 and work2, respectively. Figure 4 shows the log result that *deriveMaterial* was successfully called and the correct transaction information is stored in the system.

5 Discussion

Currently, collaboration for using existing resources to create TM largely relies on the commonly agreed exemption for educational purpose. Yet not all useful resources have this exemption. So we proposed a system that provides authorship information and contribution share of the materials reused. For open collaboration activities, this system provides an alternative to the Creative Commons license that so will encourage knowledge sharing. Blockchain is suitable in this case because it provides an immutable public ledger to record the authorship for the teachers who share their materials. Yet blockchain can be expansive in terms of miner cost. In addition, due to its immutable nature, scalability should be taken into consideration when designing the system. Accordingly, we propose that the data stored in blockchain to be just the bare minimum with only authorship and contribution shares of the finished material and not the edit history created in compiling the material.

To allow TM to be used by various teachers, we propose to register each material with blockchain together with transactions that record authorship. When such a material is used or exists in other TM, the system uses the *deriveMaterial* function to create a transaction that records the multiple authorship and contribution shares of each author. This function is also used when a TM is updated. The *deriveMaterial* function treats an update as a new transaction as so records the authorship and distribution of the latest version.

With the core on-chain functionality design, off-chain functions can be added to call the data in the blockchain such as notifying the author when his/her TM is used, or implement royalty distribution. When a TM is distributed to students, an off-chain access control function can be added to let the teacher manage the distribution of his/her material as well as count the number of access to know how many times a TM has been distributed. In addition, there are many existing blockchain platforms that the proposed blockchain system can built on. Security and scalability in general are supported by the blockchain technology we used.

The goal of this research is to propose a system to facilitate collaboration in creating TM that allows royalty sharing. Our system's functionality can record the authorship and calculate contribution share when a teacher's TM reuses other teacher's material. In addition, our system can handle the hierarchical reuse of TMs as well as their updates. Our add on contribution share calculation function can truthfully record each teacher's contribution in a TM, and the information can be used for distributing royalties or other benefits.

6   Conclusion

Our work addresses the challenges of creating TM when making use of people's work protected by copyright. We consider a smart contract among teachers who are willing to share their materials and collaborate by the automatic recording of authorship when other teachers' materials are used. Therefore, we propose a system that supports multiple authorships and records contribution shares to encourage collaboration in creating TM. In addition, we exploit the benefits of blockchain technology to create a smart contract among teachers with a public ledger that offers secure authorship records without the need for centralized management. The authorship records held on blockchain can be combined with many existing solutions, such as cryptography to secure access control, large file storage and other off-chain functions to support the TM delivery process.

We designed two blockchain functions to register material and compile multiple authorships and determine contribution shares. They are *createMaterial* to add a material's authentication information to the blockchain and *deriveMaterial* which determines multiple authorships and the contribution share of each author. For the latter, *deriveMaterial* calls the *getProportions* function to calculate contribution shares. We used the Ethereum Remix platform to implement a smart contract prototype and tested the functionality of the two proposed functions. Transactions were executed successfully and verify the achievement of our research goal. To conclude, this work provides a system framework that supports collaboration beyond OER so that TM creation can be enhance with the use of copyright restricted resources. The proposed blockchain system supports royalty sharing in the open collaboration of TM by providing records of authorship and contribution shares of material. The blockchain records can be used to acknowledge ownership or as evidence for royalty sharing. Our prototype implementation on Ethereum IDE demonstrated the feasibility of put such records into a blockchain system.

Acknowledgment. This research was partially supported by a Grant-in-Aid for Scientific Research (A) (17H00759, 2017–2020), a Grant-in-Aid for Scientific Research (B) (18H03341, 2018–2020), and a Grant-in Aid for Challenging Research (Exploratory) (20K21833, 2020–2022) from the Japan Society for the Promotion of Science (JSPS).

References

1. Hylén, J.: Open educational resources: opportunities and challenges. In: Proceedings of open education 4963 (2006)
2. Nakamoto, S.: Bitcoin: a peer-to-peer electronic cash system. (2008)
3. Creative commons. https://creativecommons.org. Accessed 04 Apr 2020
4. Crosby, M., Pattanayak, P., Verma, S., Kalyanaraman, V.: Blockchain technology: beyond bitcoin. Appl. Innov. Rev. **2**(6–10), 71 (2016)
5. Ellervee, A., Matulevicius, R., Mayer, N.: A comprehensive reference model for blockchain-based distributed ledger technology. In ER Forum/Demos, pp. 306–319 (2017)
6. Niya, S.R., et al.: A blockchain-based scientific publishing platform. In: International Conference on Blockchain and Cryptocurrency. IEEE-ICBC, Seoul, pp. 329–336 (2019)
7. Novotny, P., et al.: Permissioned blockchain technologies for academic publishing. Inf. Serv. Use **38**(3), 159–171 (2018)
8. Orvium. http://orvium.io. Accessed 04 Apr 2020
9. Mohd Pozi, M.S., Muruti, G., Abu Bakar, A., Jatowt, A., Kawa, Y.: Preserving author editing history using blockchain technology. In: Proceedings of the 18th ACM/IEEE on Joint Conference on Digital Libraries, JCDL, Texas, pp. 165–168 (2018)
10. Hilton III, J., Wiley D.A.: The creation and use of open educational resources in Christian higher education. Christian Higher Educ. **9**(1), 49–59 (2009)
11. Putnik, Z., Budimac, Z., Ivanović, M.: A practical model for conversion of existing teaching resources into learning objects. MASAUM J. Comput. **12**, 205–214 (2009)
12. Nizamuddin, N., Hasan, H.R., Salah, K.: IPFS-blockchain-based authenticity of online publications. In: Chen, S., Wang, H., Zhang, L.-J. (eds.) ICBC 2018. LNCS, vol. 10974, pp. 199–212. Springer, Cham (2018). https://doi.org/10.1007/978-3-319-94478-4_14
13. Steichen, M., Fiz, B., Norvill, R., Shbair, W., State, R.: Blockchain-based, decentralized access control for IPFS. In 2018 IEEE International Conference on Internet of Things (iThings) and IEEE Green Computing and Communications (GreenCom) and IEEE Cyber, Physical and Social Computing (CPSCom) and IEEE Smart Data (SmartData) Halifax, pp. 1499–1506 (2018)

14. Belotti, M., Božić, N., Pujolle, G., Secci, S.: A vademecum on blockchain technologies: when, which, and how. IEEE Commun. Surv. Tutorials **21**(4), 3796–3838 (2019)
15. Wood, G.: Ethereum: a secure decentralised generalised transaction ledger. Ethereum project yellow paper 151 (2014)
16. Günther, V., Chirita, A.: Scienceroot. Whitepaper (2018)
17. Calvaresi, D., Dubovitskaya, A., Retaggi, D., Dragoni, A.F., Schumache, M.: Trusted registration, negotiation, and service evaluation in multi-agent systems throughout the blockchain technology. In: IEEE/WIC/ACM International Conference on Web Intelligence (WI), pp. 56–63 (2018)
18. Zheng, Q., Yi, L., Chen. P., Dong, X.: An innovative IPFS-based storage model for blockchain. In: IEEE/WIC/ACM International Conference on Web Intelligence (WI), pp. 704–708 (2018)
19. Ethereum Foundation: "Remix-IDE," Oct 2018. https://github.com/ethereum/remix-id
20. Wikipedia. https://en.wikipedia.or. Accessed Aug 2020
21. Massive Open Online Courses (MOOCs). https://www.mooc.org. Accessed Aug 2020

Using Interactive Technology for Learning and Collaboration to Improve Organizational Culture: A Conceptual Framework

Tone Lise Dahl[✉] , Lisa S. Græslie , and Sobah A. Petersen

Dep. Technology Management, SINTEF Digital, S.P. Andersens veg 5,
7034 Trondheim, Norway
{tone.lise.dahl,lisa.graslie,sobah.petersen}@sintef.no

Abstract. Learning and collaboration are of major importance for organizations to be able to change and improve continually. Interactive learning technologies offer new opportunities for organizations to facilitate sharing of experiences and organizational learning by engaging employees in collaborative and reflective processes. This paper was initiated through an ongoing research project—seeking models or frameworks that could be used to support and analyze these types of processes. We have reviewed the literature to explore how the use of interactive learning technologies can support learning in organizations to improve organizational culture by addressing dilemmas that employees might face in their work-life. Our work revealed that key concepts to achieve this are knowledge sharing, experiential learning, and learning at the individual, group, and organization levels. Furthermore, crowdsourcing is considered as a means of engaging and gathering the inputs and feedback from the employees using learning technologies. The main contribution of this paper is a conceptual framework that addresses a research gap in enhancing the support for reflection processes and organizational learning to improve organizational culture by applying the affordances of methods such as interactive learning technologies, planned group events, and crowdsourcing.

Keywords: Interactive technologies · Organizational culture · Organizational learning · Crowdsourcing

1 Introduction

A work-life characterized by a rapid pace of change due to globalization, new technology, and the movement from an industrial society to a knowledge society requires organizations to continually be adaptable, creative, and innovative. The importance of improving organizational culture to achieve organizational change is widely acknowledged [e.g., 1, 2], and there is also a significant proportion of literature which argues that organizational culture can be managed [3]. Particularly, sharing knowledge and organizational learning is important in order to utilize knowledge and information for changing and improving organizations continually [4, 5]. While there are many benefits of having a strong and clear organizational culture [3], organizations often strive in their quest to identify and use optimal methods for improving their culture.

P. Zaphiris and A. Ioannou (Eds.): HCII 2021, LNCS 12784, pp. 15–30, 2021.
https://doi.org/10.1007/978-3-030-77889-7_2

The significant increase in the development and use of interactive learning technologies may offer attractive opportunities for organizations to facilitate knowledge sharing and learning, which in turn may shape the attitudes, beliefs, and behaviors of workers. While there are several models, frameworks, and guidelines related to knowledge management [e.g., 3, 6], technology-enhanced learning [e.g., 7], and technology-mediated learning [e.g., 8], there is a lack of guidelines and frameworks that address the whole process of how technology-enhanced learning activities could be used to build organizational culture by supporting organizational learning where the use of learning technologies are combined with social group processes and culture practices. To our knowledge, the lack of models or frameworks that support the use of technology to support knowledge sharing, reflection and learning within groups and the whole organization is noticeable.

In this paper, we explore how learning technologies can contribute to support the improvement of an organization's culture through organizational learning by addressing dilemmas that employees might face. Specifically, we aim to answer the following research question: *How can the use of interactive learning technologies support learning in the organization to improve organizational culture?* The main contribution of this paper is a conceptual framework for guiding interactive and collaborative technology-enhanced learning processes in organizations by supporting knowledge sharing, reflection and learning. The framework also illustrates how learning technologies can support learning at the individual, group and organization levels, and across these levels, to enhance organizational learning [9], and emphasizes the processes and activities beyond single events or activities, such as timebound single workshops.

The rest of this paper is organized as follows: First, Sect. 2 describes the research and development project that provides the research context of this paper. Second, in Sect. 3 we provide a theoretical background on dilemmas and organizational culture building, organizational learning experiential learning, knowledge sharing and knowledge transfer, and crowdsourcing. Third, in Sect. 4 the conceptual framework for guiding organizational change activities is presented, followed by discussion and concluding remarks.

2   Research Context

Besides the synthesis of the literature for investigating how learning technologies can improve organizational culture, this study was initiated in and informed by a research context of a multidisciplinary Research and Development project, financed by the Norwegian Research Council. In this project, the use of an interactive learning technology facilitates to bring forth the dilemmas that employees face in their daily work, by facilitating exchange of experiences and learning within the organization. Employees' concerns are considered as dilemmas, which may be resolved in several alternative ways, and each individual or group may choose to resolve them in different ways. The aim is, thus, to use learning technologies to support sharing of experiences and reflective thinking among the employees. New technologies are combined with new principles for management and governance to create change readiness in organizations.

While the activities for designing the interactive learning technology is based on Design Science Method [10] and Participatory Design (PD) [11], the overall research approach for the project is Action Research. This approach involves communities of inquiry action that evolve and address questions and issues that are significant for those who participate as co-researchers [12]. Action Research is a participatory process concerned with developing practical knowing that seeks to bring together action and reflection, and theory and practice, in participation with others in the pursuit of practical solutions to issues of pressing concern to people, and more generally the flourishing of individual people and their communities. It is a research approach that primarily arises as people try to work together to address key problems in their communities or organizations [12].

This paper focuses on the development of a conceptual framework that addresses the challenge of supporting knowledge sharing and learning from individual and group levels to the organization to improve organizational culture. See Fig. 1. We have reviewed the literature to explore how such a process can be supported using technologies for learning and collaboration.

Fig. 1. Learning and collaboration process from timebound workshops to improved organizational culture.

3 Theoretical Background

3.1 Dilemmas and Organizational Culture Building

The culture of the organization affects how much individuals identify with their organization, and it is also regarded to be one of the main elements for promoting an innovative environment [13]. The essence of organizational culture is the "values, beliefs, and norms or behavioral practices that emerge in an organization" [14, p. 247], which affects how problems are defined by individuals in the organization and the strategies they use to solve them [15].

There is a significant proportion of literature that argues that there are many benefits from having a strong, clear organizational culture and that organizational culture can, and should, be managed [3]. However, this is often challenging. Larger organizations may consist of several co-existing and conflicting subcultures [14], creating divergent interpretations and influencing the nature of relationships within the organization [15]. Furthermore, the context of the recent Covid-19 crisis has challenged the conditions for performing and evaluating work—creating conflicting orientations about issues at stake —also known as *dilemmas*.

Dilemmas occur at the individual and group levels and offer the potential to reflect on issues at stake from different perspectives. Dilemmas manifest in decision-making when actors need to make a choice and the available options exclude one another and have consequences that make them equally desirable and undesirable [16]. Decision-making in organizations is pervaded with various dilemmas that employees face every day in their work lives. The explication of dilemmas is therefore crucial for experiential and organizational learning [16]. Critical outcomes of barriers related to organizational dilemmas may involve divergent visions carried by the employees and by the management and misinterpretation of employees' metaphors by management, leading to an organizational culture that is fragmented and unable to support the organizational strategy. Dilemmas particularly impede organizational effectiveness if employees are forced to act instead of being allowed to reflect on the issue and reconsider their actions, which are necessary for learning to take place and taking the best decision [16].

Building an organizational culture requires a reconciliation of opposites through increased reflection and understanding about the different values, norms, and behavioral practices that exist in the organization. Directing attention to the dilemmas that workers are facing will force workers to examine these aspects [16], and communicating about dilemmas is also argued to increase collaboration [17]. This enables organizations to discover inconsistencies between individual needs, aspirations and behaviors, and the organization's culture and strategies.

Collaboration tools for explicating dilemmas in organizations (i.e., multi-actor context) were, before the study of Castaño et al. [16] scarcely in the literature. The literature on collaboration tools emphasizes that collaboration in teams is improved through the cooperative use of objects [18]. According to Castaño et al. [16, p. 38], such tools need to "(1) support actors to voice their interpretations and (2) represent the interrelatedness of issues at stake", to increase engagement and collaboration among individuals.

Steiner [p. 193, 19] argues that organizational learning "concerns growing competence among individuals in communicating and solving dilemmas and problems successfully, both in the short and the long term". According to Castaño et al. [16], finding solutions that bridge competing demands that are the origin of dilemmas is encouraged by revealing and debating dilemmas. Creating awareness of dilemmas (i.e., looking at issues from different angles) is critical since individuals may feel paralyzed or locked-in if they do not know what to do in specific situations, which also can lead to avoiding or ignoring deliberation and exploitation of opposites [16, 20].

3.2 Organizational Learning

The aim of organizational learning is to utilize knowledge and information to change and improve continually [5]. The literature points to primarily three levels of organizational learning in every organization: the individual level, the group level, and the organizational level [9]. Individual-level learning involves employees creating, understanding, interpreting, and experimenting with new ideas and information [9]. Individual learning might involve an adjustment of behavior through conceptual and cognitive processes [9]. Group-level learning is considered important for organizational learning to occur [21]. A group-level perspective on organizational learning highlights interpersonal perceptions and behavior. The focus shifts towards interactions among a limited group of employees and how these interactions enhance or hinder the process of creating new knowledge and initiating new actions. At a group level, employees share their learning with others, make interpretations together and a group assumption is achieved [9]. However, for learning to occur on higher levels in organizations (i.e., achieving organizational learning), it is necessary to systematically embed individual- and group-level learning in organizational structures and processes [4]. Hence, organizational learning is a change process that seeks to enhance an organization´s capability to acquire and develop new knowledge [3].

3.3   Experiential Learning and Reflective Learning in the Workplace

The Experiential Learning Theory (ELT) has had a major influence on the design and conduct of educational programs in management training and development and in formal management education [22], e.g., experiential learning in teams [23] and reflective learning processes in the workplace [24]. Experiential learning is described as a process where knowledge is created through the transformation of experience and knowledge results from the combination of grasping, reflecting, and transforming experiences. Approaches such as Kolb's experiential learning theory [25], which describe the processes from a concrete experience, and through reflection to transformed action, can enrich the management of better human performance in organizations.

Learning technologies can enable users to recognize, engage with, and reflect on experiences, which can enhance the learning effect. Reflective learning is a mechanism to turn the experience into learning opportunities. It is viewed as "the conscious re-evaluation of experience for the purpose of guiding future behavior" [24, p. 2]. Reflective learning has been found to be critical for success at work and as a mechanism for self-directed learning, but it has been emphasized that there is little work regarding the connection of reflection on individual, group and organization levels [24]. Activities at the individual level are important when recognizing that individual changes occur within the context of facilitating organizational changes [26] while organizational learning aims to help organizations to use knowledge and information to change and improve continually [2].

Krogstie and colleagues propose a model for Computer Supported Reflective Learning (CSRL-model), which describes both individual and collaborative learning and learning that impacts larger parts of an organization [24]. The CSRL-model aims to inform the design and implementation of technology to support reflective learning at work [24]. The CSRL-model, influenced by ELT, contains four stages of reflection: Plan and do work (1), initiate reflection (2), conduct reflection session (3) and apply the outcome from the reflection session (4). An event or experience while doing work triggers the need for a reflection session, which is a planned activity. The outcome(s) of a reflection session is the change that could be applied during work, i.e., learning to perform better during work as a consequence of the reflection activity (Fig. 2).

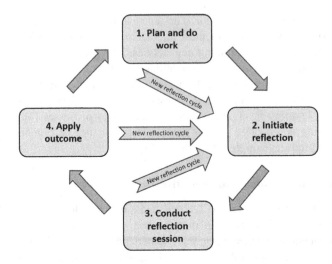

Fig. 2. The CSRL model adapted from Krogstie et al. 2013.

Reflection models are also influenced by the concept of Schön of a reflective practitioner [27], who reflects "in action", while performing a task as well as "on action" after performing the task, as addressed in the CSRL-model, amongst others. In addition, critical reflection [28] is considered important in transformative learning, decision making and changing behaviours and habits. Transformations in individuals, groups or organizations are often outcomes of a series of experiences that span beyond one event or often an individual. The reflection continuum model [29] considers reflection and learning as a continuous process, where an individual or a group of individuals, critically examine the current situation at hand and how they got there (looks back on the series of previous actions) and anticipates the consequences of potential actions before making a choice. The ability to reflect as such can be important in dealing with the dilemmas that arise in the workplace.

Most of these theories focus on individual reflection, although they can be applied to groups and the organization. Krogstie et al. [24] describes how the CSRL-model could be applied, where an individual's experience could be shared and reflected within a group, or indeed one group's experience could be shared and reflected among several groups.

3.4   Knowledge Sharing and Knowledge Transfer in Organizations

Knowledge sharing provides an important link between the individual employees and the rest of the organization and sharing experiences within and across groups is necessary to be able to support learning within an organization [30]. Knowledge transfer in organizations is referred to as "the process through which one unit (e.g., group, department, or division) is affected by the experience of another" [p. 151, 31]. Knowledge transfer thus reflects knowledge moving within or between organizations [e.g., 32, 33], and is argued to have happened when the recipient unit's knowledge or performance changes [31]. Hence, while sharing of knowledge entails the provision of knowledge by a source, it is also critical that a recipient acquires and applies the knowledge [30]. Notably, this should be regarded as a process of reconstruction [34], as knowledge is information interpreted and applied by the individual recipient [35].

When recognizing that knowledge exists at multiple levels within organizations, several factors that influence knowledge sharing in organizations can be identified. For instance, motivation to share, opportunities to share, and the culture of the work environment has been identified as major factors that influence knowledge sharing between individuals in organizations [36]. Sense of group identity and personal responsibility may help groups to shift towards a cooperative mode and help organizations to stimulate social dynamics that increase overall knowledge sharing [37]. Organizational culture and reward systems are two examples of organizational factors, and poor usability and information overload are examples of technological factors [38]. Liyanage et al. [35] emphasize four factors as prerequisites of a knowledge transfer process, including being able to identify where the knowledge resides, that individuals are willing to share their knowledge, that individuals are willing to acquire knowledge, and that the receiver is able to understand and use the knowledge [35].

Spreading and managing the knowledge of an organization's workforce can be achieved via a wide range of methods—either directly using ICT, or more indirectly through the management of social processes, the structuring of organizations, or via the use of culture and people management practices [3]. Technology-enhanced learning aims to design, develop, and test socio-technical innovations to support and enhance learning practices of both individuals and organizations [39]. However, combining computer-based knowledge sharing with experiential learning is argued to be a major dilemma because promoting the former implies less of the latter [40]. Even so, computer-based knowledge may have a mediating role by facilitating or impeding experiential knowledge, e.g., tasks can be solved, and knowledge can be spread efficiently by making use of the skills and knowledge of large groups of people by enabling crowdsourcing [41].

3.5 Crowdsourcing and Organizational Learning

Crowdsourcing has been analyzed as a contribution to organizational learning [41]. It presents a potential mode of learning that can be embraced by many or most organizations. However, how organizations can use crowdsourcing for learning is a one of the more unexplored questions in crowdsourcing [41]. Different terminologies have been used to describe what crowdsourcing is. Estellés-Arolas and González-Ladrón-de-Guevara [42] analyzed and synthesized 40 definitions extracted from 209 documents. As a result, they identified eight common characteristics to any given crowdsourcing initiative: a defined crowd, a delineated task, a clear recompense for the crowd, the identified crowdsourcer, defined benefits for the crowdsourcer, an online process, the open call, and internet usage. Thuan, Antunes, and Johnstone [43], define crowdsourcing as "an online strategy, in which an organization proposes defined task(s) to the members of the crowd via a flexible open call, in order to harness their work, knowledge, skills, and/or experience" [43, p. 42]. Three literature streams of crowdsourcing can be identified. The first stream is in computer science where the focus is on technically new implementations where non-technical aspects of crowdsourcing are often neglected. The second literature stream focuses on crowdsourcing participants' behavior, while the third and smaller stream is concerned with crowdsourcing on an organizational level of analysis [41].

Geiger, Rosemann, and Fielt [44] have classified the variety of crowdsourcing systems in four types of open systems that illustrates how crowdsourcing could support learning and collaboration in organizations: Crowd processing, crowd rating, crowd solving, and crowd creation. *Crowd processing systems* combine individual contributions to deliver a correct solution or result for a task. *With crowd rating systems* every contribution represents a specific vote where there is no right or wrong result. *Crowd solving systems* can enable people to get as close as possible to the best solution. With *crowd creations systems*, contributions are put in relation to each other instead of being evaluated isolated. Even though these systems provide one distinct service each, crowdsourcing projects are often built on systems that combine crowd services, and quantitative and qualitative components. The choice of the type of crowd system, depends on what the specific goals of a crowdsourcing project are [44].

Schlagwein and Bjorn-Andersen [41] consider organizational learning theory to be a suitable theoretical basis for understanding crowdsourcing as an organizational practice. Some of the early applications of crowdsourcing to engage learners to contribute and create their own learning material can be seen in the mobile apps Cloudbank [45] and Lingobee [46]. Both these applications were designed to crowdsource and share language learning content among the learners to support contextualized, collaborative learning. Organizational learning through crowdsourcing represents an effective form of organizational learning. It constitutes a legitimate and complementary form compared to traditional organizational learning, therefore Schlagwein and Bjorn-Andersen [41] propose "ambient organizational learning" as a framework to integrate both IT-enabled, non-member-based organizational learning with crowdsourcing and traditional, member-based organizational learning.

4   Conceptual Framework

We propose a conceptual framework for guiding interactive and collaborative technology-enhanced learning processes where the aim is for employees to collaborate and reflect on dilemmas and their beliefs and values, and to think beyond time-bound and planned group activities. The conceptual framework, *Improving Organizational Culture Using Interactive Learning Technologies (ICULT),* is designed to guide and evaluate the use of interactive learning technologies in organizations. It may also help future research to classify and analyze influencing factors for improving organizational culture and practice more systematically.

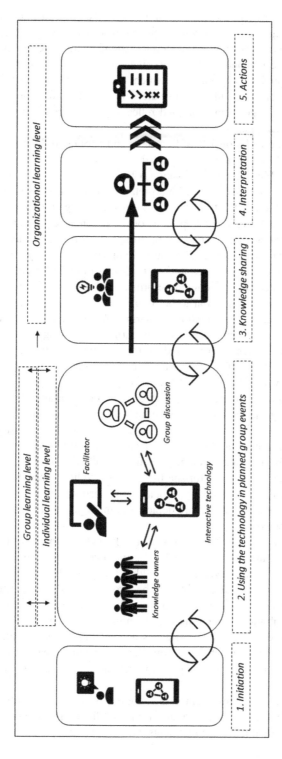

Fig. 3. The ICULT framework

The framework illustrates the steps from initiating the use of a learning technology and using a learning technology within planned activities such as a time-bound workshop, to informing decisions for concrete actions to improve organizational culture (see Fig. 3). The planned activities involve reflection and learning activities for individuals, groups and the organization, which are similar to the "initiate reflection" and "conduct reflection" steps identified in the CSRL model [24]. The outcomes from such activities could range from continued reflection processes to concrete actions to improve organizational change.

The ICULT framework consists of five steps and applies to three levels within an organization: the individual, the group, and the organization. The five steps, starting from the left side of Fig. 3 are: (1) Initiation, (2) conducting events (e.g., time-bound workshops), (3) knowledge sharing, (4) interpretation, and (5) actions for improvement.

The first step in the ICULT framework involves initiating and planning a time and space-bound event, such as a workshop, in an organization. The group activities would naturally involve several participants, i.e., a group of people. This step may be conducted by a team manager or a human resource manager. In this step, the status quo of the organizational culture is assessed to select relevant topic for discussing dilemmas. Also, the employees need to be recruited, information about the goal of a group activity needs to be shared, and the material to be used in the workshop needs to be created.

The second step directs the attention to sharing knowledge and experiences among the participants. Here, the employees use the learning technology in a planned time-bound event to encourage sharing and reflection about different dilemmas that employees are faced with. The participants in this event include the initiator and knowledge owners who take part in the workshop to enable experience sharing and reflection. This step of the framework involves individual learning through reflection on dilemmas, sharing individual knowledge and experiences through the technology, and individual reflection on the shared knowledge. Furthermore, this step also facilitates group-level learning through group discussions and reflection on the shared knowledge. Ideas from crowdsourcing, particularly gathering knowledge and experiences from individual participants for sharing, are applied here through the affordances of the interactive learning technology. Notably, the second step may include several events or several workshops, which are depicted in the figure by the circular arrows in the conceptual framework.

The third step emphasizes the sharing of the knowledge created in group events with others in the organization outside of the group event. This step will be a critical point in the process of going beyond the individual and group levels and for knowledge and experiences to become accessible at the organizational level. The knowledge created during a workshop can be shared through data collection, data analysis, and crowdsourced contributions saved in the learning technology, and/or through the participants who may share their experiences and lessons learned to their colleagues through personal interaction. Utilizing both the systematic spreading of information combined with self-initiated social interactions among individuals could contribute to accelerating organizational learning.

The fourth step is where information is being received, read, and interpreted by the targeted recipients in the rest of the organization who did not participate in the planned events. On the individual level, the recipients would be colleagues of the facilitator and the participants of the workshop who are interested in the topic. On the group level, the recipients are key individuals responsible for synthesizing the knowledge generated in step three to receive information shared outside of the planned activities, either through reading documents generated by the learning technology and/or by communicating with colleagues that participated in the facilitated event. These key individuals can be decision-makers, such as team leaders, or human resource managers, or directors who are responsible for deciding action points based on the knowledge created in the workshops and information shared. This step emphasizes the importance of how the knowledge could be shared beyond group events. The synthesized knowledge should be visualized and presented to targeted recipients such that they find it relevant, interesting, and easy to assimilate. This could, for example, be in the form of a structured report with graphics.

Finally, the fifth step focuses on the actions for improvement that have been identified from the planned event (e.g., a workshop) to embed individual- and group-level learning in organizational structures and processes. Here, decision-makers associate the knowledge with the internal needs of the organization, recognize the potential benefits, and decide what actions should be implemented for the organization to be able to improve the organizational culture and learn from the process. The decision-makers of actions for improvement on an individual level could be the participants themselves who create personal goals and actions for their development, and other individuals in the organization that could benefit from it. On a group level, this might involve the team manager and, on an organizational level this might be the human resource managers or directors.

5   Discussion

With this paper, we have explored how the use of interactive learning technologies could facilitate improvement of an organization's culture through individual-level, group-level, and organization-wide learning activities.

Our conceptual framework ICULT addresses the challenge of knowledge sharing, reflection, and learning from individual and group levels to the organization with the aim to improve organizational culture. The conceptual framework leverages on existing models such as the CSRL model [24] to support planned reflection and learning processes for individuals and groups within an organization. Furthermore, it addresses a research gap in enhancing the support for learning and reflection beyond individual and group levels, by applying the affordances of methods such as crowdsourcing and interactive learning technologies to trigger reflection processes through planned events and support the continuation of these processes after the planned, timebound workshops. While discussing dilemmas enables tapping into the organizational culture through bringing forth individual values and beliefs, the continuation of support for these processes is important to improve organizational culture. Technologies for learning and collaboration can provide a platform to support a structured way of managing the crowdsourced content from planned group events, and across the organization. An overview of how learning technologies could support the different steps of the conceptual framework are summarized in Table 1.

Table 1. Overview of how a learning technology supports the different steps of the conceptual framework.

Step	Activity	Technology support	Aim
1	Initiation of learning process	Gathering relevant information from different sources in the organization for assessing the status quo of the organizational culture. Support invitations and preparation of material for the event	Prepare for creating content to the interactive technology, such as identification of relevant dilemmas
2	One or more planned events (e.g., timebound workshops)	A platform to crowdsource contributions from participants e.g., by incorporating elements from systems of crowd processing, crowd rating, crowd solving, and/or crowd creation, and share the crowdsourced content among all participants. Furthermore, use mechanisms to obtain feedback on the crowdsourced contents from all the participants, which could support group discussions and the creation of summaries and reports related to the contents and outcomes of the event	Individual- and group-level learning and reflection. Sharing knowledge and experiences among individuals in a group
3	Knowledge sharing	Crowdsourced contents from workshops and automatically generated summaries and reports	Enable reflection at individual and group levels. Making the knowledge and experiences accessible at the organizational level
4	Knowledge interpretation	Automatically generated summaries and reports, which are customizable. Crowdsourced content from the workshops	Reflection at individual level. Organizational learning. Making the knowledge and experiences accessible at the organizational level. Visualize and present relevant knowledge to targeted recipients effectively
5	Actions for improvement	Customized reports which include a list of follow up actions	Enable decision- makers to effectively embed individual- and group-level learning in organizational structures and processes

In addition to using crowdsourcing as a method for promoting organizational learning, the learning technology could support experiential learning by enabling employees to share and reflect on issues at stake from different perspectives. The explication of dilemmas could further be supported by visualization of the crowd-sourced dilemmas and by adding interactive elements in the learning technology that requires employees to actively engage with and solve colleagues' dilemmas individually. This could be useful to support employees to voice their interpretations and represent the interrelatedness of dilemmas at work to explicate organizational dilemmas.

The ICULT framework emphasizes the use of learning technologies in planned group events to facilitate reflection, collaboration, and learning. The available options of dilemmas have consequences that make them equally desirable and undesirable [16], therefore discussing the individual contributions in groups might be of particular importance when the topic at hand requires employees to reflect upon values and beliefs instead of learning factual knowledge where correct answers are given. By using crowdsourcing and facilitating group discussions in a workshop, an organization can discover inconsistencies between its' culture and strategies, and the individual needs, aspirations and behaviors that affect employees' choices and decisions in their daily work life.

The three levels illustrated in the conceptual framework are individual, group and organization. By analysing the process divided into these levels, several important influencing factors can be identified. For instance, on an individual level of analysis, influencing factors to take into consideration when both initiating the process as well as evaluating its effect, could be motivation and opportunities to share [36]. On a group level, group identity may have an impact on the process [37]. Furthermore, organizational culture and reward systems are examples of influencing factors on an organizational level [38]. Learning technologies may support and strengthen influencing factors through functionalities like data collection and analysis, and by incorporating interactive elements such as crowdsourcing, and gamification strategies.

6   Concluding Remarks

This paper focuses on the development of the ICULT framework that addresses the challenge of knowledge sharing and learning from individual and group levels to the organization with the aim to improve organizational culture. We have reviewed the literature to explore how such a process can be supported by using technologies for learning and collaboration.

The use of interactive learning technologies creates new opportunities for organizations to facilitate experience and knowledge sharing by engaging employees in collaborative and reflective processes, such as workshops, which may facilitate organizational change. Identified key concepts for achieving an interactive and collaborative approach to improve organizational culture and change readiness are (1) knowledge sharing, (2) experiential learning, and (3) reflection at the individual, group, and organization levels. Furthermore, (4) crowdsourcing is considered as a means of engaging and gathering the inputs and feedback from the employees using a learning technology.

The main contribution of this paper is a conceptual framework that supports organizational culture practices and change through supporting learning and reflection at the individual, group and organization levels. Our focus has been on the role of interactive learning technologies that could support the gathering and sharing of knowledge and experiences within groups and organizations. In particular, we have used ideas from crowdsourcing to gather and share the knowledge in an organization, using mobile and interactive learning technologies.

The conceptual framework is based on the experiences of using a learning technology in workshops within organizations. We are currently conducting more systematic evaluations of the technology and the process outlined in the conceptual framework. The main focus so far has been the knowledge gathering and sharing within planned activities such as timebound workshops (step 2 of the conceptual framework) and how the knowledge from those could be leveraged both to support the participants of the workshops as well as the organization as a whole (in steps 3–5). So far, the benefits of crowdsourcing have been applied mostly in step 2. Some of our ongoing studies explore additional benefits that could be harnessed from the crowdsourced knowledge that could support the steps 3–5 of the conceptual framework.

A closer investigation of influencing factors is needed in further research on the role of the use of interactive technologies in organizations. The ICULT framework could help guide such investigation.

Acknowledgments. The ongoing research project and this work is funded by the Norwegian Research Council (#309829).

References

1. Schein, E.H., Schein, P.A.: The Corporate Culture Survival Guide. John Wiley & Sons, Hoboken, NJ (2019)
2. Cummings, T.G., Worley, C.G.: Organization development and change. Cengage learning (2014)
3. Hislop, D.: Knowledge Management in Organizations: A Critical Introduction. Oxford University Press, Oxford (2013)
4. Argote, L., Miron-Spektor, E.: Organizational learning: from experience to knowledge. Organ. Sci. **22**(5), 1123–1137 (2011)
5. Cummings, T.G., Worley, C.G.: Organization Development and Change. 9th edn. South-Western, Mason Ohio (2009).
6. Wang, K., Hjelmervik, O.R., Bremdal, B.: Introduction to Knowledge Management: Principles And Practice. Tapir Academic Press (2001)
7. Čudanov, M., Savoiu, G., Jaško, O.: Usage of technology enhanced learning tools and organizational change perception. Comput. Sci. Inf. Syst. **9**(1), 285–302 (2012)
8. Alavi, M., Leidner, D.E.: Research commentary: technology-mediated learning—a call for greater depth and breadth of research. Inf. Syst. Res. **12**(1), 1–10 (2001)
9. Odor, H.O.: A literature review on organizational learning and learning organizations. Int. J. Econ. Manag. Sci. **7**(1), 1–6 (2018)

10. Bichler, M.: Design science in information systems research. Wirtschaftsinformatik **48**(2), 133–135 (2006). https://doi.org/10.1007/s11576-006-0028-8
11. Sanders, E.B.-N., Stappers, P.J.: Co-creation and the new landscapes of design. Co-design **4** (1), 5–18 (2008)
12. Reason, P., Bradbury, H.: Introduction. In: Reason, P., Bradbury, H. (eds.). The SAGE Handbook of Action research and participative inquiry and practice. 2nd edn. Sage Publications (2008)
13. Chang, W.-J., Liao, S.-H., Wu, T.-T.: Relationships among organizational culture, knowledge sharing, and innovation capability: a case of the automobile industry in Taiwan. Knowl. Manag. Res. Pract. **15**(3), 471–490 (2017)
14. Flamholtz, E.G., Randle, Y.: Implications of organizational life cycles for corporate culture and climate. In: Schneider, B., Barbera, K.M., (eds.) The Oxford handbook of organizational climate and culture. Oxford University Press Oxford, pp. 235–256 (2014)
15. Howard-Grenville, J.A.: Inside the "black box" how organizational culture and subcultures inform interpretations and actions on environmental issues. Organ. Environ. **19**(1), 46–73 (2006)
16. Castaño, J.M., van Amstel, F., Hartmann, T., Dewulf, G.: Making dilemmas explicit through the use of a cognitive mapping collaboration tool. Futures **87**, 37–49 (2017)
17. Northcraft, G.B., Tenbrunsel, A.E.: Effective matrices, decision frames, and cooperation in volunteer dilemmas: a theoretical perspective on academic peer review. Organ. Sci. **22**(5), 1277–1285 (2011)
18. Rahman, N., Cheng, R., Bayerl, P.S.: Synchronous versus asynchronous manipulation of 2D-objects in distributed design collaborations: implications for the support of distributed team processes. Des. Stud. **34**(3), 406–431 (2013). https://doi.org/10.1016/j.destud.2012.11. 003
19. Steiner, L.: Organizational dilemmas as barriers to learning. Learn. Organ. **5**(4), 193–201 (1998)
20. Höijer, B., Lidskog, R., Uggla, Y.: Facing dilemmas: sense-making and decision-making in late modernity. Futures **38**(3), 350–366 (2006)
21. Balbastre, F., Oltra, V., Martinez, J.F., Moreno, M.: Individual, group, and organizational learning levels and their interactions: an integrative framework. Manage. Res. J. Iberoamerican Acad. Manage. **1**, 253–267 (2003)
22. Kolb, A., Kolb, D.: Experiential learning theory: a dynamic, holistic approach to management learning, education and development. In: Armstrong, S.J., Fukami, C. (eds.) Handbook of Management Learning, Education and Development (2011)
23. Kayes, A.B., Kayes, D.C., Kolb, D.A.: Experiential learning in teams. Simul. Gaming **36**(3), 330–354 (2005)
24. Krogstie, B.R., Prilla, M., Pammer, V.: Understanding and supporting reflective learning processes in the workplace: the CSRL model. Paper presented at the EC-TEL, Berlin, Heidelberg (2013)
25. Kolb, B.: Functions of the frontal cortex of the rat: a comparative review. Brain Res. Rev. **8** (1), 65–98 (1984)
26. Singh, R., Ramdeo, S.: Individual-Level OD Interventions. Leading Organizational Development and Change. Palgrave Macmillan, Cham. pp. 33–66 ((2020))
27. Schön, D.A.: The Reflective Practitioner: How Professionals Think in Action. Basic Books, New York (1987)
28. Mezirow, J.: How critical reflection triggers transformative learning. In: Associates JMa, editor. Fostering critical reflection in adulthood. Jossey-Bass, San Fransisco, pp. 1–20 (1990)

29. Petersen, S.A., Oliveira, M.: The use of Reflection Continuum Model to support digital game-based learning for the development of cognitive skills. In: Paper presented at the 11th European Conference on Games Based Learning, Graz, Austria (2017)

30. Wang, S., Noe, R.A.: Knowledge sharing: a review and directions for future research. Hum. Resour. Manag. Rev. **20**(2), 115–131 (2010)

31. Argote, L., Ingram, P., Levine, J.M., Moreland, R.L.: Knowledge transfer in organizations: learning from the experience of others. Organ. Behav. Hum. Decis. Process. **82**(1), 1–8 (2000)

32. Szulanski, G.: Exploring internal stickiness: Impediments to the transfer of best practice within the firm. Strateg. Manag. J. **17**(S2), 27–43 (1996)

33. Easterby-Smith, M., Lyles, M.A., Tsang, E.W.: Inter-organizational knowledge transfer: current themes and future prospects. J. Manage. Stud. **45**(4), 677–690 (2008)

34. Szulanski, G.: The process of knowledge transfer: a diachronic analysis of stickiness. Organ. Behav. Hum. Decis. Process. **82**(1), 9–27 (2000)

35. Liyanage, C., Elhag, T., Ballal, T., Li, Q.: Knowledge communication and translation – a knowledge transfer model. J. Knowl. Manag. **13**(3), 118–131 (2009). https://doi.org/10.1108/13673270910962914

36. Ipe, M.: Knowledge sharing in organizations: a conceptual framework. Hum. Resour. Dev. Rev. **2**(4), 337–359 (2003)

37. Cabrera, A., Cabrera, E.F.: Knowledge-sharing dilemmas. Organ. Stud. **23**(5), 687–710 (2002)

38. Razmerita, L., Kirchner, K., Nielsen, P.: What factors influence knowledge sharing in organizations? A social dilemma perspective of social media communication. J. Knowl. Manag. **20**(6), 1225–1246 (2016). https://doi.org/10.1108/JKM-03-2016-0112

39. Manouselis, N., Drachsler, H., Vuorikari, R., Hummel, H., Koper, R.: Recommender systems in technology enhanced learning. In: Ricci, F., Rokach, L., Shapira, B., Kantor, P.B. (eds.) Recommender systems handbook, pp. 387–415. Springer, Boston, MA (2011). https://doi.org/10.1007/978-0-387-85820-3_12

40. Matsuo, M., Easterby-Smith, M.: Beyond the knowledge sharing dilemma: the role of customisation. J. Knowl. Manag. **12**(4), 30–43 (2008)

41. Schlagwein, D., Bjorn-Andersen, N.: Organizational learning with crowdsourcing: the revelatory case of LEGO. J. Assoc. Inf. Syst. **15**, 754–778 (2014)

42. Estellés-Arolas, E., González-Ladrón-de-Guevara, F.: Towards an integrated crowdsourcing definition. J. Inf. Sci. **38**(2), 189–200 (2012)

43. Thuan, N.H., Antunes, P., Johnstone, D.: Factors influencing the decision to crowdsource: a systematic literature review. Inf. Syst. Front. **18**(1), 47–68 (2015). https://doi.org/10.1007/s10796-015-9578-x

44. Geiger, D., Rosemann, M., Fielt, E.: Crowdsourcing information systems: a systems theory perspective. Paper presented at the Proceedings of the 22nd Australasian Conference on Information Systems (ACIS 2011), Sydney, Australia (2011).

45. Pemberton, L., Winter, M., Fallahkhair, S.: Collaborative mobile knowledge sharing for language learners. J. Res. Centre Educ. Technol. **6**(1), 144–148 (2010)

46. Procter-Legg, E., Cacchione, A., Petersen, S.A.: LingoBee and social media: mobile language learners as social networkers. In: Paper Presented at the IADIS International Conference on Cognition and Exploratory Learning in Digital Age (CELDA 2012), Madrid, Spain (2012)

A Social, Virtual and Open Model for Measuring Creativity

Carlos Guillem-Aldave[1] and Rafael Molina-Carmona[2](✉)

[1] Communication Office, University of Alicante, Alicante, Spain
carlos.guillem@ua.es
[2] Smart Learning Research Group, University of Alicante,
C/San Vicente del Raspeig sn, Alicante, Spain
rmolina@ua.es

Abstract. The creativity of individuals is manifested through the products they are able to create, so that the attributes of a product also characterize the individual who created it. Therefore, a way of measuring the creativity of an individual is evaluating and measuring the creative attributes of the products he or she created. This is the basis of the new model we propose to measure creativity. The main elements of the model are the product, its creator and the evaluators that assess it. The products and their creators are characterized by an open set of measurable attributes, identified from the literature. We have also introduced a social way of evaluation, so that large amounts of evaluators could participate in the process. The work of the evaluators is assessed by assigning them a level of confidence. This level of confidence is assigned and updated considering the expertise of the evaluator but also his or her behaviour during the evaluation process. The combination of a large set of evaluators, their anonymity, and their assessment, have led to a more objective and unbiased system of evaluation and measuring.

Keywords: Creativity · Measurement of creativity · Social measurement

1 Introduction

Creativity can be understood intuitively as the ability to generate new ideas or concepts that produce original and useful solutions. It is, therefore, a High-level human capacity in which many cognitive processes of very diverse nature take part. The complexity of human thinking in general and of creative ability in particular makes it difficult to be measured.

In the literature two main areas of study are presented in relation to the measure of creativity. The most studied way of measuring assumes that creativity is a personal trait of the individual that can be measured through the qualities of the person. Over the past century, numerous tests have pursued evaluating the individual's creativity by analysing the skills and abilities that lead him or her to be creative. However, there is a second perspective that studies creativity based on the products that the individuals create. Various tests are been designed to analyse the different attributes of a product and evaluate its degree of creativity. From the analysis of many products created by the

© Springer Nature Switzerland AG 2021
P. Zaphiris and A. Ioannou (Eds.): HCII 2021, LNCS 12784, pp. 31–45, 2021.
https://doi.org/10.1007/978-3-030-77889-7_3

same person, it is possible to conclude whether that person is more or less creative. This second research area is less explored. We consider that it is worth deepening its study, pursuing the goal of achieving a more objective measure of creativity.

Furthermore, the current development of information technologies is allowing digital access to a huge number of individuals who, increasingly, share opinions, collaborate and evaluate information through digital media. The most paradigmatic example is the growing use of social networks. In many of these networks the information offered is qualified by users in a massive way through different mechanisms (like/dislike buttons, scores…), which generates currents of opinion, new trends and other opportunities that can be exploited. In this area many studies and research have been developed that can be transferred to other areas. In particular, we wonder if it is possible to use these collaborative and social mechanisms to measure the creativity that certain products incorporate and, consequently, the creative traits of their creators.

In this paper we propose a new model, to be developed on digital tools in the future, that incorporates an evaluation of the creativity through the connection of the creative individuals with a wide number of users who act as evaluators. Based on the analysis of previous studies on creativity measurement, this study aims at proposing a formal model for the social assessment of the products and their specific creative characteristics, rather than general creative skills at an abstract level.

In Sect. 2, a wide background of the topic is presented, mainly focused on creativity and how to measure it, as well as on social rating systems that will inspire our proposal. The objectives of the research are presented in Sect. 3. Our proposal is deeply described in Sect. 4, including the main components of the proposed model and the dynamics of the system. Finally, conclusions and some open questions are presented in Sect. 5.

2 Background

This study tries to establish a social system of creativity measurement based on the participation of a large number of evaluators. Therefore, a tour is necessary on the existing antecedents related to the three basic pillars of the work: creativity as an attribute of the human being, the existing proposals to measure the creativity and the social systems of evaluation.

2.1 Creativity as an Attribute of the Human Being

There are numerous definitions of creativity in the field of research, although it is not the purpose of this article to discuss or propose a new one. However, it is important to choose one that suits our purposes. We chose the definition of Sternberg, Lubart, Kaufman and Pretz [1] since it is complete and very well accepted among researchers: "Creativity is the ability to produce work that is novel, original, or unexpected; and also appropriate, useful, of high quality, or otherwise meets task constraints".

2.2   Measures of Creativity

During the last century there have been many studies that have addressed the problem of measuring the level of creativity. In general, we can establish two main lines of work. The first is to measure creativity as a personal and intrinsic trait or attribute of the individual through tests, somehow similar to intelligence tests. The second trend measures the individuals' creativity through the characteristics of the solutions they bring to the problems they solve. Next, we focus on this second area.

The research on the characteristics of creative solutions or products is not as extensive as the literature focusing on the measure of creativity as a personal trait, as Besemer and O'Quin [2] indicate, especially if we think of transferring the properties of the products to their creators.

However, researchers wonder what means that a product is creative. MacKinnon [3] states that "the starting point, indeed the bedrock of all studies of creativity, is an analysis of creative products, a determination of what it is that makes them different from more mundane products." According to Horn and Salvendy [4], "product creativity appears to be not only subject to the person who is judging the product but also subject to when and where the product exists", which allows to extract that utility of a solution is one of the signs of creativity. For Stenberg and Lubart [5] a product can be defined as creative when it is original and appropriate. Along the same lines, Amabile [6] states that the product has to be appropriate, useful and correct. Another interesting work that studies the properties of creative products, is that of Taylor and Sandler [7] with their model Creative Product Inventory, in which a group of experts evaluates seven criteria for the measurement of creativity in scientific products, using a Likert scale of 7 points. The qualities are: generation, reformulation, originality, relevancy, hedonics, complexity and condensation.

Finally, the work of Besemer and Treffinger [8] is particularly interesting since it is the basis of our proposal. They present their Creative Product Analysis Matrix, which proposes 3 dimensions (novelty, resolution and style) and 9 subscales (surprising, original, logical, useful, valuable, understandable, organic, well-crafted and elegant). This model will be studied deeply in next sections since it is the basis of our proposal.

2.3   Social Rating Systems

A social rating system can be defined as a mechanism or tool that allows the evaluation of a product, in the broadest sense, based on the opinions of a large group of people that we will call evaluators. This is the case of surveys. In essence, a survey is a procedure that seeks to collect data through a previously designed questionnaire, to obtain the opinions or reactions about what is intended to study [9]. Social networks have introduced mechanisms such as "likes" or other rating systems to evaluate products, very simple but very effective type of survey. Different alternatives have been proposed: like/dislike, stars, bubbles, scales, marks…

We focus on Scales: it is possible to rate the product on a scale of values, very frequently between 1 and 5, where 3 would be a neutral score and, below or above, negative or positive, respectively. This type of scale corresponds to the widespread Likert scale [10].

2.4   Discussion About the Background Study

The aim of this section is to identify which aspects of the background study are more widely developed and accepted and which require further research.

The first controversial aspect in the study of creativity is the definition of the term itself. Although we have assumed the definition of Sternberg [1], it is still a very broad and interpretable definition. In this sense, an aspect to be explored is how to complete the definition of creativity, so that all aspects that make an individual, object or idea creative are defined in a complete and deep manner. A first approach could be an open, explicit and measurable definition so that each attribute or characteristic that is an indicator of creativity could be included in this new definition now or in the future. A clear relationship with the scale of the degree of creativity should be established.

One of the most difficult aspects of this new definition is that it states the attributes of creativity must be measurable. The most frequent studies on the measurement of creativity have always been those focused on creativity as an individual trait, generally trying to measure the extent of divergent thinking. However, there is also a growing trend that studies how to measure creativity in products, emphasizing this to be a more tangible and objective measure. MacKinnon [3] already advanced that the starting point of studies of creativity, is the analysis of the features that make creative products different from the common ones. In this case, the attributes to be determined refer, fundamentally, to the objects or ideas that are the result of the creative process. Considering this second trend, the work of Besemer and Treffinger [8] is particularly interesting because of its wide acceptance among researchers and the adaptation to the objectives of our proposal.

Another interesting aspect that emerges from the background study is the problem of obtaining reliable evaluations of the product attributes. Tests have been developed for this evaluation, but the lack of consensus regarding the attributes to be assessed, the difficulty to find experts to perform the evaluation, and the lack of assessment of the evaluators themselves, ballast such tests. In addition, it is necessary to rely on human evaluators (nowadays it does not seem easy to develop automatic evaluation systems) and finding reliable evaluators willing to evaluate tests is not an easy task. The emergence of social networks and their rating systems can be an inspiration for the development of a social evaluation system, based on the opinion of a large number of evaluators, facilitating participation through the use of technological tools. These tools facilitate anonymity so that certain biases can be avoided. An unavoidable difficulty in this field is the generalized perception of the subjectivity of the measurement of creativity. However, if creativity is well defined, the definition is broken down into well-organized attributes, and there are a high number of participants, it is highly defensible that the measurement is considerably objectivized.

3   Objectives

Our initial hypothesis is considering that the creativity of individuals is manifested through the products they are able to create, so that the attributes of a product also characterize the individual who created it. So, the general objective of this work is proposing a new model to evaluate and measure creativity of the individuals from the attributes of the products they created. To fulfil this general objective, we set out the following specific objectives for the evaluation model:

- Identify the set of attributes that make a product creative and how to measure them. This set will be obtained from the literature but the model will be open, so that this set could be extended in the future.
- Introduce a social way of evaluation, so that large amounts of evaluators could participate in the process.
- Assess the work of the evaluators, so that they are assigned a different level of confidence. This level of confidence is assigned and updated considering the expertise of the evaluator but also his or her behaviour during the evaluation process.
- Take advantage of the possibilities and the resources that can offer the new digital tools, which bring a social level with a spectacular potential.

4 Proposed Model

The proposed model is based on the idea that a product is the result of the activity of a creative individual and, therefore, the tangible element resulting from his creativity. In this way, the product (it can be an object, an idea, a service, a process, or any result of a creative process) becomes the central element of the model that will be evaluated in such a way that the creative individual will be characterized by the assessment of his or her products.

In order to carry out these evaluations we will need the participation of the evaluators, the other fundamental participant in the proposed measurement model. At the same time, the evaluators will be characterized by the quality of their evaluations, demonstrated throughout their participation in the system.

In short, the elements the system has are:

- Entities:
  - Product: it is the result of the creative process and it can be any object, idea, service or process to be evaluated. It is characterized by a set of attributes. Attributes are the characteristics of the product that we can measure and which indicate the extent to which the product is creative.
  - Creative individuals: they are the individuals who perform the creative process and create the product as a result of that process. The attributes of the product will also characterize the individuals who created it. The evaluation of the attributes of the individuals is calculated from the evaluation of the products they have created.
  - Evaluator: is the person who evaluates the products through an evaluation questionnaire. In turn, the proposed model allows the evaluation and characterization of the work of the evaluators.
- Relationships:
  - Create: it relates the creative individuals to the products they create.
  - Evaluate: it relates the evaluators to the products they evaluate.

In Fig. 1 we see a general outline of the different elements that make up the proposed system.

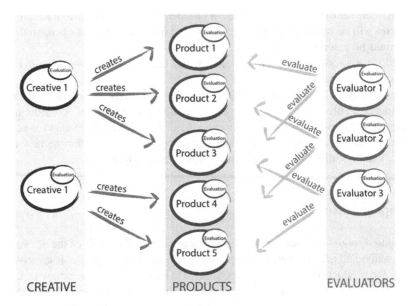

Fig. 1. Elements of the proposed system.

To complete the general explanation of the model, it is important to explain the dynamics of the system. The model works iteratively, and it is formed by two cycles: the one of creation and the other one of evaluation:

- Creation cycle: the creative individual creates a product and makes it available to the evaluation system. The system remains on the look-out for new products that are created.
- Evaluation cycle: when there is a product to evaluate the evaluation cycle begins, which in turn consists of the following steps:
- Evaluate: the evaluator evaluates the product according to an evaluation procedure that will be explained later. The result of this procedure is incorporated as an evaluation of the product.
- Update the individual evaluation: the result of the evaluation of the product contributes to the evaluation of its creator (the creative individual), in the form that is explained below.
- Update the evaluator evaluation: the result of the evaluation of the product contributes to the evaluation of the evaluator. In the following sections we will explain how this update is performed.

In short, after performing the different cycles with the work of the different creators and evaluators, an evaluation for each of the three entities of the system is obtained. The Fig. 2 presents schematically the dynamics of the system.

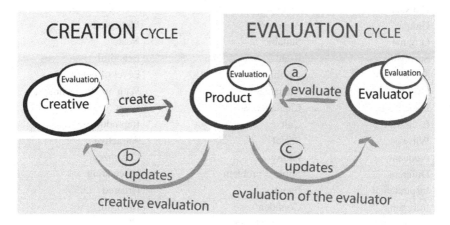

Fig. 2. Dynamics of the system.

4.1   The Product

The product, that is, the object, idea, service or process resulting from the creative process is the central element of our model. It is characterized by a set of attributes that we must measure and that indicate whether the product is creative or not, and to what extent.

The starting point for the attributes that determine a product's creativity is Besemer's Creativity Product Semantic Scale (CPSS) [11]. The CPSS model measures through several evaluators the creativity of a product through many attributes well classified into three groups or dimensions: novelty, resolution and style.

Each product gets an assessment in each of the three dimensions discussed. The three dimensions are, in turn, broken down into several facets. This model has undergone several changes so that different researchers, including its authors, have considered different facets in various studies.

In our case, we have taken as a basis the original model and other studies to propose a total of 66 facets, classified in the same three dimensions. Table 1 shows, classified in the three dimensions, the 66 facets of our adaptation of the CPSS model.

Table 1. Dimensions and facets of our model based on the CPSS.

Dimension new	Dimension resolution	Dimension style
Cool	Logical	Skilled
New	With sense	Well done
Unusual	Relevant	Well elaborated
Unique	Appropriate	Meticulous
Original	Suitable	Neat
Surprising	Right	Beautiful
Spontaneous	Useful	Level of detail
Striking	Valuable	With artistic technique
Interesting	Capitalizable	Clear Simple
Exciting	Cult	Reproducible
Witty	Social	Attractive
Frequent	Funny	Organized
Different	Solve a problem	Fascinating
Inspirational	Funny	Ordered
Intriguing	Confident	Colorful
Extravagant	Historical value	Cleansed
Modern	Viral potential	Level of improvisation
Break with the traditional	Facilitates a creative atmosphere	Careful
Desirable	Transcendent	Feeling
Eye-catching	Relevant	Rhythm
Significant	Conveys feeling	Deliberate
Extraordinary	Popularity	Elegant

Since we want the model to be open, our proposal allows this list to be expandable or redefinable depending on the needs of each study and the characteristics of each evaluated product. The high number of facets considered and their more precise definition are motivated by the need to objectify the measure of the creativity of the products. Moreover, this proposal of facets is generic for any product. For a particular one, some facets may not be applicable.

For evaluation of each attribute, Besemer and O'Quin [2] use a 7-value Likert scale, while Taylor and Sandler [7] propose a scale of 5 values. In our model, we will consider a Likert scale of 5 values, since there is no consensus regarding the number of points to be used on a Likert scale [12], and we have considered that 5 is enough to be able to perform a good measurement. However, this aspect does not condition the model at all and could easily be adapted to a Likert scale with different numbers of values.

As a result of the evaluation process, the product is characterized by the value assigned to the set of attributes, structured in the three dimensions (Fig. 3).

Fig. 3. Attributes of the product.

4.2 The Creative Individual

The individual who performs the creative process is the final object of the evaluation. As a product creator, the attributes of the product will also characterize the individual, so that the evaluation of their attributes is obtained from the evaluation of the products that he or she has created. Although in the model we speak of a creative individual, in fact the product can be the result of the work of a whole team of creatives. In that case the term creative individual refers to the whole team.

The model considers that these users can make the products available for evaluation. The creative individual is evaluated, like the products, in the three dimensions: originality, resolution and style (Fig. 4). His or her evaluation will depend on the evaluation of his or her products, the quantity of products to be evaluated and the upward or downward trend of the evaluations over time, as will be explained in a later section.

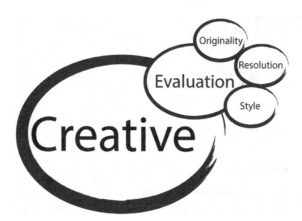

Fig. 4. Attributes of the individual.

4.3   The Evaluator

The evaluators are the people in charge of evaluating the products through an evaluation questionnaire. In almost all models of measurement of creativity, the evaluators are experts in the subject. However, in some studies, such as Besemer's [11], any user is worth assessing, thus facilitating the measurement of the tests since it is usually difficult to find experts available and willing to perform evaluations.

In our proposal anyone can contribute their opinion in the evaluation of the products. For that reason, we will have a set of experts on the subject, a wider set of initiates, and a greater number of novices. All the evaluators are anonymous, so that the evaluation is more complete and prejudices are avoided. In the proposed model, the evaluators will be classified according to their level of experience and their degree of success with the resulting consensus in each evaluation in which they participate. For this, levels of confidence are considered in the evaluators, as explained below.

The model classifies the evaluators in 5 levels of confidence according to their education, experience and the quality of their evaluations. Evaluations carried out by a higher level evaluator are more influential than those of a lower level, on a defined scale. It is the model itself that is responsible for presenting the product to evaluate to different evaluators of different levels of confidence. Figure 5 represents the process of evaluation of a product by several evaluators of different levels.

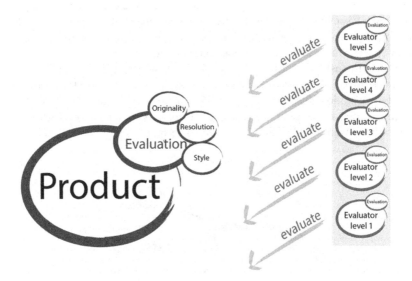

Fig. 5. Evaluation of a product by evaluators of different levels.

4.4   The Evaluation Process

This section presents the main contributions of the paper: how the individual is assessed from the product evaluation and how the levels of confidence of the evaluators are updated.

Evaluation of Facets. Each facet is classified in one of the three dimensions considered in the model, having a total of 66 facets, so that we will formulate 66 different questions so that each facet is evaluated in a Likert scale from 1 to 5. Thus, the score of a facet is the mean of the score given by the evaluators, weighted by the confidence level of the evaluators (the higher the level, the higher the weight). More formally, given a product $p \in P$ (P is the set of all the products), we define the set F of n facets to be evaluated (since we have selected 66 facets, $n = 66$), and a set E of m evaluators. Each evaluator $e_j \in E$ is assigned a confidence level $l_j \in \{1, 2, 3, 4, 5\}$. In addition, given a facet $f_i \in F$, we define $E_i \subset E$ as the subset of evaluators that have evaluated the facet f_i. For each evaluator $e_j \in E_i$, we define $v_{ij} \in \{1, 2, 3, 4, 5\}$ as the evaluation given to facet f_i by the evaluator e_j. Finally, we can define the evaluation v_i of the facet f_i as:

$$v_i = \frac{\sum_{\forall e_j \in E_i} v_{ij} \cdot l_j}{\sum_{\forall e_j \in E_i} l_j} \tag{1}$$

Evaluation of Creative Individuals. From the evaluation of the facet of a product we can obtain the evaluation of this facet for the creative individual. At this point it is necessary to have the temporal aspect into account: the creativity of a person evolves with time, according to their abilities and the experience acquired. Therefore it is not reasonable to obtain the evaluation of a creative as the average of the evaluations of its products: the last creations should have more weight in the evaluation. To take into account this aspect we introduce a temporal ordering in the product evaluations (time is here not considered strictly, but to establish a sequence), so that we denote as $v_i^{(k)}$ and $v_i^{(k+1)}$ two evaluations of the same facet corresponding to two products of the same creator, generated at instants k and $k + 1$. According to this order, $v_i^{(k)} < v_i^{(k+1)}$ since instant k is prior to $k + 1$.

The formulation that allows calculating the evaluation of an individual is recursive and instant dependent, so that the evaluation at instant k depends on the previous evaluations. In order to gradually reduce the weight of the older evaluations, a temporary reduction factor, denoted as $\rho \in [0, 1]$, is introduced, so that each new evaluation of a product implies an updating of the evaluation of its creator, reducing the weight of the previous evaluations in that reduction factor. The value chosen for ρ allows us to modulate the weight of the oldest evaluations, so that if $\rho = 1$, all the evaluations have the same weight independent from the instant, while is $\rho = 0$, only the last evaluation is considered. The formulation of the creativity evaluation of an individual c_i for facet v_i is:

$$\begin{cases} c_i^{(1)} = v_i^{(1)} \\ c_i^{(k)} = \frac{c_i^{(k-1)} \cdot (k-1) \cdot \rho + v_i^{(k)}}{(k-1) \cdot \rho + 1} \end{cases} \tag{2}$$

Update of Evaluator Confidence Levels. The confidence level of an evaluator represents how good is this evaluator at evaluating the creativity of the products. Previously, we are going to define the difference between evaluations as a measure on which the other measures will be based (Eq. 3). Let a product p be evaluated by two evaluators e_j and e_k, and let v_{ij} and v_{ik} be the evaluations given by these evaluators for each facet f_i of that product. We define the difference d_{jk} between evaluators e_j and e_k as:

$$d_{jk} = \frac{\sum_{\forall f_i \in F} |v_{ij} - v_{ik}|}{n} \tag{3}$$

where F is the set of facets and n the number of facets ($n = 66$ in our model).

Now, we must define the confidence degree DC_j of an evaluator e_j as a real value in the interval $[0, 4]$ that estimates the quality of his or her evaluations. The confidence degree is a continuous version of the confidence level of the evaluator l_j, so that $l_j = round(g_j)$. The confidence degree of an evaluator is initialized at instant 0 with a first approximation of the confidence level given by the managers of the system. Typically, this value is obtained from the expertise of the evaluators, so that experts in creativity should be assigned a level of 5, and novices in this field a level of 1. The confidence degree is now updated for every new evaluation, depending on how good the evaluator is at evaluating. In other words, if the difference d_j between his or her evaluation and the canonical one is close to 0, the evaluator is accurate and his or her confidence degree should be incremented. On the contrary, if the d_{jc} has a high value, the confidence degree should be decremented. To do so, we propose classifying this difference into three possible ranges, so that the confidence degree is updated in a quantity depending on the value of d_{jc}:

$$DC_j = d_{jc} = \frac{\sum_{\forall f_i \in F} |v_{ij} - v_{ic}|}{n} \tag{4}$$

This would be the formula for the canonical evaluation (based on the judgment of only level 5 experts):

$$v_{ic} = \frac{\sum_{\forall e_j \in E_c} v_{ij}}{m_c} \tag{5}$$

Where E_c is the set of evaluators for the canonical evaluation (equivalent to level 5, that of experts) and m_c is the size of this group.

The degree of agreement, as occurs with the difference with the canonical evaluation, is an individual measure for each evaluator and not a global one and consists of the average of the differences between the evaluations of the evaluated evaluator and those of all the others. Based on the definition of the difference between evaluations in Eq. 3, we define degree of agreement GAj for a given evaluator e_j as the mean of the differences between its evaluation v_{ij} of each facet of a product and the evaluations of the other evaluators of the system:

$$GA_j = \frac{\sum_{\forall e_k \in E^*} d_{jk}}{m - 1} \tag{6}$$

Where E^* is the total set of evaluators eliminating the evaluator himself and m is the total number of evaluatos. GA_j measures, in short, how close the evaluation of a certain evaluator is to the evaluations of the other evaluators. As in the case of DC, GA can take values in the interval $[0, 4]$ so that $GA_j = 0$ means complete agreement in the evaluation with the other evaluators of the same product and $GA_j = 4$ means that the evaluation carried out by the evaluator is totally different from that of his peers. As for the DC measure, the degree of agreement can be normalized to define it in the interval $[0.4]$.

The average difference is the mean of the differences between the evaluations of each evaluator and the canonical evaluation, that is, that of the experts, as we see in Eq. 7.

$$\overline{DC_j} = \frac{\sum_{\forall f_i \in F}\left(v_{ij} - v_{ic}\right)}{n_j} \tag{7}$$

The standard deviation of the above measurement is calculated according to Eq. 8 in the usual way.

$$s_{DCj} = \sqrt{\frac{\sum_{\forall f_i \in F}\left(v_{ij} - DCj\right)^2}{n_j - 1}} \tag{8}$$

5   Conclusions

The general objective of this work was proposing a new model to evaluate and measure creativity of the individuals from the attributes of the products they created. To fulfil this objective we have defined a social model of measurement of creativity with the following features:

- The result of a creative process, that is, the product, is the central element of the model so that it is evaluated and its creator is evaluated according to its assessment. The product is characterized by a set of measurable attributes, indicators of its degree of creativity. The set of attributes is an adaptation of the dimensions and facets proposed by Besemer's CPSS [11].
- However, the model is proposed to be open so that the set of dimensions or facets are expandable or redefinable depending on the needs of each study and the characteristics of each evaluated product.
- The evaluation of the products is extended to its creators considering all the results of the individual or team. A temporal factor is introduced so that the last creations can have a higher weight in the assessment of the creatives. The way the different evaluations are integrated and how to obtain the final evaluation of the individuals are two of the main contributions of this paper.

- The attributes of creativity are evaluated by a large and anonymous set of evaluators of different levels of expertise. The model proposes a social evaluation, somehow similar to the rating system of social networks.
- Although all the opinions are considered during the evaluation process, the evaluations from experts have a higher weight in the final evaluation of the product and its creator. The evaluators are classified in five levels of confidence, so that the ones at level 5 are the most prestigious experts and the ones at level 1 are novices.
- The evaluators are assessed based on their expertise and their behaviour in the system. The level of confidence is then updated according to this assessment. This is another main contribution of this work.

As a consequence, we have obtained an open and social model for creativity assessment. Moreover, the combination of a large set of evaluators, their anonymity, their classification in levels of confidence and the assessment of the evaluators, have led to a more objective and unbiased system of evaluation and measuring.

We also consider that we can take advantage of digital tools, which bring a social level with a spectacular potential. This is why we plan to develop a digital tool that implements this model automatically. This tool will leverage the advantages of this technology: easy and massive access, anonymity, automation, and so on. As a consequence, a validation experiment will be done, to obtain evaluation data and to validate the dynamics of the process. A deeper insight in the formulation and the empiric determination of the parameters (for instance, the reduction factor ρ) will be possible thanks to the digital tool.

References

1. Sternberg, R.J., Lubart, T.I., Kaufman, J.C., Pretz, J.E.: Creativity. In: Holyoak, K.J., Morrison, R.G. (eds.) The Cambridge Handbook of Thinking and Reasoning, pp. 351–370. Cambridge University Press, New York (2005)
2. Besemer, S.P., O'Quin, K.: Confirming the three-factor creative product analysis matrix model in an American sample. Creat. Res. J. **12**, 287–296 (1999). https://doi.org/10.1207/s15326934crj1204_6
3. MacKinnon, D.W.. : In Search of Human Effectiveness. Creative Education Foundation, Buffalo (1978)
4. Horn, D., Salvendy, G.: Product creativity: conceptual model, measurement and characteristics. Theor. Issues Ergon. Sci. **7**, 395–412 (2006). https://doi.org/10.1080/14639220500 0078195
5. Sternberg, R.J., Lubart, T.I.: La creatividad en una cultura conformista/Creativity in a Conformist Culture: UN Desafio a Las Masas (Spanish Edition). AbeBooks. ISBN: 8449303400. https://www.abebooks.com/9788449303401/creatividad-cultura-conformista-Creativity-Conformist-8449303400/plp. Accessed 06 May 2018
6. Amabile, T.M.: Social psychology of creativity: a consensual assessment technique. J. Pers. Soc. Psychol. **43**, 997–1013 (1982). https://doi.org/10.1037/0022-3514.43.5.997
7. Taylor, I.A., Sandler, B.E.: Use of a creative product inventory for evaluating products of chemists. Proc. Annu. Conv. Am. Psychol. Assoc. **7**, 311–312 (1972)
8. Besemer, S.P., Treffinger, D.J.: Analysis of creative products: review and synthesis. J. Creat. Behav. **15**, 158–178 (1981). https://doi.org/10.1002/j.2162-6057.1981.tb00287.x

9. Johnson, R., Kuby, P.: Elementary Statistics. Brooks/Cole, CENGAGE Learning (2012)
10. Likert, R.: A technique for the measurement of attitudes. Arch. Psychol. **22**(140), 55 (1932)
11. Besemer, S.P.: Creating Products in the Age of Design: How to Improve Your New Products Ideas! New Forum Press, Stilwater (2013)
12. Krosnick, J.A., Presser, S.: Question and questionnaire design. In: Marsden, P.V., Wright, J.D. (eds.) Handbook of Survey Research. Emerald, Bingley (2010)

Towards a New Tool for Individualized Content Delivery in Classrooms

Markus Maageng Jakobsen[1] ⓘ, Mads Nyborg[2] ⓘ,
and Andrea Valente[3(✉)] ⓘ

[1] Software Engineering, Maersk Mc-Kinney Moller Institute,
University of Southern Denmark (SDU), Odense, Denmark
[2] DTU Compute, Department of Applied Mathematics and Computer Science,
Technical University of Denmark, Lyngby, Denmark
manyb@dtu.dk
[3] Game Development and Learning Technology, Maersk Mc-Kinney Moller
Institute, University of Southern Denmark (SDU), Odense, Denmark
anva@mmmi.sdu.dk

Abstract. This paper focuses on orchestration in the digital, augmented classroom, and in particular the challenges involved with content individualization, and on individualized content delivery to a live classroom. The lack of widely adopted efficient digital tools in this area is established via a systematic e-learning literature review and a survey of existing software tools. Mixed methods are used to investigate current orchestration practices and tools adopted by teachers in secondary education institutions in Denmark and Norway. Based on these initial findings, a prototype for a distributed orchestration tool was designed, implemented, and tested using a variation of an A/B experiment, with a group of university students. Test data and post-test interviews showed that the tool was well received and usable even at this early development stage. An interesting discrepancy emerged in our triangulated data about the efficiency in the test tasks: the participants' perceived, and self-reported, that performance efficiency was lower than what we measured, a phenomenon common when investigating tacit knowledge in practices. These results are discussed, as well as problems with the current prototype and future lines of research.

Keywords: Content delivery · Orchestration · e-learning · Tool · Support teachers · Higher education · Augmented classroom

1 Introduction

Modern classrooms are full of technology, such as digital projectors, interactive whiteboards, and student devices. However, classroom teaching rarely utilizes the potential provided by the available technology. Lessons are often driven by linear slides presented by the teacher through a central projector, leaving little room for interactivity or individualization. While many teaching tools exist within this space (as discussed in Sect. 2.1), there appears to be a lack of solutions and research looking to utilize the augmented classroom to facilitate individualized learning for the students.

© Springer Nature Switzerland AG 2021
P. Zaphiris and A. Ioannou (Eds.): HCII 2021, LNCS 12784, pp. 46–64, 2021.
https://doi.org/10.1007/978-3-030-77889-7_4

Moreover, existing research often leans towards automation of assessments and quiz-related activities, without direct interaction with a teacher. And while there is an increasing amount of presentation tools with reasonable facilities for attendee interaction, they lack forms of content individualization, and are primarily designed based on a philosophy that "one size fits all". Even the recent increase of distant learning, supported by video-conference tools such as Zoom and Google Meet, does not appear to address these issues and instead it presents a more complex landscape where the augmented classroom is partially or completely distributed.

In this paper we focus on individualized content delivery to a live classroom; in particular, we are interested in what can be considered individualized lesson content, and what constitutes a usable and efficient delivery of such content.

Our first step was to systematically survey existing tools and related literature (see Sect. 2). To learn about current orchestration practices we then conducted an investigation through a questionnaire, addressing 22 teachers from Danish and Norwegian educational institutions, focusing on the adopted tools and approaches. From our literature we identified a range of approaches to orchestrating individualized content, while the analysis of questionnaire data revealed that teachers mainly use presentation tools such as PowerPoint alongside other exercise-focused tools. The findings suggested that it could be possible to design and implement a usable and efficient classroom orchestration tool, capable of facilitating the delivery of individualized content in a live classroom setting. Our working hypothesis is that such a tool can be developed using data from existing classroom orchestration and teacher's experiences with existing tools and techniques. To test this hypothesis, we proceeded by defining requirements, then design and iteratively implement a minimum viable product (MVP) of this new tool. Finally, we performed and analyzed data from a task-based comparative experiment, complemented by post-test interviews. This mixed methods approach was designed to capture both subjective experiences about the efficiency of our MVP, and objective parameters, such as the amount of work and time required to complete the test tasks.

The rest of the paper is organized as follows: Sect. 2 presents related work and a survey of existing software tools; Sect. 3 presents our findings from the preliminary study about current orchestration practices. Section 4 discusses requirements, design, and implementation of the MVP. The experiment and general discussion of the findings are found in Sects. 5 and 6. Section 7 concludes the paper.

2 Related Work

According to recent research, during the last decade digital classroom environments have reached the point where each student has access to one or more devices connected to a wireless network [3–[5]. Harper and Milman [6] reported in their review of 10 years of literature, that by utilizing this potential, it is possible to achieve more meaningful individualized instruction. They reported positive findings with regards to learner achievement, and that these environments can provide a more enriched learning experience. However, they found mixed results regarding student engagement partially attributed to the initial motivation of using new software (see [6]).

Adapting to new, digital tools is typically a complex process for both learners and teachers, and in this context it becomes important to evaluate the effects of digital presentations against that of traditional oral instruction. Moulton, Türkay and Kosslyn [7] for instance compare Microsoft's PowerPoint and the online alternative Prezi, against oral instruction. They provisionally conclude that software-aided presentations are more effective than oral presentations for persuading audiences, but found no evidence indicating benefits towards learning outcome, recollection, or understanding of the content. Moreover, Apperson, Laws and Scepansky found in their study [9] that the use of PowerPoint had a positive effect on learners' engagement and that teachers' likeability was improved. However, in another study, Chou, Chang and Lu [10] could not reject the possibility that the positive findings on long term knowledge acquisition were due to the novelty effect [11].

Other research into increasing engagement and learning through digital tools such as Kahoot![1] reported positive findings with regards to learner-teacher engagement and capturing learners' interest. Kahoot's quizzes also provide a break from long learning sessions, allowing for reflection and discussion of content. The novelty effect could play a major role with an online tool like Kahoot!, designed to be colorful and playful, however, we found little research focusing on it. Moreover, other studies about the use of Kahoot! have found non-conclusive indications of increased learning [14], and no correlation between perceived students' engagement and resulting assessment grade [13].

Moving from digital tools to the process of running a live classroom, we considered the concept of classroom orchestration, defined as "How a teacher manages, in real-time, multi-layered activities in a multi-constraints context" [18]. However, Roschelle, Dimitriadis, and Hoppe [18] remark the lack of a consensus on this definition; in addition, they describe how aspects of classroom orchestration deserve more attention, particularly with regards to typical teachers' problems within the domain of orchestration, such as curriculum design, deployment of assessment (formative as well as summative), and the use of time and spatial resources. An important find in [18] is that classrooms are complex environments, and that teachers' role is often to adapt materials to their specific classroom's configuration. We have observed similar roles in teachers also in our research on primary schools in Denmark [2]. According to [18] orchestration is becoming more structured, moving away from ad-hoc solutions invented by individual teachers, and showing instead a "diffusion of innovation" perspective.

The complexities of orchestration are mirrored in the diversity and specificities of learners. This project focuses on the idea of individualized content delivery, which in turn is based on differentiated instruction. According to [19] "differentiation is responsive instruction designed to meet unique individual student needs", and it enables students to learn in the same environment using the same curriculum, by differentiating the learning tasks, outcomes, and entry-points to the students' needs (see also [8]). The findings in [19] also point to the importance of appropriate grouping of learners, as a central feature of the learning environment; the authors also observe "working with students in small groups is often aligned with differentiated content or

---

[1] Kahoot! official website: https://kahoot.com/.

products of instruction", and this alignment extends to text selection (or more in general in our case, content selection), so that learners are faced with relevant contents, appropriate to their level of expertise.

While in literature differentiated instruction appears to be the most used label, both individualized and personalized instruction or learning is also found in the same context, and there appears to be mixed consensus on its use. This paper will therefore use individualized learning as an umbrella term.

2.1 Existing Software Tools

There is a variety of tools intended to aid teaching, ranging from pure presentation tools, to quiz and assessment tools, as well as classroom management software. The latter has not been included in this analysis as it typically deals with the planning and orchestrating of classes in general, and not live content delivery.

This evaluation is based on the systematic literature reviews method, and in particular on the approach discussed in [16] which pertains the review of technical and software-related papers. The software tools in this evaluation were identified through online searches for a wide range of related terms, as well as based on the recommendation from a focus group of teachers, acting as experts; the final list of software includes: Kahoot!, PowerPoint, Google Slides, Zoho, Show, Prezi, Nearpod, Creedoo, Peardeck, SlideDog, Socrative, Quizlet, Quizziz, Mentimeter, Storyline, and Zzish. A set of data points was gathered for each software tool, identifying its presentation options, non-linearity, content and interaction individualization, attendee management, and other relevant features. From the constructed feature matrix (an excerpt of the matrix is visible in Table 1), it is apparent that many tools have overlapping goals and features since they address many of the same problems. For example, the interactivity within Google Slides and PowerPoint is limited at the authoring activity, since real-time collaboration and interaction is possible only through the presentation and only when it is not in active presentation mode; this makes these tools less viable for large scale individualization and interactivity. Some of the tools in our matrix are primarily quizzing and assessment tools, with limited or no options for content presentations, while others are more traditional slide-based presentation tools.

Overall, the two most significant shortcomings of the identified software are the lack of support for presenting individualized content to participants, and to organize groups of attendees (as in Table 1). No tool appears to support individualisable contents, with the exception of only Zzish, that offers a very limited support, enabling teachers to specify some additional content for students depending on how they did in a quiz. Interestingly, some tools do offer interactivity features, mostly in the form of an option to register the individual user's interactions; however, the interactions themselves are not individualisable. An important aspect of attendees' management is grouping, and in our review only Socrative provides a presenter-managed organization of learners' groups, while Quizlet and Quizziz have an automatic grouping option.

Table 1. Excerpt from the feature matrix with key findings.

FEATURE	REMOTE DISPLAY VIEWING	REMOTE INTERACTION	REMOTE DISPLAY INTERACTION	INDIVIDUALISED INTERACTION	INDIVIDUALISED CONTENT	NONLINEAR PROGRESSION	GROUPABLE ATTENDEES
KAHOOT!	Limited	Full	None	Full	None	None	No
POWERPOINT	Limited	None	None	None	None	Limited	No
GOOGLE SLIDES	Limited	Limited	Limited	None	None	Limited	No
ZOHO SHOW	Full	Limited	Limited	Limited	None	Limited	No
PREZI	None	None	None	None	None	Full	No
NEARPOD	Full	Full	None	Full	None	Limited	No
CREEDOO	Full	Full	N/A	N/A	None	Limited	N/A
PEARDECK	Full	Full	None	Full	None	Full	No
SLIDEDOG	Full	Full	Limited	Full	None	Limited	No
SOCRATIVE	Full	Full	None	Full	None	None	By Presenter
QUIZLET	Full	Full	None	Full	None	None	Automatic
QUIZZIZ	Full	Full	None	Full	None	None	Automatic
MENTIMETER	Full	Full	Full	Full	None	None	No
STORYLINE	None	None	None	Full	None	Full	No
ZZISH	Full	Full	None	Full	Limited	Limited	No

3   Preliminary Study: Orchestration Practices

We conducted a preliminary field study on the practices and tools used in the orchestration of augmented classroom live lectures, with focus on individualization. The resulting questionnaire was sent to Danish and Norwegian teachers, and we collected responses from 22 teachers: 5 working in primary schools, 6 in middle schools, 9 in high-schools and 4 university teachers. The main purpose of the questionnaire was to identify what tools teachers use to individualize their lesson content, what content gets individualized, and what factors affect how they individualize it; most questions were in the form of multiple choice and Likert scales, with additional text answers to further elaborate where necessary.

The range of different approaches to orchestrating individualized content identified through the questionnaire shows that teachers mainly use presentation tools, such as PowerPoint, alongside other exercise-focused tools, to piece together a teaching toolset which works well for each individual teacher. While these teachers appear to share much of their pedagogical theories and reasons behind individualization approaches, we could see little consensus on how to put this knowledge into practice. Individual teachers' choice seems to be the norm, suggesting a lack of an up-to-date, theoretically founded consensus concerning digital educational tools in teachers' training.

Figure 1 shows at which institutions the respondents are currently teaching; since some respondents were involved in both primary and middle school levels, Fig. 1 shows the resulting 24 data points.

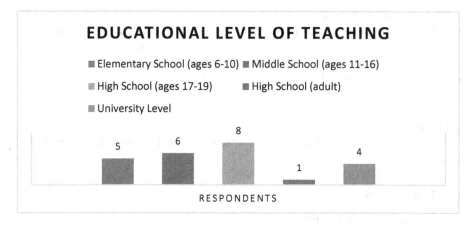

Fig. 1. Educational level of teaching for respondents.

All 22 respondents reported that they use digital tools to aid their teaching; of these, PowerPoint and Kahoot! are the most used for teaching in general, with 19 (86%) and 18 (82%) respondents respectively using them. These were followed by interactive whiteboards with 10 respondents (45%). All university teachers use PowerPoint, complemented by other tools, such as Kahoot!. PowerPoint is also the most used tool for delivering individualized lesson content, with 9 respondents (41%), followed by Quizlet with 5 respondents (23%). A summary of these findings is visible in Fig. 2. In Fig. 2 each value represents usage by one respondent, with multiple unique responses allowed per respondent; university teachers' responses are highlighted in blue; among university teachers the most used tools were PowerPoint and Google Slides (75%).

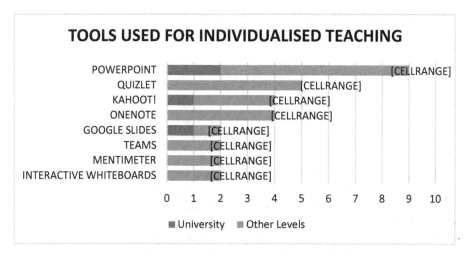

Fig. 2. Tools used specifically for delivering individualized lesson content.

The respondents were also asked to indicate what types of content they normally individualize. We found that 19 respondents (86%) individualize questions, exercises, and assignments; furthermore, 10 (45%) individualize informative content, such as concepts and general theory, but 9 of these responses were in both categories. All university teachers reported that they individualize questions, exercises, and assignments, and half of them also the informative content.

In conclusion, our data shows that PowerPoint is the most used tool for teaching, as well as being the used most tool to deliver individualized content, followed by Quizlet. These findings formed the basis for the design our final experiment, discussed in Sect. 5.

3.1 Requirements

Based on the data from the questionnaire and the systematic review of software tools, we established the core requirement for the new tool: being able to deliver individualized content to students in a classroom. Use cases were used to collect essential requirements (see Fig. 3). We further specified the actors by constructing personas for the relevant stakeholders (following the approach in [17]) i.e., teacher and student, and integrated the personas directly with feedback from stakeholders. Table 2 shows the two resulting personas.

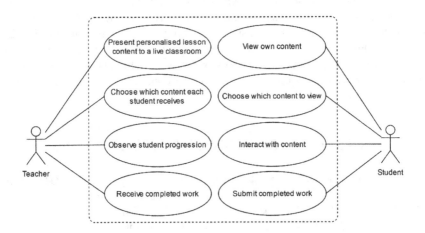

Fig. 3. Use-case diagram summarizing requirements.

From the analysis of our data and the personas, a set of functional requirements was defined, along with a set of quality attribute scenarios (QAS), which addressed the non-functional requirements of the software. A quality attribute is a testable property of a system which is used when measuring how well a system delivers its functionality; while there are several categories of quality attributes, the key ones for our new e-learning tool are performance and usability. Performance quality attributes typically measure how long it takes to complete a given task when a particular event occurs. In our case, we are addressing performance by considering the delay times in our distributed e-learning tool: for example, we require that when the teacher moves the presentation forward one slide, this change should be visible by all students in less than one second (i.e., a loose definition of real-time, that fits with the web-based nature of our new tool). Also, when a student is working on an interactive slide (e.g., a short quiz or an exercise to be solved), the time required for her solution to be submitted to the teacher through our tool, should take no more than one second. Considering that the data exchanged by our actors are rather simple, and that a class is usually composed of a small number of users, using the software at the same time, meeting the timings specified in the QAS's did not pose a challenge for the MVP.

The other important quality attribute we considered is usability, defined as the ease with which users interact with the system to achieve a desired task; usability is strongly correlated with the users' experience of a system, and in particular with the sense of how efficiently it operates. The response measures associated with usability are typically dependent on the interactions of individual users, which make them more complex to test and verify (as discussed in Sect. 5, where our main test is presented).

Table 2. Teacher and student personas: definitions and objectives.

Teacher	
Who?	The teacher is the conductor of the lesson. They are responsible for delivering the lesson content to the students and the pacing of the class progression
What do they want?	The teacher wants to be able to deliver individualized content to their students depending on their interests, abilities, and other needs; to control the class as a whole and ensure everyone progresses at a similar pace; to receive the completed work of students
Student	
Who?	The student is a participant of the lesson. They receive the lesson content and perform any activities accordingly with an aim to learn
What do they want?	The student wants to receive individualized content to make learning more interesting and engaging; to be able to interact with the lesson content; to make independent choices of what content to experience

Having defined functional and non-functional requirements, we also wanted to have a user story for our tool. In the scenario, a teacher can create sessions during a lecture, and the students will join these sessions using online devices; the students are then presented with individualized content. This content is organized as a semi-linear presentation, i.e., a linear sequence of slides with each slide potentially consisting of multiple variations, to account for classroom diversity and individual student problems or skill levels. Different students will therefore be shown different variations of the same slide, with varying degrees of complexity and support in the examples and explanations. Control over which parts of the content are accessed is either given to the teacher, or optionally to the students themselves. Students can be dynamically grouped in real-time, to simplify the distribution of contents and to provide a collaborative experience. The individualized content can offer various degrees of interactivity, ranging from reading a text to simple exercises, eventually allowing students to submit results to the teacher. Teachers are able to observe students' progress either in real-time, during in-lecture activities; moreover, in our scenario specific content can also be selected and delivered to the individual student as part of preparation for a lecture, allowing the teacher use more of lecture time for discussion and reflection, in line with the flipped classroom approach.

4   Design and Implementation of Prototype

A typical three-tier architecture was chosen for the new tool, which was designed considering the requirements and the scenario (Fig. 4). The main components are a server, a database, and two specialized clients: a teacher and a student client (a need discussed also in [2]).

The student client provides students with an individualized view into the session created by a teacher, which is handled and synchronized through a server. Any related data such as lesson content and persistent user data is stored in the database. The teacher client enables control of what content is being shown to each attending student using a semi-linear presentation structure in addition to tools for managing the class-room session.

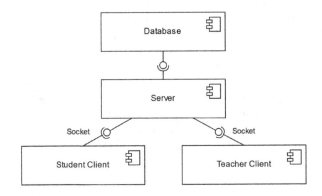

Fig. 4. Design-level component diagram of the e-learning tool.

4.1   Presentation Format

In order to facilitate the individualization of lesson content efficiently and flexibly, we need to reconceptualize sequential presentations. Existing presentation formats such as PowerPoint are entirely linear, and every student is presented the same material in the same sequence. Instead, we propose to enrich the structure of a presentation so that it can still be considered an almost-linear sequence, but we allow each slide to consist potentially of multiple versions, to account for learners' diversity (as depicted in Fig. 5). Some slides of the sequence can be simple slides, while other are allowed to be slide collections, i.e., vertically stacked slides meant to explain the same concept in multiple ways from more formal to more practical, for instance.

With this format a teacher can anticipate the need to explain the same concept at 2 or 3 different levels or use examples at various degree of complexity to cover a particular topic. According to our scenario, during class, each student uses our client application, and gets assigned individual sub-indexes for a slide collection: the result is that students see different content, while the presentation remains on the same overall slide index. In Fig. 5, when the whole class is working on slide 2 (which is in fact a slide collection), some students will see slide 2a, while others will see slide 2b on their client application. Each simple slide inside a slide collection can then be assigned by the teacher, or optionally requested by students themselves, in an attempt to ensure that all students see the content which is most suited to them.

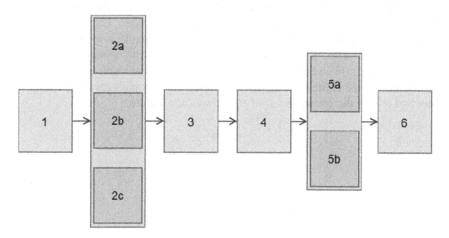

Fig. 5. Presentation format: each column indicates a slide in a presentation. Slide 2 and 5 are *slide collections* containing simple slides, to allow for individualization.

From a technical point of view, in our format a presentation contains slides of two types: simple slides and slide collections (which can contain other simple slides). Slides are implemented via a composite design pattern, and that also allows for easy extensions of the simple slides, such as multiple-choice slides, slides with embedded animations or interactive simulations. Simplified versions of these interactive slides are in fact implemented in our prototype.

4.2   Implementation

The design is implemented as an MVP prototype, capable of running online as a client-server system, and with enough functionalities to allow for testing.

Of the components in Fig. 4, the server is the one providing the majority of the required functionalities. It is responsible for sessions created by a teacher and acts as a communication relay between all clients connected to a particular session, through communication protocols that were derived from our requirement. The server keeps a centralized global state of all sessions, including a session identifier, presentation slides and current viewing state, and a list of attendees. The server manages individualization by keeping track of the specific slide that is presented to each attendee, as well as the dynamic state of the interactive slides (e.g., the answers generated when a learner engages with one of the multiple-choice slides). After every interaction received from a client, the server updates the client's state.

The system also has two types of clients (visible in Fig. 6): the teacher and student client. They are both implemented to be lightweight and capable of displaying the relevant session data and managing the receiving and sending of events to the server. Both clients maintain a reference to the server, which is used to publish and subscribe to events to and from the server. A client also maintains a local state to make the system more responsive, however, the local state is overwritten whenever newer data is received from the server. The student client allows its user to view the current slide in a live presentation, and also to interact with the interactive slides. The teacher client is designed to behave similarly to the student client and therefore includes the same functionalities. However, it also keeps information about the session id, the list of connected attendees (including the dynamic state of their assignments and interactions), and an outline of the entire presentation. A dashboard view presents these data to the teacher and allows the orchestration of the flow of the lecture.

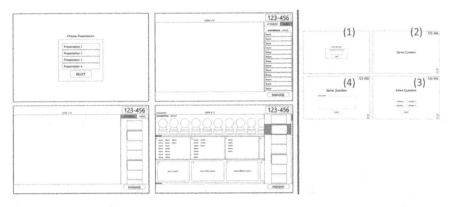

Fig. 6. Initial GUI mockup for the teacher (on the left) and student client (on the right).

The left part of Fig. 6 shows the teacher client. In clockwise sequence, starting from the top-left screen:

- the list of all available presentations;
- the main presentation view with the list of attending students on the right;
- the bottom-right screen shows the *content assignment* window, where the students can be assigned to the slides of the current presentation;
- finally, the bottom-left screen shows the *presentation view* along with an overview of the presentation: a stacked rectangle indicates a slide collection.

The right part of Fig. 6 shows instead the mockup of the user interface for the student client: the student can login (marked as 1 in Fig. 6), then she could be shown a simple slide (marked as 2), a multiple-choice slide (marked as 3), or a "text answer" (a simple kind of interactive slide we used in the test, as discussed in Sect. 5).

Figure 7 is a composite image showing five student clients and one teacher client (in the bottom-right corner). The teacher client shows the assignment screen, while the 5 students are all assigned to one of two possible sub-slides, indexed 4a and 4b. The slides 4a and 4b are interactive and Fig. 7 shows that some students have already submitted their answers and received automatic feedback.

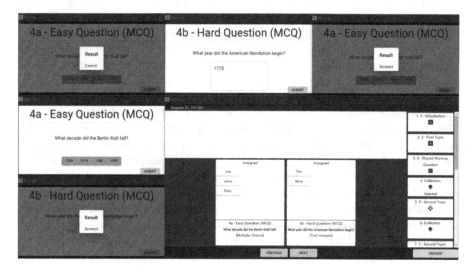

Fig. 7. The two kind of clients in the implemented prototype.

The prototype was developed by one of the authors, following an agile approach, with a backlog, sprints, and milestones; GitHub was used as code repository and for version control. The tool prototype is composed of a Node.js backend server managing all active sessions and clients. The backend server and clients are written in TypeScript and communicate using a custom communication protocol over the Socket.IO framework. Moreover, both clients are implemented in React. Functional testing was performed periodically during sprints, and the system performed adequately with all technical tests achieving well within their set targets (see requirements in Sect. 3).

After the final sprint, the final prototype was deployed to a cloud service provider with a combined teacher and student frontend client, and a backend server managing each session and all necessary data persistence. The prototype ran on virtualized server hardware called a Droplet on the cloud computing service DigitalOcean. The server used Ubuntu 18.04.1 and ran on a single virtual CPU core with 1 GB RAM and 25 GB disk space. Moreover, Docker was used to manage the builds during sprints, and to run them on the servers. Finally, the database functionality was initially implemented using a database-as-a-service product from MongoDB called Atlas. However, due to the need for persistence only extending to the actual presentation content at this stage, data persistence through local files was used instead, storing the presentations as JSON files.

5 Experiment

After finishing the development of the initial MVP prototype, an experiment was conducted to assess the usability and performance of our prototype. The test participants were a focus group of 14 university students (from the University of Southern Denmark). The participants were chosen in part because they represent a convenience sample for the authors, given that Corona restrictions were in effect during the development of this project. However, according to our experience with e-learning at the University level, and according to what stated by Boelens et al. [12], these students are highly diverse in interests, competencies, and readiness for learning. They are, consequently, an appropriate sample when investigating better and more efficient tools to manage individualized learning.

The experiment was organized as a variation of A/B testing [1], with the participants performing predefined tasks divided in groups, with or without our tool; we added an element of role-play to the test, by asking some participant to act as teacher and others as student. Simple scripts-like instructions were provided to prime the participants in their roles, called "presentation brief for teachers" and "for students"; they were introduced to the participants during the pre-test meeting. The students-participants were asked to select a specific role among: Strong Student, Slow Student, Lazy Student, and Normal Student. Roles were explained in the brief, so that each student-participant could role-play the chosen role appropriately. Each session was recorded, observational notes were taken by the authors, and all participants were given a follow-up survey focusing on perceived usability and efficiency of the tool.

5.1 Test Preparation and Setup

To perform this experiment, we needed an actual presentation that could take advantage of our new semi-linear presentation format, so we developed one covering some historical and some technical topics (in order to show the potential of semi-linear presentations in both the humanistic and the technical context).

The systematic survey and the questionnaire were the basis to decide which parts of the presentation should be individualized, and how this individualization was to be controlled: by either the teachers-participants or the students-participants. We then manually converted the presentation to both our new tool's format, and PowerPoint, with the interactive content delivered through separate documents representing each slide collection, with each student assigned one slide from each of these documents. Student responses were handled through a Zoom session's chat. Effort was taken to ensure minimal deviation from the original presentation, for both formats, which is why, while used by most teachers, we did not use Quizlet as it did not have suitable functionality for this scenario. The resulting structure of the presentation is visible in Fig. 8, and the tasks were designed to show that with our MVP both teachers and students can be in control of a presentation's flow at different times.

The experiment was executed in four separate groups, where two were test groups, and two were control groups. Each group consisted of one participant acting as the teacher, and three acting as students. The "teachers" were selected randomly within each group, and for the second session of each group, one random "student" was asked to repeat the experiment as a "teacher". The test group used the new software tool, while the teachers-participants of the second group (i.e., the control group working with the currently used tools) presented the same material and performed the same tasks with their student-participants. All participants were physically present during the experiment, with the exception of two who attended remotely via a Zoom meeting.

Through two test group sessions and two control group sessions data was gathered from three points of views: each session's duration was recorded, and both the teacher and student participants were surveyed upon completion of the session, asking for their perceived efficiency of the system.

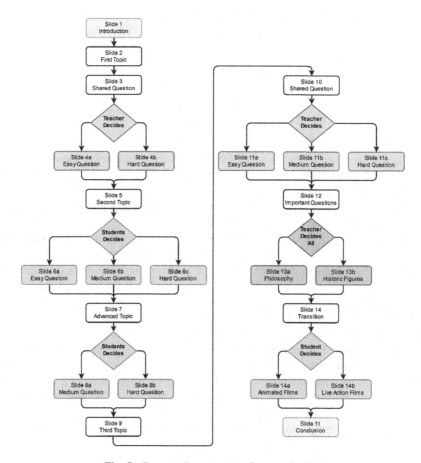

Fig. 8. Presentation structure for experiment.

5.2   Findings

The desired outcome of both groups is to successfully deliver individualized content. Hence, we decided that measuring the time it takes to achieve the desired result would indicate its efficiency: shorter time is regarded as an indication of higher efficiency. However, as it is critically important for a classroom orchestration tool to be adopted by its users, both students' and teachers perceived, subjective opinion on the system's efficiency is also be considered. Data triangulation was therefore used to combine task-completion timing, used as a quantitative efficiency measure, with the qualitative, self-reported post-test surveys.

The first quantitative data we collected is the session duration, visible in Table 3. According to the table, the prototype tool behaved measurably more efficient than the currently used tools (i.e., PowerPoint), with the test groups on average completing their sessions 37.6% faster than the control groups.

Table 3. Session duration measurements and descriptive statistics.

Session duration data		
	Test group	Control group
1	8 m 40 s	13 m
2	9 m 4 s	13 m 48 s
Mean	**8 m 52.1 s**	**13 m 24 s**
Range	**24 s**	**48 s**

The subjective measurements made by the participants regarding the efficiency of the system were recorded using a 5-point Likert scale ranging from "Very inefficient" (scored as -2) to "Very efficient" (scored as 2). Both teachers and students-participants were asked to rate various aspects of a session's efficiency, with a final overall efficiency at the end. Students in the test group reportedly considered their session more efficient than those in the control group; as for receiving exercises, the test group reported higher efficiency, with a mean 0.33 higher than the control group. With regards to submitting answers, the control group reported a marginal lead on efficiency, with the mean difference being 0.17 in favor of the control group. However, in the final question of overall efficiency the test group reported a mean of 0.17 higher than the control group.

Given the small number of teachers-participants, a quantitative analysis of the data from their post-test interviews would not lead to statistically significant data; nevertheless, we computed four key statistics: Efficiency of showing content to students (a), efficiency of assigning content to individual students (b), efficiency of observing student progress (c), and overall efficiency (d). Each of these were rated from -2 "Very inefficient" to 2 "Very efficient", and a compound statistic was created by averaging them, as shown in the diagram of Fig. 9. The figure also shows a similar statistic for students, based on four perceived efficiency measures: Efficiency of getting started with a session (a), efficiency of receiving exercises (b), efficiency of submitting answers (c), and overall lesson efficiency (d). An interesting find was a clear separation between the two teacher groups with respect to the overall measurement of perceived efficiency (d): both teachers of the test group reported the same overall efficiency of "Somewhat inefficient", which resulted in a mean score of -1, a total of 3 points less than the control group, where both teachers reported the overall lesson as "Very efficient". This is a negative result for our prototype, therefore, we decided to conduct informal interviews with the participants acting as teachers, in order to possibly gain more qualitative data. We found that the teachers of the control groups thought our tool performed very efficient in the tests, but voiced concerns as to its scalability, in particular with respect to managing large numbers of answers from the students. Also, the teachers-participants in the test groups said that the prototype was efficient, but complained about the user experience, the unfamiliarity with the tool, and that the lack of visibility of what each student-participant was seeing and doing, explaining how these problems were responsible for the low overall efficiency score they had self-reported. One of them stated that the unfamiliarity with the process of assigning students to groups with the prototype, in particular having little familiarity with neither the content nor the students, made the experience "overwhelming".

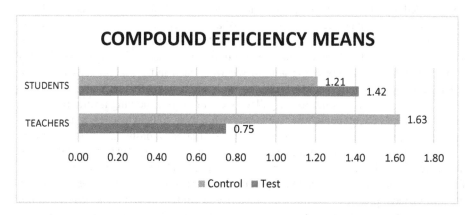

Fig. 9. Perceived efficiency: test and control groups.

Figure 9 shows the result of compounding all the self-reported data regarding efficiency into a single statistic. While the students in the test group reported better perceived efficiency, for the teachers we found the opposite, with the control group perceiving better efficiency with the current tools.

6   Discussion

From the results in Sect. 5, it is of course not possible to draw a clear conclusion circa the efficiency of our MVP. However, the goal of this project is to establish the requirements, design criteria and feasibility of a digital, live classroom orchestration tool to facilitate the delivery of individualized content. Moreover, the experiment presented in the previous section is only an early test, with a convenience sample of users. It provided insights into the usability of the current design of the prototype, but more experiments will be needed, involving our network of primary and secondary school teachers in Denmark.

Being aware of the limitations of this first experiment, we complemented efficiency with other parameters, such as technical performance, usability for both teachers and students, and perceived efficiency. The performance requirements, such as fast delivery of presentation to the students and of assignments' solutions back to teachers, were easily achieved by our prototype, mainly because of the limited number of users in our experiments, which in turn resulted in a low load on the system. Benchmark testing performed during development showed that the current architecture of the prototype, based on Node.js, React and Socket.IO, has the potential to scale up to a realistic number of participant (e.g. primary school classrooms in Demark range typically from 15 to 30 pupils, and university classrooms usually do not exceed 50 students); however, some effort would be needed to streamline the structure of the semi-linear presentations and the storing of individuals' assignments and interactions.

Considering the limited user interface, the unfamiliarity of the new tool, and the fact that the contents (i.e., the presentation in Fig. 8) were created by the authors and not decided by the test participants, the prototype did satisfy our main usability requirements, as supported by our analysis and observations. However, teachers-participants reported that the user interface was "confusing", as they struggled to find some of the information they felt they needed during their tasks. They also reported that a major hindrance was not being able to see what each individual student was seen, dynamically, as the presentation proceeded. This suggests that adding a "group view" to the teacher's client (similar to the gallery view in Zoom) showing a simplified view of each student's client, could improve clarity. Moreover, to help teachers manage large numbers of presentations, the teacher client should adopt a dashboard design pattern.

The analysis of the data we collected during the development and testing of the MVP also revealed that teachers have a practice of individualizing content, which involves forms of content differentiation, to adapt it to the students in a class. To assess our MVP, we formulated a practical definition of efficiency of content delivery, measured by both objective timings of the session and subjective, self-reported experiences by both types of users (teachers and students). In the process of defining how a presentation can be individualized by a teacher, we defined a semi-linear presentation format, with simple slides and slide collections; simple slides can also be interactive, for example containing multiple-choice questions. Interviews and our early observations show that the participants of our experiment responded positively to the idea and could work with these semi-linear presentations. We have not yet investigated the editing of the semi-linear presentations, but the data so far collected on our prototype supports the need to be conservative and provide consistent and known user interfaces to teachers; we are therefore considering a variation of existing presentation-authoring tools, to avoid the problems that teachers could face by having to adapt to an unfamiliar interface.

Finally, an interesting discrepancy emerged in our triangulated data about the efficiency in the experiment's tasks: all participants reported a lower efficiency than what we measured. In previous research with e-learning and Scandinavian teachers, this phenomenon is typically associated tacit knowledge in skill practices (as in [20] and [1]). That in turn suggests that to improve our prototype further, we should rely on ethnographic methods and long-term observations not only of the experts in orchestration practices (i.e. teachers), but also of the socio-material relations that exist in the educational institutions, among teachers and other stakeholders (such as administrators, pedagogy specialists and technology experts working for schools), because tacit knowledge is embedded in the processes and can require to look at the actors and roles in organizations.

7 Conclusion

In this paper we focus on individualized content delivery to a live classroom, in particular, we are interested in what can be considered individualized lesson content, and what constitutes a usable and efficient delivery of such contents. A knowledge gap is identified, in the lack of widely adopted efficient digital tools in this domain, and a working hypothesis is that a new tool for individualized content delivery can be designed and implemented, that is based on data from existing classroom orchestration and teacher's experiences with existing tools and techniques. We developed a testable minimum viable product and performed a preliminary experiment that compares the identified current approach against our new tool. Most teachers that answered our questionnaire do deliver individualized content, following various criteria as to how and what to differentiate in their contents; moreover, teachers currently adopt a presentation tool as well as an interactive testing/quizzing tool for individualization. Based on these findings, we realized the need for a different kind of presentation structure; we therefore defined a novel semi-linear presentation format that allows for grouping of slides, as well as interactive, quiz-like slides.

Our MVP was tested with encouraging results for an early prototype, and the negative feedback we received was mainly focused on unfamiliarity and the rather crude user-interface. However, the MVP is fully functional and fulfils the majority of the technical requirements; and this early evidence supports our belief that the new tool has the potential to help teachers in orchestrating lectures with individualized contents in the augmented classroom, including the increasingly relevant blended scenario where part of a class attends remotely.

Future work includes better usability and improved UI, especially for the teacher client. Further tests are needed to explore the computer-supported collaborative learning potential of the tool. We are currently developing more examples of semi-linear presentations, across different school subjects, and planning further tests involving classes in local Danish institutions.

References

1. Preece, J., Sharp, H., Rogers, Y.: Interaction Design: Beyond Human-Computer Interaction. Wiley, Hoboken (2015)
2. Marchetti, E., Valente, A.: It takes three: re-contextualizing game-based learning among teachers, developers and learners. In: Proceedings of the European Conference on Games Based Learning, pp. 399–406 (2016)
3. Niramitranon, J., Sharples, M., Greenhalgh, C., Lin, C.P.: Orchestrating learning in a one-to-one technology classroom. In: 6th IEEE International Conference on Wireless, Mobile and Ubiquitous Technologies in Education, WMUTE 2010, Mob. Soc. Media Learn. Educ. Form. Informal Settings, pp. 96–103 (2010). https://doi.org/10.1109/WMUTE.2010.32

4. Bergström, P., Mårell-Olsson, E., Jahnke, I.: variations of symbolic power and control in the one-to-one computing classroom: Swedish teachers' enacted didactical design decisions. Scand. J. Educ. Res. **63**(1), 38–52 (2019). https://doi.org/10.1080/00313831.2017.1324902
5. Higgins, K., BuShell, S.: The effects on the student-teacher relationship in a one-to-one technology classroom. Educ. Inf. Technol. **23**(3), 1069–1089 (2017). https://doi.org/10.1007/s10639-017-9648-4
6. Harper, B., Milman, N.B.: One-to-one technology in K-12 classrooms: a review of the literature from 2004 through 2014. J. Res. Technol. Educ. **48**(2), 129–142 (2016). https://doi.org/10.1080/15391523.2016.1146564
7. Moulton, S.T., Türkay, S., Kosslyn, S.M.: Does a presentation's medium affect its message? PowerPoint, Prezi Oral Presentations **12**(7) (2017). https://doi.org/10.1371/journal.pone.0178774
8. Hall, T., Strangman, N., Meyer, A.: Differentiated instruction and implications for UDL implementation. National Center on Accessing the General Curriculum, Wakefield (2003)
9. Apperson, J.M., Laws, E.L., Scepansky, J.A.: The impact of presentation graphics on students' experience in the classroom. Comput. Educ. **47**(1), 116–126 (2006). https://doi.org/10.1016/j.compedu.2004.09.003
10. Chou, P.N., Chang, C.C., Lu, P.F.: Prezi versus PowerPoint: the effects of varied digital presentation tools on students' learning performance. Comput. Educ. **91**, 73–82 (2015). https://doi.org/10.1016/j.compedu.2015.10.020
11. Burke, L.A., James, K.E.: PowerPoint-based lectures in business education: an empirical investigation of student-perceived novelty and effectiveness. Bus. Commun. Q. **71**(3), 277–296 (2008). https://doi.org/10.1177/1080569908317151
12. Boelens, R., Voet, M., De Wever, B.: The design of blended learning in response to student diversity in higher education: instructors' views and use of differentiated instruction in blended learning. Comput. Educ. **120**, 197–212 (2018). https://doi.org/10.1016/j.compedu.2018.02.009
13. Cameron, K.E., Bizo, L.A.: Use of the game-based learning platform KAHOOT! To facilitate learner engagement in animal science students. Res. Learn. Technol. **27**(1063519), 1–14 (2019). https://doi.org/10.25304/rlt.v27.2225
14. Göksün, D.O., Gürsoy, G.: Comparing success and engagement in gamified learning experiences via Kahoot and Quizizz. Comput. Educ. **135**, 15–29 (2019). https://doi.org/10.1016/j.compedu.2019.02.015
15. Dillenbourg, P.: Design for classroom orchestration. Comput. Educ. **69**, 485–492 (2013). https://doi.org/10.1016/j.compedu.2013.04.013
16. Budgen, D., Brereton, P.: Performing systematic literature reviews in software engineering. In: Proceedings of the 28th International Conference on Software Engineering (2006)
17. Miaskiewicz, T., Kozar, K.A.: Personas and user-centered design: how can personas benefit product design processes? Des. Stud. **32**(5), 417–430 (2011). https://doi.org/10.1016/j.destud.2011.03.003
18. Roschelle, J., Dimitriadis, Y., Hoppe, U.: Classroom orchestration: synthesis. Comput. Educ. **69**, 523–526 (2013). https://doi.org/10.1016/j.compedu.2013.04.010
19. Watts-Taffe, S., Laster, B.P., Broach, L., Marinak, B., Connor, C.M.D., Walker-Dalhouse, D.: Differentiated instruction: making informed teacher decisions. Read. Teach. **66**(4), 303–314 (2012). https://doi.org/10.1002/TRTR.01126
20. Grant, K.A.: Tacit knowledge revisited–we can still learn from Polanyi. Electron. J. Knowl. Manag. **5**(2), 173–180 (2007)

Open Educational Resources for Language Education: Towards the Development of an e-Toolkit

Panagiotis Kosmas[1]([✉]) [iD], Antigoni Parmaxi[1], Maria Perifanou[2] [iD],
and Anastasios A. Economides[2] [iD]

[1] Cyprus Interaction Lab, Cyprus University of Technology,
3075 Limassol, Cyprus
`panayiotis.kosmas@cut.ac.cy`
[2] University of Macedonia, Thessaloniki, Greece

Abstract. The Open Educational Resources (OER) movement is overgrowing over the last 15 years, as many institutions adopt the idea of openness and universal access to educational content. Thus, the research and educational material must be open to everyone interested, including students, adult learners, teachers, professionals, managers, and policymakers. With this in mind, the creation and use of OER is a current educational practice for educators around the world. This manuscript aims to provide an overview of all the core elements for creating, using, and sharing quality multilingual and interactive OERs for Language Education. Specifically, the paper provides an extensive summary of existing language OERs and Open Educational Practices (OEPs), including some important definitions, highlighting the most significant characteristics and challenges in adopting OERs for educational purposes. This review will help language teachers, students, and researchers to create, share, and use quality multilingual and interactive OERs for language learning in their teaching practices.

Keywords: Language education · Language learning · OEP · OER · Open education · OPENLang Network

1 Introduction

The Open Educational Resources (OER), a term coined during a UNESCO Forum, refers to the openness and provision of different resources for educational purposes giving users free access to the educational material and resources to be used in various educational contexts. The OER concept is growing rapidly over the last 15 years, as distance education practices and online learning methodologies have been developed and implemented worldwide. Given that, many institutions adopt the idea of openness and universal access to educational content and provide freely an enormous number of resources to the public. Thus, a lot of educational material and resources are now open and available to everyone interested (i.e., students, adult learners, teachers, professionals, managers, policymakers, etc.) and also accessible for revision and adaptation to a specific context [1].

P. Zaphiris and A. Ioannou (Eds.): HCII 2021, LNCS 12784, pp. 65–79, 2021.
https://doi.org/10.1007/978-3-030-77889-7_5

OERs are increasingly playing a critical role in distance/online learning systems in many countries. Distance learning methods have been facilitated by the available OER, as they offer enhanced access for groups customarily constrained from attending traditional institutions, such as secondary school graduates who fail to gain admission to a university, women with domestic responsibilities, learners residing in remote rural areas, and impoverished or socially marginalized communities [2].

Nowadays, although there are plenty of resources available on the web, it is sometimes difficult to find an adequate OER to use for specific purposes. This manuscript aims to provide a comprehensive overview of all the main aspects of the creation, use, and sharing of OER material for language learning and teaching. The overview will further develop our knowledge about OER and help us create an OER e-toolkit to be used by teachers, researchers, and students. This e-toolkit which is developed in the context of the European project "Open European Languages and Cultures Network", covers the basic steps of finding, using and creating an OER for Language Education.

Furthermore, this e-Toolkit will help language teachers, researchers, and others in this field on creating, sharing and using quality multilingual and interactive OERs for language learning in their teaching practices. Also, many institutions and other stakeholders (e.g., Universities, Schools, Educational organisations, Businesses, etc.) would benefit from possibly adopting this e-Toolkit in their educational practices, promoting openness, multilingualism, collaboration, and quality among others.

In this paper, we first provide an overview of OER, highlighting the most significant characteristics of OER and focusing on benefits and challenges mentioned in the literature. Then, we present an overview of existing OER guidelines for creating/sharing/using language materials and language OER databases, based on the previous successful examples of OER guidelines. Finally, we provide some information regarding the development of the e-toolkit and conclude with some important considerations and future implications.

2 An Overview of Open Educational Resources

2.1 Definitions

The concept of OER was developed in 2002 during an online discussion hosted by UNESCO. OERs are defined "as technology-enabled, open provision of educational resources for consultation, use, and adaptation by a community of users for non-commercial purposes" [3]. According to this definition, OERs refers to freely available digital resources and educational material to support the teachers and the students. These resources usually include learning objects, course materials, textbooks, experiments and demonstrations, and syllabuses, curricula, and teachers' guides [3].

The Organization for Economic Co-operation and Development defined OER as: "digital learning resources offered online ...freely and openly to teachers, educators, students, and independent learners in order to be used, shared, combined, adapted, and expanded in teaching, learning and research" [4, 5]. In this context, OERs are teaching, and learning materials/resources/tools offered freely and openly to anyone and are available under a license that allows users to retain, reuse, revise, remix, and redistribute. The opportunity for remixing, reusing and redistributing OERs developed further the OERs' concept, as this opportunity allows teachers to share the resources with colleagues and students, edit and adjust the material based on their specific needs and local context. Each OER has a Creative Commons or GNU license that states specifically how the material may be used, reused, adapted, and shared.

In the literature, there are two different types of OERs: informal OERs (e.g., social media, mobile calling, texting) and formal OERs (e.g., classroom prescribed learning tools and lectures) on specific development outcomes of functional literacy and perceived employability [6]. Some digital learning contents can be accessed and used freely as OERs in the public domain or introduced with an open license which means that anyone can legally and freely copy, use, adapt, and re-share them [7]. According to many scholars/authors Massive Open Online Courses (MOOCs) are a special case of OERs [8]; others believe MOOCs to be a progressive step in the evolution of OER [9]. In the last decade, the European Union has intensified the promotion of OERs since they can facilitate policy dialogue, knowledge sharing, and collaboration between states and institutions internationally [10].

Sometimes, OERs are interconnected or combined with Open Educational Practices (OEP). According to Ehlers [11] OEP: "is the use of Open Educational Resources for teaching and learning to innovate the learning process". With this in mind, OEPs could be defined as some practices which promote and enhance the use and development of OER following some rules, policies or pedagogical models and frameworks. Specifically, the Open Educational Quality (OPAL) Initiative defines OEPs as: "the use of OER to raise the quality of education and training and innovate educational practices on an institutional, professional and individual level" [12].

In a nutshell, OERs are the educational material freely available on the web while an OEP is actually the implementation, reuse and adjustment of an existing OER. For example, according to Ehlers [11], the pure usage of OERs in a traditional closed and top-down learning environment is not OEP.

2.2 OERs' Principles and Characteristics

OERs' general characteristics and principles, based on the literature, include amongst others, the accessibility to everyone, the openness, the open license for the reusing and modification of the material, the easiness to adapt and adjust in any context and the inclusion of all types of digital media and multimedia applications [13]. Wiley and Green [14] state that OERs should promote the following "4R" activities:

1. Revising which is adapting the OER to meet the needs of the end-user,
2. Remixing – combining or "mashing up" the OER with another OER to produce new materials,
3. Reusing – using the original or derivative versions of the OER in a wide range of new contexts, and
4. Redistributing – sharing the original work or derivative versions with others.

There are numerous OERs examples and categories. Based on the functionality and usage of OERs, there are three major categories of OERs: Directories, Repositories and

Databases. Directories provide resources that are available elsewhere on the Web. Repositories are platforms that offer specific educational material or digital tools designed and developed in the context of OER. Databases are the collection of OER, usually ones created by a particular institution.

Some examples of OERs available to the Web include learning content (i.e., course materials, content modules, learning objects, videos, assignments, journals, etc.), interactive learning environments, digital tools (i.e., software for the creation, use, and improvement of open learning content), digital textbooks, lesson plans for all the educational levels, worksheets, adaptations of previously published OER.

In this context, Economides and Perifanou [15] proposed the OPEN FASUCICESA-CPT model defining the following Open Capabilities for an OER:

- Open to Find (Seek, Locate, Discover);
- Open to Access (View, Watch, Read, Listen, Hear);
- Open to Store (Save, Retain, Download, Copy, Duplicate, Print);
- Open to Use (Control, Manage, Select);
- Open to Create (Design, Develop, Produce, Construct, Build, Calculate, Solve, Modify, Alter, Change, Adapt, Revise, Translate, Mix, Integrate, Combine);
- Open to Interact (Communicate);
- Open to Collaborate (Cooperate, Co-Create);
- Open to Evaluate (Assess, Review, Critique, Rank);
- Open to Share (Distribute, Teach, Publish, Display, Present, Present, Display, Show);
- Open to Abandon (Quit, Drop Out, Leave, Depart) without any penalties, charges, fines, obligations, punishments etc.;
- Open Cost (allow anyone to participate at no cost);
- Open Place (allow anyone to participate from anywhere);
- Open Time (allow anyone to participate anytime).

2.3   Benefits and Challenges in Using OER in Education

OERs offer great opportunities for learners, students, teachers, and educational institutions as OERs give access to a plethora of resources and content. Nowadays, learning materials can be easily distributed, shared, and adapted to meet learners' needs and interests. There is evidence from the literature that there are some important benefits of using and sharing OERs.

First of all, OERs could increase learners' motivation and engagement [16]. Shmueli [16] claims that the use and sharing of OERs can enhance education and research, reduce the costs of educational resources' development by reusing existing resources, enhance the demand for life-long learning, and allow adjusting of existing educational materials for local needs. It is also argued that OERs create opportunities for more personalised learning experiences and increase students' engagement [17]. For example, OERs can engage and motivate students with different socio-cognitive backgrounds in the learning process [17]. Some studies revealed that OERs increase students' productivity by boosting their confidence, interest, and satisfaction while other studies show that OERs' awareness is growing [18]. The use of OER is a way to enrich and enhance traditional course content in every subject and specifically in language learning. The conventional classroom can be enriched using OERs multi-media material, presenting information in multiple formats, and helping students earn the material being taught more easily. The digital resources (e.g., applications, tools, etc.) that OERs offer should be considered valuable OERs in language learning and teaching [19]. Indeed, OERs can facilitate the teaching based on some pedagogical approaches creating language awareness.

Furthermore, students anywhere in the world can access OERs at any time, and they can access the material repeatedly. This means that many people can benefit from the educational content, which is a good thing for both learners and teachers. In that way, OERs increase access to educational materials for a wider range of learners, predominantly those underserved by traditional educational opportunities. Also, OERs help teachers to expand their roles and find innovative ideas to implement in their classes [18, 20], support teaching and learning practices [21] and finally reduce costs for teachers and students during the course [22]. Also, previous studies [5, 23] claimed that teachers use OERs to enrich their teaching methods and practices as well as to interact with other colleagues [24]. According to [25], the use of OERs promotes innovation in teaching practice enriching the teaching methods, strategies and existing curriculum and content, increases educators' reflection on current practice, and creates opportunities for more collaborative methods of working [25].

Despite the benefits and advantages of using OER in educational contexts, several studies indicated some challenges and obstacles on the use of OERs. One big challenge is the lack of knowledge by educators regarding the usage of OERs, including issues of language, the lack of ICT skills, some materials are confined within the e-learning institutions, the limited free time and the lack of reward systems to account for the efforts invested in creating and using OERs [24, 26].

Even more, a lot of work should be done regarding disseminating OERs amongst the educational world to become more accessible to everyone. The use of OERs in the EU is still far behind other countries such as the USA except for the UK [10]. Given the teachers' limited knowledge, there is plenty of room for disseminating OERs that promote language learning experiences (1) geared towards a more integrated view of language learning skills and (2) favor more personalized learning experiences.

Hodgkinson-Williams [27] talking about the challenges and adaptation of using OERs, claims that the absence of students and learners' technical skills, the difficulties in covering the cost for developing or sustaining OERs, the unwillingness to share, use or give away intellectual property, the lack of incentives for the creation of OERs, and the difficulty to assure quality in open content are some of the basic challenges that researchers should be aware.

3 Use, Create, and Share of OER: Mapping the Existing Guidelines

Generally, there are numerous articles and reports which include guidelines in relation to OER. These guidelines were developed to help people interested in creating, using, and finding OER. Most of these guidelines are targeted to specific groups such as teachers, students, organisations, schools, etc. Some of these guidelines were created in the context of Erasmus + projects to enhance or promote the use of OER for specific purposes. This section presents some important existing guidelines regarding the use, creation, and sharing of OER. It also provides some important considerations that could help us create step-by-step guidelines for Language Education.

According to the literature [13], there are some concrete steps for the OERs' creation and share, as Fig. 1 shows. The first step is the design and development of the OER. In this step, it is important to consider the copyright restrictions in order to provide as much openness as possible. The second step is the choice of a specific license, for example based on the popular Creative Commons framework. Attribution is always a requirement, and the author can decide whether or not to open the OER up to remixing and/or commercial use. The next step is the publication of the OER on the web and the final step is sharing the OER with others. In the final step, there are many available choices and ways to promote and disseminate the OER in many groups of people who might be interested in using this OER (i.e., social media, email, blogs, YouTube etc.).

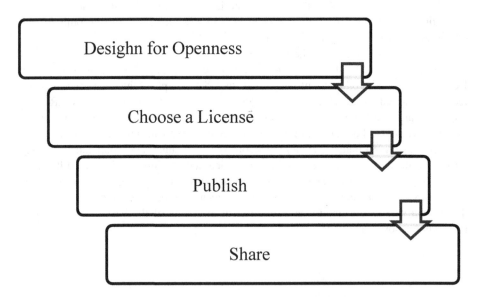

Fig. 1. Concrete steps of the OER' creation

Regarding the development and sustainability of an OER, Wiley and Henson [23] proposed a model with seven phases/steps as follows:

- Get: The first stage includes searching and finding OERs;
- Create: Generating the OER, preferably using open source tools;
- Localise: Making the OER more targeted to the specific group of people and to the particular context;
- Remix: Taking two OERs, editing and merging them to a new OER;
- Licensing: Choosing the appropriate license;
- Use: Implementing the OER in your context;
- Redistribute: Publishing the OER and making it available for a wider range of people and communities within the educational sector.

However, as many researchers stated, before finding, creating or remixing OERs you need to seriously consider the OERs' quality. Orr, Rimini and Van Damme [4] highlight some specific policy considerations and recommendations for supporting the use, sharing and adaptation of OER. According to them, for the creation of OERs, the main objectives should be to aligning the OER to key educational challenges, to ensure the sustainability of OER, to integrate OER into the whole learning setting, to support teachers and learners, to save costs, and to improve the quality of educational resources. Specifically, some of the OERs' policy actions that Orr, Rimini, and Van Damme [4] propose are the provision of open license materials, the establishment of new communities of practice within the education field, the promotion of new digital tools, and the promotion of research on how OERs are produced and used in certain contexts.

Several studies in the area of OER claim that OER can facilitate learning and lead to pedagogical change and more learner-centred experiences [18, 21, 25]. There are many examples and cases mentioned in the literature on integrating and using OER in the teaching practice to create more engaging and interactive lessons [25]. Some examples include the support of peer learning between learners using Khan Academy materials, the use of a digital course to support hybrid forms of teaching and learning, the use of a simulation to support problem-based learning, and Augmented Reality to present the learning resource etc.

In this context, Kawachi [28] developed the TIPS Framework consisting of four basic pillars: Teaching and learning process; Information and material content; Presentation product and format; System technical and technology. This framework includes some specific criteria mainly for teachers as creators of OER, as presented in Fig. 2. Each pillar provides some basic suggestions/recommendations to be taken into consideration by teachers when creating an OER. The first pillar has to do with the teaching methodologies, processes and approaches, while the second pillar focuses on the content that is included in the OER. The third pillar refers to the presentation of the material focusing on formatting and designing, and the fourth pillar is about the technical part of the OER.

Additionally, McGreal [29] indicates that the use of previously created materials is almost always more efficient than creating your own and recommends taking advantage of the online freely and legally accessible OER. The report also suggests that mixing and matching from different sources can be more effective than creating them from

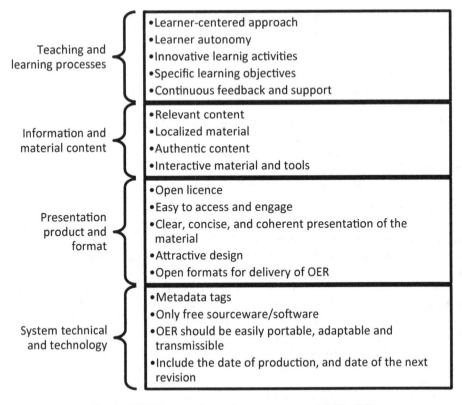

Fig. 2. TIPS framework: teachers as creators of OERs [28]

scratch. This also provides flexibility for reuse and repurposing. Similarly, Zimmermann [30] reports some general hints for creating OER highlighting the importance of copyright when using an existing available material by selecting the license carefully based on the OER's content and purpose. It is also important to think about how you would like to distribute your OER to maximize the number of people who can benefit from it. Regarding the sharing of an OER, Butcher [31] proposed four ways of sharing OER with others. The first way is to use the institutional repository. The second way is to select an open repository to share the OER and make it available to more people. The third way is to build the OER online since there are sites that encourage the development of OER within their online environments (e.g., Connexions, WikiEducator). The last way is to share the OER through social networks such as Twitter, Facebook, Linkedin, etc.

Given the potential of OER to improve higher education systems, UNESCO and the Commonwealth of Learning (COL) have proposed some guidelines to support governments, higher education institutions/providers, academic staff, student bodies, and quality assurance/accreditation and recognition bodies [32]. Below the specific guidelines for academic staff are presented:

- Develop skills to evaluate OER;
- Consider publishing OER: working collaboratively with peers and publishing materials openly that are already routinely produced as part of teaching and learning;
- Assemble, adapt, and contextualise existing OER;
- Develop the habit of working in teams;
- Seek institutional support for OER skills development;
- Leverage networks and communities of practice;
- Encourage student participation;
- Promote OER through publishing about OER;
- Provide feedback about, and data on the use of, existing OER;
- Update knowledge of IPR, copyright and privacy policies.

To conclude, there are plenty of open resources available on the web for educational usage in all educational institutions, from schools to universities. Based on the literature review and the findings from the online survey completed by Erasmus+ participants [33] will help us to create an e-toolkit for language education. In the next section, we provide some basic guidelines for the use, creation, and sharing of OER. We also present some well-known and successful databases with a focus on open resources for language learning and teaching. Language teachers and trainers can use those open resources to improve their existing teaching practices. These resources may allow them to adopt innovative strategies/methodologies and bring technology to the classroom.

4   Towards the Development of an OER e-Toolkit for Language Education

As mentioned before, many previous reports offer comprehensive guidelines on how teachers can create, use, and share OERs. Taking in consideration the insights from those reports we developed an e-Toolkit for the creation/share/use of quality multilingual and interactive OERs for language learning. This e-toolkit has been developed with regards to the OPENLang Network project (https://www.openlangnet.eu/), an Erasmus+ KA2 project. It has a concrete structure, and it combines theory and practice. More specifically, the e-Toolkit includes:

- Useful material (basic authoring tools for the creation of OERs, language OER databases, etc.),
- Specific examples of OERs,
- Useful tips for the creation/sharing of language OERs,
- Examples of good Open Educational practices in Language education,
- Self-evaluation assessment at the end of each section.

This toolkit is a step-by-step guide for Language education to equip language learning instructors and trainers with the skills they need to find, use, create, and share language OER. The e-toolkit is composed from six sections covering important aspects of working with OER, as Fig. 3 shows. Particularly, in the introduction part, the purpose of the e-toolkit is explained, the target group that the toolkit is designed for and some instructions on how to use the toolkit. The next chapter is the literature review where we provide some definitions of OERs and OEPs, some characteristics, categories, benefits, and challenges of using OERs and also an overview of existing guidelines for OERs. The rest of the e-toolkit focuses on finding, using, creating and sharing an OER. In these sections, we explain where and how to find language OERs and OEPs, how to create OER (basic authoring tools for the creation of OERs, language OERs databases). We provide specific examples of OERs and OEPs in Language education and offer useful tips for the creation and sharing of language OERs. Last, we provide some guidelines regarding copyright licensees. It is important to mention that each of the above sections/chapters include specific learning objectives and self-assessment quizzes at the end.

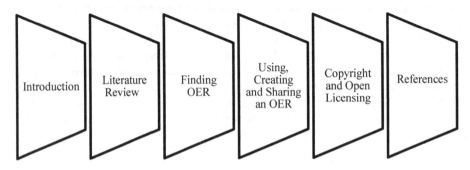

Fig. 3. Structure of the e-toolkit

The main purpose of this e-toolkit is to get language teachers and trainers involved in the adoption, creation, use, and sharing of OERs for language learning and teaching. The e-toolkit will help language teachers find, use, create, and share quality multilingual and interactive OERs for language learning in their teaching practices. All teachers/trainers/researchers of language education are expected to benefit from possibly adopting this e-toolkit in their educational practices.

4.1 Finding OER Related to Language Education

In this section, some searching tips are presented for finding an OER in the area of language education. Also, some available repositories, best OEPs for Language Learning and resources are listed to help teachers and trainers find the appropriate OERs. This section's main learning objective is to provide some basic information on conducting a preliminary search for OER related to language education.

There is a growing interest in OER use in language learning contexts [19]. OERs is a powerful tool for language learning as they promote personalized learning experiences. There are many free textbooks available in many languages. There are also many repositories and databases in relation to language education. For example, there is a series of useful material to be used in foreign language teaching, in second language teaching, in Computer Assisted Language Learning etc. A list of useful OERs databases in language learning is presented in the following Table 1.

Table 1. Some indicative OER databases for language education

a/a	OER for language education
1	Center for Open Educational Resources & Language Learning (COERLL)
2	OER Commons
3	IRIS
4	MERLOT
5	The CEELBAS Language Repository
6	AbulÉdu Data
7	OpenLearn

4.2   Using, Creating and Sharing OER

This section aims to provide useful information for language teachers and trainers on how a teacher can use an OER in the classroom, how to create and share an OER identifying the main steps and considerations of the OER creation process. Based on the previous research, some useful tips on how you can use OER in your classroom include:

- Find the most appropriate OER for your lessons.
- Integrate an OER into the whole learning setting.
- Use an OER in a collaborative way.
- Create spaces within the curriculum for this collaborative type of learning.
- Create new forms of learning within the OERs to provide learners with a learning experience that better facilitates personal development and success.
- Consider giving a study guide to your students on how to integrate the specific OER into the classroom.
- Use a learner-centred approach.
- The OER material that you use should align with local wants and needs and anticipate your students' current and future needs.

In terms of creating an OER, teachers/researchers/trainers should take into account some specific key considerations before starting the process of creating. The first thing is to identify who your audience will be (level of language, nationality, age, interests, etc.). A second important consideration has to do with the changes that need to be done in the OER if this is an existing material and mainly which types or formats of OER will be used. Last, the third consideration is related to the design challenges that need to be under consideration (i.e., content, size, formatting, etc.).

In terms of sharing, which is the final stage, the necessary steps that a teacher should follow to share its own resource are:

- Use Creative Commons to find openly licensed content to remix;
- Choose a License;
- Assign a license to the OER;
- Demonstrate best practices in the attribution of authorship, for both the authors of the OER and for your own creations.

After that, one important step is the information about Copyright and Open Licensing. It is crucial for those who would like to create an OER to understand the copyright and open licenses, be aware of the different options that the Creative Commons License framework provides, and choose the appropriate license based on the content and learners' needs.

At the end of each section, one self-assessment quiz is provided (see Fig. 4). This is a simple test or quiz that includes some questions (e.g., true/false, multiple choise questions) and some practice exercises based on the specific content and information provided in the section. This test will help people to reflect on what they have learned and test their knowledge.

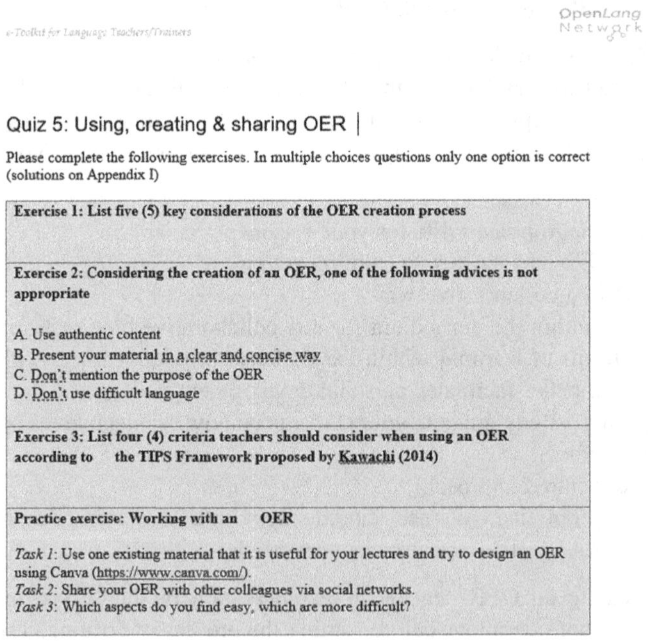

OpenLang
Network

e-Toolkit for Language Teachers/Trainers

Quiz 5: Using, creating & sharing OER |

Please complete the following exercises. In multiple choices questions only one option is correct (solutions on Appendix I)

Exercise 1: List five (5) key considerations of the OER creation process

Exercise 2: Considering the creation of an OER, one of the following advices is not appropriate

A. Use authentic content
B. Present your material in a clear and concise way
C. Don't mention the purpose of the OER
D. Don't use difficult language

Exercise 3: List four (4) criteria teachers should consider when using an OER according to   the TIPS Framework proposed by Kawachi (2014)

Practice exercise: Working with an   OER

Task 1: Use one existing material that it is useful for your lectures and try to design an OER using Canva (https://www.canva.com/).
Task 2: Share your OER with other colleagues via social networks.
Task 3: Which aspects do you find easy, which are more difficult?

Fig. 4. An example of a self-evaluation assessment included in the e-toolkit

5 Conclusions

Based on our research, there are plenty of open resources available on the web for educational usage in most educational institutions, from schools to universities. In this paper we provided some important considerations regarding the creation, use, and sharing of OERs with a focus on open resources and practices for language learning and teaching. These OERs can be used by language teachers and trainers to improve their existing teaching practices. Usually, these OERs give them opportunities to adopt innovative strategies/methodologies and bring technology to the classroom. Finally, taking into account the insights from previous reports and studies, we developed an e-toolkit with step-by-step guidelines on how teachers/researchers can create, use and share quality multilingual and interactive OER for language education.

Acknowledgements. This work has been partially funded by the European Union's Eras-musPlus programme, grant agreement: 2018-1-EL01-KA203-047967 (Project: OPENLang Network). This publication reflects the views only of the authors, and the European Commission cannot be held responsible for any use which may be made of the information contained here.

References

1. McGreal, R.: Special report on the role of open educational resources in supporting the sustainable development goal 4: quality education challenges and opportunities. Int. Rev. Res. Open Distrib. Learn. **18**(7), 292–305 (2017)
2. Saint, W.: Tertiary distance education and technology in Sub-Saharan Africa. Afr. High. Educ. Int. Ref. Handb. **5**(1), 93–111 (2003)
3. Wiley, D.: Defining the "open" in open content and open educational resources. (2014). http://opencontent.org/definition/
4. Orr, D., Rimini, M., Van Damme, D.: Open Educational Resources: A Catalyst for Innovation, Educational Research and Innovation. OECD Publishing, Paris (2015). https://doi.org/10.1787/9789264247543-en
5. Hylén, J.: Open educational resources: opportunities and challenges. In: Proceedings of Open Education. http://www.knowledgeall.com/files/Additional_Readings-Consolidated.pdf . Accessed 14 May 2020
6. Chib, A., Wardoyo, R.J.: Differential OER impacts of formal and informal ICTs: employability of female migrant workers. Int. Rev. Res. Open Distance Learn. **19**(3), 94–113 (2018). https://doi.org/10.19173/irrodl.v19i3.3538
7. United Nations Educational, Scientific and Cultural Organization: What are open educational resources (OERs)? Unesco.org, Paris (2012). http://www.unesco.org/new/en/communication-and-information/access-to-knowledge/open-educational-resources/what-are-open-educational-resources-oers/
8. Rhoads, R.A., Berdan, J., Toven-Lindsey, B.: The open courseware movement in higher education: unmasking power and raising questions about the movement's democratic potential. Educ. Theory **63**(1), 87–109 (2013). https://doi.org/10.1111/edth.12011
9. Boga, S., McGreal, R.: Introducing MOOCs to Africa: New Economy Skills for Africa Program – ICT (2014). http://oasis.col.org/handle/11599/613
10. Sabadie, J., Muñoz, J., Punie, Y., Redecker, C., Vuorikari, R.: OER: A European policy perspective. J. Interact. Media Educ. 1–12 (2014). https://doi.org/10.5334/2014-05

11. Ehlers, U.-D.: Extending the territory: from open educational resources to open educational practices. J. Open Flex. Distance Learn. **15**(2), 1–10 (2011)
12. Open Educational Quality (OPAL) Initiative. https://www.icde.org/open-educational-quality-initiative
13. Camilleri, A.F., Ehlers, U.D., Pawlowski, J.: State of the Art Review of Quality Issues Related to Open Educational Resources (OER), p. 54. Publications Office of the European Union, Luxembourg (2014)
14. Wiley, D., Green, C.: Why openness in education? In: Oblinger, D. (ed.) Game Changers: Education and Information Technologies, pp. 81–89. Educause, Washington, DC (2012). https://library.educause.edu/resources/2012/5/chapter-6-why-openness-in-education
15. Economides, A.A., Perifanou, M.: Dimensions of openness in MOOCs & OERs. In: EDULEARN 2018 Proceedings of the 10th International Conference on Education and New Learning Technologies, Palma, Spain, 2–4 July 2018, pp. 3684–3693. IATED Digital Library (2018). https://doi.org/10.21125/edulearn.2018.0942
16. Shmueli, E.: MERLOT - a reliable framework for OER. In: Proceedings of the International Computer Software and Applications Conference, pp. 697–699. IEEE Computer Society (2017). https://doi.org/10.1109/COMPSAC.2017.280
17. Mossley, D.: Open Educational Resources and Open Education. The Higher Education Academy (2013). http://dspace.vn/bitstream/11461/305/1/oer_toolkit_0.pdf
18. Farrow, R., Pitt, R., Delos-Arcos, B., Perryman, L., Weller, M., McAndrew, P.: Impact of OER use on teaching and learning: data from OER Research Hub (2013–2014). Br. J. Edu. Technol. **46**, 972–976 (2015). https://doi.org/10.1111/bjet.12310
19. Thomas, M., Evans, M.: Guest editorial. Comput. Assist. Lang. Learn. **27**, 107–108 (2014). https://doi.org/10.1080/09588221.2014.874101
20. Petrides, L., Jimes, C., Middleton-Detzner, C., Howell, H.: OER as a model for enhanced teaching and learning. In: Open ED 2010 Proceedings. UOC, OU, BYU, Barcelona, September 2010. http://hdl.handle.net/10609/4995. Accessed 17 Mar 2016
21. Bradshaw, P., Younie, S., Jones, S.: Open education resources and higher education academic practice. Campus-Wide Inf. Syst. **30**, 186–193 (2013). https://doi.org/10.1108/10650741311330366
22. Bliss, T., Robinson, T., Hilton, J., Wiley, D.: An OER COUP: college teacher and student perceptions of open educational resources. J. Interact. Media Educ. **1**, 1–25 (2013)
23. Wiley, D., Henson, H.: An initial characterization of engagement in informal social learning around MIT OCW. In: Proceedings of the 7th International Conference on Learning Sciences, ICLS, Bloomington, Indiana, pp. 832–837, June 2006. ISBN: 0-8058-6174-2
24. Conole, G., Alevizou, P.: A literature review of the use of Web 2.0 tools in higher education (2010). https://core.ac.uk/download/pdf/5162.pdf. Accessed 30 Dec 2016
25. Beetham, H., Falconer, I., McGill, L., Littlejohn, A.: Open practices: briefing paper. Briefing paper, JISC (2012). https://oersynth.pbworks.com/w/page/51668352/OpenPracticesBriefing
26. Abeywardena, I.S., Dhanarajan, G., Chan, C.S.: Searching and locating OER: barriers to the wider adoption of OER for teaching in Asia. In: Proceedings of the Regional Symposium on Open Educational Resources: An Asian Perspective on Policies and Practice, Penang, Malaysia, September 2012
27. Hodgkinson-Williams, C.: Benefits and challenges of OER for higher education institutions. Centre for Educational Technology, University of Cape Town (2010). https://libguides.library.cpp.edu/ld.php?content_id=13268187
28. Kawachi, P.: Quality Assurance Guidelines for Open Educational Resources: TIPS Framework, Version-2.0. Commonwealth Educational Media Centre for Asia New Delhi (2014). http://oasis.col.org/bitstream/handle/11599/562/TIPSFramework_Version%202%205b1%5d%20Copy.pdf?sequence=1&isAllowed=y

29. McGreal, R.: Creating, Using and Sharing Open Educational Resources. OER initiative with the help of S. D'Antoni (Athabasca University), W. Mackintosh (OER Foundation) and C. Green (Creative Commons) (2013)
30. Zimmermann, C.: Guideline for the Creation of Open Educational Resources. Information and Practical Exercises for Lecturers in Higher Education (2018)
31. Butcher, N.: A Basic Guide to Open Educational Resources (OER). Prepared by for the Commonwealth of Learning & UNESCO (2011). Edited by Kanwar, A., Uvalic'-Trumbic, S. https://drive.google.com/drive/u/0/folders/1bVEKaMFFTDPCGJiTb5lW4Mh4LCdRqdJM
32. Guidelines for Open Educational Resources (OER) in Higher Education: A report by the Commonwealth of Learning (COL) and The United Nations (2011)
33. Kosmas, P., Parmaxi, A., Perifanou, M., Economides, A.A., Zaphiris, P.: Creating the profile of participants in mobility activities in the context of Erasmus+: motivations, perceptions, and linguistic needs. In: Zaphiris, P., Ioannou, A. (eds.) HCII 2020. LNCS, vol. 12205, pp. 499–511. Springer, Cham (2020). https://doi.org/10.1007/978-3-030-50513-4_37

Optimization to Automated Phonetic Transcription Grading Tool (APTgt) – Automatic Exam Generator

Jueting Liu, Marisha Speights, Dallin Bailey, Sicheng Li,
Yaoxuan Luan, Ishaan Mishra, Yang Cao, and Cheryl Seals[✉]

Auburn University, Auburn, AL 36930, USA
{jzl0122,mls0096,djb0053,szl0072,yzl0219,
ishaan.mishra,yzc0020,sealscd}@aubrun.edu

Abstract. The Automated Phonetic Transcription Grading Tool (APTgt) is an online exam system developed by Auburn University HCI group. This application aims to support faculty in communications disorders to improve their pedagogy and timely feedback for students. This article discusses an attempt to improve teacher's experience by providing an automated method for exam generation, which can significantly save time while creating exams. The exam entry is created with the AU IPA (International Phonetic Alphabet) keyboard and system that grades the exams upon student completion of the exam. The exam is composed of several linguistics words with their pronunciation. Students need to answer the questions by inputting the correct phonetic spells during the exam. The core part in the auto-exam generator is the classification module, which can classify the input words into different difficulty levels. In this paper, we proposed two classification algorithms in the classification module: Rule-based algorithm and Classification and Regression Trees (CART).

Keywords: E-learning · Linguistics words · International phonetic alphabet · Phonetic transcription · Decision tree classifier · Multiclass classification

1 Introduction

The Internet has become more prominent in all aspects of human work and life. The Internet has also been used to support learning and with our current state of emergency, there has never been a greater need for E-learning tools in the education field, especially since the world is under a global pandemic now [1–3]. The definition of E-learning is learning utilizing technologies to access educational courses outside of a traditional classroom, and this helps users access the course materials or electronic devices anytime, anywhere with few limitations [2]. Canvas, Udemy, and W3C are all examples of platforms that provide strong support for E-learning.

The Automated Phonetic Transcription Grading Tool (APTgt) is a web-based linguistics courses E-learning system that provides functions of creating interactive examinations, taking and saving exams' results, automatically grading submitted exams, and analyzing the grades distribution for students in the Department of Communication Disorder (CMDS) at Auburn University [4]. APTgt system aims to help the

P. Zaphiris and A. Ioannou (Eds.): HCII 2021, LNCS 12784, pp. 80–91, 2021.
https://doi.org/10.1007/978-3-030-77889-7_6

disordered student in learning phonetic transcription. This system supports the improved quality of teacher's pedagogical experience by reducing the task of manually grading with the help of grading tools [1, 4]. This paper proposed an optimization to our existed APTgt system with an auto-exam generator module.

In the initial version of the system APTgt1.0, creating an exam was time-consuming and arduous for teachers [4]. After accessing the Manage Exam page, teachers need to create questions by adding scores and difficulty levels to each word with an IPA (International Phonetic Alphabet) keyboard. All the scores and difficulty levels are manually calculated by teachers. All the created questions in our original APTgt system are not reusable, which means a created word in one exam with its score and difficulty level cannot be directly called to another exam.

To optimize the system and improve the user experience, we proposed an automatic question difficulty classification module and an automatic exam generation module based on the teacher's requirements. The classification module automatically classifies input words into three difficulty levels: easy, medium, and advanced. After classification, all the words will be stored in a public question bank/word bank. The exam generation module supports teachers to generate exams by selecting difficulty level and the number of questions. With our optimization, the whole system can provide a better user experience and has greater storage efficiency in that it reduces the space utilization in the exam question database.

We also proposed two different approaches of classifying words into three different levels: a rule-based classifier and classification and regression tree classifier (CART). In the rule-based algorithm, each class of phonetic character has a specified weight. We received the total score and difficulty level by calculating the total weight. With the CART classifier, all the data are required from advisors from the Communications Disorders department, we have identified three fundamental classes phonemes with seven types of data features. Each solution has its advantage and disadvantage, the details will get discussed in the fourth section.

2   Background

Compared with orthographic transcription, in the process of phonetic transcription, the transcriber notes how the words are pronounced, using visual characters to represent sounds [5]. The International Phonetic Alphabet (IPA) characters are the most commonly used to do the phonetic transcription. For example, 'ɔːdɪˌəʊ is the phonetic spelling of "audio". The purpose of our system is to support students with communication disorders and provide them training in the process of transcribing speech phonetically, and we support students by providing them more opportunities to practice and reinforce their learning of phonetic transcription. The traditional phonetic transcription practice for students is to write phonetic symbols with pencils/pens with speech sound, which is difficult because the phonetic symbols are always hard to remember and like learning a new language. So, the demand for an E-learning system to help students with their phonetic transcription skills is high.

Currently, there are many popular web-based E-learning systems such as Canvas, Coursera, W3C. Most of them can provide general learning contents, including variable courses, interactive quizzes and comfortable user experience [3]. After investigating different E-learning systems, we decided to develop our APTgt system because most of the existing systems cannot support phonetic transcription which is our core target. Other innovations of our APTgt system include the auto-exam generating module and auto-grading module.

The APTgt system is an interactive E-learning system developed by the Auburn University HCI group in a participatory design process with the faculty from the Department of Communication Disorders to facilitate phonetic transcription training for CMDS students [1]. APTgt provides many supportive features such as the following: phonetic course content, lessons in the form of videos, practice sessions, and exam sessions. With this system, teachers can easily upload course materials, generate and manage the course, grade exams online. Students will abandon the shackles of pencils/ pen, and they do not need to remember the complex phonetic symbols, taking exams or practices can be completed with a higher user experience because of the design of the system and being supported to just need to recognize, and not have to recall all of the IPA characters. The user can just select the characters needed on our Auburn developed IPA keyboard [1, 4]. Next, we will briefly illustrate the functions of the APTgt system. There are two main roles: the teacher's role and the student's role (See Fig. 1 and Fig. 2).

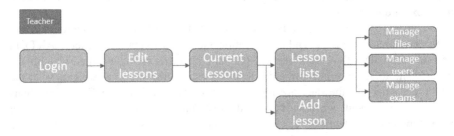

Fig. 1. Dataflow in teacher's part

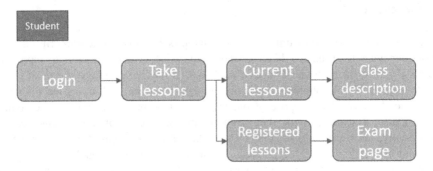

Fig. 2. Dataflow in student's part

In teacher's part (Fig. 1) [1, 4], each teacher has his/her own account which leads to his/her own courses, the different account will lead to separate space, which means teachers cannot share lesson materials and students' information, this aims to protect student's privacy. After logging into the system, teachers can create/manage lessons, exams as well as practices, and review the answers submitted by students. The lessons are formed by videos and exams are formed by audios.

A student will have to register to the system and access the functions [1, 4]. Students need to get enrolled to some lessons to get access to the lesson materials and exams related to the phonetic transcription. During the exam, each question is a word pronunciation. The student simply needs to assemble the phonetic characters from the IPA keyboard (See Fig. 3) to generate an answer that best represents the speech sound from the question. The tool also provides solutions and results analysis from students' exams, and the students will know how their grades distribute in the overall grading pole.

There is one big challenge in our existed system. When a teacher is creating an exam, he/she needs to input several questions/words with their difficulty levels and scores with the IPA keyboard. The problem is that the difficulty level and scores of each question need to be manually calculated by the teacher, there is no function to help teacher calculate the score of the questions in the old system. Even worse, the created question in one exam cannot be called to another exam. This inconvenient exam generating process took a lot of trouble to teacher and caused the waste of space utilization. In this paper, we focused on this problem and proposed some solutions to avoid the manual calculation process and optimize the whole system.

Fig. 3. IPA keyboard

3 Method

3.1 Exam Generating Tool

As discussed in prior sections, the exam generating function was developed to improve user experience and optimize space utilization by providing commonly reused words in the form of a reusable database. In the second version of APTgt software, our development effort was to provide greater support for teachers by introducing an automated approach to the generation of exams. In the original system, teachers have the arduous task that every time they need to reuse a question, and they must recreate and recalculate the difficulty level. This labor-intensive process diminishes the user experience for teachers (See left part of Fig. 4).

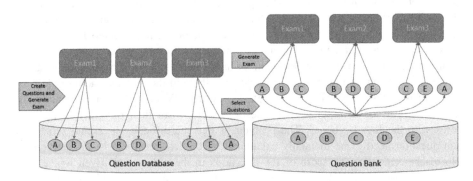

Fig. 4. A figure compared two different of generating exams.

For example, in the left part of Fig. 4, Exam1 and Exam2 have the same question "B" which means "B" needs to be calculated and uploaded twice to generate these two exams. To generate these three exams (Exam1, Exam2, Exam3) with five questions (A, B, C, D, E), question A, B, C and E needs to be uploaded multiple times. This repeat work will cause a bad user experience. Even worse, teachers must waste time thinking about the difficulty level for each question every time they upload it.

To build a smarter system, the APTgt should have the ability to automatically calculate the difficulty level of each question when it is uploaded, and the question with its difficulty level should be reused when a new exam is created with the same questions. In our proposed solution (right part of the Fig. 4), a question bank (word bank) has been built to save all the questions, and we introduced a new difficulty-classification module to calculate all the input words' score and level.

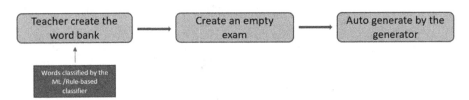

Fig. 5. Flow chart of auto-exam generator

From our new module (See Fig. 5), the teacher needs to pre-build a question/word bank. This bank will be the library for all the questions. There is a classification module in the word bank that can automatically classify the input questions into three different difficulty levels: easy, medium and advanced. During the exam generating progress, a teacher only needs to input the number of questions of each difficulty level, and the system will randomly select questions from the question bank and generate a new exam. Compared with the original system, teacher with auto-exam generator can create a new exam in 1 min without any calculating problem. Also, all the newly created questions are stored in the word bank and all the questions in the word bank are reusable regardless how many times. One teacher account can only access one word bank because different teacher may have different classification rules. This module will significantly save the teacher's work.

3.2 Decision Tree Classification

For the difficulty-classification module, according to the teachers' requirements, all the questions/words stored in the question bank need to be classified into three classes: easy, medium and advanced. It is apparent that we need a multi-class classification algorithm to match this demand. The classifier incorporates regression functionality to support new question classification and supports the prediction of appropriate word class. And the classifier should deal with the continuous value because the attributes for a question are always continuous values. Finally, we proposed two solutions for the classification module: the rule-based algorithm and the Decision tree algorithm.

Decision tree learning is one of the most popular machine learning methods for classification and regression [6–8]. It's a kind of non-parameter supervised learning, the goal is to create a model that predicts the value of a target variable by learning simple rules from data features. In the tree structure, leaves represent class labels and branches represent conjunctions of features that lead to those class labels. Famous decision tree algorithms include ID3, C4.5 and Classification and Regression Tree (CART) [9]. ID3 is a top-down greedy algorithm that helps build the decision tree by iteratively selecting the best features at each step from the root node. C4.5 is an extension of ID3, C4.5 can handle both continuous and discrete attributes. Compared with ID3 and C4.5, the tree structure for CART is binary tree, CART can be used in classification and regression while it can also handle numeric values. That's the reason we choose CART as our classification algorithm.

If all data belong to a single class, it can be called pure. This dataset's degree should be 0 and 1, 0 means all data belong to the single class while 1 means all data belong to another class. In CART, we use Gini index to measure the uncertainty, the less Gini index is, the purer the dataset is [9].

Assume there are K classes, p_k is the probability of an object being classified to that class [9].

$$Gini(p) = \sum_{k=1}^{K} p_k(1 - p_k) = 1 - \sum_{k=1}^{K} p_k^2$$

For a binary classification problem, the probability of the first sample is p[11]:

$$Gini(p) = 2p(1 - p)$$

For sample D, the number of D is $|D|$, suppose there are K classes, the number of one particular class is $|C_k|$, the function will be [11]:

$$Gini(D) = 1 - \sum_{k=1}^{K} (\frac{|C_k|}{|D|})^2$$

For sample D, the number of D is $|D|$, if divide D into $|D1|$ and $|D2|$ based on one attribute A, we can find:

$$Gini(D, A) = \frac{|D_1|}{|D|} Gini(D_1) + \frac{|D_2|}{|D|} Gini(D_2)$$

CART algorithm will iteratively do binary classify to one feature, so based on CART algorithm, the decision tree model will be a binary tree [6, 7].

3.3 Exam Grading Tool

APTgt exams mainly focus on phonetic transcription which means in the students' part, students need to represent how the phonetic sound format [4]. With an International Phonetic Alphabet (IPA) keyboard [1], students can input their answers to the system. The grading tool should have the ability to calculate the difference between the student's answer and the correct answer. That becomes a String-to-String correction problem [10], also known as an edit distance problem.

The definition of minimum edit distance is the minimum number of insertions, deletions and substitutions that required to transform one string into another [4]. Different definitions may use a different set of operations, in our algorithm, we operations are insertion, deletion and substitution.

Define two strings A and B as two sequences of characters, A has the length of n and B has the length of m (m and n can be different). D(i, j) is the minimum edit distance between A[1...i] and B[1...j], thus the minimum edit distance between A and B is D(n, m).

There are four cases during the dynamic implementation [10, 11]:

- If the last character of A and B is the same, ignore the last character and recur the length of A and B to n − 1 and m − 1.
- For insert operation, recur the length of A and B to n and m − 1.
- For delete operation, recur the length of A and B to n − 1 and m.
- For substitute operation, recur the length of A and B to n − 1 and m − 1.

For every operation, a cost of that operation should be added, and all the costs can be regarded as the same value in our system.

The recurrence relation:

1. For each i = 1...M
2.   For each j = 1...N
3. $D(i,j) = \min(D(i-1,j) + cost, D(i,j-1) + cost, D(i-1,j-1) + cost)$

4 Classification Solutions

To solve the classification part, we proposed two different solutions: the rule-based algorithm and classification and regression tree classifier.

4.1 Rule-Based Algorithm

According to the phonetic transcription, we divided the phonetic characters into 12 classes: *front vowel, back vowel, central vowel, stress, r-color vowel, diphthong, consonant, affricate, allophone, diacritics, two phoneme and other*. All the alphabets in one dictionary have the same weight. For all created words, the classification module will calculate the total weight of each word and store the word with its score in the question bank (word bank). The overall difficulty level of a word can be classified by the word's weight to easy, medium and hard (Tables 1 and 2).

Table 1. Rule-based classification module

Class	Characters	Weight
FrontVowels(FV)	"i","ɪ","e","ɛ","æ"	1
BackVowels(BV)	"u","ʊ","o","ɔ","a"	1.5
CnetralVowels(CV)	"ɝ","ʌ","ɚ","ə"	2
Stress(ST)	"eɪ", "oʊ"	3
RColoredVowels(RCV)	"ɪɹ","ɛɹ","aɹ","ɔɹ","ʊɹ","oɹ"	2.5
Diphthong(DT)	"aʊ", "ɔɪ", "aɪ"	2
Consonants(CO)	"ɹ", "θ", "ð", "ʒ", "ʃ"	1
Affricates(AF)	"d͡ʒ", " t͡ʃ"	2
Allophone(AL)	"ɾ", "ʔ"	2
Diacritics(DI)	"ː", "‖", "˺", "˜", "ˇ", "˚", "̟", "̠", "˔", "˕", "̺", "̪", "ɫ"	2
TwoPhonemes(TP)	"mj","kw","ks"	2
JSound(JS)	"j"	1
Others(OT)	p","t","k","b","d","g","s","z","f","v","h","n","m","ŋ","l","r","w","ɫ","n̩","m̩"	1

We supposed the range for difficulty level is easy: 0–11.5, medium: 12–22, adv: 22+. The rule is not simply accumulating the total weight of characters but also consider the total length of the word. Some classes with multiple characters need to be treated carefully. For example, the score for "mji" is 3 while "nji" is 2.5 because "mj" belongs to TwoPhonemes which score is 2, it is not correct by just using the score of "m" plus the score of "j" and plus the score of "i". Here is an image of created words stored in the question bank (See Fig. 6).

Word File	File Pronunciation	Correct Word Pronunciation	Word Difficulty Score	Word Difficulty Level	Listen	Edit	Delete
1597114331645_file_example_WAV_1MG.wav	bbdθf	bbdθf	5.0	easy 1	Listen	Edit	x

Fig. 6. Word in the question bank

The rule-based algorithm is easy to understand and implement.

4.2 CART Classifier

Data Prepared. We received about 120 words with their difficulty level from advisors from department of speech, Auburn University, all the difficulty level is judged by advisor's experience. 70% of the dataset are used for model training and rest of the words are used for testing. Since the CART algorithm can handle the continuous value, we can utilize the number of different phonetic characters to be the data features in the decision tree model [12–14]. We select the number of Vowels (VO), Allophones (AL), Affricates (AF), Consonants (CO), Diacritics (DI), Two Phonemes (TP) and Diphthongs (DP). Here are some samples of our training dataset.

Table 2. Examples of dataset

Words	VO	AL	AF	CO	DI	TP	DP	Difficulty Level
ptk	0	0	0	3	0	0	0	easy
fjaũɔu	2	0	0	2	0	0	1	medium
tʃg̊ðæʔ	1	1	1	2	0	0	0	easy
wjaũʌtʃiõʊə̥	3	0	1	2	1	0	2	hard
refitʃaũʔ	2	2	1	1	0	0	1	medium
θa.lə̃ʔeĩẽ	3	2	0	2	3	0	1	hard
rɪre.ð	2	2	0	1	1	0	0	easy
ãjaks	2	1	0	0	1	1	0	medium
wjaũʌtʃiõʊə̥	3	0	1	2	1	0	2	hard

Model Trained. We used python sklearn library [12] to train the classification and regression tree model and pydotplus to draw the decision tree model (Fig. 7).

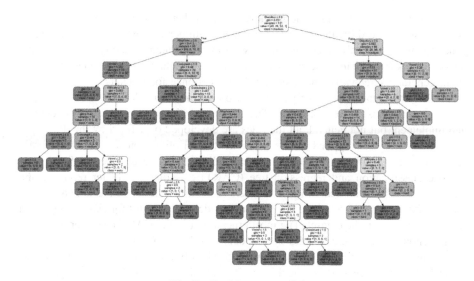

Fig. 7. Decision tree model

After finishing creating decision tree model, the *predict()* method can be used to predict which class should a new input word be. The parameters in the *predict()* are the data features of the word [12] (Fig. 8).

```
print(clf.predict([[1, 0, 0, 1, 0, 1, 1]]))
['easy']
```

Fig. 8. Predict the new input word

5   Conclusion

In this paper, we introduced an auto-exam generator to optimize our existed APTgt system (See Fig. 9). This exam generating module can significantly improve the user experience including save teacher's work and improve the space utilization.

Fig. 9. Auto-exam generator

From the Fig. 9, the illustration indicates a teacher generating an exam, he/she needs to select the difficulty level and input the number of the questions. The exam generator will randomly select questions with that indicated difficulty level from the question bank (word bank). Teachers can additionally manually edit the questions. This exam generator effectively improved the user experience for teachers.

In the classification part, we proposed two classification solutions. The rule-based classifier and decision tree classifier. The rule-based algorithm is easy to understand and implement but not general, all the rules are developed or defined by the developer which may not well applied to the phonetic transcription courses. If the different teachers have the different criteria, that means all the rules need to be redefined.

The classification and regression tree (CART) classifier can better represent the teacher's ideas. We can treat different teachers as the different dataset, as long as we got the data from a teacher, a unique decision tree model will be built for classification and regression based on the dataset. The most crucial part in the CART classifier is data, if we get enough data, we can build tree models with better accuracy.

In this paper, seven labels have been set to classify all the data into three classes, about 120 words were added to the dataset, 70% of them were used for training and rest of the words were used for testing. Finally, we got about 84% of correctness. We believe the correct rate will be improved by adding more words into the dataset.

References

1. Seals, C.D., et al.: Applied webservices platform supported through modified edit distance algorithm: automated phonetic transcription grading tool (APTgt). In: Zaphiris, P., Ioannou, A. (eds.) HCII 2020. LNCS, vol. 12205, pp. 380–398. Springer, Cham (2020). https://doi.org/10.1007/978-3-030-50513-4_29
2. Berge, Z.L.: Active, interactive, and reflective eLearning. Q. Rev. Distance Educ. 3(2), 181 (2002)
3. Cerna, M.: Modified recommender system model for the utilized eLearning platform. J. Comput. Educ. 7(1), 105–129 (2019). https://doi.org/10.1007/s40692-019-00133-9
4. Li, S., Atkins, M.S.: Software engineering to develop online phonetics educational training: interdisciplinary research with communications sciences and disorders. In: ASEE-SE 2020, p. 11, Auburn (2020)
5. Shriberg, L.D.: A procedure for phonetic transcription by consensus. J. Speech Lang. Hearing Res. 27, 456–465 (1984)
6. Qawqzeh, Y.K., Otoom, M.M.: A proposed decision tree classifier for atherosclerosis prediction and classification. IJCSNS Int. J. Comput. Sci. Network Secur. 19(12), 23 (2019)
7. Altaf, T., Anwar, S.M.: Multi-class Alzheimer's disease classification using image and clinical features. Biomed. Signal Process. Control. 43, 64–74 (2018)
8. Patel, H., Prajapati, P.: Study and analysis of decision tree based classification algorithms. JCSE 6(10), 14 (2018)
9. Leo, B.: Classification and Regression trees. Wadsworth and Brooks/Cole Advanced Books and Software, New York
10. Wagner, R.A., Fischer, M.J.: The string-to-string correction problem. J. ACM 21, 168 (1974)

11. Ristad, E.S., Yianilos, P.N.: Learning string-edit distance. IEEE Trans. Pattern Anal. Mach. Intell. **20**(5), 522–532 (1998)
12. https://scikit-learn.org/stable/modules/tree.html
13. https://towardsdatascience.com/decision-tree-algorithm-for-multiclass-problems-using-python-6b0ec1183bf5
14. Rutkowski, L., Jaworski, M.: The CART decision tree for mining data streams. Inf. Sci. **266**, 1–15 (2014)

Designing an App for Remotely Children's Spelling Assessment

Jaline Mombach[1,2] and Fabrizzio Soares[2,3(✉)]

[1] Farroupilha Federal Institute – Alegrete Campus, Porto Alegre, RS, Brazil
`jaline.mombach@iffarroupilha.edu.br`
[2] Instituto de Informática, Universidade Federal de Goiás, Goiânia, GO, Brazil
`fabrizzio@ufg.br`
[3] Computer Science, Southern Oregon University, Ashland, OR, USA

Abstract. A type of spelling test is a regular activity in children's literacy classes. This traditional paper-based test has application details that need in-person administration. However, the pandemic period required several class adjustments to distance learning and did not exist a digital solution to aid professionals in this assessment. Therefore, our goal is to provide a method to perform spelling assessments for children, even remotely. Using the Design Science Research Methodology, we describe the design study to develop an artifact for children's spelling tests in this work. We report as findings expectations of literacy professionals and parents for that, and a usability inspection by experts in the artifact developed. The prototype evaluation indicates approximately 73% adherence to specific children's design recommendations guidelines, more outstanding adhesion than those previously evaluated by the literature using the same guideline. These results indicate our artifact is feasible and can aid children's literacy in remote learning.

Keywords: Children · Literacy · Spelling assessment

1 Introduction

In the last year, we have experienced a crisis with no precedence, caused by the COVID-19 pandemic. As a result, teachers and other professionals, who work with children, had been required to adjust all learning activities to remote environments. Emergent literacy was one of the most challenging areas because young children – no-literate – are even more dependents on adults than other students to understand homework requirements [1].

A routine task in literacy classrooms is spelling tests. Educational researchers report the possibility of classification children's thoughts about how the writing system works while learning it. Children go through different comprehension phases of *phonemes* and *graphemes* during the literacy process, and because of that, professionals perform tests to recognize the child's writing hypothesis [2–4].

© Springer Nature Switzerland AG 2021
P. Zaphiris and A. Ioannou (Eds.): HCII 2021, LNCS 12784, pp. 92–107, 2021.
https://doi.org/10.1007/978-3-030-77889-7_7

Teachers, speech therapists, psychologists, and other professionals perform individual tests for children's spelling level identification. These assessments support plan literacy activities that better meet personal learning needs for each child. Usually, traditional spelling tests use paper, pencil, and handwriting in dictation sessions [5].

Professionals must perceive essential details while the children write, such as trace direction, mirrored letters presence [6], phonemes pronunciation, and gestures in how they read what they write. These strategic signals are an essential part of the evaluation, as much as letter choice. However, capture that in a distance learning context is not a simple assignment [7].

Hence, we aim to provide a method to perform traditional spelling assessments for children, even in remote contexts. In this work, we describe the design study to develop an app for children's spelling tests. The rest of the paper is organized as follows: First, we overview the related works - technologies that possible dictation sessions configuration. Then, we describe our proposal's concept and development, adopting the Design Science Research Methodology (DSRM). Next, we present a heuristic evaluation to validate the prototype. Finally, we discuss the evaluation results as a proof of concept and ideas about future work regarding this alternative method.

2   Related Works

Technology can aid teachers in literacy classes, and there is growing attention of the Child-Computer Interaction community for that. Additionally, the mobile application market has been designing solutions for children, especially in the face of remote teaching [1,8]. Thus, we investigate the previous works focused on children's spelling. The Fig. 1 reveals the graphical interfaces by the principal solutions investigated.

A game called DysEggxia [9] integrates a method to improve the spelling of children with dyslexia through playful and targeted exercises. The principal distinction between the proposal and the others is the non-use of correct words or positive examples to follow. It presents for the child with a misspelled word as an exercise to solve.

ABRACADABRA [10] is a web-based literacy program, which provides resources and tools for teachers and parents. The spelling test section uses the Wide Range Achievement Test [13], and it asks children to write single words on dictation. Although the original test [13] is using handwriting, ABRACADABRA adopted a model of choice of letters, as shown in Fig. 1b.

Some paid applications intended to perform children's dictation tasks have been developed. One available one is the "DoodleSpell" [11]. The app presents some activities, such as the original dictate (audio asking to write something), also picture-based dictation, and exercises of copying words and finding them in word search puzzles. The tool increases the difficulty level according to the skills acquired by the child.

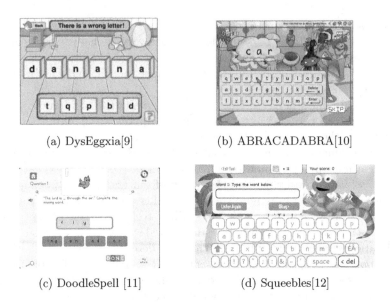

(a) DysEggxia[9]   (b) ABRACADABRA[10]

(c) DoodleSpell [11]   (d) Squeebles[12]

Fig. 1. Children's spelling apps related to our proposal.

Although it presents several options for the teacher, it does not provides children handwriting records. The Fig. 1c shows the screenshot of DoodleSpell. Finally, another paid application is "Squeebles Spelling Tests" [12]. This app is a specific tool for parents and teachers to create customized spelling tests. Among the main features, there are set up tests for multiple users, upload spelling lists recording audio of the word for children to hear, and send the tests created to the cloud, allowing sharing on different family devices. As well as other apps, also it does not provide capture of handwriting.

Therefore, several works provide ways to spelling assessment. The main observed features are the teacher's possibility of word customization, support for the voice user interface, reports, and creation of dictation sessions. Nevertheless, just one study reports pedagogical foundation or theories support. Moreover, interactions for spelling are using a keyboard or a selection of letters on the screen. Consequently, these solutions do not solve professionals' new demand to perform tests similar to traditional face-to-face in a remote learning context.

Furthermore, in the Brazilian scenario, any of these apps would be used because it lacks assistance in the Portuguese language and the spelling theories common in Brazilian literacy classrooms. No previous study focused on supporting teachers to perform spelling tests automated through children's handwriting to the best of our knowledge. Thus, in the next section, we describe more details about our approach to working that.

3   Study Design

Facing the perspective of solving a real problem using computational technology, we adopted the Design Science Research Methodology (DSRM) as the methodology to delineate the project. DSRM provides an iterate process containing phases to identify the problem, define objectives of a solution, artifact design and development, demonstration, evaluation, and communication [14]. The Fig. 2 shows the design process, described as follows.

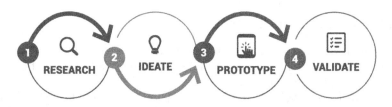

Fig. 2. The design process: (i) user research and spelling technologies review; (ii) brainstorming session for ideation; (iii) wireframes build and hi-fi prototype; (iv) experts validate. The design process: (i) user research and spelling technologies review; (ii) brainstorming session for ideation; (iii) wireframes build and hi-fi prototype; (iv) experts validate.

3.1   User Research

First, we needed to learn how users do spelling tests in a traditional environment; what steps they performed at in-person classes before the pandemic period? Thus, we interviewed teachers and conducted an online survey for parents and professionals in the infant's area. The scope was limited to Brazilian users.

In a partnership with the CEPAE/UFG, the school belonging to our university, we received experts' contributions in contextual interviews. Three literacy teachers told us about the emergent literacy period and usual spelling activities. For that, we ask: (i) What are the most common activities in literacy classes? (ii) How is children's writing assessed? (iii) Are there difficulties with individual spelling assessments? (iv) Does school use technologies regularly in the classroom?

Survey. From April to June 2020, we applied two online questionnaires to understand users' pain points and overall necessities in the spelling assessments during the pandemic period.

Parents/guardians of children 4–7 years answered questions about expectations and difficulties in the remotely learning period in an online questionnaire.

We asked: (i) Do schools maintain remote school activities? (ii) What digital resources schools use for communication among teachers, parents, and children? (iii) Which content format teachers adopt most frequently? (iv) Is the teacher evaluating the children's activities? (v) Do you identify difficulties for the child to perform remote activities during this period? Additionally, the questionnaire provided an open box for comments.

There was another questionnaire we applied to children's literacy professionals. Our interest in this questionnaire was to understand how spelling evaluations occur, the most notable theories that teachers use, session dictation duration, what is most important to observe in the dictation sessions, and whether teachers maintained evaluations during the remote teaching period. We also provided an open box for opinions.

3.2   Ideation and Prototyping

After the user research step, we conduct a systematic review to analyze the main related works. We also reviewed similar apps and made a list of functional requirements to plan the method.

Inspired by the children's writing development theories and how professionals manage spelling assessments, our research group idealized the "Children Literacy Aid Tool" (CLAT) method. CLAT simulates a spelling assessment equivalent as teachers perform the face-to-face activity in classrooms. An app must support collecting children's handwriting on touchscreen devices and a platform for professionals and parents to follow each child's progress data.

3.3   Expert Validation

A focus group discussion supports identifying participants' perceptions, feelings, perspectives, and ideas about a particular subject, product, or activity. Thus, as a first concept validation, we showed the hi-fi prototype to teachers and collected their opinion in a focus group discussion. We asked them what the benefits and limitations of the method proposed. For that, we used two devices in that test: (i) Samsung Galaxy Tab 10.1 (2010) model P7500 - Android 4.2.2; (ii) Samsung Galaxy Note 10.1 (2013) model GT-N8000, Android 7.1.2, including the S pen. The participants were the same as the contextual interview before.

Using the TIDRC framework [8] as a guideline, we invite five computer experts to inspect these design guidelines analytically in our prototype [15].

Guidelines. The TIDRC is a guideline of developmental suitability for children's touch screen interfaces evidenced-based design recommendations, resulting from a comprehensive literature review by Soni et al. It presents structured guidelines in three interface dimensions: cognitive, physical, and socio-emotional.

The socio-emotional dimension analyzes items about customization options, activity structure, and social sharing and privacy. The physical dimension analyzes gesture and target features, such as type of gestures, gesture family, and target size. Finally, the cognitive dimension evidences visual design and audio features, interactive and informational features, and application responsiveness.

The original conceptual framework has 57 evidence-based design recommendations, distributed in 4 items to socio-emotional, 11 items to physical, and 47 items to cognitive dimension. However, we adapted it, adjusting to specificities of the target audience (4 to 7 years old) and the literacy context. Thus, we consider just 53 items for the questionnaire of evaluation.

Thus, we designed an online form for the evaluators to answer the prototype's adherence level regarding those items. We have adopted a Likert scale of 5 points: strongly disagree, disagree, neutral, agree, and strongly agree. Additionally, there were text input boxes for relevant raters' observations to each item category.

Procedure. We instructed the participants to access the application and explore it openly. Next, they received the address of the online evaluation form. Because of the COVID-19 pandemic, we were unable to experiment face-to-face with the evaluators. Then, we configured a cloud testing service for remote evaluation to ensure access to all and the same environment for the test. Genymotion Cloud provides Android virtual devices to run apps on the web, ensuring all features, including audio and text-to-speech configuration. Consequently, we created a virtual tablet device, Android version 10.0, 1536 × 2048 size with 320 DPI, and sent an invitation to evaluators to online access.

During the design process, we achieved some results and shared them in the following section.

4   Results and Discussion

After teacher interviews, parents questionnaires, prototyping steps, and tests with specialists, we achieved some results. Thus, in this section, we report the main findings during the artifact design process.

4.1   User Insights

We began the project by interviewing three literacy teachers. As for the most common literacy activities, they showed tasks to writing and reading skills. Generally, the activities involve a central theme, such as an infant story and exploring words about that.

As for writing assessment, there are several types of activities, collective and individual moments. Furthermore, teachers differ "spontaneous writing" from "guided writing." The spontaneous way is when the children choose what they want to write, while guided is when an adult dictates something to children, usually from a word list. About technologies used in school, they said that exist a few tablet devices at school. For this reason, teachers need to use them collectively. Nonetheless, an interesting point is the teachers observe children's greater interest in carrying out activities in this type of device than traditional ways using paper and pencil.

They indicated that there are several methodologies for literacy in Brazil, and therefore, different modes of conducting spelling tests. The choice of test type depends on the theory supported by each school. Because of this reporting, we conducted an online questionnaire to receive more teachers' answers. We conducted a survey using two questionnaires: one for professionals and the other for parents.

Professionals Overview. The professionals' questionnaire received the contribution of 104 people from all Brazilian regions. The first question we asked was if they applied word dictations for children. The majority, about 83% of participants, answered yes against 17% of them that said not. Thus, we asked these professionals which theoretical basis they adopted. Approximately 79% of respondents said that they classify children's writing according to the theory of Ferreiro et al. [2]. Another 13% indicated that they label writing on levels created by themselves, based on their experience. Only 3% pointed to Linnea's theory [3], and another 3% registered that they do not classify children's spelling.

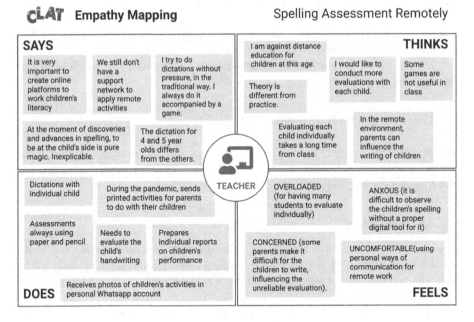

Fig. 3. Empathy mapping example - professionals.

In addition to these indicators, most professionals spend up to 30 min performing the individual dictations. When we asked them what challenges there are in applying individual dictation, they reported: number of children in the same class, keeping other children in school activity while applying individual dictation, lack of an appropriate environment for individual dictation, difficulty in manually organizing the children's records, and evaluation of results. Only 13% of the professionals reported that they do not see difficulties in this activity. By uniting the professionals' perceptions in the interviews and the survey, we created an empathy map for the teacher user profile, illustrates in Fig. 3. The empathy map deals with teachers' pain and desires regarding the possibility of evaluating spelling remotely, especially during the pandemic period.

Understanding Face-to-Face Spelling Tests. During the contact with the professionals, we try to understand how the individual evaluation works. Therefore, we describe below the steps to teachers performing spelling assessments based on Ferreiro's theory [2], one of most practiced in Brazil.

Teachers plan a list of four words and a sentence to be dictated. These words differ in the number of syllables and must be from the same semantic context. At the test time, the environment must be conducive to the child's concentration. This test is a silent and individual moment with the professional.

Hence, children had to follow some instructions:

1. The professional asks the child to write on the paper as he thinks how to spell the first dictated word.
2. After the child has finished, professionals ask him to read what he has just written, pointing with his finger to the register (finger-point reading).
3. In the sequence, the professional observes what movements the children have made with their finger while reading and draws the gesture made below the child's writing. This strategic sign is essential to identify a phonetic connection with letters' choice and if the child has syllabic perception.
4. The steps are repeated until the professional dictates all the words and the final sentence. Then, the professional analyzes the child's record and classifies which level is appropriate.

Parents Overview. The parents' questionnaire received the contribution of 119 people, guardians from children 4 to 7 years (literacy period). Likewise the professionals' questionnaire, there were participants from all Brazilian regions[1].

This specific questionnaire aimed to understand the parents' view of literacy activities during the remote classes period. To the guardians who responded that remote activities were normally occurring at the child's school (76% of respondents), we asked about the most commonly used resources, the format of content sent, and how evaluations of children's productions were happening.

The Fig. 4 illustrates in a graph the responses received regarding resources used. Parents responded to social networks such as Whatsapp, Facebook, and Instagram regarding the most used resources (56% choices). Furthermore, they chose the use of the Learning Management System (LMS), such as Google Classroom, Edmodo, Moodle, among others (51% choices). Video platforms (Youtube and Vimeo) are also a widely used resource, with approximately 44%

---

[1] The project website presents the detailed survey data: http://fabrizziosoares.me/clat.

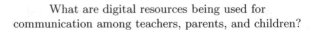

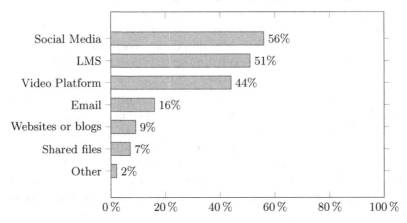

Fig. 4. The responses received regarding resources used by schools during the pandemic period to remote learning.

of choices. Likewise, email (16%) is often mentioned, and websites or blogs (9%). Additionally, parents indicated cloud shared folders (7%), such as Google Drive, Dropbox, and One Drive. In the "Other," they mentioned Microsoft Teams and also a school platform.

Already on the content format sent, the main is recorded video (33%). In the recorded video, teachers film lessons and send them to children - asyn-

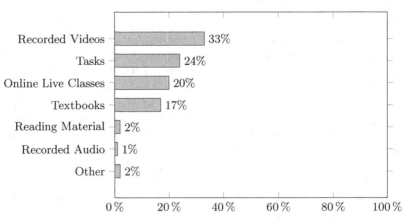

Fig. 5. Type of content format most used during the remote learning period.

chronously). Many schools adopted printed tasks (24%), and others have opted for online live classes (20%). The textbook also appears as a content option in this period, with approximately 17% of choices. Among the less mentioned items are the use of reading material and recorded audio. In the "Other" option, one person described "small videos with proposals of games, and storytelling" and another that the school made a mix of all content formats. The graph of Fig. 5 reveals the data received in this question.

We asked how teachers were evaluating the activities done by the child during the pandemic. Most of those guardians indicated that they send a photo of the activity or a digitalized paper task version by social networks, approximately 42% of the users. However, the number of responses describing that teachers not doing evaluations in this period was also significant (40%), at least in parents' understanding. Some of them also indicated that teachers correct in the digital platform of school, almost 16% of the answers. The Fig. 6 demonstrates a graph with detailed data on this issue.

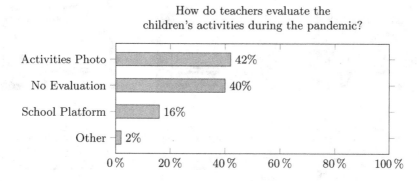

Fig. 6. Teachers' evaluation approaches for children's writing records

Finally, we asked all parents what the main difficulties for spelling remote activities were. About 68% of the participants registered an adult's dependence to perform activities as a crucial factor. In the sequence, the lack of direct communication between teachers and children (29%), difficulty in restricting children's access to the digital environment for study purposes only (15%), and the reduction of teachers' feedback. Additionally, they indicated the need to access children to social networks and communication difficulties among all professionals who attend the child (teacher, speech therapist, among others). Furthermore, 13% of respondents said there are no difficulties in this process. From parents' and professionals' comments, we have designed an artifact to solve remote spelling evaluations, detailed below.

4.2 Solution Designed

After contextualization and analysis of requirements emerge the Children Literacy Aid Tool (CLAT) project. Firstly, we develop a prototype for the Android system. The graphical interface is based on previously evaluated applications, including the free spelling area. The teacher's report is currently the same as the paper version (including markings on how the child read). This prototype has limited functionality since its function was only to test children's interaction. Therefore, we intend to amplify the proposal, allowing access to conventional browsers. Consequently, it will be possible to use in different touch-sensitive devices, regardless of operational systems.

The initial prototype follows the approach of Ferreiro et al. [2], which was the one that had the most significant prominence in the survey we conducted for literacy teachers. The Fig. 7 demonstrates the step by step hi-fi prototype developed. In this approach, the app dictates four words from the same semantic field, which differ in the number of syllables. Next, it dictates a sentence using one of the previous words.

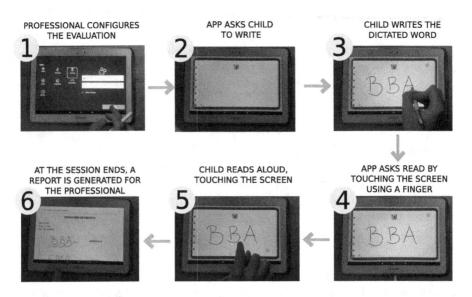

Fig. 7. Steps of the dictation on the mobile device.

The professional chooses one of the available themes and writes the child's name and age. Afterward, he passes the device to the child, who will be evaluated. The app dictates (by text-to-speech) the word for the child. In the sequence, the child writes - using his own finger or a pen for touch-sensitive devices. The app recognizes that the child has finished spelling and asks him to read aloud and touch with the finger on the screen. This process is repeated until all the words, and the sentence has been dictated. In the end, the app generates the report for the professional in PDF format. To evaluate the prototype designed, we evaluate it with experts using a specific guideline and the results are describe below.

4.3   Heuristic Evaluation

The COVID-19 pandemic did not allow interaction tests with children since the schools canceled face-to-face activities. Therefore, to demonstrate that our proposal is child-friendly and feasible for utilization, we made a preliminary validation of the prototype with specialists of Human-Computer Interaction, through usability inspection using the TIDRC conceptual framework [8].

Firstly, the experts reported about the socio-emotional dimension. The graph in Fig. 8 illustrates 46.7% of agreement with items evaluated, 13.3% neutrality, and 40% of disagreement. Most positive assessments were in the item "Provides choice and customization features to enhance children's intrinsic motivation and task engagement." Evaluators indicated the possibility of teachers choosing themes and words as compatible with this item. However, some evaluators disagree because it is not possible for customization by children.

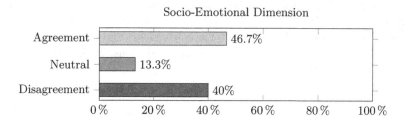

Fig. 8. Percentage of adherence to three items evaluated in socio-emotional dimension

The item "Uses an open-ended app structure to support children's engagement and creativity" was a few nonspecific because in this type of spelling test is not possible an open-ended structure for children since that sequence is crucial for a correct assessment by the teacher. Thus, the majority of experts classified it as neutral adherence. The last item, "Avoids computer-automated social interactions for children," received the severest disagreement since the app uses text-to-speech technology to dictate words for children.

Next, the physical dimension had eleven items to appreciate, generally about gestures and targets area. The graph in Fig. 9 demonstrates 74.5% of adherence for these items, 14.5% of neutrality, and just 11.3% of disagreement by evaluators.

The specialists assessed the determined gesture family as well as the size of the gesture area and button choices. However, the framework addresses possibilities of scrolling that the application does not provide. Consequently, items "Supports full-hand gestures for scrolling instead of thumb and index finger

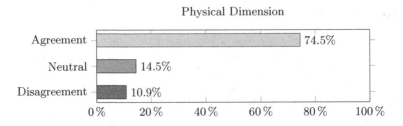

Fig. 9. Percentage of adherence to eleven items evaluated in physical dimension

gestures" and "Uses horizontal scrolling instead of vertical scrolling, which is conceptually difficult for children" were the ones that received the lowest adherence appraisers. However, we did not include scrolling precisely because the writing area occupies the whole screen without considering these options.

The cognitive dimension is the one with the most significant number of recommendations because it understands features of visual design, audio, interactivity, informational options, and application responsiveness. The Fig. 10 demonstrates almost 75% of the app adherence with recommendations, 13.8% neutrality, and just 11% disagreement.

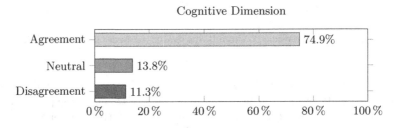

Fig. 10. Percentage of adherence to thirty-nine items evaluated in cognitive dimension

The evaluators strongly agree that the application adheres to visual design guidance: graphics, backgrounds, and text font are ideals to an infant proposal. To the audio features, they consider appropriate sounds to feedback uses. However, there was a negative assessment about the item "Avoids using background music with videos" because the intro video had a song background.

About interactive features, the specialists approve the clickable options, labels, and low menu complexity items. Nevertheless, they reported the no-existence of explicit scaffolding such as interaction prompts to help children remember how to accomplish tasks. Informational features received a favorable assessment as well, save the presence of a tutorial that was contradictory. Due to the recommendation "Avoids using in-app tutorials for children; the interface should provide some form of guidance during tasks," this aspect held strong disagreement assessed by experts.

Soni et al. [8] reported that apps evaluated in their study adhere to only 51% of items in the cognitive dimension and 67% in the physical dimension. At the same time, our prototype adheres to up to 74.9% of the cognitive dimension items and 75% in the physical dimension. As for the socio-emotional dimension, the study indicates that, on average, 72% of apps adhere to these items. In CLAT, these items need to be improved since the application adheres to 47% of the socio-emotional recommendations. However, CLAT disagrees with some TIDRC items due to teachers' pre-literacy requirements, mainly in the socio-emotional dimension. Therefore, the expansion of specific guidelines for children's touch-sensitive applications regarding early literacy, including pedagogical resources, is evident.

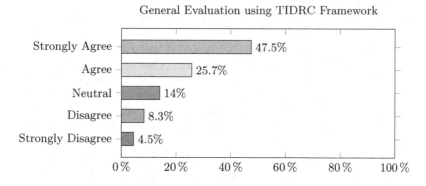

General Evaluation using TIDRC Framework

Fig. 11. Percentage of adherence to all fifty-three items evaluated by five experts

In general, the evaluation of the prototype was entirely satisfactory. The Fig. 11 illustrates a graph with the total percentage of app adherence to the fifty-three TIDRC framework items. There were approximately 47% of the experts' strong agreement, followed by almost 26% of agreement, 14% neutrality, 8% disagreement, and 4.5% strong disagreement. If we consider fidelity to the recommendations, adding the percentages of strong agreement and agreement, we reached 73.2% of positive assessment against just 12.8% of inconsistency and the rest in neutrality. The heuristic evaluation results show an essential validation to the solution designed concerning evidence-based design recommendations for children.

5   Concluding Remarks

Teachers perform children's spelling tests in literacy classes. However, during the pandemic period, emerged need to perform this traditional face-to-face assessment remotely. The work goal was to understand the main design requirements for this type of task and develop a digital solution to support teachers, children, and parents.

Complementing previous solutions focused on children spelling activities, we presented a solution for mobile devices that promote teachers' customization of dictation sessions and capture children's handwriting. Our proposal, named Children Literacy Aid Tool, presents an artifact using an educational theoretical basis as the teachers practice in traditional paper-based tests. As steps in methodology, we performed context interviews and a survey for parents and literacy professionals. We designed an artifact and assessed it in a usability inspection for experts.

As the results, we report findings of how Brazilian parents face the remote period with children in the literacy phase and the main difficulties of this. Furthermore, we mapped out how professionals usually performed the traditional face-to-face paper-based assessment process and created a method to do it remotely, with digital support. We also describe the main themes that emerged from the children's literacy in a distance learning context - teachers' expectations, roles, perceived benefits, and concerns.

After developing a prototype, we evaluated it using the TIDRC conceptual framework, and we obtained satisfactory results. Overall, our app has achieved 73% approval on guidelines from evidence-based design recommendations for children used. These results suggest that the new solution is feasible to support children's spelling tests. Thus, we conclude that our goal was achieved, and the next steps are to correct the items pointed out by the evaluators and test with children.

A significant advantage of the proposed method over the others is the teacher's possibility of remote evaluation, capturing the child's handwriting. Other apps use the keyboard or visible letters to choose the writing, which does not simulate the classroom's real context.

Moreover, we intended to offer an advanced writing experience for the child, reproducing the paper and pencil experience adapted in different touch-sensitive devices and promoting greater engagement of the learner during the spelling sessions through gamification strategies.

References

1. Dong, C., Cao, S., Li, H.: Young children's online learning during Covid-19 pandemic: Chinese parents' beliefs and attitudes. Child. Youth Serv. Rev. **118**, 105440 (2020)
2. Ferreiro, E., Teberosky, A., Lichtenstein, D.M.: Psicogênese da língua escrita. Artes Médicas (1986)
3. Ehri, L.C.: Phases of development in learning to read words by sight. J. Res. Reading **18**(2), 116–125 (1995)
4. Ganske, K.: The developmental spelling analysis: a measure of orthographic knowledge. Educ. Assess. **6**(1), 41–70 (1999)
5. Cardoso-Martins, C., Corrêa, M.F., Lemos, L.S., Napoleão, R.F.: Is there a syllabic stage in spelling development? Evidence from Portuguese-speaking children. J. Educ. Psychol. **98**(3), 628 (2006)

6. Mombach, J., Ferreira, C., Felix, J., Salvini, R., Soares, F.: Mirrored and rotated letters in children spellings: An automatic analysis approach. In: 2020 IEEE Canadian Conference on Electrical and Computer Engineering (CCECE), pp. 1–4 (2020). https://doi.org/10.1109/CCECE47787.2020.9255765

7. Mombach, J., Rossi, F.D., Felix, J., Soares, F.: Remote assessing children's handwriting spelling on mobile devices. In: 2020 IEEE 44th Annual Computers, Software, and Applications Conference (COMPSAC), pp. 1279–1284. IEEE (2020)

8. Soni, N., Aloba, A., Morga, K.S., Wisniewski, P.J., Anthony, L.: A framework of touchscreen interaction design recommendations for children (TIDRC) characterizing the gap between research evidence and design practice. In: Proceedings of the 18th ACM International Conference on Interaction Design and Children, pp. 419–431 (2019)

9. Rello, L., Bayarri, C., Otal, Y., Pielot, M.: A computer-based method to improve the spelling of children with dyslexia. In: Proceedings of the 16th International ACM SIGACCESS Conference on Computers and Accessibility, pp. 153–160 (2014)

10. Savage, R.S., Erten, O., Abrami, P., Hipps, G., Comaskey, E., van Lierop, D.: Abracadabra in the hands of teachers: the effectiveness of a web-based literacy intervention in grade 1 language arts programs. Comput. Educ. **55**(2), 911–922 (2010)

11. EZ Education Ltd., Doodlespell (2020). https://www.doodleenglish.com/doodlespell/

12. Key Stage Fun. Squeebles spelling test (2020). https://keystagefun.co.uk/literacy-apps/squeebles-spelling-test/

13. Wilkinson, G.S.: WRAT-3: Wide range achievement test administration manual. Wide Range Inc. (1993)

14. Peffers, K., Tuunanen, T., Rothenberger, M.A., Chatterjee, S.: A design science research methodology for information systems research. J. Manag. Inf. Syst. **24**(3), 45–77 (2007)

15. Mombach, J., et al.: A new approach to performing paper-based children's spelling tests on mobile devices. In: 2020 IEEE International Conference on Systems, Man, and Cybernetics (SMC), pp. 4346–4351. IEEE (2020)

Digital Technologies Assisting Migrant Population Overcome Language Barriers: The Case of the EasyRights Research Project

Eleftheria Nteliou[1](✉) , Jacques Koreman[2] , Inna Tolskaya[3] ,
and Olga Kehagia[1]

[1] University of Thessaly, Volos, Greece
{enteliou, ok}@uth.gr
[2] Norwegian University of Science and Technology, Trondheim, Norway
jacques.koreman@ntnu.no
[3] Capeesh, Trondheim, Norway
inna@capeesh.com

Abstract. The issue of migrant integration in host communities is of major importance, because its effectiveness can influence employment opportunities, social cohesion, and economic welfare, creating equal opportunities among citizens. One of the greatest challenges towards this goal is the limited knowledge of the language of the host community, which can create miscommunication and additional difficulties to migrants. Basic language training is important, but it is of little help when migrants are confronted with the language used in complex procedures that are required for their inclusion in the new country of residence. This paper, which is descriptive and explorative in nature, focuses on the targeted digital solutions offered by the EU-funded easyRights research project that can help migrants effectively communicate and receive guidance, in order to handle the demands of various inclusion-related procedures that may differ from one country to the other. One of the digital tools presented in the paper aims at facilitating familiarization with the required domain-specific vocabulary, while the second one intends to offer pronunciation training, including training for the domain-specific words, in order to equip migrants with the knowledge and skills they need to communicate effectively. The two digital tools, which could act synergistically, employ advanced technology and are part of a technological pathway, whose aim is to assist migrants exercise their rights in the process of their integration in a new country. Implications are also discussed.

Keywords: Digital · Mobile-based language training · Migrant integration

1 Introduction

The fast pacing technological evolution that has occurred in recent years paved the way for unprecedented changes in human life and communication and brought promises for solutions to problems that relate to various fields of human action. One of these fields that have always been challenging and where technology can provide effective solutions is social organization and active citizenship [1], especially in cases in which

P. Zaphiris and A. Ioannou (Eds.): HCII 2021, LNCS 12784, pp. 108–124, 2021.
https://doi.org/10.1007/978-3-030-77889-7_8

societies consist of multicultural and plurilingual populations, as a result of the rising migration trends. This paper focuses on the European context and on the technological solutions that can be employed with the purpose of assisting the migrants' social inclusion in new places of residence, by helping them overcome the language barrier and exercise their rights.

1.1 Migration and Integration in Europe: Facts and Trends

The issue of migration in Europe has attracted increasing attention in recent years, because there is a great number of people from various countries and nationalities that have been constantly crossing the EU (European Union) borders in an effort to chase opportunities for a better life. In fact, it has been estimated that more than 1 million people have entered the EU borders during the 'refugee crisis' in 2015 [2] and this number keeps growing with even more third country (non-EU) nationals from various parts of Africa, the Middle East or the Black Sea countries constantly reaching the European continent and following different routes [3–5].

The reasons for migration vary and may also determine the status of the 'moving person', who is generally called a 'migrant', but falls, in fact, into one of the three following categories [6, 7]:

1. Asylum seeker: A third-country (non-EU country) national or stateless person who has usually been forced to leave the country of origin, mainly for reasons of war, persecution or human rights violation, and has made an application for protection to another country, in respect of which a final decision has not yet been taken and as a consequence, he/she has not been legally recognized as a refugee yet.
2. Refugee: A third-country national or stateless person who has voluntarily left the country of former residence and is unwilling or unable to return, because of fear of persecution for reasons of race, religion, political opinion or membership to a particular social group and to whom the right of international protection is recognized.
3. Migrant: A person who has usually been a resident in a third country and establishes his/her usual residence in the territory of an EU Member State for a period that is, or is expected to be, at least 12 months and is neither a refugee nor an asylum seeker.

The term 'migrant' is going to be used as an umbrella term in this paper to refer to all these three categories.

Regardless of the reasons for moving to another country, migrants have acknowledged human rights that should be respected in any case, so that violations and marginalization can be avoided [6, 8]. Consequently, the migrants' integration in host communities should be a priority. However, this also seems to be a challenge, since there is not always a clear perception of what the process of integration entails and how it can be achieved. In fact, integration is sometimes considered as a one-way process of adaptation, that refers to the migrants' 'acculturation' or 'assimilation' to the host community's culture, way of life and mentality [9]. Instead, the definition provided in [10] describes migrant integration as "a two-way process of adaptation", during which both the migrants but also the host communities should become aware of their exact rights and obligations and collaborate towards shared goals, some of which are the respect for common values as well as access to services and the labor market. This definition manages to include the concept of the 'social engineering of integration' that is likely to lead to functional multi-cultural societies [11].

Apart from the definitional ambiguities, it seems without doubt that the issue of migrant integration is closely related to the migrant's human rights, safety and legal identity, thus rendering it necessary for host countries to design migration policies and specify criteria for integration, such as the 'Zaragoza integration indicators', which examine the level of integration in the areas of education, employment, social inclusion and active citizenship [12]. These initiatives are directed towards the confrontation of the practical challenges involved in the integration process, which include, among others, information poverty [13], bureaucratic, legal and cultural barriers as well as limited proficiency in the local language [14].

In fact, the migrants' limited knowledge of the language of the host community seems to be a serious issue, since it may create miscommunication and feelings of disappointment, making migrants miss opportunities to familiarize themselves with the host culture, expand their social contacts and match their skills with the local labor market [9, 15, 16]. Therefore, the language gap could hinder the migrants' active participation in host communities and prolong the process of their social inclusion, thus rendering language learning "a first-priority intervention for the general migrant and refugee community" [17, p. 100]. This explains the need for the design of language and education policies that carefully consider the issue of language diversity and recognize the migrants' literacy as an essential right and a prerequisite for their actual integration in a society that regards them as citizens with equal rights [18].

All these challenges that relate to migrant integration can be confronted to a great extent by the means of digital technology tools, such as automation, digitalization, robotics, artificial intelligence, the Internet of Things (IoT), web-based platforms and location-based applications, which have changed the landscape of economic transactions and social processes on a global scale in recent years [14, 19, 20]. In addition to the management of migration flows and border control, digital connectivity can also provide valuable solutions in the newly arrived migrants' information about local administrative and housing services, labor market and entrepreneurship opportunities as well as educational and training courses [21, 22].

The section that follows describes how the migrants' knowledge gap in the language of the host country can be covered by innovative training practices that involve digital technology, as part of the process towards their social inclusion.

1.2 Digital Technological Solutions for Migrant Language Training

On a global level, the ownership and use of mobile phones and social media connectivity have been following a rising trend which can be partly justified by the increased investment in advanced technologies as well as by the availability of low-cost smartphones and data consumption offers [23]. Meanwhile, smartphones are widely recognized as an essential tool for migrants to keep contact with their country of origin and survive in the new country, since web sites, phone-based applications and social media are the main sources of information about the pre-migration, settlement as well as integration stages [24, 25]. Despite the fact that mobile-based internet connectivity may still not be feasible for all migrant populations and in particular for refugees found in rural areas [26], the facilitating role of technology and particularly the digital connectivity offered by mobile phones is also emphasized in the 2030 Agenda for Sustainable Development, since it can help toward migrant integration, which can contribute to the economic and social development of both the destination countries and the countries of origin [27].

Among the technologies that have been commonly employed with the purpose of supporting migrants' social inclusion, employability, education and training in the language of the host country, those that relate to mobile-based digital connectivity are the most popular, such as Free Digital Learning (henceforth referred as FDL), Massive Open Online Courses (henceforth referred as MOOCs) and gamified learning platforms [17, 28–31]. These technologies, whose educational benefits have already been confirmed in various settings that do not always relate to migrant integration purposes [32–35], seem likely to offer great potential, especially in cases where there is no funding or opportunities for formal education or live training courses and can also help migrants handle any difficulties or language issues even long before starting their journey to a foreign country.

Concerning the migrants' language training, in particular, Colucci et al. [28] provide examples of several apps, MOOCs and FDL online courses, that primarily appear as language learning initiatives, but they also serve as a means of assisting civic integration (e.g. guiding migrants to cope with administrative procedures). The authors support that these tools can adapt the content of learning and the related vocabulary to specific situations that relate to the migrants' needs, following an approach that is very close to "Content and Language Integrated Learning" (CLIL) [36].

In the same vein, Castaño-Muñoz et al. [30] point out that MOOCs and FDL can be effectively used towards assisting not only migrant civic integration and employment, but also language learning and participation in higher education, offering great potential and many options in terms of the mode of learning. Concerning the FDL intended for language learning, the authors point out that there are several initiatives that target the migrants' language learning needs, whose development has been favored by the widespread use of mobile phones, the great number of translation apps, commercial mobile apps (such as Duolingo and Babbel) and educational videos that can be watched on line for free as well as the possibility to readapt many open resources, MOOCs and university language courses to create free material that can be used either online, off line or in a face-to-face context of language instruction. Some digital applications that are mentioned as examples are Welcomm![1], which promotes non-formal language learning and Kiron[2], which addresses refugee students and prepares them for admission in the German Higher Education system, by offering online language courses in combination with online practice in other competencies.

Moreover, the combination of FDL with gamification, that is the "use of game-design elements in non-game contexts" [37, p. 2425], can effectively contribute to educational purposes, since gamification has been found to make the whole learning

---

[1] https://welcomm-europe.eu/.

[2] https://kiron.ngo/en/.

process more enjoyable and motivating, reducing learners' anxiety and building confidence in the foreign language [29, 34, 35]. In fact, the combination of mobile learning with gamified activities, could offer several benefits in language immersion programmes where migrants are the target users, by promoting learner autonomy and maximizing the benefits of informal situated learning.

In relation to mobile learning, in particular, Kukulska-Hulme et al. [29] review three projects that use mobile learning technology to achieve contextualized language learning beyond the classroom in language immersion programs. The first one is the MASELTOV project (Mobile Assistance for Social Inclusion and Empowerment of Immigrants with Persuasive Learning Technologies and Social Network Services), which is based on a context-aware smartphone application that combines language learning with game playing services, social interaction, navigation and information [32, 38]. In the SALSA project (Sensors and Apps for Languages in Smart Areas), mobile language lessons attain a game playing character, since they are triggered by bluetooth beacons and also include a treasure hunt or trail [39]. The third project reviewed is the 'Mobile Pedagogy for English Language Teaching', which explores learners and teachers' views on the use of phones and tables for language learning, on the basis of which a Mobile Pedagogy framework has been developed that can guide efforts to design mobile-based language learning practices.

The benefits of digital language learning for migrants of different age groups have also been confirmed by other studies, in which digital tools have the potential to promote familiarization in the vocabulary and pronunciation of the host country along with cultural training [40], expressive L2 vocabulary acquisition in children from low-income families [41], personalized L2 training of illiterate adult migrants, which can also lead to increased learner motivation and self-esteem [42] as well as learner autonomy through a dynamic, task-based approach [43].

Given the major contribution of technology in the field of migrant integration, language migration policies and research have been focusing on the improvement of the synergies between technological innovations and social integration schemes. In what follows, there will be a presentation of an EU initiative, the easyRights research project that intends to provide further solutions in this field.

1.3   The EasyRights Research Project

The Research Executive Agency (REA), which was established by the European Union, has organized the 2018–2020 call on Migration, whose aim is the production of innovative solutions, which include ICT, for the effective governance of issues that relate to migrant integration in host communities. Part of this Call is the EasyRights Horizon 2020 research project, which basically intends to satisfy the needs of migrants, who encounter several difficulties in relation to administrative procedures and the documentation of their arrival in host countries and also help towards the deeper integration of already established migrants, by providing solutions based on advanced artificial intelligence technology.

In an effort to make migrants aware of the required actions and their rights during this transitional stage before their inclusion in host communities, the easyRights project has designed a Natural Language Processing (NLP) intelligent system that presents administrative procedures as a series of steps that migrants need to take, thus creating workflows of action for specific administrative requests that can be frequently updated any time political or administrative changes might occur. This system is partly based on personalized learning and automated technologies that combine machine learning and gamified activities, which are employed for the creation of a vocabulary training mobile app (Capeesh) as well as for a pronunciation training platform (CALST) that can provide migrants with domain-specific knowledge that is required for the completion of different procedures. These digital tools are designed for migrant needs in four European cities, namely Birmingham (UK), Malaga (Spain), Larissa (Greece) and Palermo (Italy), for different purposes (see Table 1). What is interesting is that these digital tools are adapted to different languages, given that the native languages in the four pilot cities are not the same and the migrant populations under study come from various cultural and language backgrounds.

Table 1. The four pilot cities and the different migrant needs the easyRights digital tools intend to provide assistance for.

Pilot city	Migrant needs related to integration
Birmingham (UK)	- Checking vehicle compliance with the city's Clear Air Zone - Participating in public consultation - Registering and completing an online assessment tool for access to learning English
Larissa (Greece)	- Applying for residence permit - Applying for certification of nationality
Malaga (Spain)	- Applying for asylum - Searching for employment
Palermo (Italy)	- Registering at the Registry Office - Searching for employment

In the sections that follow there will be a description of the methodology followed in order to construct the task-specific language learning app (Capeesh) and the pronunciation training tool (CALST) as well as an exemplification of how they work.

2 The EasyRights Digital Tools for Migrant Language Training

2.1 Capeesh: A Digital Tool for Vocabulary Training

The growing availability of mobile technologies has contributed to an increase in mobile-assisted language learning in which learners can autonomously study a second language (L2) anytime or anywhere [44]. To help migrants learn the language required to understand critical information provided in authentic situations, the Capeesh Language Learning mobile application offers exercises that teach the domain-specific language used in such authentic situations. The Capeesh Language Learning application is a self-directed, gamified and asynchronous language learning application designed to teach progressive language skills with an emphasis on teaching domain-specific language and providing any language combinations (L1-L2) for the unique learners. Capeesh language learning application combines communicative didactics, cognitivism, and constructivism with game theory and spaced repetition training [45]. The content in the easyRights project consisting of domain-specific vocabulary, sentences and dialogues is built up using natural language processing technologies to analyze text material provided by the municipalities of Birmingham, Malaga, Palermo and Larissa. Boulton and Cobb [46] had earlier conducted a meta-analysis that found corpus-based or data-driven learning to result in better learning outcomes than traditional approaches. The corpora provided by the municipalities in the easyRights project enable Capeesh to create numerous contextualized examples of how any given word, phrase, sentence, or concept is described in the target languages (i.e. English, Spanish, Italian and Greek), thus enabling the migrant learners to learn the language corpus that is most critical or salient to them in the process of accessing and understanding their rights (see Fig. 1).

The migrant learners in the easyRights project can be categorized as second language learners (SLLs) because they are speaking their maternal language first, for instance Arabic, while learning the language spoken in their host country. More shaming occurs with second language learners than foreign language learners and the SLLs are therefore often pushed to relinquish their primary language and learn the dominant language in the host state [47, 48]. In the easyRights pilot cities Birmingham, Malaga, Palermo and Larissa, the languages of English, Spanish, Italian and Greek are respectively promoted as official languages. Government policies that globally promote official languages over others create language hierarchies either overtly or covertly [48]. If the language used in legal procedures and immigration processes is only made available in English, Spanish, Italian or Greek, this can invalidate and devalue heritage and minority languages in the mainstream society. In order to support the migrants in bridging this language gap, Capeesh provides personalization in terms of the language app experience and also in the onboarding experience for the migrant learner. Capeesh does this by enabling the addition of multiple minority languages as display languages for all four language courses (English, Spanish, Italian and Greek) and the language learning app automatically sets the display language to be the same language as the language setting on the learners' smartphone. When adding minority languages or indigenous languages to the app, one of the main challenges is making sure that there exists a digital alphabet that is globally understood by the native speakers and that can be imported and visualized in the Capeesh application.

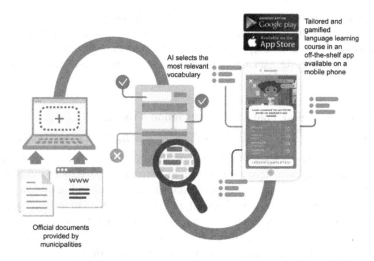

Fig. 1. A schematic representation of the Capeesh AI pipeline[3]

The Capeesh technology enabling efficient creation and publication of domain-specific language courses with multiple (L2) display languages has been developed by Capeesh AS and utilized by organizations in the private and public space since 2018. Although the app is able to provide all language combinations and a highly customizable language learning corpus, there are situations where a direct translation of either vocabulary or expressions taught does not exist in the maternal language and therefore requires either cultural or creative interpretation. Examples are compound words such as "working environment", where a direct translation in maternal languages such as Tirginya does not exist, due to cultural differences. Legal processes in different countries are highly likely to differ due to culture. That is why Capeesh has also added manual steps in the translation process in order to provide translators with explanations of certain vocabulary or expressions that are culture-specific so that the translator can create an explanation or new translation of the expression or vocabulary taught.

Another challenge the Capeesh technology addresses is the analysis of legal documents. For example, analyzing legal documents in Greek language requires state-of-the-art natural language processing algorithms to be developed to work for the Greek alphabet. In 2020 no open natural language processing algorithms (NLP) for Greek language existed. Capeesh has therefore since spring 2020 worked to build Greek NLP in order to enable authentic language learning needed to help the Greek migrants access and learn their rights.

While many of the above problems are addressed in Capeesh, little is known about the migrant learners' motivation for language study in terms of preferred context of learning, desired learning outcomes, cultural preferences and needs to learn pragmatic competences and domain-specific language. A final challenge in the language corpus creation process is to ensure that there is no information asymmetry between the

---

[3] The figure is adapted from the Capeesh website (https://www.capeesh.com/) after permission.

problem experienced by the content provider (municipalities, NGOs) and the problem experienced by the learners (the migrants). There is therefore a need for continuous and collective work between the corpus creators and learners to overcome such information asymmetry by conducting hackathons, surveys and extensive user testing in the creation process.

2.2   CALST: A Digital Tool for Pronunciation Training

The vocabulary training tool presented in the previous section complements basic language training. It teaches vocabulary for specific topics which are related to complex procedures which migrants need to deal with in order to achieve inclusion in the new country of residence, e.g. the application for a residence permit in Larissa, as presented in Sect. 1.3. To apply for a residence permit, migrants may need to interact with public authorities using spoken communication, for example an interview. It is therefore important to put migrants in a position where they not only know the vocabulary of the new language, but they also know how to pronounce the words.

Speaking a new language is a difficult task. Complex patterns of articulatory control in the native language that have been learned over a lifetime must be adapted to those of the new language. Like any other skill, a lot of training is required to improve one's pronunciation. As long as this process is ongoing, speakers will have a foreign accent, which is not necessarily a problem. The goal for second language learning has therefore shifted from native-like pronunciation to intelligibility and comprehensibility [49].

Incorrect pronunciation can reduce intelligibility and lead to misunderstandings [50]. Many misunderstandings can be resolved because the listener can use the context in which a word is used to come to a correct understanding of the migrant's intended message. Nevertheless, research has shown that listeners often are prejudiced when a speaker has a strong accent. For example, speakers may be considered less trustworthy [51]. This is true even if the listener is aware of the prejudice. It is therefore in migrants' own interest to reduce their foreign accent. This underlines the importance of pronunciation as a skill that enables migrants to communicate successfully to achieve their goal of inclusion in the host society.

To support migrants to achieve this goal, the Computer-Assisted Listening and Speaking Tutor (CALST) [52] offers exercises for all words in the domain-specific vocabulary that contain challenging sounds. The exercises consist of pronunciation exercises, in which the migrant compares his/her pronunciation of a word with that of a tutor, and spelling exercises which include feedback to the migrant. Languages differ greatly in the correspondence between spelling (letters) and pronunciation (sounds): while their relation is relatively straightforward in Spanish or Italian, it is very complex in Greek or English. The pronunciation and spelling exercises "prep" migrants for their interactions with native speakers, for instance, a conversation with administrative personnel about the application of a residence permit.

Whether sounds are challenging or not depends on the differences between the sound inventory of the migrant's native language (L1) and that of the target language spoken in the host country (L2). This is demonstrated in Fig. 2, which shows a comparison of the consonant inventories of Kurdish (left figure) and standard Arabic (right figure) with Greek. The sounds on a dark grey background in the figure are likely to present problems for migrants with these native languages when they learn Greek. Despite substantial overlap, we can also recognize differences: for instance, since standard Arabic does not have /p, v, x/ or /ɣ/, which Kurdish does have. These sounds can present problems for Arabic speakers learning Greek, while Kurdish speakers probably will not have any problems with these sounds (but with several others). It should be noted that not all expected mispronunciations of these sounds are equally detrimental to comprehensibility.

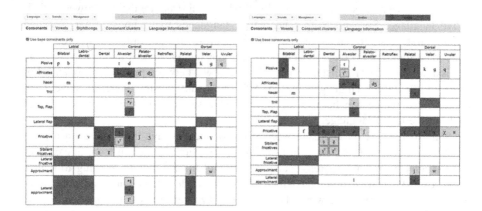

Fig. 2. Comparison of (parts of the) sound inventories of Kurdish and Arabic with Greek

The above figure was generated using L1-L2 map [53], which is based on language information collected by Maddieson [54] and extended with more languages. It now contains the sound inventories of over 500 languages. As part of the easyRights project, the sound inventories of native languages spoken by larger migrant groups will be added to the database so that pronunciation exercises can be tailored to their needs.

But besides "prepping" exercises for domain-specific vocabulary, CALST also offers more comprehensive exercises for any pronunciation problem language learners may encounter. Often, migrants find it difficult to pronounce some sounds of the target language (Greek in the example) because they cannot hear the difference between that sound and another, more familiar sound. Particularly sounds that are similar to a sound in the migrant's native language are difficult to learn because they are easily confused perceptually [55]. That is why CALST also offers two types of listening exercises in which phonetically similar sounds are contrasted, in addition to pronunciation and spelling exercises. These comprehensive exercises do not use the domain-specific vocabulary, but instead learning material is used that is based on linguistic criteria. The listening exercises focus on so-called minimal pairs, i.e., word pairs which contrast a word containing a specific challenging sound with a similar word in which that sound is replaced by one which is familiar for the language learner, like in the English word pair "shell – sell" which differs in the first sound.

Problems in learning to pronounce a new language are not restricted to individual sounds (consonants, as in the figures above, or vowels). Learners also find it difficult to pronounce sounds which occur in unfamiliar positions, even if they have the sound in their own language. A simple example is that of final devoicing, as in Syrian Arabic, where for example voiced syllable-final /d/ is replaced by its voiceless counterpart /t/ (but cf. [56]). To deal with such challenges, CALST offers exercises for consonants in both word-initial and word-final positions.

Depending on the allowed syllable structures in the migrant's native language, consonant clusters may be difficult to pronounce. A Farsi speaker may have difficulty with pronouncing a Greek word starting with 'sp', and solve this by adding an epenthetic vowel before the cluster; the effect of this is that the vowel together with the s makes up a separate syllable, the results of which is a structure that is allowed in their native language. Speakers with other native languages may choose other so-called "repair strategies" to create admissible structures, for example cluster reduction (deleting a sound in the cluster), substitution (replacing a sound by another to create an admissible cluster) or for instance insertion of a vowel between the two consonants. For some of the target languages in CALST, consonant cluster exercises have been implemented which can help to un-learn syllable structure restriction which do not apply in the target language.

Some languages do not have word stress or they always have stress on a fixed syllable in the word (the first or last, or the one-but-first or one-but-last). Speakers of these languages are often stress-deaf [57] and will have difficulty learning to realize stress correctly, as for example, in Greek where stress is lexical and not predictable from the syllable structure of the word. The correct realization of stress is important for the perception of rhythm and is a major hindrance for comprehensibility if realized wrongly.

Finally, intonation or sentence melody is important to get across the intention of the speaker. It is also a language property that lingers longest when learning a new language, and it is difficult to teach in online systems.

Many of the above problems are addressed in CALST, although not equally for all languages. Because little of the knowledge we have about the influence of a migrant's native language on the acquisition of a new language can be implemented in a hands-on pronunciation training system like CAST, all exercise results in CALST are logged together with the learner's native (L1) and target language (L2). In this way, the system can learn from previous users and adapt the selection of exercises to the combination of L1 and L2 to tailor pronunciation training more and more to the learner and reduce unnecessary exercises for mi-grants learning a new language.

Moving to a new country is in itself a very taxing experience. Language learning should be as effective and enabling as possible, helping migrants to achieve their goal of social inclusion.

3   Digital Language Learning for Migrants: Implications

One of the main challenges migrants experience in the easyRights project is the lack of both foreign language skills and the pragmatic competences needed to perform necessary administrative procedures and communicate effectively. This seems to be a major problem, since the migrants' awareness and learning of domain-specific knowledge required by the host country actually affects their ability to access and understand their rights in a target country. In fact, the importance of sociolinguistic knowledge is also addressed in [58], by showing that on the lower levels of language competence, sociolinguistic and pragmatic competences were considered important in compensating for lacking linguistic competence. Moreover, Kärkkäinen's [59] study of learning, teaching and integration showed that both trainers and migrants associate difficulties in learning, teaching and integration with the existence of cultural differences and poor language skills. While language learning is viewed as a lifelong process, new technologies can help provide opportunities that substantially support effective language learning by enabling the creation of learning activities, tasks and experiences that are truly authentic to the migrant learner, take place in authentic contexts, involve authentic language in order to optimize language learning [60] and also assist towards social awareness. With context playing a critical role in the foreign language (FL) learning, context-aware technology is a promising tool for support of FL learning [61]. The digital tools presented in the previous section can help migrants improve their knowledge of domain-specific vocabulary and exercise their pronunciation skills, through tasks that are personalized and adapted to specific migrant needs, by taking into consideration language and procedural factors that relate to the context of communication. As a result, when the migrants use these tools, they will be trained to properly communicate in the language of the host community and exercise their rights.

However, the compelling and challenging task of accessing and understanding critical information in a new and foreign country, particularly while lacking formal language knowledge and pragmatic skills, does not only concern the migrant population. Castañeda [62] suggests that such learning has ceased to be considered a personal challenge and, instead, has become a socio-economic imposition of a hypercompetitive society. An important presumption when investigating digital technologies' ability to assist migrant populations overcome domain-specific language barriers is therefore that the migrants are aware of the problem and that they experience a need for better information. According to Kessler [63], the new worldwide participatory culture presents FL teaching with limitless opportunities to create for learners meaningful, authentic language practice experiences that situate learning in truly compelling contexts. This implies a need to provide migrants with opportunities for foreign language training that situates the learning process in the context of accessing and understanding their rights in authentic situations like job seeking, asylum processes and processes of applying for social benefits.

In contexts where technological solutions are targeted towards complex social and civic challenges, an important factor that should be taken into consideration is the issue of testing and validating the technological prototypes that are designed for these purposes. This can actually happen if the end users of the technological solutions are actively involved in the design and implementation process, providing substantial feedback in relation to their needs and the extent to which they are satisfied by the digital tools that are offered. In fact, this kind of interaction among the experts in the field of technology and various stakeholders that may range from public administrators, business people to the actual end users of the technological products, is found at the heart of the concept of "participatory design", which is people-centered and close to a humanitarian approach regarding the use of technology [64, 65]. This kind of collaboration among various stakeholders that all have a common goal in relation to the use of technology can take place in hackathon events, which initially had a purely technological orientation, but have gradually acquired a social dimension, aiming to bring together experts from different disciplines as well as citizens in order to exchange opinions and find effective solutions to common problems [66–68]. In fact, the technological tools that have been designed within the frame of the easyRights project are currently being tested in organized hackathon events that take place in the four pilot cities, where technology experts collaborate with local administration stakeholders, academics and migrants, in order to examine the extent to which the vocabulary and pronunciation tools work effectively towards the integration of migrant populations with different needs. Based on the feedback received during the hackathons, improvements or alterations to the existing digital tools might occur, with the purpose of properly adapting them to the needs of the end users in each pilot city.

4   Conclusion

The technological solutions that are described in this paper aim not only at equipping migrants with the language knowledge and skills they need for important everyday transactions, but also with specific guidance regarding the administrative procedures they are required to perform in the process of their actual integration in the host communities. This is an effort that is embedded within the wider goal of creating societies based on active citizenship and equal opportunities by the means of digital tools that facilitate public procedures and serve humanitarian purposes. As suggested in [31], the migrants' involvement in learning designs that involve technological innovations can inspire new perspectives in relation to other mobile populations as well, such as students and business people. Within the same frame of thought, the globalization of migration and its related social challenges should be faced as an opportunity for technology to demonstrate its full potential, by exploiting the human and digitalization interface for the benefit of the former. In the world of 'human-technology symbiosis' [1], technology is expected to adapt itself to the needs of multicultural societies, by mitigating social differences and providing opportunities for active democratic citizenship.

Acknowledgement. The project is funded by the EU Horizon 2020, grant agreement ID: 870980. However, the full responsibility of the paper and the opinions expressed herewith are solely of the authors and do not necessarily reflect the point of view of any EU institution.

References

1. Stephanidis, C.C., et al.: Seven HCI grand challenges. Int. J. Hum. Comput. Interact. **35**(14), 1229–1269 (2019). https://doi.org/10.1080/10447318.2019.1619259
2. United Nations High Commissioner for Refugees. http://www.unhcr.org/afr/news/latest/2015/12/5683d0b56/million-sea-arrivals-reach-europe-2015.html. Accessed 19 Jan 2020
3. Migration Data Portal. https://migrationdataportal.org/regional-data-overview/europe. Accessed 19 Jan 2020
4. Frontex. https://frontex.europa.eu/along-eu-borders/migratory-map/. Accessed 19 Jan 2020

5. European Council. https://www.consilium.europa.eu/en/infographics/migration-flows/. Accessed 29 Jan 2020
6. Amnesty International. https://www.amnesty.org/en/what-we-do/refugees-asylum-seekers-and-migrants/. Accessed 20 Jan 2020
7. European Commission: Migration Whitepaper: a new approach to digital services for migrants. https://ec.europa.eu/digital-single-market/en/news/migration-whitepaper-new-appr oach-digital-services-migrants. Accessed 29 Jan 2020
8. UnitedNations. https://www.ohchr.org/EN/Issues/Migration/Pages/MigrationAndHumanRig htsIndex.aspx. Accessed 19 Jan 2020
9. Hamberger, A.: Immigrant integration: acculturation and social integration. J. Identity Migr. Stud. **3**(2), 2–21 (2009)
10. Migration Data Portal. https://migrationdataportal.org/themes/migrant-integration. Accessed 19 Jan 2021
11. Favel, A.: Integration nations: the nation-state and research on immigrants in Western Europe. Multicultural Challenge Comp. Soc. Res. **22**, 13–42 (2003)
12. Huddleston, T, Niessen, J., Tjaden, J.D.: Using EU Indicators of Immigrant IntegrationFinal Report for Directorate-General for Home Affairs, Brussels: European Commission (2013). https://ec.europa.eu/home-affairs/. Accessed 23 Jan 2021
13. Caidi, N., Allard, D., Quirke, L.: Information practices of immigrants. Ann. Rev. Inf. Sci. Technol. **44**(1), 491–531 (2012). https://doi.org/10.1002/aris.2010.1440440118
14. Brown, D., Grinter, R.E.: Designing for transient use: a human-in-the-loop translation platform for refugees. In: Proceedings of the 2016 CHI Conference on Human Factors in Computing System, pp. 321–330. ACM (2016). https://doi.org/10.1145/2858036.2858230
15. Adserà, A., Pytliková, M.: The role of language in shaping international migration. Econ. J. **125**(586), F49–F81 (2015). https://doi.org/10.1111/ecoj.12231
16. Lochmann, A., Rapoport, H., Speciale, B.: The Effect of Language Training on immigrants' Economic Integration: Empirical Evidence from France. IZA Discussion Papers 11331, Institute of Labor Economics (IZA) (2018)
17. Colucci, E., Castaño Muñoz, J., Devauz, A.: MOOCs and free digital learning for the Inclusion of migrants and refugees: a European policy study. In: Proceedings of EMOOCs 2017: Work in Progress Papers of the Experience and Research Tracks and Position Papers of the Policy Track. pp. 96–103 (2017). http://ceur-ws.org/Vol-1841/P02_114.pdf
18. Collins, J.: Migration, language diversity and educational policy: a contextualized analysis of inequality, risk and state effects. Policy Features Educ. **13**(5), 577–595 (2015)
19. Biagi, F., Grubanov-Boskovic, S., Natale, F., Sebastian, R.: Migrant workers and the digital transformation in the EU. JRC Technical report EUR 29269 EN. Publications Office of the European Union, Luxembourg (2018). https://doi.org/10.2760/561934
20. Berg, J., Furrer, M., Harmon, E., Rani, U., Silberman, M.S.: Digital Labour Platforms and the future of work: Towards decent work in the online world. ILO, Geneva (2018). https://www.ilo.org/global/publications/books/WCMS_645337/lang–en/index.htm. Accessed 23 Jan 2021
21. Lupiañez, F., Codagnone, C., Dalet, R.: ICT for the employability and integration of immigrants in the European Union: Results from a survey in three Member States. In: Carretero, S., Centeno, C. (eds.) JRC Technical report EUR 27352 EN. Publications Office of the European Union, Luxembourg (2015). https://doi.org/10.2791/271816
22. Benton, M., Glennie, A.: Digital Humanitarianism: How Tech Entrepreneurs are supporting refugee integration. Migration Policy Institute, DC (2016). https://www.migrationpolicy.org/sites/default/files/publications/TCM-Asylum-Benton-FINAL.pdf. Accessed 23 Jan 2021

23. Research and Markets: Mobile Data Consumption Trends Market to 2027 - Global Analysis and Forecasts by Subscribers, Technology and Geography. Report ID: 4769858 (2019). https://www.researchandmarkets.com/reports/. Accessed 23 Jan 2021

24. Mancini, T., Sibilla, F., Argiropoulos, D., Rossi, M., Everri, M.: The opportunities and risks of mobile phones for refugees' experience: a scoping review. PLoS ONE **4**(12), e0225684 (2019). https://doi.org/10.1371/journal.pone.0225684

25. Gillespie, M., et al.: Mapping Refugee Media Journeys: Smartphones and Social Media Networks. The Open University/France Médias Monde (2016). https://doi.org/10.13140/RG.2.2.15633.22888

26. GSMA. The Importance of Mobile for Refugees: A Landscape of New Service and Approaches (2017). https://www.gsma.com/mobilefordevelopment. Accessed 25 Jan 2021

27. Gelb, S., Krishnan, S.: Technology, migration and the 2030 Agenda for Sustainable Development. Overseas Development Institute (ODI) (2018). https://www.odi.org/sites/odi.org.uk/files/resource-documents/12395.pdf. Accessed 25 Jan 2021

28. Colucci, E., Smidt, H., Devaux, A., Vrasidas, C., Safarjalani, M., Castaño Muñoz, J.: Free Digital Learning Opportunities for Migrants and Refugees. Report number: JRC106146 EUR 28559 EN, European Union JRC Science Hub, (2017). https://publications.jrc.ec.europa.eu/repository/bitstream/JRC106146/kjna28559enn.pdf. Accessed 25 Jan 2021

29. Kukulska-Hulme, A., Gaved, M., Jones, A., Norris, L., Peasgood, A.: Mobile language learning experiences for migrants beyond the classroom: Some lessons from research/Les enseignements de la recherché, pp 219–224 (2017). https://doi.org/10.1515/9783110477498-030

30. Castaño-Muñoz, J., Colucci, E., Smidt, H.: Free digital learning for inclusion of migrants and refugees in Europe: a qualitative analysis of three types of learning purposes. Int. Rev. Res. Open Distrib. Learn. **19**(2) (2018). https://doi.org/10.19173/irrodl.v19i2.3382

31. Kukulska-Hulme, A.: Mobile language learning innovation inspired by migrants. J. Learn. Dev. **6**(2) (2019). https://jl4d.org/index.php/ejl4d/article/view/349. Accessed 28 Jan 2021

32. Kukulska-Hulme, A., Norris, L., Donohue, J.: Mobile pedagogy for English language teaching: a guide for teachers. ELT Res. Papers **14**(07) (2015). https://www.teachingenglish.org.uk/sites/teacheng/files/E485%20Mobile%20pedagogy%20for%20ELT_v6.pdf. Accessed 25 Jan 2021

33. Castaño Muñoz, J., Punie, Y., Inamorato dos Santos, A.: MOOCs in Europe: Evidence from pilot surveys with universities and MOOC learners. JRC-IPTS Brief (2016). https://ec.europa.eu/jrc/sites/jrcsh/files/JRC%20brief%20MOOCs_JRC101956.pdf. Accessed 25 Jan 2021

34. Dehghanzadeh, H., Fardanesh, H., Hatami, J., Talaee, E., Noroozi, O.: Using gamification to support learning English as a second language: a systematic review. Comput. Assist. Lang. Learn. 1–24 (2019). https://doi.org/10.1080/09588221.2019.1648298

35. Figueroa-Flores, J.: Using gamification to enhance second language learning. Digit. Educ. Rev. **27**, 32–54 (2015). https://files.eric.ed.gov/fulltext/EJ1065005.pdf. Accessed 25 Jan 2021

36. Urmeneta, C.: An introduction to content and language integrated learning (CLIL) for teachers and teacher educators. CLIL. J. Innov. Res. Plurilingual Pluricultural Educ. **2**(1), 7–19 (2019). https://doi.org/10.5565/rev/clil.2

37. Deterding, S., Sicart, M., Nacke, L., O'Hara, K., Dixon, D.: Gamification: using game-design elements in non-gaming contexts. In: Proceedings of the 2011 Annual Conference Extended Abstracts on Human Factors in Computing Systems, vol. 66, pp. 2425–2428 (2011). https://doi.org/10.1145/1979742.1979575

38. Gaved, M., Jones, A., Kukulska-Hulme, A., Scanlon, E.: A citizen-centred approach to education in the smart city: incidental language learning for supporting the inclusion of recent migrants. Int. J. Digit. Literacy Digit. Competence **3**(4), 50–64 (2012). https://doi.org/10.4018/jdldc.2012100104

39. Gaved, M., Greenwood, R. Peasgood, A.: Using and appropriating the smart city for community and capacity building amongst migrant language learners. In: Proceedings of the 7th International Conference on Communities and Technologies, pp. 63–72. The Open University, UK (2015). http://oro.open.ac.uk/43783/

40. Hashemi, S.S., Lindstrom, N.B., Bartram, L., Bradley, L.: Investigating mobile technology resources for integration. In: Proceedings of the 16th World Conference on Mobile and Contextual Learning-mlearn, pp. 1–8 (2017). https://doi.org/10.1145/3136907.3136930

41. Verhallen, M.J.A.J., Bus, A.G.: Low-income immigrant pupils learning vocabulary through digital picture storybooks. J. Educ. Psychol. **102**(1), 54–61 (2010). https://doi.org/10.1037/a0017133

42. Kluzer, S., Paolis, R.: Using tablets for L2 learning with illiterate adult migrants: results from experiments in Piedmont and Emilia Romagna: Some lessons from research/Les enseignements de la recherché (2017). https://doi.org/10.1515/9783110477498-048

43. Schiepers, M., et al.: Creating a dynamic and learner-driven online environment for practicing second language skills: guiding principles from second language acquisition and online education. In: Beacco, J.C., Krumm, H.J., Little, D., Thalgott, P. (eds.) The Linguistic Integration of Adult Migrants/L' intégration linguistique des migrants adultes: Some lessons from research/Les enseignements de la recherché, pp. 225–232. Walter de Gruyter. https://doi.org/10.1515/9783110477498-031

44. Reinders, H., Benson, P.: Research agenda: Language learning beyond the classroom. Lang. Teach. **50**(4), 561–578 (2017). https://doi.org/10.1017/S0261444817000192

45. Ertmer, P.A., Newby, T.J.: Behaviorism, cognitivism, constructivism: comparing critical features from an instructional design perspective. Perform. Improv. Q. **6**(4), 50–72 (1993). https://doi.org/10.1111/j.1937-8327.1993.tb00605.x

46. Boulton, A., Cobb, T.: Corpus use in language learning: a meta-analysis. J. Lang. Learn. **67**(2), 348–393 (2017). https://doi.org/10.1111/lang.12224

47. Hélot, C., Young, A.: The notion of diversity in language education: policy and practice at primary level in France. Lang. Cult. Curric. **18**(3), 242–257 (2008). https://doi.org/10.1080/07908310508668745

48. Wang, C., Winstead, L.: Handbook of research on foreign language education in the digital age. ICI Global (2016). https://doi.org/10.4018/978-1-5225-0177-0

49. Derwing, T., Munro, M.: Accent, intelligibility and comprehensibility: evidence from Four L1s. Stud. Second. Lang. Acquis. **19**(1), 1–16 (1997)

50. Munro, M.J.: Intelligibility: buzzword or buzzworthy? In: Levis, J., LeVelle, K. (eds.) Proceedings of 2nd Pronunciation in Second Language Learning and Teaching Conference (PSLLT) Iowa State University, pp. 7–16 (2011)

51. Lev-Ari, S., Keysar, B.: Why don't we believe non-native speakers? The influence of accent on credibility. J. Exp. Soc. Psychol. **46**(6), 1093–1096 (2010). https://doi.org/10.1016/j.jesp.2010.05.025

52. CALST [Computer-Assisted Listening and Speaking Tutor, Computer software] (2017). https://www.ntnu.edu/isl/calst

53. Koreman, J., Bech, Ø., Husby, O., Wik, P.: L1-L2*map*: a tool for multi-lingual contrastive analysis. In: Proceedings of 17th International Congress of Phonetic Sciences (ICPhS2011), Hong Kong, pp. 1142–1145 (2011)

54. Maddieson, I.: UPSID: UCLA phonological segment inventory database. Phonetics Laboratory, Department of Linguistics (1980)

55. Best, C.T., Tyler, M.D.: Non-native and second-language speech perception: commonalities and complementarities. In: Munro, M.J., Bohn, O.-S. (eds.) Second Language Speech Learning: The Role of Language Experience in Speech Perception and Production, pp. 13–34. John Benjamins, Amsterdam (2007)
56. Barry, M., Teifour, R.: Temporal patterns in Syrian voicing assimilation. In: Proceedings of 14th International Congress of Phonetic Sciences, San Francisco, pp. 2429–2432 (1999)
57. Peperkamp, S., Dupoux, E.: A typological study of stress "deafness". In: Gussenhoven, C., Warner, N. (eds.) Laboratory Phonology 7. de Gruyter, Berlin, pp. 203–240 (2002)
58. Härmälä, M.: Linguistic, sociolinguistic, and pragmatic competence as criteria in assessing vocational language skills: the case of Finland. Melbourne Papers Lang. Test. **15**(2) (2010)
59. Kärkkäinen K.: Learning, Teaching and Integration of Adult Migrants in Finland. University of Jyväskylä (2017). https://jyx.jyu.fi/handle/123456789/55745
60. Egbert, J., Hanson-Smith, E., Chao, C.: Introduction: Foundations for teaching and learning. In: 2nd CALL Environments: Research, Practice, and Critical, pp. 19–28 (2007)
61. Lee, S.M.: A systematic review of context-aware technology use in foreign language learning. Comput. Assist. Lang. Learn. (2019). https://doi.org/10.1080/09588221.2019.1688836
62. Castañeda, S.B.: Lifelong learning and limiting factors in second language acquisition for adult students in post-obligatory education. Cogent Psychol. **4**(1), 1404699 (2017). https://doi.org/10.1080/23311908.2017.1404699
63. Kessler, G.: Technology and the future of language teaching. Foreign Lang. Ann. **51**(1), 205–218 (2018). https://doi.org/10.1111/flan.12318
64. Björgvinsson, E., Ehn, P., Hillgren, P.: Participatory design and "democratizing innovation". In: Proceedings of the 11th Conference on Participatory Design, PDC 2010, Sydney, pp. 41–50 (2010). https://doi.org/10.1145/1900441.1900448
65. Simonsen, J., Robertson, T.: Routledge International Handbook of Participatory Design, 1st edn. Routledge, New York (2013)
66. Concilio, G., Molinari, F., Morelli, N.: Empowering citizens with open data by urban Hackathons. In: 2017 Conference for E-Democracy and Open Government (CeDEM), Krems, pp. 125–134. IEEE (2017)
67. Götzen, A., Simeone, L., Saad-Sulonen, J., Becermen, B., Morelli, N.: The hackathon format: an analysis of its possible interpretations under a service design perspective. In: Proceedings of NordDesign 2020. Technical University of Denmark, Lyngby (2020). https://doi.org/10.35199/NORDDESIGN2020.6
68. Saad-Sulonen, J., Götzen, A., Morelli, N.: Service design and participatory design: time to join forces? In: Proceedings of the 16th Participatory Design Conference 2020, vol. 2, pp. 76–81 (2020). https://doi.org/10.1145/3384772.3385133

Learning Theories and Teaching Methodologies for the Design of Training in Digital Competence for Language Teachers: A Narrative Review

Antigoni Parmaxi[1]([⊠]) [iD], Anna Nicolaou[1] [iD],
Elis Kakoulli Constantinou[1] [iD], Maria Victoria Soulé[1] [iD],
Salomi Papadima Sophocleous[1] [iD], and Maria Perifanou[2] [iD]

[1] Cyprus University of Technology, Limassol, Cyprus
antigoni.parmaxi@cut.ac.cy
[2] University of Macedonia, Thessaloniki, Greece

Abstract. This paper provides a narrative review of learning theories and teaching methodologies that can be used to design training activities for an online or blended training workshop addressed to language teachers. The review was performed in a traditional, narrative manner and revolved around the exploration of recent, influential learning theories, such as Connectivism, Social Constructionism, and Ecological Theory. It also involved an exploration of contemporary teaching methodologies, such as game-based learning, problem-based learning, and virtual exchange, which were deemed important for language teachers in order to get an up-to-date overview of theoretical perspectives and improve their teaching. This review is part of the *Digital Competence for Language Teachers (DC4LT)* Erasmus+ KA2 project and its ultimate objective was to delineate an array of learning theories and teaching methodologies in order to enable trainers to select the ones that are most suitable for training workshops in digital competence for language teachers. The specific review concludes with implications for the design of a training workshop with replicability and transferability potential for future trainers.

Keywords: Digital competence · Language instruction · Learning theories · Teaching methodologies

1 Introduction

1.1 Background

Digital competence has been recognised as a fundamental skill in education for the 21st century and a number of frameworks have been developed so as to align this priority with the empowerment of educators. However, in spite of the various efforts towards the transformation of education in light of the new, highly digitised era we are living in, many of these endeavours seem to be focused on teachers of various disciplines in general, with only a few exceptions that are directed to specific teaching specialties. One discipline of education in which digital competence is of utmost importance is

© Springer Nature Switzerland AG 2021
P. Zaphiris and A. Ioannou (Eds.): HCII 2021, LNCS 12784, pp. 125–139, 2021.
https://doi.org/10.1007/978-3-030-77889-7_9

language instruction whereby the focus is to enable learners to effectively communicate in the target language. Since communication and interaction mostly occur in digital environments in the current situation of remote teaching and distance learning, the need to train language educators towards the enhancement of their digital competence seems to be pressing. Language educators today are in need of specific training so as to be able to update their Information and Communications Technology (ICT) knowledge and skills and adequately support their learners to communicate in the foreign language. However, providing such training in a methodical way, one needs to consider current learning theories and teaching methodologies so as to effectively connect pedagogy and technology in language teaching and learning. With this in mind, this paper reviews current learning theories and teaching methodologies that can be used to design training activities for an online or blended training workshop addressed to language teachers. The ultimate objective of the review was to outline selected learning theories and contemporary teaching approaches that can guide the design of a set of replicable training activities addressed to language educators towards the enhancement of their digital competence and the integration of technology in their teaching in a pedagogically sound manner.

1.2   Digital Competence in Education

During the last two decades there has been a continuous debate on defining what digital competence, digital skills or digital literacy are, along with a strong effort on developing a framework that could encompass all key elements needed in order to assess teachers' digital competence successfully. To that end, extensive research [1–17] has been carried out in this area which proposed various digital literacy frameworks and assessment tools that could facilitate the assessment of teachers' digital competence. In most cases, the proposed frameworks have many differences (i.e., structure, proficiency levels, overall perspective) but also similarities (i.e., common components, focus on skills development). A well known framework that nowadays is widely used by European educators is the *Digital Competence Framework for Educators* (DigCompEdu) which classifies the main components of the digital competence - twenty-two (22) various competences - in six (6) basic areas: i) Professional Engagement; ii) Digital Resources; iii) Teaching and Learning; iv) Assessment; v) Empowering Learners, and vi) Facilitating Learners' Digital Competence [18]. The DigCompEdu research study is built on previous work [19–22] which aimed at defining the European citizens' Digital Competence (DigComp1.0; DigComp2.0; DigComp2.1) in general, and the Digitally Competent Education Organizations (DigCompOrg). Other frameworks which are also used by many educators worldwide are: the *Framework for ICT literacy* proposed by the American Educational Testing Service [23]; the *SAMR Framework* [2], the *Technological Pedagogical Content Knowledge TPACK Framework* [3], the *UNESCO ICT Competency Standards for Teachers* [24], the *JISC's Digital Literacies Framework* [10], the *Common Digital Competence Framework for Teachers* [25], the *Professional Digital Competence Framework for Teachers in Norway* [13], the *UNESCO ICT Competency Framework For Teachers* [4, 5], and the *Teacher Digital Competency (TDC) Framework* [17]. Besides the frameworks that target teachers' digital competence, there are also tools that focus mostly on the assessment of students' ICT skills, such as the *PISA 2021 ICT Conceptual Framework* [15], which aims at documenting the students' use of ICT and understand the diverse ways in which ICT is introduced in schools, or *the British Columbia's Digital Literacy Framework* [11], which defines the digital competencies of children age 5–18.

1.3   Digital Competence in Language Instruction

With regard to digital literacy frameworks and assessment tools designed specifically for language teachers, there is limited research. *The Framework for Online Language Teaching Skills* [26] is a well known framework that proposes three (3) assessment dimensions (technology, pedagogy and evaluation) and three (3) different competence levels aiming at orientating language teachers online training programmes. This framework is built on Hampel and Stickler's [27] 'skills pyramid' framework, which intended to identify the key competences of an online language tutor proposing a pyramid of skills with seven key competences ranging from lower level general skills (e.g. basic ICT competence) to higher level skills (i.e. facilitation of communicative competence). Most of the proposed digital literacy frameworks and tools have a common perspective and were designed for English Language Teachers. Such frameworks include the *BALEAP Competency Framework for Teachers of English for Academic Purposes* [28], the *TESOL Technology Standards Framework* [29], the *Framework for Quality Professional Development for Practitioners Working with Adult English Language Learners* by the Center for Adult English Language Acquisition (CAELA) Network [30], the *CPD Framework for Teachers of English* by the British Council [31], and the *Cambridge English Teaching Framework* [32]. On the contrary, both the *2digi Digital Literacy Assessment Tool* created by the 2digi project [33] and the *EAQUALS Framework* (Evaluation and Accreditation of Quality in Language Services) [34] addressed the training needs of teachers of different languages. More specifically, the 2digi project offers a self-assessment tool that applies for all language teachers who wish to assess and document their digital literacy, while the EQUALS Framework describes a variety of skills and competences that language teachers need to acquire during their professional development including digital skills.

Despite the current interest in developing frameworks and tools directed towards the empowerment of language educators in upgrading their ICT skills, the current situation of remote teaching and distance learning calls for a pressing need for training language teachers towards the enhancement of their digital literacy. The design and implementation of relevant training workshops has lately proliferated across the world. However, such activities can be especially useful if they are informed by theoretical perspectives so as to effectively connect pedagogy and technology integration in learning. The present paper adds to this discussion by reviewing relevant learning theories, i.e. Connectivism, Social Constructionism, and Ecological Theory while providing an overview of current teaching methodologies, i.e. game-based learning, problem-based learning, and virtual exchange or telecollaboration.

2 Method

2.1 Review Strategy

This study aims at providing a synthesis of literature on learning theories and teaching methodologies in the specific field of language learning. Following a non-systematic/narrative methodology, we identified and summarised what has been published on the specific topic with an eye to providing a summary of recent, published research. Narrative literature reviews are useful tools especially for identifying concepts and ideas that change rapidly and have a multidisciplinary nature [35, 36]. As noted by Ferrari [37], non-systematic/narrative methodologies do not have acknowledged guidelines, and the selection process followed is not concrete. For the completion of this review, the IMRAD (Introduction, Methods, Results, Discussion) format was followed as suggested by Ferrari [37]. The framework of this narrative review is depicted in Table 1.

Table 1. General framework of this narrative review (adapted from Ferrari 2015).

Introduction	Method/Literature search	Central body/Discussion	Conclusion
Description of rationale	Search strategy	Discussion/summary of basic concept 1	Highlight main points
Definition of objectives and scope	Description of selected studies	Discussion/summary of basic concept 2	Link with research scope
Necessity of this review	Compilation of list of selected research studies	Discussion/summary of basic concept 2	Demonstrate the meaning of research design

2.2 Search Strategy

Initially, we aimed at establishing a general understanding of the topic through a preliminary search in Google Scholar. This preliminary search allowed us to capture the scope of the existing literature and refine the topic and selection criteria for the studies to be included. Our review was guided by the following criteria:

1. The work describes a learning theory/methodology that is aligned with the use of technologies in the specific field of language learning.
2. The work is published in English.
3. The work is published after 2004, as we aimed at collecting theories and methodologies that align with the use of recent technologies.

The studies that did not meet the aforementioned criteria were excluded. After completing our search to locate relevant resources, we compiled our list of selected research studies that comprised the corpus of this manuscript. In the following section, the results are presented in the format of a short summary of key notions and aspirations of each learning theory and teaching methodology and are demonstrated in a descriptive/qualitative rather than a quantitative level.

3 Discussion

3.1 Exploration of Influential Learning Theories

Nowadays, the view about the way people acquire knowledge has changed, as theories of learning and research progress through the years. Contemporary theories of learning extend their roots into the past, and many questions that research aims to answer today are not new, since they were first the subject of philosophy and later on of psychology [38]. In recent years the developments brought by the advancement of technology have had a great influence on all aspects of our everyday life, including education, and have unavoidably affected the way knowledge is acquired. This has had an impact on training methodologies that can be used for language learning and also training methodologies that can be utilised for language teacher training, amongst other things.

Looking back at psychology in the first half of the 20th century, behaviouristic theories of learning prevailed. These theories viewed learning "as a change in the rate, frequency of occurrence, or form of behavior or response, which occurs primarily as a function of environmental factors" [38, p. 21]. Behaviourism regarded learning as model and stimuli based, and pattern drilling, repetition and immediate correction of error were the major characteristics of learning processes. Behaviourism was criticised mainly because the concept of learning it supported violated "the human right to self-determination and self-expression" [39, p. 14]. Later on, cognitive theories of learning emerged as a response to behaviourism. Cognitivism viewed learning "as an internal mental phenomenon inferred from what people say and do. A central theme is the mental processing of information: its construction, acquisition, organization, coding, rehearsal, storage in memory, and retrieval or non retrieval from memory" [38, p. 22]. Cognitivism recognised that with instruction alone learning cannot be achieved; nevertheless, it was criticised for "considering the essence of human action to reside in its alleged source in mental processes at the expense of the social surroundings of the action" [40, p. 3]. In more recent years, research concentrated more on the learner and how knowledge is constructed rather than acquired; this is referred to as constructivism, influenced mainly by the theories of Piaget and Vygotsky. Constructivism "does not propound that learning principles exist and are to be discovered and tested, but rather that learners create their own learning" [38, p. 230]. Constructivist theories of learning brought major changes in the learning and teaching processes with learners becoming actively involved in the learning procedure.

All these advancements in research on learning had a major influence on the teacher training methodologies used in teacher education. At the beginning of the 20th century, the "craft model" of professional development evolved, according to which the expert figure, the master trained the potential teachers by showing them what to do, which they later had to imitate [41, 42]. This model of teacher training was influenced by the behaviouristic theories of learning, and was later rejected, since it was based on pure imitation. The craft model was replaced by the "applied science model" for professional development, which is considered to be the traditional model for teacher development. According to this model, teachers are trained drawing from the findings of empirical science; in other words, they are requested to apply the scientific knowledge obtained from research in their practice [41]. The major criticism of the applied science model was the difficulty of bridging the gap between science and practice, which, according to Burns and Richards [43], still constitutes a problem. A more modern model for teacher training was the "reflective model" for professional development, initiated firstly by Schön [44]. This model placed great emphasis on the value of reflection. According to Wallace [41], the knowledge that the trainee receives interacts with previous experiential knowledge, and through practice and reflection professional competence is achieved. With the prevalence of learning theories such as constructivism and social constructivism, sociocultural perspectives on teacher training developed. According to these perspectives of professional development, "professional knowledge (coded through theories and procedures), personal knowledge (tacit and explicit), and community knowledge (embedded in the day-to day practices of the community as "ways of doing") converge to help community members develop" [42, p. 12]. Recent perspectives of learning and the impact of technology have brought about new theories which will be discussed in the next part.

Connectivism

Apart from social constructivist approaches, another contemporary influential learning theory today is connectivism, introduced by George Siemens [45]. Connectivism stresses the influence of technology and networking in the discovery of knowledge. According to Siemens [45, p. 5], "[l]earning can reside outside of ourselves". As Kop and Hill [46] suggested, for Siemens "knowledge is actuated through the process of a learner connecting to and feeding information into a learning community". Such view of learning has contributed to the evolvement of online communities of practice (CoPs), which, according to Wenger and Trayner-Wenger [47, p. 1], "are groups of people who share a concern or a passion for something they do and learn how to do it better as they interact regularly". Even though research involving connectivist approaches to language learning is limited, there are researchers and language instructors who embrace this learning theory viewing their classes as learning communities. Senior [48] discusses effective language learning and teaching in both face-to-face and online learning environments elaborating on connectivism and the notion of connectivity in a broader sense. In addition, Al-Shehri [49] examines students' collaborative language learning experiences through the use of mobile phones and social networking in the formulation of networked learning environments. Similarly, Kakoulli Constantinou [50, 51] describes the integration of cloud technologies, and more specifically the G Suite for Education, in English for Specific Academic Purposes courses following social constructivist and connectivist approaches.

Social Constructionism

The learning theory of Constructionism [52–54] was defined as: "Including, but going beyond, what Piaget would call 'constructivism.' The word with the *v* expresses the theory that knowledge is built by the learner, not supplied by the teacher. The word with the *n* expresses the further idea that this happens especially felicitously when the learner is engaged in the construction of something external or at least shareable… a sand castle, a machine, a computer program, a book." [54, p. 1]. Based on Papert's framework, Resnick [55] proposes 'distributed constructionism', as the design and construction of meaningful artefacts by more than one person. The use of computer networks to facilitate interactions between people and knowledge construction plays a pivotal role in distributed constructionism. Rüschoff and Ritter [56, p. 219] point out that "construction of knowledge and information processing are regarded as key activities in language learning". Furthermore, since the integration of new media into language learning is a necessary step to ensure the acquisition of the kind of language skills and competencies needed for living and working in the knowledge society, Rüschoff [57] suggests the implementation of Constructionism as the appropriate paradigm for language learning. Recent studies [58, 59] have adopted this paradigm for language learning practices tasking small groups of learners to construct shareable artifacts. In particular, these studies propose the use of social technologies for collaborative construction of shareable artefacts. According to Parmaxi and Zaphiris [58, p. 34], social technologies include "social network sites such as Facebook, Twitter, Linkedin and Google+; social software, such as blogs and wikis; and digital artifacts sharing platforms, such as Dropbox, Evernote and Google Drive".

Ecological Theory

Another way of exploring language learning is Ecological Theory. Drawing from biological theories, language ecology places importance to the dynamic relations between elements in an environment [60]. Ecological Theory recognises that learning does not occur in isolation from its environment but is rather emergent in the environment and interconnected to the environment's components [61]. "An ecological approach aims to look at the learning process, the actions and activities of teachers and learners, the multilayered nature of interaction and language use, in all their complexity and as a network of interdependencies among all the elements in the setting, not only at the social level, but also at the physical and symbolic level" [62, p. 3]. In language learning, an ecological approach can be adopted through "symbolic mediation, collaborative learning, participation, and the achievement of common activities around real-world tasks" [60, p. 4]. This can be particularly important in computer-mediated environments whereby the learning context becomes a lot more dynamic encompassing components such as users, spaces, tools and digital artefacts. This is illustrated in recent studies, such as a study by Palalas [63] which adopted an ecological perspective in mobile-assisted language learning placing emphasis on the role of the learning context and the interaction with that context. In addition, among the major characteristics of Ecological Theory are critical activism and democratic participation [64]. These echo the concept of critical digital literacy manifested in the use of technology as social praxis [65]. Pangrazio [66] explains that critical digital literacy is based upon a view which links digital activity to the concepts of freedom, democracy and civic engagement. In this sense, the acquisition of digital competences is used to effect positive change both at the individual and the collective, social level.

3.2   Exploration of Contemporary Teaching Methodologies

In the context of this review, a number of contemporary teaching methodologies and approaches have been explored with a view to evaluating their potential in developing language teachers' digital competences. The overall aim was to select the most suitable teaching methodologies for assisting language educators in aligning their pedagogical aims with technological integration in their instruction. Through the development of their own digital skills, language educators can be empowered to enhance their learners' active learning, collaboration, autonomy, communication skills, as well as intercultural competence and global citizenship. The teaching methodologies and approaches explored in this study included web-quests [67] immersive technologies for language learning [68], virtual reality games in language learning [69], game-based learning [70], problem-based learning [71], and virtual exchange or telecollaboration [72]. Among these approaches, the last three will be described below, highlighting their potential in developing language educators' digital competences while supporting their students' learning in a highly digitised world.

Game-Based Learning

Game-based learning increasingly receives attention in language learning mainly because of its potential to support the use of the target language creatively and purposively [70]. Several definitions of game-based learning emphasise the use of games and/or play for supporting teaching and learning and achieving certain learning outcomes [73–75]. Although game-based learning often makes use of digital games, this is not always a rule, whilst scholars often debate on a concrete definition of game. Salen and Zimmerman [76, p. 80] define a game as "a system in which players engage in an artificial conflict, defined by rules, that results in a quantifiable outcome". Games are an exciting and appealing tool for learners of all ages, and gain attention as a means that can foster collaboration and provide opportunities for scaffolded language learning [see 77]. Currently, a variety of technologies have been employed for supporting game-based learning. For example, Yukselturk, Altıok, and Başer [70] examined the effects of game-based learning with Kinect technology demonstrating its positive effects on learning quality and motivation. On the same line, Palomo-Duarte et al. [78] delineate how mobile technologies have been employed for supporting game-based learning, demonstrating its potential to support active learning.

Problem-Based Learning

Problem-based learning (PBL) is a type of student-centred educational approach where students learn a topic via their experience in solving open-ended problems. In PBL, elements of active, interactive, and collaborative learning are incorporated to allow teachers to observe their students' learning process [79]. PBL is a student-driven process that uses a bottom up approach to bring the students from a problem to the theory [71]. Sevilla-Pavón [80] proposes the following steps for the process: (1) a problem is introduced to the students, (2) students find and analyse information from different sources, (3) students come to the problem and try to solve it by applying the autonomously acquired knowledge. In order to solve a problem, students work collaboratively using multiple tools. In online and blended learning environments, Web 2.0 tools can be employed to enhance teamwork, independent learning, communication skills, problem-solving skills, interdisciplinary learning, and information-mining skills [81].

Virtual Exchange

"Telecollaboration, or virtual exchange, are terms used to refer to the engagement of groups of learners in online intercultural interactions and collaboration projects with partners from other cultural contexts or geographical locations as an integrated part of their educational programmes" [72, p. 1]. Guth and Helm [82] have defined telecollaboration in language learning contexts as an Internet-based exchange aimed at developing both language skills and intercultural communicative competence. Research studies have documented the continuing development of virtual exchange along with the benefits of this pedagogical paradigm which include the enhancement of language skills and intercultural communicative competence [82], critical media literacy [83], as well as social, digital, and entrepreneurial skills [84]. Recently, virtual exchange has been directed towards the development of critical digital literacies that guide participants beyond the functional uses of technology [85] by involving them in action-oriented, global citizenship activities. For example, a study by Nicolaou and Sevilla-Pavón [86] which adopted an ecological perspective in the design and implementation of a virtual exchange project, connected the classroom with mentors from the local community in an effort to enhance learners' intercultural collaboration and global citizenship while promoting equality, social justice and awareness of critical social issues [87].

4   Conclusion

4.1   Summary

This study followed a narrative review of learning theories and teaching methodologies that can be used for designing training activities in online or blended format for language teachers. The review revolved around the exploration of recent learning theories and contemporary teaching approaches, which align well with the computational culture and are important for language teachers in order to gain an up-to-date overview of theoretical and methodological perspectives. The design of the training workshop for language teachers builds on the theoretical aspirations of Connectivism, Social Constructionism and Ecological Theory as well as on the practical recommendations of game-based learning, problem-based learning, and virtual exchange in order to provide new working methods and tools to practising or prospective language practitioners. With regard to theoretical aspirations, Connectivism can feed into the design of digital learning activities enhancing networking and the development of communities of practice. Social Constructionism directs towards the co-construction of shareable digital artefacts, while Ecological Theory presents opportunities for a multilayered nature of interaction and language use as well as for the critical use of technology. As for methodological recommendations, game-based learning and problem-based learning can direct towards the use of online playful activities and the exploration of solutions around open-ended problems, respectively. Finally, virtual exchange can provide a useful terrain for online intercultural collaborative projects.

Figure 1 provides an overview of the theoretical aspirations and methodological recommendations as well overall design recommendations for training activities addressed
to language educators:

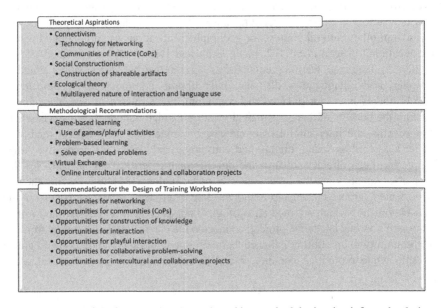

Fig. 1. Overview of the learning theories and teaching methodologies that inform the design of
the training workshop.

The recommendations provided in this review might raise questions regarding the
working practices of practising teachers and how the existing practices can be informed
by the most current theoretical and methodological approaches. As technology is
rapidly changing and the technologies that are prominent in today's language classroom might be considered outdated in a few years, we suggest training workshops to
place emphasis on transferrable skills and practices that can be applied to achieve a
specific learning outcome, rather than on the innovation of a specific technology.
Technology on its own can both enhance and degrade a learner's skills, as well as
support or hinder a language teacher in regard to his/her teaching. This review shows
that the successful design of a training workshop depends on grounding the use of
technologies on specific theoretical and methodological aspirations. The teaching and
learning culture is expected to evolve only if teaching practices are updated bottom-up
rather than top-down due to technological advancements.

4.2 Limitations

This study does not aim to provide a holistic view of learning theories and teaching
methodologies for the design of training for language teachers. This study followed a
narrative review, and the subjective inclusion criteria is a common limitation of

narrative studies according to Ferrari (2015). We aimed at mitigating this limitation by having concrete research questions and inclusion and exclusion criteria.

Acknowledgements. The work presented in this publication has been partially funded by the European Union's Erasmus Plus programme, grant agreement 2018-1-NO01-KA203-038837. This publication reflects the views only of the authors, and the European Commission cannot be held responsible for any use which may be made of the information contained therein.

References

1. Bundy, A.: Australian and New Zealand Information Literacy Framework: Principles, Standards, and Practices, 2nd edn. New Zealand Institute for Information Literacy and Council of Australian University Librarians, Adelaide (2004)
2. Hippasus. http://hippasus.com/resources/tte/puentedura_tte.pdf. Accessed 15 Dec 2020
3. Mishra, P., Koehler, M.: Technological pedagogical content knowledge: a framework for teacher knowledge. Teach. Coll. Rec. **6**, 1017–1054 (2006)
4. United Nations Educational, Scientific and Cultural Organisation (UNESCO). https://unesdoc.unesco.org/ark:/48223/pf0000265721. Accessed 18 Jan 2021
5. United Nations Educational, Scientific and Cultural Organisation (UNESCO). https://unesdoc.unesco.org/ark:/48223/pf0000213475_eng. Accessed 18 Jan 2021
6. Reedy, K., Goodfellow, R.: Digital and Information Literacy Framework. Open University, UK (2012)
7. Hinrichsen, J., Coombs, A.: The five resources of critical digital literacy: a framework for curriculum integration. Res. Learn. Technol. **21**, 1–16 (2013)
8. Klebansky, A., Fraser, S.: A strategic approach to curriculum design for information literacy in teacher education: implementing an information literacy conceptual framework. Austr. J. Teach. Educ. **38**(11), 103–125 (2013)
9. Krumsvik, R.J.: Teacher educators' digital competence. Scand. J. Educ. Res. **58**(3), 269–280 (2014). https://doi.org/10.1080/00313831.2012.726273
10. JISC. https://www.jisc.ac.uk/guides/developing-digital-literacies. Accessed 11 Dec 2020
11. Government of British Columbia. https://www2.gov.bc.ca/gov/content/education-training/k-12/teach/resources-for-teachers/digital-literacy. Accessed 11 Dec 2020
12. DBE, Republic of South Africa. https://www.education.gov.za/Portals/0/Documents/Publications/Digital%20Learning%20Framework.pdf?ver=2018-07-09-101748-95. Accessed 11 Jan 2021
13. Kelentrić, M., Helland, K., Arstorp, A.T.: Professional digital competence framework for teachers in Norway. The Norwegian Centre for ICT in Education, 1–74 (2017)
14. International Society for Technology in Education. https://www.iste.org/standards/for-educators. Accessed 10 Oct 2020
15. OECD. https://www.oecd.org/pisa/sitedocument/PISA-2021-ICT-framework.pdf. Accessed 19 Nov 2020
16. NAACE. https://www.naace.co.uk/si-srf.html. Accessed 19 Nov 2020
17. Falloon, G.: From digital literacy to digital competence: the teacher digital competency (TDC) framework. Educ. Technol. Res. Dev. **68**, 2449–2472 (2020)
18. Redecker, C.: European framework for the digital competence of educators: DigCompEdu (No. JRC107466). Joint Research Centr, Seville site (2017)
19. Ferrari, A.: DIGCOMP: a framework for developing and understanding digital competence in Europe. EC JRC IPTS, Seville, Spain (2013)

20. Kampylis, P., Punie, Y., Devine, J.: Promoting effective digital-age learning. A European framework for digitally-competent educational organisations (No. JRC98209). Joint Research Centre, Seville site (2015)
21. Vuorikari, R., Punie, Y., Carretero Gomez S., Van den Brande, G.: DigComp 2.0: the digital competence framework for citizens. Update Phase 1: The Conceptual Reference Model. Publication Office of the European Union, Luxembourg (2016)
22. Carretero, S., Vuorikari, R., Punie, Y.: The digital competence framework for citizens. Publications Office of the European Union (2017)
23. Panel, I.L.: Digital transformation: a framework for ICT literacy.Educational Testing Service, 1–53 (2002)
24. United Nations Educational, Scientific and Cultural Organisation (UNESCO). https://unesdoc.unesco.org/ark:/48223/pf0000156207. Accessed 10 Jan 2021
25. INTEF. https://intef.es/Noticias/common-digital-competence-framework-for-teachers/. Accessed 07 Sept 2020
26. Compton, L.K.L.: Preparing language teachers to teach languages online: a look at skills, roles, and responsibilities. Comput. Assist. Lang. Learn. 22(1), 73–99 (2009). https://doi.org/10.1080/09588220802613831
27. Hampel, R., Stickler, U.: New skills for new classrooms: Training tutors to teach language online. Comput. Assist. Lang. Learn. 18(4), 311–326 (2005). https://doi.org/10.1080/09588220500335455
28. BALEAP. http://www.baleap.org.uk/teap/teapcompetencyframework.pdf. Accessed 28 Sept 2020
29. TESOL. https://www.tesol.org/docs/default-source/books/bk_technologystandards_framework_721.pdf?sfvrsn=4bd0bee6_2. Accessed 07 Nov 2020
30. Center for Adult English Language Acquisition (CAELA) Network. http://www.cal.org/caelanetwork/profdev/framework/index.html. Accessed 02 Feb 2021
31. British Council. https://www.teachingenglish.org.uk/article/british-council-cpd-framework. Accessed 20 Jan 2021
32. Cambridge English. https://www.cambridgeenglish.org/blog/how-and-why-the-framework-was-developed/. Accessed 26 Jan 2021
33. 2digi. https://2digi.languages.fi/. Accessed 26 Jan 2021
34. EAQUALS. https://www.eaquals.org/our-expertise/teacher-development/the-eaquals-framework-for-teacher-training-and-development/#:~:text=The. Accessed 13 Dec 2020
35. Collins, J.A., Fauser, C.J.M.: Balancing the strengths of systematic and narrative reviews. Hum. Reprod. Update 11(2), 103–104 (2005)
36. Minichiello, A., Hood, J.R., Harkness, D.S.: Bringing user experience design to bear on STEM education: a narrative literature review. J. STEM Educ. Res. 1(1), 7–33 (2018)
37. Ferrari, R.: Writing narrative style literature reviews. Med. Writ. 24(4), 230–235 (2015)
38. Schunk, D.H.: Learning Theories: An Educational Perspective, 6th edn. Pearson Education Inc., Boston (2012)
39. Roberts, J.: Language Teacher Education. Arnold, London (1998)
40. Arponen, V.P.J.: The extent of cognitivism. Hist. Hum. Sci. 26(5), 3–21 (2013). https://doi.org/10.1177/0952695113500778
41. Wallace, M.J.: Training Foreign Language Teachers: A Reflective Approach. Cambridge University Press, Cambridge (1991)
42. Maggioli, G. D.: Teaching Language Teachers: Scaffolding Professional Learning. Rowman & Littlefield Education, Plymouth (2012)
43. Burns, A., Richards, J.C.: Introduction. Second language teacher education. In: Burns, A., Richards, J.C. (eds.) The Cambridge Guide to Second Language Teacher Education, pp. 1–8. Cambridge University Press, New York (2009)

44. Schön, D.A.: The Reflective Practitioner: How Professionals Think in Action. Temple Smith, London (1983)
45. Siemens, G.: Connectivism: a learning theory for the digital age. Int. J. Instruc. Technol. Dist. Learn. **1**, 1–8 (2005). https://doi.org/10.1.1.87.3793
46. Kop, R., Hill, A.: Connectivism: learning theory of the future or vestige of the past? Int. Rev. Res. Open Distance Learn. **9**(3), 1–13 (2008). https://doi.org/10.19173/irrodl.v9i3.523
47. Wenger-trayner.com. https://wenger-trayner.com/wp-content/uploads/2015/04/07-Brief-intr oduction-to-communities-of-practice.pdf. Accessed 31 Jan 2021
48. Senior, R.: Connectivity: a framework for understanding effective language teaching in face-to-face and online learning communities. RELC J. **41**(2), 137–147 (2010). https://doi.org/10.1177/0033688210375775
49. Al-Shehri, S.: Connectivism: a new pathway for theorising and promoting mobile language learning. Int. J. Innov. Leadersh. Teach. Hum. **1**(2), 10–31 (2011)
50. Kakoulli Constantinou, E.: Teaching in clouds: using the G Suite for Education for the delivery of two English for Academic Purposes courses. J. Teach. Eng. Spec. Acad. Purp. **6**(2), 305–317 (2018). https://doi.org/10.22190/jtesap1802305c
51. Kakoulli Constantinou, E.: Revisiting the cloud: reintegrating the G Suite for Education in English for Specific Purposes teaching. In: Giannikas, C.N., Kakoulli Constantinou, E., Papadima-Sophocleous, S. (eds.) Professional Development in CALL: A Selection of Papers, pp. 55–69 (2019). https://doi.org/10.14705/rpnet.2019.28.870
52. Papert, S.: Mindstorms: Children, Computers and Powerful Ideas. Basic Books, Nueva York (1980)
53. Papert, S.: The Children's Machine: Rethinking School in the Age of the Computer. Basic Books, Nueva York (1993)
54. Papert, S., Harel, I.: Situating constructionism. Constructionism **36**(2), 1–11 (1991)
55. Resnick, M.: Distributed constructionism. In: Edelson, D.C., Domeshek, E.A. (eds.). Proceedings of the 1996 International Conference on Learning Sciences, pp. 280–284 (1996)
56. Rüschoff, B., Ritter, M.: Technology-enhanced Language Learning: construction of knowledge and template-based learning in the foreign language classroom. Comput. Assist. Lang. Learn. **14**(3), 219–223 (2001)
57. Rüschoff, B.: Language. In: Adelsherger, H., Collis, B., Pawlowski, J. M. (eds.) Handbook on Information Technologies for Education and Training, pp. 523–539. Springer, Heidelberg (2004). https://doi.org/10.1007/978-3-540-74155-8
58. Parmaxi, A., Zaphiris, P.: Developing a framework for social technologies in learning via design-based research. Educ. Media Int. **52**(1), 33–46 (2015)
59. Parmaxi, A., Zaphiris, P., Ioannou, A.: Enacting artifact-based activities for social technologies in language learning using a design-based research approach. Comput. Hum. Behav. **63**, 556–567 (2016)
60. Steffensen, S.V., Kramsch, C.: The ecology of second language acquisition and socialization. Lang. Soc. 1–16 (2017)
61. Larsen-Freeman, D.: Looking ahead: Future directions in, and future research into, second language acquisition. Foreign Lang. Ann. **51**(1), 55–72 (2018)
62. van Lier, L.: The ecology of language learning: practice to theory, theory to practice. Procedia Soc. Behav. Sci. **3**, 2–6 (2010)
63. Palalas, A.: The ecological perspective on the 'anytime anyplace' of Mobile-Assisted Language Learning. Technologie mobilne w kształceniu językowym, 29–48 (2015)
64. van Lier, L.: The semiotics and ecology of language learning. Utbildning Demokrati **13**(3), 79–103 (2004)

65. Ávila, J., Pandya, J.Z.: Critical digital literacies as social praxis: intersections and challenges. In: New Literacies and Digital Epistemologies, vol. 54. Peter Lang, New York (2013)

66. Pangrazio, L.: Reconceptualising critical digital literacy. Disc. Stud. Cult. Polit. Educ. **37**(2), 163–174 (2016)

67. Perifanou, M., Mikros, G.: 'Italswebquest': a wiki as a platform of collaborative blended language learning and a course management system. Int. J. Knowl. Learn. **5**(3–4), 273–288 (2009)

68. Legault, J., Zhao, J., Chi, Y.A., Chen, W., Klippel, A., Li, P.: Immersive virtual reality as an effective tool for second language vocabulary learning. Languages **4**(1), 13 (2019)

69. Alfadil, M.: Effectiveness of virtual reality game in foreign language vocabulary acquisition. Comput. Educ. **153**, 103893 (2020)

70. Yukselturk, E., Altıok, S., Başer, Z.: Using game-based learning with kinect technology in foreign language education course. J. Educ. Technol. Soc. **21**(3), 159–173 (2018)

71. Abdullah, J., Mohd-Isa, W. Samsudin, M.: Virtual reality to improve group work skill and self-directed learning in problem-based learning narratives. Virt. Real. **23**, 461–471 (2019). https://doi.org/10.1007/s10055-019-00381-1

72. O'Dowd, R.: From telecollaboration to virtual exchange: state-of-the-art and the role of UNICollaboration in moving forward. J. Virt. Exchange **1**, 1–23 (2018)

73. Squire, K.: Video game-based learning: an emerging paradigm for instruction. Perform. Improv. Q. **26**(1), 101–130 (2013). https://doi.org/10.1002/piq.21139

74. Shaffer, D.W., Halverson, R., Squire, K.R., Gee, J.P.: Video games and the future of learning. Phi Delta Kappan **87**(2), 105–111 (2005)

75. Plass, J.L., Homer, B.D., Kinzer, C.K.: Foundations of game-based learning. Educ. Psychol. **50**(4), 258–283 (2015)

76. Salen, K., Zimmerman, E.: Rules of Play: Game Design Fundamentals. MIT Press, Cambridge (2004)

77. Papastergiou, M.: Digital game-based learning in high school computer science education: impact on educational effectiveness and student motivation. Comput. Educ. **52**(1), 1–12 (2009)

78. Palomo-Duarte, M., Berns, A., Cejas, A., Dodero, J. M., Caballero, J. A., Ruiz-Rube, I.: Assessing foreign language learning through mobile game-based learning environments. Int. J. Hum. Cap. Inf. Technol. Profess. (IJHCITP) **7**(2), 53–67 (2016)

79. Donnelly, R.: Blended problem-based learning for teacher education: lessons learnt. Learn. Media Technol. **31**(2), 93–116 (2006). https://doi.org/10.1080/17439880600756621

80. Sevilla-Pavón, A.: Implementing technology-supported problem-based learning in a context of English for Specific Purposes. In: Zúñiga, T., Schmidt, L.T. (eds.) New Methodological Approaches to Foreign Teaching, pp. 167–186. Cambridge Scholars Publishing, Cambridge (2017)

81. Tan, O.S.: Problem-based learning innovation: using problems to power learning in the 21st century. Gale Cengage Learning (2021)

82. Guth, S., Helm, F.: Telecollaboration 2.0: language, literacies and intercultural learning in the 21st century, vol. 1. Peter Lang. (2010)

83. Müller-Hartmann, A.: Learning how to teach intercultural communicative competence via telecollaboration: a model for language teacher education. Internet-Mediated Intercultural Foreign Language Education, pp. 63–84 (2006)

84. Vinagre, M.: Developing key competences for life-long learning through virtual collaboration: teaching ICT in English as a medium of instruction. In: Handbook of Research on Foreign Language Education in the Digital Age, pp. 170–187. IGI Global (2016)

85. Hauck, M.: Virtual exchange for (critical) digital literacy skills development. Eur. J. Lang. Policy **11**(2), 187–210 (2019)
86. Nicolaou, A., Sevilla-Pavón, A.: Expanding a telecollaborative project through social entrepreneurship. In: Colpaert, J., Aerts, A., Cornillie, F. (eds.) XIXth International CALL Research Conference: Call Your Data 2018, pp. 295–302. University of Antwerp, Antwerp (2018)
87. Sevilla-Pavón, A., Nicolaou, A.: Artefact co-construction in virtual exchange: 'Youth entrepreneurship for society'. Comput. Assis. Lang. Learn., 1–26 (2020)

The OPENLang Network Pedagogical Framework: Designing an Open and Collaborative Language Learning Environment for Erasmus+ KA1 Mobility Participants

Maria Perifanou(✉) and Anastasios A. Economides

University of Macedonia, Egnatia 156, 546 36 Thessaloniki, Greece
maria.perifanou@uom.edu.gr, economid@uom.gr

Abstract. The design of an online open and highly interactive language learning environment is quite challenging as it entails a variety of specific factors to be carefully considered. One of the main challenges of the OPENLang Network project is to create an open and collaborative language learning environment for networking between language learners and teachers across Europe. The OPENLang Network platform envisages to bring together Erasmus+ mobility participants that wish to improve their language skills and cultural knowledge as well as volunteer educators who would like to offer support to all learners and share open language learning resources. This initiative is funded by the Erasmus+ programme and aims at raising language awareness of mobility participants, as well as fostering the Open Education European multicultural and multilingual vision via Open Educational Resources (OERs) and Massive Open Online Courses (MOOCs). The development of the OPENLang Network language learning environment is based on the design of the OPENLang Network's Pedagogical Framework. This paper first analyses the pedagogical theories, frameworks, and models applied in the Online Language Learning and Teaching context. Then, it presents the major research findings of the initial OPENLangNetwork's needs analysis survey which aimed to map and analyse the language needs of the participants involved in long-term mobility activities supported under Erasmus+ Key Action 1. Finally, it presents and analyses the OPENLang Network pedagogical framework which drives the design and development of the OPENLang Network language learning environment.

Keywords: Online language learning · Pedagogical framework · OPENLang network

1 Introduction

Designing an open and highly interactive language learning environment is a big challenge. Interaction-based learning is a cornerstone of many socially oriented approaches to L2 learning [1]. As it is known, increasing contact with the target language appears to be one of the most critical factors for successful Language

P. Zaphiris and A. Ioannou (Eds.): HCII 2021, LNCS 12784, pp. 140–160, 2021.
https://doi.org/10.1007/978-3-030-77889-7_10

Learning. Language is about communication and there is nothing more motivating than being able to use one's newly acquired language skills in an authentic environment [2, 3]. In fact, learner's participation and interaction are at the center and of crucial importance for successful language learning, whether it involves face-to-face, blended or fully online teaching. This is because "language learning is a skill-based process rather than a content-based one. Skills' development, such as the acquisition of speaking and listening skills, require constant synchronous interaction in the target language" [4]. In fact, fostering real-time synchronous interaction is an important principle in distance language teaching as synchronous oral and visual interaction is a crucial component in online language learning. Furthermore, a successful online language learning environment should support learners' autonomy and should give them sufficient time for practice and the possibility to get feedback and guidance when they need them [5].

Taking into consideration all the aforementioned factors a research has been initiated which aims at creating an open and collaborative language learning environment for bringing together language teachers and learners from different parts of Europe who wish to learn and practice the European language of their preference as well as to explore its rich and unique culture. This research initiative is conducted in the context of the OPENLang Network project (https://www.openlangnet.eu/) which is funded by the Erasmus+ programme under the Key Action 2 (KA2). Its main research goals include raising language awareness of mobility European languages, as well as fostering the Open Education European multicultural and multilingual vision via Open Educational Resources (OERs) and Massive Open Online Courses (MOOCs). More concretely, the OPENLang Network project aims at developing the OPENLang Network platform which envisages to connect Erasmus+ mobility participants that wish to improve their language skills and cultural knowledge, as well as volunteer educators who would like to offer support to all learners and share open language learning resources. As it was aforementioned, designing an online open and highly interactive language learning environment is quite challenging as it entails a variety of specific factors to be carefully considered. To that end, our research team explored first the pedagogical theories, frameworks, and models applied in the Online Language Learning and Teaching context. Based on the outcomes of the literature review as well as on the research findings emerged by a needs analysis survey which was conducted in the context of the project, it was proposed a pedagogical framework which drove the design and development of the OPENLang Network language learning environment. All these pedagogical design process phases will be analysed in the following sections.

2   Online Language Learning and Teaching Practice: Theoretical Background

2.1   Computer Assisted Language Learning Theoretical Overview

During the last four decades there are a plethora of studies which attempt to address the pedagogical aspects of online, bended and hybrid language teaching. The research area which investigates in general the digital language learning and teaching is known as

CALL and was defined by [6] as "the search for an study of applications of the computer in language teaching and learning". This area has undergone quite dramatic changes in pedagogical paradigms in the wake of technological changes first with the advent of the web, and later with the e-learning platforms and apps, and web 2.0 technologies.

But is there a CALL theory? Researchers have tried to define what is a CALL theory. Hubbard [7] emphasised the importance of deep understanding of the impact of technology on the learning environment and the learning process. He defined CALL theory as "the set of perspectives, models, frameworks, and specific theories that offer generalizations to account for phenomena related to the use of computers and the pursuit of language learning objectives, to ground relevant research agendas, and to inform effective CALL design and practice.... a CALL theory is a set of claims about the meaningful elements and processes within some domain of CALL, their interrelationships, and the impact that they have on language learning development and outcomes [7]. On the other hand, Egbert and Hanson Smith [8] claimed that there is no need for a "CALL theory": "... educators do not need a discrete theory of CALL to understand the role of technology in the classroom; a clear theory of SLA and its implications for the learning environment serves this goal".

The fact is that since 1960 there is a huge body of research in the field of CALL which shows that there are no prevailing CALL theories but only a group of theories which include a mix of the known learning theories, Second Language Acquisition theories, linguistic theories, and human-computer interaction theories. Many researchers [1, 9–12] described how the different approaches such as behaviorist, cognitivist, and sociocultural (constructivist) have influenced theories and research on the second language acquisition.

In fact, Warschauer and Healey [13] classified the history of CALL in three main phases: a) First phase: *"Behaviorist and later structural CALL"* (1960s to 70s); b) Second phase *"Communicative CALL"* (1970s to 80s); and c) Third phase *"Integrative CALL"* (2000 onwards).

More specifically, the first phase was characterised by its focus on the behaviorist approach in language acquisition and has mostly promoted behaviorist language learning approaches such as practice tasks and drills. As Warschauer [13] sustained "Essential in *behaviorist CALL* is the understanding that repeated exposure to the same material is beneficial or even essential to learning".

In the second phase, prevailed mostly the communicative approach in CALL which emphasized the important role of interaction and promoted the cognitivist approaches both in second language acquisition and learning theories. Such approaches focus on the importance of thinking processes in learning and language learning. In fact, language learning is seen as a process which involves memory, thinking, reflection, abstraction, and metacognition. In this case, research has shown that the way the learning content and tasks are presented in the online environment can have a major impact on how this material will be stored in the learner's long-term memory [14, 15].

Finally, in the third phase, the "Integrative CALL" phase [13], prevailed mostly the use of web, multimedia, Computer-mediated Communication (CMC) [12] and was encouraged both the project and task based language learning, as well as the tandem language learning. Tandem learning is a very powerful use of CMC especially in second language pedagogy as it gives the opportunity of instant communication to two native speakers of different languages to communicate regularly with one another, each one with the purpose of learning the other's language. In this CALL phase, it is also observed the arrival of MOOs ("Multi-user domain, Object-oriented"), an online social community where you can interact with other users in a text-based virtual reality. It is clear that a MOO provides a potentially highly useful and cost-effective way of bringing students together for tandem learning [16]. This offers the benefits of authentic, culturally grounded interaction, while also promoting a pedagogical focus among participants.

In "Integrative CALL" phase, sociocultural approaches, which draw heavily on Vygotsky and Bakhtin, are promoted in Second Learning Acquisition (SLA), which see language learning as an "interpersonal process situated in a social and cultural context and mediated by it" [17]. Vygotsky claimed that learning resulted from social inter-action rather than through isolated individual effort, and that engagement with others was a critical factor in the process [18]. Generally, when sociocultural theory is applied in CALL, it means that new and different forms of social interaction can occur, both online and in the classroom. The terms 'situated learning' and 'communities of prac-tice' derive from this perspective and are often used to highlight the importance of active learner participation in the community of the classroom or in online community settings [19]. Warschauer [20] also argued about cooperative or collaborative learning in online language classrooms where teachers could work with students on purposeful activities and could learn in social groups and communities of practice.

In fact, Constructivist or Socio-Cultural Approaches in second language learning theories see as essential the possibility for learners to construct their own knowledge and the importance of social contexts as preconditions for learning a language. As a consequence, learners in online second language learning environments should be allowed to construct knowledge rather than being given knowledge through instruction.

Furthermore, learners should be given the possibilities to interact with both online teachers and other online learners [9, 14, 21]. Sociocultural SLA approaches encom-pass a number of known terms: Zone of proximal development (ZPD), scaffolding, mediation, identities, interculturalism, affordances, community of practice, participa-tory learning, situated learning theory, co-construction, ecology, dialogism, critical theory, discursive practices, activity theory, private speech, peer response, collabora-tion, networking, etc. [22]. The sociocultural approach to CALL has a better com-patibility with the Web 2.0 tools. Of course, each technology has its own affordances that govern differently the ways in which interactions occur [23, 24]. The technology does not determine the interaction, but its attributes do help shape them. New emerging technologies of this new web era have opened new opportunities of interconnection and interaction and have brought new learning theories that apply to CALL. Recently, the connectivist theory was named as "the learning theory for the digital age" [25]. It perceives learning as a process that is not entirely under the control of the individual and occurs within complex and lacking definite form environments [25]. Downes [26] argued that "to learn in a connectivist course is to grow and develop, to form a network of connections in one's own self. Connectivist learning is a process of immersion in an environment, discovery and communication – a process of pattern recognition rather than hypothesis and theory-formation".

This has led to the current phase of CALL as it brings new educational challenges in the area of online language learning in terms of the nature of networks connecting people but also in terms of the quantity and the availability of knowledge. Examples of these new practices in online Language Learning are the Massive Open Language Learning Courses (LMOOCs or MOOLCs) which aim at unlimited participation and open access via the web and they are largely divided into behavioristic-based xMOOCs and connectivist-based MOOCs. According to the literature, the connectivist MOOC type (cMOOC) is ideal for language learning courses since cMOOCs encourage openness, autonomy, interactivity, peer-to-peer learning, social networking, and emergent knowledge [2, 27]. Furthermore, it is worth mentioning that many advanced technologies (i.e., advanced computer-mediated communication tools, artificial intelligence, augmented reality, smart mobile apps) which have been used in the language teaching process during the last decade have also implemented known teaching approaches in innovative ways such as webquests 2.0 [28], problem-based language learning [29], mobile assisted language learning [30], game-based language learning [31, 32], augmented reality in language learning [33].

2.2 Theories, Frameworks and Models in Online Language Teaching and Learning

From the analysis of the evolution phases of CALL in the previous section, it is clear that there is no common CALL theory and that technology and pedagogy are closely interconnected and one drives the other.

Recently, this was also confirmed by [34] who examined 166 research papers in order to detect the pedagogical theories used in the context of CALL. They found that there were no clearly 'dominant' theories showing up with any consistency except from a small number of general labels (SLA theory, learning theory, linguistic theory). They identified four primary sources for the theories: (1) language learning–centred extensions of human-computer interaction or technology in education theories, (2) technology-centred extensions of second language acquisition theories, (3) learning theories from psychology and education, and (4) linguistic theories. Across twenty-five years of articles, they identified just one solid reference to a theory developed specifically for this field [34]. Generally, literature reveals that there are a number of theories (Major theories, SLA theories, Foreign Language Acquisition theories, e-learning theories) that clash with one another and emerge in new combinations according to the affordances of novel online language learning environments.

In regards to frameworks and models which have been used in online language teaching and learning there is not so much research evidence. According to literature, there are not many frameworks and models which specifically addressed the needs of online language teaching and learning. On the contrary there are numerous models and frameworks (i.e., Merrill's instructional design principles [35]; Kolb's learning cycle [36]; Mayes and Fowler's framework [37]; Laurillard's conversational framework [38]; Community of Inquiry framework, Garrison and Anderson [39]; Collis and Moonen's '4Es' pedagogical model' [40]; Jonassen's constructivist model [41]; n-Quire model by Dewey [42]; Activity Theory by Kuuti [43]; Wenger's community of Practice [44]; Salmon's 5 stage e-moderating model [45]; Connectivism by Siemens [25]; Preece's framework for online community [46]; The 8 Learning Events Model (8LEM) by Leclercq and Poumay [47]) which were used for the design of online language courses and mostly adopted from the e-learning field. Each model has a particular focus and emphasis, and is aligned with a particular set of theoretical perspectives which are based on the major learning theories.

As far as frameworks and models for online language teaching is concerned, there has been some research that addresses technology integration in language teaching from different perspectives and frameworks [48–53]. Technology integration is defined as 'the process of determining which electronic tools and which methods for implementing them are the most appropriate responses to given classroom situations and problems' [54]. For example, Hoven [55] offered theoretically grounded models for computer-based listening. Salaberry [51] outlined the pedagogical principles of using technologies in teaching second language, while Bax [49] presented the process of 'normalization' of CALL and ways of how 'technology could become invisible and embedded in everyday practice'. Tudor [52]. on the contrary, proposed an ecological perspective of language teaching highlighting 'the various human and contextual factors which influence the use and likely effectiveness of this technology' [52] without addressing the role of technology. He emphasized that teaching and learning processes involve teachers, students, and all others who influence the practices in each classroom, as well as the dynamic interaction between participants, methodology, and context. Later, Plass and Jones [50] proposed a model of cognitive processing in second-language acquisition supported by multimedia. This model provides only insights on how teachers can use multimedia to support language learners but does address the factors that could affect the use of technology by teachers. Hampel and Hauck [53] described a pedagogical framework for integrating audio-conferencing effectively in distance language courses at their institution.

Known theories and concepts that have supported the process of designing instructional technology for language learning are the following: "The Content-Based Lesson Plan", "Bloom's Taxonomy", "Constructivism"," Metacognition", "Schema Theory". Perhaps the most elaborated design framework is that of Colpaert (2004), which is pedagogy-driven and creatively blends engineering principles and pedagogical approaches and is specifically focused on the creation of language courseware. As most of the pedagogy-driven approaches, this is also inspired by the learner centered or constructivist pedagogical approach. Colpaert [56] has explored the boundaries of pedagogy-driven research in the context of online language learning. This design framework consists of two phases: (a) define first what is needed in terms of functionalities, and (b) evaluate to what extent available technologies allow them to be implemented. It is similar to the instructional design model "ADDIE" (Analysis, Design, Development, Implementation, Evaluation). In contrast to the other alternative approaches for the development of an online learning environment (technology-driven, attributes-based and affordance-based), this approach involves "a detailed specification of what is needed for language-teaching and language-learning purposes in a specific context, defines the most appropriate method, and finally attempts to describe the technological requirements to make it work". The goal of this research was to try to prove that sufficient linguistic/ didactic functionality can be realized online by applying an adequate design plan.

Furthermore, it is worth mentioning that there are also specific theories of Foreign Language Acquisition which have provided one rationale for instruction and for the design of online language learning environments such as the "Monitor theory" [57], the "Input Processing Model" [58], "Interaction Theory" and "Sociocultural Theory" [18, 59–61]. "Monitor Theory" [57] emphasizes the importance of comprehensible linguistic input in the acquisition process. It proposes an initial silent period in which students listen, but do not speak, as a way to promote acquisition. "Monitor Theory" indicates that a series of activities emphasizing listening comprehension should precede even the most simple production activities.

The "Input Processing Model" [58] differentiates between input (the language to which the learner is exposed) and intake (the language that actually gets processed by the learner). This model emphasizes the importance of binding the form of a word to its meaning. If it is used as a rationale, it would indicate that early input activities ought to be simple recognition activities that require students to attend to one important detail and connect form to meaning. Activities would progress from simple to complex activities along a continuum ranging from recognition to simple one word production to sentence level and discourse level production in a logical order.

"Interaction Theory" and "Sociocultural Theory" emphasize the importance of the social aspect of language learning [18, 59–61]. Within these frameworks, language is negotiated and socially mediated or assisted. Paraphrasing, requests for repetition, clarification requests, verification checks, and comprehension checks are tools used by the novice learner to achieve proficiency during interaction with an expert speaker. Promoting social interaction through the computer and providing opportunities for the production of both oral and written language that may be negotiated would be indicated in a design organized around these theories. These two theories also imply that a completed educational program should be designed so that paired and group-learning opportunities are afforded to the student.

Theories are linked to a variety of language teaching methods (i.e., Community Language Learning Method, Communicative Approach, Multiple Intelligences -Based Instruction, Content-Based Instruction, Task-Based Instruction, Interactive-Integrated Approach) which also influence the design of instructional material and of online language learning environments.

In conclusion, the literature reveals that there is a variety of theories such as Major Learning Theories, SLA theories, Foreign Language Acquisition theories, e-learning theories that are applied in different combinations to Online Language Learning and Teaching Practice according to the technical affordances and the pedagogical goals in every case. There are also interesting frameworks and models which can be applied in the context of Computer Assisted Language Learning (CALL), depending on different educational goals. Frameworks and models related to social constructivism theories and connectivism are preferred in the context of CALL, because they promote task based learning, social interaction, authentic learning, collaborative learning, personalised autonomous and self-directed learning, social learning which are crucial for learning a second or a foreign language.

3   OPENLang Network Needs' Analysis Survey

During the first semester of 2019, the consortium of the OPENLang Network Erasmus+ project (https://www.openlangnet.eu/) conducted a needs' analysis survey in order to identify the language and cultural needs as well as the motivations of the Erasmus+ KA1 mobility participants who were involved or planned to be involved in an Erasmus+ mobility for at least one month. There were also taken several interviews with a number of Erasmus+ stakeholders from 3 European countries (Greece, Cyprus, and Italy). The research findings of the survey have shown that learning a new language and exploring a new culture were the two main reasons for participating in an Erasmus+ mobility, as it was also mentioned by other researchers in literature [62]. Improving or gaining language skills for a fluent or at least basic communication level or even for specific purposes were the most important educational priorities for the participants. In fact, most of the participants characterised their communication with local people during their mobility as the biggest linguistic challenge. Other important linguistic challenges for them include the difficulty to understand the regional accents/dialects and the comprehension of the academic language. Though, for many of them, advancing their listening skills and enriching their general vocabulary was still a very important factor, while improving their reading and writing skills was a less important one [63, 64]. Participants also had different views regarding the language level needed by the Erasmus+ participants during their mobility. Based on their linguistic priorities, some participants claimed that the C1-C2 levels (based on CEFR classification) were the ideal language levels to have in order to cope with material that is academic or cognitively demanding, while for everyday communication a lower level was enough. Participants were also asked to express their preferences regarding the type of learning content, the online language learning environment and the mode of learning. Regarding the content, most of the participants preferred multimedia material (images, video, etc.) and an interactive user-friendly online language learning environment with less text and more visual representations.

Regarding the mode of learning most participants preferred the social way of learning. Combining the results of questionnaires and interviews it was shown that there is a big need for linguistic support via training, seminars or language courses for both outcoming and incoming participants. Furthermore, there is a need for networking and collaboration between participants in the Erasmus+ KA1 mobility in order to achieve cultural understanding and intercultural communication, as well as to build friendships or even professional opportunities for the future. The findings of the OPENLang Network survey have confirmed previous research findings that have shown that the development of language proficiency and learning a different culture are the main reasons to participate in an Erasmus+ mobility [62, 65–68]. Other research findings, that were also really important for the design of the OPENLang Network Pedagogical Framework, were first that the participants gave priority in advancing specifically their listening and communication skills as well as their general vocabulary, and secondly that the participants preferred social learning, intercultural communication and networking in an interactive multimedia environment.

4   OPENLang Network Pedagogical Framework: Dimensions and Process

The OPENLang Network's Pedagogical Framework is designed based on the questionnaire and interviews answers which were conducted to explore the language and culture awareness needs of the Erasmus+ KA1 mobility participants involved in long-term mobility activities, as well as on the literature review on the theoretical background of the online language education.

Designing an open language learning environment which could provide multiple types of interaction for the learners is a challenging task. Interaction-based learning is a cornerstone of many socially oriented approaches to L2 learning" [65]. As it is known, increasing contact with the target language appears to be one of the most critical factors for successful Language Learning. Language is about communication, and there is nothing more motivating than being able to use one's newly acquired language skills in an authentic environment [69, 70]. In fact, learner's participation and interaction are at the center and of crucial importance for successful language learning, whether it is face-to-face, blended or fully online teaching. This is because "language learning is a skill-based process rather than a content-based one. Skills' development, such as the acquisition of speaking and listening skills, required constant synchronous interaction in the target language" [4]. In fact, fostering real-time synchronous interaction is an important principle in distance language teaching since synchronous oral and visual interaction is a crucial component in online language learning. A successful online language learning environment should support learners' autonomy and should give them sufficient time for practice and the possibility to get feedback and guidance when they need them [2, 27, 69]. Each learner of the OPENLang Network is seen as an autonomous learner but also as a learner who can interact with other peers and/or the teacher in pairs or in small groups or even in a big community.

One of the main challenges of the design of the OPENLang Network's Pedagogical Framework was to provide the opportunity to each learner for social interaction, Language Learning input/output, authenticity, exposure, feedback, and learner autonomy which are key factors for a successful language learning [70].

More concretely, the philosophy behind the design of the OPENLang Network's Pedagogical Framework was inspired by a learner-centered, social-constructivist and connectivism pedagogical paradigm blending a variety of pedagogical approaches and instructional strategies derived from the areas of CALL, elearning, SLA and FLL (i.e. Autonomous learning, Self-regulated learning, Personalised learning, Collaborative learning, Cooperative learning, Community learning, theory of transactional distance, Language Communication theory, Second Language Acquisition theories, Interaction and Socio-cultural theory, Social Constructivism and Connectivism, Activity theory, Situated Learning theory, Language Acquisition Theory, Tandem Learning theory, Wenger's Theory of communities of practice).

The OPENLang Network open and collaborative language learning environment is designed to provide multiple types of interaction to learners who belong in a community of language practice. Each learner of this environment is seen as an autonomous learner who can use the open educational material content (OERs), but also as a learner who can interact with other peers and/or the teacher in a one-to-one pair or in small groups or even in a big community. Learners are placed at the center of the OPENLang Network online language learning environment and are free to take their own personalised learning paths as it presented in the following diagram below which showcase the OPENLang Network Pedagogical Framework (Fig. 1).

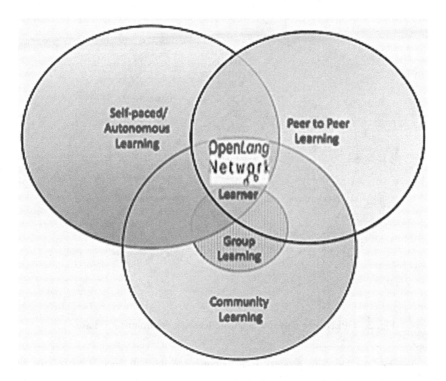

Fig. 1. OPENLang network pedagogical framework

The learners can select the mode of interaction and collaboration that they prefer (autonomous, one-to-one, pair-to-pair, one-to-many), choose among the available tools and services offered by the platform, and control the amount of open material (OERs) they want to use, reuse, share as well as the duration of time that they need to spend for studying or practicing the target language or exploring a new culture. Each learner can practice the language of his/her choice by choosing a language partner such as a peer, a group or a teacher. A learner in the OPENLang Network belongs to a large community and has access to an open forum where he/she can start an interesting discussion about any topic he/she likes. This aspect is very important because the target group of users are Erasmus+ students who face many challenges and difficulties in every phase of their mobility. Teachers play also a significant role in this network as they can support the community with their contribution either as language partners, or as members of the discussion area or as content contributors as they can create, share, evaluate or recommend their language OERs. The following diagram (Fig. 2) presents the active role of the OPENLang Network learner.

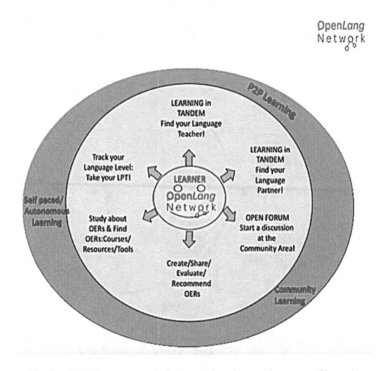

Fig. 2. OPENLang network language learning environment (Phase 1).

In general, the learning process is in accordance with the principles of the self-paced self-regulated learning and autonomous learning, personalised learning, tandem learning, cooperative and collaborative learning, community learning, social constructivism and connectivism.

4.1 Self-placed, Self-regulated and Autonomous Learning

Each learner of the OPENLang Network is seen as an autonomous learner who is at the center of the learning process. A number of known theories are connected to autonomous learning and the learner-centred approaches. According to the literature, in a learner-centered approach the learner is considered as the key agent of the learning process [71], and a defining element in online learning [4]. The choices regarding the pedagogical design of the OPENLang Network language learning environment were driven by the learners' interests and needs. From this pedagogical perspective, our research team aims to create a diverse learning environment which could enable personalized learning that could allow learners to make decisions about how to choose tools and configure the learning environment to best suit their learning goals and needs [72]. Personalised and autonomous learning are in line with self-paced and self-regulated learning (SRL). Naidu [73] defines self-paced learning as "a mode of learning that enables individuals to study online or with the help of portable technologies in their own time, at their own pace, and from their own place" (p. 260). Self or learner paced distance and e-learning courses are based on increased learner independence and flexibility, as learners can start their courses at any time during the year, and complete them at their own pace [74]. Self-regulated learning (SRL) is a known distance education theory, which is defined as the ability of learners to control the factors or conditions affecting their learning [75]. Pintrich [76] defined self-regulated learning as "an active and constructivist process whereby learners attempt to monitor, regulate, and control their cognition, motivation and behaviors after setting goals for their learning, are guided and restricted by their own goals and the learning environment they are in". Social context plays an important role in self regulated learning [77]. Instructors or peers are external factors who become models to guide learners in self-regulation activities and provide feedback [78]. Because of the social processes, learners can develop their competencies to meet challenges, for content and context. Consequently, they become self-regulated learners [78].

The OPENLang Network language learning environment aims to be a social language learning environment where each learner is a self-paced and self-regulated learner who can have multiple opportunities for authentic interaction (input and output). This pedagogical approach offers also other important opportunities to learners such as the free choice to set their own goals, their own learning strategies, the time of study, with whom to study and the possibility to monitor and reflect on their learning progress [77]. Some studies have shown that self-regulated learners are more successful in distance learning [79] sustained that distance learning is more flexible, learner-centered, and autonomous than face-to-face as it requires learners to be self-regulated and use their self-regulated learning skills more frequently. In general, self-regulated learning skills are critical for success in self-paced distance learning environments where learners study on their own.

4.2   Peer-to-Peer or Tandem Learning

Following the needs of the OPENLang Network's survey participants, about multiple opportunities for interaction, we have introduced tandem learning services in the OPENLang Network Platform as it was originally planned. Tandem language learning has a lot to do with collaborative language learning. This type of learning takes place when two people share the idea of improving their communicative competence in the target language, and establish a negotiation to reach an agreement on how they will deal with the tasks they have to face together [80]. The overarching principles of tandem learning are: a) The principle of autonomy: Being responsible for your own learning; and b) The principle of reciprocity: Being responsible for ensuring mutual benefit [81]. More specifically, "Autonomy" implies that both partners are responsible for their own learning, so they decide "what they want to learn, how and when, and what sort of help they need from their partner". "Reciprocity" means that each partner brings certain skills and abilities which the other partner seeks to acquire and in which both partners support each other in their learning in such a way that both benefit as much as possible from their working together [81]. Both principles are closely related to the views some scholars have on autonomy in foreign language learning [82–84], as a mutual collaboration among students with a view to improving their linguistic competence in the target language but also their intercultural communicative competence by learning of the way people live and behave within the target language community [85].

Other studies [86, 87] have explored the application of Tandem learning by Erasmus students. In the first study [86] Erasmus students preferred Tandem learning to other ways for practicing the language and learning the new culture. The students from other European Union countries, studying under the Erasmus scheme, reported that tandem learning was a real opportunity for them to get to know English students and to practice English as this was the best way to socialise closely with them since it was much more difficult to make English friends when they came to study in the UK. According to the findings of another study [87], Tandem learners may gain almost as much as learners immersed in the L2 environment, in this case Erasmus Tandem students. Interactive situations such as Tandem learning, which are typically friendly and of low anxiety, assist the development of automaticity in second language use, and thus the ability to produce longer and more fluent speech units. For the Erasmus students, who were immersed in the L2 environment, tandem learning has activated and automated some of the language that had been learnt formally in their country.

During the last 20 years, many researchers [88–92] have explored the potentials of tandem learning in the area of language learning. Tandem learners have practiced a variety of languages such as English, German, Spanish, Japanese, Chinese, Russian, Brasilian using first the traditional email and later several Web 2.0 tools such as *Skype, Adobe Connect, Google instant messaging, QQ, WeChat,*wiki, etc.

All these researches on tandem learning practices have explored mostly the use of tandem learning between specific groups of learners such as two university language classes [91] and usually on the acquisition of two specific languages. Rarely, we have seen a web-based tandem language exchange environment in which more than two languages were practiced such as the ETR web based tandem learning environment which included three languages [88].

Based on the research findings aforementioned, Tandem Learning was selected by the OPENLang Network team as an ideal pedagogical approach for Erasmus+ students to acquire linguistic and intercultural competence by interacting in synchronous and asynchronous ways in pairs or in small groups of tandem pairs. The research in this area is quite limited and the OPENLang Network team aims to explore the benefits of tandem learning practices in an open multilingual European community which is not limited to few languages but it will support and promote every European language. The research will focus first on finding ways to support the tandem pairs and at a later stage will research small groups of participants. One idea would be connecting tandem pairs participating in a common discussion and debate on specific topics that a teacher or a peer would propose. Discussion topics for the Tandem communication could be also proposed in the discussion area by the OPENLang Network community. Learners' linguistic or intercultural needs that may emerge during the different phases of the Erasmus+ mobility could be discussed in the discussion area and in this way could enrich the linguistic and intercultural competences of all the participating learners. Small group learning is based on a cooperative learning approach while community learning promotes collaborative learning and is based on social-constructivism learning theories and the connectivism theory.

4.3   Small Group Learning: Cooperative and Collaborative Learning

More specifically, the pedagogy which lies behind the small group learning is cooperative learning which shares the same basic set of principles with the widespread Communicative Language Teaching. Cooperative language learning responds to the trend in foreign language teaching methods with focusing on the communicative and effective factors in language learning because language learners need to know how to use the knowledge in practice and to express or narrate their thoughts and ideas. Cooperative learning can create an effective learning climate as it offers a relaxed climate in the classroom, can increase student motivation [93, 94] and increase learner's self-confidence and self-esteem [95]. It also provides various chances of Input and Output as it creates natural, interactive contexts, where students listen to each other, ask questions, and clarify issues and this is valuable in the oral practice and listening comprehension. They also produce more accurate and appropriate language, which itself provides input for other students [95]. Cooperative learning also increases a variety of language functions as it creates a real-life social setting in which language is normally used (i.e., clarifying, making suggestions, encouraging, disagreeing, negotiating of meaning, etc.). Furthermore, cooperative learning promotes learners' responsibility and independence to help students become more autonomous and self-controlled [96].

In the case of the OPENLang Network, the project's team will explore informal cooperative learning tasks where in each task there will participate up to three (3) tandem pairs, preferably with the support of the language teacher who could guide the specific task. In traditional class, the informal or formal group works are supported by the teacher in multiple ways via specific activities (i.e., webquest, think-pair-share, peer instruction jigsaw, etc.). In the context of the open language learning community we will explore how language learners could work either in one tandem pair, or in two or three tandem pairs together. Cooperative learning in an online context has different challenges and can be facilitated also by various advanced technologies.

4.4   Community Learning: Communities of Practice and Connectivism

Additionally to tandem learning and small group learning, learning in an online community is also a challenging opportunity for OPENLang Network learners. Social constructivism, situated learning, communities of practice and connectivism are theories which lie behind learning in an online community. Since 2005, most of the Second Language Acquisition (SLA) research explored sociocultural and social cognitive theories such as "activity theory, socio-constructivism, community of practice, social cognitive theory" [1]. Social constructivism conceptualises learning as participation in shared activities where the context and the situated nature of learning are integral considerations. From this perspective, knowledge is distributed among members of a community, and learning involves individuals' abilities to participate successfully in community of practices [44]. Wenger [44] describes Communities of Practice (CoP) as "groups of people who share a concern or a passion for something they do and learn how to do it better as they interact regularly." This learning that takes place in a CoP is not necessarily intentional as it occurs in a community. Situated Learning Theory also emphasizes that learning is unintentional and situated within authentic activity, context, and culture, known as the "process of legitimate peripheral participation" [97]. It occurs when students work on authentic tasks that take place in a real-world setting [98]. Social interaction is a critical component of situated learning—learners become involved in a "community of practice" which embodies certain beliefs and behaviors to be acquired [44].

Social interaction is also a critical component in connectivism, the theory of the digital world according to Siemens [25] who argues that what is more important is the ability to learn (create and understand connections) than the current amount of knowledge. Connectivism is a logical development of social constructivist theory in a digitally-mediated world that views learning as a process of developing networks of information, contacts, and resources that are applied to real problems [25]. According to the theory of Connectivism, learning occurs when a learner connects to a learning community and feeds information into it. Connectivism "is built on an assumption of a constructivist model of learning, with the learner at the centre, connecting and constructing knowledge in a context that includes not only external networks and groups but also his or her own histories and predilections" [99].

Connectivism, outlines four foundations for learning, which include autonomy, connectedness, diversity, and openness [100]. According to Nattoch Dag [101] connectivism has similar principles with adult learning and "the main difference between adult learning and connectivism, however, is that whereas adult learning principles focus on the individual learner, connectivism focuses on the aspect of connectivity, and how the learner himself or herself connects the nodes".

As far as language learning is concerned, it is important to use a variety of information resources (books, Internet, mass media, ICT, etc.) and this is in line with connectivism which defines learning as a process of creating connections among the nodes or information resources. Language learning is also a long-life activity and it cannot be learnt just as a set of words and phrases and this follows into the principles of lifelong learning in adult education and connectivism's connectedness. A connectionist-based course is based on autonomy, diversity (different countries, different cultures and backgrounds) connectedness and interactivity. 'Autonomy' gives priority to learners' own goals, purposes, objectives or values. 'Diversity' ensures that creativity is fostered among members of a community. 'Openness' emphasizes the lack of barriers, ensures the free flow of ideas and content sharing and gives freedom to choose between different technologies. A connectionist-based course which promotes connectedness, interactivity, autonomy, diversity, and openness are also highly important characteristics for an efficient online language learning environment because they are key factors for a successful language learning [2, 69, 70].

To sum up, a number of learner-centered and social-constructivist & connectivist learning theories and pedagogical approaches have inspired the design of the OPEN-Lang Network's Pedagogical Framework.

5 Conclusions and Future Steps

The research findings of the OPENLang Network's needs analysis survey as well as the literature review on existing pedagogical theories, frameworks and models applied in Online Language Education led to the creation of the OPENLang Network's Pedagogical Framework. Based on this framework the OPENLang Network team has also developed the OPENLang Network's Design Framework and the OPENLang Network online platform which will be presented in future publications.

One first conclusion that the literature review revealed is that there is not a single CALL theory which is applied to Online Language Learning and Teaching but a variety of theories such as Major Learning Theories, SLA theories, Foreign Language Acquisition theories, e-learning theories that are applied in different combinations to Online Language Learning and Teaching Practice according to the technical affordances and the pedagogical goals in every case. Furthermore, it was found that the pedagogical models and frameworks which are applied for the design of online language learning environments are mostly adopted from the field of e-learning and inspired by a blend of theories as it was aforementioned. The major conclusion here is that the design of a highly interactive online language learning environment is quite challenging as it entails to take under consideration a number of factors such as the needs of the target group, the pedagogical implications and the technical affordances of the online environment.

Furthermore, the findings of the OPENLang Network survey shown that the development of language proficiency and learning a different culture are the main reasons to participate in an Erasmus+ mobility and that Erasmus+ participants need to be able to have access to a continuous language training before, during, and after their mobility.

Currently, the OPENLang Network team is getting prepared for piloting the OPENLang Network platform and all its available services. The team is organising a 4 weeks MOOC which will offer a full training course to language teachers with a focus on the use, creation, and share of language OERs. This course also aims to test the multilevel interaction scenarios of the OPENLang Network's Pedagogical Framework and, additionally, to explore the possibility of creating small working language groups in which a teacher could facilitate the discussion of max 6 students (or 3 tandem pairs). Based on the valuable feedback that will be received by all the participants, the OPENLang Network team will make all the changes needed.

Acknowledgements. This work has been partially funded by the European Union's ErasmusPlus programme, grant agreement: 2018-1-EL01-KA203-047967 (Project: OPENLang Network). This publication reflects the views only of the authors, and the European Commission cannot be held responsible for any use which may be made of the information contained here.

References

1. Wang, S., Vasquez, C.: Web 2.0 and second language learning: what does the research tell us? CALICO J. **29**(3), 412–430 (2012). https://doi.org/10.11139/cj.29.3.412
2. Perifanou, M.A.: How to design and evaluate a massive open online course (MOOC) for language learning. In let's build the future through learning innovation! no. **1**, pp. 283–290 (2014)
3. Perifanou, M.A.: Key factors for designing a successful massive open online interactive language learning environment (MOILLE) **IX**(1), 89–104 (2016)
4. Wang, Y., Chen, N.-S.: Criteria for evaluating synchronous learning management system: arguments from the distance language classroom. Comput. Assist. Lang. Learn. **22**(1), 1–18 (2009)
5. Perifanou, M.: Designing strategies for an efficient Language MOOC. In: Proceedings of the EUROCALL 2016 Conference, Limassol, Cyprus, pp. 380–385 (2016). https://doi.org/10.14705/rpnet.2016.eurocall2016.592
6. Levy, M.: Computer-Assisted Language Learning: Context and Conceptualization. Oxford University Press, New York (1997)
7. Hubbard, P.: Developing CALL theory: a new frontier. In: Thomas, M. (ed.) New Frontiers in CALL: Negotiating Diversity, pp. 1–6. JALT CALL SIG, Japan (2009)
8. Egbert, J., Hanson-Smith, E.: CALL Environments: Research, Practice, and Critical Issues. Teachers of English to Speakers of Other Languages, Alexandria (2007)
9. Chapelle, C.A.: The relationship between second language acquisition theory and computer-assisted language learning. Mod. Lang. J. **93**, 741–753 (2009)
10. Gass, S.M., Selinker, L.: Second language acquisition: an introductory course, 3rd edn. Routledge, New York and London (2008)
11. Warschauer, M.: Computer assisted language learning: an introduction. In: Fotos, S. (ed.) Multimedia Language Teaching. Logos International, Tokyo (1996)
12. Warschauer, M.: Foreword. In: Thomas, M. (ed.) Handbook of Research on Web2.0 and Second Language Learning. Information Science Reference, Hershey (2009)
13. Warschauer, M., Healey, D.: Computers and language learning: an overview. Lang. Teach. **31**, 51–71 (1998)
14. Ally, M.: Foundations of educational theory for online learning. In: The Theory and Practice of Online Learning, 2nd edn., pp. 15–44. Athabasca University Press, Athabasca (2008) http://www.aupress.ca/index.php/books/120146
15. Mitchell, R., Myles, F.: Second Language Learning Theories, 2nd edn. Hodder Arnold, London (2004)
16. O'Rourke, B.: Form-focused interaction in online tandem learning. CALICO J. **22**(3), 433–466 (2013). https://doi.org/10.1558/cj.v22i3.433-466
17. Lamy, M.-N., Hampel, R.: Online Communication in Language Teaching and Learning. Palgrave McMillan, Basingstoke (2007)
18. Vygotsky, L.: Mind in Society. The Development of Higher Psychological Processes. Harvard University Press, Cambridge (1978)
19. Donato, R., McCormick, D.: A sociocultural perspective on language learning strategies: the role of mediation. Mod. Lang. J. **78**(4), 453–464 (1994)
20. Warschauer, M.: Sociocultural perspectives on CALL. In: Egbert, J., Petrie, G. (eds.) CALL Research Perspectives, pp. 41–52. Lawrence Erlbaum, Mahwah (2005)
21. Thomas, L.: Improving student retention in higher education: improving teaching and learning. Austr. Univ. Rev. **51**(2) (2009)

22. Zuengler, J., Miller, E.R.: Cognitive and sociocultural perspectives: two parallel SLAworlds? TESOL Q. **40**(1), 35–58 (2006)
23. Hutchby, I.: Conversation and Technology: From the Telephone to the Internet. Blackwell, Malden (2001)
24. Smith, B.: Computer-mediated negotiated interaction: an expanded model. Mod. Lang. J. **87**, 38–57 (2003)
25. Siemens, G.: Connectivism: a learning theory for the digital age. Int. J. Instruc. Technol. Dist. Learn. **2**(1), (2005). http://www.itdl.org/Journal/Jan_05/article01.htm
26. Downes, S.: Connectivism and connective knowledge: essays on meaning and learning networks. National Research Council Canada (2012). http://www.downes.ca/files/books/Connective_Knowledge-19May2012.Pdf
27. Perifanou, M., Economides, A.: MOOCs for language learning: an effort to explore and evaluate the first practices. In: Proceedings of the INTED2014 Conference, Valencia, Spain, pp. 3561–3570 (2014). http://library.iated.org/view/PERIFANOU2014MOO
28. Perifanou, M., Mikros, G.: 'Italswebquest': a wiki as a platform of collaborative blended language learning and a course management system. Int. J. Knowl. Learn. **5**(3–4), 273–288 (2009). https://doi.org/10.1504/IJKL.2009.0312
29. Lee, S.-Y., Lo, Y.-H.G., Chin, T.-C.: Practicing multiliteracies to enhance EFL learners' meaning making process and language development: a multimodal Problem-based approach. Comput. Assis. Lang. Learn. (2019). https://doi.org/10.1080/09588221.2019.1614959
30. Morgana, V., Kukulska-Hulme, A. (eds.): Mobile Assisted Language Learning Across Educational Contexts. Routledge Focus on Applied Linguistics. Routledge (2021)
31. Perifanou, M.A.: Language micro-gaming: fun and informal microblogging activities for language learning. In: Lytras, M.D., Ordonez de Pablos, P., Damiani, E., Avison, D., Naeve, A., Horner, D.G. (eds.) WSKS 2009. CCIS, vol. 49, pp. 1–14. Springer, Heidelberg (2009). https://doi.org/10.1007/978-3-642-04757-2_1
32. Godwin-Jones, R.: Augmented reality and language learning: from annotated vocabulary to place-based mobile games. Lang. Learn. Technol. **20**(3), 9–19 (2016). http://llt.msu.edu/issues/october2016/emerging.pdf
33. Fan, M., Antle, A.N., Warren, J.L.: Augmented reality for early language learning: a systematic review of augmented reality application design instructional strategies, and evaluation outcomes. J. Educ. Comput. Res. **58**(6), 1059–1100 (2020)
34. Hubbard, P., Levy, M.: Theory in computer-assisted language learning research and practice. In: The Routledge Handbook of Language Learning and Technology (2016). https://www.routledgehandbooks.com/doi/10.4324/9781315657899.ch2. Accessed 26 Feb 2021
35. Merrill, M.D.: First principles of instruction. Educ. Technol. Res. Dev. **50**(3), 43–59 (2002)
36. Kolb, D.: Experiential Learning: Experience as the Source of Learning and Development. Prentice Hall, Englewood Cliffs (1984)
37. Mayes, J.T., Fowler, C.J.H.: Learning technology and usability: a framework for understanding courseware. Interact. Comput. **11**, 485–497 (1999)
38. Laurillard, D.: Rethinking University Teaching: A Framework for the Effective Use of Educational Technology. Routledge/Falmer, London (1993)
39. Garrison, D.R., Anderson, T., Archer, W.: Critical inquiry in a text-based environment: computer conferencing in higher education model. Internet High. Educ. **2**(2–3), 87–105 (2000)
40. Collis, B., van der Wende, M.: Models of technology and change in higher education: an international comparative survey on the current and future uses of ICT in higher education. University of Twente, CHEPS (2002)

41. Jonassen, D.: Designing constructivist learning environments. In: Reigeluth, C.M. (ed.) Instructional Theories and Models, 2nd edn., pp. 215–239. Lawrence Erlbaum Associates, Mahwah (1999)
42. Dewey, J.: Democracy and Education. An Introduction to the Philosophy of Education. The Free Press, New York (1916, c. 1966)
43. Kuutti, K.: Activity theory as a potential framework for human-computer interaction research. In: Nardi, B. (ed.) Context and Consciousness: Activity Theory and Human-Computer Interaction, pp. 17–44. MIT Press, Cambridge (1996)
44. Wenger, E.: Communities of Practice: Learning, Meaning, and Identity. Cambridge University Press (1998). https://doi.org/10.1017/CBO9780511803932
45. Salmon, G.: E-moderating: The Key to Teaching and Learning Online, 2nd edn. Routledge, New York (2003)
46. Preece, J.: Online Communities: Designing Usability, Supporting Sociability. Wiley, Chichester (2000)
47. Leclercq, D., Poumay, M.: The 8 learning events model and its principles. LabSET. University of Liège (2005). http://www.labset.net/media/prod/8LEM.pdf
48. Hoven, D.: Improving the management of flow of control in computer-assisted listening comprehension tasks for second and foreign language. Unpublished doctoral dissertation, University of Queensland, Brisbane, Australia (1997)
49. Bax, S.: CALL - Past, Present and Future. System. Elsevier Ltd. (2003). https://doi.org/10.1016/S0346-251X(02)00071-4
50. Plass, J., Jones, L.: Multimedia learning in second language acquisition. In: Mayer, R. (ed.) The Cambridge Handbook of Multimedia Learning. Cambridge University Press, Cambridge (2005)
51. Salaberry, M.R.: The use of technology for second language learning and teaching: a retrospective. Modern Lang. J. **85**, 39–56 (2001)
52. Tudor, I.: Learning to live with complexity: towards an ecological perspective on language teaching. System **31**, 1–12 (2003)
53. Hampel, R., Hauck, M.: Computer-Mediated Language Learning: Making Meaning in Multimodal Virtual Learning Spaces. Language Learning & Technology (2004)
54. Roblyer, M.D., Doering, A.H.: Integrating Educational Technology into Teaching, 5th edn. Allyn & Bacon, Boston (2010)
55. Hoven, D.: A Model for listening and viewing comprehension in multimedia environments. Lang. Learn. Technol. **3**(1), 88–103 (1999)
56. Colpaert, J.: Editorial: transdisciplinarity. Comput. Assist. Lang. Learn. **17**(5), 459–472 (2004)
57. Krashen, S.M.: Principles and Practice in Second Language Acquisition. Pergamon Press, Oxford (1982)
58. Lee, J.G., VanPatten, B.: Making Communicative Language Teaching Happen. McGraw-Hill, New York (1995)
59. Doughty, C.J., Long, M.H.: Optimal psycholinguistic environments for distance foreign language learning. Lang. Learn. Technol. **7**(3), 50–80 (2003)
60. Long, M.H.: Input, interaction, and second language acquisition. Ann. N. Y. Acad. Sci. **379**, 259–278 (1981)
61. Lantolf, J.-P.: Sociocultural Theory and Second Language Learning. Oxford University Press, Oxford (2000)
62. Gallarza, M.G., Fayos-Gardó, T., Arteaga-Moreno, F., Servera-Francés, D., Floristán-Imizcoz, E.: Different levels of loyalty towards the higher education service: evidence from a small university in Spain. Int. J. Manage. Educ. **14**(1), 36–48 (2019)

63. Kosmas, P., Parmaxi, A, Perifanou, M., Economides, A.A.: Mapping the language learning profile of the Erasmus+ KA1 Mobility Participants. Research report, OPENLangNet Erasmus+ project (2020). https://www.openlangnet.eu/outputs/

64. Kosmas, P., Parmaxi, A., Perifanou, M., Economides, A.A., Zaphiris, P.: Creating the Profile of participants in mobility activities in the context of Erasmus+: motivations, perceptions, and linguistic needs. In: Zaphiris, P., Ioannou, A. (eds.) HCII 2020. LNCS, vol. 12205, pp. 499–511. Springer, Cham (2020). https://doi.org/10.1007/978-3-030-50513-4_37

65. Van Maele, J., Vassilicos, B., Borghetti, C.: Mobile students' appraisals of keys to a successful stay abroad experience: hints from the IEREST project. Lang. Intercult. Commun. 16(3), 384–401 (2016)

66. Aslan, B., Jacobs, D.B.: Erasmus student mobility: some good practices according to views of Ankara University exchange students. J. Educ. Future (5), 57 (2014)

67. Borghetti, C., Beaven, A.: Lingua francas and learning mobility: reflections on students' attitudes and beliefs towards language learning and use. Int. J. Appl. Linguist. 27(1), 221–241 (2017)

68. Llanes, À., Tragant, E., Serrano, R.: The role of individual differences in a study abroad experience: the case of Erasmus students. Int. J. Multiling. 9(3), 318–342 (2012)

69. Perifanou, M.: PLEs & MOOCs in language learning context: a challenging connection. In: Proceedings of the PLE Conference 2014, Tallinn, Estonia, (2014). http://pleconf.org/2014/files/2014/06/paper-34.pdf

70. Perifanou, M.: Personalized MOOCs for language learning: a challenging proposal. Elearning Papers 45, 1–13 (2015)

71. White, C.: Language Learning in Distance Education. Cambridge University Press, Cambridge (2003)

72. McLoughlin, C., Lee, M.J.: Personalised and self-regulated learning in the Web 2.0 era: International exemplars of innovative pedagogy using social software. Australas. J. Educ. Technol. 26(1), 28–43 (2010)

73. Naidu, S.: Enabling time, pace, and place independence. In: Spector, J.M., Merill, M.D., Merrienboer, J., Driscoll, M.P. (eds.) Handbook of Research on Educational Communications and Technology, pp. 259–268. Lawrence Erlbaum Associates, New York (2008)

74. Anderson, T., Annand, D., Wark, N.: The search for learning community in learner paced distance education: or, 'Having your cake and eating it, too!' Australas. J. Educ. Technol. 21(2), 222–241 (2005)

75. Dembo, M.H., Junge, L.G., Lynch, R.: Becoming a self-regulated learner: implications for web-based education. In: O'Neil, H.F., Perez, R.S. (eds.) Web-Based Learning: Theory, Research, and Practice, pp. 185–202 (2006)

76. Pintrich, P.R.: The role of goal orientation in self-regulated learning. In: Boekaerts, M., Pintrich, P.R., Zeidner, M. (eds.) Handbook of Self-regulation, pp. 451–502. Academic Press (2000). https://doi.org/10.1016/B978-012109890-2/50043-3

77. Zimmerman, B.J.: Self-regulatory cycles of learning. In: Straka, G.A. (ed.) Conceptions of Self-Directed Learning, pp. 221–234. Waxmann, Münster (2000)

78. Hadwin, A.F., Oshige, M., Gres, C.L.Z., Winne, P.H.: Innovative ways for using gStudy to orchestrate and research social aspects of self-regulated learning. Comput. Hum. Behav. 26(5), 794–805 (2010)

79. Kuo, Y.C., Walker, A.E., Schroder, K.E.E., Belland, B.R.: Interaction, internet self-efficacy, and self-regulated learning as predictors of student satisfaction in online education courses. Internet High. Educ. 20, 35 (2014)

80. Alonso, C.: Learning diaries to foster learner autonomy in mixed-ability groups. Tejuelo 11, 47–63 (2011)

81. Brammerts, H.: Autonomous language learning in tandem: the development of a concept. In: Lewis, Walker (eds.), pp. 27–36 (2003)
82. Benson, P., Voller, P. (eds.): Autonomy and Independence in Language … Classroom. Cambridge University Press, Cambridge (1996)
83. Little, D.: Learner Autonomy 1: Definitions, Issues and Problems. Authentik, Dublin (1991)
84. Nunan, D.: Research Methods in Language Teaching. Cambridge University Press, Cambridge (1992)
85. Byram, M.: Teaching and Assessing Intercultural Communicative Competence. Multilingual Matters Ltd., Philadelphia (1997)
86. Woodin, J.: Cultural categorisation: what can we learn from practice? An example from tandem learning. Lang. Intercul. Commun. **10**, 225–242 (2010). https://doi.org/10.1080/14708470903348556
87. Morley, J., Truscott, S.: Incorporating peer assessment into tandem learning. Lang. Learn. J. **33**(1), 53–58 (2006). https://doi.org/10.1080/09571730685200111
88. Appel, C., Mullen, T.: Pedagogical considerations for a web-based tandem language learning environment. Comput. Educ. **34**, 291–308 (2000)
89. Appel, C., Mullen, T.: A new tool for teachers and researchers involved in email tandem language learning. ReCALL **14**(2), 195–208 (2002). https://doi.org/10.1017/S0958344400200022
90. Nazarenko, A.: Learning languages via telecollaboration: "Variation on the Theme." In: 12th International Conference Innovation in Language Learning, pp. 160–164. Filodiritto Editore (2019)
91. Pomino, J., Gil-Salom, D.: Integrating E-tandem in higher education. Procedia. Soc. Behav. Sci. **228**, 668–673 (2016). https://doi.org/10.1016/j.sbspro.2016.07.102
92. Telles, J.A., Zakir, M.deA., Funo, L.B.A.: Teletandem e episódios relacionados a cultura. DELTA Documentacao de Estudos Em Linguistica Teorica e Aplicada **31**(2), 359–389 (2015). https://doi.org/10.1590/0102-445084549183239327
93. Brown, H.: Principles of Language Learning and Teaching, 4th edn. Longman Pearson Education Limited, London (2000)
94. Crandall, J.: Content-Based Instruction (CBI). Concise Encyclopedia of Educational Linguistics, pp. 208–604. Cambridge University Press, Oxford (1999)
95. Zhang, Y.: Cooperative language learning and foreign language learning and teaching. J. Lang. Teach. Res. **191**, 81–83 (2010). https://doi.org/10.4304/jltr.1.1.81
96. Johnson, D., Johnson, R.: What we know about cooperative learning at the college level. Coop. Learn. **13**(3) (1993). http://www2.emc.maricopa.edu/innovation/CCL/whatweknow.ht
97. Lave, J., Wenger, E.: Situated Learning: Legitimate Peripheral Participation. Cambridge University Press, Cambridge & New York (1991)
98. Winn, W.: Instructional design and situated learning: paradox or partnership? Educ. Technol. **33**(3), 16–21 (1993)
99. Anderson, T., Dron, J.: Learning technology through three generations of technology enhanced distance education pedagogy. Cognitivist/behaviourist pedagogy. Eur. J. Open Distance E-Learn. **2**, 1–14 (2012)
100. Corbett, F., Spinello, E.: Connectivism and Leadership: Harnessing a Learning Theory for the Digital Age to Redefine Leadership in the Twenty-First Century. Elsevier Ltd., Heliyon (2020). https://doi.org/10.1016/j.heliyon.2020.e03250
101. Nattoch Dag, K.: A scholar-practitioner perspective on a leadership development program in health care: integrating connectivism theory. Adv. Develop. Hum. Resour. **19**(3), 295–313 (2017)

Research on the Design of E-education Application Interface Based on Kansei Engineering

Zhimeng Qi[(⊠)]

East China University of Science and Technology, Shanghai 200000, China

Abstract. With the rapid development of the Internet and the improvement of people's demand level in recent years, E-education has become an industry with great development potential, and E-education applications have become the first choice for young people to improve themselves. More and more Internet companies have been aiming at this potential market, developing various forms of E-education applications to seize the market. However, the fierce market competition leads to the appearance of homogeneous product design and the lack of user preference in interface design. For E-education applications, the design of interactive interface and user experience is a very important part, and a good user experience is the key to users' continuous use of the application. This paper uses the research method of Kansei engineering to study the interface design of the existing E-education apps, finds out the demand preference of young people for the interface design of E-education applications, and puts forward the theoretical guidance and the design trend that can be used in the future electronic education products.

Keywords: E-education · APP interface design · Kansei engineering · User experience

1 Introduction

In recent years, the rapid development of the world's economy and the rapid take-off of the Internet are external factors; people's growing desire for learning and rising consumption ability are internal factors. Under the influence of these two factors, the consumption structure of consumers has undergone tremendous changes, and is now transforming from survival type to self-realization type. Research shows that more and more consumers are willing to pay time and money to improve their self-worth. As a good way to promote self-improvement and development, knowledge acquisition has been greatly promoted in the economic environment, which also gives birth to the development and evolution of E-education products. From the beginning of the rise of E-education applications in 2016 to the full bloom of E-education industry in recent years, E-education products have changed from single type to diversified type. In the new pattern of knowledge consumption, the new requirements of users also put forward new requirements for the development of E-education industry.

P. Zaphiris and A. Ioannou (Eds.): HCII 2021, LNCS 12784, pp. 161–171, 2021.
https://doi.org/10.1007/978-3-030-77889-7_11

2   Research Background

2.1   The Concept of E-education

E-education, as the name suggests, is the product of the combination of knowledge and the Internet. Different from the traditional offline paid courses, today's E-education relies on the mature development of the Internet and has a strong Internet attribute. In a broad sense, e-education is to turn knowledge into products or services, and realize its commercial value by selling these knowledge products or services; in a narrow sense, it is to use the information gap between information producers and consumers, package information into products or services, and sell them through the Internet [1]. The E-education app and online education website which have developed rapidly in recent years. Many product forms form a new business form of knowledge productization. This paper will mainly focus on the narrow sense of E-education, that is, the research of E-education applications, and put forward the guiding methods.

2.2   Development Trend of E-education Industry

E-education industry is a very promising industry. As an extension of school and classroom, E-education applications have the characteristics of flexible time and unlimited geographical location, which is very in line with the fast-paced and busy lifestyle of today's young people. The rise of E-education is a good opportunity to improve themselves. Consumers can often get good knowledge sharing through the network and mobile applications. At the same time, due to the sudden epidemic, many people's pace of life has been broken. A large number of staff and students are facing unemployment, dropout and other situations. The improvement of self-ability has become a group demand, and E-education just meets the opportunity of this era. It gives consumers a good opportunity to improve themselves during the epidemic period, and online access to knowledge has become a hot topic among young people.

2016 is called "the first year of E-education" by the media [1]. E-education products break the boundary between the dissemination and acquisition of knowledge. E-education apps, led by Iget, Himalaya, etc., rapidly layout the industry market, leading the rapid rise of E-education market. At the same time, with the development of the market, E-education applications will be launched after 2016, and the product competition is fierce. In 2017, the scale of China's E-education industry was about 4.91 billion yuan, nearly tripled year on year. In the next three years, the scale of E-education industry will maintain high growth and continue to expand. It is estimated that by 2020, the scale of E-education industry will reach 23.5 billion yuan.

With the rapid development of E-education applications in recent years, the major companies have realized that not only the basic form, but also the deep connotation are needed to make applications. In other words, E-education applications should not only capture users' minds in terms of content differentiation and professionalism, but also make continuous efforts in user experience to increase users' stickiness. With richer functions and more optimized experience, facing the user groups with more complex needs, we will transform from product-oriented to service-oriented.

2.3 The Influence of Interface Design of E-education Application on User Experience

As more and more E-education applications are designed with in-depth consideration of user needs, deep cultivation of user experience. Therefore, while providing consumers with knowledge, designers are also committed to providing them with a perfect knowledge service. Such as social experience to increase communication, emotional incentive to promote learning enthusiasm, perfect feedback mechanism to enhance the user's persistence and loyalty [2]. The most direct way to present these service-oriented contacts is in the user interface of the product. Good and appropriate visual language can better enhance the user's perception and attract users to use them, so as to provide cognitive space and development opportunities for the whole service process.

At the same time, after the continuous polishing and polishing of the market, many E-education apps are very rich in content, mainly in the form of audio, video, graphics and so on. Complex forms often need appropriate interface design to satisfy the sense of use, which also provides new ideas and challenges for the interface design of E-education app. Therefore, as the "window" of products and services, the interface design of app is a very important part in the process of user experience. If the interface design is more in line with user preferences and habits, it will greatly improve the user's preference and user stickiness. Based on the importance of interface design for E-education products, this paper studies user preferences for E-education products to guide the design, so that E-education products can better serve users.

3 Research Method

3.1 Kansei Engineering and the Application of E-education

Kansei engineering [3] is proposed by Mitsuke Nagmachi of Hiroshima University in Japan. It combines the engineering technology of design, computer, psychology, statistics and other disciplines. It can refine users' perceptual needs into product design direction, namely perceptual clustering. Kansei engineering is a subject based on experiments. It can transform people's subjective feelings and emotional intentions into design language and design elements, and quantify users' emotional expression as the key data to guide the design.

Based on the investigation of many research methods in Kansei Engineering, this study decided to use semantic difference analysis method to study E-education applications. Semantic Differential is a method of psychological measurement, also known as feeling recording method, mentioned by Charles Egerton Osgood (1916–1991) in his paper the measurement of meaning in 1957 [4]. It analyzes the semantics of the product through the perceptual vocabulary description of the sample by the interviewees, and finally obtains the guidance for the design practice from the data collation and analysis. Therefore, using the method of Kansei engineering to study the interface design of E-education products can effectively rationalize and digitize the perceptual cognition of the target users, and provide guidance for the future design trend with quantitative indicators.

3.2 Sample Selection

According to the research of iResearch in the 《2018 China online E-education Market Research Report》 [5], the main consumers of E-education products are young people under the age of 30. They have a certain consumption ability, and can effectively screen and evaluate E-education applications. After investigating the popular E-education applications among young people, the author selects a series of E-education apps to determine the sample range. Then, through the market research of E-education apps, four top products in E-education industry are selected based on the degree of market exposure, the intensity of E-education attributes and the professionalism of knowledge content, and then analyzed. The four samples are: Himalaya, a paid knowledge platform based on audio, Overdrive, which is famous for "e-library", Iget, a paid audio knowledge platform based on "knowledge network celebrities", and Blinkist, a reading app combining audio listening with e-reading, as shown in Fig. 1.

3.3 Perceptual Vocabulary Extraction

In order to make this study objective, rigorous and professional, the author collected a sample of perceptual intention vocabulary from the main user groups of E-education apps. The respondents meet the following conditions: (1) they are between 25 and 30 years old; (2) they have certain understanding and experience in using E-education applications; (3) they have certain aesthetic and experiential requirements for the interface design of E-education apps, mainly users engaged in art design-related professions. Each respondent will describe the perceptual vocabulary in four aspects: overall feeling, color matching, interface layout and using experience, combined with the above four samples, and each person will provide no less than eight words. At the same time, experts in the fields of perceptual engineering and E-education were invited to classify the collected perceptual vocabulary and eliminate similar words and remote words. Finally, the above four categories were matched and filtered, and each category contained two pairs of perceptual words.

Fig. 1. Collection of knowledge payment samples.

The study finally identified two groups of perceptual intention words under each category, namely: "modern - traditional, professional - amateur" for respondents to describe their first impression of the sample, i.e., the overall feeling part; "fashionable - conservative, calm - flamboyant" is used to describe the perceptual perception of the sample's color, i.e. the color matching part; "harmonious - cluttered, simple - redundant" can reflect the respondents' subjective feelings about the interface layout, i.e. the interface layout part; "feature rich - single function, easy to use - difficult to use" can help respondents describe how the interface design presents functionality and how it reflects the user experience, i.e. the user experience section, as shown in Table 1.

Table 1. Perceptual vocabulary selection in knowledge payment applications

Category	Perceptual vocabulary
Overall feeling	1. Modern - Traditional
	2. Professional - Amateur
Color matching	3. Fashionable - Conservative
	4. Calm - Flamboyant
Interface layout	5. Harmonious - Cluttered
	6. Simple - Redundant
Using experience	7. Feature rich - Single function
	8. Easy to use - Difficult to use

3.4   Questionnaire Design and Distribution

This study used the semantic differential method combined with a Seven Grades Likert Scale to create a questionnaire, which was designed in two parts. The first part was the respondents' basic information and use of E-education products, which was used to screen and evaluate the validity of the questionnaire at a later stage. The second part is the respondents' scores for the perceptual words of each sample, which consists of 4 samples with 8 sets of perceptual words to form a 7-level scale. The scale values are $-3, -2, -1, 0, 1, 2$, and 3. The middle value is 0, and the smaller the value, the closer the respondent's perception is to the left-side perceptual words, and vice versa. In order to reduce the probability of invalidity, this questionnaire was distributed in a small area, and mainly to art and design related professionals. The scale part of the questionnaire is shown in Table 2.

Table 2. Questionnaire design

Sample Image	Perceptual Vocabulary Values
Himalaya	Modern -3 -2 -1 0 1 2 3 Traditional
	Professional -3 -2 -1 0 1 2 3 Amateur
	Fashionable -3 -2 -1 0 1 2 3 Conservative
	Calm -3 -2 -1 0 1 2 3 Flamboyant
	Harmonious -3 -2 -1 0 1 2 3 Cluttered
	Simple -3 -2 -1 0 1 2 3 Redundant
	Feature rich -3 -2 -1 0 1 2 3 Single function
	Easy to use -3 -2 -1 0 1 2 3 Difficult to use

4 Results and Discussion

At the end of the survey, 40 questionnaires were collected. The age range and the degree of use of E-education applications were used as indicators to screen invalid questionnaires, and 34 valid questionnaires were finally determined for the statistics and discussion of the results. The data of each perceptual vocabulary group were combined with the Likert scale for the mean statistics, as shown in Table 3.

Based on the four indicators, the samples are compared in horizontal and vertical dimensions. The horizontal comparison is based on the perceptual vocabulary score of each sample to find out the characteristics of each sample; the vertical analysis is based on the score of each perceptual vocabulary to find out the sample with the highest score and analyze its characteristics.

Table 3. Statistics of the average number of perceptual words in the questionnaire

Perceptual vocabulary group	Sample			
	1. Himalaya	2. Overdrive	3. Iget	4. Blinkist
Overall feeling				
Modern - Traditional	−0.5	−1	−0.24	−1.18
Professional - Amateur	−0.97	−0.94	−0.76	−1.38
Color matching				
Fashionable - Conservative	0.03	−0.76	0.12	−1.15
Calm - Flamboyant	−1.32	−0.62	−0.53	−0.71
Interface layout				
Harmonious - Cluttered	−0.76	−1.03	−0.71	−1.15
Simple - Redundant	−0.35	−1.29	−0.5	−1.12
Using experience				
Feature rich - Single function	−1.18	−0.71	−0.79	−0.97
Easy to use - Difficult to use	−0.85	−1.18	−0.56	−0.91

4.1 Comparison of Vertical Indicators

Overall Feeling. In the category of "overall feeling", Blinkist has the lowest total score, which means that its interface is more modern and professional; Iget has the highest total score, which makes people feel more traditional and amateur in the four samples.

Color Matching. The lowest score of "color matching" is still Blinkist, which fits the perceptual word "fashion". But Himalaya is the closest to "calm" in the color matching plate, but because of its low degree of fashion, the overall color feeling is not as good as Blinkist.

Interface Layout. In the category of "interface layout", Overdrive is the closest to "concise", and Blinkist is the most harmonious. However, the total score of overdrive was the lowest, and the page layout gave respondents the best feeling.

Using Experience. Himalaya has the lowest overall score in the "using experience" section, that is, the best performance. Although Himalaya does not bring outstanding feelings to the respondents in other sections, it is closest to "functional composite", indicating that its interface design can better highlight functions. But Overdrive is closest to the emotional word "easy to use."

4.2   Comparison of Horizontal Indicators

Himalaya. Himalaya is most close to "calm" and "feature rich" in various perceptual indicators. In terms of color matching, Himalaya uses white background with orange as the main tone, with moderate lightness, non-jumbled elements, and fine control of proportion and white space, so it gives users a sense of stability. At the same time, due to its rich contacts on each page, it shows more kinetic energy entrance through icon and function module, and brings users more complex functional experience. It is a stable and functional electronic education product.

Overdrive. Overdrive is characterized by a "simple" interface layout and an "easy-to-use" user experience. To be specific, Overdrive makes the layout loose and simple by leaving more white space and reducing the visual elements and colors of the interface. The reading page banner is narrow and long, at the same time, it is equipped with fewer icon and function modules, which brings users the most concise interface layout experience and convenient use experience.

Iget. Iget is characterized by its "professional" overall experience and close to the "feature rich" use experience, but the color matching is relatively conservative. Iget home page framework is more detailed, from the title bar, banner to live broadcast and headlines of the plate is rich but not pondering, with a certain sense of professionalism. But because its icon and other page elements are mostly gray background, orange is only the page embellishment, it seems that the color collocation is more conservative and monotonous.

Blinkist. Blinkist brings the most "professional and modern" overall feeling. With its simple colors and unified content modules, the overall feel of the interface is simple and clear, with modern design features that make it easy for users to understand the product and get started quickly. The simple colors and fonts can also better show the professionalism of the application. At the same time, Blinkist is no less colorful, with a dark blue background and white characters, accented by a blue-green progress bar and icon of the same color, making the color scheme very simple and stylish.

5   Guidance for Design

After detailed analysis of the questionnaire and the sample, I have a deeper understanding of the perceptual preferences of the young user group, mainly in the following four areas.

5.1   Overall Feeling

The target users of E-education prefer a sense of modernity and professionalism on the whole, which also reflects that people's requirements for education application are still serious. The designer is required to have a comprehensive control over the overall elements and layout in the design, and show the overall feeling of the interface in the principle of simplicity and consistency. All elements should be orderly and unified in the design. For E-education applications, it is necessary to have a sense of modernity and professionalism, which is also conducive to users' long-term use of the application, enhancing users' trust, and facilitating users' later cognition and use of the product.

5.2   Color Matching

It can be seen from the questionnaire that the color matching of E-education application is fashionable and calm. With the development of Internet, the application of E-education is the combination of knowledge and Internet, which is no longer serious knowledge sharing. The combination of fashion and calmness represents the appropriate liveliness, while retaining the original conscientiousness and preciseness of E-education applications. Only by combining the two can we design E-education applications that are popular with target users and young people. Designers can fit the sensory experience of target users through color control, and can use no more than three colors to match the interface. In normal mode, white or simple solid color can be used as the background, and the main visual color is presented in the main elements, or highlighted in the details of the interface. Finally, gold or gray can be used as embellishment to enhance the overall interface texture and sense of hierarchy.

5.3   Interface Layout

Young people's preference for app interface layout is harmonious and concise. Because the E-education applications are often accompanied by more functions and components, such as the selection of education projects, the view of progress, the communication with other users and so on. Therefore, the harmonious and simple interface layout can reduce the user's use burden and memory burden, make every function clearly visible, and also easy to guide the next step of the use experience. This requires designers to arrange the functional modules of the interface in order to make it more complex with the user's sensory experience and actual needs. The most commonly used parts and the functions to guide users to use are clearly and concisely displayed in the interface, so that users do not need to spend extra time and energy to identify information. Secondly, we can refer to the simple collocation of colors to make the interface orderly and neat. The presentation of interface layout has a great relationship with the brightness, intensity and contrast of colors. Only simple functional module design and reasonable color proportion can present an easy-to-use interface layout.

5.4   Using Experience

Rich functions and easy-to-use experience are the current user groups' preferences for E-education application experience. Due to the electronic education app currently has text, audio and video expansion, the function is relatively rich, so in the design, we should consider how to make the rich function easy and practical, so as to be more in line with the user's habits. This is not a small challenge for designers. Designers need to cultivate user experience design, combine the above elements, and layout the overall use process from the user's habits. Such as reading and audio switch freely, watching video at the same time can record text and other functions are updated, but to really put into the user's scene will appear messy and flustered. Then we need to start from the users' habits, find users' subconscious use actions, facilitate users' contact and use of the app, strengthen the professionalism of the use experience, and reduce the possibility of users' wrong choice.

6 Summary

As an innovation of future education mode, e-education application is now developing towards a more mature and experience oriented direction, which has great development prospects and value. Based on the Kansei Engineering Research of E-education application interface design, this paper finally determines the future design direction from the overall feeling, color matching, interface layout and user experience. It aims to provide guidance for the future design of E-education app, make it more adapt to the changing needs of users, and create a more user-friendly experience in the future development.

References

1. Liu, S.: Research report on e-education field .36 Krypton (2017)
2. Liu, S.-S., Zhang, T.: Research on interaction design of e-education class application. Popular Lit. Arts, 119–120 (2019)
3. Wang, T., Xu, Z.: Optimized design of automobile driving space interior based on perceptual engineering. Pack. Eng., 1–7 (2020)
4. Jiao, M.Y., Gao, F., Hao, P.Y., Dong, L.: Study on the evaluation of urban strip park plant landscape based on SD method. J. Northwest Forestry College **28**(05), 185–190 (2013)
5. China online e-education market research report 2018: Ariadne Consulting Series Research Report (Issue 3, 2018): Shanghai Ariadne Market Consulting Co., 297–352 (2018)

Create Children's Programming Teaching Aids with Chinese Characteristics: Provide a Method Framework to Assist Designers in Designing

Zhijuan Zhu, Xinjun Miao[✉], Yan Qin, and Wenzhen Pan

School of Mechanical Science and Engineering, Huazhong University of Science and Technology, Wuhan, People's Republic of China

Abstract. China is gradually deepening its education reform. Children's programming education in STEAM education has caused widespread concern, however, there is no corresponding method for teaching aids design. In this paper, we conducted a comprehensive review of literatures on the development and application of STEAM education in China and globally. After analyzing current situation of children's programming education in China, primary design principles of children's programming teaching aids are summarized. Service design theory was utilized during the research. Five elements of the children's programming curriculum system were summarized and design method of children's programming teaching aids were proposed with analyzing the common points of service design and children's programming courses. This research integrated service design concepts into children's programming education, summarized design methods of Chinese children's programming aids through the relationship of five elements including people, media, scenes, actions, and goals. In addition, this research proposed a new design framework named "Children – Technology – Traditional culture – Children". The results have positive value for improving the current homogenization of the Chinese programming market, and can promote the emergence of more children's programming teaching aids with Chinese characteristics.

Keywords: Teaching aids design · Chinese characteristics · Service design · Children programming · STEAM

1 Introduction

With the deepening of China's education reform, STEAM education has been promoted wave after wave due to its compliance with the policy of China's deepening education reform. Children's programming education in STEAM education is gradually known and respected. However, the practice of the STEAM concept in major regions of China was still stuck in the basic curriculum of schools such as labor technology and general technology, less research is made on the content of curriculum integration, teaching forms, teaching tools, and so on. As a result, designers become difficult when designing teaching aids. The purpose of this article is to summarize the

P. Zaphiris and A. Ioannou (Eds.): HCII 2021, LNCS 12784, pp. 172–190, 2021.
https://doi.org/10.1007/978-3-030-77889-7_12

design method of Chinese children's programming teaching aids and develop a prototype framework to help designers design Chinese children's programming teaching aids smoothly.

Designers generally respect their own design methods in the process of designing products, and these methods have evolved from the general methods of teaching guidance when they were junior designers. For junior designers, it is necessary to have a methodological framework for product design. More specifically, junior designers are often confused and overwhelmed when they are new to design in a new field. A basic design method of the general public is to guide them in design. However, for the design of teaching aids, it is often confused with toys or products, so that the demand for new classroom forms for STEAM education has not been adapted. Therefore, designers need to have a deeper understanding of the design methods for children's teaching aids.

For the purposes of this paper, the term "teaching aids" means "ordinary objects used in a class for teaching purposes" (New Century English-Chinese Dictionary). The term "product" means "a thing that is grown or produced, usually for sale" (Oxford Advanced English-Chinese Dictionary 2018). The term "toy" means "an object for children to play with" (Oxford Advanced English-Chinese Dictionary 2018). Therefore, there is a fundamental difference between teaching aids and the other about "teaching". At the same time, Classroom interactive teaching and subject integration are more emphasized in STEAM education. This shows that designers need to understand the design methods applicable to teaching aids in order to make use of "teaching" and "learning" fusion and produce the desired user experience design.

literature searches in research databases (Design and Applied Arts Index, Web of Science and EBSCO) did not lead to the clear design method to enable designers to carry out the design smoothly, nor to much discussion was caused. Different categories of products have different characteristics. At least for inexperienced designers, this may mean that the factors that need to be considered when designing this type of product are ignored. And in some cases, common product design methods are used, resulting in unsatisfactory results. From an educator perspective, when teaching the subject to design students, separate explanations and training on teaching aid categories are available. To address these issues, this paper defines a framework that defines the design method of Chinese children's programming teaching aids.

The main focus of this paper is on programming education for Chinese children. This delimitation has been imposed in order to put focus on the discussions of the paper. In terms of culture, regional characteristics may be involved. However, its contribution may also be relevant for other types and geographical designs.

The remainder of the paper is structured as follows. First, relevant literature on STEAM education and children's programming education is reviewed. On this basis, the paper then proposes a framework on design method of Chinese children's programming teaching aids. Hereafter, the application of the framework is discussed. The paper ends with final conclusions being drawn.

2 Literature Review

2.1 STEM and STEAM Education in Children

As the knowledge and capabilities required for solving technological problems have become increasingly integrated and complex, the capability to apply interdisciplinary knowledge to solve complex problems is highly needed [1, 2]. In traditional classrooms, the preparation of students is unable to solve real-world problems because of the division of disciplines [3]. In order to address this concern, Integrated Science, Technology, Engineering, and Mathematics (STEM) education has received widespread attention as a plausible solution for developing a better instructional approach to aid students in developing capabilities for solving complex real-world problems [4].

With the increasing popularity of technology, people are beginning to realize that in STEM education, which is full of engineering thinking, children's learning and creativity may be stifled. Although design has been a feature of technology education since the 1990s, its contributions to mathematics and science education have received less attention particularly in the elementary grades [5, 6]. Regarding the relationship between art and science, many scholars believe that science cannot be completed without art, and have long proposed suggestions for integrating art into science [7]. Therefore, the integration of STEM disciplines through design is recognized as an increasingly important area of research [8, 9]. Integration with other disciplines, such as art, can help teachers more easily consider the use of technology to encourage young children's creativity [10]. In order to do this, a newer acronym called "STEAM" (Science, Technology, Engineering, Arts, Mathematics) has expanded on STEM and is growing in popularity [11].

STEAM education originated in the United States. Since the 1990s, it has gradually become popular in South Korea, Britain and other countries and regions. In 2016, President Obama unveiled a plan to give students all across the U.S. a chance to learn computer science [12]. Outside the United States, STEAM education continues to evolve with its own characteristics in various countries. For example, in Finland, all elementary students have to learn programming since 2016 [13]. The UK has also established clear policies and frameworks for introducing technology and computer programming to young children [14, 15]. In 2015, the Singapore government launched the "PlayMaker Programme" initiative to introduce technology to young children [16].

In China, with the gradual deepening of education reform, STEAM education has been promoted wave after wave due to its own compliance with the policy of deepening reform of Chinese education. Children's programming education in STEAM education is gradually known. In 2017, the State Council of China issued a notice on the development of a new generation of artificial intelligence development plans (Guo Fa [2017] No. 35). The "new generation of artificial intelligence development plans", which clearly pointed out that artificial intelligence will become the new focus of international competition, and it needs to be carried out step by step. The intelligent education project, that is, the artificial intelligence-related courses should be widely opened in primary and secondary schools, to promote programming education in place, and to train batches of compound talents, thus forming a highland of artificial intelligence talents in China [17]. In the era of continuous technological development, new terms such as "Internet+", "crowd space", and "shared regulation" are constantly appearing. Chinese scholars have begun to pay attention to how to integrate STEAM education with these new terms, and children in this new era. New ways to cultivate innovation ability [18]. In the research database (China Knowledge Network), a comprehensive study of the current literature of Chinese scholars shows that the current STEAM education-related research in China is focused on practical research, of which the research on the construction of the STEAM curriculum system mainly includes teaching models, methods, strategies, Course design and more [19].

2.2   Children's Programming Teaching Aid Design

Traditionally, STEAM topics are taught in an ex-cathedra format. In this mode, the teacher talks and the students just listen. However, the researchers found that under this mode, students' learning enthusiasm was not high, and the teaching effect was not satisfactory. At this time, a project-based learning model (PBL) was proposed to teach through projects or specific topics. Under this model, teaching aids became an indispensable element.

In PBL mode, teachers frequently choose robotics as a topic for STEAM and PBL [20]. One of the reasons for the increasing use of robots in education is that robots stimulate the imagination of children and adults because they look like humans, or they replace humans when doing different tasks [21]. In addition to more and more research focusing on the potential of educational robots in the teaching process, we also need to pay attention to the difficulties and limitations of robot technology in the implementation of education. Robots are usually complex machines, consisting of many parts and control modules, including knowledge of mathematics, engineering, science and other aspects. Therefore, when students are too young or lack relevant knowledge, such programs are not effective for them. In the choice of robots, one of the most common methods is to use commercial robot kits. LEGO Mindstorms is a common system of LEGO Technic blocks combined with sensors, motors and programmable logic blocks, and is a popular example of such kits [20, 22]. Although such a commercial robot can be put into use quickly and has a public course description, its fixed and closed attributes also limit the more possibility of student operation.

In China, it is only relevant research on children's enlightenment aids, such as the application of Montessori's aids theory to children's enlightenment aids, or the impact of different aids on children's visual function [23, 24]. In particular, research on teaching aids in China is mainly concentrated on the experimental teaching aids in science subjects in junior and high schools. For children's teaching aids, it is often confused with toys, and there is still a lack of research on emerging teaching aids for children. Nowadays, most teaching institutions in China only introduce foreign programming tools such as Scratch to carry out related programming teaching. They have not studied the innovation, logic and interest of the programming curriculum themselves, and the related programming teaching aids are even more varied. Most institutions choose to embezzle directly from existing foreign products, which is not entirely suitable for the educational ideas of Chinese children. In general, there are the following problems exist in the design of Chinese children's programming aids:

1. Single form

   The current teaching aids market lacks formal innovation in the products of children's programming courses. As long as programming is mentioned, people's first idea is often robots. In teaching aids, only different types of robots are used, which lacks the possibility of application to different carriers and the needs of children of different ages.

2. Serious homogenization

   At present, China's entire children's programming education environment has a low threshold, serious homogeneity, and uniform curriculum. Teaching aids are just stiff embezzlement. Although some institutions have begun to do research on teaching aid innovation, they have not really considered the needs of children and different courses and localization, which is contrary to the original intention of programming education in "innovation".

3. Lack of artistry

   At present, most educational institutions spend less thought on the design of teaching aids, but only meet the needs of the curriculum functionally. Especially neglecting the cultivation of the art part of children. The product lacks artistic research on colors, forms, and craftsmanship.

In general, in the field of studying STEAM education, the research on the development and design of related teaching aids is still in a relatively single environment. Research scholars focus on how to develop more suitable educational robots to meet the needs of STEAM education, without realizing the possibility that besides robots, there are other carriers that can be used as teaching aids. This provides more space for thinking about the design of the teaching aid method architecture later in this article.

The following section summarizes the basic design principles for the design of Chinese children's programming teaching aids through comprehensive field observations and related literature analysis.

3   Design Principles of Chinese Children's Programming Teaching Aids

3.1   Cultural Connotation with Chinese Characteristics

For China, children's programming education was originally introduced from abroad. At present, the most important thing is how to create a programming classroom and programming aids suitable for Chinese children, rather than just copying. As a teaching aid, it first needs to have educational attributes. In programming aids, scientific and technological education is essential, and cultural education is also indispensable for Chinese children. If you want to reflect Chinese characteristics, starting with Chinese traditional culture is a good starting point for children's education. The traditional Chinese symbols in the form and connotation will bring great inspiration to the designer, and also make the society more and more agree that this is the source of modern Chinese design [25]. For programming teaching aids, it is necessary to inherit a certain degree of cultural connotation in traditional culture, extract cultural themes suitable for children, integrate with innovative thinking, times, forward-looking and technology, and keep up with the trend of the times the traditional culture is better inherited.

3.2 Sustaining Children's Emotional Needs with Sustainability

According to Maslow's theory of human needs hierarchy, children's demand for products in different periods is analyzed. It can be seen from Fig. 1 that the requirements of the initial level of physiology and safety correspond to the basic safety, practicality, and ease of use of the product. When it rises to middle-level respect and social needs, it corresponds to the interactivity, entertainment, creativity, and intellectuality of the product. When it reaches the highest level of self-actualization, it corresponds to the learnability and explorability of the product [26].

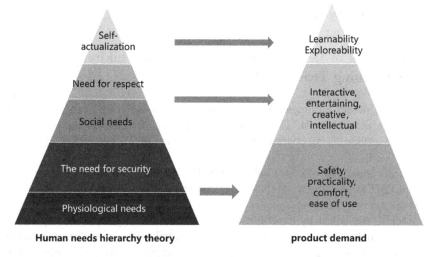

Fig. 1. Maslow's theory of hierarchy of human needs and product demand for children's programming teaching aids

The age range for children is defined as 6–12 years [27]. At the age of 6–12, children are affected by their learning and living environment, their emotions and personalities are developed, and their sense of responsibility and collective honor appear. They are more likely to rate themselves based on adult and peer reviews. The demand for products has begun to rise to intermediate society and the need for respect, and even the highest self-realization stage. Therefore, in the design of children's programming teaching aids, on the basis of meeting the basic safety and physiological needs of products, more attention needs to be paid to products the high-level needs of the company are more important in terms of interactivity, creativity, and learnability. Because of the special nature of programming, the product itself has certain intellectuality and creativity, but at the same time, it is easy to ignore the interaction between children in the learning process with peers, teachers, parents and the sustainability of the product That is, the possibility of continuous exploration and learning.

3.3 Innovative Thinking, Multiple Ways of Fun

The distinction between toys and teaching aids lies in "teaching", but in terms of function, teaching aids should also have a certain interest. And for children at this age, they already have some more complicated psychological and behavioral reactions, and their attention is improved, but they are single. It is difficult for them to pay attention to multiple things at the same time or to pay attention to one thing for a long time. Children's perception ability is mainly divided into five aspects: sight, hearing, touch, proprioception, and vestibular sense. Among them, the most basic vision, hearing, and touch can be used as innovative ideas to attract children's attention, thereby increasing the interest of teaching aids. At the same time, in the design process of teaching aids, it is necessary to break away from the traditional robot-led thinking limitations and develop the possibility of different carriers.

4   Framework of Design Method for Chinese Children's Programming Teaching Aid

This section provides a framework for designers on how to design Chinese children's programming teaching aids. The framework is proposed based on the relationship between the service design concept and the design of children's programming teaching aids.

The earliest method of education about STEM education is to integrate constructivism into STEM teaching methods. Constructivism is a theory about how people learn [28]. It describes learning as a process in which people build their understanding and knowledge of the world by experiencing things and reflecting on those experiences [21]. Based on this, Papert [29] proposed a constructivist learning theory based on which students learn meaningfully when they construct actual physical objects that are meaningful to them and can be shared with others (such as friends or parents). In simple terms, students can learn by doing things instead of listening. This form can stimulate students' enthusiasm and deeper understanding of the topic at hand [30].

In the development of constructivist learning theory, an integrated STEM education method was proposed. Integrated STEM education is a teaching method where students can participate in engineering design and/or research. And they can experience meaningful learning through the integration and application of mathematics, technology and science [31]. The theory of integrated STEM is an in-depth exploration of constructivist learning theory from a certain point of view, and it is also the teaching method advocated by ordinary classrooms at present.

By understanding the constructivist learning theory and integrated STEM education, you will find that they have one thing in common, emphasizing the degree of student participation in the learning process, and more emphasis on interaction in learning. And this kind of interaction needs teaching aids as a medium to achieve the purpose of improving learning effects. Such a statement has something in common with the American scholar Sampson's definition of service as an activity aimed at achieving the interests of customers as the work purpose of the provider [32]. Therefore, this article links the design of STEAM teaching aids with the concept of service design. In China, this concept was first introduced by Xin Xiang yang, who believed that service is often a service provider's professional expertise, material or time resources to achieve the task or experience goal of the serviced person. Therefore, service design can be summarized as an activity for the benefit of others.

Most of the STEAM education is presented in the form of courses. For the courses, it can be defined as the activity of the teacher to provide resources such as professional expertise and time that he has mastered to achieve the goal of obtaining knowledge for students. This definition is consistent with the philosophy of service design. In STEAM education, the children's programming curriculum is different from the traditional curriculum. The children's programming curriculum pays more attention to the students' own practical experience and experience goals. There are similarities between the "student-oriented" and "people-oriented" of service design for children's programming courses. The introduction of the service design concept can provide a set of operable methods and processes for the design of children's programming teaching aids.

Cao Jianzhong and Xin Xiangyang started from the "five-in-one" theory of American rhetoric Kenneth Burke in the 20th century, and summarized people, action, purpose, scene, and media into the five basic elements of service design, and built a foundation Five-element service design framework (Fig. 2) [33, 34]. Although these five service design elements have their own points, they are also like the five fingers of a person. They are related to each other and indispensable, and together form the basic framework of service design. Based on this framework, the five elements corresponding to children's programming courses are students and teachers, teaching aids, maker space and classrooms, and the integration, learning and practice of various disciplines in STEAM. In this way, a framework for children's programming curriculum design based on the five elements of service design is constructed (Fig. 3). Under this framework, the service design concept is integrated into the children's programming curriculum system. The relatively vague children's programming curriculum system has become five variables that can be clearly grasped in actual operation, and the corresponding five problems. Corresponding to this framework, it can be clearly seen that the curriculum teaching aids mainly studied in this article belong to one of the five elements, and the other four elements are the variable factors that affect the curriculum teaching aids. Based on the relationship between the four variable factors and the common factor, the children's programming course is summarized. The design framework of teaching aids, and proposed a new model of "children-technology-traditional culture-children" can be recycled (Fig. 4).

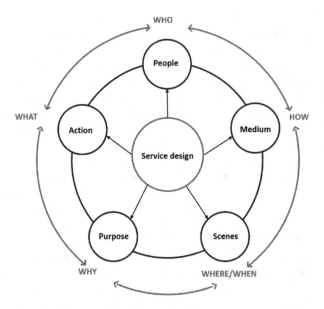

Fig. 2. Five elements based service design framework (2019)

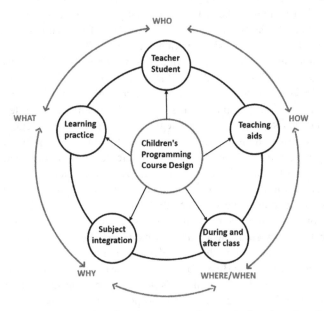

Fig. 3. Design framework of children's programming curriculum based on five elements

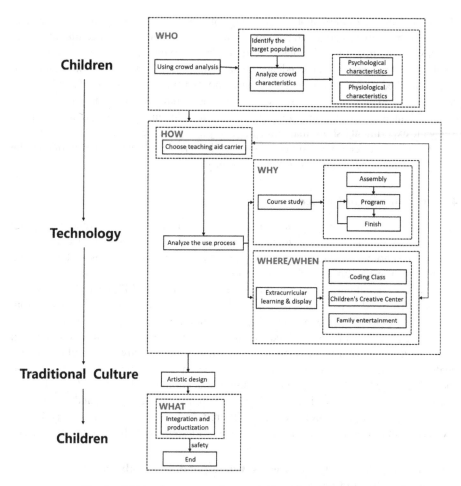

Fig. 4. Children's programming curriculum design framework

4.1 Using Crowd Analysis

"People" is the most important factor in service design and children's programming curriculum design, as well as in teaching aid design. Therefore, when facing the design of children's programming teaching aids, the first consideration is the use of the crowd. The definition of children has been mentioned in the previous design principles. It is positioned at the age of 6–12, and the development of children's sensory integration ability. In terms of characteristics, children can be divided into two stages, 6–8 years old and 9–12 years old.

After the use of the population is determined, the physical and psychological characteristics of the target population need to be analyzed. 6–8 years old is an advanced sensory integration stage for children. Children already have some complicated psychological and behavioral responses, and their language skills have improved. The development of physical muscles has significantly improved children's athletic ability, and they can participate in a variety of labor and games in their studies and lives. Children have a certain amount of attention but are single, and it is difficult to pay attention to multiple things at the same time [35]. Children aged 9–12 transitioned to youth, and their sense of independence began to increase. At this stage, children are no longer satisfied with the knowledge obtained simply from textbooks, and have begun to continuously explore the mysteries of society and nature. At this time, the children's emotions fluctuate greatly, and it is easy to be impulsive in handling transactions [36]. Relevant experiments show that from the analysis of the auditory, tactile, vestibular, visual, and proprioceptive abilities of sensory integration ability, vision is one of the strongest aspects of children's perception ability.

4.2 Pick the Right Carrier

After determining the target population of the product, and the psychological and physiological characteristics of the target population, it is necessary to select a suitable carrier. The choice of the carrier is closely related to the use scene. Most of the existing children's programming teaching aids are only for class learning, and ignore the communication and interaction after class. Li YiRu and others [37] have shown in their research that the development of the STEAM curriculum has gradually changed from constructivism to pragmatism, humanism, and utility. Yuan Lei [38] even pointed out that the emergence of STEAM education neglected the close connection between students 'internal spiritual development and social practice activities, resulting in students' weak social responsibility and social utilitarianism. Various research results also show that the use of children's programming aids should no longer be limited to the classroom. The use of teaching aid carriers should be extended to life, and increase the frequency of communication between children and their peers, parents and even society. So that STEAM education can improve children's core literacy in a true sense.

4.3 Analyze Product Use Processes, Corresponding to Subject Knowledge and Components

After selecting the suitable carrier, in order to make the teaching aids truly achieve the purpose of disciplinary integration, it is necessary to study the process of using teaching aids and correspond the process to the subject knowledge of STEAM education. STEAM education is based on the interdisciplinary knowledge fusion, shifting the focus of the problem from a single subject to a specific problem, and using mathematical, scientific, engineering, art, and technical content and knowledge to solve the problem, so as to achieve subject integration and improve knowledge Apply effects [39]. For multi-disciplinary integration, component teaching aids can be used to encourage children to make teaching aids from scratch in the form of material packages. The use of each component corresponds to the knowledge system of different disciplines, combining problems with surrounding environments and materials.

4.4 Expand Artistic Design

Artistic design is a key factor ignored by most programming teaching aids in China. Most programming teaching aids are transplanted imitations. Simply copying the development experience of other countries will hinder the speed and quality of China's basic education curriculum reform [40]. From an artistic point of view, China has a history of 5,000 years, and its culture has been passed down. Excellent traditional culture is the essence that every citizen of China should learn and inherit, which also provides unique inspiration to the Chinese design field source. For educational products such as children's programming aids, traditional cultural elements can be incorporated. Extracting the artistic image from traditional culture and designing the appearance and function of children's programming aids will help the integration of technology and culture and allow children to feel the influence of traditional culture in a subtle way. At the same time, we can better explore a road of reform and development of STEAM curriculum with Chinese characteristics and Chinese characteristics.

4.5 Integration and Productization

All products need to go through the process of integration and productization from the final production to sales and use, and the factor of learning and practice in the design of children's programming courses is closely related. The final integration and productization process is the most critical for the design of children's programming teaching aids. The design of safety for children's products is very important. At present, many products may have security risks. For example: the small parts on the product are easy to be accidentally eaten; the sharp edges of the product are easy to be cut during use; the use of unfriendly materials or the presence of harmful gases in the production process of the product will cause certain effects on children's bodies. For teaching aids, the frequency of use will be greatly increased, so the final design of children's programming curriculum teaching aids needs to be optimized for safety to ensure safety during use.

5 Application of the Framework

The design process of "Zodiac Signs" programmable night light is the application of the framework as described above. They are a series of teaching aids for children's programming courses to help students master programming knowledge in the classroom better and understand the Chinese traditional cultural knowledge of the Zodiac signs.

According to the children's programming teaching aid design framework described above, the specific design flow of the "Zodiac Sign Night Light" is shown in Fig. 5. First the target population is determined for children who are 6–12 years old. 6–12 years old children have gradually complicated psychological and behavioral responses, and their consciousness of independence have gradually increased. They have begun to explore knowledge outside the curriculum. Visual perception is the strongest ability of sensory integration, thus the lamp is selected as the carrier of teaching aids. It then analyzes the use of processes, and the subject knowledge corresponding to the three steps of assembly, programming and completion during the course teaching, which integrates knowledge in four fields: technology, mathematics, engineering, and art. In terms of product appearance optimization, the Chinese zodiac, one of the most classic traditional cultures, is used as the source of design form. The zodiac is a symbol that accompanies each person's life, and because the image of the animal is a child's favorite element, the image of the zodiac is re-created, combining material characteristics, and combining modern design styles to form a set of teaching aids (Fig. 6). Finally, the product details are integrated for security, and finally a box (Fig. 7) is formed to cooperate with the course teaching.

The "Zodiac Night Light" is mainly divided into two parts: one is the lamp surface and the other is the base. The size of the lamp surface is controlled in a rectangle of 133×196 mm, a 5 mm thick acrylic plate is used, and the base is a $145 \times 60 \times 43$ oval column. In the design of the lamp surface, the zodiac image is merged with modern design elements to simplify the redesign. At the same time, the design of the supporting knowledge card (see Fig. 8). While learning scientific knowledge, children also learned about the Chinese zodiac. The entire set of boxes requires children to follow the course step by step. The use process is divided into three steps: assembly, programming, and completion. There are 5 lessons for teaching, of which the two steps of programming and completion are cyclic. The assembly part is to take out the material package and assemble the light strips. This step allows children to learn circuit knowledge. It belongs to the first two lessons of the supporting course teaching. They learn the circuit knowledge and their own actual operation to realize the function. It involves STEAM education "Engineering". The second part is the programming part. It is for children to learn programming knowledge. They can design the frequency, form, and brightness of the lighting. It belongs to the three or four class hours of the supporting course teaching. It is the teaching of programming knowledge and the practice of children's personal skills The STEAM knowledge involved in this part is "Technology", "Mathematics" and "Art". In the last part, the children design their favorite lights. In one lesson, the design is completed to achieve the final effect, which corresponds to "Art". The use process can enable teachers and children to interact well in teaching and can also be used in family teaching, increasing the interaction between children and parents.

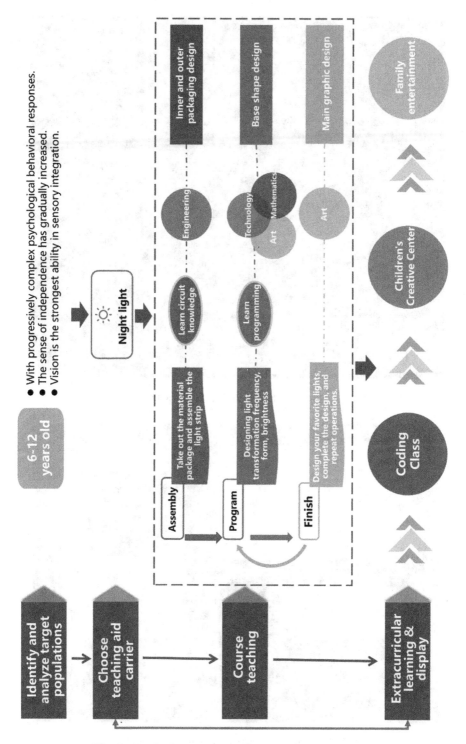

Fig. 5. "Zodiac" programmable night light design process

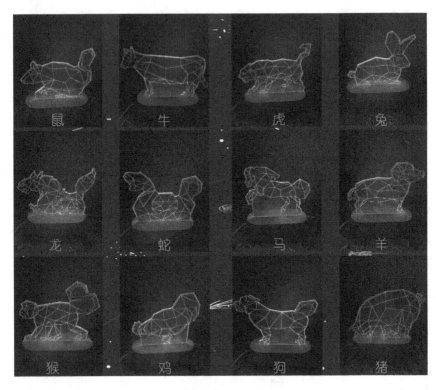

Fig. 6. Chinese Zodiac Night Light

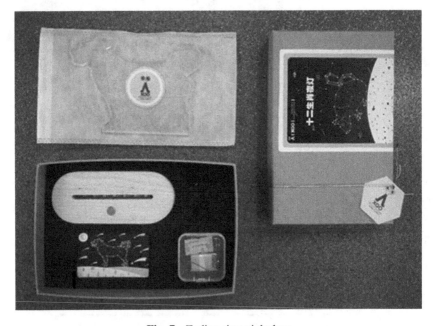

Fig. 7. Zodiac sign night box

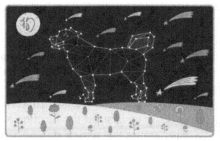 

Fig. 8. Zodiac knowledge card (front and back)

The design of teaching aids using the design methods for children's programming aids summarized in the previous section also conforms to the design principles of children's programming aids. The traditional culture of the "twelve zodiac signs" is incorporated into teaching aids, which influences children's cognition in a subtle way, so that children's programming teaching aids have cultural connotations with Chinese characteristics. The use of lamps as a carrier conforms to the principle of sensory integration ability mentioned above. For children, visual perception is the strongest of the five aspects of sensory integration. It is feasible to continue to attract children's attention with lights. The broken traditional design thinking of programming teaching aids is in line with the principle of innovative thinking and fun multi-exploration channel. Because the brightness and darkness of the light and the frequency of change can be designed and implemented by the children themselves, the exploration of the product is enhanced. Children's own initiative to develop different possibilities, which meets the highest point of children's emotional needs-self-realization, in the learning process, allowing children to actively explore and learn is a point that needs to be considered in the design of teaching aids, which is in line with emotions The principle of demand. The carrier of lamps also increases the use of products, making teaching aids not only limited to classrooms, but also used in homes, activity spaces, etc., which increases the entertainment of the product and improves the sustainability of the product.

6 Conclusion

This paper has proposed a framework for designers to design children's programming teaching aids. Based on the literature review, this paper first defines the differences between teaching aids and toys and products to distinguish the unique attributes of teaching aids. Next, analyze the current status of the design of children's programming teaching aids (covering disciplines, vectors, and functions), and summarize the existing problems, and propose design principles for Chinese children's programming. Hereafter, the constructivist learning theory and integrated STEM education used in STEM education have been extended to service design concepts, and the analysis of the children's programming curriculum system from the perspective of service design has an inseparable relationship. By combining the concept of service design, a set of frameworks for the design methods of children's programming teaching aids has been developed.

The literature research conducted did not lead to the universal use of methods for designing teaching aids for children. This is very important, because the cultural gap between countries, education methods, and other factors affect the design of children's programming teaching aids has its advantages and limitations.

The proposed framework illustrates a general approach to designing children's programming aids. Using such a method helps to better understand the function and applicability of teaching aids. On this basis, the paper argues that design students (and designers) would benefit from acquiring skills that will enable them to apply targeted design methods to designing children's programming aids. Therefore, the framework may be a useful starting point for teaching design methods for design educators.

As this article proves, designers' mastery of design methods for children's programming aids involves many aspects of design research. Considering the perspective provided by the framework on the concreteness of the curriculum concept, future research may use the framework as a pointer to different design topics for further exploration and to organize and connect existing insights related to design methods.

References

1. Bybee, R.W.: The Case for STEM Education: Challenges and Opportunities. NSTA Press, Arlington (2013)
2. Havice, W.: The power and promise of a STEM education: thriving in a complex technological world. In: The Overlooked STEM Imperatives: Technology and Engineering, pp. 10–17. ITEEA, Reston (2009)
3. Fan, S.-C., Yu, K.-C.: How an integrative STEM curriculum can benefit students in engineering design practices. Int. J. Technol. Des. Educ. 27(1), 107–129 (2015). https://doi.org/10.1007/s10798-015-9328-x
4. Thibaut, L., Knipprath, H., Dehaene, W., Depaepe, F.: How school context and personal factors relate to teachers' attitudes toward teaching integrated STEM. Int. J. Technol. Des. Educ. 28(3), 631–651 (2017). https://doi.org/10.1007/s10798-017-9416-1
5. Jones, A., Buntting, C., de Vries, M.J.: The developing field of technology education: a review to look forward. Int. J. Technol. Des. Educ. 23, 191–212 (2013)
6. Kelley, T.R., Brenner, D.C., Pieper, J.T.: Two approaches to engineering design: observations in STEM education. J. STEM Teacher Educ. 47(2), 5–40 (2010)
7. Braund, M., Reiss, M.J.: The 'Great Divide': how the arts contribute to science and science education. Can. J. Sci. Math. Technol. Educ. 19(3), 219–236 (2019)
8. Crismond, D.P., Adams, R.S.: The informed design teaching and learning matrix. J. Eng. Educ. 101(4), 738–797 (2012)
9. McFadden, J., Roehrig, G.: Engineering design in the elementary science classroom: supporting student discourse during an engineering design challenge. Int. J. Technol. Des. Educ. (2018). https://doi.org/10.1007/s10798-018-9444-5
10. Sullivan, A., Bers, M.U.: Dancing robots: integrating art, music, and robotics in Singapore's early childhood centers. Int. J. Technol. Des. Educ. 28(2), 325–346 (2017). https://doi.org/10.1007/s10798-017-9397-0

11. Yakman, G.: STEAM education: an overview of creating a model of integrative education. In: Pupils' Attitudes Towards Technology (PATT-19) Conference: Research on Technology, Innovation, Design & Engineering Teaching, Salt Lake City, Utah, USA (2008)
12. White House, Office of the Press Secretary: FACT SHEET: President Obama announces computer science for all initiative [Press release] (2016). https://www.whitehouse.gov/the-press-office/2016/01/30/fact-sheet-president-obama-announces-computer-science-all-initiative-0.
13. Pretz, K.: Computer science classes for kids becoming mandatory. The Institute: The IEEE News Source (2014)
14. Siu, K., Lam, M.: Technology education in Hong Kong: international implications for implementing the "'Eight Cs'" in the early childhood curriculum. Early Childhood Educ. J. **31**(2), 143–150 (2003)
15. U.K. Department for Education: The National Curriculum in England: Framework Document. The Stationery Office, London (2013)
16. Digital News Asia: IDA launches $1.5m pilot to roll out tech toys for preschoolers (2015). https://www.digitalnewsasia.com/digital-economy/ida-launches-pilot-to-roll-out-tech-toys-forpreschoolers
17. Yang, Q.X., Jia, F.S., Hao, W.Z., et al.: Exploration and practice of scratch children's programming education. J. Sci. Teach. **2019**(22), 134–135 (2019)
18. Tao, L.X., Yan, G.H., Ren, Z.J., et al.: The change from STEAM education to maker education in the "Internet" background: from project-based learning to the cultivation of innovation ability. Dist. Educ. J. **34**(01), 28–36 (2016)
19. He, W.Y., Chang Xin, Y., Wen, W.J., et al.: "Learning-Research-Career Development" oriented STEAM education curriculum design research. China Electr. Educ. **2019**(02), 51–56 (2019)
20. Vandevelde, C., Wyffels, F., Ciocci, M.-C., Vanderborght, B., Saldien, J.: Design and evaluation of a DIY construction system for educational robot kits. Int. J. Technol. Des. Educ. **26**(4), 521–540 (2015). https://doi.org/10.1007/s10798-015-9324-1
21. Barak, M., Assal, M.: Robotics and STEM learning: students' achievements in assignments according to the P3 Task Taxonomy—practice, problem solving, and projects. Int. J. Technol. Des. Educ. **28**(1), 121–144 (2016). https://doi.org/10.1007/s10798-016-9385-9
22. Church, W., Ford, T., Perova, N., Rogers, C.: Physics with robotics-using LEGO MINDSTORMS in high school education. In: Association for the Advancement of Artificial Intelligence Spring Symposium (2010)
23. Run, W., Jin, Z.X.: Implications of montessori teaching aids theory and its implications for children's toy selection. Educ. Rev. **2014**(06), 112–114 (2014)
24. Mei, X.Y., Li, W., Feng, J., et al.: Effects of different teaching aids on children's visual function. Chinese School Health **2001**(06), 499–500 (2001)
25. Yu, T.B., Dong, T.X.: Research on chinese traditional educational design of children's toys. Pop. Lit. **2017**(21), 120–121 (2017)
26. Shi, W.X.: Research on children's product design based on children's physiological and psychological needs level. Ind. Technol. Forum **17**(04), 69–70 (2018)
27. De, S.H.: On children's programming education. China Inf. Technol. Educ. **2019**(11), 104–105 (2019)
28. Piaget, J.: The Moral Judgment of the Child. Free Press, New York (1965)
29. Papert, S.: Mindstorms: Children, Computers and Powerful Ideas. Basic Books, New York (1980)
30. Stager, G.: Papertian constructionism and the design of productive contexts for learning. In: Proceedings of EuroLogo 2005 (2005)
31. Moore, T.J., Smith, K.A.: Advancing the state of the art of STEM integration. J. STEM Educ. Innov. Res. **15**(1), 5–10 (2014)

32. Ping, D.F., Yang, X.X.: Research on definition of service design based on phenomenological method. Decoration **2016**(10): 66–68 (2016)
33. Yang, X.X.: Interaction is micro organizational design behavior. Design **32**(08), 44–46 (2019)
34. Zhong, C.J., Yang, X.X.: The five elements of service design: exploration based on the theory of dramatistic pentad. Des. Educ. Expl. (2018)
35. Lei, P.Z., Qin, F.Q., Qun, W.Y.: Research on design of children's educational products based on sensory integration theory. Beauty Times (1) **2019**(05), 106–109 (2019)
36. Tong, D.B., Hua, T., Ci, L.H.: A literature review of research on children's sensory integration training. Med. Inf. **2006**(12), 2239–2242 (2006)
37. Ru, L.Y., Yuan, P.Y.: Development course, value orientation and localization of STEAM curriculum. Mod. Educ. Technol. **29**(09), 115–120 (2019)
38. Lei, Y.: Classroom teaching reform of STEAM education from the perspective of core literacy. China Electri. Educ. **2019**(11), 99–103 (2019)
39. Lei, Y., Xin, Z.Y.: Subject curriculum projectization: STEAM course content design. Open Educ. Res. **25**(01), 92–98 (2019)
40. Qing, S.N., Xin, G., Shan, C.: Analysis on the path of STEAM curriculum reform in basic education. Courses teaching materials. Teach. Methods **39**(07), 27–33 (2019)

Learning, Teaching and Collaboration Experiences

Auto-Assessment of Teamwork and Communication Competences Improvement Applying Active Methodologies. Comparing Results Between Students of First Academic Year in Architecture, Economics and Engineering Degrees

Marian Alaez[1] , Susana Romero[1] , David Fonseca[2](✉) ,
Daniel Amo[2] , Enric Peña[2] , and Silvia Necchi[2]

[1] University of Deusto, 48007 Bilbao, Spain
{marian.alaez, sromeroyesa}@deusto.es
[2] La Salle, Ramon Llull University, C/ Sant Joan de la Salle 42,
08022 Barcelona, Spain
{fonsi, daniel.amo, enric.pc,
silvia.necchi}@salle.url.edu

Abstract. In the first years of a university degree it is very important to maintain student motivation in order to avoid possible risks of early dropout. To this end, the design of practices focused on the improvement of transversal competences such as Teamwork and Oral Communication allows students to make more motivating progress in their specific knowledge. At the same time, students improve in skills that are highly recognized and required in the professional world. The practical awareness of the student's level and the current context of hybrid teaching (face-to-face and virtual) derived from the pandemic increase student motivation to improve these competences. These skills are based on work in specific subjects and in a way that is independent of the type of degree/studies being studied, with a homogeneous profile at a national level.

Keywords: Team work · Oral communication · Improving competences · Motivation · Educational data analytics

1 Introduction

The first years of an undergraduate programme are usually generic courses where students are trained in the basic concepts of specific subjects. The heterogeneity of the entry profiles [1–3], which is at present even harder due to the closing of the pre-university cycle in a pandemic context with virtual training, can lead to a decrease in student motivation, which is a fundamental parameter in their follow-up and interest [4, 5]. In this sense, one approach to mitigate the initial impact of undergraduate studies may be to design the most introductory subjects, activities and/or practices focusing on

P. Zaphiris and A. Ioannou (Eds.): HCII 2021, LNCS 12784, pp. 193–209, 2021.
https://doi.org/10.1007/978-3-030-77889-7_13

generic competences. This may help to increase the student's motivation to study, which directly correlates with an increase in academic performance [6–10].

The present research focuses on analysing, in three different degrees (Law, Architecture and Building Construction, and Engineering), how activities focused on the improvement of such important generic competences as Teamwork and Oral Communication, transversally worked on to the specific competences, can help to improve students' motivation. This progress will not only be limited to their specific studies, but also in autonomy, as they will become more aware of their learning of these competences. In order to ensure that future graduates have a better and broader labour market insertion, this type of transversal -or generic- competences require initial training that is progressively incorporated into all subjects, enabling the student to achieve the best possible skills [9, 11, 12].

On the basis of the design and implementation of a standardised rubric for the competences described as well as the use of a standardised instrument for measuring motivation, the research presents the three activities designed and the exploratory results obtained on the basis of the students' answers to two questionnaires, one before the practical experience and the other at the end.

2 Theoretical Framework

2.1 The Relevance of Generic Competences: Teamwork and Communication

Employers are considered a very important stakeholder in the university context. One of the goals of the degree programmes is the employability of their students. Therefore, the competences-based curricula will have to consider how they perceive the profile of the graduate who enters their organisations to work [13–16]. Competences such as Teamwork and Communication have been identified as key in student empowerment. To ensure this, it is essential to motivate students and to start their training from an early stage and in a transversal way to their more specific training.

Employers in our universities have been pointing out for several years that students are graduating without sufficient development of these competences [11], which is an obstacle to their employment insertion. Even those students with brilliant academic records often have poor communication and interpersonal skills and prefer the control provided by individual work to the potential offered by teamwork.

Consequently, in this project we decided to develop an educational pill on Teamwork that could be used either separately or together with instructions to improve the student's communication skills. The aim was to share it with first-year students so that, from the very beginning of their university studies, they would be aware of the enormous potential of teamwork, based on synergies, as well as of the keys that favour its effectiveness. The underlying idea is that teamwork must be carefully nurtured from the beginning of the group's formation to its final evaluation process [17]. Its implementation has been carried out in different universities and degrees through a group work in a subject.

Three levels of mastery can be distinguished in this competence [18]. The first, which has been considered appropriate for first-year students, refers to the responsibility that team members must show in completing tasks on time and in giving priority to the team's objectives over individual interests. The second and third levels, which would be left for higher courses, relate, respectively, to participation and involvement in the team's objectives, ensuring a good climate, and to team leadership.

It was then decided to formulate the generic competence Teamwork, in its first level, as "Actively participating and collaborating in team tasks and promoting confidence, cordiality and focus on shared work" [18]. The educational pill is designed to be delivered in five phases, following the Learning Model of the University of Deusto [19]:

- Contextualisation. In this stage, students are asked to identify their previous experiences in teamwork in order to build on them. According to the design of the pill, the students presented their testimonies about positive and negative experiences in Teamwork.
- Reflective Observation. The aim is to promote reflection through the formulation of questions on the subject being dealt with. In the didactic pill, an extract from Alan Turing's film, Enigma Code, was presented, from which the students were asked to express their reflections by asking questions.
- Conceptualisation. This stage was developed in a teacher-led conversation, in which the key factors that condition the effectiveness of teamwork, such as the size of the group, the roles of the members, the communication skills, the attitude, the conflict resolution or the decision-making process, were explained.
- Active experimentation. Students were asked to follow the established guidelines for the group work assigned in the subject.
- Evaluation. Assessment was introduced in several moments. The first one was an initial assessment, based on the students' perception of the development of this competence; the following ones were throughout the team work, as teachers monitored students through tutorials and, finally, after the delivery and presentation of the work, students were asked to answer a final assessment questionnaire.

To assess the competence at the chosen level "Actively participating and collaborating in team tasks and promoting confidence, cordiality and focus on shared work" the following three indicators were chosen:

- Completes assigned tasks within deadline as group member
- Participates actively in team meetings, sharing information, knowledge and experiences
- Collaborates in defining, organising and distributing group tasks.

To measure progress on these indicators we used the evaluation rubrics that can be seen in the results section. These rubrics describe the behaviours associated with each rating in each of the indicators.

On the other hand, we have been learning to speak since we were children. As adults, we usually think that we can communicate effectively. Nevertheless, it is easy to prove without much effort that this assumption is not right. We believe that when we talk to others we are being understood in what we want to say but daily experience -

both at home and at work- shows us that there is usually a big difference between what we try to convey and what is understood [20].

A presentation is effective if it is designed and prepared to tell not just a story but something specific to a specific public. Therefore, it is necessary to have information about the audience in a way that allows us to clearly and specifically define the objective of the communication, without forgetting its design and its redaction.

Oral communication competence means being effective in transmitting ideas, knowledge and feelings through words, both in conversations and in group activities of any size. It is easy to find people who have a passive attitude, even in situations that require your active participation. The causes of such behavior should be sought in psychological factors, such as extreme shyness or a complete lack of self-confidence. This type of people can also have problems associated with rambling, and an unclear expression that hinders and even prevents the understanding of others. In their communications there may be a lack of structure, contradictions between what is expressed in words and what is transmitted through the body language, or even poor examples and means of support that are inappropriate for what is said or to whom it is said.

At the opposite end we find people who dominate this competence, that is, people who speak clearly. A well-structured speech adapted to the audience, a body language that agrees with the message and a good tone of voice and means of support, generate a better general ability to communicate effectively what you want to transmit. Therefore, we are talking about a better education of the person in today's society mediated around communication.

On these bases, it was decided to formulate the generic competence Oral Communication at its first level of mastery as "Expressing own ideas in a structured, intelligible way, participating opportunely and significantly in informal, formal and structured conversations and discussions" [18]. The educational pill was designed to be delivered in different phases, following the University of Deusto Learning Model [19]. In this case study we have focused on the following three indicators:

- Conveying important information.
- Delivering structured talks meeting any specified requirements that may exist.
- Using visual aids in giving talks.

2.2   The Student's Motivation in the First Undergraduate Courses

Numerous studies show that students entering universities today are very different from the students who are now teaching them both in terms of previous skills and in terms of attitude and motivation to acquire new ones. This leads universities to consider the need to take into account students' own characteristics and opinions in order to enable them to succeed in their studies [21]. Motivation-enhancing aspects include methodologies for maintaining their attention, which must be active [22] to substantially improve students' performance [23]. And according to Partanen's studies [24], this improvement is even greater with direct interaction with peers and teachers. In other words, although students may initially be reluctant to work in teams and fearful of presenting their ideas to their peers, the development of these competences improves not only their motivation but also the final experience and results.

In this project we have taken the MUSIC® model (eMpowerment, Usefulness, Success, Interest, and Caring) [25, 26] as a reference. This model considers the different variables that can influence motivation, both those considered as positive -which produce an increase- and those that prevent dissatisfaction. It also considers the role played by the different agents, such as the university-faculty and the teachers, and the intrinsic factors of the students themselves, such as whether or not they like the challenges and tasks assigned to them.

This model consists of different questionnaires. We have chosen the one most appropriate to the context and, within this, the questions that have been considered appropriate to the experience to be developed, as well as the guidelines for its implementation. The purpose of this questionnaire is to measure the students' perception based on a number of variables related to the motivation of the activities to be carried out. The aim is to identify strengths and weaknesses of the educational actions from the point of view of student motivation and commitment.

The questions that have been chosen take into account the student's perception of the usefulness of the activities and the importance of the knowledge acquired for their future, their ability to do them successfully and to obtain a high grade, the attractiveness of the teaching methods used, the enjoyment they will derive from the activities, their control over the activities, and the role of the teacher's attitude in their performance. The parameters obtained are quantitative and widely validated, although the model stresses that they should be considered independently.

3 Experimental Framework

3.1 Case 1: Group A, Law Degree

The project has been carried out in the subject Introduction to Economics, which forms part of the Basic Training module of the first year of the Law degree. The educational pills designed to improve motivation, as well as the generic competences of teamwork and oral communication have been "transversalized" to a subject-specific competence. The aim of this specific competence is to interpret the major current economic problems articulated through the Sustainable Development Goals (SDGs), in order to identify the economic facet that impregnates the current socio-political-humanitarian reality and its consequences [27].

The subject is taught in the first semester, so the group of students is new to the university and comes from different centres and places. Their previous experience of working in a team, their previous training in oral communication and their motivation are very varied. The curriculum assigns the first level development in the Generic Competence of Teamwork to this subject, so it has been the axis around which both the Oral Communication pill and the motivation study have pivoted. Firstly, the students were given a questionnaire asking them to self-assess their initial level of motivation, as well as their initial level of development of the two Generic Competences. For this purpose, they were offered the indicators designed for the evaluation of the competences, with their descriptive rubric of evident behaviours.

The Teamwork pill was presented and put into practice on several consecutive days. After a first meeting in which some students' testimonies of their good and bad experiences of teamwork were shared, students' roles were identified and groups were formed, taking care to include one student with each predominant role. Key issues of teamwork were shared in a participatory way through a classroom discussion method. The teacher then presented the document with the instructions for the work on the SDGs to be carried out as a team. The students met in their groups for the first time to agree on the logo and the motto that identified them. Then they proceeded to carry out the work according to the instructions. Once the work had been completed and before the oral presentation, the teacher presented the Oral Communication educational pill, also addressing issues related to non-verbal communication.

The oral presentation of the group work took place in the classroom. As they went along, the students received feedback from the teacher pointing out the strengths and weaknesses found in their communication. After the experience, the students filled in a final evaluation questionnaire in which they re-assessed themselves on motivation, teamwork and communication. The results are very satisfactory as they show a better perception of their motivation and development of the competences worked on.

3.2   Case 2: Group B, Architecture and Building Construction Degrees

In the School of Architecture, the experience has been carried out in the "Aula BCN" activity, a cross-cutting activity in the first year that is developed through three exercises with the participation of all the subjects. Specifically, the activity presented here was the first of the course, carried out as an introductory visit to the Borne district of Barcelona with the participation of the subjects of Construction, History, Graphic Expression and Computer Tools [28, 29].

The main objective of the activity is the proposal to open one's eyes, learning how to look, and how to represent the imbalances that burst into space. Listening to what is out of place, it is easier to analyze the agents involved and their ways of relating, revealing with them the factors involved in architecture. Through a historical and constructive look, under a graphic representation, the aim of this exercise is to explore and communicate the "violated intimacies" of Passeig del Born and its surroundings, where the church of Santa María del Mar, the Borne Market and the "Fossar de las Moreres" are located, as well as the interesting urban axis, from the historical and constructive point of view.

The visit took place one month after the start of classes, so that the groups of three or four students (freely grouped) could get to know each other and work in a coordinated way according to their presence (bearing in mind that the students can follow the course both face-to-face and online). Prior to the visit, subject-specific training sessions were held, as well as a session on how to improve training and motivation in the generic competences of Teamwork and Communication that are going to be worked on. They were also asked about their perception of their level of preparation for teamwork, their communication skills and their motivation to improve in these aspects.

The practice focuses on making a video (.mp4) of 5 min' maximum, where, through different chapters, the "violated intimacies" in the location identified and its surroundings must be shown. The video has to explain in 5 chapters the critical view of the architectural and urban space of Paseo del Born. During the visit, the keys to look and analyze the space will be given. The visit will have enough time to clarify doubts and open a debate. Each chapter of the video will try to record the "violated intimacies" of the space through 5 items: in relation to a specific PLACE of the visited space (building or urban environment); in relation to a CONCEPT that appeared in the comments of the visit (beauty, inhuman, fear, absence, transparency, liquid ...); in relation to an IMAGINARY related to some reality of Passeig del Born (social imaginary of progress, of traditions and beliefs...); in relation to a WILL represented in some spatial intention (in this sense, the "violated intimacies" will be affected by this "will", understood as the human capacity to freely decide what is desired and what is not); and in relation to a specific FUNCTION of a visited space (commercial, religious, family, symbolic, etc.). The audiovisual must be able to tell the "violated intimacy" without being explicitly explained but using the poetics of audiovisual language as a way of communication. Only if the chapter has an audio of a narrative nature based on a fictional, a real story an interview or a thought as a revealed private diary, will be a narrator allowed.

Audiovisual language is totally free since it is itself a creative act justified by communication skills. In this sense, the use of archive and/or real images, both photographic and drawing or reference, as well as audios recorded in situ, interviews, songs or manipulated sounds is something that is part of creativity, and also the ability to communicate and to analyze the work. Not only it is an exercise with a deep and interesting analysis at the spatial level expected, but also with a clear intention of development of the creativity and communication skills.

In order to carry out the evaluation, they were provided with the rubric used in the previous training, and in addition to the video, they were given a template to fill in with the distribution of tasks and the communicative script of the video. On the basis of the video and the filled-in template, all the videos were viewed and commented by both the teachers and the rest of the class, before the final survey was carried out.

3.3 Case 3: Group C, Engineering Degree

In the Faculty of Engineering, the experience was carried out in the second-year subject of Electronics, as part of the double degree in Design+Mechanics. In the first weeks of this subject, various competences were worked on as a basis for the final project, where the pills designed to improve the transversal competences of teamwork, communication and increased motivation were put into practice.

This is a second-year subject with only 18 students. The group already knew each other, as they had previously worked on other projects. There were no problems with oral communication that usually occur in earlier groups. However, the biggest challenge in this subject tends to be that of motivation. Being a double degree, the orientation of each student may be more towards one degree or the other, and some students consider Electronics to be "out of place".

As a first step in the experience, students were asked to answer a series of questions about their previous experience of teamwork and co-communication, as well as to position themselves on the motivation with which they started the assignment. They were then asked to divide into three teams to work on the two competences and the motivational element. The division was free and the reasons for opting for one team or another could be diverse: to know the subject in more depth, to feel some interest, to find it more difficult... On this basis, they had to draw up a collaborative document shared with the rest of their colleagues in which they would list difficulties, advantages, disadvantages and guidelines for teachers and students to improve oral communication skills, teamwork, or to increase motivation when carrying out a project.

The resulting document had to be agreed upon by the team working on it. This began in a class hour guided by the teacher and had to be completed outside the classroom. After the students' previous elaboration, the teacher made the pills prepared for the experience available to them, and the different teams contrasted their information, completed, modified, etc. until they reached a consensus again, among themselves and with the teacher. The final documents were explained to the class as a whole by the teams themselves, and they all agreed on the guidelines, recommendations, procedures, forms of action and evaluation to be applied during the project, which they would begin to develop in the following session.

The composition of the teams for the project was different and was carried out according to the guidelines that they themselves had set. The project itself was also developed according to their rules, and once it was finished, it was presented to the rest of the classmates, taking into account their recommendations. Likewise, the teacher respected the agreement on the distribution of the group mark.

After the presentation, in the same session, the students were invited to re-fill in the second part of the questionnaire, in order to get their perception of their evolution in terms of teamwork and communication, as well as their motivation for how the experience had developed. In their answers, a clear overall improvement can be seen in all of them.

4   Results

4.1   PRE-Questionnaire

Before each group experience was carried out, a session was held to explain how to work in a group and what actions are necessary for effective communication. The aim of this session was to familiarise students with the rubric system used in the assessment of teamwork and communication competences, according to the proposal developed at the University of Deusto. As it can be seen from the proposal, competences are usually assessed at different levels of mastery and with different indicators for each level. In our approach, and given that we were working with first-year undergraduate students, we selected the first level (out of three) for each competence. We also selected half of the indicators referred to in this level, selecting the ones that were transversally suitable for the three study groups and adapted to the activities designed.

The three indicators surveyed in relation to teamwork competence (TW1, TW2, and TW3) and their rubric (based on five levels) are:

- TW1: Performs the tasks assigned to you within the required deadlines.
    - R1_TW1: I don't fulfill the assigned tasks
    - R2_TW1: I partially fulfill the assigned tasks or delay in their delivery

- R3_TW1: I give in time the tasks assigned to me
- R4_TW1: The quality of the task I perform is a remarkable contribution to the team
- R5_TW1: In addition to fulfilling the assigned task, my work guides and facilitates that of the rest of the team members.
- TW2: Actively participate in the team's meeting spaces, sharing information, knowledge and experiences.
  - R1_TW2: Into the group work I am easily absent and my presence is irrelevant.
  - R2_TW2: I intervene little, rather at the request of others.
  - R3_TW2: In general, I am active and participatory in group meetings.
  - R4_TW2: With my interventions I promote the participation and improvement of the quality
  - R5_TW2: My contributions are fundamental to both the group process and the quality.
- TW3: Collaborates in the definition, organization and distribution of group tasks.
  - R1_TW3: I show resistance to the organization of teamwork.
  - R2_TW3: I merely accept the work organization proposed by the other members of the group.
  - R3_TW3: I participate in the planning, organization and distribution of teamwork.
  - R4_TW3: I am organized and I distribute the work effectively.
  - R5_TW3: I Promote a work organization by leveraging the resources of team members.

The same procedure was followed for the Communication competence. The three common indicators applicable transversally to the experience (CC1, CC2 and CC3) were selected on the basis of a five-level rubric:

- CC1: Transmission of relevant information.
  - R1_CC1: I express myself in a poor or confusing way.
  - R2_CC1: I present some basic ideas.
  - R3_CC1: I explain fundamental ideas.
  - R4_CC1: I communicate clear reasons and/or values/attitudes.
  - R5_CC1: I stand out for clarity in my communication of reasoning and/or feelings.
- CC2: The presentations are structured, meeting the required requirements.
  - R1_CC2: My presentations have a lack of intelligible structure.
  - R2_CC2: The structure of the presentation is not effective, or does not meet the requirements.
  - R3_CC2: The presentation is structured, meets the required requirements, if defined.
  - R4_CC2: I link ideas and arguments easily.
  - R5_CC2: I make a very effective and organized communication.
- CC3: Media support in presentations.
  - R1_CC3: I do not use the required or reasonably necessary systems of support.
  - R2_CC3: The media support is not appropriate for presentation.
  - R3_CC3: I use required media support or reasonably necessary.

- R4_CC3: The use of media support helps the audience to be placed in the speech.
- R5_CC3: The use of media support makes it possible to emphasize the keys of the communication.

Once each exercise and the two competences to be worked on had been presented, the students were asked about their current degree of perception for each of the indicators (for both TW and CC), as well as which of the different indicators they perceived as having the greatest possibility of improvement with the proposed work. Finally, in the same questionnaire, students were asked about their degree of motivation with respect to the proposal, in this case using a reduced sample of questions based on the MUSIC [26].

The first step in the analysis of the results of the PRE-questionnaire was to compare the responses in order to analyze the degree of homogeneity between the three groups in the experiment. To this end, the arithmetic means of the answers related to the degree of training in group work competence, communication competence and MUSIC were compared. PRE-questionnaire average scores are similar in all groups. To estimate the probability that groups were significantly similar, we used the Student's t-test (Gosset, 1908), using a null hypothesis (H0) that there were no differences in scores between groups (see Table 1).

Table 1. Statistically significance (Two-tailed) - p

Compared groups	TW	CC	MUSIC
A-B	0,1609	0,0513	0,7774
A-C	0,7547	0,4358	0,1296
B-C	0,1855	0,2285	0,2798

Due the results, which exceed the threshold of $p = 0.05$, which means that there is a very low probability that the groups are different in their skills and previous training about their level of competences and motivation. The null hypothesis, which states that there are no significant differences between groups, is accepted.

Focusing on the results on the students' previous level of teamwork competence, the results obtained were (see Table 2 for TW and Table 3 for CC):

Table 2. TW average results by group and its Standard Deviation (SD) for each teamwork average indicator in the PRE-Questionnaire (n = sample by group).

Group	n	TW1	SD	TW2	SD	TW3	SD
A	26	4,19	0,69	3,50	0,65	3,77	0,65
B	19	3,88	1,16	3,56	0,30	4,07	0,70
C	14	3,93	0,73	3,64	0,63	4,07	1,00
Global	69	4,00	0.86	3,57	0,53	3,97	0,78

Table 3. CC average results by group and its Standard Deviation (SD) for each teamwork average indicator in the PRE-Questionnaire (n = sample by group).

Group	n	CC1	SD	CC2	SD	CC3	SD
A	26	3,96	0,77	3,85	0,67	3,88	0,82
B	19	3,93	0,78	3,71	0,44	3,76	0,36
C	14	3,86	0,86	3,57	0,51	3,86	0,95
Global	69	3,92	0,81	3,71	0,54	3,84	0,71

Analysing firstly the results of TW (Table 2), we can clearly observe that, in general, students rate themselves as highly skilled (with values of around 4/5). The TW2 indicator stands out as the one with significantly lower values than TW1 and TW3 (3.57/5) for all the groups in the study. As we will see later (Table 6), TW2 is explicitly identified as an aspect to be improved in groups B and C, and also in group A, but in the same way in this case as TW3.

The results of the CC indicators show a greater homogeneity in the three groups. With an average value centred on 3.85/5, no indicator in any group exceeds the limit of 4/5 and the potential for improvement is distributed between CC3 and CC1 depending on the groups, as we will see in the comparison with the results after the experience.

The results of motivation will be analysed comparatively in Sect. 4.3, but in order to be able to compare the results after each educational pill, we can see a quite similar prior development of the students at a competence level, with a significant potential to improve the indicators and a proactive attitude in all the groups.

4.2 POST-Questionnaire

Once the different educational pills (explained in Sect. 3) had been carried out, and after the corresponding delivery of each case, a POST-questionnaire was conducted. It followed the same study parameters as the PRE-questionnaire, but with a broader question in the specific case of the evaluation of teamwork: for each initial indicator, a homonymous question was added about each student's perception of the work carried out by the rest of the members of the team. In this way, the questions presented were as follows:

- TW1_a: I have performed the assigned tasks within the group within the required time frames.
- TW1_b: In general, my group members have carried out the tasks assigned within the group within the required timeframes.
- TW2_a: I have actively participated in the team's meeting spaces, sharing information, knowledge and experiences
- TW2_b: In general, my group members have actively participated in the team's meeting spaces, sharing information, knowledge and experiences
- TW3_a: I have collaborated in the definition, organization and distribution of group tasks.
- TW3_b: In general, my team members have collaborated in the definition, organization and distribution of group tasks.

The results obtained were as follows:

Table 4. TW average results by group and its Standard Deviation (SD) for each teamwork average indicator in the POST-Questionnaire (n = sample by group). In Bold the averages with a major value than in the PRE-Questionnaire.

Group	n	TW1_a	SD	TW2_a	SD	TW3_a	SD
A	26	4,08	1,26	**4,15**	0,78	**4,12**	0,82
B	19	3,57	1,27	**4,01**	0,86	3,85	1,09
C	14	**4,07**	1,21	**4,07**	0,62	**4,21**	0,89
Global	69	3,91	1,25	**4,08**	0,75	**4,06**	0,93

As can be seen, up to 6 averages (marked in bold) have improved with respect to the initial survey, highlighting TW2 with positive increases for all study groups. It should be remembered that this indicator was identified as the one with the lowest initial preparation by all the groups, and also as the one with the greatest potential for improvement. Its increase is significant ($p = 0.003$), since after the educational experience it has become the one with the highest perception of readiness on the part of the students, rising from 3.57/5 to 4.08/5. In addition, and as can be seen in Table 5 below, it is the indicator on which the students have observed the greatest competence in their work colleagues.

Table 5. TW average results by group and its Standard Deviation (SD) for each teamwork average indicator in the POST-Questionnaire (n = sample by group). In Bold the averages with a major value than in the Pre-test.

Group	n	TW1_b	SD	TW2_b	SD	TW3_b	SD
A	26	3,73	1,31	**4,19**	0,69	3,73	0,96
B	19	3,29	1,52	3,88	1,09	3,85	1,13
C	14	3,93	1,33	3,79	0,80	4,21	0,70
Global	69	3,65	1,39	3,95	0,69	3,93	0,93

On the other extreme, we find TW1. Although the personal perception of the students has remained practically unchanged (from 3.92 to 3.91), it is remarkable the decrease they observe in the competence of their co-workers, which drops to 3.65/5 (see Table 5). This overall decrease is particularly noticeable in the results of group B, where the perception of the TW1 indicator is the lowest of the whole process, going from an initial value of 3.93 (see Table 3), to 3.57 (see Table 4 for personal change), and to 3.29 (Table 5, for group change).

As can be seen, the distribution and completion of tasks in the times defined within the group (TW1) continues to be a difficulty to be considered in the design of future group work, especially due to the impact it has on the final deliverable of any activity. Although this indicator is considered critical in the evaluation of the activities, it is not identified as an aspect to be improved. In this case, TW2, as can be seen in Table 6, continues to be the indicator that the students identify as an aspect to be improved (PRE) and an aspect improved (POST). In this sense, and in view of the results, it is necessary that in the design of future educational activities to be worked on in groups, a monitoring of the distribution of tasks and their timing should be designed to enable control and guidance by the teaching staff, since although the pupils do not identify it as a value to be improved (Table 6), the results refute this perception (Tables 4 and 5).

Table 6. Indicators perceived to be improved by the students (PRE vs. POST perception), related with Teamwork Competence (TW)

Group	A-Pre	A-Post	B-Pre	B-Post	C-Pre	C-Post	Global PRE	Global POST
TW1	0	**3**	2	**3**	4	1	6	**7**
TW2	13	**14**	10	**11**	8	7	31	**32**
TW3	13	9	7	5	2	**6**	22	20

By similarly analysing the variation of the indicators referring to communication competence (CC), in Table 7 we can see that CC3 is the indicator that has obtained the greatest overall increase, going from an average of 3.84/5 to 4.05/5. CC2 has also increased overall, and the only indicator that has experienced a decrease is CC1, from 3.92 to 3.84, although this decrease is not significant.

Table 7. CC average results by group and its Standard Deviation (SD) for each communication average indicator in the POST-Questionnaire (n = sample by group). In Bold the averages with a major value than in the PRE-questionnaire.

Group	n	CC1	SD	CC2	SD	CC3	SD
A	26	3,96	0,92	3,73	0,78	**4,27**	0,87
B	19	3,76	0,47	**3,91**	0,48	**3,87**	0,81
C	14	3,79	0,47	**3,64**	0,74	**4,00**	1,18
Global	69	3,84	0,70	**3,76**	0,67	**4,05**	0,95

CC3 was the indicator on which the PRE-Questionnaire identified the greatest need for improvement (see Table 8), especially for Group A, which obtained the highest increase (from 3.88 to 4.27/5). This demonstrates the correct design and usefulness of the activity carried out for this group. Likewise, and as can be seen for this group, CC2 is the only indicator that decreases. In this way, it is directly identified as an indicator to be improved in future work on the student's perception. Group 1 also reflects a coherent result, with CC1 being the only indicator that has decreased with respect to the initial perception and the one that has been identified with the greatest increase in the need for improvement in future activities. Group C is the one that distributes the results more widely, identifying CC1 and CC3 as indicators to be improved. However, in accordance with the results and being the only one that decreases in evaluation, it is clear that CC1 should be the one on which future efforts should be focussed (it has the same number of identifications (5), without reduction (CC3 has reduced from 6 to 5)).

Table 8. Indicators perceived to be improved by the students (PRE vs. POST perception) related with Communication Competence (CC)

Group	A-Pre	A-Post	B-Pre	B-Post	C-Pre	C-Post	Global PRE	Global POST
CC1	6	**8**	8	**10**	5	5	19	**23**
CC2	6	**13**	5	3	3	**4**	14	**20**
CC3	14	5	6	6	6	5	26	17

4.3 Student's Motivation

We used the validated MUSIC instrument for the study of student motivation, as indicated above. In our case, we have made a simplification based on 9 questions covering all the dimensions studied by the instrument ("M": M3, "U": Average M1 and M8, "S": Average M2 and M5, "I": Average M3 and M4, and "C": Average M6 and M9), using:

- M1: In general, the planned activities of the course are useful.
- M2: I am confident in my ability to successfully carry out the established activities.
- M3: The teaching methods described actively involve me in the course.
- M4: I think I'm going to enjoy the course activities.
- M5: I consider myself able to get a high grade on the activity.
- M6: I have control over how I learn the contents of the course/activity.
- M7: The teacher cares about my performance in the course.
- M8: I believe that the knowledge achieved in this course is important for my future.
- M9: The teacher is friendly/understandable.

The comparative results of MUSIC can be seen in Table 9 below:

Table 9. MUSIC values comparison (based on a Likert scale of 6 levels). In Bold values with an increment and in italic significate increments and decrements.

	Pre-questionnaire					Post-questionnaire				
Group	M	U	S	I	C	M	U	S	I	C
A	4,88	5,44	5,10	5,00	5,40	**4,96**	5,33	**5,10**	4,83	**5,54**
B	4,63	5,43	4,43	4,68	4,94	*4,26*	*4,82*	*5,03*	4,57	4,63
C	4,64	4,68	4,79	4,75	5,61	*5,36*	*5,61*	*5,61*	*5,79*	*6,00*
Global	4,72	5,18	4,77	4,81	5,32	**4,86**	**5,25**	**5,25**	**5,06**	**5,39**

As can be observed, there has been an overall increase in student motivation, both with the educational proposal and with the system of improvement and monitoring of the competences worked on. It is worth highlighting the significant increase in all levels in group C. At the other extreme, there was a significant decrease in levels M and U in group B, the only ones with significant statistics. These decreases centred on eMpowerment and the Usufulness of the practice of group B are related to the type of exercise carried out. This exercise is less focused and the transversality of both the content and the proposal reduces the degree of comfort of the student, who does not perceive its applicability equally in all subjects. At the other extreme, we find the variable S related to the ability to successfully carry out the exercise, which was the only variable that increased overall for all the groups, especially in the case of groups B and C.

5 Conclusions

In order to reduce early drop-out rates, the need to motivate students in the first years of undergraduate studies is essential. Designing training strategies that increase student motivation has been demonstrated to improve academic results and thus reduce the risk of early dropout. In this sense, focusing activities on exercises that actively improve transversal competences is a first step to motivate students in specific contents. The improvement of two transversal competences as important as teamwork and communication, and the students' perception of their level and their need for improvement, will help teachers in the design of courses and activities, and therefore in the distribution of contents and tasks in a successful way.

The results of the study carried out show how, as a whole, the proposals for educational pills based on active methodologies implemented have improved both student motivation and their degree of training in the generic competences on which the work focuses. The analysis of results has identified the need to continue training students in the aspects linked to TW1 (organisation of tasks and timings), as this has been shown to be a critical aspect according to the exercise. Globally, the study groups have improved ostensibly in the TW2 indicator referring to the ability to provide ideas and solutions at work, being identified by all of them as an aspect to continue improving and which is linked to the second of the competences dealt with in the study, that of effective communication.

In this sense, a differentiation by type of studies can be observed. The more technical studies, such as Architecture or Engineering, identify CC1 (Transmission of relevant information) as a key indicator, while in the Law Degree, the key indicator is CC2 (Presentations well-structured and meeting the required requirements).

As a conclusion, the study leaves the door open for further replication by focusing on an improved design of the educational pills in order to assess the improvement in the identified key indicators as well as in student motivation.

Acknowledgments. This research was funded by the project "Improving social and collaborative competences of undergraduate students using active methodologies. A mixed assessment approach", granted at the VI Call of ACM (Aristos Campus Mundus) Research Projects—2020, with the grant number ACM2020_02.

References

1. Hutchison, M.A., Follman, D.K., Sumpter, M., Bodner, G.M.: Factors influencing the self-efficacy beliefs of first-year engineering students. J. Eng. Educ. **95**(1), 39–47 (2006). https://doi.org/10.1002/j.2168-9830.2006.tb00876.x
2. Beqiri, M.S., Chase, N.M., Bishka, A.: Online course delivery: an empirical investigation of factors affecting student satisfaction. J. Educ. Bus. **85**(2), 95–100 (2009). https://doi.org/10.1080/08832320903258527
3. Rodenbusch, S.E., Hernandez, P.R., Simmons, S.L., Dolan, E.L.: Early engagement in course-based research increases graduation rates and completion of science, engineering, and mathematics degrees. CBE Life Sci. Educ. **15**(2), ar20 (2016). https://doi.org/10.1187/cbe.16-03-0117
4. García-Peñalvo, F.J., Corell, A., Abella-García, V., Grande, M.: La evaluación online en la educación superior en tiempos de la COVID-19. Educ. Knowl. Soc. (2020). https://doi.org/10.14201/eks.23013
5. García-Peñalvo, F.J., Corell, A.: La COVID-19: ¿enzima de la transformación digital de la docencia o reflejo de una crisis metodológica y competencial en la educación superior? Campus Virtuales **9**(2), 83–98 (2020)
6 Fonseca, D., Martí, N., Redondo, E., Navarro, I., Sánchez, A.: Relationship between student profile, tool use, participation, and academic performance with the use of Augmented Reality technology for visualized architecture models. Comput. Human Behav. **31**, 434–445 (2014). https://doi.org/10.1016/j.chb.2013.03.006
7. Fonseca, D., García-Peñalvo, F.J.: Interactive and collaborative technological ecosystems for improving academic motivation and engagement. Univers. Access Inf. Soc. **18**, 423–430 (2019)
8. Fonseca, D., Redondo, E., Villagrasa, S.: Mixed-methods research: a new approach to evaluating the motivation and satisfaction of university students using advanced visual technologies. Univers. Access Inf. Soc. **14**, 311–332 (2015). https://doi.org/10.1007/s10209-014-0361-4
9. Necchi, S., Peña, E., Fonseca, D., Arnal, M.: Improving teamwork competence applied in the building and construction engineering final degree project. Int. J. Eng. Educ. **36**, 328–340 (2020)
10. Sanchez-Sepulveda, M.V., Marti-Audi, N., Fonseca Escudero, D.: Visual technologies for urban design competences in architecture education. In: Proceedings of 7th International Conference on Technological Ecosystems for Enhancing Multiculturality, pp. 726–731. ACM New York, NY, USA, Leon, Spain (2019). https://doi.org/10.1145/3362789.3362822
11. Peña, E., Fonseca, D., Marti, N., Ferrándiz, J.: Relationship between specific professional competences and learning activities of the building and construction engineering degree final project. Int. J. Eng. Educ. **34**, 924–939 (2018)
12. Peña, E., Fonseca, D., Martí, N.: Relationship between learning indicators in the development and result of the building engineering degree final project. In: ACM International Conference Proceeding Series, pp. 335–340 (2016). https://doi.org/10.1145/3012430.3012537
13. Iglesias-Sánchez, P.P., Jambrino-Maldonado, C., de las Heras-Pedrosa, C.: Training entrepreneurial competences with open innovation paradigm in higher education. Sustain (2019). https://doi.org/10.3390/su11174689
14. Abelha, M., Fernandes, S., Mesquita, D., Seabra, F., Ferreira-Oliveira, A.T.: Graduate employability and competence development in higher education-a systematic literature review using PRISMA. Sustain **12**(15), 5900 (2020). https://doi.org/10.3390/SU12155900

15. Wagenaar, R.: Competences and learning outcomes: a panacea for understanding the (new) role of Higher Education? Tuning. J. High. Educ. **1**(2), 279–302 (2014).
16. Asonitou, S., Hassall, T.: Which skills and competences to develop in accountants in a country in crisis? Int. J. Manag. Educ. **17**(3), 100308 (2019). https://doi.org/10.1016/j.ijme.2019.100308
17. Barkley, E., Cross, K.P., Major, C.H.: Técnicas didácticas de colaboración: manual para profesores universitarios. Ulacit (2005)
18. Villa, A., Poblete, M.: Aprendizaje basado en competencias. Una propuesta para la evaluación de las competencias genéricas. Editorial Mensajero, Bilbao (2007)
19. de Deusto, U.: Teamwork Competence Assessment. https://www.deusto.es/cs/Satellite/deusto/es/modelo-de-formacion-de-la-universidad-dedeusto/documento?i=1340094971726. Accessed 15 Jan 2021
20. Mikkelson, A.C., York, J.A., Arritola, J.: Communication competence, leadership behaviors, and employee outcomes in supervisor-employee relationships. Bus. Commun. Q. **78**(3), 336–354 (2015). https://doi.org/10.1177/2329490615588542
21. Kahu, E.R., Nelson, K.: Student engagement in the educational interface: understanding the mechanisms of student success. High. Educ. Res. Dev. **37**(1), 58–71 (2018). https://doi.org/10.1080/07294360.2017.1344197
22. Bunce, D.M., Flens, E.A., Neiles, K.Y.: How long can students pay attention in class? A study of student attention decline using clickers. J. Chem. Educ. **87**(12), 1438–1443 (2010). https://doi.org/10.1021/ed100409p
23. Freeman, S., Eddy, S.L., McDonough, M., Smith, M.K., Okoroafor, N., Jordt, H., Wenderoth, M.P.: Active learning increases student performance in science, engineering, and mathematics. Proc. Natl. Acad. Sci. U. S. A. **111**(23), 8410 (2014). https://doi.org/10.1073/pnas.1319030111
24. Partanen, L.: How student-centred teaching in quantum chemistry affects students' experiences of learning and motivation - a self-determination theory perspective. Chem. Educ. Res. Pract. **21**(1), 79–94 (2020). https://doi.org/10.1039/c9rp00036d
25. Jones, B.D.: Motivating Students by Design: Practical Strategies for Professors. CreateSpace, Charleston (2018)
26. Jones, B.D.: Motivating students to engage in learning : the music model of academic motivation. Int. J. Teach. Learn. High. Educ. (2009)
27. Romero, S., Aláez, M., Amo, D., Fonseca, D.: Systematic review of how engineering schools around the world are deploying the 2030 agenda. Sustainability **12**(12), 5035 (2020)
28. Centeno, E., et al.: A comparative study of the application of lesson study in different university learning environments. In: Zaphiris, P., Ioannou, A. (eds.) Learning and Collaboration Technologies. Designing, Developing and Deploying Learning Experiences, pp. 425–441. Springer International Publishing, Cham (2020)
29. Fonseca, D., et al.: Evaluación mixta de actividades transversales en el grado de Arquitectura basadas en la metodología de la "Lesson Study." In: de Madrid, U.P. (ed.) Proceedings of CINAIC 2019 - Congreso Internacional sobre Aprendizaje, Innovación y Cooperación. pp. 331–336, Madrid (2019). https://doi.org/10.26754/CINAIC.2019.00071

Usability of Learning Management Systems for Instructors – The Case of Canvas

Weiqin Chen[✉], Norun C. Sanderson, Anna Nichshyk,
Way Kiat Bong, and Siri Kessel

Oslo Metropolitan University (OsloMet), P.O. Box 4,
St. Olavs Plass, 0130 Oslo, Norway
{weiche,nsand,annani,wayki,sirik}@oslomet.no

Abstract. The past 30 years have seen increased adoption of learning management systems (LMSs) in education. Several studies have investigated the usability of LMSs for students. However, very few studies have assessed the usability from the instructors' perspective. Usability issues can pose challenges for instructors who use LMSs to create, manage and deliver courses. These challenges require instructors to spend extra time and energy on tackling the challenges rather on teaching-related tasks, which will have negative impacts on learners' experiences and learning outcomes. This paper aims to identify usability challenges in LMSs for instructors. We used Canvas as an example and conducted user testing with 35 university instructors in computer science and engineering disciplines. Pre- and post-interviews were transcribed and analyzed together with the observation data during their use of Canvas to carry out tasks. The results show that, although Canvas has made continuous efforts to improve its usability, instructors still face some usability challenges. Instructors are a diverse user group for LMSs. Further research should consider recruiting participants from other disciplines and investigating other LMSs to identify possibilities for improving general usability of digital tools for instructors.

Keywords: Learning management system (LMS) · Usability · Instructor · Canvas

1 Introduction

Learning management systems (LMSs) are widely used for creating, administrating, delivering courses and learning materials, not only in higher educational institutions, but also in schools and companies for employee training purposes. LMSs provide tools and functions such as course management, online group chats and discussions, documents (e.g., lecture material, homework, and assignments), PowerPoint presentations, and video clips uploading, grading, and course evaluations to support teaching and learning [1]. LMSs hold the promise of increased efficiency of teaching and enriched student learning and are having and will increasingly have profound impacts on teaching and learning [2]. The increase in digital learning is driving the adoption of LMSs. According

P. Zaphiris and A. Ioannou (Eds.): HCII 2021, LNCS 12784, pp. 210–223, 2021.
https://doi.org/10.1007/978-3-030-77889-7_14

to a recent report,[1] the LMS market is expected to grow at a compound annual growth rate (CAGR) of 20.5% from 2019 to 2025 to reach USD 28.1 billion by 2025.

The increasing complexity of LMS functions and interaction possibilities has raised concerns among researchers regarding the quality of the interface and the ways in which activities are performed by students and instructors in these systems [3]. After reviewing usability evaluation methods in usability for e-learning platforms, Freire et al. [3] stated that the perspective of the user, not of the system, should be focused on when evaluating usability of LMSs.

Several studies have investigated the usability of LMSs for students [4–6], including commercially available products such as Blackboard, Desire2Learn, open source LMSs such as Moodle, Sakai, and custom-made LMSs developed for specific institutions or organizations. Most recently, Alhadreti [7] conducted a comparative usability study of Blackboard and Desire2Learn with 20 students who were first-time users of LMSs at one university. The findings show that that usability problems in navigation, layout, content, and functionality were found in both systems, although Blackboard has more severe usability issues than Desire2Learn.

Usability issues can pose challenges for instructors who use LMSs to create, manage and deliver courses. If left unaddressed, these challenges will affect their experience negatively and require them to spend extra time and energy on tackling the challenges rather than on teaching-related tasks. However, very few studies have assessed usability of LMSs from the instructors' perspective [8]. The usability challenges for instructors also have indirect impacts on learners' satisfaction and learning experiences. For example, Leone et al. [9] studied students' perceptions of usefulness and usability of two LMSs (Moodle and Sakai) at two universities. Based on the analysis of data from focus groups and usage log data from both students and instructors, they conclude that when an instructor knows how to use LMSs, students are more satisfied and have a better learning experience.

This paper aims to identify and understand usability challenges in LMSs for instructors. We used Canvas as an example and conducted user testing with 35 university instructors. Canvas is one of the most popular learning management systems, with more than 30 million global users by 2019.[2] It is also one of the LMS platforms recommended for higher education institutions in Norway.

2   Related Research

Studies that focus on the instructors' perspectives mostly concern acceptance of LMSs [1, 10] and motivating factors for faculty members' acceptance and use of LMSs [11, 12]. Focusing on the newly introduced Canvas LMS, Fathema et al. [1] collected survey data from 560 individuals with teaching responsibilities at two universities. The results indicated that system quality of LMS (usability, availability, reliability,

---

[1] Learning management system (LMS) market report by Meticulous Research: https://www.meticulou sresearch.com/product/learning-management-system-market-5052.

[2] Our Story | Instructure: https://www.instructure.com/about/our-story.

adaptability and response time) has significant impacts on perceived usefulness, perceived ease of use, and on faculty attitudes toward LMS use. Fathema and Sutton [10] also collected recommendations for Blackboard in their survey of 100 individuals with teaching responsibilities. Many respondents identified design issues in Blackboard, including poor interface design, lack of flexibility and complexity of features.

Although usability has been identified as one of the most important factors that affect instructors' acceptance of and motivation to use LMSs, very little research has focused on usability of LMSs for instructors. Phongphaew and Jiamsanguanwong [13] conducted a usability evaluation of myCourseVille, a custom-made LMS, focusing on the interfaces for both students and instructors at one university. The participants were three students and five instructors. In the interface for instructors, they found diverse usability issues, such as too small font size, confusing/ambiguous icons, too much information and too many options. Lalande and Grewal [14] studied two LMSs (Desire2Learn and Blackboard) from the administrators' perspective. In their study they collected quantitative data including number of mouse clicks, pages traversed, and data fields inputted based on 14 administrative tasks performed by one of the authors. The tasks included user creation, user enrolment, user management, course creation, course transportability, semester/team management and department management. Although Desire2Learn was found to require fewer mouse clicks and pages than Blackboard, the study identified usability challenges for administrators in both LMSs.

3   Method

In this study we conducted user testing of Canvas with pre- and post- interviews to understand the difficulties and challenges instructors met when performing tasks.

3.1   Participants and Data Collection

Participants were mainly recruited through emails to members of faculties in computer sciences and engineering subjects. We argue that instructors in computer science and engineering faculties are expected to have higher levels of digital competence than those in other disciplines and are therefore better equipped to understand, learn and use digital tools in teaching.

We recruited 35 participants (P1–P35) from two countries: 17 instructors (one female and 16 male) in Poland, mainly from computer science and electronic engineering subjects, and 18 instructors (five female and 13 male) in Norway, mainly from computer science and complementary subjects. Table 1 presents details of the participants. Five participants (one in Norway and four in Poland) had no experience of LMSs as instructors, but four of them had used LMSs as students. All the other participants used the LMSs configured by their universities. Only two had experience with Canvas, one as an instructor and the other as a student.

Table 1. Participants in user testing

Country	Number	Age (Mean ± SD)	Years of ICT use (Mean ± SD)	Years of LMS use (Mean ± SD)
Poland	17	36 ± 7	22 ± 5	5 ± 2
Norway	18	43 ± 11	27 ± 6	8 ± 6

After introducing the study, each participant was asked to sign a consent form and complete a pre-interview focusing on demographic information, experience in teaching and particularly online teaching, and experience in using learning management systems. After the pre-interview, each participant was asked to perform a set of pre-prepared tasks in Canvas.

- adding a module to a course
- publishing course material
- creating and publishing a quiz
- adding an announcement
- creating and publishing an assignment
- creating and publishing a discussion forum

The areas/tools in Canvas that were necessary to do these tasks were Announcement, Assignment, Discussion, Module, and Quiz. The built-in Text editor is used in all of these except Module.

The participants were encouraged to think aloud, and observation notes were taken on how they carried out the tasks, whether they were successful, on any difficulties they faced, and on hints given to the participants during the tasks. The post-interview aimed to better understand the participants' experiences of Canvas and to identify key issues and possibilities to address them. All the interviews were audio-recorded and transcribed verbatim. The audio recordings were deleted immediately after they were transcribed. All collected data were anonymized before analysis.

3.2 Data Analysis

The analysis of observation notes and post-interviews focused on identifying usability issues experienced by participants and where in the Canvas platform and in which tasks these issues were encountered, as well as on identifying any additional challenges the participants mentioned or experienced. Any positive and negative statements from participants concerning their experiences with Canvas tools were also noted.

Jacob Nielsen's 10 usability heuristics[3] were used for categorizing usability issues. In addition, other issues mentioned in the post-interviews that are not covered by these heuristics, such as accessibility issues related to contrast and use of colors, and those related to novice user experiences, were summarized as additional challenges.

---

[3] 10 Usability Heuristics for User Interface Design: https://www.nngroup.com/articles/ten-usability-heuristics/.

4 Results

Although most of the participants had not used Canvas before, they were able to carry out most of the tasks. However, our study also revealed usability challenges.

4.1 Usability Issues by Heuristics

In the following sections we will provide details of the challenges and usability issues categorized based on the usability heuristics.

Heuristic 1: Visibility of System Status. This heuristic concerns showing users correct information about the system status and whether the user receives appropriate and timely feedback on system status, for example after s/he has performed an action, such as selecting a menu item or clicking on a button. One issue related to the visibility of system status that was encountered by the participants was that the font size menu item does not reflect the actual font size for the selected text in the Text editor. A few users also expressed feeling uncertain about the results of their actions:

"In some moments I was confused that maybe my actions didn't do what I expected" (P13).

Heuristic 2: Match Between System and the Real World. This heuristic deals with how the system parallels the real world, including the familiarity of concepts, symbols and terms used and whether information appears in an order that is natural or logical to the user. The user testing showed that many participants, when creating a quiz, seemed puzzled at having to configure quiz details before they could add questions, which often is considered the main purpose of creating a quiz.

"When I create a quiz, I expect to create a quiz and it is to create questions, not change the settings. The settings, in my workflow, would come last, and they in some ways are kind of optional." (P18)

Another issue many participants expressed confusion about was the use of the plus (+) symbol for adding or creating a new item such as a new module or assignment, or for adding an element to a module. This plus sign is sometimes used together with the name of what is to be created, as in "+Module" or "+Quiz", and sometimes alone ("+") for adding new elements to a module. Several participants found this confusing.

"This '+' symbol does not exactly tell you what... what it does. Like, for me I don't know what it does, and why it is different from '+Module'" (P18)

When using the Text editor in rich text mode, a line below the editor window displays information about the HTML tag for the text item where the cursor is at in the editor. For example, "p" indicates a paragraph and "h2" indicates a level 2 heading. Some participants who were unfamiliar with HTML found this information confusing.

"This letter "p" was very confusing because I didn't know what it meant." (P13)

Heuristic 3: User Control and Freedom. Enabling users to go back a step to where they were previously, and providing options for undoing or cancelling their actions can promote a feeling of control and freedom. Canvas offers users these options and clicking the browser's back button works well. It also offers "breadcrumbs" at the top of the page to support easy navigation, and observation notes from the user testing show that many users used these breadcrumbs for navigating back to the main course page. The notes, however, also show that many users did not easily find their way back to the main page of the course from, for example, editing a module element. A few participants expressed in the post-interview that they found it difficult to move from a tool, such as Announcement or Assignment, back to the main course page.

"It was a bit confusing, how to get back to the main page." (P32)

Heuristic 4: Consistency and Standards. Following standards and ensuring consistency with external systems as well as ensuring consistency internally between the different parts (user interfaces) of the system can make it easier to use and learn, since the user can recognize features and ways of doing things from other systems or other parts of the same system. Overall, Canvas was considered easy to use by most of the participants, suggesting adherence with established conventions, but many also encountered difficulties. For example, when selecting a date for a deadline or a time for publishing, e.g., an assignment, many were unfamiliar with having to click "Done" after selecting the date, which some commented that they did not have to do in another system they often used.

"During the picking of the date, ... I assumed that the window would close after choosing the date, because this is how the calendar in Windows, for example, works." (P13)

Many also clearly expected to be able to create an announcement as an element in a module by using the plus button, as they would do to add a quiz or an assignment. However, creating an announcement can only be done via the course main menu, which can seem inconsistent, especially for novices unfamiliar with the Canvas concepts and terminology.

When moving a module element using drag and drop, many also expected to be able to do this from anywhere on the element (listed in the module), but this can only be done via a symbol/icon showing two vertical lines of dots on the far left in the element.

"When I was moving items under the modules, there was only one special place on the left where I should click and then drag the mouse. I expected that it would be available on the whole area of the item." (P13)

Heuristic 5: Error Prevention. Helping users avoid making mistakes through warnings or through the design is another important aspect of usability, and can spare users much frustration in cases where they risk losing the work they have done. In Canvas, users risk losing their updates to questions in a quiz. After users have changed one or more questions, the system does not require them to click on "Update question" before saving. Instead, they can select "Save" or "Save and publish", which does not save the changes to the questions. No warning is given about losing these changes by clicking "Save". Several participants experienced this issue during the user testing, and some also commented on it in the post-interviews.

"It was quite good, except when the question disappeared, when I saved, so there should be some kind of warning." (P32)

Heuristic 6: Recognition Rather than Recall. Canvas has a graphical interface with visible menus and icons that can be recognized by returning users and is to some extent recognizable for users familiar with similar systems. For example, the Text editor in Canvas uses icons commonly used in most text editors, e.g., "B" for bold text, in addition to menus. The various areas/tools in Canvas have similar layout and can be operated in much the same manner, which promotes recognition rather than recall. Furthermore, since all but two of the participants were new to Canvas, we did not find any issues related to this heuristic.

Heuristic 7: Flexibility and Efficiency of Use. Canvas offers some flexibility in use and many options, as well as some use of accelerators (shortcut keys), promising relatively efficient use for a returning user. The use of common accelerators in the Text editor is one example of supporting efficiency of use. Another example is that the user has opportunity to create, e.g., a quiz or an assignment directly when adding a module item via the Module "plus" button, or alternatively creating them via the course main menu, in which case they would not be linked to a specific module. There were no indications in the user testing or the post-interviews of participants missing anything regarding flexibility or support for efficient use. Some participants did however comment that they were a little uncertain about which alternative to use in two of the tasks where they were asked to create and publish respectively a quiz and an assignment. This may be related to the fact that almost all the participants were new to Canvas and had not experienced the many different options Canvas offers. We therefore did not find any issues related to this heuristic.

Heuristic 8: Aesthetic and Minimalist Design. This heuristic concerns reducing the user's cognitive load by focusing the design and content on what is necessary for the intended purpose of the interface, while simultaneously having an appealing design. Canvas offers many useful functionalities and options to the user. The instructor can control what course menu items are visible to the students, but all options and course menu items are available to the instructor. Novices can find this overwhelming. The observation notes from the user testing indicated some participants spent much time trying to find certain functions, and several expressed sometimes having difficulties in orienting themselves in Canvas and that the layout did not help much in this respect.

"Some things are hard to figure out from the layout." (P20)

"It was difficult to find where to go ... it was... everything looks alike, the same." (P27)

Heuristic 9: Help Users Recognize, Diagnose, and Recover from Errors. Communicating clearly and understandably to the user that an error has occurred and what the problem is, as well as offering guidance to recover from the error, can be of great help to the user and avoid moments of user uncertainty and frustration. Overall, error messages in Canvas are communicated relatively clearly and in plain language, but some participants found that the error messages were not descriptive enough for them to understand what the problem was or what they needed to do to recover from it. In addition, a few participants experienced situations where no error message appeared in cases where this would have been expected, particularly where the user tried to select "Add item" before selecting the "New..." field (in Page, Quiz, etc.).

Heuristic 10: Help and Documentation. The Canvas community[4] provides good documentation in the form of guides and help for troubleshooting. However, the

---

[4] The Canvas Community: https://community.canvaslms.com/t5/Canvas/ct-p/canvas.

Canvas interface itself provides no help buttons or tooltips for users except in Text editor, indicating very little proactive help. The tasks in the user testing did not specifically address documentation or availability of help while using the interface, but it seems clear that some of the issues that were experienced by users related to understanding the meaning of symbols/icons and terminology, and that some activities, such as moving a module element or adding an announcement, could have benefitted from some context-relevant help in the interface.

4.2   Summary of Usability Issues Identified in User Testing and Post-Interviews

Table 2 provides an overview of the number of issues that occurred during the testing tasks and that were highlighted by participants during the post-interviews per usability heuristic.

Table 2. Number of issues identified in user testing and post-interviews related to the 10 heuristics.

Heuristics	Number of issues in user testing	Number of issues post-interviews
1. Visibility of system status	3	1
2. Match between system and the real world	17	32
3. User control and freedom	1	2
4. Consistency and standards	12	39
5. Error prevention	3	3
6. Recognition rather than recall	0	0
7. Flexibility and efficiency of use	0	0
8. Aesthetic and minimalist design	0	6
9. Help users recognize, diagnose, and recover from errors	2	0
10. Help and documentation	1	0

Most issues the participants encountered while performing the tasks were related to expectations of where to find tools or how to use tools, such as where to create an announcement, or how to edit a module item. Their expectations were often based on their experience with other, similar (LMS) platforms, indicating a possible breach with conventions for such platforms. As the majority (33 of 35) of the participants were new to the Canvas platform, we did not find any issues in Heuristic 6, recognition versus recall, and Heuristic 7, flexibility and efficiency in use.

Considering which areas/tools in Canvas the participants reported difficulties (Fig. 1), the results from the user testing and post-interviews indicate that most of the issues were related to the interface in general ("General"), such as moving between tools, locating tools, or functions or information, and editing modules ("Module") such as adding new items to a module or rearranging the order of items in a module. Comments on the general layout of Canvas or on several tools, or that participants did not specifically relate to a tool or area, were also included in the General category. Many also mentioned that they expected to be able to add an announcement as an element to a module using the plus icon instead of having to use the course main menu. Other Canvas areas/tools where participants mentioned experiencing difficulties include Quiz, Assignment, Text editor, and Discussions. The user testing indicated many experienced problems with the Quiz tool, especially when creating a Quiz. One example is that the area for the settings is shown before the questions area, so they had to locate and click on the questions tab before they could add any questions, which many experienced as confusing. They also had to click on "Update question" before saving the Quiz, which were not communicated clearly in the interface. Assignment and Announcement were other tools where many participants experienced difficulties during user testing.

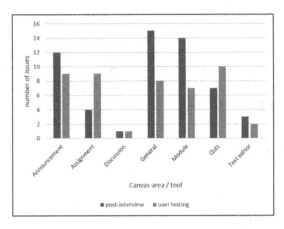

Fig. 1. Overview of relevant Canvas area/tool and number of identified usability issues in user testing and post-interviews.

Relating the areas/tools in Canvas and the number of reported difficulties to relevant usability heuristics (Fig. 2 and Fig. 3), it appears that many issues are related to how the system matches the real world (Heuristic 2), such as unfamiliarity with the symbols and terminology and with some of the Canvas concepts. Although the "+" symbol is well known from mathematics to mean addition of two numbers, and probably well known to the participants, the use of this symbol in the Canvas context to mean the adding of a new module item, seemed unfamiliar to participants, and some had to spend more time trying to figure out how to add module items. Some concepts in Canvas, such as Module, were found difficult to understand. This may however have been influenced by the fact that none of the participants' institutions are located in English-speaking countries and that, consequently, all participants were to some extent unfamiliar with concepts and terms commonly used in educational settings in English-speaking countries.

Many also encountered and reported difficulties finding where to add an Announcement, which is not an element that can be added to a Module, such as an Assignment or a Quiz, and could only be reached through the course main menu. This can be attributed to internal consistency (Heuristic 4), but is also most probably influenced by the participants' previous experiences of similar systems, suggesting a possible lack of external consistency with similar platforms (Heuristic 4) and perhaps a lack of understanding of the "Module" concept (Heuristic 2). It is also worth bearing in mind that this was the very first time most of the participants used Canvas, and that this most probably influenced the number of issues identified and reported in the user testing and post-interviews.

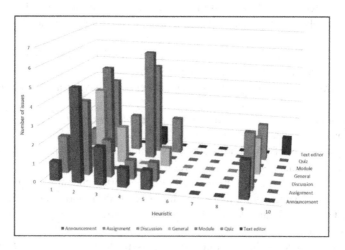

Fig. 2. Overview of issues related to heuristic for each relevant Canvas area/tool (from user testing).

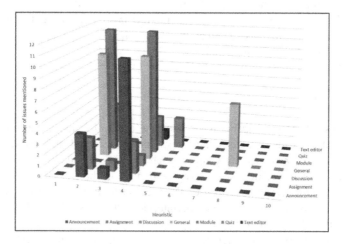

Fig. 3. Overview of issues related to heuristic for each relevant Canvas area/tool (from post-interviews).

4.3   Additional Usability Issues and Participants' Opinions

Other issues mentioned by participants in the post-interviews were mainly related to font size, colors used, and the contrast of text. Although influencing the usability of the system, their comments concerning difficulties perceiving the text were clearly related to accessibility.

"Everything is white here, so maybe it will be better if some parts will be ... contrast, I guess." (P11)

"I had a little problem viewing it. I would have needed more contrast, or maybe a larger font size." (P34)

Some participants also reported that they considered the difficulties they encountered to be related to not having used Canvas before, such as general difficulties in orienting themselves in Canvas, and that it would be easier once they had had more time to learn.

"It was the first time. I think it would be easier after I try it for sometimes, because it was easier at the end, when I had used it." (P31)

In the post-interviews only one participant reported having a negative (*"frustrating"*) experience with Canvas.

"Frustrating, yes, because I have never seen it before, and every program has a different, you know... way to do it." (P27)

The majority (28 of 35) reported aspects which they found positive while using Canvas. Some participants (6 of 35) expressed neither positive nor negative opinions. Fewer than one third of the participants (10 of 35) reported encountering no difficulties at all during user testing, while more than half (24 of 35) reported encountering some difficulties. One participant did not clearly state whether s/he experienced any difficulties using Canvas.

When asked whether they would use Canvas in their courses, about half of the participants (16 of 35) stated clearly that they would, only one participant stated clearly that s/he would not, while more than half (18 of 35) were uncertain or said they would only use it for parts of their course or that it would depend on certain aspects not covered in the user testing, such as handling grading tasks, attendance, functionality for communicating with students, whether it was required by their university, and data security and encryption requirements.

5   Discussion

Although most of the participants were first-time users of Canvas, they were able to perform the tasks without many challenges. They considered possibilities for more interactive activities provided by Canvas, such as quizzes and discussions, as interesting and potentially useful. The majority responded in the post-interviews that they found Canvas intuitive and easy to use. This demonstrates that Canvas has generally good usability. However, observations and interviews have also shown that participants encountered usability challenges.

The teaching is organized differently in Canvas compared with the LMSs they were familiar with. The differences resulted in a mismatch between the participants' expectations and what Canvas actually offers, particularly in terms of terminology and the workflow for organizing teaching. For example, participants found it confusing having to configure quiz details before adding questions because such workflow in Canvas is different from that they use in their own teaching practice or in LMSs they have previously used. Several participants expected Announcements to come under Module, not directly under Course. Although most of the participants were able to adapt quickly to the new way of organizing teaching in Canvas, some after receiving hints, we found that some were unable to adapt, even after receiving hints and guidance from the researchers. One participant who had used another LMS for many years was found to have the most difficulties during testing. While it is natural for instructors to draw on their previous experience of LMSs when faced with a new LMS, intuitive design of and training in a new LMS is important for instructors to be able to quickly adjust to and accept it [15, 16].

Usability issues in LMSs experienced by instructors and a lack of training can result in extra time and effort being required of instructors. This extra workload also contributes to the low motivation to actively use LMSs [17]. Our study was conducted after the Norwegian universities decided to migrate from an old LMS to Canvas. Instructors needed to reorganize their teaching according to the new workflow in Canvas. Some instructors had a negative attitude towards Canvas during the transition period and tried to defend the old LMS rather than embrace the new one. Although most LMSs, including Canvas, provide possibilities for active teaching and learning in an interactive learning environment, many instructors consider LMSs a delivery mechanism for posting teaching plans, assignments, and teaching materials and resources. LMSs are rarely used as an integrated pedagogical tool for engaging students in active learning [18]. In addition to the complexity of LMSs and to usability issues, lack of facilitation such as training and technical support often result in instructors having to spend extra time on learning and solving technical problems, when they would prefer to spend that time on activities more closely related to teaching the subjects. This has led to negative attitudes towards LMSs [1]. More and more digital tools, including LMSs, are deployed in educational institutions, particularly during the COVID-19 pandemic. When making decisions on which digital tools instructors should use, have institutions considered the usability of the tools? Have instructors been involved in the decision-making process? Have institutions provided adequate training to instructors before instructors must use the new tools? The answers to such questions have implications for instructors' acceptance and use of digital tools and impact the effective implementation of these tools in educational institutions [15, 16].

The participants in our study provided some contradictory comments and feedback. For example, some responded that they were overwhelmed by the many options and menu items in Canvas, while others considered this a positive feature. Instructors are a diverse user group of LMSs with different abilities, experience, preferences, usage styles, and levels of digital competence and skills. This diversity calls for adaptive or individualized configuration. The one-size-fits-all approach adopted by educational institutions, where the whole institution has the same configuration of an LMS, is unable to address these differences. Making use of artificial intelligence and data analytics approaches to provide personalization and just-in-time support that adapt to individual instructor's needs, preferences and usage profiles may provide instructors with more engaging experiences of LMSs [19].

6 Conclusion and Future Work

Although Canvas has made continuous efforts to improve its usability, instructors still face some usability challenges. Our study and other related research have shown that learning management systems in general have usability problems which create difficulties for instructors and affect their user experience.

Usability issues are considered one of the main factors that impede the comprehensive adoption of LMSs among instructors [1]. For LMSs to be used to their fullest capacity, it is essential that they be designed with high levels of usability for the diversity of users, including students, instructors and administrators. The participants in our study were limited to computer science and engineering disciplines, which may hinder the generalizability of the results. Further research should consider recruiting participants from other disciplines and study other educational tools and platforms to identify possibilities for improving general usability of digital tools for instructors.

Some usability issues can only be identified after having used the system for some time. For example, when copy and pasting text from outside Canvas to Canvas Text editor, the font type information will disappear. Nearly all the instructors participating in our study were first-time users of Canvas, and the tasks they carried out during the testing were limited to those most commonly in their normal working practice. Thus, the range of usability issues found in our study is limited. Future research should consider longitudinal study allowing instructors to use a LMS for a longer period in order to fully understand the usability challenges.

Acknowledgements. The authors would like to thank all participants in this study. The project is funded by Faculty of Technology, Art, and Design at Oslo Metropolitan University.

References

1. Fathema, N., Shannon, D., Ross, M.: Expanding the technology acceptance model (TAM) to examine faculty use of learning management systems (LMSs) in higher education institutions. J. Online Learn. Teach. **11**, 210–232 (2015)
2. Coates, H., James, R., Baldwin, G.: A critical examination of the effects of learning management systems on university teaching and learning. Tert. Educ. Manage. **11**, 19–36 (2005)
3. Freire, L.L., Arezes, P.M., Campos, J.C.: A literature review about usability evaluation methods for e-learning platforms. Work **41**, 1038–1044 (2012)
4. Goh, W.W., Hong, J.L., Gunawan, W.: Exploring students' perceptions of learning management system: an empirical study based on TAM. In: Proceedings of the IEEE International Conference on Teaching, Assessment and Learning for Engineering (TALE), pp. 367–372 (2013)

5. Nakamura, W.T., Oliveira, E.H.T., Conte, T.: Usability and user experience evaluation of learning management systems: a systematic mapping study. In: Proceedings of the 19th International Conference on Enterprise Information Systems (ICEIS), pp. 97–109 (2017)
6. Orfanou, K., Tselios, N., Katsanos, C.: Perceived usability evaluation of learning management systems: empirical evaluation of the system usability scale. Int. Rev. Res. Open Distrib. Learn. **16**, 227–246 (2015)
7. Alhadreti, O.: A comparative usability study of blackboard and Desire2Learn: students' perspective. In: Zaphiris, P., Ioannou, A. (eds.) HCII 2020. LNCS, vol. 12205, pp. 3–19. Springer, Cham (2020). https://doi.org/10.1007/978-3-030-50513-4_1
8. Alturki, U., Aldraiweesh, A., Kinshuck.: Evaluating the usability and accessibility of LMS "Blackboard" at King Saud University. Contemp. Issues Educ. Res. **9**, 33–44 (2016)
9. Leone, R., Mesquita, C., Lopes, R.: Use of Learning Management System (LMS): a study in a brazilian and portuguese universities. In: Proceedings of the 12th International Conference on Computer Supported Education (CSEDU), vol. 2, pp. 352–358 (2020)
10. Fathema, N., Sutton, K.: Factors influencing faculty members' learning management systems adoption behavior: an analysis using the technology acceptance model. Int. J. Trends Econ. Manage. Technol. **2**, 20–28 (2013)
11. Garrote, R., Pettersson, T.: Lecturers' attitudes about the use of learning management systems in engineering education: a Swedish case study. Australas. J. Educ. Technol. **23**, 327–349 (2007)
12. Gautreau, C.: Motivational factors affecting the integration of a learning management system by faculty. J. Educators Online **8**, 1–25 (2011)
13. Phongphaew, N., Jiamsanguanwong, A.: Usability evaluation on learning management system. In: Ahram, T., Falcão, C. (eds.) International Conference on Applied Human Factors and Ergonomics (AHFE), pp. 39–48. Springer, Cham (2018)
14. Lalande, N., Grewal, R.: Blackboard vs. Desire2Learn: a system administrator's perspective on usability. In: Proceedings of the International Conference on Education and E-Learning Innovations, pp. 1–4. IEEE (2012)
15. Ge, X., Lubin, I., Zhang, K.: An investigation of faculty's perceptions and experiences when transitioning to a new learning management system. Knowl. Manage. E-Learning Int. J. **2**, 433–447 (2010)
16. Ryan, T., Toye, M., Charron, K., Park, G.: Learning management system migration: an analysis of stakeholder perspectives. Int. Rev. Res. Open Distance Learn. **13**, 220–237 (2012)
17. Weaver, D., Spratt, C., Nair, C.S.: Academic and student use of a learning management system: implications for quality. Australas. J. Educ. Technol. **24** (2008)
18. Rhode, J., Richter, S., Gowen, P., Miller, T., Wills, C.: Understanding faculty use of the learning management system. Online Learn. **21**, 68–86 (2017)
19. Eden Dahlstrom, D., Brooks, C., Bichsel, J.: The Current Ecosystem of Learning Management Systems in Higher Education: Student, Faculty, and IT Perspectives. Research report, EDUCAUSE Center for Analysis and Research (ECAR) (2014)

Goals Matter: Changes in Metacognitive Judgments and Their Relation to Motivation and Learning with an Intelligent Tutoring System

Elizabeth B. Cloude[1]([⊠]) [iD], Franz Wortha[2], Megan D. Wiedbusch[1] [iD],
and Roger Azevedo[1]

[1] Department of Learning Sciences and Educational Research,
University of Central Florida, Orlando, FL 32816, USA
{elizabeth.cloude,meganwiedbusch}@knights.ucf.edu,
roger.azevedo@ucf.edu
[2] Department of Psychology, University of Greifswald,
Franz-Mehring-Str. 47, 17489 Greifswald, Germany
franz.wortha@uni-greifswald.de

Abstract. Research suggests metacognition enhances performance with emerging technologies (e.g., intelligent tutoring systems [ITSs]), where learning goals guide metacognitive processes (e.g., judgments of learning and feelings of knowing). A growing body of evidence has found significant relationships between motivation, metacognitive process use, and performance with ITSs. Yet, most studies do not define metacognition based on its relevance to achieving a learning goal (or multiple learning goals). In this study, we examined 186 undergraduates' multimodal data captured during learning with an ITS called MetaTutor to analyze whether the stability of change in the proportion of metacognitive judgments initiated on pages containing information relevant to achieving either learning goals 1 or 2. Latent growth curves suggested that the stability of page-irrelevant metacognitive judgments from the first to second learning goal was positively related to performance, but there were no relations between achievement goal orientation. We describe implications for contextualizing metacognition to the model of metamemory and multiple learning goals with an ITSs. Future research utilizing this method could provide insight into designing effective interventions based on what personally motivates learners to engage in metacognition to augment their learning and performance with emerging technologies.

Keywords: Metacognition · Motivation · Intelligent tutoring systems

Supported by the National Science Foundation and the Social Sciences and Humanities Research Council of Canada.

P. Zaphiris and A. Ioannou (Eds.): HCII 2021, LNCS 12784, pp. 224–238, 2021.
https://doi.org/10.1007/978-3-030-77889-7_15

1   Introduction

Self-regulated learning (SRL) is critical for improving performance across a variety of settings and emerging technologies (e.g., intelligent tutoring systems [ITSs]) [1,9,32]. There is agreement among the scientific community that metacognition resides at the heart of SRL [1,8–10]. A metamemory framework by [11] (see Fig. 1) is commonly used to explain the dynamics of metacognition to study its relation to learning and performance with ITSs [1]. This framework assumes learners initiate metacognition, i.e., monitoring and controlling cognitive processes, in service of learning goals [11]. Further, one could easily argue that learning including metacognition is an innately goal-driven process and goal pursuit is directly related to motivation (e.g., achievement goal orientation), suggesting that motivation and/or learning goals steer metacognition during learning with ITSs [3,4,14]. However, few studies examine metacognition based on its relevance to motivation or a learning goal (or multiple learning goals; i.e., does the learners' metacognition relate to achieving learning goals presented within the learning environment?) *during* a learning session using multimodal data, illustrating major gaps in our understanding of metacognition with ITSs.

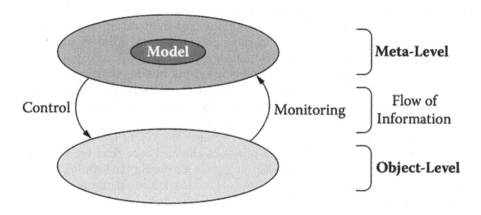

Fig. 1. Model of metamemory [11].

1.1   Related Work

Motivation refers to the act of both initiating and sustaining behaviors [18,19]. The model of metamemory [11] emphasizes that before learning can occur, two components must take place in the learner: (1) determining a goal and (2) formulating a plan to achieve that goal. A number of studies find significant relationships between metacognition, motivation, and performance [3–7,12]. A study by [4] found the degree to which learners engaged in metacognition during learning with an ITS was significantly related to their achievement goal orientation–a construct of motivation that describes how a learner is oriented toward achieving a goal [13]. While results did not suggest significant relationships between performance and achievement goal orientation, the time and frequency of engaging in metacognitive processes such as judgments of learning and feelings of knowing were significantly related to achievement goal orientation and performance, potentially suggesting these constructs may have a complex interacting relationship. Similar results were found by [3]. They examined relationships between achievement goal orientation and performance that were related to two learning goals set during a learning session with an ITS. Their findings suggested there were significant differences in performance related to the first learning goal set during the session between achievement goal orientations; but, their models did not reveal significant differences in performance related to the second learning goal. These findings suggest that there may have been changes in achievement goal orientation after completing the first learning goal. Conversely, they did not find significant relationships between achievement goal orientations and the frequency of using metacognitive processes with an ITS [3].

The mixed findings in literature regarding relationships between motivation, metacognition, and performance may be a result of fluctuating motivation over the course of learning with an ITS. For example, if achievement goal orientation was measured prior to learning, then learners would have been placed into a particular orientation that may no longer be relevant to their orientation during the learning activity. Additional limitations exist in literature as few studies define metacognition in relation to learning goals (e.g., is the learner initiating metacognitive judgment to gauge their understanding of the circulatory system?) or the context in which they are used, missing key information that could illuminate the complex and potentially interacting relationships between motivation, metacognition, and performance with emerging technologies. In this study, we sought to address these gaps by defining metacognition based on its relevance to two learning goals during learning an ITS called MetaTutor [2]. We examined if and to what extent metacognitive processes changed over time based on its relevance to achieving the first two learning goals set during the learning session and examined its relation to achievement goal orientation and performance using latent growth curve analysis.

1.2   Current Study

In the current study, we addressed the issues highlighted above by examining page-relevant and page-irrelevant metacognitive processes across learning goals 1 and 2 during learning about the human circulatory system with MetaTutor, an ITS. Specifically, we estimated whether the proportion of metacognitive processes initiated on pages either relevant or irrelevant to achieving both learning goals 1 and 2 changed (or remained stable) and its relation to achievement goal orientation [13], and performance using a latent growth curve modeling approach. Our research questions include: **(1) To what extent is the stability or change in page-relevant metacognitive processes used across learning goals 1 and 2 during learning with MetaTutor relate to achievement goal orientation and performance while controlling for prior knowledge**

and experimental condition? We hypothesize there will be significant relationships between the stability or change in page-relevant metacognition across learning goals 1 and 2, achievement goal orientation, and performance, based on the assumptions in the model of metamemory which explains that motivation and learning goals guides metacognition while learning [11] as well as empirical findings [5–7,12]. More specifically, studies find relationships between achievement goal orientation and metacognitive process use [4] as well as metacognitive process use and performance [3], but we do not propose a directional hypothesis due to the mixed findings in literature. **(2) To what extent does the stability or change in page-irrelevant metacognitive processes across learning goals 1 and 2 during learning with MetaTutor relate to achievement goal orientation and performance scores while controlling for prior knowledge and experimental condition?** We hypothesize there will be significant relationships between the stability or change in page-irrelevant metacognitive processes used across learning goals 1 and 2, achievement goal orientation, and performance that are aligned with the model of metamemory [11] as well as previous empirical findings [5–7,12]. Again, we do not propose a directional hypothesis based on the nature of mixed findings illustrated in previous studies [3,4].

2 Methods

2.1 Participants and Materials

186 undergraduates ($M_{Age} = 20.39$, $SD = 2.67$; 52% female) were recruited from three large North American university and completed a 2-day study with MetaTutor, a multi-agent ITS [2] designed to enhance self-regulation and knowledge of the human circulatory system using 47 pages of text and diagrams (Fig. 2). Most of the sample identified as 'White/Caucasian' (58%) and participants were compensated $10/h for their time where the study lasted up to three hours total. The Institutional Review Board approved of this study prior to recruitment and data collection. A series of questionnaires were administered prior to learning with MetaTutor to capture emotions, self-efficacy, and motivation[1] such as the Achievement Goal Questionnaire-Revised (AGQ-R) [13], a 12-item self-report measure designed to capture two dimensions of goal orientation: (1) mastery/performance and (2) approach/avoidance. A 4-option multiple choice, 30-item knowledge assessment was administered before and after learning with MetaTutor to gauge changes in knowledge of the human circulatory system. The pre/post-tests were counterbalanced and randomized across both conditions.

2.2 MetaTutor: A System Designed to Enhance Metacognition

MetaTutor was built to enhance self-regulated learning (SRL) and knowledge of the human circulatory system using 47 pages of text and diagrams (see Fig. 2) [2].

---

[1] We do not provide more information on the other questionnaires administered to maintain brevity. Readers are encouraged to email the corresponding author to inquire more information.

Four pedagogical agents (PAs; Pam the Planner, Gavin the Guide, Mary the Monitor, Sam the Strategizer) were designed into the system to intervene and scaffold performance by mirroring human tutoring interactions that were triggered using event- and time-based production rules [2,30]. At the beginning of the learning session, participants were instructed to follow the overall objective: *Learn as much as possible about the human circulatory system within a 90-min time frame.* From this, participants were required to set two learning goals that were related to the overall objective with help from Pam the Planner. Pam the Planner assisted participants in setting learning goals based off of their performance on the pre-test assessment such that if participants did not do well on certain topics of the human circulatory system (e.g., heart components), then Pam suggested the participant set specific learning goals related to those topics. However, participants had the agency to choose which learning goals they set for themselves over the course of their learning with MetaTutor. Upon starting the learning session with MetaTutor, participants had opportunities to initiate SRL processes (e.g., summarizing or monitoring progress toward achieving their set learning goals) which they did so by selecting buttons on the SRL palette built into the right-hand side of the interface (Fig. 2).

2.3 Experimental Design

Participants were randomly assigned to one of the two conditions: prompt and feedback (P+F; $n = 93$) or control ($n = 93$). In the P+F condition, participants were prompted to use SRL processes via the SRL palette and received feedback on performance from the PAs (Fig. 2). Participants in the control condition did not receive performance feedback or prompts. Each of the PAs were built toward a specific SRL strategy and/or process for participants in the P+F condition. For instance, Mary the Monitor was built to prompt participants to use metacognitive processes such as monitor their progress toward goals, while Pam the Planner assisted participants in setting meaningful learning goals that were related to their prior knowledge, i.e., performance on the pre-test assessment, in relation to the overall learning objective (regardless of experimental condition). Sam the Strategizer was triggered to intervene participants to initiate cognitive strategies such as summarizing content or taking notes, while Gavin the Guide presented participants to the system (e.g., how to use tools, navigate the pages using the table of content, etc.) and administered self-report questionnaires measuring emotions throughout the learning session.

2.4 Procedure

On the first day of the study, participants were randomly assigned to a condition, and following informed consent, they were instructed by a researcher to sit in front of a computer and complete demographic questions, self-report questionnaires and a 30-item, 4-option, multiple-choice pre-test assessment on the human circulatory system. This task typically lasted 30–60 min. On day 2, participants were instrumented with an electrodermal activity bracelet and calibrated

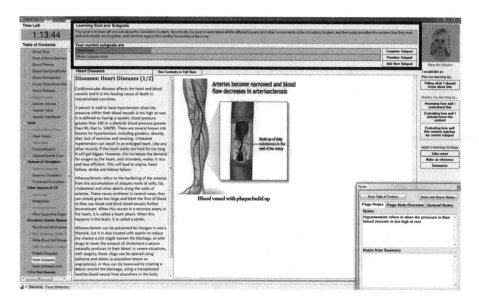

Fig. 2. MetaTutor interface. *Note 1.* SRL palette on the right-hand side; learning goals highlighted at top in black rectangle; PA in top-right hand corner of interface.

to an eye-tracker and facial recognition software[2] before learning with MetaTutor. Regardless of the condition participants were assigned to, they were required to set two learning goals (e.g., learn about the malfunctions of the circulatory system). Once two learning goals were set, they began viewing biology content presented within MetaTutor. Once the learning session was over, participants completed post-test questionnaires that were similar to the pre-test questionnaires as well as a 30-item, 4-option, multiple-choice assessment on the human circulatory system. Afterwards, participants were paid, debriefed, and thanked for their time.

2.5 Coding and Scoring

Page-Relevant and Page-Irrelevant Metacognition. The two learning goals that participants set at the beginning of the session (i.e., before engaging with biology content) served as the basis for defining whether metacognition was relevant or irrelevant by assessing which page a metacognitive process was initiated on (e.g., content evaluation [CE]; e.g., 'did the page provide information relevant to achieving learning goal 1?'). For example, if a learner set a goal to learn about the malfunctions of the circulatory system and then initiated a CE on a page covering blood vessels, the CE would be defined as irrelevant to meeting their goal. If the learner initiated a CE on a page covering sickle-cell

---

[2] We do not provide details about these data channel since they were not included in our analysis. Readers are encouraged to email the corresponding author for more information.

disease, the CE would be defined as relevant to meeting their goal. This approach generated a total of (1) page-relevant and (2) page-irrelevant metacognitive processes for learning goals 1 and 2 for each participant. Next, we created proportions by summing the total number of metacognitive processes initiated during learning, which included: judgments of learning, content evaluations, monitoring progress toward goals, and feelings of knowing that were initiated using the SRL palette [33]. Afterwards, we computed four proportions for each participant by dividing the total number of page-relevant metacognitive process by learning goal 1 or learning goal 2 over total metacognitive processes used. We did the same for page-irrelevant metacognitive processes (see Table 1 for descriptive statistics by condition).

Performance. To define performance, we calculated the proportion of correct answers over total items for both pre/post-test assessments. As such, the pre-test ratio score represented prior knowledge of the circulatory system, while the post-test ratio scores represented the knowledge acquired after learning with MetaTutor. Reliability metrics for both assessments ($\alpha = 0.79$) indicated satisfactory results [24].

Achievement Goal Orientation. AGQ-R scores were computed from data captured using the Achievement Goal Questionnaire-Revised [13]. This instrument operationalizes motivation using a 2×2 framework that captures four goal orientation constructs: (1) mastery, (2) performance, (3) approach, and (4) avoidance. Specifically, participants data were summed into a total of four scores for a combination of each dimension: (1) mastery-approach, (2) performance-approach, (3) mastery-avoidance, and (4) performance-avoidance. These scores ranged from 1–30. Reliability metrics ($\alpha = 0.77$) indicated satisfactory results [24].

2.6   Statistical Analysis

We calculated latent growth models using a structural equation framework for (1) page-relevant metacognition and (2) page-irrelevant metacognition across learning goals 1 and 2 during learning with MetaTutor to examine whether page-relevant or page-irrelevant metacognitive processes toward learning goal 1 (latent intercepts), and its stability or change toward learning goal 2 (latent slopes), were related to AGQ-R and post-test scores while controlling for pre-test scores and experimental condition. The latent growth curve approach was built using confirmatory factor analysis models with an imposed factor mean structure and constraints to yield estimates of change, such that each participant received random-effect estimate(s) to assess whether (and to what extent) their change (or lack thereof) differed from the trajectory of all participants (see Eqs. 1–2) [17].

$$Y_i = \Lambda\eta_i + \epsilon_i, \tag{1}$$

$$\eta_i = \alpha + \gamma(X_i) + \zeta_i \tag{2}$$

Note that Λ represents matrix factor loadings to fit a particular change trajectory; η is a vector for individual change factors (i.e., intercepts and slopes); ϵ reflects a vector of residuals; α is a vector of change factor means and γ is a matrix of coefficients for the predicted effect on latent change factors; and, X represents the predictor variable under investigation, while ϵ is a vector of random for each individual.

3 Results

Data were extracted from log files using 'Numpy' [22] and 'Pandas' [23] packages in Python. The dataset was processed and analyzed using R Studio (R version 3.5.1) [26] with several packages: 'utils' [26], 'readxl' [27], 'dplyr' [21], 'reshape' [20], 'psych' [29], and 'ggplot2' [25]. We used the 'lavaan' package to compute the structural equation model [28].

3.1 Preliminary Analyses

Prior to building the latent growth models, we generated descriptive statistics to assess the state of each predictor variable and its relation to the outcome variable (see Table 2). Homogeneous variance and normality assumptions were met prior to conducting the analyses. Next, we calculated paired t-tests to control for the potential effect of condition on the proportion of page relevant/irrelevant metacognitive processes and post-test scores. The analyses suggested there were only significant differences in the proportion of learning goal 1 page-relevant metacognitive processes, $t(156.59) = 3.41$, $p < 0.05$. Specifically, participants in the P+F condition demonstrated a higher proportion of page-relevant metacognitive processes for learning goal 1 ($M = 0.41$) compared to the control condition ($M = 0.30$). However, we did not find significant differences for other predictor variables between conditions.

3.2 To What Extent Does the Stability or Change in Page-Relevant Metacognitive Processes Across Learning Goals 1 and 2 During Learning with MetaTutor Relate to Achievement Goal Orientation and Performance Scores While Controlling for Prior Knowledge and Experimental Condition?

A latent growth model was calculated and suggested that the data fit the model. The findings revealed no relationships existed between the proportion of page-relevant metacognition, AGQ-R scores, and post-test scores ($ps > 0.05$) with the exception of pretest scores ($\beta = 0.646$, $p < 0.05$). This finding was inconsistent with our hypothesis and previous literature suggesting metacognition and motivation were related to performance [3–7,11,12,14].

Table 1. Descriptive statistics.

Variables	M (SD)	Range
Pre-test scores	0.57 (0.15)	0.93
Post-test scores	0.68 (0.15)	0.97
Proportion of learning goal 1 relevant metacognition	0.36 (0.23)	1.0
Proportion of learning goal 2 relevant metacognition	0.23 (0.19)	1.0
Proportion of learning goal 1 irrelevant metacognition	0.51 (0.24)	1.0
Proportion of learning goal 2 irrelevant metacognition	0.65 (0.23)	1.0
Mastery-approach	13.00 (2.18)*	15.0
Performance-approach	11.00 (3.01)*	15.0
Mastery-avoidance	12.00 (3.03)*	15.0
Performance-avoidance	12.00 (3.34)*	15.0

Note 2. * = median.

Table 2. Fit indices for models.

Variables	χ	df	CFI	TLI	RMSEA
Page-relevant metacognition	32.162*	16	0.884	0.782	0.074
Page-irrelevant metacognition	41.926*	16	0.814	0.652	0.093

Note 3. CFI = comparative fit index; TLI = Tucker–Lewis index; RMSEA = root mean square error of approximation; SRMR = standardized root mean residual. *$p < 0.05$.

3.3 To What Extent Does the Stability or Change in Page-Irrelevant Metacognitive Processes Across Learning Goals 1 and 2 During Learning with MetaTutor Relate to Achievement Goal Orientation and Performance Scores While Controlling for Prior Knowledge and Experimental Condition?

A second latent growth model was estimated and found statistically significant relationships between post-test scores, the intercept (or stability) in the proportion of page-irrelevant metacognition initiated across learning goals 1 and 2 ($\beta = 2.55$, $p < 0.05$), as well as pre-test scores ($\beta = 0.640$, $p < 0.05$; see Figs. 3 and 4). That is, the average proportion of page-irrelevant metacognition across learning goals 1 and 2, while controlling for pre-test and condition, had a positive relationship with post-test scores. This finding was consistent with our hypothesis and previous literature suggesting metacognition and motivation were related to performance [3–7,11,12,14]. However, it is important to note that changes in the proportion of page-irrelevant metacognition over learning goals 1 and 2 and AGQ-R scores were unrelated to post-test scores. This finding was inconsistent with our hypothesis.

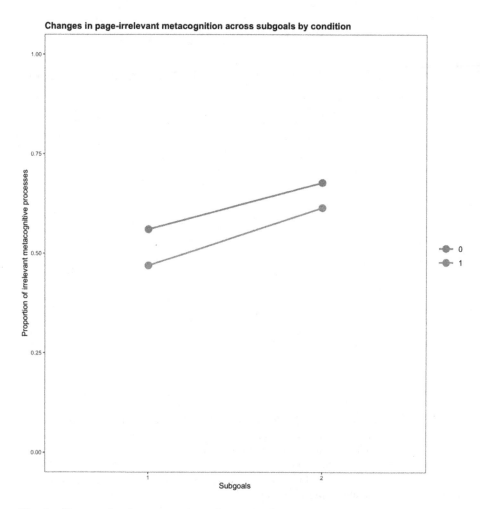

Fig. 3. Changes in the proportion of page-irrelevant metacognition across learning goals 1 and 2. *Note 4.* Legend on right-hand side: 0 = control; 1 = P+F condition.

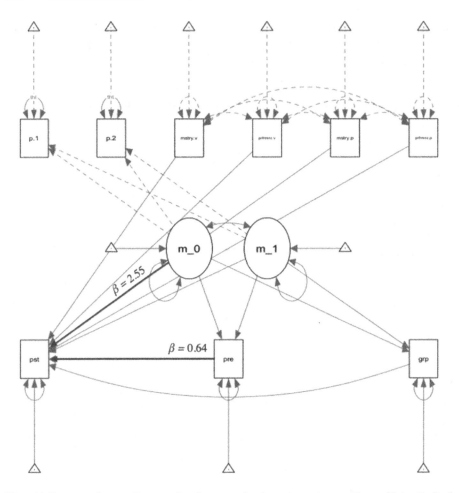

Fig. 4. Structural equation paths for page-irrelevant metacognition. *Note 5.* Red arrows = ps < 0.05; pst = post-test scores; pre = pre-test scores; grp = condition; p. 1 = proportion of irrelevant metacognition for learning goal 1; p. 2 = proportion of irrelevant metacognition for learning goal 2; m_0 = intercept; m_1 = slope; mastry.av = mastery avoidance; performance.v = performance avoidance; mastry.p = mastery approach; performance.p = performance approach. (Color figure online)

4   Discussion

In this study, we sought to address gaps in literature by defining metacognition based on its relevance to learning goals during learning an ITS called MetaTutor. Specifically, we examined if and the extent to which page-relevant and page-irrelevant metacognitive processes changed from learning goals 1 to 2 related to the overall objective of the learning session. Our first research question examined the extent to which the stability or change in page-relevant metacognitive processes across learning goals 1 and 2 during learning with MetaTutor were related to achievement goal orientation and performance scores while controlling for prior knowledge and experimental condition. The model suggested no relationships existed between the stability or change in proportion of page-relevant metacognitive processes across learning goals 1 and 2, AGQ-R scores, and post-test scores, with the exception of pre-test scores being related to post-test performance. This finding was inconsistent with our hypothesis, previous literature, as well as the model of metamemory [11] which suggests that metacognition and motivation are related to performance. A possible explanation could be because few studies have examined metacognition in relation to multiple (or changing) learning goals, motivation, and performance. Additionally, capturing achievement goal orientation before learning (i.e., on the first day of the study), defined motivation as a static trait and failed to capture motivational changes (e.g., metamotivation [14]). Studies provide evidence suggesting motivation fluctuates over the course of learning [3,4,14]. Since the model of metamemory assumes motivation drives goal setting which steers the degree to which learners engage in metacognition [11], motivation could have changed during the learning session and impacted metacognitive process use. Future studies should assess multi-channel data such as eye-gaze, verbalizations, and physiology to capture more information which may provide insight into motivational constructs (and their changes) (e.g., expectancy-value theory, self-determination theory, self-efficacy theory) [34,35,37] that go beyond self-report measures administered once during the study. Multimodal data may provide more information on the role of motivational changes and its relation to metacognition and performance. A noteworthy direction for researchers may be to adopt a goal systems theory perspective in order to examine learning goals and motivation as dynamical systems [36].

The second research question examined the extent to which the stability or change in page-irrelevant metacognitive processes across learning goals 1 and 2 during learning with MetaTutor were related to achievement goal orientation and performance scores while controlling for prior knowledge and experimental condition. The model suggested that the stability in the proportion of page-irrelevant metacognitive processes used across both learning goals 1 and 2 was positively related to post-test scores; however, this effect was not found for motivation. This suggests that the average proportion of page-irrelevant metacognitive processed used across learning goals 1 and 2 (rather than the change), had a positive relationship with post-test scores. This finding emphasizes that changes in the proportion of page-irrelevant metacognition across learning goals 1 to 2 was not related to performance or motivation. However, we did not include cognitive processes in our models which could have been used to compensate for changes in page-relevant metacognition. This effect is further illustrated in Fig. 3, where there was an increase in the proportion of page-irrelevant metacognition from learning goal 1 to 2. Further, we suspect again that no relationships were found between the proportion of page-irrelevant metacognitive processes and motivation because of administering self-report items before learning engaged with biology content. This methodological approach assumes that motivation does not fluctuated (i.e., metamotivation), where studies provide evidence suggesting motivation fluctuates during learning and its impact on performance [3,4,14].

4.1 Limitations

Limitations of this study include only capturing metacognition using the SRL palette, missing any internal judgments learners may have initiated outside of the SRL palette. We also examined count data using the proportional frequency of metacognitive processes, where most studies focus on metacognitive accuracy and so analyzing count data might explain the difference in our findings from previous studies. We also captured motivation using self-report data administered before learners engaged with learning materials, potentially missing any fluctuations in their motivation over the course of the learning session.

4.2 Future Directions and Implications

Future studies should prioritize using multi-channel data to capture metacognition and define it in relation to learning goals. For example, what might eye-gaze add in capturing learners' metacognition [31], i.e., what were learners' fixating on before a judgment of learning was initiated and were these data aligned with performance on the judgment of learning (e.g., learner reports understanding the information, yet the learner did not fixate on the content where the information resided and scored poorly on the pre/post-test)? What might a combination of log files, eye gaze, and concurrent verbalizations offer to examine metacognition and its change over time, especially in relation to multiple learning goals? Further, investigating the same learner across multiple domains could advance our understanding of relations between motivation, SRL, and performance. Ideally, we would have the learner engage in a domain that they find interesting as well as a domain that they find little interest in engaging with. The data captured across the two domains may pave a way to illustrate how motivation constructs (e.g., interest) is reflected in SRL processes such as metacognition and its relation to performance with ITSs. To design ITSs which scaffold effective metacognition and SRL, future research should also focus on capturing how prevalent and relevant metacognitive processes are using multi-channel data, which might also inform the learner's motivation and understanding (or misunderstanding) of information in real-time. Thus, it is essential that future studies contextualize their analyses to gain a more accurate insights to inform design implications for building ITSs, which have the capacity to self-modify its production rules to trigger interventions based on what personally motivates the learners to engage in metacognition. Our findings provide implications for capturing metacognition that is contextualized to learning goals and aligned with the model of metamemory [11] in real-time using multi-channel data to build ITSs and pedagogical agents which provide interventions sensitive to what personally motivates learners to use metacognition [15,16].

References

1. Azevedo, R.: Reflections on the field of metacognition: issues, challenges, and opportunities. Metacognition Learn. **15**, 91–98 (2020). https://doi.org/10.1007/s11409-020-09231-x

2. Azevedo, R., Taub, M., Mudrick, N.-V.: Using multi-channel trace data to infer and foster self-regulated learning between humans and advanced learning technologies. In: Schunk, D.H., Greene, J.A. (eds.) Handbook of Self-Regulation of Learning and Performance, 2nd edn, pp. 254–270. Routledge, New York (2018)
3. Cloude, E.B., Taub, M., Azevedo, R.: Investigating the role of goal orientation: metacognitive and cognitive strategy use and learning with intelligent tutoring systems. In: Nkambou, R., Azevedo, R., Vassileva, J. (eds.) ITS 2018. LNCS, vol. 10858, pp. 44–53. Springer, Cham (2018). https://doi.org/10.1007/978-3-319-91464-0_5
4. Cloude, E.B., Taub, M., Lester, J., Azevedo, R.: The role of achievement goal orientation on metacognitive process use in game-based learning. In: Isotani, S., Millán, E., Ogan, A., Hastings, P., McLaren, B., Luckin, R. (eds.) AIED 2019. LNCS (LNAI), vol. 11626, pp. 36–40. Springer, Cham (2019). https://doi.org/10.1007/978-3-030-23207-8_7
5. Cromley, J.G., Kunze, A.J.: Metacognition in education: translational research. Transl. Issues Psychol. Sci. **6**(1), 15–20 (2020). https://doi.org/10.1037/tps0000218
6. Hong, W., Bernacki, M.L., Perera, H.N.: A latent profile analysis of undergraduates' achievement motivations and metacognitive behaviors, and their relations to achievement in science. J. Educ. Psychol. https://doi.org/10.1037/edu0000445
7. McDowell, L.D.: The roles of motivation and metacognition in producing self-regulated learners of college physical science: a review of empirical studies. Int. J. Sci. Educ. **41**(17), 2524–2541 (2019). https://doi.org/10.1080/09500693.2019.1689584
8. Dunlosky, J., Rawson, K.A.: The Cambridge Handbook of Cognition and Education. Cambridge University Press, Cambridge (2019)
9. Järvelä, S., Bannert, M.: Temporal and adaptive processes of regulated learning-What can multimodal data tell?. Learn Instr. **72**, 101268 (2021)
10. Koriat, A.: Confidence judgments: the monitoring of object-level and same-level performance. Metacognition Learn. **14**(3), 463–478 (2019). https://doi.org/10.1007/s11409-019-09195-7
11. Nelson, T.O., Narens, L.: Metamemory: a theoretical framework and new findings. In: Bower, G.H. (ed.) The Psychology of Learning and Motivation, 2nd edn., pp. 125–141. Academic Press Inc., Cambridge (1990)
12. Özcan, Z.Ç.: The relationship between mathematical problem-solving skills and self-regulated learning through homework behaviours, motivation, and metacognition. Int. J. Math. Educ. Sci. Technol. **47**(3), 408–420 (2016). https://doi.org/10.1080/0020739X.2015.1080313
13. Elliot, A.J., Murayama, K., Pekrun, R.: A 3 × 2 achievement goal model. J. Educ. Psychol. **103**(3), 632–648 (2011). https://doi.org/10.1037/a0023952
14. Miele, D.B., Scholer, A.A., Fujita, K.: Metamotivation: emerging research on the regulation of motivational states. In: Elliot, A.J. (ed.) Advances in Motivation Science, pp. 1–42. Elsevier, Amsterdam (2020)
15. Du Boulay, B., Del Soldato, T.: Implementation of motivational tactics in tutoring systems: 20 years on. Int. J. Artif. Intell. Educ. **26**(1), 170–182 (2016). https://doi.org/10.1007/s40593-015-0052-1
16. Du Boulay, B.: Towards a motivationally intelligent pedagogy: how should an intelligent tutor respond to the unmotivated or the demotivated? In: Calvo, R., D'Mello, S. (eds.) New Perspectives on Affect and Learning Technologies. LSIS, vol. 3, pp. 41–52. Springer, New York (2011). https://doi.org/10.1007/978-1-4419-9625-1_4

17. McNeish, D., Matta, T.: Differentiating between mixed-effects and latent-curve approaches to growth modeling. Behav. Res. Methods **50**, 1398–1414 (2018). https://doi.org/10.3758/s13428-017-0976-5

18. Ryan, R.M., Deci, E.L.: Self-determination theory and the facilitation of intrinsic motivation, social development, and well-being. Am. Psychol. **55**(1), 68–78 (2000)

19. Ryan, R.M., Deci, E.L.: The darker and brighter sides of human existence: basic psychological needs as a unifying concept. Psychol. Inq. **11**(4), 319–338 (2000). https://doi.org/10.1207/S15327965PLI110403

20. Wickham, H.: Reshaping data with the reshape package. J. Stat. Softw. **21**(12), 1–20 (2007)

21. Wickham, H., François, R., Henry, L., Müller, K.: dplyr: a grammar of data manipulation. R package version 1.0.2 (2020). https://CRAN.R-project.org/package=dplyr

22. Oliphant, T.E.: A Guide to NumPy, vol. 1, p. 85. Trelgol Publishing (2006)

23. McKinney, W.: Pandas: a foundational Python library for data analysis and statistics. Python High Perform. Sci. Comput. **14**(9), 1–9 (2011)

24. Cronbach, L.J.: Coefficient alpha and the internal structure of tests. Psychometrika **16**(3), 297–334 (1951). https://doi.org/10.1007/BF02310555

25. Wickham, H.: ggplot2: Elegant Graphics for Data Analysis. Springer, New York (2016). https://doi.org/10.1007/978-3-319-24277-4

26. R Core Team: A language and environment for statistical computing. R Foundation for Statistical Computing, Vienna, Austria (2019). www.R-project.org/

27. Wickham, H., Bryan, J.: readxl: Read Excel Files. R package version 1.3.1 (2019). https://CRAN.R-project.org/package=readxl

28. Rosseel, Y.: Lavaan: an R package for structural equation modeling. J. Stat. Softw. **48**(2), 1–36 (2012). www.jstatsoft.org/v48/i02/

29. Revelle, W.: psych: procedures for personality and psychological research. Northwestern University, Evanston, Illinois, USA (2020). https://CRAN.R-project.org/package=psych

30. Taub, M., Azevedo, R., Rajendran, R., Cloude, E.B., Biswas, G., Price, M.J.: How are students' emotions related to the accuracy of cognitive and metacognitive processes during learning with an intelligent tutoring system? Learn. Instr. **72**, 101200 (2021)

31. Mudrick, N.-V., Azevedo, R., Taub, M.: Integrating metacognitive judgments and eye movements using sequential pattern mining to understand processes underlying multimedia learning. Comput. Hum. Behav. **96**, 223–234 (2019)

32. Lajoie, S.-P., Pekrun, R., Azevedo, R., Leighton, J.-P.: Understanding and measuring emotions in technology-rich learning environments. Learn. Instr. **70**, 101272 (2020)

33. Greene, J.-A., Azevedo, R.: A macro-level analysis of SRL processes and their relations to the acquisition of a sophisticated mental model of a complex system. Contemp. Educ. Psychol. **34**(1), 18–29 (2009)

34. Wigfield, A., Eccles, J.-S.: Expectancy-value theory of achievement motivation. Contemp. Educ. Psychol. **25**(1), 68–81 (2000)

35. Deci, E.-L., Ryan, R.-M.: Self-determination theory. In: Van Lange, P.-A.-M., Kruglanski, A.-W., Higgins, E.-T. (eds.) Handbook of Theories of Social Psychology, vol. 2, pp. 416–436. Sage Publications Ltd., London (2012). https://doi.org/10.4135/9781446249215.n21

36. Kruglanski, A.-W., Shah, J.-Y., Fishbach, A., Friedman, R., Chun, W.-Y., Sleeth-Keppler, D.: A theory of goal systems, pp. 208–250 (2002)

37. Schunk, D.-H., DiBenedetto, M.-K.: Motivation and social cognitive theory. Contemp. Educ. Psychol. **60**, 101832 (2020)

WhatsApp or Telegram. Which is the Best Instant Messaging Tool for the Interaction in Teamwork?

Miguel Á. Conde[1]([✉]) [iD], Francisco J. Rodríguez-Sedano[2] [iD],
Francisco J. Rodríguez Lera[1] [iD], Alexis Gutiérrez-Fernández[1] [iD],
and Ángel Manuel Guerrero-Higueras[1] [iD]

[1] Department of Mechanics, Computer Science and Aerospace Engineering,
Robotics Group, Universidad de León–Campus de Vegazana S/N,
24071 León, Spain
{mcong, fjrodl, alexis.gutierrez,
am.guerrero}@unileon.es
[2] Department of Electric, Systems and Automatics Engineering,
Robotics Group, Universidad de León – Campus de Vegazana S/N,
24071 León, Spain
francisco.sedano@unileon.es

Abstract. Instant Messaging tools are a part of our technified daily life. Tools such as WhatsApp or Telegram have millions of users that send continuously billion of messages. This can be used in different context and one of them is in Education. An important part of education is students' interaction and specially how they interact when working together as a team. This paper deals with an analysis of which of this tool is better in this specific context, especially when students are developing teamwork competences. To facilitate the analysis of the messages two Learning Analytics tools were developed and applied in the context of a Computer Science degree subject, with an important increment in students' number of messages regarding previous years but several issues to explore, such as: how to deal with the students that employs other tools different to this for interacting with peers, how to encourage students to employ instant messaging tools as real communication mechanisms, how to measure messages content and not only quantity or how to identify the acquisition of other competences analyzing the conversations.

Keywords: Teamwork · Interaction · Conversation · Instant messaging · WhatsApp · Telegram

1 Introduction

Teamwork assessment as one of the competences more demanded by the labor market has become also a key competence to be developed in the educational institutions [1]. The acquisition of such competences requires students to work together, in groups as they will do possibly in their future work. Working in groups involves different type of activities, as can be work distribution, planning, development, review and publication

P. Zaphiris and A. Ioannou (Eds.): HCII 2021, LNCS 12784, pp. 239–249, 2021.
https://doi.org/10.1007/978-3-030-77889-7_16

of the results, etc. All of them have something in common, they require team members interaction and collaboration [2, 3].

If the educational institutions aim to facilitate the development of teamwork competence it is necessary to assess how students acquire it. In order to do so, several research works have shown that this cannot be evaluated only by considering each team results, but their interaction as a key element in Team Work Competence (TWC) development [4].

The interaction of the team members in face-to-face environments will probably carried out by talking. However, in an educational context collaboration is not something that will take place only in this way because: 1) discussions with peers are not always possible in classes specially with big groups; 2) in many cases collaboration goes beyond the educational institution where students are not together; and 3) students use other type of tools to interact between them, something that has been specially highlighted by the pandemic situation.

Taking this heterogeneity into account it seems clear that the evaluation of students' interactions during the teamwork activities is something hard specially with big groups, so, it is necessary to use tools that facilitate such work. In [5] Fidalgo et al. the researchers describe a Learning Analytics (LA) tool that allows analyzing students' interactions in forums. This was later tested successfully in other contexts [4–10]. However, a common complaint of the students involved was that they do not use commonly the forums to interact, that they employ other tools such as instant messaging tools. This leads to the implementation of two LA tools to evaluate instant messaging tools, one for analyzing students' WhatsApp interactions and the other one for Telegram [11, 12]. They were successfully applied in two experiences and with this paper, we would like to compare both systems and to discuss which could be better for the evaluation of the individual acquisition of TWC.

In order to do so, the paper is structured as follows. Next section describes the research context describing and comparing WhatsApp and Telegram. Section 3 will explore and compare the LA tools developed for the analysis. Section 4 will discuss the implementations, comments on some preliminary evaluation results, and presents the conclusions.

2   Research Context

This section describes the concept of Instant Messaging tools (IM) and specially WhatsApp and Telegram apps.

2.1   Instant Messaging Tools

Nowadays one of the most common ways of communication is IM tools. These are online tools that facilitate synchronous communication among users that has become very popular with their inclusion in smartphones and the popularization of this kind of devices [13]. In fact, they are one of the most significant tools in our daily life and especially relevant for young people. They even prefer using IM apps than other communication tools such as phone calls or email [14, 15].

The popularity of these tools can be shown by the number of users they have. Considering stadista.com last report (October of 2020 - data based on We are Social, Kepios and other sources [16]), the most popular apps for IM were: WhatsApp with 2 billion users, Facebook messenger with 1.3 billion, WeChat with around 1.2 billion, QQ mobile with 648 million, Snapchat with 433 and Telegram with 400.

In education, it is the most popular communication among students. They consider IM tools as very straightforward apps [17] with which they can chat individually or in groups, share images, videos, voice, talk, etc. [13]. In educational contexts, IM tools have been applied for different purposes although the most common aim is to improve communication experience among students and teachers [18–23]. These experiments have shown that IM facilitates knowledge sharing and enhances interactivity between peers; increases the sense of being present at a place; support collaboration and makes possible to interact anywhere and anytime [23, 24]. There are nonetheless tradeoffs, the use of IM tools can distract students from learning because it can be used for educational purposes, but it is not something easy to control [25, 26]. So, if we want to apply these tools in education, which can be really interesting given the above describe advantages, it is necessary to control how students are using them.

There are different possible ways to apply IM in education but the most common are using them as a communication channel for students' groups. Such interaction can be later analyzed from a quantitative perspective [24] or taking into account the contents of the messages [27]. In the case of this work, the idea is to use it for assessing teamwork which has been seen as a possibility in other of the authors works, but that is not very common.

2.2 WhatsApp vs Telegram

Given this context, we can understand that can be possible and positive to employ IM tools in education. Now it is time to decide which tool to use. The present authors have carried out experiments and adaptations both for WhatsApp and for Telegram, so now we compare both technologies and later how they can be adapted for the educational contexts.

WhatsApp

It was created as a free instant messaging tool that uses Internet to allow users to send texting messages without character limits and share with other images, audios, videos, weblinks, documents, etc. [28]. WhatsApp also provides additional social information to its users, e.g., contacts can see when their friends are online, when they are typing and when they last accessed the application. Finally, WhatsApp provides delivery notifications, highlighting when a message is sent and when it is delivered to the recipient's device [29]. Recently it was acquired by Facebook.

As we have seen before it is the most popular IM app but, why is people adopting it? Among other reasons because: it is free; the possibility to send unlimited messages; the sense of synchronous communication; it is trendy; to interact with a group of persons and because of the sense of privacy compared with other social networks [29].

Regarding the application of WhatsApp in education, there are several studies describing the possibilities it provides in this field [30–32], samples about how to use it for students and teachers communication [20, 24], and others related to the development of specific competences [33, 34] which also could include the works of the authors about teamwork interaction assessment.

Telegram
Telegram is another very popular and free IM service based on an open-source platform. Services are similar to those provided by WhatsApp, although there are differences that we will comment later. Telegram was developed in August 2013 by russian-born entrepreneur Pavel Durov [35]. Telegrams users have grown in the last years, passing from 200 million users in 2018 to 400 in 2020 [36].

The use of Telegram includes several specific services such as the use of Telegram ID so someone can contact the user without a phone number, the use of bots, the presence of an open API to integrate the tool and messages with other systems, the access through a great number of platforms as it is stored in the cloud, etc. [35].

Regarding the possible uses of Telegram in Education it, as WhatsApp and other IM tools is mainly used as communication channel to support educational activities in several fields [37–40], although in this case, the possibility to use channels or bots [41] changes the typical way in which IM tools used to be employed.

Differences Among Telegram and WhatsApp
It is necessary to point out that these two IM platforms share a lot of functionalities but also present important differences. Although, as they are continuously evolving, the functionalities included in each of them, tend to include what their users demands, which means that what now is not present in one of the platforms could be included in the near future. For instance, WhatsApp does not include stickers or animated gifs but they have been recently implemented or Telegram that does not include video calls but have included them in August 2020.

The following issues are based on several comparisons, we are only focused on differences defined by tech web pages [42–44], similarities are ignored:

Privacy and Security. Although both IM tools end-to-end encryption, so conversations can only be available for the receiver and sender, Telegram adds a functionality that are secret chats where screenshots are not possible and messages are self-destructed after a time.

Compatible platforms. Telegram is defined as a cloud-based system, so it is easier to access it from any platform and from different devices at the same time. WhatsApp also includes this functionality as WhatApp web, but it can be only used in a device at the same time and it is linked to a phone number.

- Telegram ID. Telegram provides to the users an ID, so the user account does not need to be linked to a phone number (it is only necessary on the installation) and it is possible to share only the TelegramID and not the phone number with other contacts.
- Groups and Channels. WhatsApp facilitates groups for 256 users while Telegram allows in the last versions up to 200.000. In addition, Telegram allows the user to be subscribed or to create Channels. They are a tool for broadcasting public messages to large audiences, where the message is signed with the channel name and not the username.

- API. WhatsApp is a proprietary tool so if you want to use its API it is necessary to pay for it, it is called WhatsApp Bussiness API [45]. On the contrary, Telegram is open source, so it provides an API [46] that facilitates access to different functionalities and the definition of tools that use it.
- Bots. WhatsApp is developing currently bots, but they have this functionality available as part of the WhatsApp Bussiness API commented above. Telegram facilitates the definition of bots [47] and their integration in the groups and channels, there exist a wide number of bots with different functionalities.
- Polls. Telegrams provide a functionality to include polls as messages in your chats. In Whatsapp it is necessary to define them externally and embed the result as a message.
- Other. There are other functionalities different in both tools, as the type of emojis, the way in which backups are carried out, the possibility to pin or edit messages, etc.

It should be noted that, independently of the differences, nowadays WhatsApp is the most popular IM tool. Although Telegram has duplicated the number of users in one year as shown by statista reports [36, 48].

3   LA Solutions Based on Telegram and WhatsApp

In order to evaluate TWC individual acquisition we have employed CTMTC in several experiments but, as commented above, the students claim that their conversations using a forum were not natural. This leads to the definition of tools to facilitate this assessment when the interactions are carried out using WhatsApp or Telegram. In this section, we describe and compare both solutions. In any of them, the idea is to gather the messages and explore them with a LA tools in order to reduce the time required to evaluate the individual work in each group [5].

3.1   LA Solution for WhatsApp

This solution has been described in two previous works. It consists of the implementation of two different components, a web plugin included in a Learning Management Course – LMS (Moodle in this case) and a LA tool. The idea is that the teacher will instantiate a TW activity and the students can use the plugin to upload a text file with their WhatsApp conversation. The plugin parses the information and stores it in a new table on Moodle database. The information stored can be later accessed by a LA tool using Moodle web services layer. The teacher could check what the students have done in the LA and evaluate them according to a rubric. The data shown by the LA will be the same for Telegram and for WhatsApp. Figure 1 shows the component distribution for this option.

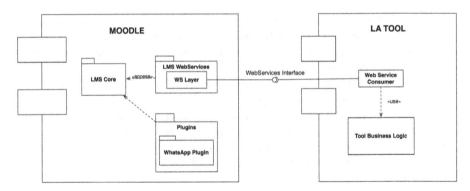

Fig. 1. Description of the components involved in the LA tool implementation for WhatsApp (obtained from [11]).

3.2 LA Solution for Telegram

In this case the solution is based on Telegram bots technology, and it is independent of any LMS. In order to develop it a bot was created that uses webhook methods to gather the messages and facilitate a real-time analysis of the activity that take place in the conversations where the bot is included. So, the teacher only needs to provide the students with some guides to use the bot, they include them in their group and the messages can be gathered and later analyzed in the LA. In this case the LA includes the same date considered in the WhatsApp experience but there will be no integration with the LMS. The deployment diagram of this solution is shown in Fig. 2.

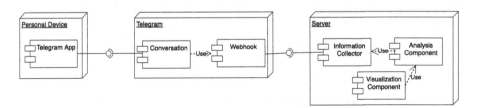

Fig. 2. Deployment diagram with the different components (obtained from [12]).

3.3 Differences Between Both Solution

Technically, both solutions are ok and in both cases the LA is an external component that should present the data to facilitate the teacher making decisions. Regarding the differences we can find several:

- Isolated component or integration with the LMS. In the WhatsApp solution the component is integrated into Moodle. This means that the teacher should instantiate the activity and the students should access to it to parse their conversations. In addition, this implies that the information parsed is stored in the institutional LMS (commented below). In the case of Telegram there is not a component in this sense beyond the bot. The integration of the component into Moodle presents several advantages, as the centralization of all the activities and data, but also means that it is necessary that teachers and students interact with it. In the case of Telegram, it is more straightforward. The teachers need only to explain how the bot works and the students to include it into the group and execute some commands.

- Data stored in the LMS or on an external Server. This can be interesting because the information will be stored in the LMS and transferred via web services to the LA tool, so the institution could "control" the data. The problem is that this data could be attacked when it is transferred. In the case of Telegram this attack it is also possible, but the information is going to be stored in an external server that we can control. In this case WhatsApp drawback could be that the educational institution does not allow to access to the LMS database.
- Parse the information or not. In the case of WhatsApp, we need to parse the data, because the text conversation includes phone numbers and in the case of teachers it is not necessary nor desirable this information but a student id in order to know the author of each message. In the case of Telegram, as it uses TelegramIDs, the phone number is not included in the data and the student only needs to execute a command in the group to associate their PersonalID with the TelegramID. This means less work to be done by the student and more privacity as the phone number is not present in any part of the evaluation process.

4 Discussion and Conclusions

This work has explored two very popular IM Tools that can be used by students and teachers to interact in teamwork tasks. The evaluation of the TWC requires to explore such interaction so, in order to do this, we developed two different LA tools. The paper has analyzed both the technical differences of the IM tools and the differences between the LA Tools. Is this enough to answer the question about which is the best tool? We have tested both tools in two experiments carried out with students from a second course subject of Computer Science degree. We are still analyzing the results of the second experiment, but with more than 100 students involved per each of them, we can say that the question cannot be answered flatly, and it depends on several issues:

1. What tool or tools are the students using to interact? Using WhatsApp or Telegram can be seen as a trendy solution, but they are not the only possible communication ways of the students. If they employ other tools, then the interaction cannot always be tracked or analyzed. As we are applying this in a controlled educational context, we have allowed the students to use an asynchronous tool for communication (Moodle forums) or a synchronous (WhatsApp). Most of the students involved decide to use the synchronous tool (more than a 90%) although, especially those with less interaction, comment that they employ other tools to chat with their team partners, such as Skype, Discord, Facebook, etc.
2. If the students were used to employ WhatsApp or Telegram they were happy using them, but if they have not used these tools before they say that this cause them more effort.

3. Students suggested the analysis of audio as a possible research work and although WhatsApp and Telegram allow audio and videocalls, they were not defined as voice channels. Anyway, this functionality should be taken into account in future developments
4. The average number of messages per student has been increased in comparison with forums with an average of 216.3 messages per student in WhatsApp vs 164.3 in Telegram.
5. Some of the conversations seem artificial and only to answer to the assignment requirements, that is, the students were not using these tools for a real interaction.
6. Teachers consider that any of the tools can help the to assess students' interaction, however, it would be useful to include emojis analysis and the application of natural language processing techniques over the messages, so it was possible to take into account other competences related to TWC or with leadership [49, 50].
7. From the programmers' point of view they prefer a Telegram solution because in this way there is not constraints related with the educational institution databases. Although this requires securing properly the data in the server where it is going to be stored.

Given these issues, it is clear that it is necessary to continue working in this line, taking into account the different suggestions and promoting among the students that they should interact using the IM as they are interacting in real conversations, which use to be one of the hardest parts of the work.

Answering the question raised by this paper is not easy, the use of synchronous tools is very interesting in the context of teamwork, but in anyway the students should be motivated. If we use WhatsApp or Telegram probably is not they key issue, but how to enhance and promote real students' interactions.

References

1. Colomo-Palacios, R., Casado-Lumbreras, C., Soto-Acosta, P., García-Peñalvo, F.J., Tovar-Caro, E.: Competence gaps in software personnel: a multi-organizational study. Comput. Human Behav. **29**, 456–461 (2013)
2. Leidner, D.E., Jarvenpaa, S.L..: The use of information technology to enhance management school education: a theoretical view. MIS Quarterly **19**, 265–291 (1995)
3. Vogel, D.R., Davison, R.M., Shroff, R.H.: Sociocultural learning: a perspective on GSS-enabled global education. Commun. Assoc. Inf. Syst. **7** (2001)
4. Conde, M.Á., Rodríguez-Sedano, F.J., Sánchez-González, L., Fernández-Llamas, C., Rodríguez-Lera, F.J., Matellán-Olivera, V.: Evaluation of teamwork competence acquisition by using CTMTC methodology and learning analytics techniques. In: Proceedings of the Fourth International Conference on Technological Ecosystems for Enhancing Multiculturality, pp. 787–794. ACM, Salamanca, Spain (2016)
5. Fidalgo-Blanco, Á., Sein-Echaluce, M.L., García-Peñalvo, F.J., Conde, M.Á.: Using learning analytics to improve teamwork assessment. Comput. Human Behav. **47**, 149–156 (2015)

6. Séin-Echaluce, M.L., Fidalgo-Blanco, Á., García-Peñalvo, F.J., Conde, M.Á.: A knowledge management system to classify social educational resources within a subject using teamwork techniques. In: Zaphiris, P., Ioannou, A. (eds.) Learning and Collaboration Technologies: Second International Conference, LCT 2015, Held as Part of HCI International 2015, Los Angeles, CA, USA, 2–7 August 2015, Proceedings, pp. 510–519. Springer International Publishing, Cham (2015)

7. Fidalgo, A., Leris, D., Sein-Echaluce, M.L., García-Peñalvo, F.J.: Indicadores para el seguimiento de evaluación de la competencia de trabajo en equipo a través del método CTMT. Congreso Internacional sobre Aprendizaje Innovación y Competitividad - CINAIC 2013, Madrid, Spain (2013)

8. Sein-Echaluce, M.L., Fidalgo-Blanco, Á., García-Peñalvo, F.J.: Students' knowledge sharing to improve learning in engineering academic courses. Int. J. Eng. Educ. (IJEE) **32**, 1024–1035 (2016)

9. Conde, M.A., Colomo-Palacios, R., García-Peñalvo, F.J., Larrucea, X.: Teamwork assessment in the educational web of data: a learning analytics approach towards ISO 10018. Telematics Inform. **35**, 551–563 (2018)

10. Conde, M.Á., Hernández-García, Á., García-Peñalvo, F.J., Fidalgo-Blanco, Á., Sein-Echaluce, M.: Evaluation of the CTMTC methodology for assessment of teamwork competence development and acquisition in higher education. In: Zaphiris, P., Ioannou, A. (eds.) Learning and Collaboration Technologies: Third International Conference, LCT 2016, Held as Part of HCI International 2016, Toronto, ON, Canada, 17–22 July 2016, Proceedings, pp. 201–212. Springer International Publishing, Cham (2016)

11. Conde, M.Á., Rodríguez-Sedano, F.J., Rodríguez-Lera, F.J., Gutiérrez-Fernández, A., Guerrero-Higueras, Á.M.: Assessing the individual acquisition of teamwork competence by exploring students' instant messaging tools use: the WhatsApp case study. Univ. Access Inf. Soc. (2020)

12. Conde, M.Á., Rodríguez-Sedano, F.J., Fernández, C., Gutiérrez-Fernández, A., Fernández-Robles, L., Limas, M.C.: A Learning Analytics tool for the analysis of students' Telegram messages in the context of teamwork virtual activities. In: Eighth International Conference on Technological Ecosystems for Enhancing Multiculturality, pp. 719–724. Association for Computing Machinery, Salamanca, Spain (2020). https://doi.org/10.1145/3434780.3436601

13. Conde, M.Á., Rodríguez-Sedano, F.J., Rodríguez-Lera, F.J., Gutiérrez-Fernández, A., Guerrero-Higueras, Á.M.: Analyzing students' whatsapp messages to evaluate the individual acquisition of teamwork competence. In: Zaphiris, P., Ioannou, A. (eds.) HCII 2019. LNCS, vol. 11591, pp. 26–36. Springer, Cham (2019). https://doi.org/10.1007/978-3-030-21817-1_3

14. Carnevale, D.: Email is for old people. The Chronicle of Higher Education 53 (2006)

15. Junco, R., Mastrodicasa, J.: Connecting to the net.generation: what higher education professionals need to know about today's students. NASPA, National Association of Student Personnel Administrators, Student Affairs Administrators in Higher Education, US (2007)

16. Most popular global mobile messenger apps as of October 2018 Statista. https://www.statista.com/statistics/258749/most-popular-global-mobile-messenger-apps/. Última vez accedido 5 Feb 2019

17. Lewis, C., Fabos, B.: Instant messaging, literacies, and social identities. **40**, 470–501 (2005)

18. Edman, A., Andersson, F., Kawnine, T., Soames, C.-A.: Informal math coaching by instant messaging: two case studies of how university students coach K-12 students AU - Hrastinski. Stefan. Interact. Learn. Environ. **22**, 84–96 (2014)

19. Cifuentes, O.E., Lents, N.H.: Increasing student-teacher interactions at an urban commuter campus through instant messaging and online office hours. Electron. J. Sci. Educ. **14** (2010)

20. Smit, I., Goede, R.: WhatsApp with BlackBerry; can messengers be MXit? A philosophical approach to evaluate social networking sites. Cape Peninsula University of Technology (2012). https://repository.nwu.ac.za/handle/10394/13628

21. Sweeny, S.M.: Writing for the instant messaging and text messaging generation: using new literacies to support writing instruction. J. Adolesc. Adult Literacy **54**, 121–130 (2010)

22. Lauricella, S., Kay, R.: Exploring the use of text and instant messaging in higher education classrooms. Res. Learn. Technol. **21** (2013)

23. Klein, A.Z., da Silva Freitas Jr., J.C., Vieira-Mattiello-Mattiello-da-Silva, J.V., Victoria-Barbosa, J.L., Baldasso, L.: The educational affordances of mobile instant messaging mim: results of whatsapp used in higher education. Int. J. Distance Educ. Technol. **16**, 51–64 (2018)

24. Bouhnik, D., Deshen, M.: WhatsApp goes to school: mobile instant messaging between teachers and students. J. Inf. Technol. Educ. Res. **13**, 217–231 (2014)

25. Fox, A.B., Rosen, J., Crawford, M.: Distractions, distractions: does instant messaging affect college students' performance on a concurrent reading comprehension task? **12**, 51–53 (2009)

26. Junco, R., Cotten, S.R.: Perceived academic effects of instant messaging use. Comput. Educ. **56**, 370–378 (2011)

27. Gronseth, S., Hebert, W.J.T.: GroupMe: investigating use of mobile instant messaging in higher education courses. TechTrends **63**, 15–22 (2019)

28. Lantarón, B.S.: Whatsapp: su uso educativo, ventajas y desventajas. Revista de Investigación en Educación **16**, 121–135 (2018)

29. Church, K., De Oliveira, R.: What's up with WhatsApp? comparing mobile instant messaging behaviors with traditional SMS. In: Proceedings of the 15th International Conference on Human-computer Interaction with Mobile Devices and Services, pp. 352–361 (2013)

30. Willemse, J.J.J.C.: Undergraduate nurses reflections on Whatsapp use in improving primary health care education. **38**, 1–7 (2015)

31. Barhoumi, C.: The effectiveness of WhatsApp Mobile Learning Activities Guided By Activity Theory on Students' Knowledge Management. Contemp. Educ. Technol. **6**, 221–238 (2015)

32. Aljaad, M., Hamad, N.J.E.: Whatsapp for educational purposes for female students at college of education-king Saud university. Education **137**, 344–366 (2017)

33. Awada, G.: Effect of WhatsApp on critique writing proficiency and perceptions toward learning AU - Awada, Ghada. Cogent Educ. **3**, 1264173 (2016)

34. Andújar-Vaca, A., Cruz-Martínez, M.-S.: Mobile instant messaging: WhatsApp and its potential to develop oral skills. Comunicar **25**, 43–52 (2017)

35. Sutikno, T., Handayani, L., Stiawan, D., Riyadi, M.A., Subroto, I.M.I.: WhatsApp, viber and telegram: Which is the best for instant messaging? Int. J. Electr. Comput. Eng. **6**, 2088–8708 (2016)

36. Most popular global mobile messenger apps as of October 2020, based on number of monthly active users https://www.statista.com/statistics/258749/most-popular-global-mobile-messenger-apps/. Última vez accedido 03 Feb 2020

37. Iksan, Z.H., Saufian, S.M.: Mobile learning: innovation in teaching and learning using telegram. Int. J. Pedagogy Teacher Educ. **1**, 19–26 (2017)

38. Iqbal, M.Z., Alradhi, H.I., Alhumaidi, A.A., Alshaikh, K.H., AlObaid, A.M., Alhashim, M. T., AlSheikh, M.H.: Telegram as a tool to supplement online medical education during COVID-19 crisis. Acta Informatica Medica **28**, 94 (2020)

39. Dargahi Nobari, A., Reshadatmand, N., Neshati, M.: Analysis of Telegram, an instant messaging service. In: Proceedings of the 2017 ACM on Conference on Information and Knowledge Management, pp. 2035–2038 (2017)
40. Faraji, S., Valizadeh, S., Sharifi, A., Shahbazi, S., Ghojazadeh, M.: The effectiveness of telegram-based virtual education versus in-person education on the quality of life in adolescents with moderate-to-severe asthma: a pilot randomized controlled trial. Nursing Open **7**, 1691–1697 (2020)
41. Martínez Rolán, L.X., Dafonte Gómez, A., Garcia Miron, S.: Usos de las aplicaciones móviles de mensajería en la docencia universitaria: Telegram. 6° Congreso Internacional sobre Buenas Prácticas con TIC, Málaga, España, 18–20 octubre 2017. Comunicación audiovisual e publicidade (2017)
42. Telegram Features that WhatsApp Does Not Have (Updated 2021). https://cutt.ly/HkfvQaB. Última vez accedido 03 Feb 2021
43. Telegram VS Signal, With WhatsApp Comparison Table. https://meganvwalker.com/telegram-vs-signal-with-whatsapp-comparison-table/. Última vez accedido 03 Feb 2021
44. Telegram vs WhatsApp: en qué se parecen y en qué se diferencian ambas aplicaciones. https://www.xataka.com/basics/telegram-vs-whatsapp-en-que-se-parecen-y-en-que-se-diferencian-ambas-aplicaciones. Última vez accedido
45. WhatsApp Bussiness API. https://www.whatsapp.com/business/api/?lang=en. Última vez accedido 03 Feb 2021
46. Telegram APIs. https://core.telegram.org/. Última vez accedido 03 Feb 2021
47. Bots: An introduction for developers. https://core.telegram.org/bots/. Última vez accedido 13 Sept 2020
48. Most popular global mobile messenger apps as of October 2019, based on number of monthly active users. https://www.statista.com/statistics/258749/most-popular-global-mobile-messenger-apps/. Última vez accedido 12 Feb 2020
49. Tasa, K., Taggar, S., Seijts, G.H.: The development of collective efficacy in teams: a multilevel and longitudinal perspective. J. Appl. Psychol. **92**, 17–27 (2007)
50. Sein-Echaluce, M.L., Fidalgo-Blanco, A., Esteban-Escano, J., García-Peñalvo, F.J.G., Conde-González, M.Á.: Using learning analytics to detect authentic leadership characteristics in engineering students. Int. J. Eng. Educ. **34**, 851–864 (2018)

Effectiveness of System-Facilitated Monitoring Strategies on Learning in an Intelligent Tutoring System

Daryn A. Dever[1(✉)], Franz Wortha[2], Megan D. Wiedbusch[1], and Roger Azevedo[1]

[1] University of Central Florida, Orlando, FL 32816, USA
{ddever,meganwiedbusch}@knights.ucf.edu,
roger.azevedo@ucf.edu
[2] Universität Greifswald, Greifswald, Germany
franz.wortha@uni-greifswald.de

Abstract. To effectively process complex information within intelligent tutoring systems (ITSs), learners are required to engage in metacognitive monitoring micro-processes (content evaluations [CEs], judgments of learning [JOLs], feelings of knowing [FOKs], and monitoring progress towards goals [MPTGs]). Learners' average monitoring micro-process strategy frequencies were used to examine learning gains using a person-centered approach as they interacted with MetaTutor. Undergraduates (n = 94) engaged in self-initiated and system-facilitated self-regulated learning (SRL) strategies as they studied the human circulatory system with MetaTutor, a hypermedia-based ITS. Using hierarchical clustering, results showed a difference in learning between clusters differing in metacognitive monitoring process usage. Specifically, learners who used both CEs and FOKs for a greater proportion of monitoring strategy usage had significantly greater learning gains than learners who used MPTGs. Implications for monitoring strategy usage across different micro-processes and the development of ITSs to facilitate and scaffold learners' interactions with these micro-processes via prompting are discussed.

Keywords: Monitoring · Self-regulated learning · Intelligent tutoring systems

1 Introduction

To effectively process complex instructional materials while learning with intelligent tutoring systems (ITSs), learners are required to efficiently engage in and accurately deploy self-regulated learning (SRL) strategies [1]. SRL involves learners monitoring and modulating their cognitive, affective, metacognitive, and motivational processes to effectively process information while interacting with complex instructional materials such as the human circulatory system [2]. However, most learners typically lack the SRL abilities required to successfully learn with an ITS [3, 4]. Because of this, ITSs have incorporated scaffolding techniques (e.g., prompting) to support learners in sufficiently utilizing SRL strategies (e.g., increased frequency, higher accuracy). For example, MetaTutor [2] is a hypermedia-based ITS consisting of several pages of text

© Springer Nature Switzerland AG 2021
P. Zaphiris and A. Ioannou (Eds.): HCII 2021, LNCS 12784, pp. 250–263, 2021.
https://doi.org/10.1007/978-3-030-77889-7_17

and diagrams to guide learners' understanding of the anatomy and function of the human circulatory system. The environment facilitates learners' SRL by prompting learners to engage in specific strategies based on how frequently a learner uses a strategy (i.e., low user-initiated frequency = more frequent SRL prompts) and for how long the learner was engaged in the strategy (i.e., prompt to engage in the strategy for a longer period of time). This study examines how system-facilitated prompts aid learners' engagement in SRL, specifically metacognitive monitoring strategy use, during learning about the human circulatory system with MetaTutor.

1.1 Metacognitive Monitoring and SRL

Metacognitive monitoring is essential to learners' ability to engage in SRL and achieve set goals by accounting for their progress during learning, achievement of sub-goals, and the effectiveness of previously used strategies [5]. These strategies are some of the most important SRL processes as behavior regulation is based on information obtained through monitoring. Monitoring one's own progress through strategy use has been integrated into multiple models of SRL, emphasizing the importance of this facet of SRL [6]. Zimmerman's [7] SRL model highlights monitoring within the performance phase where learners are required to monitor their progress, understanding, and cognitive engagement as the task is executed. Within Pintrich's [8] model, monitoring is a critical phase for learners to engage in throughout SRL. Efklides [9] introduced the metacognitive and affective model of SRL (MASRL) in which SRL consists of two levels - the Person level and the Task x Person level. Within the Task x Person level, monitoring is promoted as the main process where learners' performance on a task is dependent on the ability for learners to monitor and control the interaction between their cognition, metacognition, affect, and self-regulation of affect and effort throughout the task. Within this Task x Person level, monitoring is particularly important as the level is often data-driven where bottom-up processes are required to be controlled via monitoring for successful performance. The conditions, operations, products, evaluations, and standards (COPES) model [10, 11] identifies monitoring as occurring during both the operations and standards phases where learners actively and consistently monitor their progress towards goals during information processing and as products are evaluated via self-assessment. Within COPES, monitoring is considered a central controller that moderates learners' cognitive evaluations and the control of cognitive conditions, operations, and standards. The progression of SRL models throughout the past couple decades have consistently expressed the importance of monitoring to guide and control cognition during a learning task. Overall, monitoring is an essential process during SRL that occurs throughout the entirety of a learning activity, influencing how learners select information, deploy other SRL processes and strategies, and adapt these strategies to achieve the overall goal.

Monitoring consists of several micro-processes that contribute to learners' ability to oversee their progress during learning, evaluate instructional materials that are being read, and tracking their overall understanding of the instructional materials within their environment [12, 13]. For instance, learners deploy judgments of learning (JOLs), feelings of knowing (FOKs), and content evaluations (CEs) as well as monitoring progress towards goals (MPTGs) to monitor their learning. JOLs are deployed by learners to evaluate understanding of complex instructional materials within an ITS. FOKs require learners to evaluate their current understanding of previously encountered information. FOKs often correspond to learners' feeling of familiarity with information, but can also demonstrate an inability to recall certain pieces of information. That is, FOKs reveal to what extent learners remember concepts or topics that were introduced while they evaluate which information they may need to revisit for a deeper understanding that better meets the learning standards or goals the learner has set. CEs refer to judging information from instructional materials as relevant or irrelevant to set goals. By examining learners' engagement in micro-processes during monitoring, researchers may account for how learners identify inconsistencies between information and prior knowledge, evaluate information in reference to set goals, and achieve these goals by comprehending the information within the environment and employing appropriate SRL strategies.

1.2   Monitoring in Intelligent Tutoring Systems

Monitoring SRL processes during learning is critical to how learners process information from their environments, specifically ITSs. A study by Paans and colleagues [14] examined learners' temporal SRL activities during hypermedia learning. Results showed that more successful learners demonstrated a more even distribution of cognitive and metacognitive activity use whereas less successful learners used cognitive strategies significantly more than metacognitive strategies. Further, Paans et al. [14] also found that more successful learners utilized metacognitive strategies at the beginning of the task and less at the end where less successful learners did not demonstrate a temporal variation in SRL strategy use. This study highlights the need for learning environments to facilitate adequate SRL strategy use, where multiple strategies are used throughout the full learning task.

To foster and support learners' SRL strategy use, ITSs can externally facilitate learning by employing pedagogical agents to prompt and scaffold learners' interactions [15, 16]. Gaze Tutor is an ITS promoting biology-related content knowledge that adapts pedagogical agents' interactions with learners based on learners' gaze behavior [17]. This ITS was successful in increasing learning gains for deep processing by directing learners towards important information from instructional materials that should be attended to [17], further encouraging learners' engagement in SRL. MetaTutor has the ability for learners to be prompted to engage in SRL strategies, including metacognitive monitoring micro-processes, via pedagogical agents to increase learners' use of these strategies at appropriate points in time contextualized to the task (e.g., CE prompted during reading; JOL prompted after reading). Previous studies have noted the success of this type of scaffolding in strategy use and learning. Bouchet, Harley, and Azevedo [18] found that as learners used MetaTutor to learn about the human circulatory system, adaptive prompting aided learners in self-initiating SRL processes over time, but the quality of the SRL prompts decreased when learners self-initiated the processes versus when they were prompted. Trevors, Duffy, and Azevedo [19] showed that during learning with MetaTutor, learners with low prior knowledge used less SRL strategies, such as note-taking, than learners with high prior knowledge; yet, when pedagogical prompting and feedback was introduced, the gaps in SRL strategy use diminished.

While the scaffolding present in Gaze Tutor [17] indirectly supports SRL strategy use by adaptively re-engaging learners in processing critical information, MetaTutor's prompting system explicitly and dynamically supports learners' interactions with the environment while externally facilitating SRL by prompting learners to engage in metacognitive strategies throughout the learning session. It is important to note that MetaTutor promotes learners' use of specific SRL strategies, such as monitoring micro-processes, further encouraging learners to use strategies that are aimed at specific outcomes. For example, a prompted CE aims at aiding the learner in identifying information that is important to their learning goal versus information that is critical for a different learning goal. Therefore, it is essential to not only account for the temporal alignment of SRL processes, as denoted by Winne's [10] information-processing theory (IPT) of SRL, but also acknowledge the micro-processes that are encompassed within macro-processes (e.g., monitoring), as shown by Greene and Azevedo's [12] framework.

1.3 Theoretical Framework

To fully explain learners' use of metacognitive monitoring processes within MetaTutor, two models were considered as the theoretical grounding for this study. Winne's [10] IPT of SRL model, similar the models mentioned previously, describes learning as occurring throughout four phases: (1) defining the task; (2) setting goals and plans to achieve those goals; (3) deploying strategies throughout information processing; and (4) adapting goals, plans, and strategies if the overall learning goal has not been achieved. This model states that additional processes – i.e., conditions, operations, products, evaluations, standards (COPES) – exist within each phase so the learner identifies task and cognitive conditions (e.g., task constraints, prior knowledge), deploys operations (e.g., searching, monitoring, assembling, rehearsing, translating) that result in products, and evaluate these products against standards. From this model, monitoring is identified as occurring throughout learning, from learners monitoring their own understanding of task constraints to comparing products and standards for examining how current understanding achieves the set goals.

In conjunction with the IPT model [10], we considered Greene and Azevedo's [12] SRL macro- and micro-processes framework which details the SRL processes that occur throughout the four phases of IPT. The four macro-processes include planning, monitoring, strategy use, and task difficulties and demands, each containing several micro-processes. JOLs, FOKs, CEs, and MPTGs are considered micro-processes for monitoring. The effectiveness of specific micro-level processes is dependent on characteristics of the learning task (e.g., the learning domain) [20]. Previous studies have shown that micro-processes used while learning history could differ from those used to learn a different domain [20, 21], driving our research in examining how the use of multiple micro-level processes are related to learning and to each other. For example, do individual or pairs of micro-processes emerge from learners' data and are they associated with learning outcomes? Few studies have investigated how the joint use of multiple micro-level metacognitive processes is related to learning within ITSs (see

[14]). Addressing this gap, we use a person-centered approach to examine how learners, when assisted by prompts from the system, engage in SRL monitoring strategies. While previous studies have used this approach to examine learner interactions with MetaTutor (see [22]) examining learner profiles based on metacognitive monitoring variables and their relationship to learning has not been addressed. Using a person-centered approach, we aim to examine emerging patterns of how individual or paired monitoring micro-processes are related to learning.

1.4   Current Study

The goal of this study was to examine how learners engaged in metacognitive monitoring strategies throughout learning with MetaTutor, a hypermedia-based ITS, that were both self-initiated and externally-facilitated through prompts by pedagogical agents. While previous studies have examined metacognitive monitoring strategies, few studies have examined the influence of both self- and externally-facilitated instances on learning outcomes using a person-centered approach. To address the goal of this current study, we examined three research questions: (1) Can proportional metacognitive monitoring strategy be used to identify groups of learners?; (2) Do the selected clusters differ in learning outcomes?; and (3) How do clusters differ in proportional metacognitive monitoring strategy use?

The first research question examines how learners can be identified by their similar interactions with SRL strategies that are both self-initiated and system-facilitated. As other studies have used this approach to examine learner interactions with MetaTutor (see [22]), we hypothesize that individual groups of learners who differ in their monitoring micro-process strategy usage will be identified from the data. The second research question examines how clusters differing in their monitoring micro-process usage vary in their learning outcomes. While a difference in learning gains is expected, we do not provide a directional hypothesis as (1) the clusters depend on the data-driven results of the first research question and (2) all micro-processes are essential to learning. The purpose of the third research question is to narrow down the comparison between the groups that differ in their learning outcomes. For this research question, we hypothesize that learners that have greater learning gains will demonstrate a greater distribution of strategy use across all four monitoring micro-processes [14, 19].

2   Methods

2.1   Participants and Materials

Data from 94 ($M_{age} = 20$, $SD_{age} = 2.10$; 56% female) undergraduate students from three large public North American universities were analyzed for this current study. Originally, 190 students participated in this study, but as our study examines self-initiated SRL strategies in addition to system-facilitated strategies, participants from the control condition only containing self-initiated strategies were removed from analyses, resulting in our final dataset of 94 participants. Participants were randomly assigned to one of two conditions. In the Prompt and Feedback Condition, participants were prompted by the system to engage in SRL processes and provided feedback on their success. Participants within this condition were also able to self-initiate these processes. In this experimental condition, learners were strongly influenced to utilize both cognitive and metacognitive SRL strategies as they completed their subgoals and attained appropriate domain-specific information by pedagogical agents which played a role in the type of strategy that was prompted (e.g., Mary the Monitor prompted monitoring strategies; Pam the Planner prompted planning strategies). In the control condition, learners were not prompted by the system nor received feedback, but self-initiated all SRL strategy interactions. After being randomly assigned to either of the two conditions, the participants completed a 30-item multiple-choice pre- and post-test related to the content presented in MetaTutor. After the post-test, participants were compensated \ $10 per hour. As a t-test revealed that these conditions did not differ in their learning gains ($p > .05$) calculated from the pre- and post-test scores (see Coding and Scoring).

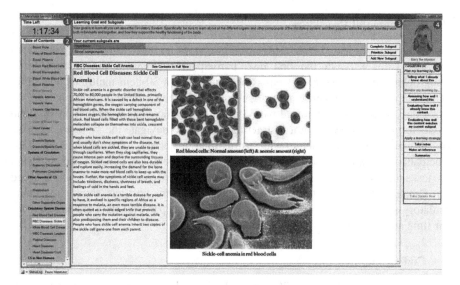

Fig. 1. Screenshot of MetaTutor environment with a countdown timer (1), table of contents (2), current subgoal (3), pedagogical agent (4), and SRL palette (5).

2.2   MetaTutor

Within this study, participants learned about the human circulatory system with MetaTutor [2], a hypermedia-based ITS, which contains 47 pages of text and diagrams about sub-topics and -systems related to the human circulatory system. Participants had the overall goal to learn as much as possible about the human circulatory system (e.g., anatomy, purpose, how different components work together). There are several features available within MetaTutor (Fig. 1) including a countdown timer from 90 min, table of contents with hyperlinks to different pages of the environment, an overview of learning (sub-)goals, the pedagogical agent, and the SRL palette which allows participants to self-initiate different SRL strategies.

To foster learners' use of SRL strategies (i.e., note-taking, summarizing, planning, inference-making, prior knowledge activation, JOLs, FOKs, MPTGs, and CEs), the MetaTutor system can prompt learners to engage in specific processes through production rules that are enacted based on (1) learners' monitoring and control of their understanding of text content and ability to evaluate the content and (2) time between SRL strategy usage. In addition to prompting learners to use these strategies, the system also provides performance feedback on the strategy. For example, learners are informed by a pedagogical agent that their summary of text is too long, short, or acceptable. It is important to note that learners may also self-initiate as well as be prompted to engage in these processes. Within MetaTutor, there are four pedagogical agents that assist learners with different types of SRL strategies: Gavin the Guide, Pam the Planner, Mary the Monitor, and Sam the Strategizer. Within this study, we specifically examined the monitoring processes that are initiated by Mary the Monitor – i.e., JOLs, MPTGs, FOKs, and CEs.

2.3   Experimental Procedure

This study was conducted over a period of two days to study how participants learn with MetaTutor [2]. On the first day, participants completed the consent form, demographics questionnaire, self-report measures, and a 30-item multiple-choice pre-test developed by a domain expert regarding the human circulatory system. On the second day, participants interacted with MetaTutor. Participants were first provided an introductory video to MetaTutor instructing on how to navigate the system and chose two sub-goals prior to interacting with instructional materials. After setting their goals, participants were able to read texts, examine diagrams, complete quizzes, and engage in SRL tasks throughout learning with MetaTutor. After the learning session which lasted approximately 90 min, participants completed a 30-item post-test about the human circulatory system. Upon completion of the post-test, participants were thanked for their time and compensated $10 per hour (up to $40).

2.4   Coding and Scoring

Pre- and post-test scores on the 30-item multiple-choice human circulatory tests were used to calculate normalized change scores [23]. These equations (see Eqs. 1–2) calculate the learning gains of each participant while accounting for their prior knowledge.

$$\frac{post - pre}{100 - pre} \tag{1}$$

$$\frac{post - pre}{pre} \tag{2}$$

If the post-test score is greater than the pre-test score, participants' normalized change score is calculated using Eq. 1. When participants' pre-test score is greater than their post-test score, the normalized change score is calculated using Eq. 2. If the pre- and post-test scores are the same, participants received a normalized change score of 0.

Metacognitive monitoring strategies used for this study included CEs, FOKs, JOLs, and MPTGs, recorded from participants' log files during data collection. Usage was defined by the proportion of participants' metacognitive monitoring frequency in each of the micro-processes relative to their total frequency of all monitoring processes. For example, if a participant had a total number of 50 monitoring strategies used, and engaged in CEs 25 times, then that participant would be characterized as using CEs for 50% of their metacognitive monitoring strategy usage. By using this proportion, we are able to assess how each type of strategy was used relative to the total number of times participants engaged in metacognitive monitoring. By using clustering methodology for these variables, we are able to examine how participants were similar in their proportional use of specific micro-processes.

2.5 Data Processing

Several packages in R [24] were used for analyses including 'stats' and 'graphics' packages from R, 'dendextend' [25], and 'psych' [26]. Clustering methodology using Ward's method on the Euclidian distance matrix was utilized for this study as this allows the analyses to be driven by a person-centered approach to understand how learners grouped by similar characteristics differ from each other to potentially use learner profiling in future studies.

3 Results

3.1 Research Question 1: Can Proportional Metacognitive Monitoring Strategy Be Used to Identify Groups of Learners?

Learners' average CEs, FOKs, JOLs, and MPTG frequency proportions were used as variables for hierarchical clustering. By using an average, the number of times each learner used a specific metacognitive monitoring strategy was isolated to uniformly examine the relationship between each micro-process. Using this method, four clusters of participants were identified (see Fig. 2) differing in their metacognitive monitoring strategy usage. The four clusters of participants were initially identified as: (Cluster 1) greater CE and JOL usage, (Cluster 2) greater CE and MPTG usage, (Cluster 3) greater JOL usage, or (Cluster 4) greater FOK usage (see Table 1). Cluster 4 was removed from subsequent analyses as there were less than 10 participants. The remaining clusters, Cluster 1 (N = 35), Cluster 2 (N = 37), and Cluster 3 (N = 15), were used in further analyses.

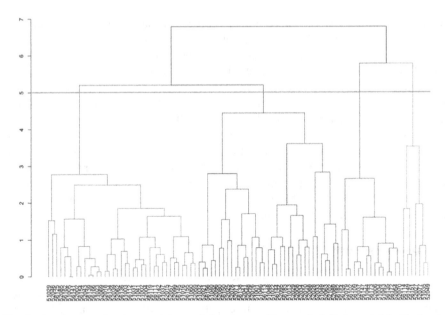

Fig. 2. Dendogram showing participants belonging to Clusters 1–4 (left to right). Horizontal line depicts the number of clusters chosen.

Table 1. Mean (SD) proportion of metacognitive monitoring strategy usage for Clusters 1–4.

Cluster	Monitoring micro-process			
	CE	FOK	JOL	MPTG
Cluster 1	0.36 (0.22)	0.16 (0.16)	0.40 (0.13)	0.08 (0.04)
Cluster 2	0.43 (0.13)	0.07 (0.10)	0.15 (0.13)	0.34 (0.16)
Cluster 3	0.19 (0.05)	0.07 (0.08)	0.58 (0.17)	0.17 (0.13)
Cluster 4	0.21 (0.07)	0.56 (0.10)	0.10 (0.05)	0.13 (0.07)

3.2   Research Question 2: Do the Selected Clusters Differ in Learning Outcomes?

An ANOVA identified the differences in learning gains between Clusters 1, 2, and 3. One leveraging outlier for Cluster 2 was removed. While clusters significantly differed ($F(2,83) = 3.94$, $p < .05$), post hoc pairwise t-tests with a Bonferroni correction for multiple tests ($p < .0125$) identified participants in Clusters 1 ($M = 0.32$, $SD = 0.21$) had significantly greater learning gains than participants in Cluster 2 ($M = 0.20$, $SD = 0.18$; $t(67) = 3$, $p = .01$). Cluster 3 was not significantly different from the other clusters ($p < .0125$).

3.3   Research Question 3: How Do Clusters Differ in Proportional Metacognitive Monitoring Strategy Use?

A two-way mixed ANOVA was calculated to identify how Clusters 1 and 2 differed in terms of both user- and system-initiated metacognitive monitoring strategy usage.

A significant interaction between clusters and strategies $(F(3,207) = 27.6, p < .0001;$ see Fig. 3) and t-test pairwise comparisons with correction $(p < .0125)$ showed learners in Cluster 1 used CEs and FOKs significantly more whereas Cluster 2 used significantly more MPTGs (see Table 2). However, JOL usage did not significantly differ between clusters. A second two-way mixed ANOVA isolating proportional user-initiated strategy usage yielded a significant interaction between clusters and strategies $(F(3,195) = 13.8, p < .0001)$ and replicated the learner profiles found when examining both self- and system-initiated strategies (see Table 2).

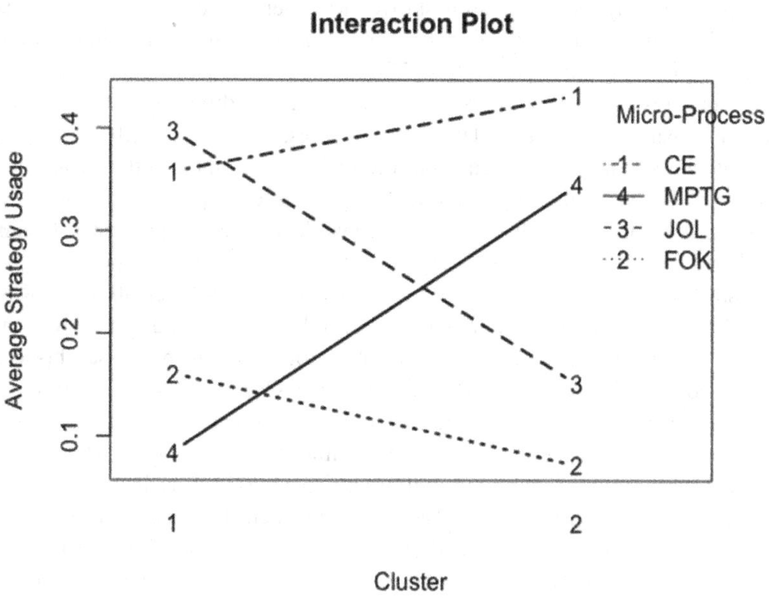

Fig. 3. Interaction plot of overall average micro-process usage between Clusters 1 & 2.

Table 2. Comparisons of strategy usage between initiators and Clusters 1 & 2.

Initiator		Monitoring micro-process			
		CE	FOK	JOL	MPTG
System & User	Cluster 1	0.48 (0.17)	0.11 (0.11)	0.19 (0.15)	0.22 (0.10)
	Cluster 2	0.36 (0.08)	0.04 (0.05)	0.14 (0.11)	0.46 (0.10)
	t(df)	$t(48) = 4.0*$	$t(49) = 3.0*$	$t(48) = 2.0$	$t(48) = -11.0*$
User	Cluster 1	0.11 (0.23)	0.10 (0.16)	0.19 (0.27)	0.59 (0.29)
	Cluster 2	0.01 (0.05)	0.01 (0.05)	0.06 (0.15)	0.92 (0.16)
	t(df)	$t(33) = 2.0*$	$t(34) = 3.0*$	$t(45) = 2.0$	$t(39) = -4.0*$

Note. Mean(SD) proportion of metacognitive monitoring strategy use. * denotes significance at $\alpha = 0.0125$.

4 Discussion

The goal of this study was to use a person-centered approach to understand how learning is related to self-initiated and system-facilitated metacognitive monitoring strategy usage during learning about complex instructional material with MetaTutor. The first research question examined how learners can be identified by their similar interactions with SRL strategies. Through hierarchical clustering, we identified 4 groups of learners based on their strategy usage. The first research question shows profiles of learners that had singularly occurring micro-processes (e.g., Clusters 3 and 4) and profiles with multiple equally-occurring micro-processes (e.g., Clusters 1 and 2). Confirming the first hypothesis, results showed that there are distinct groups of learners who differ in their monitoring micro-process strategy usage while interacting with MetaTutor, supporting previous studies [22].

The second research question examined how clusters differing in their monitoring micro-process usage vary in their learning outcomes. Consistent with our hypothesis, results showed a significant difference between Clusters 1 and 2 in their learning gains where Cluster 1 demonstrated greater learning gains than participants in Cluster 2. Results from the third research question narrows down the comparison between both Clusters 1 and 2 to examine how these specific clusters differ in their monitoring micro-process usage. Because we only examined Clusters 1 and 2, results from Research Question 3 partially confirmed our hypothesis. While results did not show a greater distribution of strategy use across all four monitoring micro-processes between all clusters, we identify significant differences between Clusters 1 and 2 in how participants within these clusters used monitoring micro-processes.

When examining the significantly different micro-processes solely between Clusters 1 and 2, we profile participants belonging to Cluster 1 as having significantly greater CE and FOK usage when examining both system-facilitated and user-initiated strategies as well as only user-initiated strategies. Participants belonging to Cluster 2 had significantly greater MPTG usage, with no differences between clusters when examining JOL usage. By understanding how these clusters differ in terms of metacognitive monitoring strategy usage and learning, we infer that participants who use more monitoring micro-processes demonstrate greater learning than those who, for majority of their time monitoring, primarily use only one monitoring micro-process, partially confirming our hypotheses [14, 19]. This finding is in line with SRL models (i.e., IPT) as different processes are effective at different stages of learning. Additionally, we consider the nature of CEs and FOKs compared to MPTGs contextualized to MetaTutor. CEs and FOKs require learners to make judgments based on the content where instructional materials presented within the environment are evaluated for relevance (CE) which directly relates to how much information participants believe they carry over from the readings within MetaTutor (FOKs). FOKs have a direct impact on selecting necessary learning strategies where negative FOKs may influence participants' decisions to use cognitive strategies (e.g., note-taking) more frequently to increase learning. In contrast, MPTGs require learners monitor their progress through a progress bar to determine if they have interacted with enough instructional materials to continue on to their next goal. This is expected to occur less frequently have a more indirect impact on strategy selection where immediate use of a control strategy is not required. These processes and their contribution to learning and SRL can significantly enhance current models of SRL [10, 27] by specifying the role of micro-level processes and their feedback loops in supporting SRL with ITSs.

5   Limitations

There are a few limitations to this study that should be considered. First, this study used a combination of both self-initiated and system-facilitated monitoring strategies within the analyses. However, we decided to not separate these processes as they are inter-linked due to the production rules which set the prompting. For example, a participants' interactions with one micro-process may have been influenced by prior promptings of the system to engage in the same or a different micro-process. Additionally, our aim within this study was to examine how system-facilitated strategy use supplemented self-initiated processes in order to analyze how learning gains may have been attributed to system prompts on individual monitoring micro-processes. Second, this experimental study used an exploratory method (i.e., hierarchical clustering) which examines how the data reveals individual differences in how participants engaged in strategy use. As such, this study does not more deeply examine exactly how and when these monitoring micro-processes influence learning, but rather sets the stage of examining which processes are attributed to increased learning gains based on the dynamic interactions between learners and ITSs across time.

6   Conclusions and Future Directions

The results of this study explain how learners varying in their learning gains use metacognitive monitoring micro-processes throughout learning with MetaTutor, a hypermedia-based ITS covering a complex topic, the human circulatory system. From the results, we conclude that increased learning gains are associated with the quantity of strategies used as well as the depth of effort the strategy requires contextualized to the learning environment. Future studies can examine how system-facilitated monitoring strategies supplement learners' self-initiated strategies over time during learning and how the duration of these strategies, not just the frequency, are related to learning gains. Our study indicates that future systems should be designed to promote a balanced use of different metacognitive monitoring strategies, prompting the expansion of this study's approach in future studies to examine other areas of SRL (e.g., cognitive, emotional, and motivational regulation processes). Future ITSs and other learning technologies can incorporate a person-centered approach to dynamically scaffold individual learners as they use metacognitive monitoring strategies while learning about complex topics [28].

Acknowledgements. This research was supported by funding from the National Science Foundation (DRL#1661202, DUE#1761178, DRL#1916417, IIS#1917728), the Social Sciences and Humanities Research Council of Canada (SSHRC 895-2011-1006). The authors would also like to thank members of the SMART Lab at UCF for their contributions.

References

1. Winne, P.H., Azevedo, R.: Metacognition. In: Sawyer, K. (ed.) Handbook of the Learning Sciences. 3rd edn. Cambridge University Press, Cambridge, MA (in press)
2. Azevedo, R., Taub, M., Mudrick, N.V.: Understanding and reasoning about real-time cognitive, affective, and metacognitive processes to foster self-regulation with advanced learning technologies. In: Schunk, D.H., Greene, J.A. (eds.) Handbook of Self-regulation of Learning and Performance, 2nd edn., pp. 254–270. Routledge, New York (2018)
3. Josephsen, J.M.: A qualitative analysis of metacognition in simulation. J. Nursing Educ. **56**, 675–678 (2017)
4. Molenaar, I., Roda, C., van Boxtel, C., Sleegers, P.: Dynamic scaffolding of socially regulated learning in a computer-based learning environment. Comput. Educ. **59**, 515–523 (2012)
5. Schunk, D.H., Greene, J.A.: Handbook of Self-Regulation of Learning and Performance, 2nd edn. Routledge, New York (2018)
6. Panadero, E.: A review of self-regulated learning: six models and four directions for research. Front. Psychol. **8**, 1–28 (2017)
7. Zimmerman, B.J.: Attaining self-regulation: a social cognitive perspective. In: Boekaerts, M., Pintrich, P.R., Zeidner, M. (eds.) Handbook of Self-regulation, pp. 13–40. Academic Press, CA (2000)
8. Pintrich, P.R.: The role of goal orientation in self-regulated learning. In: Boekaerts, M., Pintrich, P.R., Zeidner, M. (eds.) Handbook of Self-regulation, pp. 452–502. Academic Press, CA (2000)
9. Efklides, A.: Interactions of metacognition with motivation and affect in self-regulated learning: the MASRL model. Educ. Psychol. **46**, 6–25 (2011)
10. Winne, P.: Theorizing and researching levels of processing in self-regulated learning. Br. J. Educ. Psychol. **88**, 9–20 (2018)
11. McCardle, L., Hadwin, A.F.: Using multiple, contextualized data sources to measure learners' perceptions of their self-regulated learning. Metacogn. Learn. **10**, 43–75 (2015)
12. Greene, J., Azevedo, R.: A micro-level analysis of SRL processes and their relations to the acquisition of a sophisticated mental model of a complex system. Contemp. Educ. Psychol. **34**, 18–29 (2009)
13. Azevedo, R.: Multimedia learning of metacognitive strategies. In: Mayer, R.E. (ed.) Handbook of Multimedia Learning, 2nd edn., pp. 647–672. Cambridge University Press (2014)
14. Paans, C., Molenaar, I., Segers, E., Verhoeven, L.: Temporal variation in children's self-regulated hypermedia learning. Comput. Human Behav. **96**, 246–258 (2019)
15. Azevedo, R., Gašević, D.: Analyzing multimodal multichannel data about self-regulated learning with advanced learning technologies: issues and challenges. Comput. Human Behav. **96**, 207–210 (2019)
16. Johnson, W.L., Lester, J.C.: Face-to-face interaction with pedagogical agents, twenty years later. Int. J. Artif. Intell. Educ. **26**, 25–36 (2016)
17. D'Mello, S., Olney, A., Williams, C., Hays, P.: Gaze tutor: a gaze-reactive intelligent tutoring system. Int. J. Human-Comput. Stud. **70**, 377–398 (2012)
18. Bouchet, F., Harley, J., Azevedo, R.: Can adaptive pedagogical agents' prompting strategies improve students' learning and self-regulation? In: 13th International Conference on Intelligent Tutoring Systems, pp. 368–374 (2016)

19. Trevors, G., Duffy, M., Azevedo, R.: Note-taking within MetaTutor: interactions between an intelligent tutoring system and prior knowledge on note-taking and learning. Educ. Technol. Res. Dev. **62**, 507–528 (2014)
20. Greene, J.S., Bolick, C.M., Jackson, W.P., Caprino, A.M., Oswald, C., McVea, M.: Domain-specificity of self-regulated learning processing in science and history. Contemp. Educ. Psychol. **42**, 111–128 (2015)
21. Poitras, E., Lajoie, S.: Using technology-rich environments to foster self-regulated learning in the social studies. In: Schunk, D.H., Greene, J.A. (eds.) Handbook on Self-regulation of Learning and Performance, 2nd edn., pp. 254–270. Routledge, New York (2018)
22. Bouchet, F., Harley, J.M., Trevors, G.J., Azevedo, R.: Clustering and profiling students according to their interactions with an intelligent tutoring system fostering self-regulated learning. J. Educ. Data Min. **5**, 104–146 (2013)
23. Marx, J., Cummings, K.: Normalized change. Am. J. Phys. **75**, 87–91 (2007)
24. R Core Team: R: A language and environment for statistical computing. R Foundation for Statistical Computing (2020)
25. Galili, T.: dendextend: an R package for visualizing, adjusting, and comparing trees of hierarchical clustering. Bioinformatics (2015)
26. Revelle, W.: psych: Procedures for Personality and Psychological Research, Northwestern University (2018)
27. Azevedo, R., Dever, D.: Multimedia learning and metacognitive strategies. In: Mayer, R.E., Fiorella, L. (eds.) The Cambridge Handbook of Multimedia Learning, 3rd edn. Cambridge University Press, New York (in press)
28. Graesser, A.C., Fiore, S.M., Greiff, S., Andrews-Todd, J., Foltz, P.W., Hesse, F.W.: Advancing the science of collaborative problem solving. Psychol. Sci. Public Interest **19**, 59–92 (2018)

Digital Competence Assessment Survey for Language Teachers

Mikhail Fominykh[1]([⊠]) [iD], Elizaveta Shikhova[2]([⊠]) [iD],
Maria Victoria Soule[3]([⊠]) [iD], Maria Perifanou[4]([⊠]) [iD],
and Daria Zhukova[2]([⊠])

[1] Norwegian University of Science and Technology, Trondheim, Norway
mikhail.fominykh@ntnu.no
[2] ITMO University, Saint Petersburg, Russia
{e.shikhova, dzhukova}@itmo.ru
[3] Cyprus University of Technology, Limassol, Cyprus
mariavictoria.soule@cut.ac.cy
[4] University of Macedonia, Thessaloniki, Greece
maria.perifanou@uom.edu.gr

Abstract. In this paper, we present the results of the digital competence assessment survey for language teachers. The survey assessed how language teachers use digital technologies, their attitude towards these technologies, their related skills and competencies, their satisfaction and training needs, and the institutional support they receive. In total, 283 language teachers from 43 countries participated in the survey. The data were collected in 2019. The results indicate that language teachers use various computer-assisted language learning instructional methods. They generally consider that digital technologies are beneficial for the classroom. The lack of training prevents them from using specific technology-based methodologies, in contrast to the lack of technical infrastructure. The majority of the participants are not satisfied with their level of digital language teaching expertise. Two-thirds of those who receive digital competency training at their organizations, report that the training sessions happen irregularly or rarely. At the same time, the majority of the teachers confirm these training to be effective and the skills they received are applied in practice. We discuss the results of the survey in relation to the previous research, policies and practical challenges of the digitalization of language education. The major contribution of the paper is a representation of the teacher's perspective on the role of digital technologies in their practice. We assume that the new realia of teaching in the context of COVID-19 have changed the overall need in digital language teaching skills among the teachers, as well as the share of the teaching staff who teach online on a regular basis. The future work includes a new survey in order to evaluate the scope of this change.

Keywords: Digital competences · Language learning · Teacher education

© Springer Nature Switzerland AG 2021
P. Zaphiris and A. Ioannou (Eds.): HCII 2021, LNCS 12784, pp. 264–282, 2021.
https://doi.org/10.1007/978-3-030-77889-7_18

1 Introduction

Digital skills and competencies are widely acknowledged as essential for modern citizens. Digital literacy was also highlighted as one of the key competencies for lifelong learning for more than a decade, for example, in the Digital Agenda for Europe in 2010 [1], and the Partnership for 21st Century Skills [2]. However, there is still a long way to integrate digital technologies or Information and Communication Technologies (ICT) to their full potential in language classrooms. The key findings of a large survey of schools in Europe were that the biggest percentage of European schools lacked the appropriate infrastructure, had low-frequency use of digital technologies in the classroom, and 70% of the teachers did not consider themselves as 'digitally' confident or able to teach digital skills effectively [3].

Furthermore, one of the major outcomes of the same survey was the urgent need to invest in training teachers, in addition to the investment in the digital infrastructure. The results of the same survey, published in 2019, indicated that around 60% of European students are taught by teachers that engage in professional development activities about digital technologies in their own time. The pandemic that started in 2020 has strongly influenced the teaching practices in a very short time. Learning shifted to an emergency mode, while the teachers had to quickly acquire new skills, especially in effectively using digital technologies. During these events, the results of studies and strategic recommendations to invest in training teachers can be seen in a new light.

Language proficiency is a key tool for common understanding between citizens, especially in culturally diverse regions, such as Europe. Language teachers need to acquire new skill sets regularly in order to become digitally competent. Those who aim to organize online language courses, need different skills than those trained to teach in a face-to-face classroom [4]. This modern educational reality even prior to the pandemic required innovative pedagogies, open digital learning environments, and open educational resources.

The application of technologies to language learning, and particularly the use of computers in language teaching has a history of half a century [5]. In his critical examination of the history and future of Computer Assisted Language Learning (CALL), Bax envisaged that CALL was going to be truly integrated into the classroom and into teachers' practices. He posited that the end goal for CALL should be 'normalisation' defined by the author as "the stage when the technology becomes invisible, embedded in everyday practice and hence normalised" [6]. Despite the progression observed in the last twenty years towards technology integration in language teaching, Bax's vision for CALL still remains an illusion. The present study aims to understand key factors that might play a role in technology integration, focusing on the language teachers and their digital skills. For this purpose, the research objectives of the study presented in this paper are:

1. to identify to what extent and how language teachers integrate novel technologies and methodologies in their teaching practices
2. to map their level of digital competences and skills
3. to understand their training needs on digital technologies to later prepare adequate and valuable training materials

Furthermore, the study presented in this paper was designed to support higher education institutions and other private and public organizations that need to improve the quality of their language study programs by providing a useful set of recommendations for language teaching in the digital era.

The survey presented in this paper was designed to provide the teachers' perspective on the digital competences in language learning. In a context of a larger study, the teachers' perspective was complemented by employers' expectations and a reflection on the European and national policies [7–9].

The paper is structured as follows. Section 2 describes the context of the study and the background. Section 3 presents the questionnaire that was designed for the study, the target groups, data collection process, and the data analysis methods. Section 4 presents the results of the study, structured by eight sections of background, level of teaching, instructional models, attitude towards digital technologies, competences in digital teaching, satisfaction with digital competences and need for training, institutional support for enhancing digital competences, and institutional aid for personal development. In Sect. 5, we discuss the results, analyzing how they fulfill the objectives outlined above. In Sect. 6, we present the limitations of the study, draw conclusions, and outline future work directions.

2 Background

2.1 Integration of Technologies and Methodologies in Language Teaching Practice

With the rapid development of technology in the last twenty years, the need for the inclusion of digital tools in second language practices has been addressed in several studies [10–13]. Research on teachers' integration of technologies started becoming stronger in the 2000s. An example can be found in Lam's qualitative study conducted in the USA to explore teachers' perceptions towards technological developments on education [11]. Lam reported that the main reasons that influence the adoption of technology are related to teachers' personal belief in benefits of technology, or lack thereof, rather than to a resistance to technology. She concludes stating that teachers should not be considered 'technophobic', and institutions, defined by Lam as 'technophilic', should not rush to obtain the latest innovations without considering the needs of teachers and students.

Albirini examined the attitudes of high school English as a foreign language teachers in Syria toward digital technologies [10]. His quantitative study investigated the relationship between computer attitudes and five independent variables: computer attributes, cultural perceptions, computer competence, computer access, and personal characteristics (including computer training background). Albirini concludes claiming that Syrian teachers have positive attitudes toward digital technologies in education. In particular, teachers' attitudes were predicted by computer attributes, cultural perceptions and computer competence. His results pointed to the importance of teachers' vision of technology itself, their experiences with it, and the cultural conditions that surround its introduction into schools in shaping their attitudes toward technology and its subsequent diffusion in their educational practice.

More recently, Sullivan and Bhattacharya carried out a qualitative study and analyzed how technology has been perceived and used by a language teacher in her span of twenty-year career as a foreign language educator [13]. The results revealed a complex negotiation process, a thoughtful reflection of advantages and disadvantages of technology integration in foreign language classrooms, and the value of understanding the cyclical nature of technology integration in education.

The successful integration of technologies in the foreign and second language classroom was and continues to be a very challenging task as it entails the selection of the appropriate teaching methodologies which can address specific linguistic needs. In fact, in order new educational technologies to be effective they need to be well supported by innovative pedagogical approaches which in turn could enable collaboration, communication and mobility [14]. To that end, there is a large body of research that investigates the use of computers and emerging technologies in the foreign and second language classroom known for the last 40 years as the field of CALL. What it revealed, though, is that there are no prevailing CALL theories. It is clear that the arrival of new technologies has driven the use of a "set" of theories which include a blend of known learning theories, linguistic theories, Second Language Acquisition theories, and human-computer interaction theories.

An effort to map the "CALL theories" was done by Warschauer and Healey [15] who divided 30+ years of history from 1960s to 1990s into three main phases: a) behavioristic CALL, b) communicative CALL, and c) integrative CALL matching different technologies to certain pedagogical approaches. The first phase stressed mostly the importance of behavior and promoted behaviorist language learning approaches such as drills and practice tasks. The second phase promoted mostly the communicative approach and the cognitivist approaches in both education theory and second language acquisition theories. Finally, in the third phase prevailed mostly the importance of the social contexts as preconditions for learning a language promoting the Computer Mediated Communication technologies along with Constructivist and Socio-Cultural Approaches and methods in foreign as well as second language learning such as the situated learning theory, the activity theory, scaffolding learning, collaborative learning, project-based learning, etc.

The third phase defined by Warschauer and Healey led soon to a more recent CALL phase which emphasised the use of web 2.0 tools, networking and the creation of communities of practice promoting Connectivism, an influential contemporary learning theory which "perceives learning as a process that is not entirely under the control of the individual and occurs within complex and lacking definite form environment knowledge needs to be connected with the right people in the right context in order to be classified as learning" [16]. A characteristic application of Connectivism is the connectivist type of Massive Open Online Language Courses which offer open access language courses to a massive number of language learners supporting interactivity, peer-to-peer learning, autonomy, social networking, openness and emergent knowledge [17].

During the last decade, CALL integrated many novel technologies (i.e., virtual learning environments, augmented reality, artificial intelligence, smart mobile apps, advanced computer-mediated communication tools) in the language teaching process and introduced various innovative teaching approaches such as problem-based learning [18], webquests 2.0 [19], game-based learning [20, 21] mobile assisted language learning [22], virtual reality games in language learning [23], and tandem learning in telecollaboration [24].

Language teachers need to be well and constantly informed and trained on how to organize online, distance or hybrid language courses to be able to make best use of all these emerging technologies applying efficient and novel teaching approaches.

2.2   Language Teachers' Digital Competences and Skills

Language teaching is a very challenging task as it requires a sound grounding in disciplinary and pedagogical content knowledge as well as in technology knowledge obtained through constant professional development and practical experience. With the advent of technologies, the need for hybrid, online or distant language learning and for digitally competent language teachers has grown significantly. In fact, competency in the use of ICT is nowadays an integral part of a foreign language teachers' professional competency' [25].

Digital skills include technical and pedagogical use of ICT in education and training teachers with these skills contributes to improve the teaching-learning process [26]. Since 2005, Hampel & Stickler stressed that "teaching language online requires skills that are different from those used to teach language in face-to-face classrooms. It is also different from teaching other subjects online" [27]. To that end, Hampel and Stickler's proposed a "skills pyramid" framework, which intended to identify the key competences of an online language tutor proposing a pyramid of skills with seven key competences ranging from lower-level general skills (e.g., basic ICT competence) to higher level skills (i.e. facilitation of communicative competence).

Many more researchers investigated language teachers' distance training and tried to define the digital competencies and skills that language teachers should acquire [28–33]. Digital competence encompasses a set of skills that are associated with several areas of knowledge. For example, Zhao et al. proposed three knowledge areas which must be integrated: a) technology proficiency, b) pedagogical compatibility and c) social awareness [34]. Ferrari later defined digital competence as the "set of knowledge, skills, and attitudes [...] required when using ICT and digital media to perform tasks; [...] and build knowledge" [35].

Many researchers also discussed the role of distance language tutors emphasizing that they should be able to provide accurate feedback, encouragement, and support in such a way that the student feels 'reassured, valued and respected' [30, 31, 36]. A recent study [32] has shown that several factors such as collaborative learning, linking theories with practice, access to support and resources, scaffolding learning experiences, modeling ICT integration and assessment with ICT, practice through reflection-on-action, and collaborative learning can lead language teachers to obtain an advanced level of digital competence. This study has also shown that language teachers are "digital role models" and need to reflect on the ways they use digital technologies.

Even though digitally skilled language teachers are needed, there is still a reluctance towards the use of ICT. This seems to be a major barrier for the integration of digital technologies and their use in the language classroom [37]. In fact, in many cases (e.g., [26]) teachers still use the traditional method where the teacher is the transmitter of knowledge and the student is a mere passive recipient. Further analysis follows in the next section.

2.3   Language Teachers' Training Needs on Digital Technologies

Language teachers' integration of digital technologies in their teaching practices can be influenced by many factors [38]. Son and Windeatt consider teachers' training on the use of digital technologies as a key element in teachers' attitudes towards their use of these technologies in the classroom [39].

Several studies investigated the impact of training in digital technologies on language teaching practices from different perspectives [40–42], which include technology workshops, lectures on CALL, online courses, face-to-face courses specifically designed for a CALL certificate, and CALL master's degrees [43, 44]. Despite the wide range of language teacher training programs in digital technologies, Hong criticized that the number of courses and workshops are insufficient, and their quality is inadequate [45]. In the same line, Ertmer and Ottenbreit-Leftwich point out that even though teachers receive training on the use of technology, they are often incapable of integrating it in their teaching practices [46]. An explanation of this phenomenon was provided by Guichon who proposes that the technologies discovered during digital technology education programs become obsolete after teachers obtain certification and have the possibility to put into practice what they learnt during training [47].

In his study conducted with 108 TESOL master's degree graduates, Kessler found that not only informal training in digital technology through conference workshops, in-service training, personal reading and other forms of self-edification, but also formal instruction obtained during undergraduate courses as well as Masters' courses on the use of digital technologies do not serve the teachers' pedagogical needs, specifically when they need to create their own digital educational materials [48].

More recently, Soulé and Papadima-Sophocleous investigated CALL practices in the Cypriot Higher Education system and their relation to teachers' education in CALL and professional development [12]. The study was designed to assess CALL training, training for technology integration into the educational process, and CALL practices among second language instructors from public and private universities. The analysis of the data revealed a considerable variety in instructors' training, which ranged from in-service training, seminars, conferences, and lectures on CALL or CALL training as part of master's or doctorate programs. Despite this variety, the perception of instructors towards the training received for technology integration was generally positive, particularly in terms of its usefulness for the evaluation, selection, and use of computer-based instructional material. However, statistically significant differences were found among instructors according to their CALL training in terms of their perception towards effectiveness of training, leading to the creation of computer based instructional materials. Similarly, differences were found in the frequency of usage of mobile devices, website creators, wikis, and other social technologies.

The purpose of the present study is, therefore, to contribute to the description of the current situation of language teachers' integration of technologies and methodologies in their teaching practices, language teachers' digital competences and skills, and language teachers' training needs.

3   Method

3.1   Research Design

While designing the survey we pursued three main objectives, as described in the introduction: to describe how teachers use digital technologies in their everyday practice, to learn what their digital literacy level is, and what kind of training they need. These three objectives were transformed into five main topics of the survey. We aimed to find out the following:

- what instructional methods language teachers use in computer-supported language learning
- what attitude language teachers have towards the use of digital technologies
- how language teachers assess their digital competence level
- how satisfied language teachers are with their level of digital competences, and what their training needs are
- what language teachers think of the institutional aid in personal and professional development towards digital competences

3.2   Tool Design

The survey was designed for two target groups: (a) language teachers and (b) administrators and policymakers working in the area of language learning. Questions about the personal and professional background were included for both target groups in the same form, but all other questions were formulated differently to make them more relevant for the professional background of the respondents.

The data were collected with the digital tool EnjoySurvey. The questionnaire consisted of 48 anonymous closed multiple-choice questions. The logic of the questionnaire adjusted automatically with respect to the answers the participants gave.

Even though the survey addressed both language teachers and administrators working in the area of language learning, the number of respondents from the latter group is not sufficient to analyze the obtained data qualitatively. Therefore, in this paper we consider only data received from language teachers. The teachers answered in total 32 questions structured in eight topics (Table 1).

Table 1. Survey topics and question codes

Topics	Question codes
1. Personal and professional background	Q1, Q2, Q13
2. Level of teaching	Q3a-c, Q4a-d
3. Language learning instructional models	Q5a-k
4. Attitude towards digital tech in language teaching	Q6a-c
5. Competencies in digital language teaching	Q7, Q8
6. Satisfaction with digital competencies training & required improvement	Q9, Q10, Q10a-c
7. Institutional support for enhancing digital competencies	Q11
8. Institutional aid for personal development towards digital competencies	Q12

3.3   Participants

In total, 283 language teachers answered the questions of the survey. The respondents were predominantly female (85%), while others were male (15%). The age distribution of survey respondents changed through five age groups: age bracket 17–25 year (4% of respondents), 26–35 (24%), 36–45 (36%), 46–55 (24%), and 56–65 (12%).

The majority of the teaching staff surveyed (46%) have indicated a master's degree as their highest level of education attained. Another significant cohort of the respondents (29%) have PhD-level education and other Doctoral degrees (9%). The next largest cohort (8%) have bachelor-level education. The option Certified/licensed professional was selected by 7% of respondents. Other options were selected by less than one percent.

The larger part of the teaching staff surveyed (40%) has been in the profession for 1120 years. The second-largest cohort of the respondents (22%) have been teaching for 2130 years. Close to the latter, with 19% of the respondents, is the group with 610 years in service. The respondents with 5 or fewer years in service represented 10%. And the respondents with more than 30 years in service - 9%.

The predominance of the teaching staff surveyed (69%) works at a university. A smaller but still sizable group of the respondents (19%) work at a secondary, middle, or primary school. Other respondents represent colleges (3%), vocational educational institutions (3%), self-employed (3%), policy-making organizations (1%), and lifelong learning and distant/online education institutions (1%).

The respondents stated that their employment organizations are located in 43 different countries. The largest number of participants located in Russia (36.7%), Czech Republic (8.1%), Cyprus (6.0%), Austria (4.9%), Italy (3.5%), Greece (2.8%), Serbia (2.8%), Norway (2.8%), Lithuania (2.5%), Finland (2.5%), Spain (2.1%), Japan (1.8%), Romania (1.4%), India (1.1%), Iran (1.1%), Portugal (1.1%), Turkey (1.1%), and in 26 other countries (less than 1% in each).

In this survey, we asked the language teachers about the cohort of students they teach (in respect of their language acquisition), and the majority of the teaching staff surveyed (63%) are foreign language teachers. Almost a quarter of the participants (24%) teach both students' first language and foreign language cohorts. And 13% of the respondents teach only students' first language.

3.4   Data Collection and Analysis

The data were collected from March to July 2019. The survey was promoted in the professional networks of the study collaborators, at their universities, and on social media.

The collected data were processed in R-programming software. The method of descriptive statistics was used for the data analysis.

4   Results

The results of the survey provide the language teachers' perspective on the digital competences in language teaching. This section is structured by the sections of the survey and refers to the codes of specific questions where necessary (Table 1).

4.1   Instructional Models

The majority (78%) of the teaching staff who participated in the survey teach their students face-to-face. More than half (59%) of the respondents in this category practice the blended learning model of instruction. A third of this category's respondents use the online/distance instructional model (Fig. 1). The participants could choose multiple options.

Fig. 1. Instructional models used within the last two years (Q4)

4.2   Language Learning Instructional Methods

In Sect. 3 of the survey (Table 1), we evaluated the instructional methods that language teachers use in their daily practice. Survey question Q5 included 10 instructional methods most commonly used in CALL (Fig. 2). The response options included two positive alternatives, formulated as follows: "Use as the core methodology" and "Use as an auxiliary methodology". The response options also included three alternatives for not using the methods (see legend on Fig. 2).

The survey proved content-based learning and task-based learning to be the most used as core language learning methodologies. Game-based learning and project-based learning are the most used as auxiliary methodologies (Fig. 2).

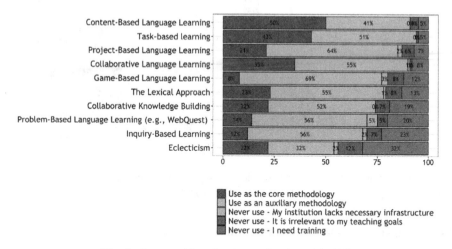

Fig. 2. Language learning instructional models (Q5)

The larger part of respondents has stated that they use all the educational technologies under consideration in their teaching practice, with eclecticism being used the least.

The lack of necessary infrastructure proved to have little influence on the teachers' motivation to use language teaching methodologies.

4.3 Attitude Towards Digital Tech in Language Teaching

In Sect. 4 of the survey (Table 1), the teachers were asked to state their overall attitude towards digital technologies in language teaching, as well as in the role these technologies play in the students' progress. The results showed that generally they agree that digital technologies enhance language learning and are beneficial for the classroom (Fig. 3, left). Nevertheless, the respondents rated the role of digital technologies in academic performance of their students as less positive (Fig. 3, right).

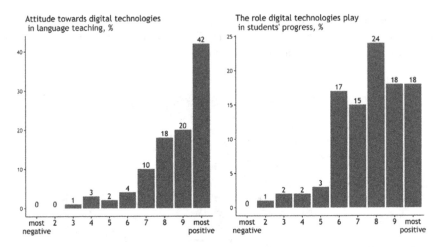

Fig. 3. Attitude towards digital technologies in language teaching (Q6b, left) and The role digital technologies play in students' progress (Q6c, right)

4.4 Competencies and Satisfaction with Competencies

In Sect. 5 of the survey (Table 1), language teachers who responded to the survey self-assessed their level of proficiency in using digital technologies, choosing from six levels (Fig. 4, left). A question in Sect. 6 of the survey (Table 1) about the kind of training the participants are interested in contained the same six levels (Fig. 4, right). Each of the six levels contained a detailed description for the participants (for example, Intermediate: *I am capable of using technically specific tools and devices [...]. I also understand how to implement digital technologies in language teaching [...]. I also try to enrich the variety of digital tools that I use in my language lessons and to introduce innovative teaching methodologies*).

The majority of the teaching staff surveyed (34%) identify themselves as belonging to the Intermediate group of digital language teaching experts (Fig. 4, left). The second-largest group of respondents (27%) identify their digital language teaching expertise as that of the Pre-Intermediate level, while the third-biggest percentage (22%) consider themselves as belonging to the Advanced group. Only 5% describe themselves as Proficient digital language teaching experts.

A relatively small number of language teachers identify themselves as complete novices (4%) and beginners (8%). In addition, very few require training at the beginner level (5%) and pre-intermediate level (6%).

Assessing if the participants are satisfied with the level of digital language teaching expertise, we suggested only two options in question Q9 (yes, satisfied and no, not satisfied). More than two-thirds of the teachers (71%) responded not satisfied to this question. The survey also asked if the participants believe that they can improve their digital language teaching expertise by participating in an external digital literacy training program in question Q10. The questions also included two answer alternatives: yes and no. The majority of the participants (95%) responded positively to this question.

Among those who believe that they can improve their digital language teaching expertise by participating in an external digital literacy training program, a majority (43%) are interested in Advanced-level training and 18% in Proficient, while almost a third (29%) would opt for intermediate-level training (Fig. 4, right).

The teachers who highly value the role of technology in teaching (those who opted to 8, 9 or 10 on a scale from 1 "negative" to 10 "positive", Fig. 3, left), noted more often that they need advanced training than those who believe that technology plays a mediocre role in teaching (those who have chosen 6 and 7 on the same scale).

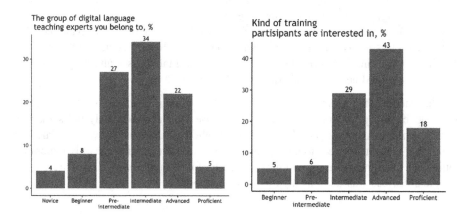

Fig. 4. The groups of digital language teaching experts you belong to (Q7, left) and Kinds of training participants are interested in (Q10a, right)

4.5 Institutional Support and Aid

In Sect. 7 of the survey (Table 1), we assessed the institutional support for enhancing digital competences of language teachers by asking about the availability and frequency of the digital literacy training provided by the respondents' employers.

Sizable part of the respondents (27%) reported that their employers never organize training for advancing digital skills, while approximately half of the participants (47%) responded that they have access to such kind of training in their workplace. (Q11). However, two-thirds of the respondents, who receive such training at their organizations, report that the training sessions happen irregularly (36%) or as rarely as once per year (29%). Only 21% of the teachers stated that their employers organize training regularly. At the same time, 63% of the teachers describe the training held at their employing organizations as effective and the skills they received are applied in practice.

Among the most preferable and effective ways to improve their level of digital literacy apart from the formal training, the language teachers named experience exchange sessions (34%). Other options included participation in CALL conferences (23%), participation in special interest groups (22%), and mentoring programs organized by the educational institutions (21%).

In Sect. 8 of the survey (Table 1), we studied the institutional aid for personal development towards digital competencies that the participants expect from their employing institutions.

The survey participants expressed their opinions on how their employment organization could contribute to improvement of their digital literacy level, additionally to training. The suggested means to facilitate the advancement of digital literacy were selected by the participants as follows. It was possible to select multiple answers:

- Allocate working hours for language teacher digital literacy development 54%
- Arrange a technical support service or equivalent 54%
- Create a digital literacy mentoring program 52%
- Ensure there is an adequate quantity of modern, reliable digital tools available 51%
- Provide classrooms fully equipped with latest technological devices 50%
- Allocate working hours for the development of digital courses and programs 50%
- Grant unlimited access to the equipped classrooms 30%

The teaching staff surveyed tended to choose the additional methods for achieving a higher level of digital language teaching expertise with approximately the same frequency, where two means slightly ahead of the others (see the list above). The method of granting unlimited access to the equipped classrooms emerged as the only unpopular option. At the same time, providing classrooms fully equipped with the latest technological devices was rated as high as other methods.

5   Discussion

5.1   Use of Instructional Methods and Attitude Towards Digital Technologies

Evaluating the instructional methods language teachers use in their daily practice, we received rather positive results. The participants replied that they use (either as a core or an auxiliary method) all 10 suggested instructional methods most commonly used in CALL (Fig. 2). The answers varied from the least used method Eclecticism (22% of participants use it as a core method and 32% use it as an auxiliary method, Fig. 2) to Task-based learning (43% of participants use it as a core method and 51% use it as an auxiliary method, Fig. 2). This means that language teachers use multiple and varied CALL instructional methods.

The data confirm that the most common reason for not using specific instructional methods was the need for training. It varied from only 5% for Content-based language learning and Task-based learning to nearly one third –32% for Eclecticism. Out of the ten instructional methods most commonly used in CALL, we identified four that require more training: Collaborative knowledge building, Problem-based language learning, Inquiry-based language learning, and Eclecticism.

The results might postulate a correlation between the data we collected and the problem of inadequate quality or level of courses and training that might still exist today, after it has been identified in multiple studies as early as a decade ago Hong [45] and even earlier by Kessler [48].

The results generally confirm the challenge of integrating digital technologies into language teaching practices that was identified earlier [46] and confirmed in multiple studies [3].

We evaluated the integration and use of different instructional methods together with the digital competences of language teachers. We followed the definition of digital competences by Ferrari [35] and considered that this set of skills includes both technical and pedagogical use of ICT [26]. And yet, the previous research shows that the integration of digital technologies and their use in the language classroom is a long process where many teachers are still reluctant to use digital technologies, which seems to be a major barrier [37]. Needless to say, the integration of digital technologies into language teachers' praxis can be influenced by many factors [38].

In the past, the *lack of digital infrastructure and services* has been considered a serious challenge [3]. The data we collected did not confirm that this is an important reason for not using specific instructional methods. According to the results of our survey, language teachers do not consider this obstacle to be essential, hence only 5% or fewer participants choosing it (Fig. 2). This discrepancy can possibly be related to the fact that the predominant majority of our survey participants (69%) were employed at universities, and only 19% worked at a secondary, middle, or primary school. In general, universities might have better digital infrastructure than schools, and thus overall results did not reflect lack of infrastructure as an important barrier. According to the data, the *need for training* is a much more common motive for not using specific instructional methods.

Exploring the attitudes of language teachers towards the use of digital technologies, we evaluated two main constituents: the frequency of use and the perceived effectiveness.

In a general question: "Your attitude towards digital technologies in language teaching", the responses were very positive – 80% in the most positive end of the Likert-scale (steps 8, 9, and 10 on Fig. 3, left). Language teachers generally see digital technologies as something that enhances learning and is beneficial for the language classroom. On this background, the results from a more specific question "The role digital technologies play in your students' progress", provide further insights. The respondents are still optimistic, but much lower than in the previous question: 60% answering in the most positive end of the Likert-scale (steps 8, 9, and 10, Fig. 3, right). Therefore, these results may point that language teachers did not use digital technology to its full potential. This can also mean that there is a gap between the current use and the potential that teachers believe that digital technologies should have for teaching and learning purposes. This confirms the need for training as a means to unitize the full potential of digital technologies.

The results of the survey presented in this paper (Fig. 3 and 4) correspond to the findings of Son and Windeatt [39], who perceive teachers' training in the use of digital technologies as a key element in teachers' attitude towards their use of these technologies in the classroom. The respondents who confirmed the high value of technology in teaching also were more certain that they want to advance their level of digital literacy, than those whose general attitude towards technology was less positive.

5.2 Language Teachers' Training Needs on Digital Technologies

The key finding that contributes to defining the training needs of language teachers is the *level of required training*. The analysis of the results of two survey questions: the proficiency level the respondents identify themselves with and the level of training the respondents are interested in (Sect. 4.3), both indicate that most language teachers have all basic digital competencies. This means that the demand for the basic CALL or digital literacy training is low among language teachers.

A recommendation on the level of digital competence training that is in demand among language teachers can be derived from the same results. The majority of the respondents identify themselves with the pre-intermediate and intermediate level, while the levels of training the majority of respondents are interested in are intermediate and advanced. These levels of digital language teaching expertise were defined as:

- Intermediate: *I am capable of using technically specific tools and devices, i.e. technical aspects and uses of interactive whiteboards, software for creating media, audio/video files and images, main uses of digital equipment, mobile devices, software for language learning, etc. I also understand how to implement digital technologies in language teaching using the right teaching methodology for every language need, i.e. collaborative tools like Padlet to enhance writing skills, video editing tools like Toondoo to enhance oral and writing skills, etc. I also try to enrich the variety of digital tools that I use in my language lessons and to introduce innovative teaching methodologies.*
- Advanced: *I feel confident using more advanced digital technologies, i.e. learning management systems (LMS), web 2.0 tools, mobile learning devices and applications for languages learning, etc. following the right language teaching methodology, e.g. I can independently create a blended LMS-based module on Moodle, Canvas, edX, etc. platform and train my students and colleagues in using the proposed technology.*

By looking at the level of satisfaction that language teachers show towards digital tools and the associated learning approaches (Sect. 4.4) and the improvement they consider necessary (Sect. 4.5), we can get further insight into the level of demand and characteristics of the required training.

In particular, most of the language teachers report that they are not satisfied with their level of digital language teaching expertise. At the same time, the majority of teachers believe that they can improve their digital language teaching expertise by participating in an external digital literacy training program. This result confirms previous findings by Soulé and Papadima-Sophocleous [12], who different training modes are seen as useful by language teachers (not only formal certified programs).

The result that the respondents, although generally positive towards using digital technologies in teaching, are not fully convinced about their usefulness for the progress of students (Sect. 4.3), indicates that they have not reached the full potential in using these technologies, as was previously reported [4]. These indicators correlate with the results for the *training needs of the teachers* (Sect. 4.4), from which we can conclude that organizing digital competence training for language teachers is potentially in high demand.

Furthermore, language teachers show interest (Sect. 4.5) in taking part in different training activities apart from formal training, specifically in experience exchange sessions. This indicates that language teachers need to have access to various kinds of training in order to implement novel technology-enhanced learning methodologies.

6 Conclusions

The major contribution of study presented in this paper is the description of the teachers' perspective on the use of digital technologies in language teaching.

For the objective of identifying to what extent and how language teachers integrate novel technologies and methodologies in their teaching practices, our results demonstrate (a) that language teachers use multiple and varied instructional models and (b) provide details on the use and challenges related to 10 CALL methods.

For the objective to map the level of digital competences and skills of language teachers, our results show that (a) most language teachers have all basic digital skills and (b) language teachers are positive towards using digital technologies in general but are less certain about the role of digital technologies in student progress, which indicates a gap between the current use and the potential that teachers see for digital technologies.

For the objective to understand the training needs of language teachers on digital technologies, our data show that (a) most language teachers are not satisfied with their level of digital language teaching expertise, which is most often pre-intermediate and intermediate and (b) the greatest majority of the teachers believe that they can improve their digital language teaching expertise, requiring most often intermediate and advanced-level training.

The limitations of the study include a relatively low number of participants. Although the participants represented 43 countries, more than a third of all responses came from a single country, while 26 countries were represented by only one or two respondents. In addition, many of the survey questions were asking the respondents to self-assess their skills, needs and practices. This should be considered when interpreting the results.

The study was designed and conducted before the start of the COVID-19 pandemic. We assume that the new realia of teaching in the context of COVID-19 have changed the overall need in digital language teaching skills among the teachers, as well as the share of the teaching staff who teach online on a regular basis. Future work should evaluate the scope of this change, investigating how language teachers use digital technologies in the new context, their updated attitude towards these technologies, and status of the related skills and competencies they have. We also propose to use qualitative methods to get a deeper understanding of the factors that facilitate and the challenges that hinder and ultimately prevent language teachers from integrating digital technology in their day-to-day practice. We propose conducting a comparative study of pre- and post-pandemic use of digital technologies by language teachers and their attitude towards technologies, analyzing how the global lockdown affected the use of digital technologies and the development of digital competencies.

Acknowledgements. The work presented in this paper has been supported by the Digital Competences for Language Teachers project (DC4LT https://www.dc4lt.eu/). The project was funded by the European Union's Erasmus Plus programme, grant agreement 2018-1-NO01-KA203-038837.

References

1. European Commission: Communication from the Commission to the European Parliament, The Council, The European Economic and Social Committee and The Committee of the Regions. A Digital Agenda for Europe. (2010) https://eur-lex.europa.eu/LexUriServ/LexUriServ.do?uri=COM:2010:0245:FIN:EN:PDF
2. Partnership for 21st Century Skills: P21's Framework for 21st Century Learning (2009). https://files.eric.ed.gov/fulltext/ED519462.pdf
3. European Commission: 2nd survey of schools: ICT in education. final report - Study (2019). https://ec.europa.eu/digital-single-market/en/news/2nd-survey-schools-ict-education
4. Redecker, C., Punie, Y.: European Framework for the Digital Competence of Educators: DigCompEdu (2017). https://ec.europa.eu/jrc/en/publication/eur-scientific-and-technical-research-reports/european-framework-digital-competence-educators-digcompedu
5. Ng, K.L.E., Olivier, W.P.: Computer assisted language learning: an investigation on some design and implementation issues. System **15**(1), 1–17 (1987)
6. Bax, S.: CALL—past, present and future. System **31**(1), 13–28 (2003)
7. Talmo, T., Fominykh, M., Giordano, A., Soule, M.V.: Digital searchlight – a study on digital skills being sought amongst language teachers. In: 14th International Technology, Education and Development Conference, Valencia, Spain, 2–4 March, pp. 4956–4965 (2020)
8. Talmo, T., et al.: Digital competences for language teachers: do employers seek the skills needed from language teachers today? In: Zaphiris, P., Ioannou, A. (eds.) HCII 2020. LNCS, vol. 12205, pp. 399–412. Springer, Cham (2020). https://doi.org/10.1007/978-3-030-50513-4_30
9. Fominykh, M., et al.: Digital competences in language education: teachers' perspectives, employers' expectations, and policy reflections (2019). https://www.dc4lt.eu/
10. Albirini, A.: Teachers' attitudes toward information and communication technologies: the case of Syrian EFL teachers. Comput. Educ. **47**(4), 373–398 (2006)
11. Lam, Y.: Technophilia vs. technophobia: a preliminary look at why second-language teachers do or do not use technology in their classrooms. Can. Modern Lang. Rev. **56**(3), 389–420 (2000). https://doi.org/10.3138/cmlr.56.3.389
12. Soulé, M.V., Papadima-Sophocleous, S.: Exploring the influence of teachers' education and professional development in Cypriot higher education CALL practices. In: Giannikas, C.N., Kakoulli Constantinou, E., Papadima-Sophocleous, S. (eds.) Professional development in CALL: a selection of papers, pp. 25–37 (2019)
13. Sullivan, N.B., Bhattacharya, K.: Twenty years of technology integration and foreign language teaching: a phenomenological reflective interview study. Qualitative Report **22**(3), 757–778 (2017)
14. Webster, L., Murphy, D.: Enhancing learning through technology: challenges and responses. In: Enhancing Learning Through Technology, pp. 1–16 (2008)
15. Warschauer, M., Healey, D.: Computers and language learning: an overview. Lang. Teach. **31**(2), 57–71 (1998)
16. Siemens, G.: Connectivism: a theory for the digital age. Int. J. Instr. Technol. Distance Learn. **2**(1) (2005). http://www.itdl.org/Journal/Jan_05/article01.htm

17. Perifanou, M., Economides, A.: MOOCs for language learning: an effort to explore and evaluate the first practices. In: 8th International Technology, Education and Development Conference, Valencia, Spain, 10–12 March, pp. 3561–3570 (2014)
18. Hwang, G.-J., Hsu, T.-C., Lai, C.-L., Hsueh, C.-J.: Interaction of problem-based gaming and learning anxiety in language students' English listening performance and progressive behavioral patterns. Comput. Educ. **106**, 26–42 (2017)
19. Perifanou, M., Mikros, G.: "Italswebquest": a wiki as a platform of collaborative blended language learning and a course management system. Int. J.Knowl. Learning **5**(3–4), 273–288 (2009)
20. Godwin-Jones, R.: Augmented reality and language learning: from annotated vocabulary to place-based mobile games. Lang. Learn. Technol. **20**(3), 9–19 (2016)
21. Hwang, G.-J., Chiu, L.-Y., Chen, C.-H.: A contextual game-based learning approach to improving students' inquiry-based learning performance in social studies courses. Comput. Educ. **81**, 13–25 (2015)
22. Burston, J.: MALL: the pedagogical challenges. Comput. Assist. Lang. Learn. **27**(4), 344–357 (2014)
23. Dalton, G., Devitt, A.: Irish in a 3D world: engaging primary school children. Lang. Learn. Technol. **20**(1), 21–33 (2016)
24. Canals, L.: The effects of virtual exchanges on oral skills and motivation. Lang. Learn. Technol. **24**(3), 103–119 (2020)
25. Sysoyev, P.V., Evstigneeva, I.A., Evstigneev, M.N.: The development of students' discourse skills via modern information and communication technologies. Procedia. Soc. Behav. Sci. **200**, 114–121 (2015)
26. Rodríguez, B.R., Gómez Zermeño, M.G.: Digital competences in English language teaching and learning at high. Campus Virtuales **6**(2), 51–59 (2017)
27. Hampel, R., Stickler, U.: New skills for new classrooms: training tutors to teach languages online. Comput. Assist. Lang. Learn. **18**(4), 311–326 (2005)
28. Cadorath, J., Harris, S., Encinas, F.: Training for distance teaching through distance learning. Open Learn. J. Open, Distance e-Learning **17**(2), 139–152 (2002)
29. Compton, L.K.L.: Preparing language teachers to teach language online: a look at skills, roles, and responsibilities. Comput. Assist. Lang. Learn. **22**(1), 73–99 (2009)
30. White, C., Murphy, L., Shelley, M., Baumann, U.: Towards an understanding of attributes and expertise in distance language teaching: tutor maxims. In: Evans, T., Smith, P., Stacey, E. (eds.) Research in Distance Education (RIDE), vol. 6, pp. 83–97. Deakin University, Geelong (2005)
31. Shelley, M., White, C., Baumann, U., Murphy, L.: "It's a unique role!" Perspectives on tutor attributes and expertise in distance language teaching. Int. Rev. Res. Open Dist. Learn. **7**(2), 1–15 (2006)
32. Røkenes, F.M., Krumsvik, R.J.: Prepared to teach ESL with ICT? A study of digital competence in Norwegian teacher education. Comput. Educ. **97**, 1–20 (2016)
33. Oksana, B.K., Olha, V.P.: Future english language teachers' digital competence development by means of storyjumper software tool. Inf. Technol. Learn. Tools **79**(5), 126–138 (2020)
34. Zhao, Y., Pugh, K., Sheldon, S., Byers, J.L.: Conditions for classroom technology innovations. Teach. Coll. Rec. **104**(3), 482–515 (2002)
35. Ferrari, A.: Digital competence in practice: an analysis of frameworks. Joint Research Centre, European Commission, Luxembourg, Report EUR 25351 EN (2012). https://ec.europa.eu/digital-single-market/en/news/digital-competence-practice-analysis-frameworks
36. Murphy, L.M., Shelley, M.A., White, C.J., Baumann, U.: Tutor and student perceptions of what makes an effective distance language teacher. Distance Educ. **32**(3), 397–419 (2011)

37. Raman, K., Yamat, H.: Barriers teachers face in integrating ICT during English lessons: a case study. Malays. Online J. Educ. Technol. **2**, 11–19 (2014)
38. Lin, C.-Y., Huang, C.-K., Chen, C.-H.: Barriers to the adoption of ICT in teaching Chinese as a foreign language in US universities. ReCALL **26**(1), 100–116 (2014)
39. Son, J.-B., Windeatt, S. (eds.): Language Teacher Education and Technology: Approaches and Practices. Bloomsbury Academic, London (2017)
40. Davies, G.: Perspectives on Offline and Online Training Initiatives. In: Felix, U. (ed.) Language learning online: Towards best practice, pp. 193–214. Swets & Zeitlinger, Lisse (2003)
41. Rickard, A., Blin, F., Appel, C.: Training for trainers: challenges, outcomes, and principles of in-service training across the Irish education system. In: Hubbard, P., Levy, M. (eds.) Teacher education in CALL. pp. 203–218. John Benjamins, Philadelphia, PA (2006)
42. van Olphen, M.: Digital portfolios: Balancing the academic and professional needs of world language teacher candidates. In: Kassen, M.A., Lavine, R.Z., Murphy-Judy, K., Peters, M. (eds.) Preparing and developing technology-proficient L2 teachers. pp. 265–294. CALICO, San Marcos, TX (2007)
43. Hubbard, P., Levy, M.: The scope of CALL education. In: Hubbard, P., Levy, M. (eds.) Teacher Education in CALL. John Benjamins (2006)
44. Reinders, H.: Teaching (with) technology: the scope and practice of teacher education for technology. Prospect **24**(3), 15–23 (2009)
45. Hong, K.H.: CALL teacher education as an impetus for L2 teachers in integrating technology. ReCALL **22**(1), 53–69 (2010)
46. Ertmer, P.A., Ottenbreit-Leftwich, A.T.: Teacher technology change. J. Res. Technol. Educ. **42**(3), 255–284 (2010)
47. Guichon, N.: Training future language teachers to develop online tutors' competence through reflective analysis. ReCALL **21**(2), 166–185 (2009)
48. Kessler, G.: Assessing CALL teacher training: what are we doing and what could we do better? In: Hubbard, P., Levy, M. (eds.) Teacher education in CALL. pp. 23–43. John Benjamins (2006)

Japanese EFL Learners' Speaking Practice Utilizing Text-to-Speech Technology Within a Team-Based Flipped Learning Framework

Yasushige Ishikawa[1]([⊠]) [iD], Shinnosuke Takamichi[2] [iD],
Takatoyo Umemoto[1] [iD], Masao Aikawa[1] [iD], Kishio Sakamoto[1] [iD],
Kikuko Yui[1] [iD], Shigeo Fujiwara[3] [iD], Ayako Suto[3] [iD],
and Koichi Nishiyama[4] [iD]

[1] Kyoto University of Foreign Studies, Kyoto, Japan
{y_ishikawa, t_umemoto, m_aikawa, k_sakamoto,
k_yui}@kufs.ac.jp
[2] The University of Tokyo, Tokyo, Japan
shinnosuke_takamichi@ipc.i.u-tokyo.ac.jp
[3] Uchida Yoko Co., Ltd., Tokyo, Japan
{shigeo.f, a.suto}@uchida.co.jp
[4] Infinitec Co., Ltd., Tokyo, Japan
nishiyama-koichi@infinitec.co.jp

Abstract. This study investigated the following hypothesis. Speaking practice using text-to-speech (TTS) technology decreases students' anxiety and increases their self-efficacy toward making presentations in English in front of their classmates. It was conducted in a university EFL flipped learning course in which a team-based framework was implemented. First-year students who were enrolled in the EFL flipped learning courses at a university in Japan voluntarily participated in this study. A control group and an experimental group were created. Pre- and post-investigation questionnaires on students' anxiety and self-efficacy about making class presentations in English were conducted. A two-factor analysis of variance (two-way ANOVA) with a mixed design of time period (pre and post) and group (experimental and control groups), and a correlation analysis between the number of times they practiced, and the length of each practice (in seconds) were conducted to validate the above hypothesis. As for presentation anxiety, the main effect of timing was significant ($p < .05$, partial $\eta^2 = .14$). There was a decrease in the mean value from pre- to post-questionnaire. Second, as for the presentation self-efficacy, the interaction effect was significant ($p < .01$, partial $\eta^2 = .25$). Based on the results of the analyses, it was revealed that that speaking practice using the TTS technology decreased the students' anxiety and increased their self-efficacy toward making presentations in English. It is anticipated that speaking practice in this manner would lead to students' increased confidence in the delivery of their presentations.

Keywords: Speaking practice · Text-to-speech technology · Team-based flipped learning framework

© Springer Nature Switzerland AG 2021
P. Zaphiris and A. Ioannou (Eds.): HCII 2021, LNCS 12784, pp. 283–291, 2021.
https://doi.org/10.1007/978-3-030-77889-7_19

284 Y. Ishikawa et al.

1 Introduction: Text-to-Speech Technology for English Education

Studies have demonstrated the usefulness of text-to-speech (TTS) technology in a language learning setting. Handley and Hamel [1] reported positive results for TTS use and recommended the technology for English as a Foreign Language (EFL) learners' listening and speaking practice. TTS synthesis, which generates speech from text input, offered means of providing spoken language input to learners in Computer-Assisted Language Learning environments [2]. Liakin, Cardoso, and Liakina [3] claimed the pedagogical benefits of TTS technology for second or foreign language learning.

Exposure to input of the target language is indispensable for mastering the language. However, learners in an EFL context, such as Japanese EFL learners, are placed in input-poor environments because English is neither their native nor official language, and there is a limited number of native English teachers available. English as a native language, which is in the inner circle of the three-circle model of English proposed by Kachru [3], has been used as a source of accurate English models and the best English teaching materials for English education in Japan. However, it is possible for TTS technology to generate human-like voices. As Azuma [4] stated, "the time may have come when we can use the TTS synthesized speech as a model in educational settings focused on the teaching of foreign languages" (p. 498). Hai and Oki [4] examined the quality of TTS synthetic speech by comparing it with natural human speech. The results revealed that TTS synthetic speech was perceived to be almost as natural as human speech and the students with a low English proficiency level preferred TTS sounds to voices of native English speakers. TTS technology has the potential to enhance EFL learning by providing easily accessible spoken language input [5]. A trainee teacher in Turkey utilized a Web-based TTS tool outside class in order to improve her English pronunciation, and it was found that her accent started being perceived as native, indicating that the online TTS tool may be effective as a self-study tool for improving the trainees' English pronunciation [6]. Even in an environment where English is the first language, TTS technology has been used for English language lessons. Parr [7] conducted an eight-month survey with twenty-eight grade five students whose first language was English and revealed that the TTS technology promoted an inclusive reading practice that facilitated language learning for students with different reading abilities.

2 Purpose of the Study

This study aimed to investigate the following hypothesis: speaking practice using TTS technology decreases students' anxiety and increases their self-efficacy toward making presentations in English in front of their classmates.

To address the above hypothesis, we developed a system that supports students' speaking practice using TTS technology and implemented the system within a team-based flipped learning framework in a university EFL course in Japan.

3   Development of the System

The system we developed functions as a learning environment, which is installed on students' and teachers' mobile devices, such as laptops, tablets, and smartphones. All of its functions (see Fig. 1) were delivered using an online server. Various data, including texts, audio files, attachments, and students' performance data, were stored in MySQL (see Fig. 2).

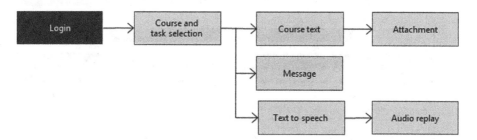

Fig. 1. Diagram of the functional components in the system

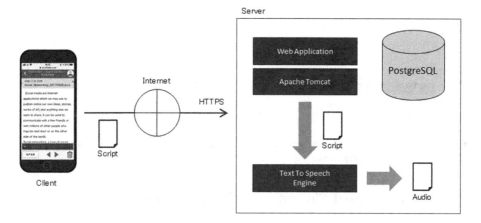

Fig. 2. MySQL system block diagram

The following are the instructions for students to generate TTS sounds in the system mentioned above.

1. Click on the "Create New" button, and when the dialog box appears, select the document you want to convert to audio, and then, click the "Start" button.
2. Click the "Convert to Audio" button at the bottom left of the screen to convert it to an audio file.
3. When the conversion is finished, a playback bar will appear in the lower left corner of the screen, and you can press the bar to listen to the audio.

4. In the converted audio, you can set the word or expression you want as an emphasis point, as shown in Fig. 3:

   (1) By double-clicking on the word or expression you want to emphasize, it will be highlighted in red and designated as an emphasis point.

   (2) After specifying the emphasis point, click on the "Convert to Audio" button to convert the speech again, and the speech will be generated with the required emphasis.

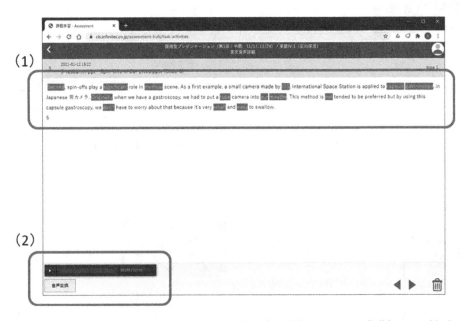

Fig. 3. Screenshot of the emphasis points (in red) and the "Convert to Audio" button with the playback bar (Color figure online)

4 The Team-Based Flipped Learning Framework

The above system was used in the university EFL flipped learning course in Japan. Several studies have reported on the effectiveness of flipped learning (e.g., [8–17]). Researchers have investigated whether adopting innovative strategies or technologies can make flipped learning more effective [18]. Therefore, we created an original team-based flipped learning framework and implemented it within the course.

The framework comprises three phases: (1) pre-class, (2) class, and (3) post-class sessions. First, within small groups, students collaborate on learning tasks outside of class. Second, after rubric-based self- and peer assessments of their out-of-class activities, the students set a goal and collaborate in small groups on learning tasks to achieve the goal. Before the end of the class, the students set a new goal for their next out-of-class activities after the self- and peer assessments of their class activities. Third, outside of class, students collaborate on learning tasks within small groups to achieve the new goal set at the end of the class session. Figure 4 illustrates the team-based flipped learning framework.

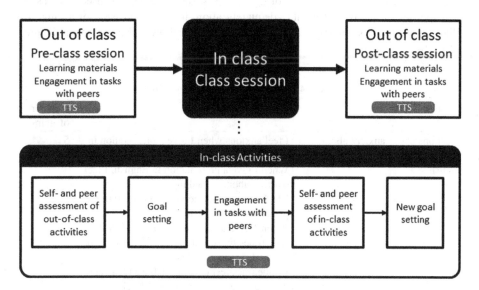

Fig. 4. Team-based flipped learning framework

The EFL flipped learning course was mandatory for first-year students at a university in Japan. It consisted of three units, each having four sessions (one session per week). The students were divided into groups of 4–5 people during the first week of the semester and were registered in the system (See Sect. 3). The weekly outline of course topics was as follows:

1. Week 1: Registration and instructions about the system
2. Week 2–Week 5: Unit 1; pre-questionnaire
3. Week 6–Week 9: Unit 2
4. Week 10–Week 13: Unit 3; post-questionnaire
5. Week 14–Evaluations, reflections, and feedback

5 The Study

5.1 Participants

Of the 39 first-year students, 30 students who were enrolled in the EFL flipped learning courses at a university in Japan in AY 2020, voluntarily participated in this study. Of those 30 students, 16 were in the experimental group and 14 were in the control group.

5.2   Method

Pre- and post-questionnaires on students' anxiety and self-efficacy about making class presentations in English were conducted in October 2020 and in January 2021. A 5-point Likert Scale (from 1: strongly disagree to 5: strongly agree) was used to measure the responses in a way that would adequately allow for the expression of a range of beliefs about students' anxiety and self-efficacy. Table 1 shows the questions in the pre- and post-questionnaires.

Table 1. Questions in the pre- and post-questionnaires

Question	Item	Number of items
Questions about anxiety about making class presentations in English	I feel anxious when I give a presentation in English When I give a presentation in English, I feel worried about something I feel anxious and nervous when I give a presentation in English When I give a presentation in English, I sometimes think that my performance is not as good as other students' I sometimes feel uncomfortable and agitated when giving a presentation in English	5
Questions about self-efficacy about making class presentations in English	I think I will be good at giving presentations in English in the future I think I can give a good presentation in English I am confident in my ability to give presentations in English I think I can give a good presentation in English if I put my mind to it I think I will get a good grade in my English presentation	5

When students used the TTS technology to practice their presentations, the number of times they practiced, and the length of each practice (in seconds) were recorded. The data were then downloaded in the CSV file format.

5.3   Results and Discussion

In order to verify the reliability of the results of the pre- and post-questionnaires, the alpha (α) coefficients for presentation anxiety and self-efficacy were calculated for each of the pre- and post-questionnaires, and each was found to be sufficient as is in Table 2.

We conducted a two-factor analysis of variance (two-way ANOVA) with a mixed design of time period (pre and post) and group (experimental and control groups) to explore the effects of the TTS technology (See Table 2). As for presentation anxiety, the main effect of timing was significant ($p < .05$, partial $\eta^2 = .14$). There was a decrease in the mean value from pre- to post-questionnaire. As for presentation self-efficacy, the interaction effect was significant ($p < .01$, partial $\eta^2 = .25$).

Multiple comparisons (Holm) were conducted. First, there was a significant difference between the two groups, with the control group having a higher mean value than the experimental group ($p < .05$). Next, there was a significant increase in mean values from the pre- to post-questionnaires in the experimental group ($p < .05$). Finally, there was a decrease in mean values from the pre- to post-questionnaires in the control group ($p = .08$).

Table 2. Mean, standard deviation, α coefficient of each subscale and results of two-way ANOVA

Subscale	Group	Pre			Post			Main effect of time	Main effect of group	Interaction effect
		Mean	SD	α	Mean	SD	α			
Presentation anxiety	Experimental group	3.56	0.71	0.77	3.34	1.01	0.88	4.71*	0.50	0.07
	Control group	3.39	0.69		3.10	0.98				
Presentation self-efficacy	Experimental group	2.68	0.67	0.89	3.04	0.84	0.89	0.98	1.41	9.39**
	Control group	3.26	0.75		3.07	0.72				

$^*p < .05$, $^{**}p < .01$

Furthermore, in the experimental group, the total number of TTS practice sessions and the total practice time (seconds) for each student's presentation were calculated (*Mean* = 65.24, *SD* = 32.11). We also calculated the difference scores for each of presentation anxiety and self-efficacy by subtracting the scores of the pre-questionnaire from the scores of the post-questionnaire. The mean difference score for presentation anxiety was -0.22 ($SD = 0.70$), and the mean difference score for presentation self-efficacy was 0.36 ($SD = 0.58$).

The correlation analysis between the difference score of presentation anxiety and the practice time per session (in seconds) showed no correlation ($r = -.29$, *n.s.*). Next, a correlation analysis was conducted to examine the relationship between the difference scores of presentation self-efficacy and practice time per session (in seconds), and a positive correlation was found ($r = .45$, $p = .08$).

Regarding presentation anxiety, the main effect of timing was significant. There was a decrease in the mean value from the pre- to post-questionnaire. Regarding presentation self-efficacy, the interaction effect was significant.

There was a significant difference between the two groups, with the control group having a higher mean value than the experimental group. Additionally, there was a significant increase in mean values from the pre- to post-questionnaires in the experimental group. Moreover, there was a decrease in mean values from the pre- to post-questionnaires in the control group.

The results of the correlation analysis between the difference scores of presentation self-efficacy and practice time per session (in seconds) showed a positive correlation, implying that the longer the students practice per session with the TTS technology, the more their self-efficacy tends to increase from the pre- to post-questionnaires.

6   Conclusion

The study's hypothesis—speaking practice using the TTS technology decreases students' anxiety and increases their self-efficacy toward making presentations in English in front of their classmates—was supported.

The results shown in Sect. 5 revealed that speaking practice using the TTS technology decreased the students' anxiety and increased their self-efficacy toward making presentations in English. Thus, it is anticipated that the practice using the TTS technology would lead to students' increased confidence in the delivery of their presentations.

7   Further Research Directions

Our next step is to validate the hypothesis, "whether practicing presentations using a TTS synthesis engine with an English model of Japanese EFL learners that contains Japanese accents but does not affect communication in English, would decrease the learners' English presentation anxiety and would increase the learners' self-efficacy for making presentations in English, compared to practicing presentations, using a TTS synthesis engine with a native English speaker's English model."

If this hypothesis is validated, it is expected that Japanese EFL learners will no longer need to worry about whether they are pronouncing English as well as native English speakers. Moreover, this will help to reduce their anxiety about speaking English and increase their confidence in making public presentations in English.

Acknowledgement. This study is supported by the Cooperative Research Project Initiative of Kyoto University of Foreign Studies, Japan. The data presented, the statements made, and the views expressed are solely the responsibility of the authors.

References

1. Handley, Z., Hamel, M.J.: Establishing a methodology for benchmarking speech synthesis for computer-assisted language learning (CALL). Lang. Learn. Technol. **9**(3), 99–120 (2005)
2. Handley, Z.: Is text-to-speech synthesis ready for use in computer-assisted language learning? Speech Commun. **51**(10), 906–919 (2009)
3. Liakin, D., Cardoso, W., Liakina, N.: The pedagogical use of mobile speech synthesis (TTS): focus on French liaison. Comput. Assist. Lang. Learn. **30**(3–4), 325–342 (2017). https://doi.org/10.1080/09588221.2017.1312463
4. Kachru, B.B.: World Englishes and English-using communities. Ann. Rev. Appl. Linguist. **17**, 66–87 (1997). https://doi.org/10.1017/S0267190500003287

5. Azuma, J.: Applying TTS technology to foreign language teaching. In: Zhang, F., Barber, B. (eds.) Handbook of Research on Computer-Enhanced Language Acquisition and Learning, pp. 497–506. Information Science Reference, Hershey (2008)

6. Hirai, A., Oki, T.: Comprehensibility and naturalness of text-to-speech synthetic materials for EFL listeners. JACET J. **53**, 1–17 (2011)

7. Moon, D.: Web-based text-to-speech technologies in foreign language learning: opportunities and challenges. In: Kim, T.-H., Ma, J., Fang, W.-C., Zhang, Y., Cuzzocrea, A. (eds.) FGIT 2012. CCIS, vol. 352, pp. 120–125. Springer, Heidelberg (2012). https://doi.org/10.1007/978-3-642-35603-2_19

8. Ekşi, G.Y., Yeşilçınar, S.: An investigation of the effectiveness of online text-to-speech tools in improving EFL teacher trainees' pronunciation. Engl. Lang. Teach. **9**(2), 205–214 (2016)

9. Parr, M.: Text-to-speech technology as inclusive reading practice: changing perspectives, overcoming barriers. LEARNing Landsc. **6**(2), 303–322 (2013)

10. Gilboy, M.B., Heinerichs, S., Pazzaglia, G.: Enhancing student engagement using the flipped classroom. J. Nutr. Educ. Behav. **47**(1), 109–114 (2015)

11. Hsieh, J.S.C., Wu, W.-C.V., Marek, M.W.: Using the flipped classroom to enhance EFL learning. Comput. Assist. Lang. Learn. **30**(1–2), 1–12 (2017)

12. Hung, H.-T.: Flipping the classroom for English language learners to foster active learning. Comput. Assist. Lang. Learn. **28**(1), 81–96 (2015)

13. Ishikawa, Y., et al.: A flipped learning approach to university EFL courses. In: Khosrow-Pour, M. (ed.) Encyclopedia of Information Science and Technology, 4th edn, pp. 3850–3860. Information Science Reference, Hershey (2017)

14. Ishikawa, Y., Tsubota, Y., Smith, C., Murakami, M., Kondo, M., Tsuda, M.: Integrating online and offline student collaboration in EFL flipped learning courses. In: Palalas, A. (ed.) Blended Language Learning: International Perspectives on Innovative Practice, pp. 303–328. China Central Radio & TV University Press, Beijing (2018)

15. Lin, C.-J., Hwang, G.-J.: A learning analytics approach to investigating factors affecting EFL students' oral performance in a flipped classroom. J. Educ. Technol. Soc. **21**(2), 205–219 (2018)

16. McLaughlin, J.E., et al.: The flipped classroom: a course redesign to foster learning and engagement in a health professions school. Acad. Med. **89**(2), 236–243 (2014). https://doi.org/10.1097/ACM.0000000000000086

17. Nouri, J.: The flipped classroom: for active, effective and increased learning—especially for low achievers. Int. J. Educ. Technol. High. Educ. **13**(33) (2016). https://doi.org/10.1186/s41239-016-0032-z

18 Hwang, G-J., Yin, C., Chu, H-C.: The era of flipped learning: promoting active learning and higher order thinking with innovative flipped learning strategies and supporting systems. Interact. Learn. Environ. **27**(8), 991–994 (2019)

Achieving Student Engagement in Learning: Utilizing a Rubric-Based Assessment System for Visualizing Learners' Self-, Peer, and Teacher Assessments

Yasushige Ishikawa[1]([✉]) [iD], Takatoyo Umemoto[1] [iD],
Yasushi Tsubota[2] [iD], Shigeo Fujiwara[3] [iD], Ayako Suto[3] [iD],
and Koichi Nishiyama[4] [iD]

[1] Kyoto University of Foreign Studies, Kyoto, Japan
{y_ishikawa, t_umemoto}@kufs.ac.jp
[2] Kyoto Institute of Technology, Kyoto, Japan
tsubota-yasushi@kit.ac.jp
[3] Uchida Yoko Co., Ltd, Tokyo, Japan
{shigeo.f,a.suto}@uchida.co.jp
[4] Infinitec Co., Ltd, Tokyo, Japan
nishiyama-koichi@infinitec.co.jp

Abstract. This research project ultimately aims to achieve high student engagement in learning by utilizing a rubric-based assessment system for students' self- and peer assessments, as well as teacher assessments and feedback. This system was applied, at a university in Japan, to an English as a foreign language collaborative learning course to improve students' presentations in English. Engagement in learning is defined in this paper as the communication in the learning process among the participants that can be measured quantitatively and evaluated qualitatively. To achieve engagement in the learning process by the participants, we created a rubric-based assessment system that enables both teachers and students to formatively assess personal performance toward the desired learning outcome by using a rubric, which, simultaneously, would visualize the assessments made by the teachers and the students on the screen of the students' smartphones. Correlation analyses clarified the relationships among peer assessments, students' motivations for continuous learning, and students' course evaluations. There were positive correlations between trust in, and usefulness of, peer assessments; and among usefulness of peer assessments, motivations for continuous learning, and course evaluations. Semi-constructed interviews were also conducted and the results show that peer assessments would lead to improved performances in the students' next presentations. These findings revealed that peer assessments and the visualization of the assessments by the participants through a rubric-based assessment system encourages the students to achieve mutual engagement in the learning process.

Keywords: Student engagement in learning · Peer assessment · Self-assessment · Rubric-based assessment system

© Springer Nature Switzerland AG 2021
P. Zaphiris and A. Ioannou (Eds.): HCII 2021, LNCS 12784, pp. 292–300, 2021.
https://doi.org/10.1007/978-3-030-77889-7_20

1 Introduction

1.1 Student Engagement in Learning

Coates [1] defined engagement as "a broad construct intended to encompass salient academic as well as certain non-academic aspects of the student experience" (p. 122). It comprises the following five facets: active and collaborative learning, participation in challenging academic activities, formative communication with academic staff, involvement in enriching educational experiences, and feeling legitimated and supported by the university's learning communities. Krause and Coates [2] defined student engagement as "the extent to which students are engaging in activities that the higher education research has shown to be linked with high-quality learning outcomes" (p. 493). Coates [3] defined student engagement as "students' involvement with activities and conditions likely to generate high-quality learning" (p. 3) and provided the following six engagement scales: (1) academic challenge: the extent to which expectations and assessments challenge students to learn; (2) active learning: students' efforts to actively construct knowledge; (3) student and staff interaction: the level and nature of students' contact and interaction with teaching staff; (4) enriching educational experience: students' participation in broadening educational activities; (5) supportive learning environment: students' feelings of support within the university community; and (6) work integrated learning: integration of employment-focused work experiences into study. Travers [4] defined learning engagement as "the ability to motivationally and behaviorally engage in an effective learning process" (p. 50). Quaye, Harper, and Pendakur [5] defined student engagement as "participation in educationally effective practices, both inside and outside the classroom, which leads to a range of measurable outcomes" (p. 3).

We adapted Travers' definition of learning engagement, defining it as a student's ability to take part in learning opportunities by using effective learning processes, based on taking responsibility for their choices. This definition also involves feedback from oneself and other participants to assess personal performance, and undertaking autonomous actions for self- and peer progress in the context of learning targets. Therefore, engagement in learning is defined in this paper as the communication in the learning process among the participants that can be measured quantitatively and evaluated qualitatively. Such engagement should be satisfying to the participants such that they perceive it to be sufficiently productive while not being overly burdensome; thus, engagement would ideally be sustained over the whole course of learning.

1.2 Rubric

It is well known that student engagement in learning is enhanced when assessment tasks and student activities are designed considering what needs to be learned [6], and when a rubric is used effectively [7]. Reddy and Andrade [8] defined a rubric as "a document that articulates the expectations for an assignment by listing the criteria or what counts, and describing levels of quality from excellent to poor" (p. 435). Stevens and Levi [9], meanwhile, defined a rubric as "a scoring tool that lays out the specific expectations for an assignment" (p. 3) and can "provide a detailed description of what constitutes acceptable or unacceptable level of performance" (p. 3). Rubrics are used by teachers to grade student performance, but they can also be used by students as a formative assessment tool for their work in progress. When used as a student-centered approach to assessment, rubrics can help students understand the standards of an assignment and their learning goals [8, 10].

1.3   Learners' Self-, Peer, and Teacher Assessments

Self-assessment is defined as "students making judgements about their own work" ([11], p. 4). Peer assessment is defined as "an arrangement whereby students evaluate and make judgements about the work of their peers and construct feedback commentary" ([12], p. 103) and peer assessment is an alternative to teacher assessment and/or feedback [12]. In addition to self- and peer assessments, co-assessment is included in the formative assessment [13] and is defined, by Deeley, as a shared system of assessment which involves self-assessment in addition to assessments by peers and the teacher [14]. An example of co-assessment is group assessment where the product of a student group work is assessed by the students from another group (inter-peer assessment) or as the product of student group work assessed by the students within that group (intra-peer assessment) as well as self-assessment by individual students [11]. Providing assessment criteria is crucial in self-, peer, and group assessments. The assessment criteria should be connected to learning outcomes; thus, a rubric is an essential tool to provide students with a clear image of what is expected as those outcomes [15]. If students receive peer assessments contradictory to what they understand, they should go back to the rubric to clarify the expectations [16]. Students can learn a lot about higher education's assessment culture if they are involved in designing the assessment criteria to be used in peer assessments [11].

In this study, therefore, we asked students which aspects of their performance they preferred to be assessed on and used their answers to create a rubric for assessing student performance in terms of desired learning outcomes. We then developed a rubric-based assessment system for mobile devices such as laptops, tablets, and smartphones that displays the assessments done by teachers and students.

2   Purpose of the Study

The purpose of this study is to achieve engagement in learning by participants with the use of a rubric-based assessment system for students' self- and peer assessments as well as teacher assessments and feedback in the English as a foreign language (EFL) collaborative learning course and, in particular, to improve students' presentation skills in English at a university in Japan.

To achieve engagement in the learning process by the participants, we created a rubric-based assessment system that enables both teachers and students to formatively assess personal performance in terms of the desired learning outcomes and also, simultaneously, visualizes the assessments on the students' mobile devices.

3   Research Question

The study was conducted to answer the following research question regarding the use of a rubric-based assessment system to enable formative assessments by the teachers and students: Would the use of a specially developed rubric-based assessment system encourage students to achieve engagement in the learning process?

4   Development of the Rubric-Based Assessment System

Research into increasing student engagement has generally focused on teaching methods and general principles. Here we explored the development of a specific practical tool, the rubric-based assessment system. The system functioned as a learning environment on students' and teachers' mobile devices. All its functions (see Fig. 1) were delivered through an online server. Various data, including texts, audio files, attachments, and students' performance data, were stored in MySQL (see Fig. 2).

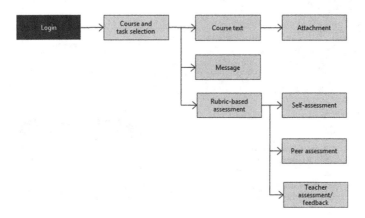

Fig. 1. Diagram of the functional components in the rubric-based assessment system

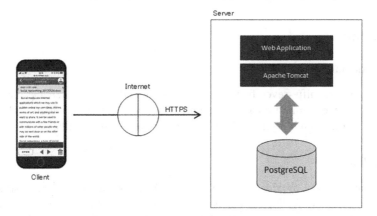

Fig. 2. MySQL system block diagram

Our system enabled both teachers and students to: (1) assess personal performance by using the created rubric, and (2) simultaneously look at the assessments provided by teachers, themselves, and peers on their devices. This system was applied to the EFL collaborative learning course to improve students' presentation skills in English at a university in Japan. Figure 3 shows a screenshot of the assessments made by a teacher and the students within the system.

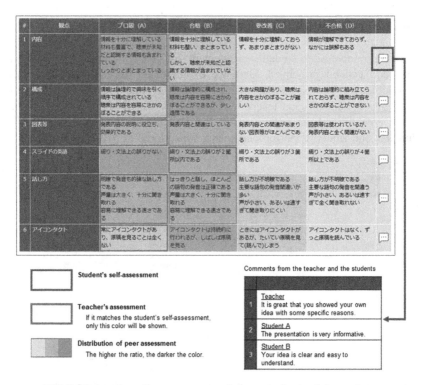

Fig. 3. Screenshot of assessments made by a teacher and the students

5   The Study

5.1   Participants

Fifty-one out of the fifty-seven first- and second-year students who were enrolled in the EFL collaborative learning courses at a university in Japan in AY 2020, voluntarily participated in this study to improve their English presentation skills.

5.2   Method

A questionnaire was provided, at the end of December 2020, to each participant ($n = 51$) to elucidate feelings about peer assessments, students' motivation for continuous learning, and students' course evaluations [17]. The questionnaire consisted of

Table 1. Questionnaire

Question	Item	Number of items
Questions about trust in peer assessments	I think the peer assessment by the participants is reliable I think the assessment given to me by the peer assessment is valid I think that peer assessment can be a hit or miss depending on who is assessing me	3
Questions about usefulness for peer assessments	I think that peer assessment will help me deepen my understanding I think it is worthwhile to be able to see various presentations through peer assessment I will try to assess all the presentations in an honest manner I think it will be useful to assess each other	4
Questions about course evaluations	What I learn in this class is important to me I like studying in this class I think that learning in this class will be useful for me I think what I will learn in this class will be useful for me to know I think it is interesting to learn in this class It is important for me to understand what I have learned in this class	6
Questions about motivation for continuous learning	Would you like to take this class again in the future?	1

four parts (see Table 1). A 5-point Likert Scale (ranging from 1–strongly disagree, to 5–strongly agree) was used for the responses, to adequately allow for the expression of a range of participants' feelings about peer assessments, students' motivations for continuous learning, and students' course evaluations.

Semi-structured interviews were conducted with ten randomly selected participants two weeks after the questionnaires were completed. How the students felt about self-assessments, peer assessments, and the visualization of the assessments to all the participants through the rubric-based assessment system was asked. Because we were trying to get comments from the students on how they were impressed with self-assessments, peer assessments, and the visualization of the assessments to all the participants through the rubric-based assessment system, we conducted interviews with them.

5.3 Results and Discussion

To verify the reliability of the results of the questionnaire, the alpha (α) coefficients were calculated for each subscale, and the values were sufficient. The mean and standard deviation were then calculated for each subscale (See Table 2 for means, standard deviations, and α coefficients for the subscales).

Table 2. Mean, standard deviation, and α coefficient of each subscale

Subscale	Mean	SD	α
Trust in peer assessments	3.55	0.69	.74
Usefulness for peer assessments	4.26	0.56	.74
Course evaluations	3.90	0.78	.94
Motivation for continuous learning	3.73	0.98	

$n = 51$

A correlation analysis was conducted to examine the relationships among the subscales. There was a positive correlation between trust in peer assessments and the usefulness of peer assessments ($p < .001$). This means that students who have trust in the peer assessments have a higher usefulness for the peer assessments. There was also a positive correlation between the usefulness of peer assessments and course evaluations ($p < .001$), and between the usefulness of peer assessments and motivations for continuous learning ($p < .001$). This indicates that students who find peer assessments highly useful value the course and are inclined to continue taking the course. Moreover, course evaluations were strongly correlated with motivations for continuous learning ($p < .001$). This shows that students who valued the course highly are more motivated to continue taking the course. Based on the above results and analyses, it is apparent that peer assessments can contribute to both motivating students regarding continuous learning and highly valuing the course, and generally engaging them in their learning (See Table 3 for the results of the correlation analyses).

Table 3. Results of the correlation analyses

		1	2	3
1	Trust in peer assessments			
2	Usefulness for peer assessments	.57***		
3	Course evaluations	.33*	.60***	
4	Motivation for continuous learning	.23	.46***	.82***

$^*p <. 05$, $^{***}p <. 001$

In the semi-structured interviews, self-assessments, peer assessments, and the visualization of the assessments to all the participants through the rubric-based assessment system were discussed with the participants.

Regarding the self-assessments, it was found that the participants had negative views on self-assessments, such as "I am too nervous to remember much during the presentation, so I cannot evaluate objectively," "I am too positive and sometimes not accurate, therefore, I cannot rely on it," and "I evaluate without properly understanding what was wrong." Regarding the peer assessments, the following comments were collected: "I thought it was good to have my presentation assessed so that I could learn in detail about areas for improvement that I would not have noticed on my own," and "The audience listens to the presentations, and the opinions from an objective point of view which will help me improve my presentation next time." These comments showed that the participants had positive feelings about the peer assessments. Regarding the visualization of assessments through the rubric-based assessment system, all participants felt the visualization would lead to confidence in their next presentations.

6 Summary of the Findings

The research question of this study—whether the use of the specially developed rubric-based assessment system would encourage students to achieve engagement in the learning process by the students—was answered positively:

- The correlation analyses indicated that peer assessments can contribute to both motivating students regarding continuous learning and course evaluation, as well as improving their engagement in their learning.
- The semi-constructed interviews showed the students felt that peer assessments would be indispensable and that it would encourage then to perform better in their next presentation.

These two results revealed that peer assessments and the visualization of the assessments, by the participants through the rubric-based assessment system, were key to achieving engagement in the learning process and ultimately students' achievement of the desired learning outcomes.

7 Conclusion

This research shows that peer assessments, with the use of a rubric-based assessment system, encourage students to achieve engagement and desired outcomes in the learning process. The usefulness of peer assessments was strongly correlated with students' course evaluations and with students' motivations for continuous learning. In the interviews conducted, the students commented that peer assessments could encourage them to perform better in their next presentations. Therefore, to enhance students' course evaluations and students' motivations for continuous learning, it is necessary to conduct course designs and teacher assessments and feedback that recognize the usefulness of peer assessments.

Further research is warranted. We are planning to investigate whether the gap between students' and teachers' rubric-based assessments is correlated with students' achievement of the desired outcomes, and if so, in what ways the gap can be visualized and corrected.

Acknowledgement. This study was supported by the Grant-in-Aid for Scientific Research (#18K00763) provided by the Japan Society for the Promotion of Science. The data presented, the statements made, and the views expressed are solely the responsibility of the authors.

References

1. Coates, H.: Engaging students for success: Australasian student engagement report, Australasian survey of student engagement. Australian Council for Educational Research, Victoria, Australia (2009)
2. Krause, K., Coates, H.: Students' engagement in first-year university. Assess. Eval. High. Educ. **33**(5), 493–505 (2008)
3. Coates, H.: A model of online and general campus-based student engagement. Assess. Eval. High. Educ. **32**(2), 121–141 (2007)
4. Travers, N.L.: Prior learning assessing handbook. Achieving the Dream, Silver Spring, Maryland (2015)
5. Quaye, S.J., Harper, S.R., Pendakur, S.L.: Student Engagement in Higher Education: Theoretical Perspectives and Practical Approaches for Diverse Populations, 3rd edn. Routledge, New York (2020)
6. Boud, D.: Associates: Assessment 2020: seven propositions for assessment reform in higher education. Australian Learning and Teaching Council, Sydney (2010)
7. Francis, J.E.: Linking rubrics and academic performance: an engagement theory perspective. J. Univ. Teaching Learning Prac. **15**(1) (2018)
8. http://ro.uow.edu.au/jutlp/vol15/iss1/3
9. Reddy, Y.M., Andrade, H.: A review of rubric use in higher education. Assess. Eval. High. Educ. **35**(4), 435–448 (2010)
10. Stevens, D., Levi, A.J.: Introduction to Rubrics: An Assessment Tool to Save Grading Time, Convey Effective Feedback, and Promote Student Learning, 2nd edn. Stylus Publishing, Sterling (2013)
11. Panadero, E., Jonsson, A.: The use of scoring rubrics for formative assessment purposes revisited: a review. Educ. Res. Rev. **9**, 129–144 (2013)
12. Race, P.: A briefing on self, peer and group assessment. Learning and Teaching Support Network (LTSN), York, UK (2001)
13. https://phil-race.co.uk/wp-content/uploads/Self,_peer_and_group_assessment.pdf
14. Nicol, D., Thomson, A., Breslin, C.: Rethinking feedback practices in higher education: a peer review perspective. Assess. Eval. High. Educ. **39**(1), 102–122 (2014)
15. Marín, V.I., Pérez Garcias, A.: Collaborative e-assessment as a strategy for scaffolding self-regulated learning in higher education. In: Caballé, S., Clarisó, R. (eds.) Formative assessment, learning data analytics and gamification: in ICT education, pp. 3–24. Academic Press, London, UK (2016)
16. Deeley, S.: Summative co-assessment: a deep learning approach to enhancing employability skills and attributes. Act. Learn. High. Educ. **15**(1), 39–51 (2014)
17. Reinholz, D.: The assessment cycle: a model for learning through peer assessment. Assess. Eval. High. Educ. **41**(2), 301–315 (2016)
18. Li, L., Liu, X., Steckelberg, A.L.: Assessor or assessee: how student learning improves by giving and receiving peer feedback. Br. J. Edu. Technol. **41**(3), 525–536 (2010)
19. Watanabe, F., Kogo, C.: The effect of learners' e-learning and peer assessment characteristics on motivation for continuous learning and course evaluation in Japan massive open online course. Japan J. Educ. Technol. **41**(1), 41–51 (2017)

Using the G Suite for Education in Language Teacher Education: Benefits and Challenges

Elis Kakoulli Constantinou[(✉)] [iD]

Cyprus University of Technology, 31 Archbishop Kyprianos, 3036 Limassol,
Cyprus
elis.constantinou@cut.ac.cy

Abstract. Even though research in the use of cloud technologies in the delivery of online courses is expanding, online language Teacher Education remains an unexplored area. This paper reports on the results of a study conducted during spring 2018 and 2019, in which the G Suite for Education was utilised for the delivery of an online Teacher Education course in English for Specific Purposes (ESP) based on social constructivism and connectivism. It specifically focuses on the benefits and the challenges encountered while using some of the core services of the suite. A total of 24 English language educators from different countries participated in the study. Data were collected through questionnaires administered to the participants before the course, the facilitator's field notes, the participants' reflective journals, comments on Google Classroom and Facebook Messenger during the course, and focus groups/interviews after the completion of the course. The results of the study revealed that the G Suite for Education may potentially create the appropriate environment and conditions for learning and professional development. The study also revealed many positive aspects of these technologies as well as challenges encountered. At a time when schools, universities and other educational institutions are moving all of their operations online, this paper can prove useful for all educators, especially language teacher educators, who wish to consider using the G Suite for Education in their practices.

Keywords: Online language teacher education · Cloud computing · G suite for education · Social constructivism · Connectivism

1 Introduction

The development of technology and the constantly changing needs of the society today have led to the rise of online education. The disruption of education and the sudden shift away from on-site learning, because of COVID-19, have brought about dramatic changes resulting in remote learning through the use of various technology tools. The reliance on online education as the only viable solution during the pandemic, has established cloud computing technologies as "an unsung hero" [1, p.1]. According to the National Institute of Standards and Technology, cloud computing "enables ubiquitous, convenient, on-demand network access to a shared pool of configurable computing resources (e.g., networks, servers, storage, applications, and services) that can be

P. Zaphiris and A. Ioannou (Eds.): HCII 2021, LNCS 12784, pp. 301–314, 2021.
https://doi.org/10.1007/978-3-030-77889-7_21

rapidly provisioned and released with minimal management effort or service provider interaction" [2, p.2]. These developments have affected all fields of education including language Teacher Education.

As research into the integration of cloud-based tools and Learning Management Systems (LMSs) in the learning and teaching process is growing, the use of tools such as the G Suite for Education in language learning and teaching is becoming more popular [3–5]. Nevertheless, despite the popularity that the G Suite for Education has been gaining the last years, the studies which report on the use of the suite for language TE are still limited.

This paper describes the experience of using the G Suite for Education for the delivery of an online English for Specific Purposes (ESP) Teacher Education course designed at the Cyprus University of Technology. More specifically, it focuses on the way some of the tools were used and elaborates on the benefits as well as some challenges encountered while using these tools.

2   Literature Review

2.1   Cloud Technologies and the G Suite for Education

Cloud computing has dominated many aspects of professional and personal life, while a decade ago, many people foresaw that cloud technologies were going to revolutionize the IT industry [6]. The potential of cloud technologies lies in their qualities, in other words their on-demand self-service, broad network access, resource pooling, and measured service [2, 6]. These affordances serve many different fields, including education.

The G Suite for Education constitutes the suite of cloud-based tools launched by Google that can be employed in education. The core services of the suite include Gmail, Calendar, Classroom, Contacts, Drive, Docs, Forms, Groups, Sheets, Sites, Slides, Chat, Meet, Vault, and Chrome Sync. Generally, the G Suite for Education has been regarded as cost effective, convenient, practical, flexible with high scalability [7]. As with every other cloud-based technology, minimal infrastructure is required; only an electronic device with access to the internet and reliable internet connection. Moreover, the G Suite applications are freely downloadable on devices such as tables or smartphones.

The benefits resulting from the use of G Suite for Education tools in the educational process reported in the literature are numerous. The ease with which these applications can be incorporated into mobile devices was one of the main reasons why the suite was selected as a LMS at Polotsk State University in Belarus, according to Barun, Dauhiala, Dauhiala, and Dziatlau [8]. The researchers investigated the perceptions of students towards the G Suite for Education, and stated that students were generally positively oriented towards the use of these Google tools in the teaching and learning processes. Some of the positive aspects of the suite they mentioned were permanent access to the materials, participation in online testing, submission of electronic assignments, possibility to pose questions, and synchronous communication. Korobeinikova et al. [9] also discussed the use of the G Suite for Education in tertiary education contexts. They supported that using mobiles, smartphones or other electronic devices in higher education "is neither entertainment nor a tribute to fashion", but an integral part of the learning process (p. 108); in this sense, cloud technologies can only facilitate access to educational material and make course management easier. Praising the affordances of the suite, the researchers stated that it can fully support "the main factors of intensification of teaching" [9, p.110].

Similarly, Bhat, Raju, Bikramjit, and D'souza [10] talked about the effectiveness of Google Classroom regarding the submission of assignments; more specifically, they referred to the ability to keep track of late submissions without facing difficulties with understanding the handwriting of students. In their study, both teachers and students commented positively on the use of such tools and appeared to understand the need to shift from the use of traditional teaching methods to e-learning tools. They emphasised however, the need for being adequately prepared to deal with the technical aspect of these technologies by receiving appropriate training. Talking about the qualities of Google Classroom, Fenton [11] expressed the view that amongst the greatest virtues of Google Classroom are its simplicity and the fact that it is connected with all the other tools of the G Suite, providing thus the course designer and the instructors with a wide variety of affordances and immediate access to G Drive. He also made reference to the fact that it allows for collaboration. Apart from research in the field of education in general, research from the field of language education in particular also proves that G Suite for Education tools have been used in ESP contexts in tertiary education, and they have been positively perceived by the students and the course facilitator [4, 5].

Despite the benefits that have been reported in the literature, there have also been some challenges associated with the use of the G Suite for Education. Abid Azhar and Iqbal's [12] research study focused on the opinion of higher education teachers on the effectiveness of Google Classroom. According to their results, teachers expressed the view that the contribution of the tool to their teaching effectiveness or the learners' engagement was not important. They even added that other platforms can be more effective than Google Classroom. Other concerns reported in the study related to difficulties encountered by the students with the use of the tool and misuse of mobile technologies in the classroom. What is interesting to note is that the researchers supported that the reason for these challenges stemmed from their lack of training, and they stressed the need for appropriate training in the use of G Suite for Education tools by both teachers and students. Additionally, Bhat, Raju, Bikramjit, and D'souza [10] expressed a concern which relates to the originality of students' work, since it is easy to share their work with each other; nevertheless, they believed that this difficulty can be overcome when plagiarism check is applied on the assignments.

2.2 The G Suite for Education in Language Teacher Education

Even though the use of the G Suite for Education has become popular the last years, only a limited number of studies have investigated the use of these tools for Teacher Education. Heggart and Yoo's [13] study is among the few. Its purpose was to examine the effectiveness of using Google Classroom with a group of 33 final year pre-service primary TE students, and the results showed that Google Classroom was very positively perceived by both the students and the instructors and that the platform was regarded as easy to access, and encouraged collaboration and the student voice. Furthermore, it provided students with the opportunity to learn autonomously and enabled the instructors to move on with a quicker pace in the class.

Basher [14] was another researcher who applied Google Classroom in a Teacher Education context. Following the experimental approach, Basher [14] divided a group of 60 students in Saudi Arabia into two groups of 30 students each, the control group and the experimental group. The researcher taught the control group in the traditional way, while the experimental group was introduced to Google Classroom, which was used to share course materials. The results of the study showed that there were significant statistical differences in the results between the experimental and controlled group when the Google classroom application was utilised, which related to teaching efficiency and academic achievement.

Another study that investigated the use of Google Classroom at Teacher Education level was that of Gupta and Pathania [15], who attempted to explore the web-based learning environments of Google Classroom and to assess its effectiveness. The sample consisted of 60 M.Ed. and M.A. Education students in a college of education in Jammu where Google Classroom was implemented. The findings of the study showed that students used Google Classroom to communicate with each other, and they felt autonomous and able to ask their instructor questions that they might have. Generally, they enjoyed learning and working collaboratively. The study also revealed that there were no gender differences between male and female students in their Google classroom learning environments. Moreover, it was found that there were no significant differences between the courses that students attended. In general, the majority of students preferred Google Classroom to more conventional methods, and they characterised Google classes as more interesting, livelier and more enjoyable. Students were also able to learn faster.

The research study described in this paper was conducted in spring 2018 and 2019 and focuses on the use of the G Suite for Education for the delivery of an online Teacher Education course in ESP. The section that follows sheds light on some of the aspects of the course in order to provide a background for the study.

2.3   The Online English for Specific Purposes Teacher Education Course

Even though ESP is an area which has been developing during the last decades, the need for ESP Teacher Education remains intense [16, 17]. An investigation of the existing ESP Teacher Education courses, shows that they are low in number, mostly offered at an MA level, on-site, demand the physical presence of the trainees, and cannot cater for the needs of ESP practitioners who cannot leave their teaching positions in order to receive Teacher Education. Sensing this need, the researcher developed an online ESP Teacher Education course, named the Reflective Teacher Education course in ESP, based on social constructivist and connectivist theories of learning. More details on the curriculum of this course can be found in Kakoulli Constantinou and Papadima-Sophocleous [18].

Having investigated various online platforms for the delivery of the course, it was decided that the G Suite for Education was the most appropriate one for this purpose. The suite was user-friendly, free of charge and there was support at no cost 24 h, seven days a week. Through the G Suite for Education administrative account, the course facilitator (and researcher) could provide all the trainees with Google usernames and passwords, and both the trainees and the course facilitator were offered limitless storage space. Furthermore, the tools that they had access to allowed for organisation of the course material, easy collaboration, administration of students' work, easy grading and feedback, and also self and group reflection. Lastly, no advertisements appeared while using the suite.

The G Suite for Education tools that were used for the delivery of the course appear in Table 1.

Table 1. The tools used for the delivery of the course.

Tools	Purpose
Google Classroom	-The platform used for classroom management purposes, where all the instructions and material for the course were uploaded and tasks were submitted and discussed. Feedback was provided by both the facilitator and the participants in the course
G Drive	-The online space directly connected to Google Classroom, where the teachers and the facilitator saved and shared the material for the course and collaborated. Teachers could share documents and work both synchronously and asynchronously on them using features such as the "Chat" or "Comment"
Google Docs	-A tool used for the creation of documents, collaboration and cooperation
Google Slides	-A tool used for the creation of presentations
Google Forms	-The tool used for registering the participants in the course and for the creation of questionnaires and quizzes
Google Sites	-The Web page-creation tool used to create a website for the course (https://sites.google.com/site/reteesponline/home-1)

Apart from G Suite for Education tools, other tools were used for the delivery of the course such as, YouTube, which was used for sharing videos with interesting material during the course. According to Szeto and Cheng [19], YouTube is one of the most common Information and Communication Technology (ICT) tools used in education with many affordances. Because of the fact that it has become extremely popular among users, it covers a wide range of topics including teaching methodology issues. Moreover, YouTube videos can be embedded in Google Classroom. Apart from YouTube, Skype was used for teleconferencing, mainly to deliver webinars/tutorials, and also at the end of the course for the focus groups/interviews. Skype was regarded as suitable for this purpose, as it is free and has many capabilities for education, as Hashemi and Azizinezhad [20] argue. In the second stage of the study, Skype was replaced by Zoom.

Furthermore, a private group was created on Facebook for sharing ideas, news, events, articles and good practices, communicating and establishing a team spirit. The group aimed at providing more interesting learning experiences to the participants [21] and also support and strengthen the network, the learning community that was created

[22, 23]. Additionally, Facebook Messenger was used for communication purposes, in case the teachers faced difficulties and wished to contact the facilitator more directly. Communication via Messenger was easier and quicker, since the majority of teachers had Facebook accounts, and they used Messenger in their everyday life. Finally, the teachers personal email accounts were also used for communication purposes.

3 The Research Study

3.1 The Purpose and Methodology of the Study

The research study aimed at addressing the neglected need for ESP Teacher Education among a group of 24 language instructors from different parts of the world through the formulation of an online community.

The methodology followed was that of Technical Action Research [24], as the purpose was for the researcher to propose a possible answer to the problem of insufficient ESP Teacher Education amongst this community of language instructors through the design of an intervention, this online ESP Teacher Education programme. The study developed in two Stages, the two spiral cycles of Technical Action Research; in Stage 1 (February 26–April 8, 2018) the intervention was designed, implemented and reflection on its implementation followed; in Stage 2 (May 20–May 31, 2019) the intervention was refined, implemented again, and final reflections were drawn.

3.2 The Participants

The 24 language instructors that participated in the study were ESP educators representing different ESP fields or English as a Foreign Language (EFL) teachers who expressed interest in educating themselves on issues pertaining to ESP teaching methodology or updating their knowledge on the latest developments in ESP teaching practices. Table 2 gives an overview of the participants in the study.

The participants in Stage 2 were from the same group of participants in Stage 1. They were less in the second stage, due to the fact that some of them did not manage to complete Stage 1, and others because they faced personal, professional or technical problems and could not participate. The fact that they were given access to the material also drove some of them to make the decision to study this material at a later stage. In order to maintain their anonymity, the participants were assigned numbers (e.g. Teacher 1–Teacher 24).

It is worth mentioning that some of the teachers were not familiar with Google Drive (12.5%) or Google Classroom (16.7%) at all, even though the majority stated that they were extremely familiar with the use of Gmail (70.83%). The majority was also well-acquainted with Skype (58.33%) and Facebook (66.7%). This was expected since Google Drive and Google Classroom are not tools that are used widely in everyday life.

Table 2. The participants in the study.

Stage 1	Place of work	%	Age	%	Sex	%
(N = 24)	Greece	37.5	20–29	12.5	Male	12.5
	Cyprus	20.83	30–39	33.33	Female	87.5
	Saudi Arabia	16.66	40–49	33.33		
	Spain	8.33	50–59	12.5		
	Sudan	4.16	No response	8.33		
	United Kingdom	4.16				
	Egypt	4.16				
	Kosovo	4.16				
Stage 2						
(N = 14)	Greece	42.8	20–29	7.14	Male	14.3
	Cyprus	28.5	30–39	28.5	Female	85.7
	Sudan	7.14	40–49	57.1		
	United Kingdom	7.14	No response	7.14		
	Egypt	7.14				
	Kosovo	7.14				

3.3 Research Tools and Analysis of Data

Data were obtained through the use of an online questionnaire administered to the teachers at the beginning of the course, the aim of which was to extract information on their profiles, their needs in terms of ESP Teacher Education, and the reasons for which they wished to attend the course. Data were also elicited from the reflective journals that the teachers kept, the facilitator's field notes, discussions on Google Classroom and Facebook Messenger (introduced in Stage 2), and finally focus groups and interviews which took place after the course was completed. These tools were used in both Stages of the study, except for the questionnaire, which was only used at the beginning of the course.

The quantitative data obtained from the questionnaire were analysed using IBM's SPSS 22 software, while thematic analysis was conducted for the qualitive data collected from the other tools using NVivo 12 software. For purposes of reliability, an external researcher recoded the data, and Cohen's kappa test was run in both Stages (in Stage 1 k = 0.67 and in Stage 2 k = 0.62). The results of the test showed that there was substantial agreement between the coders [25].

4 Results and Discussion

The large amount of data obtained generated results pertaining to different characteristics of the participants, various positive aspects of the course, challenges encountered, as well as various suggestions for future improvements and additions. Some of these results appear in Kakoulli Constantinou [26]. As mentioned earlier, this paper focuses on the use of the G Suite for Education for the delivery of this course, and it aims at delineating some benefits and challenges deriving from its use. The results are presented in two stages, the two cycles of the study.

4.1 Stage 1

Generally, the teachers and the facilitator spoke positively about the experience they had with the course in Stage 1. They enjoyed the course and characterised it as well-organised (n = 10, 41.66%), which implied that the choice of the researcher to use Google Classroom was appropriate.

Teachers were satisfied with the ways the material was presented (n = 15, 62.5%), and the fact that through Google Classroom, which was connected to the G Drive folder of the class, they would have access to the course material after the completion of the course. Generally, teachers were pleased with Google Classroom (n = 12, 50%) and Google Docs. One participant stressed the collaborative aspect of Google Docs and the practicality of cloud technology. These findings were compatible with previous research conducted on the use of the G Suite for Education [27, 28]. Through Google Docs teachers were able to send constructive feedback to each other and also receive constructive feedback by the facilitator, which they appreciated. The same tool allowed teachers to keep reflective journals in which their learning experiences and thoughts were noted. These journals, were stored in the G Drive folder of the course, and were shared with the facilitator. In general, the interactive and collaborative nature of G Suite for Education tools fostered the implementation of social constructivism, on which the course was built, a view also expressed by Denton [29].

Moreover, two of the teachers that did not have easy access to a computer found the Google Classroom mobile application very useful, as they were able to perform all the necessary tasks on their smartphone. This affordance of Google Classroom was also discussed by Barun, Dauhiala, Dauhiala, and Dziatlau [8]. Another positive aspect of the course was the fact that during the course, a sense of belonging to a CoP, as defined by Wenger and Trayner-Wenger [30], was developed, which proves that these tools can serve connectivist theories of learning.

Apart from all the benefits deriving from the use of the G Suite for Education, some challenges were encountered both with these tools as well as with some other tools used in the course. More specifically, Teacher 9, who had not used Skype for some time, did not know how to join the Webinar. For the teachers who could not attend Skype Webinars, the Webinars were scheduled on a new date and time. Skype connection difficulties were also faced by the facilitator. With regards to Google Classroom, six teachers (25%) mentioned that they came across some kind of difficulty, at least one time, with one of them stating that she did not like the interface (4.16%). Problems faced had to do with not being sure whether an assignment was submitted, figuring out how the platform worked and finding their way around the Google Classroom mobile application. As far as Google Drive was concerned, three participants had difficulties with finding the folders shared with them at the beginning (12.5%). Another problem encountered by Teacher 18 was the fact that she did not know how to access the document she worked on in Google Drive. Teacher 11 also expressed the view that moving from one folder to the other was challenging for her.

Moreover, another challenge faced was the difficulty of some of the teachers at the beginning of the course to understand where to post their first assignment.

These challenges were faced due to the fact that some of the participants were not familiar with Google Classroom or Google Drive, as the results of the questionnaire administered at the beginning showed. According to King [31], amongst the parameters for successful online teacher education and professional development is the ability of the technology to work smoothly enough so that learning is not disrupted; teachers need to feel comfortable with the technologies used. To minimize these challenges the facilitator provided constant support to the teachers and instructions were sent to them in various modes, audio-visual and written, via email, messages and Google Classroom posts.

Regarding their G Suite for Education accounts in general, only two teachers encountered some kind of difficulty (8.33%) at the beginning of the course. One of the teachers confused his personal Google account with the G Suite Google account provided to him by the facilitator and could not have access to the course material. Another teacher, on the other hand, faced problems with logging in her account, and the facilitator had to reset her password.

With regards to the Facebook closed group that was maintained for the course, this was generally well-accepted by the participants. Two of the participants however (8.33%) did not have a Facebook account, and did not wish to create one, because they considered Facebook as a tool purely for social networking that could not be used on a strict professional basis. The facilitator did not wish to impose the use of Facebook on the teachers. Nevertheless, recognising the value of social media in learning nowadays and in the creation of bonds between online community members [22, 23], the private Facebook group was maintained, despite the decision of the two teachers not to participate in it.

The teachers also faced challenges related to the communication and collaboration they had with each other, as synchronous communication was generally avoided by the teachers. As mentioned earlier, they contacted each other using tools such as Google Classroom or Google Drive or through commenting on the closed Facebook group, but this was done mostly asynchronously. This could be due to the fact that participants were not familiar with each other and hesitated to establish any form of relationship with each other outside the course boundaries, especially at the beginning of the course. However, the majority of the participants felt comfortable with sending the facilitator private messages via Messenger or emails for help, advice, clarifications or to comment on something (n = 14, 58%).

Upon completion of Stage 1 of the study, one of the most interesting suggestions expressed by the participants was the idea of organising more Webinars in the future. Teachers appeared to appreciate synchronous communication, and this was a parameter that was taken into account in the refinement of the course in Stage 2.

4.2   Stage 2

In the second cycle of the study, the course was renewed based on the feedback obtained from Stage 1. Therefore, two more weeks were added to the course, during which more Webinars were added, as suggested by the teachers. The new addition to the course was named ReTEESP Online: The Sequel, and it aimed at complementing the initial course and improve it, and to provide teachers with the opportunity to study issues in the ESP field that they did not have the opportunity to study in the first version of the course. The tools that were used for the course were the same as in Stage 1, so that teachers understand that this sequel part was a continuation of the first version of the course, and also for purposes of consistency. The only changes made were the addition of Google Calendar for Scheduling Webinars, a Facebook Messenger group for more direct communication, and the replacement of Skype by Zoom, which was regarded as more appropriate for the delivery of Webinars than Skype.

In general, participants were positively oriented towards the course characterising it as interesting and useful with new ideas (n = 7, 50%). In all their comments teachers agreed that the combination of the two courses together was successful; in this sense, it could be claimed that the addition of the sequel course was beneficial and this way the ReTEESP Online had actually improved.

With regards to challenges faced in Stage 2 of the study, it is worth mentioning that they were less than in Stage 1, and they involved technical difficulties such as poor internet connection (n = 1, 7.14%) forgotten passwords (n = 3, 21.42%) and Zoom time restrictions (40 min with an audience of more than three people for the free Basic Plan used for the delivery of this course). Additionally, after the completion of the two stages of the study, in July 2019, a notification was posted on Google Classroom by Google that, as of September 2019, a new version of Classroom would be launched, which would include a Classwork page to help teachers organise classwork. Any classes using the previous version of Classwork would be automatically converted to the new version. Unfortunately, this was a challenge that was beyond the facilitator's control, which raised concerns regarding the extent to which users can control these technologies; such concerns are in line with Sultan's [32] and Dillon, Wu, and Chang's findings [6], who expressed certain worries over the use of cloud technologies in education. Additionally, after the completion of the course, Teacher 14 mentioned that he would have liked to see the material posted on Google Classroom at least one day before the Webinar so that there would be time to study them and be engaged in discussion beforehand.

To cope with the challenges of teachers not being able to participate in all the Webinars due to lack of time and other commitments, the facilitator recorded the Webinars with the participants' permission and uploaded the videos on the Google Classroom platform for everyone to watch in case they could not attend. Furthermore, the Facebook Messenger group that was created, which served as a Chat Room, allowed for the discussion to continue after the completion of the Webinars. To address the technical difficulties teachers faced, the facilitator was always available to provide them with help and the necessary instructions (i.e. sending them emails with instructions and resetting forgotten passwords). Moreover, the same Google class that was created for Stage 1 was used in Stage 2 to make it easier for the teachers to navigate and also to allow them to have all the material for the course gathered in one place. To face Zoom time restrictions, the Webinars were scheduled for 40 min to stay within the time limit of the free Basic Plan.

Upon completion of Stage 2, the only suggestion that was expressed regarding the technologies used for the course related to the addition of an open forum that would allow the teachers to maintain the professional bonds that they had established in the context of the course. The tool that was suggested for this open forum was Facebook, as this was regarded as one of the most popular tools used by teachers in their everyday life. This is an interesting suggestion, which implies that for a day-to-day update and exchange of ideas, platforms which are used in daily life can be more easily employed than other platforms.

4.3   General Comments

In agreement with Heggart and Yoo [13], Basher [14], and Gupta and Pathania [15], the results of the study revealed that the G Suite for Education tools managed to create the appropriate environment and conditions to foster the acquisition of knowledge. The study also revealed many positive aspects of these technologies, such as the fact that the course was well-presented, well-organised and structured through the use of Google Classroom, the collaborative aspect of Google Docs, and the practicality of cloud technologies amongst others. The success of the course was not only due to the affordances of the technologies used, but also due to the pedagogies underlying the use of these technologies [33].

Furthermore, the study showed certain challenges that participants in this online TE course faced, such as difficulties in locating files and navigating through the G Drive, forgetting passwords, and generally challenges mostly of technical nature. Such challenges can exist, especially when the participants in the course are not adequately trained in the use of the technologies used for the delivery of the course. For this reason, constant monitoring of the situation by the facilitator is important, and provision of simple and effective instructions on how to cope with technicalities is necessary; this denotes that the facilitator should be comfortable with the use of these tools.

5   Limitations

Being a Technical Action Research study, the present study has certain limitations, which relate to the nature of Action Research, which operates at a local context, aiming at providing solutions to localised problems. Despite the fact that this study aims at providing a solution to the problem faced by this group of 24 language instructors, the fact that these instructors operate in different parts of the world and come from different educational contexts implies that the findings could apply in different online language Teacher Education contexts.

6   Conclusion

This paper describes the use of the G Suite for Education in the design and delivery of an online ESP Teacher Education course for language instructors that wished to receive training in teaching ESP outside the bounds of formal university education. The aim of the paper is to delineate the benefits and challenges that derive from the use of some of the tools of the suite.

The importance of the study lies in the fact that on the one hand, ESP Teacher Education is a field with very limited research, and on the other hand, the research conducted on the use of cloud technologies such as the G Suite for Education in language Teacher Education contexts is also limited. Therefore, this paper attempts to shed light on the affordances of G Suite for Education tools and the challenges that may potentially arise from its use in an attempt to contribute to the body of knowledge on the use of cloud technologies in the field of online Teacher Education in general and online language Teacher Education in particular. The results of the study may prove useful to designers of online Teacher Education courses, researchers in the field of online Teacher Education, stakeholders, decision-makers, institutions, language teachers, and generally anyone interested in this topic.

References

1. Alashhab, Z.R., Anbar, M., Singh, M.M., Leau, Y.-B., Al-Sai, Z.A., Abu Alhayja'a, S.: Impact of coronavirus pandemic crisis on technologies and cloud computing applications. J. Electron. Sci. Technol. 1–12 (2020). https://doi.org/10.1016/j.jnlest.2020.100059
2. Mell, P., Grance, T.: The NIST definition of cloud computing: recommendations of the national institute of standards and technology (2011). https://www.nist.gov/publications/nist-definition-cloud-computing
3. Esteban, D.S.G., Martínez, D.C.T.: Critical reflections on teaching ESP through constructivist, communicative and collaborative technological integrated procedures. Procedia. Soc. Behav. Sci. **141**, 342–346 (2014). https://doi.org/10.1016/j.sbspro.2014.05.059
4. Kakoulli Constantinou, E.: Teaching in clouds: using the G suite for education for the delivery of two English for academic purposes courses. J. Teaching English Specific Acad. Purposes **6**(2), 305–317 (2018). https://doi.org/10.22190/jtesap1802305c
5. Kakoulli Constantinou, E.: Revisiting the cloud: reintegrating the G Suite for Education in English for Specific Purposes teaching. In: Giannikas, C.N., Kakoulli Constantinou, E., Papadima-Sophocleous, S. (eds.) Professional Development in CALL: A Selection of Papers, pp. 55–69 (2019). https://doi.org/10.14705/rpnet.2019.28.870
6. Dillon, T., Wu, C., Chang, E.: Cloud computing: issues and challenges. In: 2010 24th IEEE International Conference on Advanced Information Networking and Applications, pp. 27–33 (2010). https://doi.org/10.1109/AINA.2010.187
7. González-Martínez, J.A., Bote-Lorenzo, M.L., Gómez-Sánchez, E., Cano-Parra, R.: Cloud computing and education: a state-of-the-art survey. Comput. Educ. **80**, 132–151 (2015). https://doi.org/10.1016/j.compedu.2014.08.017
8. Barun, A.N., Dauhiala, N.V., Dauhiala, D.A., Dziatlau, U.U.: Peculiarities of using G Suite for Education services in the educational process of Polotsk State University. J. Phys: Conf. Ser. **1691**, 1–6 (2020). https://doi.org/10.1088/1742-6596/1691/1/012161
9. Korobeinikova, T.I., et al.: Google cloud services as a way to enhance learning and teaching at university. CEUR Workshop Proc. **2643**, 106–118 (2020)
10. Bhat, S., Raju, R., Bikramjit, A., D'souza, R.: Leveraging e-learning through google classroom: a usability study. J. Eng. Educ. Trans. **31**(3), 129–135 (2018). https://doi.org/10.16920/jeet/2018/v31i3/120781
11. Fenton, W.: Google Classroom could bridge a gap in online learning. PC Mag. 27–32 (2017)
12. Abid Azhar, K., Iqbal, N.: Effectiveness of Google Classroom: teachers' perceptions. Prizren Soc. Sci. J. **2**(2), 52–66 (2018)

13. Heggart, K.R., Yoo, J.: Getting the most from google classroom: a pedagogical framework for tertiary educators. Aust. J. Teacher Educ. **43**(3), 140–153 (2018). https://doi.org/10.14221/ajte.2018v43n3.9
14. Basher, S.: The impact of google classroom application on the teaching efficiency of pre-teachers. Int. J. Soc. Sci. Educ. **2**(2), 33–48 (2017). https://doi.org/10.1016/j.compedu.2016.11.005
15. Gupta, A., Pathania, P.: To study the impact of Google Classroom as a platform of learning and collaboration at the teacher education level. Educ. Inf. Technol. **26**(1), 843–857 (2020). https://doi.org/10.1007/s10639-020-10294-1
16. Basturkmen, H.: ESP teacher education needs. Lang. Teach. **52**(3), 318–330 (2019). https://doi.org/10.1017/S0261444817000398
17. Gaye, A.: Implications of current research in ESP for ESL/ESP teacher training. In: Kenny, N., Işık-Taş, E.E., Jian, H. (eds.) English for Specific Purposes Instruction and Research: Current Practices, Challenges and Innovations, pp. 203–225. Springer, Cham (2020). https://doi.org/10.1007/978-3-030-32914-3_11
18. Kakoulli Constantinou, E., Papadima-Sophocleous, S.: Professional development in English for Specific Purposes: designing the curriculum of an online ESP teacher education course. In: Papadima-Sophocleous, S., Kakoulli Constantinou, E., Giannikas, C.N. (eds.) Tertiary Education Language Learning: A Collection of Research, pp. 89–109 (2021). https://doi.org/10.14705/rpnet.2021.51.1256
19. Szeto, E., Cheng, A.-N.: Exploring the usage of ICT and YouTube for teaching: a study of pre-service teachers in Hong Kong. Asia Pac. Educ. Res. **23**(1), 53–59 (2013). https://doi.org/10.1007/s40299-013-0084-y
20. Hashemi, M., Azizinezhad, M.: The capabilities of Oovoo and Skype for language education. Procedia. Soc. Behav. Sci. **28**, 50–53 (2011). https://doi.org/10.1016/j.sbspro.2011.11.010
21. Balcikanli, C.: Prospective English language teachers' experiences in Facebook: adoption, use and educational use in Turkish context. Int. J. Educ. Dev. Using Inf. Commun. Technol. (IJEDICT), **11**(3), 82–99 (2015). https://www.learntechlib.org/p/171323/. Accessed 26 Feb 2021
22. Dogoriti, E., Pange, J., Anderson, G.S.: The use of social networking and learning management systems in English language teaching in higher education. Campus-Wide Inf. Syst. **31**(4), 254–263 (2014). https://doi.org/10.1108/CWIS-11-2013-0062
23. Yildirim, I.: Using Facebook groups to support teachers' professional development. Technol. Pedagog. Educ. **28**(5), 589–609 (2019)
24. Grundy, S.: Three Modes of Action Research. Curriculum Perspectives **2**(3), 23–34 (1983)
25. Landis, J.R., Koch, G.G.: The measurement of observer agreement for categorical data. Biometrics **33**(1), 159–174 (1977). https://doi.org/10.2307/2529310
26. Kakoulli Constantinou, E.: Distance learning in teacher education: lessons learned from an online english for specific purposes teacher education course. In: 15th Annual International Technology, Education and Development Conference Proceedings (2021)
27. Brown, M.E., Hocutt, D.L.: Learning to use, useful for learning: a usability study of google apps for education. J. Usability Stud. **10**(4), 160–181 (2015)
28. Liu, S.H.J., Lan, Y.J.: Social constructivist approach to web-based EFL learning: collaboration, motivation, and perception on the use of google docs. Educ. Technol. Soc. **19**(1), 171–186 (2016)
29. Denton, D.W.: Enhancing instruction through constructivism, cooperative learning, and cloud computing. TechTrends **56**(4), 34–41 (2012). https://doi.org/10.1007/s11528-012-0585-1

30. Wenger, E., Trayner-Wenger, B.: Communities of practice: a brief introduction (2015). https://doi.org/10.2277/0521663636
31. King, K.P.: Identifying success in online teacher education and professional development. Internet Higher Educ. 5(3), 231–246 (2002). https://doi.org/10.1016/S1096-7516(02)00104-5
32. Sultan, N.: Cloud computing for education: a new dawn? Int. J. Inf. Manage. 30(2), 109–116 (2010). https://doi.org/10.1016/j.ijinfomgt.2009.09.004
33. Powell, C.G., Bodur, Y.: Teachers' perceptions of an online professional development experience: implications for a design and implementation framework. Teach. Teach. Educ. 77, 19–30 (2019). https://doi.org/10.1016/j.tate.2018.09.004

Nudge for Note Taking Assist System: A Learning Strategy Feedback System Among Learners Through Their Tablet

Takaki Kondo[1](✉), Kyoichi Yokoyama[1], Tadashi Misono[2], Rieko Inaba[3], and Yuki Watanabe[1]

[1] Tokyo University of Science, Tokyo, Japan
{1720509, 1719528}@ed.tus.ac.jp, wat@rs.tus.ac.jp
[2] Shimane University, Matsue, Shimane, Japan
misono@edu.shimane-u.ac.jp
[3] Tsuda University, Tokyo, Japan
inaba@tsuda.ac.jp

Abstract. In this paper, we propose a learning strategy feedback system, Nudge for Note Taking Assist System (NoTAS), developed for students to facilitate learning strategies among others in class using nudges. The system has three functions: note-taking function, learning log function, and learning visualization function. The purpose of this study is to develop software to apply nudge theory and to provide feedback on note-taking among students in class. We evaluated the effectiveness of NoTAS for high school students from two perspectives: whether the use of NoTAS interfered with the class and whether the nudges were encouraged in class. From the results of the questionnaires, we found that the students were able to concentrate on learning in the class using NoTAS, and the interface was well-received. Moreover, students can use the learning visualization function of NoTAS to see if other students are note-taking in class. This information promotes learning among students, indicating that the nudge makes achievements regarding learning awareness.

Keywords: Note-taking interface · Nudge · Realtime feedback system

1 Introduction

Recently, many countries have witnessed the growing trend of teachers using Information Technology (IT) in classes. Doing so not only enables more effective learning but also offers an environment for learning analytics by providing each learner with individual devices. In schools that have already adopted IT education, teachers are using electronic board and tablet devices to teach their classes. Heaslip et al. shows that by using response analyzers, teachers can provide feedback to students according to their level of understanding [1]. Thus, the use of IT in class is assumed to make it easier for learners to communicate their ideas in real-time and receive sequential feedback in class. Besides, Bester and Brand point out that students are more likely to concentrate in class when they use technologies in class [2]. Therefore, it can be suggested that

© Springer Nature Switzerland AG 2021
P. Zaphiris and A. Ioannou (Eds.): HCII 2021, LNCS 12784, pp. 315–331, 2021.
https://doi.org/10.1007/978-3-030-77889-7_22

there is a need to utilize systems that are less burdensome for students and allow them to concentrate in class.

Moreover, owing to the advances in technology, notes can now be taken using a pen tablet without any stress [3]. Although there are some note-taking applications available, Stacy and Cain indicate that students should use an interface that makes it easy for them to cognitively participate in the note-taking process and that facilitates revision, summarization, and emphasis [4]. Kobayashi defines note-taking as the process by which learners take notes, handouts, and highlight text in teaching-learning situations such as classes and text reading [5]. Therefore, students must utilize an interface that allows them to write notes and highlight text easily.

Beaudoin and Winne developed the nStudy system, which can be used for both individual and collaborative learning on a desktop computer. nStudy supports individual and collaborative learning with concept analysis constructed by the learner in a web browser. Additionally, it can manage learning objectives. Moreover, nStudy allows teachers and other learners to provide comments and feedback on learners' essays [6]. While nStudy can provide detailed feedback, it is difficult to use in class because it is hard for teachers to instruct students constantly on which note-taking is correct and who should be the role model. Therefore, we propose the possibility of providing feedback to each student on learning strategies such as note-taking in class. In other words, we hypothesize that students who could not take notes could be given feedback by assuming that the notes taken by the majority of students were correct. Therefore, we decided to apply "Nudge," which has been studied extensively in the field of behavioral economics in recent years.

Thaler and Sunstein define the nudge as any element of choice behavior that changes people's behavior predictably without narrowing the choice or significantly changing the economic stimulus [7]. It has been applied to educational studies [8]; however, most research is confined to nudging on teaching policies with little research on nudging the learning strategies among learners in class. Therefore, we define the educational nudge as selecting one's learning behavior from others' because we aim to learn each others' learning strategies such as note-taking in the class. We believe that nudge could be adapted to promote note-taking through an interface.

2 Purpose

The purpose of this study is to develop software to apply the Nudge theory and to provide feedback on note-taking among students in class. Specifically, we conducted a class using the developed software for high school students and evaluated the effectiveness of the software using questionnaires. There are two perspectives for the evaluation.

1. The use of the software does not interfere with the class.
2. Other students' note-taking affects students' own behavior in class. In other words, the nudge occurs in class.

3 Developed System

3.1 System Overview

Nudge for Note Taking Assist System (NoTAS) can be used in a whole class where a wireless LAN is available and where each learner and teacher has their own tablet. NoTAS is available on web browsers such as Safari and Google Chrome. The system can be used by up to 45 learners at a time, excluding the teacher. In addition, we assume a class style in which the teacher distributes class material to the learners for each class. NoTAS is a system to be used in class and the class procedure is shown in Fig. 1.

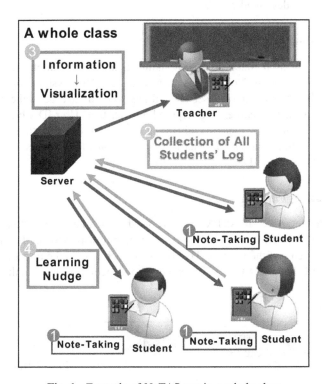

Fig. 1. Example of NoTAS use in a whole class

The details below correspond to the numbers in Fig. 1.

1. Students write notes and highlight text on the class material distributed on the tablet.
2. The system collects the information that all students have written on the material.
3. Visualization is performed based on the collected information. At this time, the visualized information is not what the students have written on the material but where and when they have written it.
4. The visualized information is displayed on all students' tablets to facilitate note-taking.

In this way, by forcibly displaying the note-taking information of all students on their tablets, students can review their own notes and reflect on how they should proceed with their learning. Assuming that the notes written and the text highlighted by a large number of learners are correct, we thought that visualizing this information would encourage learners to nudge each other in a whole class. Nudges may promote note-taking on the part of the students. In addition, the teacher can teach a lesson based on the visualized information. Therefore, we have implemented three functions in NoTAS: note-taking function, learning log function, and learning visualization function. Furthermore, we introduced user authentication so that only certain learners can access the system. The details of each function and the reasons why we implemented these functions are described below.

3.2   User Authentication Function

As a user authentication function, BASIC authentication was adopted allowing only specific learners to access NoTAS. Learners can go to the system login screen by correctly entering their common User ID and password in BASIC authentication. To access the class material, learners are required to enter their User ID which the teacher assigns to each learner in advance. Learners log in to all classes with their User ID and, since it is possible to log in with another learner's personal ID, learners must be careful when entering their User ID.

3.3   Note-Taking Function

We present the Interface of NoTAS usually used by learners (Fig. 2). Learners can write notes and highlight text directly on class material displayed on the tablet device using the tablet pen and their hands. The details of each icon in the upper menu bar are shown in Table 1. For No. 4 to No. 7, when the tapped icon is turned on, the other icons are turned off.

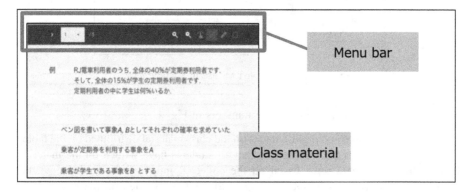

Fig. 2. Basic NoTAS screen

Table 1. Name of each function in the menu bar

No.	Icon		Name
1			Previous / Next Page Button
2			Page selection drop-down Total number of pages
3			Zoom in Button Zoom out Button
4			Swipe Button on / off
5			Pen Button on / off
6			Marker Button on / off
7			Select Button on / off
8			Delete Button

The students can use the note-taking function to write notes and highlight text in class. Here, we explain how to use the buttons on the menu bar.

After users log in to NoTAS, the first page of the class material is displayed. When the user taps the previous/next page button, they can move between pages. It is also possible to move to other pages by selecting the page you want to see using the dropdown option. The next buttons are zoom in/zoom out buttons. When the user taps these buttons, the page is enlarged or reduced by 20%. Next, is the swipe button. The swipe button is used to move the enlarged material. The user needs to select the swipe button to move a material, because they can take notes with own finger. The next button is the pen button. By selecting this button, the user can take notes in the class material. Also, they can highlight the material by selecting the marker button. The teacher can set a color and thickness for the pen and marker in advance. Next, is the select button. The user can select and move the position of notes and highlights. In addition, when the user selects the position, they can tap the delete button. Thus, they can delete the selected written notes and highlights by tapping delete.

When the user uses the note-taking function with a tablet, they can write with their fingers and a tablet pen. Regarding personal computers, if the device has a touch panel display, the user can use it in the same way as a tablet. If the device does not have a touch panel, they can operate it with a mouse.

3.4   Learning Log Function

There are two types of functions: the collection of learning log function and the confirmation of learning log function.

Collection of Learning Log Function. This function records the note-taking that learners perform on class material. Specifically, when learners write or delete notes and highlights in class material, their note-taking behavior is saved sequentially. Not only are the contents of the notes and highlighted parts saved but also the time when the notes and highlights were written. Using this function, the system converts the stored information into data for use in the learning visualization function. In addition, only teachers can view all of the stored information with the confirmation learning log function.

Confirmation of Learning Log Function. This function can only be used by teachers. Teachers can view the learning log of the learners' note-taking processes and the shading of the visualization during the note-taking by specifying the learner (User ID) and the material (Class ID). However, teachers can change the color and thickness of the lines of the pen and marker functions used by the learner, the thickness of the pen and marker functions to be visualized, the transparency per line, and the additive value settings after the class. When these settings are updated again, they are reflected in the confirmation of the learning log function. Therefore, it is easier to check the note-taking of a specific learner by setting the transparency and additive value of the pen and marker functions to 0, which were set before the class.

The learning log function also uses BASIC authentication. The User ID and password are different from those used by learners and, thus, learners cannot access this function. After BASIC authentication, when the teacher enters the User ID and Class ID, the first page of the latest material for the corresponding learner is displayed.

As with the note-taking function, the page to be viewed can be selected using the page movement button on the left side of the menu bar. In addition, teachers can see the process of note-taking, such as when and what the learner has written by selecting the time from the drop-down menu. The User ID, Class ID, and Select Learning Log of the learner who is currently viewing the learning log are displayed by tapping the menu selection button on the far right (Table 2). When you tap Select Learning Log, the learner selection screen appears, and you can again specify the learner (User ID) and the class material (Class ID) that you wish to refer to.

Table 2. Tool button of confirmation of learning log function

No.	Icon	Name	Operation / display contents
9		Menu Select Button	This is displayed only on the teacher screen. Tapping this button displays a menu on the right side of the screen.

3.5   Visualization of Learning Function

The learning visualization function is the main function of NoTAS. When a learner writes notes and highlights on the class material with this function, the approximate location of the notes and highlights written by other learners on the class material displayed on the tablet is visualized on the same material in almost real time. When using NoTAS, the teacher needs to upload the class material (.pdf) and prepare it for distribution on learners' tablet devices.

The mechanism of visualization is described below. The interface of NoTAS consists of four layers: note-taking layer, learning log layer, learning visualization layers, and class material layer (Fig. 3). The note-taking layer is designed to display the menu bar of NoTAS. The learning log layer displays the notes and highlights written by the user. The note-taking layer and learning log layer correspond to the note-taking function of NoTAS. Thus, there are personal layers. Then, the learning visualization layer shows the position and timing of other students' note-taking. Before a class using NoTAS, the teacher sets the transparency per line and the additive value for the lines drawn with pen and maker functions. The transparency here is a parameter used to set the density of the line actually drawn with the pen and maker functions. The additive value is a parameter that makes the line thicker than the line actually drawn. The notes and highlight information of learners in class collected by the collection of learning log functions of NoTAS are converted into a visualization layer based on the set transparency per line and the additive value, and then displayed on the class material of all learners. The visualization layer is updated every 5 s. Since the visualization layer overlaps with the number of learners in class, the more learners fill in the same part, the darker the color becomes. As a result, the areas written by more learners are emphasized. On the other hand, if a learner deletes notes or highlights that have been written, those areas appear lighter when the visualization layer is updated. Finally, the class material layer displays the class materials (.pdf) uploaded by the teacher in advance.

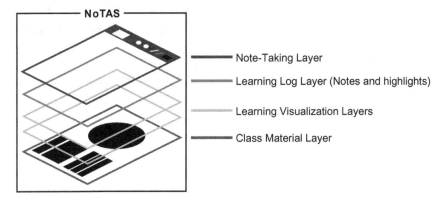

Fig. 3. Learning visualization mechanism

Here is an example of visualization when NoTAS is used in class. Time passes from Fig. 4 to Fig. 5 and then to Fig. 6. Figure 4 shows the visualization that appears when 25% of the class (about 10 learners) highlighted text. Figure 5 shows a darker visualization of the same area of highlighted text on the left interface because half of the class (about 20 learners) highlighted the text. In addition, the red area indicates that about 25% of the class has started writing notes. Figure 6 shows a darker color because more time has passed, and many learners have written notes and highlighted elsewhere. Regarding the settings of NoTAS, the visualization of pen function has a thickness of 2 (px), transparency of 0.02 per line, and an additive value of 45 (px). Also, the visualization of marker function has a thickness of 10 (px), transparency of 0.02 per line, and an additive value of 20 (px). Although this learner did not take notes or highlight anything, as the screenshots below show, when other learners in the same class took notes, the color is displayed on the class material of the learner who did not take notes.

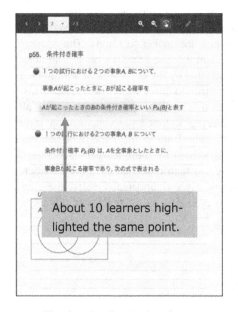

Fig. 4. Visualization interface 1

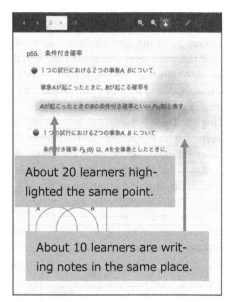

Fig. 5. Visualization interface 2

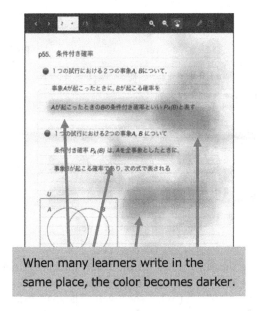

When many learners write in the
same place, the color becomes darker.

Fig. 6. Visualization interface 3

4 Method

4.1 Data Collection

For this research, we designed a class and questionnaire to discuss the effectiveness of using NoTAS in class. We collected quantitative data from questionnaires distributed to learners who took the class with and without the learning visualization function of NoTAS.

4.2 Procedure

Written informed consent was obtained from the participants, and anonymity was guaranteed for this study. The second author surveyed two mathematics classes of first-year high school students (89 students, 34 males and 55 females). The number of valid responses is 86 because students who were absent from the class were excluded. Each student and teacher had their own tablet device (Surface Go or iPad 7) and tablet pen. Since students used tablets in their daily classes, it was judged that there would be no problem with the basic handling of the devices.

Two classes were surveyed in September 2020. We conducted two classes, one with the learning visualization function of NoTAS (visualization) and the other without the learning visualization function of NoTAS (non-visualization). We designed the classes so that novelty and order effects were canceled. Before the survey parts, two classes were conducted as practice parts to familiarize the students with NoTAS. Figure 7 shows the procedure of research.

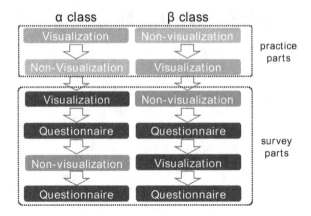

Fig. 7. Procedure of research

Before conducting the survey, we set the color, thickness, transparency per line, and additive value for the pen and marker functions of NoTAS. The pen function is RGB (255, 0, 0), 2 (px), 0.02, 45 (px), respectively. The marker function is RGB (0, 0, 255), 10 (px), 0.02, 20 (px), respectively. In this study, we did not display any specific information about the notes because we wanted to provide information to promote learning only. Therefore, the additive value setting for the pen function is much larger than that for the maker function.

4.3   Questionnaires

In this research, we surveyed questionnaires from three perspectives as follows:

Concentration in Class. We adopted 6 items to check whether students are affected by the visualization information and are able to concentrate on the class to the same extent as usual when using the learning visualization function of NoTAS. This was done after each class using a 5-point Likert scale (1 = I don't think so and 5 = I think so).

System Interface. We developed 12 items to evaluate the interface of NoTAS, focusing on the usability of NoTAS. As with the questions on concentration, we conducted this survey after each class using a 5-point Likert scale (1 = I don't think so and 5 = I think so).

Realizing the Nudge. We created the following items to investigate the factors that make students perform note-taking. We only surveyed after the class utilizing the learning visualization function. The item on notes asked about three factors: oral explanation, writing on the board, and nudges. The item on highlighting asked about two factors: oral explanation and nudges. The teacher did not write the highlighted text on the board, which is the reason for the absence of the writing on the board factor. These items were multiple choice. Then, we asked the students whether they were motivated to write notes or to highlight when they saw other students' notes or highlighted text in class according to a 5-point Likert scale (1 = I don't think so and 5 = I think so). Finally, we asked students who attempted to perform note-taking after seeing others' note-taking why they did this and students who tried to perform note-taking but eventually did not do so why they did not. The questions were open-ended.

4.4 Guidelines for Analysis

In terms of the degree of concentration, we conducted a Wilcoxon signed-rank test to compare the means of the classes with and without the visualization function of NoTAS. Then, we conducted a Wilcoxon one-sample test to compare the means after the class with the learning visualization function so that we could evaluate the interface of NoTAS. Finally, we compared the number of students for each factor to see the effect of nudges on notes and highlighting. Besides, we divided the open-ended descriptions of the behaviors into those that included the nudge factors and those that did not.

5 Results

In total, 86 participants (about 96%) answered the two questionnaires. The result of the questionnaires to evaluate the change in awareness of NoTAS and the effectiveness of using NoTAS in class are presented below. The results of the Shapiro-Wilk test show that the data were not normally distributed for all items.

5.1 Concentration in Class

Table 3 shows the results of a Wilcoxon signed-rank test for the scores of concentration in class. The class in which students used the learning visualization function is called "visual", while the class in which students did not use it is called "non-visual". The item "NoTAS interfered with my learning" was significantly higher in the class using the learning visualization function. However, the mean is small ($M_{Vis} = 2.12$).

Table 3. Comparison of concentration

	Visual		Non-visual		$M_{Vis}-M_{Non}$	Z	r
	M_{Vis}	SD_{Vis}	M_{Non}	SD_{Non}			
1. I missed the explanation while writing notes on NoTAS.	2.44	1.17	2.27	1.01	0.17	-1.38	0.15
2. I missed the explanation while looking at the material displayed on NoTAS.	2.00	0.93	2.03	0.98	-0.04	-0.30	0.03
3. I looked away from the blackboard while writing notes on NoTAS.	3.20	1.13	3.06	1.14	0.14	-0.91	0.10
4. I often looked away from the blackboard while looking at the material displayed on NoTAS.	2.79	1.17	2.73	1.23	0.06	-0.35	0.04
5. NoTAS helped me to concentrate in class.	3.51	0.93	3.58	0.95	-0.07	-0.90	0.10
6. NoTAS interfered with my learning.	2.12	1.03	1.85	0.91	0.27	-2.47*	0.27

$n = 86$, 5-point scale $^{*}p < .050$

5.2 System Interface

Table 4 shows the results of the Wilcoxon one-sample test for the score of the system interface. It is compared with the median value of 3.00 because data for these items was collected via a 5-point Likert scale. As a result, the interface of NoTAS was generally well-received.

Table 4. Evaluation of system interface

	M	SD	Median	M-3.0	W	r
1. The icons at the top of the page are easy to understand.	4.30	0.84	4.50	1.30	2933.00 ***	0.57
2. The icons at the top of the page are easy to select.	3.97	1.07	4.00	0.97	2349.00 ***	0.26
3. Pages are easy to turn.	4.07	1.06	4.00	1.07	2731.00 ***	0.46
4. Highlights are easy to draw.	3.86	1.09	4.00	0.86	2569.00 ***	0.37
5. My notes are easy to erase.	2.92	1.34	2.50	-0.08	1279.00	0.32
6. My highlights are easy to erase.	3.16	1.36	3.00	0.16	1488.00	0.20
7. It is easy to zoom in and out of the material.	3.27	1.23	3.00	0.27	1397.00 †	0.25
8. The thickness of the line in the notes I wrote is just right.	3.92	1.02	4.00	0.92	2311.00 ***	0.24
9. The thickness of the line in the highlights I wrote is just right.	3.86	1.03	4.00	0.86	2383.00 ***	0.27
10. The color of my notes is easy to see.	3.44	1.16	4.00	0.44	1607.00 ***	0.14
11. The color of my highlights is easy to see.	3.62	1.10	4.00	0.62	1782.00 ***	0.05
12. The space for notes and highlights is small. (R)	2.71	1.25	3.00	-0.29	658.00 *	0.65
$n = 86$, 5-point scale, (R): Reverse item				† $p < .100$, * $p < .050$, *** $p < .001$		

5.3 Realizing the Nudge

Figure 8 shows the number of students that agreed that certain factors encouraged them to write notes and highlight text. Regarding the notes, 65 students (76%) answered that the writing on the board was an encouraging factor, 58 students (67%) answered that the explanation was an encouraging factor, 34 students (40%) answered that the nudge was an encouraging factor, and one student (1%) did not answer. As for highlight the text, 75 students (87%) answered that the explanation was an encouraging factor, 36 students (42%) answered that the nudge was an encouraging factor, and two students (2%) did not answer.

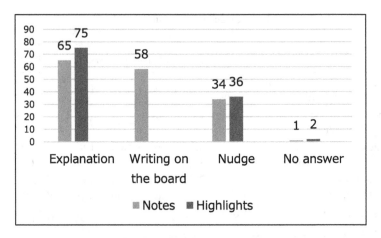

Fig. 8. Factors of note-taking

Then, Table 5 shows the results of the Wilcoxon one-sample test for the score of realizing the nudge.

Table 5. Realizing the nudge

	M	SD	Median	M-3.0	W	r
1. I was motivated to write notes and highlight texts when I saw other students' notes and highlights in class.	4.01	1.10	4.00	1.01	2688.00***	0.43

n = 86, 5-point scale   ***p < .001

Finally, Table 6 and Table 7 show the results of the open-ended questions focusing on why students did or did not take notes. Table 6 categorizes the descriptions that include nudges and those that do not include nudges. The most common reason including nudges was "because other students judged it to be important." The most common reason excluding nudges was "because I judged it to be important." Table 7 shows the three categories: interface; instruction; and other.

Table 6. Reasons for note-taking

Descriptions including nudge elements	• Because the shaded parts came out • Because I could see where everyone else was writing, and I understood that this was important • I felt that it was not good for me not to do anything while my friends were taking notes • I felt that I had to do something because everyone else was doing well in the class
Descriptions excluding nudge elements	• Because I thought that I should write down the important things • I wrote to organize the content of the class • To understand the content of the class well so that I can check it in the future • Because the teacher told us it was important • Because the teacher wrote it on the board

Table 7. Reasons for not doing (or not being able to do) note-taking

Descriptions of the interface	• Because it was difficult to write and the writing was too messy to read • The colors were too dark in places where everyone wrote, so I could not write in the same place
Descriptions of the instruction	• I could not keep up with the writing • I did not have enough time
Other	• I did not think it was necessary for me • I felt that I could understand without taking notes • Because I was not sure what to write

6 Discussion

6.1 The Use of the Software Does Not Interfere with the Class

From the results of concentration in class, it was found that there was no difference in basic behaviors such as listening and watching between the two classes with and without the learning visualization function of NoTAS. The item "NoTAS interfered with my learning" was significantly higher in the class using NoTAS. However, this result was considered appropriate because the students did not usually use NoTAS and the mean was low at 2.12. Therefore, it was suggested that students can concentrate almost as much as in a normal class even if they can see other learners' note-taking with NoTAS.

From the results of the system interface evaluation, we can interpret that the students highly appreciated the functions of NoTAS because almost all items are higher than the median. On the other hand, it was found from the students' open-ended questions that the erase and scroll functions need to be improved. Besides, some students found it difficult to see their notes and highlights. Therefore, regarding the learning visualization function, the necessity of changing the font color was suggested to differentiate one's notes from other students'.

6.2   The Nudge Occurs in Class

Regarding the realization of nudges and students' behavior, the main reason for students' note-taking was because the teacher explained or wrote on the board. Note-taking by nudges accounted for 40.7% of the total. This suggests that there are two types of students in the classroom: students who are encouraged to learn by other students' learning and students who facilitate the learning of other students. From the results, it was suggested that teachers should explain what they want to convey to students on the board or orally. Although we developed NoTAS for students to promote their learning, we suggest that NoTAS is effective not only for students who have not or cannot take notes but also for students who missed oral or written explanations.

Moreover, it was found from the result of the questionnaire and open-ended descriptions that students are motivated to take notes when they see other students' behavior on NoTAS. Therefore, it was suggested that students can promote the nudge in class in terms of awareness when they use NoTAS.

7   Conclusion

The purpose of this study is to develop software to apply nudge theory and provide feedback on note-taking among students in class. We evaluated the effectiveness of NoTAS for high school students from two perspectives: whether the use of NoTAS interfered with the class and whether the nudge was encouraged in class.

From the results of the questionnaire, it is found that the students were able to concentrate on learning in the class using NoTAS. Therefore, it was suggested that there was little resistance to the use of NoTAS in the whole class. However, many students found the deleting and scrolling functions to be difficult to use, suggesting that the note-taking function needs to be improved.

Furthermore, we found that NoTAS can promote students' note-taking. Students can see that other students are writing notes and highlighting text in class by using NoTAS. This information allows students to encourage each others' learning, thus indicating that students have achieved the nudge in terms of awareness. At first, we developed NoTAS for students who could not take notes or who did not know how to write. However, it was also shown to be effective for other students because NoTAS gave them confidence in the learning strategy and served as a reminder of which material was important. On the other hand, one of the reasons why students could not take notes even when prompted by nudges was that the learning visualization layer was too dark. To solve this problem, it is necessary to regulate the density of the learning visualization layer according to its intended use or to change the color of one's notes and those of other students.

Finally, we discuss the limitations of this study and future issues. The first is that we conducted this study in the short term. In the future, it is necessary to investigate the effects of the system when the students become familiar with it through long-term practice. The second is that we conducted this study in a high school setting. In both classes, the lesson design was the same, but from the students' responses, the teacher may have given slightly different instructions. Therefore, it is necessary to conduct a rigorous investigation by dividing the students in the same class into two groups: one group using NoTAS and the other group using different note-taking software. Third, we focus only on the awareness aspect of the nudge and evaluated it. It is necessary to analyze how the students' note-taking changed as a result of the nudges in their learning logs. For example, we should investigate whether more students take notes when they use NoTAS and whether there is a difference in when they start to write. By doing so, we may be able to encourage learning strategies changes by promoting technology that uses nudges.

Acknowledgment. This work was supported by JSPS KAKENHI Grant Number JP19K03066. We would like to thank Editage (www.editage.com) for English language editing.

References

1. Heaslip, G., Donovan, P., Cullen, J.G.: Student response systems and learner engagement in large classes. Act. Learn. High. Educ. **15**, 11–24 (2014)
2. Bester, G., Brand, L.: The effect of technology on learner attention and achievement in the classroom. S. Afr. J. Educ. **33**(2), 1–15 (2013)
3. Özcakmak, H., Sarigöz, O.: Evaluation of Turkish teacher candidates' perception of note taking concept. Educ. Res. Rev. **14**, 78–86 (2019)
4. Stacy, E.M., Cain, J.: Note-taking and handouts in the digital age. Am. J. Pharm. Educ. **79**(7), 107–112 (2015)
5. Kobayashi, K.: Note-taking and note-reviewing in a seminar class setting. Jpn. J. Educ. Psychol. **48**, 154–164 (2000). (in Japanese)
6. Beaudoin, L.P., Winne, P.H.: nStudy: an internet tool to support learning, collaboration and researching learning strategies. In: Canadian e-Learning Conference held in Vancouver, Canada (2009)
7. Thaler, R.H., Sunstein, C.R.: Nudge: improving decisions about health, wealth, and happiness. Penguin Books, UK (2009)
8. Damgaard, M.T., Nielsen, H.S.: Nudge in education. Econ. Educ. Rev. **64**, 313–342 (2018)

To Explore the Influence of Single-Disciplinary Team and Cross-Disciplinary Team on Students in Design Thinking Education

Xiao Ma and Hsien-Hui Tang[✉]

National Taiwan University of Science and Technology, Taipei, Taiwan
drhhtang@gapps.ntust.edu.tw

Abstract. Design thinking is regarded as an effective way of innovation and has a very broad prospect in the educational environment. At present, there are few studies on the influence of design thinking. This study takes the students participating in the design thinking course offered by the National Taiwan University of Science and Technology as the research object, uses the method of a questionnaire survey to explore the influence of single-disciplinary team and cross-disciplinary team on students, and discusses the characteristics and problems of different teams in design thinking education in the environment of higher education. The results show that: 1) after designing the thinking course, the students who participate in the single-disciplinary team and the students in the cross-disciplinary team have similar positive comments on the curriculum plan and its impact, 2) In terms of teamwork, we find that the two types of teams have their own characteristics, and there are also some constraints. This study is expected to supplement the research on the influence of design thinking and provide a reference for the development of design thinking education in the future.

Keywords: Design thinking · Teamwork · Design innovation education

1 Introduction

In recent years, the cultivation of innovative ability has attracted attention all over the world. University as the most important output window of talents, cultivating innovative talents will be one of the important goals of higher education. Design thinking is a human-centered and collaborative method to solve problems, which promotes innovation by improving the creative thinking ability of participants [1]. In the educational environment, design thinking has the potential to expand existing disciplines and enable more colleges and universities in creativity education [2]. Design thinking has the characteristics of encouraging tacit experience, increasing empathy, reducing cognitive bias, promoting game-based learning, flow, interdisciplinary collaboration, encouraging growth in failure, unexpected solutions and creating confidence [3]. Relevant studies have shown that design thinking education may help to cultivate students' creativity and adaptability so that they can acquire the knowledge, skills, and attributes needed to solve complex problems collaboratively [4].

© Springer Nature Switzerland AG 2021
P. Zaphiris and A. Ioannou (Eds.): HCII 2021, LNCS 12784, pp. 332–346, 2021.
https://doi.org/10.1007/978-3-030-77889-7_23

Teamwork training is a very important part of design thinking education. Students from different academic backgrounds form teams to work together to develop new product or service concepts. The mode of teamwork enables students to learn from interaction with lecturers and from communication among team members [5], students are no longer just passive participants in the educational environment but change from simple participation to dynamic, co-creative experience [6, 7].

It is worth noting that there are relatively few studies on the learning and teaching of design thinking [2], and most articles focus on discussing examples or reporting the results of a single case study, and the books are usually concepts and their constituent elements, explaining and guiding how to use a particular tool [8]. Most articles discuss design thinking at the individual or organizational level, rarely at the team level, quantitative research is rare in terms of research methods, and descriptive and normative studies are more common than interpretive studies [9].

This study recruited the students who participated in the design thinking course as the research participants, used the questionnaire survey method, including closed questions and open questions, to discuss the influence of single-disciplinary team-work and cross-disciplinary teamwork on students' learning. A single-disciplinary team means that the team members are composed of people from a single disciplinary background, while a cross-disciplinary team means that the team members are composed of people from different disciplinary backgrounds. The single-disciplinary team in this study is composed of students with a design background, and the cross-disciplinary team is composed of students with a design background and business management background. The purpose of the study is to provide a reference for the development of design thinking education in the future. In order to achieve the purpose of the study, the following objectives are drawn up:

1. Summarize the influence of single-disciplinary teamwork and cross-disciplinary teamwork on students' learning,
2. According to the results of the questionnaire, the characteristics and problems of different teams in design thinking education are discussed.

2 Literature Review

2.1 Design Thinking

Design thinking is a human-centered approach to innovation that draws from the designer's toolkit to integrate the needs of people, the possibilities of technology, and the requirements for business success [10]. The application of design thinking in different disciplines is growing and has made valuable contributions to various disciplines. In the field of design, design thinking combines theory with practice from the point of view of a designer and is correspondingly rooted in the field of design, In the field of management, design thinking is considered to be the best way to create and innovate, as a way to describe the methods of designers and to integrate them into academic or practical management discourses [11], in the field of education, Rauth et al. [12] determine the different abilities of design thinking education, such as arche-typal skills, emotional skills, the ability to choose perspective, empathy and specific ways of thinking. Design thinking skills can be learned through teaching methods that include problem-based learning, project-based learning, and inquiry-based learning in classroom activities [13].

In the educational environment, design thinking has many advantages. In the field of business and management education, Glen, R. et al. [14] believes that design thinking complements the analytical focus of business education and shows students accustomed to a structured learning environment how the seemingly chaotic design thinking process achieves the desired results, thus benefiting them. In the field of medical education, McLaughlin et al. [15] summarized 15 different case studies of design thinking in the public health sector, "*All highlighted the importance and benefit of collaboration, particularly as it related to the multidisciplinary teams and the diversity of thinking that advanced the work as well as the identification and participation of multiple stakeholders within the process*".

Although the advantages of design thinking in the educational environment should be affirmed, there is a lack of sufficient evidence for its impact. McCullagh [16] talks about "*exaggerated claims*", The applicability of design thinking has both limitations and challenges that may lead to the failure of an overall approach or a specific approach (part) [3]. Academic discussion is limited to the influence of design thinking on enterprise performance [17]. Carr et al. [18] advocate research to determine ways to measure the impact of design thinking. This study focuses on observing the problems in the actual implementation of design thinking education, summarizing its impact on students, and supplementing the research content of design thinking in the educational environment.

2.2   Teamwork

The mode of teamwork is built on the basis of skills and knowledge, and the process of teamwork is a behavior in which members depend on each other. Through cognitive, linguistic, and behavioral activities, inputs are transformed into results to organize task work to achieve collective goals [19]. In IDEO, teamwork has always been an important aspect of work, so it has become part of the discussion of design thinking put forward by Kelley and Brown [11], the integration of different perspectives inside and outside the organization is considered to be the core aspect of design thinking [20]. Building a cross-functional, multidisciplinary team can help "solve the complexity of the project and ensure that the technical, business, and personnel latitudes of the problem are reflected" [21]. Teamwork and deep learning are seen as essential skills in the industry, and universities promote teamwork as part of a flexible and transferable set of skills suitable for employment [22–25], the aim is to provide students with the opportunity to learn concepts in depth [26, 27]. From the team level, this study discusses the impact of the single-disciplinary team and cross-disciplinary team cooperation in design thinking education on students and pays attention to observing the progress of individual and collective knowledge.

2.3 Summary

With the change of the global industry and the progress of technology, the field of education, like the business field, is working to emphasize the education system led by innovation [28]. Higher education iterates and develops ways to integrate with the industry through continuous research on practice and innovation. In the predicament, higher education continues to develop to adapt to social changes, narrowing the gap between talent training and the needs of the industry. As a human-centered innovative method, design thinking considers people's needs and behavior, as well as the feasibility of science and technology or business [29], through cooperation to find solutions to problems, to develop critical thinking, innovative thinking, cooperation in solving fuzzy problems, and other skills that participants need to succeed.

The application of design thinking in the educational environment is becoming more and more frequent, and design thinking is very popular at all stages of school education, as well as short courses on design thinking and innovation. Design thinking provides a popular multidisciplinary skillset [30]. However, there are still some unexpected problems in the actual environment. In the environment of higher education, there are also some restrictive and uncertain factors in design thinking education. For example, some design thinking education is conducted in single-disciplinary teams, while others are conducted in cross-disciplinary teams. If we understand the influence of different team types on students in the education of design thinking, it will be of great help to expand the research on the influence of "the influence of design thinking". This study hopes to supplement the content of "the influence of design thinking" which is less studied in the current academic field by discussing the influence of single-disciplinary team cooperation and cross-disciplinary team cooperation on students in design thinking education. It will be very important to provide richer practical research for design thinking education in the future.

3 Methods

3.1 An Introduction to the Course of Design Thinking in This Study

This study was based on two design thinking courses offered by the Department of Design, National Taiwan University of Science and Technology. The course lecturers had 20 years of teaching experience and nearly 100 workshops on design thinking. The content of the course was to promote the participants human-centered innovation and execution ability from the aspects of thinking theory, tool practice, case sharing, and creative practice. The purpose of the course was to cultivate design thinking practitioners with "pragmatic innovation", "human-centered", "cross-domain integration" and "iteration". The task of the course was carried out in the mode of teamwork, and each group completed a service design case to address a real problem in industry through teamwork.

3.2 Subject Description

The subjects of this study came from design discipline and business management discipline respectively, in which the majors of design students covered industrial design, service design, business design, visual communication design, and design education; business management students majors included marketing, curatorial exhibition, business administration.

A total of 56 subjects were tested in this study. A total of 29 students in the single-disciplinary team were divided into 5 groups, each of which was composed of students with a design background. A total of 27 students in the cross-disciplinary team were divided into 4 groups, each of which was composed of students with a design background and business management background.

3.3 Introduction to the Method of Questionnaire Survey

The process of this study is as follows: the first step is that all the subjects fill in the Google form online at the end of the course; the second step is to analyze and collect the data after completing the answer.

In addition to the basic information used to understand the basic situation of the subjects, the types of the questionnaire include closed questions and open questions. the purpose of the questionnaire is to increase the richness of feedback information through the combination of closed questions and open questions.

The first question (Q1) to the eleventh question (Q11) is a closed question, and the answer item is set to a fixed radio, in which the type of answer is: the first question (Q1) is the Net Promoter Score (NPS) of the evaluation course, using the NPS fixed scale (0–10, 0 is impossible, 10 is highly likely). The second question (Q2) is to evaluate the importance attached to the curriculum (1–5, 1 is very unimportant, 5 is very important), and the third question (Q3) is to evaluate the degree of satisfaction with the curriculum (1–5, 1 is very dissatisfied, 5 is very satisfied). The type of answer item of the fourth question (Q4) to the eleventh question (Q11) is Likert scale 5 (1–5, 1 is very disagree, 5 is very agree). Questions 12 (Q12) to 18 (Q18) are open-ended questions. There are two types of answers: multiple-choice questions and short answer questions. Questions 12 (Q12) to 15 (Q15) are multiple-choice questions, which are composed of a combination of fixed options and short answers (multiple choices can be made), questions 16 (Q16) to 18 (Q18) are short answers. The contents of the questionnaire are shown in Table 1.

3.4 Introduction of Analysis Method

The first question is the Net Promoter Score (NPS), Calculate your NPS using the answer to a key question, using a 0–10 scale: How likely is it that you would recommend this course to classmates or friends? Respondents are grouped as follows: 1) Promoters (score 9–10) are loyal enthusiasts who will keep buying and refer others, fueling growth, 2) passives (score 7–8) are satisfied but unenthusiastic customers who are vulnerable to competitive offerings, 3) detractors (score 0–6) are unhappy customers who can damage your brand and impede growth through negative word-of-mouth. NPS is calculated by

Table 1. Contents of the questionnaire.

Question type	Question
Closed - ended question	Q1: How likely is it that you would recommend this course to classmates or friends? Q2: how much do you attach importance to the course? Q3: what is your satisfaction with the course? Q4: you feel that you are contributing to the team Q5: you feel valued on the team Q6: you think you have leading ability in the team Q7: you have a clear understanding of what the team's goals are Q8: you can understand the opinions expressed by members in different fields Q9: you can get enough trust from team members Q10: your ideas often run counter to the team consensus Q11: participation in teamwork helps improve individual abilities
Open - ended question	Q12: what are your needs for the choice of teammates? Q13: in your opinion, what is the impact of teamwork on you? Q14: what do you think is the key to teamwork? Q15: what role do you play in teamwork? Q16: what do you think are the advantages of the course? Q17: what issues or parts do you spend a considerable amount of time on in the collaborative design process? What's the solution? Q18: what is the biggest problem you encounter in teamwork? What is your opinion or suggestion?

subtracting the percentage of customers who answer the NPS question with a 6 or lower (known as "detractors") from the percentage of customers who answer with a 9 or 10 (known as "promoters").

This study corresponds to different analysis methods according to the types of questionnaire questions. The feedback information of the closed problem (Q2–Q11) was statistically analyzed by an independent sample T-test ($p < .05$, double tail). Students who participate in single-disciplinary teams and cross-disciplinary teams are independent of each other, meet the independence, and conform to the normal distribution. Therefore, an independent sample T-test is adopted.

The analysis method of open-ended problems is divided into two parts, one is presented by calculating the percentage (% = number of people who selected this option/total number of people), and the other is collated and described by qualitative research methods.

4 Results

Through the design thinking course in colleges and universities, this study discusses the impact of single-disciplinary teamwork and cross-disciplinary teamwork on students. Now the feedback information is sorted out and summarized according to the corresponding analysis methods, and the following main results are summarized:

4.1 The Similarities Between Teams

After the course of design thinking, through the quantitative survey, we can clearly see the influence of the composition of the two types of teams on the students.

First, the members of the two types of teams have similar positive comments on the course loyalty, importance and satisfaction of the course, and speculate that the composition of the team does not affect the feeling of the course. The purpose of the first, second and third questions is to understand the course loyalty, importance and satisfaction of the students in the two types of teams.

The first question (Q1) is to ask students: How likely is it that you would recommend this course to classmates or friends? The results of statistics are shown in Fig. 1. In the "single-disciplinary team", there are 25 Promoters, 4 passives, and 0 detractors. The value of NPS is 86%. In the "cross-disciplinary team", there are 21 Promoters, 5 Passives, and 1 Detractors. The value of NPS is 74%. It can be seen that both types of teams have a high degree of loyalty to the course (see Fig. 1).

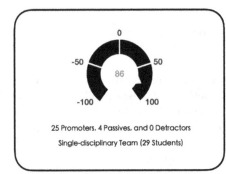 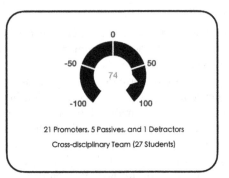

25 Promoters, 4 Passives, and 0 Detractors

Single-disciplinary Team (29 Students)

21 Promoters, 5 Passives, and 1 Detractors

Cross-disciplinary Team (27 Students)

Fig. 1. NPS calculation results of the single-disciplinary team and cross-disciplinary team.

The second question (Q2) is that students are required to evaluate the importance they attach to the curriculum. There is no significant difference between single-disciplinary team (M = 4.75, SD = 0.78) and cross-disciplinary team (M = 4.70, SD = 0.46), t(df) = 0.31, $p = 0.75 > .05$. The third question (Q3) is that students are required to assess their satisfaction with the course. Similarly, there is no significant difference between single-disciplinary team (M = 4.82, SD = 0.38) and cross-disciplinary team (M = 4.59, SD = 0.69), t(df) = 1.55, $p = 0.12 > .05$. The details of the data are shown in Table 2.

According to the statistical results, there is no significant difference in course loyalty, importance, and satisfaction between the students of the two groups. In addition, the NPS values of both courses are more than 70%, and the M values of course importance and satisfaction are higher (M > 4.00). This shows that the two types of team members have similar positive comments on the course loyalty, importance, and satisfaction of the course, and we speculate that the composition of the team does not affect the feeling of the course.

Table 2. Quantitative statistical results of Questions 2–11

Question	Single-disciplinary Team M (SD)	Cross-disciplinary Team M (SD)	T	P
Q2: how much do you attach importance to the course?	4.75 (0.78)	4.70 (0.46)	0.31	0.75
Q3: what is your satisfaction with the course?	4.82 (0.38)	4.59 (0.69)	1.55	0.12
Q4: you feel that you are "contributing" to the team	4.27 (0.75)	4.37 (0.68)	−0.49	0.62
Q5: you feel "valued" on the team	4.24 (0.68)	4.25 (0.94)	−0.08	0.93
Q6: you think you have "leading ability" in the team	3.89 (0.77)	3.29 (1.06)	2.42	0.01*
Q7: you have a clear understanding of what the team's goals are	4.58 (0.50)	4.55 (0.50)	0.22	0.82
Q8: you can understand the opinions expressed by members in different fields	4.62 (0.62)	4.48 (0.57)	0.86	0.39
Q9: you can get enough trust from team members	4.48 (0.63)	4.40 (0.88)	0.36	0.71
Q10: your ideas often run counter to the team consensus	1.89 (0.97)	1.92 (0.82)	−0.12	0.90
Q11: participation in "teamwork" helps improve individual abilities	4.55 (0.50)	4.40 (0.74)	0.84	0.40

*$P < 0.05$, Single-disciplinary Team. n = 29, Cross-disciplinary Team. n = 27

Second, the two types of team members have similar positive comments on the degree of individual contribution to the team, the degree of being valued by the team, and the degree of trust gained by the team, is speculated that team composition has little influence on the feeling of teamwork. The purpose of the fourth, fifth and ninth questions is to understand the feelings of the two types of team students in teamwork, including the individual's contribution to the team, the degree of being valued by the team, and the degree of trust gained from the team. The results showed that:

The fourth question (Q4) required students to evaluate the degree of contribution to the team, and there was no significant difference between single-disciplinary team (M = 4.27, SD = 0.75) and cross-disciplinary team (M = 4.37, SD = 0.68), t(df) = −0.49, $p = 0.62 > .05$. The fifth question (Q5) requires students to evaluate how much they are valued in the team. there is no significant difference between single-disciplinary teams (M = 4.24, SD = 0.68) and cross-disciplinary teams (M = 4.25, SD = 0.94), t(df) = −0.08, p = 0.93 > .05. The ninth question (Q9) requires students to assess the degree of trust they gain from team members. Similarly, there is no significant difference between single-disciplinary team (M = 4.48, SD = 0.63) and cross-disciplinary team (M = 4.40, SD = 0.88), t(df) = 0.36, p = 0.71 > .05. The details of the data are shown in Table 2.

According to the statistical results, there is little difference between the two types of team members in terms of individual contribution to the team, how much they are valued by the team, and how much trust they gain from the team, and M > 4.00. This can show that the two types of team members have similar positive comments on the degree of individual contribution to the team, the degree of being valued by the team, and the degree of trust gained by the team. It is speculated that team composition has little influence on the feeling of teamwork.

Third, the two types of team members have similar positive comments on understanding team goals and members' opinions, and thus we speculate that team composition has little influence on understanding team goals and members' opinions. The purpose of the seventh, eighth and tenth questions is to understand the evaluation of the two types of team students on the level of understanding team goals and members' opinions. The results showed that:

The seventh question (Q7) requires students to assess the extent to which they understand the team's goals. There was no significant difference between single-disciplinary team (M = 4.58, SD = 0.50) and cross-disciplinary team (M = 4.55, SD = 0.50), t(df) = 0.22, p = 0.82 > .05. The eighth question (Q8) requires students to assess the extent to which they understand the views of members in different fields. There was no significant difference between single-disciplinary team (M = 4.62, SD = 0.62) and cross-disciplinary team (M = 4.48, SD = 0.57), t(df) = 0.86, p = 0.39 > .05. The tenth question (Q10) requires students to assess the extent to which their ideas contradict the consensus of the team. Similarly, there was no significant difference between single-disciplinary teams (M = 1.89, SD = 0.97) and cross-disciplinary teams (M = 1.92, SD = 0.82), t(df) = −0.12, p = 0.90 > .05. The details of the data are shown in Table 2.

According to the statistical results, there is little difference between the two types of team members in the degree of understanding between collaborative projects and team members. The means of the seventh and eighth questions (Q7 and Q8) is greater than 4.00, and the mean of the tenth question (Q10) is less than 2.00. It can show that the two types of team members have similar positive comments on the degree of understanding between the understanding team goals and members' opinions. We speculate that team composition has little influence on understanding team goals and members' opinions.

4.2   The Values

Through the above quantitative survey, we find that the students of the two types of teams are satisfied with the current curriculum plan. This study continues to confirm the value and characteristics of curriculum design for participants through qualitative analysis. The goal of this case course is to train design thinking practitioners. According to the lecturers of the courses, the characteristics of design thinking practitioners are "pragmatic innovation", "human-centered", "cross-domain integration" and "iteration". After sorting out the feedback information of question 16 (Q16) through qualitative method, it is found that:

Both types of team members mentioned the help of the curriculum in the cultivation of the characteristics of "pragmatic innovation" The course provides innovative design thinking and a broad communication field, and uses appropriate tools to assist innovation, produce truly landing, beneficial or influential solutions, and cultivate the ability to solve innovative problems. For example, students from a single-disciplinary team mentioned, "*it is possible to structurally understand how an innovative design thinking needs to be implemented, and how to use appropriate tools to assist divergence convergence and verification, so as to improve the landing and feasibility of commercialization*". Similarly, Students from cross-disciplinary team also mentioned, "*the publication of results is quite practical to seek advice from operators, not only for homework, but also to listen to some suggestions from the industry, which will help to increase the feasibility of the project*".

Both types of team members mentioned the help brought by the course in the cultivation of the characteristics of the "human-centered". In the cooperation, the students mentioned to combine the stakeholders, think about the problem from different angles, emphasize the human-centered problem-solving way, and produce a solution that really meets the needs of the stakeholders. For example, students from a single-disciplinary team mentioned that "*this course stimulates many human-centered thinking*". Similarly, students from cross-disciplinary team mentioned that "*learn to develop and insight into problems from the user's point of view, explore more opportunities and solutions that design can spread, improve users' pain points and integrate needs and expectations*".

Both types of team members mentioned the help brought by the curriculum in the cultivation of the characteristics of "cross-domain integration". Students mentioned that the course provides a clear-thinking framework, assists the divergence and convergence of innovation, and combines different fields to solve fuzzy problems. For example, students from a single-disciplinary team mentioned, "*have a clearer outline of the concept and process of service design, and help them to use different tools and perspectives to come up with solutions when they encounter problems*". Similarly, the students of the cross-disciplinary team mentioned, "*the structure is orderly, and the course is very interesting, have a more complete thinking process for future design, and start a great enthusiasm for service design. A good cooperative relationship can be achieved by cooperating with students from different disciplines*".

Both types of team members mentioned the help of the course in the cultivation of "iterative ability". Students emphasize the continuous verification of the correct-ness of the solution direction at different stages of the course, as well as iterative solutions and landing methods. For example, students from a single-disciplinary team mentioned, *"in the process of creative situation creation, we use a variety of methods and discussions to achieve possible successful situations, from the point of view of user experience, through the tests conducted in the classroom at each stage of work to confirm whether the direction of input is accurate"*. Similarly, students from the cross-disciplinary team also mentioned, *"it is very practical to learn service design methods step by step and find solutions through practical tests"*.

4.3   The Differences Between Teams

Through the above quantitative and qualitative methods, we find that the two types of team members are satisfied with the curriculum plan and its impact. This study continues to explore the characteristics and key issues of the team through quantitative and qualitative methods.

Members of a single-disciplinary team feel more strongly that they have the leading ability in the team. In the sixth question (Q6), there is a significant difference between single-disciplinary team (M = 3.89, SD = 0.77) and cross-disciplinary team (M = 3.29, SD = 1.06), t(df) = 2.42, $p = .01 < .05$. The details of the data are shown in Table 2. This shows that the members of the single-disciplinary team come from the same discipline, have a relatively high degree of communication understanding and a high sense of trust, and the degree of leading ability in the evaluation team is significantly higher than that of the cross-disciplinary team. We speculate that team composition affects team leadership.

Cross-disciplinary teamwork promotes the improvement of communication, knowledge sharing, and cooperation, on the other hand, it also brings some restrictive factors, such as low efficiency of cooperation. The purpose of question 13 (Q13) is to understand the impact of teamwork. The results showed that:

On the one hand, compared with the percentage of "successfully complete the task, get twice the result with half the effort", the result is that the cross-disciplinary team (55.5%) is lower than the single-disciplinary team (72.4%). The percentage of cross-disciplinary teams is higher than that of single-disciplinary teams in choosing "efficiency is often too low", "it is easy to form dependence and hinder the exertion of individual ability" and "there is no significant effect". The details of the data are shown in Table 3.

On the other hand, in some positive impact options, cross-disciplinary teams are higher than single-disciplinary teams, for example, "enhance members' understanding and obtain good interpersonal relationships" (single-disciplinary team 75.8%, cross-disciplinary team 88.8%), "exercise their teamwork ability" (single-disciplinary team 79.3%, cross-disciplinary team 88.8%), and "expand their knowledge" (single-disciplinary team 69%, cross-disciplinary team 81.4%). The details of the data are shown in Table 3.

Table 3. Q13: In your opinion, what is the impact of teamwork on you? (% = number of choices/total number of people * 100)

Option category	Single-disciplinary Team (%)	Cross-disciplinary Team (%)
Enhance the understanding of the members and obtain good interpersonal relationships	75.80	88.80
Complete the task smoothly and get twice the result with half the effort	72.40	55.50
Exercise your teamwork ability	79.30	88.80
Expand your knowledge	69	81.40
There is no significant effect	0	3.70
It is easy to form dependence and hinder the exertion of individual ability	0	11.10
Efficiency is often too low	10.30	25.90

Single-disciplinary Team. n = 29, Cross-disciplinary Team. n = 27

In the feedbacks, students participating in cross-disciplinary teams mentioned, "*get to know each other, learn from others' strong points to offset one's weakness*", "*enhance the ability to cooperate with design professional teams*", "*exercise leadership skills*", "*learn to be led*", "*enhance professional knowledge*" and so on.

These results show that the students who participate in cross-disciplinary team cooperation think that the degree of low cooperation efficiency is higher than that of the single-disciplinary team, but the influence degree of interpersonal relationship, team cooperation ability, and knowledge breadth is higher than that of the single-disciplinary team. From the perspective of the two sides of things, cross-disciplinary team members come from different disciplinary backgrounds, which on the one hand promotes the improvement of communication, knowledge sharing, and cooperation, on the other hand, it also brings some restrictive factors, such as low efficiency of cooperation.

To sum up, this study found that: 1) the two types of team members have similar positive comments on the course loyalty, the degree of importance on the course, the degree of satisfaction with the course, the degree of contribution to teamwork, the degree of being valued by the team, the degree of trust in the team and the level of understanding of team goals and members' opinions, 2) both types of team members mentioned the help brought by the cultivation of the characteristics of design thinking practitioners, 3) In terms of teamwork, we find that the two types of teams have their own characteristics, and there are also some constraints.

5 Conclusions

With the continuous progress of society, innovative education in the environment of higher education has become an important research topic. Design thinking provides help for innovative education with its own advantages, but design thinking education has a long way to go. Based on the design thinking course, this study summarizes the impact of single-disciplinary team cooperation and cross-disciplinary team cooperation on students and discusses the characteristics and problems of different teams in design thinking education. According to the results, the two types of team members are satisfied with the current curriculum plan, and the curriculum design provides help for participants to become "design thinking practitioners". In terms of teamwork, we find that the two types of teams have their own characteristics, and there are also some restrictive factors.

The students who participate in the single-disciplinary team and the students of the cross-disciplinary team have similar positive comments on the curriculum plan and its impact, and the team composition has little difference on the students. This study is based on the design thinking course offered by the Department of Design, in which business management students are quite close to design students in learning cognition and innovation. The quantitative survey shows that: the two types of team members have similar positive comments on the course loyalty, the degree of importance on the course, the degree of satisfaction with the course, the degree of contribution to teamwork, the degree of being valued by the team, the degree of trust in the team and the level of understanding of team goals and members' opinions.

We find that the students of the two types of teams are satisfied with the current curriculum plan. Qualitative analysis confirms the value and characteristics of curriculum design for participants, both types of team members mentioned the help brought by the cultivation of the characteristics of design thinking practitioners.

In terms of teamwork, we find that the two types of teams have their own characteristics, and there are also some constraints. On the one hand, the two types of teams have their own characteristics. Students who participate in single-disciplinary teams have more profound feelings in terms of course evaluation, cooperative projects and understanding among members, sense of trust and their leading ability in the team. Cross-disciplinary teams feel more deeply in terms of "contribution" and "importance", and Students who participate in cross-disciplinary teams are deeply influenced by different subject knowledge and interpersonal interaction. On the other hand, due to the characteristics of different teams, there are also some restrictive factors. The participants of the cross-disciplinary team come from different fields, and the instability of cooperation is higher than that of the single-disciplinary team, and its communication and cooperation efficiency is weaker than that of the single-disciplinary team.

Facing the future, the education of design thinking will still be an important re-search issue. From the perspective of team collaboration, this study compares the influence of single-disciplinary team and cross-disciplinary team on students, which provides a reference for design thinking education. In the future, we should continue to pay attention to the research on different issues that influence design thinking courses to promote the development of creativity and foster excellent "T-type" talents for the society.

References

1. Aflatoony, L., Wakkary, R., Neustaedter, C.: Becoming a design thinker: assessing the learning process of students in a secondary level design thinking course. Int. J. Art Design Educ. **37**(3), 438–453 (2018)

2. Withell, A., Haigh, N.: Design thinking education: findings from the research-led, design, evaluation, and enhancement of a university-level course. In: ICERI2017 Proceedings, pp. 3290–3298. IATED (2017)
3. Panke, S.: Design thinking in education: perspectives, opportunities and challenges. Open Educ. Stud. **1**(1), 281–306 (2019)
4. Koh, J.H.L., Chai, C.S., Wong, B., Hong, H.Y.: Design Thinking and Education, pp. 1–15. Springer, Singapore (2015). https://doi.org/10.1007/978-981-287-444-3
5. Graff, D., Clark, M.A.: Communication modes in collaboration: an empirical assessment of metaphors, visualization, and narratives in multidisciplinary design student teams. Int. J. Technol. Des. Educ. **29**(1), 197–215 (2018). https://doi.org/10.1007/s10798-017-9437-9
6. Barron, B.: When smart groups fail. J. Learn. Sci. **12**(3), 307–359 (2003)
7. Lewis, S., Pea, R., Rosen, J.: Collaboration with mobile media: shifting from 'participation' to 'co-creation'. In: 2010 6th IEEE International Conference on Wireless, Mobile, and Ubiquitous Technologies in Education, pp. 112–116. IEEE, April 2010
8. Stickdorn, M., Schneider, J.: This is Service Design Thinking: Basics. Tools, Cases (2010)
9. Micheli, P., Wilner, S.J., Bhatti, S.H., Mura, M., Beverland, M.B.: Doing design thinking: conceptual review, synthesis, and research agenda. J. Prod. Innov. Manag. **36**(2), 124–148 (2019)
10. Brown, T.: IDEO. IDEO DESIGN THINKING. https://designthinking.ideo.com/
11. Johansson-Sköldberg, U., Woodilla, J., Çetinkaya, M.: Design thinking: past, present and possible futures. Creativity Innov. Manage. **22**(2), 121–146 (2013)
12. Rauth, I., Köppen, E., Jobst, B., Meinel, C.: Design thinking: an educational model towards creative confidence. In: DS 66–2: Proceedings of the 1st International Conference on Design Creativity (ICDC 2010) (2010)
13. Dym, C.L., Agogino, A.M., Eris, O., Frey, D.D., Leifer, L.J.: Engineering design thinking, teaching, and learning. J. Eng. Educ. **94**(1), 103–120 (2005)
14. Glen, R., Suciu, C., Baughn, C.C., Anson, R.: Teaching design thinking in business schools. Int. J. Manage. Educ. **13**(2), 182–192 (2015)
15. McLaughlin, J.E., Wolcott, M.D., Hubbard, D., Umstead, K., Rider, T.R.: A qualitative review of the design thinking framework in health professions education. BMC Med. Educ. **19**(1), 98 (2019)
16. McCullagh, K.: Stepping up: beyond design thinking. Design Manage. Rev. **24**(2), 32–34 (2013)
17. Gruber, M., de Leon, N., George, G., Thompson, P.: Managing by design. Acad. Manag. J. **58**(1), 1–7 (2015)
18. Carr, S.D., Halliday, A., King, A.C., Liedtka, J., Lockwood, T.: The influence of design thinking in business: some preliminary observations. Design Manage. Rev. **21**(3), 58–63 (2010)
19. Marks, M.A., Mathieu, J.E., Zaccaro, S.J.: A temporally based framework and taxonomy of team processes. Acad. Manag. Rev. **26**(3), 356–376 (2001)
20. Carlgren, L., Rauth, I., Elmquist, M.: Framing design thinking: the concept in idea and enactment. Creativity Innov. Manage. **25**(1), 38–57 (2016)
21. Glen, R., Suciu, C., Baughn, C.: The need for design thinking in business schools. Acad. Manage. Learn. Educ. **13**(4), 653–667 (2014)
22. CPA: Professional Accreditation Guidelines for Higher Education Programs. The Institute of Chartered Accountants in Australia and CPA Australia, Sydney (2012)
23. Greenan, K., Humphreys, P., McIlveen, H.: Developing transferable personal skills: part of the graduate toolkit. Education+Training **39**(2), 71–78 (1997)

24. Jackling, B., De Lange, P.: Do accounting graduates' skills meet the expectations of employers? A matter of convergence or divergence. Account. Educ. Int. J. **18**(4–5), 369–385 (2009)
25. Sin, S., Jones, A.: Generic Skills in Accounting: Competencies for Students and Graduates. Pearson Education, Sydney (2003)
26. Fearon, C., McLaughlin, H., Eng, T.Y.: Using student group work in higher education to emulate professional communities of practice. Education+Training **54**(2), 114–125 (2012)
27. Mutch, A.: Employability or learning? Groupwork in higher education. Education+Training **40**(2), 50–56 (1998)
28. Beckman, S., Barry, M.: Innovation as a learning process: embedding design thinking. Calif. Manage. Rev. **50**, 25–56 (2007)
29. Brown, T.: Design thinking. Harv. Bus. Rev. **86**(6), 84 (2008)
30. Volkov, A., Volkov, M.: Teamwork benefits in tertiary education. Education+Training **57**, 262–278 (2015)

Effect of Presenting Co-occurrence Networks that Reflect the Activeness of Face-to-Face Discussions

Taisei Muraoka[1], Naruaki Ishikawa[1], Shigeto Ozawa[2] (ID), and Hironori Egi[1](✉) (ID)

[1] Department of Informatics, Graduate School of Informatics and Engineering,
The University of Electro-Communications, Chofu, Japan
hiro.egi@uec.ae.jp

[2] Faculty of Human Sciences, Waseda University, Tokorozawa, Japan

Abstract. This paper proposes a system that presents outlines of discussions in other groups in the same classroom as co-occurrence networks that reflect the activeness of discussions. The proposed system focuses on discussions conducted by two people during a lecture. The activeness of the discussions is analyzed using nonlinguistic acoustic information, which is calculated based on participants utterances collected by wearable devices. The co-occurrence networks are drawn with emphasizing the active parts of discussions by each group. We conducted an experiment to verify the effect to the participants by applying the proposed system to a lecture, and the effect of presenting the co-occurrence networks was examined in a subjective evaluation. The participants conducted another discussion after observing the co-occurrence networks of the previous discussion, and the second discussion was scored by the lecturer. As a result, the co-occurrence networks reflecting discussion activeness were not evaluated higher than those that did not reflect discussion activeness. This suggests that the variety of topics in the co-occurrence networks may stimulate discussion participants more effectively.

Keywords: Group discussion · Co-occurrence network · Nonlinguistic acoustic information · Word embedding

1 Introduction

Tackling complex problems are difficult, with the limits in individuals' perspectives, experiences and knowledge. Creative activity grows out of the relationship between an individual and other human beings. Because complex problems require more knowledge than any single person possesses, it is essential that all involved learners participate, communicate, collaborate from each other [1].

Active learning, which is worked on a problem and actively involved its learning process, has been introduced in the education field. One active learning approach introduces a discussion style in which divide small groups are formed during a lecture. In discussions, it is important to hear and understand the opinions

© Springer Nature Switzerland AG 2021
P. Zaphiris and A. Ioannou (Eds.): HCII 2021, LNCS 12784, pp. 347–360, 2021.
https://doi.org/10.1007/978-3-030-77889-7_24

of others. However, in such small-group discussions, the opinions of participants maybe similar if the learners are in the same field of study. In such cases, the range of discussion can be limited; thus, it may be difficult to include unexpected opinions. To solve this problem, it is useful to incorporate different opinions and ideas from outside the group into the discussion.

To incorporate different ideas from outside the group, several group discussion techniques have been proposed such as jigsaw method [2], sharing comments on worksheets, and providing a list of keywords. However, these methods have problems in supporting ideas and activating discussions. For example, when sharing opinions among groups using the jigsaw [2], the degree of success depends on the level of understanding of the target learners. If the learner cannot summarize the discussion effectively, sharing opinions with other learners cannot be achieved. And stable membership groups experienced higher levels of comfort and perceived friendliness than did groups that changed membership [3]. In discussion, it is possible that changed membership prevent from discussion activeness. In addition, when using comments on worksheets, the learner requires significant time to understand the details of the discussion because a lot of information may be shared. With a list of keywords, it is possible to grasp an outline of the discussion; however, it may be difficult to understand the entire discussion because the general context is omitted. Thus, in this study, to obtain general understanding of the context of a discussion, we propose a method to present words that evoke the subject of the discussion.

The proposed method comprises three main phases, i.e., Discussion Phase 1, Support Phase, and Discussion Phase 2. After Discussion Phase 1, the proposed system presents a co-occurrence network to participants. Using the proposed system, we examine how the proposed system affects Discussion Phase 2.

2   Related Work

2.1   Visualizing Discussion Outlines

Previous studies have investigated visualizing discussion content. For example, a previous study [4] visualized discussion using extruded word clouds. Here, the authors created word clouds in consideration of the number of participants involved topic words in a given period. By looking at word clouds, it is possible to identify when the discussion topic become hot or cold. In addition, by connecting the same words in adjacent word clouds, it is possible to observe the emergence of new words, the extinction of weak words, and the existence of surviving words.

Another study proposed a method to view tags related to previous topics selected by a user [5]. As a result, the supporting system helps users remember previous conversation topics and demonstrates that viewing tags is less burdensome than checking a chat log.

2.2   Recommend Next Topic Idea

Wang [6] helps with new ideas by presenting images that is highly relevant to the word of user's input. In brainstorming, the system searches ideas in the discussion based on the corpus and presents images related to the keywords contained in the ideas. The presentation of images may let users to give information that is unrelated to the theme. Therefore, it is insufficient as a presentation method for the users to understand the outlines of the discussion.

In addition, Sunayama [7] proposed a system that recommends a next topic that is related to the current topic. This system uses the hit counts of a web search engine to evaluate the relations of the current topic, and the top-five words of the number of hit counts are presented by users. The purpose of this system is keeping the conversation. Note that the presented topics are general; thus, this system is unlikely to stimulate discussions.

3   Discussion Support Based on the Condition

3.1   Presenting Co-occurrence Networks that Reflect Activeness of Discussions

In this study, to understand an outline of a complete discussion in a short period, we proposed a system that presents words that evoke the topic of the discussion using co-occurrence networks. A co-occurrence network is a network diagram of the similarity of the patterns in which words appear. However, if the co-occurrence network is simply drawn from utterances in the discussion, the discussion topics can become dispersed, and it may be difficult to quickly understand the discussion.

Thus, to encourage participants to lead to new ideas, we introduce a method to emphasize active parts of a discussion when drawing the co-occurrence network. Active parts of a discussion are likely to be an attractive topic for the group. In addition, the participants are actively involved these parts of the discussions therefore, the participants of other groups could easily sympathize with the discussion content. We consider that these parts of a discussion well represent the overall discussion. Therefore, we consider that participants can understand discussion outlines easily by emphasizing the most active parts of a discussion.

In addition, it is necessary to consider the characteristics of the other groups. Here, we focus on a group with low relevance to the original group's discussion. We expect that using the content of a group not mentioned by the original group would be stimulating for the original group.

3.2   Nonlinguistic Acoustic Features

Here, the following features are introduced to estimate the activeness of a discussion [Anonymous, 2019]: time percentage of an utterance, percentage of silence, and coefficient of speech overlap. Note that these values are calculated using only nonlinguistic acoustic information per unit time.

Time Percentage of Utterance. The time percentage of an utterance value is the utterance duration of a participant per unit time. The time percentage of utterance is calculated for each participant in a group discussion, and the value is given in the range 0% to 100%. The degree of participation of each participant in the discussion is obtained by evaluating the transition of the time percentage of an utterance.

Percentage of Silence. The percentage of silence value is the duration in which no group member spoke per unit time, and it is calculated per group (rather than for each individual). The value is given in the range 0% to 100%. The degree of stagnation of the group is obtained by evaluating the transition of the percentage of silence.

Coefficient of Speech Overlap. The coefficient of speech overlap is the sum of the total time percentage of an utterance of all participants in and the percentage of silence of the group during a discussion, and it is calculated per group (rather than for each individual). This value is given in the range 1 to the total number of participants in the group. In addition, if there is no speech overlap, the coefficient of speech overlap is 1. The degree of activeness in the group can be determined by evaluating the transition of the coefficient of speech overlap.

3.3 Wearable Device

Wearable devices are consists in reference to previous research[9]. Here, Raspberry Pi 3B+ or Raspberry Pi 4B are attached to a unidirectional USB microphone that records the participants' utterances. Figure 1 shows the wearable device. The utterance audio data of the utterances are recorded and stored as WAVE format files in the wearable devices. In addition, the nonlinguistic acoustic features are calculated by a server using the CSV files saved in the wearable devices.

In this study, we evaluated whether the discussion was active every 20 s. Using the nonlinguistic acoustic features collected in Discussion Phase 1, the threshold to assess whether the discussion was active or inactive was determined (Sect. 5.1). Then, the weight of words in the active parts of the discussion were treated as double-counted. As a result, the active parts of the discussion can be emphasized and reflected in co-occurrence networks.

3.4 Converting Utterance into Text in the Discussions

Using the audio files collected by the wearable devices, the discussion content of each participant is to text using Google Cloud Speech-to-Text. However, Cloud Speech-to-Text could not add punctuation marks at that time, and punctuation is essential to draw the co-occurrence networks. In addition, the recognized precision was reduced by informal term in the discussions. Therefore, after performing the speech recognition process, punctuation marks were added and erroneous conversions were corrected to refine the text.

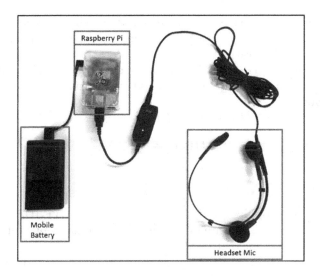

Fig. 1. Wearable device

3.5   Relevance to the Contents of the Discussion

In this study, we considered it is necessary to use the co-occurrence network of a group with low relevance to the discussion content to stimulate discussion. Using the content of another group not mentioned by the original group is expected to stimulate the original group to think about new ideas related to the target subject matter. Thus, Word2vec [9], which represents the meaning of a word using vectors, was used to compare the relevance of the discussion content. Here, the similarity of the content of the discussions was calculated between groups. In a previous study, word embedding was used to support conversation. Nishihara [10] proposed a topic switching system for unfamiliar couples in face-to-face conversations. When couples end the conversation, this system selects a new topic and presents the new topic to the couples.

In this study, the existing trained model was used. Here, the Wikipedia data are used as learning data, and the feature vector for each word is 300 dimensions. In addition, the meanings of words are considered; thus, this method is more human-friendly than word coincidence among discussions. To select the new topic, the information of both hobbies collected are vectorized using Word2vec, and then words that are highly related to those words are presented to the user as next topic words.

The original goal of Word2vec is to compare the similarities of words. However, in this study, the vector averages of words are compared. This method hardly generates the difference as the number of words increases. Thus, similarity increases even for unrelated sentences.

Here, we extract topic words in the discussion, and we employed TF-IDF to search these words, where the weight of a term that occurs in a document is proportional to the term frequency. The specificity of the term can be quantified as an inverse function of the number of documents in which it occurs. With these ideas, TF-IDF can be used to measure the importance of words in documents. TF-IDF is expressed by Eqs. (1), (2), and (3). Here, $n_{t,d}$ is the number of times words t appear in group d, n_d is the number of appearance of all words in group d, N is the total number of groups, and df(t) is the number of groups in which word t appears.

$$tfidf(t,d) = tf(t,d) \cdot idf(t,N) \tag{1}$$

$$tf(t,d) = \frac{n_{t,d}}{n_d} \tag{2}$$

$$idf(t,N) = \log \frac{N}{df(t)} + 1 \tag{3}$$

As a result, the top-five words are selected from the TF-IDF value. If the words have same values, they are ranked according to the number of links in the co-occurrence network for that word.

The discussion data converted to text were subjected to morpheme analysis using Mecab [11] to extract nouns. Then, the top-five nouns were selected as topic words using the TF-IDF method. Each topic word was then vectorized using Word2vec, and it was averaged. Thus, the feature vector in the group discussion can be calculated. When selecting topic words, we excluded words containing numbers and those that did not appear in the co-occurrence networks of the group. We estimated the discussion relevance by comparing the feature vectors in the discussions of each group using cosine similarity (Eq. (4)). Here, the feature vector of discussion content a is denoted $\overrightarrow{a}$, and the feature vector of discussion contents b is denoted $\overrightarrow{b}$. This similarity takes minimum 0 and maximum values of 0 and 1, respectively, where a higher values indicates higher similarity.

$$cos(a,b) = \frac{\overrightarrow{a} \cdot \overrightarrow{b}}{|\overrightarrow{a}||\overrightarrow{b}|} \tag{4}$$

3.6   Creating the Co-occurrence Networks

The KHcoder text analysis was used to draw the co-occurrence networks from the discussion text. Calculating the co-occurrence relationship uses the Jaccard index. The calculation of the co-occurrence relation between words X and Y is expressed in Eq. (5). Here, that X and Y are the number of appearances of each word, and we selected "sentence" as the unit of aggregation.

$$Jaccord(X,Y) = \frac{|X \cap Y|}{|X \cup Y|} \tag{5}$$

Note that we excluded several parts of speech, e.g., interjections and adverbs that have no characteristic meaning. In addition, we used the TermExtract Perl module for automatic keyword extraction to detect and extract compound words.

3.7   Flow of Co-occurrence Network Presentation

As mentioned previously, we consider that a discussion comprises Discussion Phase 1, Support Phase, and Discussion Phase 2. The content of Discussion Phase 1 for all groups is converted to text (Sect. 3.4). Then, the activeness of the discussion is reflected in the text (Sect. 3.3). Next, the co-occurrence networks are drawn (Sect. 3.6) using these data. Then relevance is then is determined using the method described in Sect. 3.5. From the results, we select the group with the lowest relevance to the original group. Then, the co-occurrence network of the selected group is presented in the Support Phase. Figure 2 shows the flow of co-occurrence network presentation.

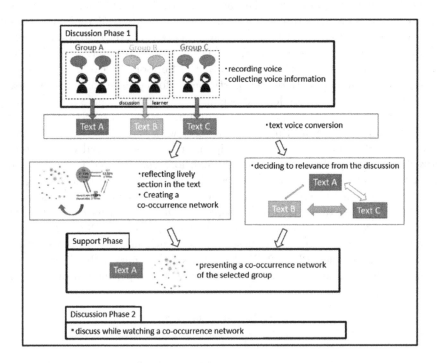

Fig. 2. Flow of co-occurrence network presentation

4   Experiment

We conducted an experiment to validate how the proposed system affects Discussion Phase 2.

4.1   Experimental Procedure

This experiment was conducted during a science lecture held at a university's interdisciplinary faculty. The participants included 36 undergraduates who gave informed consent. Note that the control condition was based on the proposed system without using discussion activeness. Each group comprised two participants. In total, there were seven groups for the experimental condition and 11 groups for the control condition. This 90-min lecture was held during the second semester of 2019. Discussion Phase 1 was held during the eleventh lecture, and Discussion Phase 2 was held in the thirteenth lecture. Note that all participants attended the lecture on both days. In addition, the group compositions were fixed throughout the experimental procedure.

In the 11th lecture on the first day, only the Discussion Phase 1 was conducted. Prior to starting the experiment, an outline of the experiment was provided, and the wearable devices were explained. In addition, teaching assistances provided a demonstration. Then, Discussion Phase 1 was conducted for 10 min. The participants engaged discussion while wearing headset microphones. Based on the content of Discussion Phase 1, the system drew and selected co-occurrence networks to be presented to each group using the procedure described in Sect. 3.7.

In the 13th lecture on the second day, the Support Phase and Discussion Phase 2 were conducted. Here, the participants formed the same groups used in Discussion Phase 1 before lecture began. Before starting the Support Phase, the experiment was explained again. In addition, the co-occurrence network was introduced. In the Support Phase, a worksheet with the selected co-occurrence network was distributed to each participant. Here, one optimal co-occurrence network for the experimental or control conditions was selected for each group. Each participant was given three minutes think about the worksheet. During this time, the participants were asked circle the parts of the co-occurrence networks that they expected to be treated as topics in Discussion Phase 2. Then, five minutes were given for Discussion Phase 2. After Discussion Phase 2, the participants were asked to answer a questionnaire to evaluate the proposed system and describe Discussion Phase 2. Table 1 shows the themes of the discussions in Discussion Phases 1 and 2, and Table 2 describes the experimental procedure.

Table 1. Discussion theme

Phase	Discussion theme
Discussion Phase 1	Explain the achievements of this faculty that you belong to
	The targets are people who do not know this faculty
	Example
	What did you grow most after entering university?
	How have you overcome your weakness?
	How would you like to use your university experience in the future?
Discussion Phase 2	What you noticed and discovered while checking the co-occurrence
	Network of the other group

Table 2. Experimental procedure

Day	Time	Contents
Day 1	5 min	Explain about experiment and demonstration
	2 min	Explain about wearable device
	10 min	Discussion Phase 1
Day 2	2 min	Explain the co-occurrence networks
	3 min	Support Phase
	5 min	Discussion Phase 2
	After discussion	Questionnaire about this system

4.2 Evaluation Item

Table 3 shows the question items of the subjective evaluation questionnaire Likert scale: "5. Strongly Agree," "4. Agree," "3. Neither Agree nor Disagree," "2. Disagree," and "1. Strongly Disagree."

Table 3. Experimental procedure

Question	Contents
Q1	You understood the contents in other group by seeing the co-occurrence network
Q2	Seeing the co-occurrence network triggered utterance
Q3	You came up with new ideas by seeing the co-occurrence network
Q4	Seeing the co-occurrence network was useful in this discussion

After Discussion Phase 2, the participants were asked to outline Discussion Phase 2 on the worksheet. In addition, the content of Discussion Phase 2 was converted to text using the method described in Sect. 3.4, and the spoken text was created. The grades of the worksheets were evaluated in three levels by the lead teacher. Here, the ratio of the high evaluation was 15%, the ratio of the middle evaluation was 70%, and the ratio of the low evaluation was 15%. The worksheets were scored according to the same criteria as the other day's lessons in other themes of the lecture. In addition, the text data were evaluated in three levels by the teachers. The ratio of the high evaluation was 30%, the ratio of the middle evaluation was 40%, and the ratio of the low evaluation was 30%. Here, the text that deepened the meaning and relationship of links in the co-occurrence network was ranked higher, and the text in which the intention of the content could not be observed in the co-occurrence network was ranked lower. The rest was standard discussion. The scoring criteria for the worksheet and spoken text are shown in Tables 4 and 5, respectively.

The participants were asked to provide a freeform response to the following: "Please state what you thought during the lecture and the reason."

Table 4. Evaluation of the worksheet

Grade	Percentage	Criteria
High	15%	Not only the facts, but also thinking deep
Medium	70%	Describes according to the set issues about the fact
Low	15%	The worksheet in which the intention of the content could not be read

Table 5. Evaluation of discussion log

Grade	Percentage	Criteria
High	30%	Spoken text that deepened the meaning and relationship of the links in the co-occurrence networks
Medium	40%	Spoken text in which based on presenting the fact about the co-occurrence networks
Low	30%	Spoken text in which the intention of the content could not be observed in the co-occurrence network

5   Result of the Experiment

5.1   Decision on Co-occurrence Networks

The threshold of discussion activeness was determined from the results of the Discussion Phase 1. Here, the nonlinguistic acoustic features of Discussion Phase 1 were analyzed. Table 6 shows the details of the nonlinguistic acoustic features for Discussion Phase 1. As mentioned in Sect. 3.3, discussion activeness was evaluated every 20 s. In reference to a previous study [8], the threshold of discussion activeness was defined as follows.

Table 6. Analysis of Discussion Phase 1

	Time percentage of utterance	Percentage of silence	Coefficient of speech overlap
Average	37.01%	31.41%	1.054
SD	6.44%	10.66%	0.039

(1) Time Percentage of Utterance for 20 s is greater than 43.45%
(2) Percentage of Silent Time for 20 s is less than 31.41%
(3) Coefficient of Speech Overlap for 20 s is the top 33% of each group

The values of the upper 33% of the coefficient of speech overlap in each group were defined based on the hypothesis that the characteristics of responses from each participant differ in existence of utterance. The threshold of the time percentage of utterance is the sum of the average and standard deviation of all groups, and the threshold of the percentage of silence is the average of all groups. Based on this threshold, we determined whether a certain part of the discussion was active for each part. Here, the weight of the words in active parts of the discussion is treated as double-counted when the system drew the co-occurrence networks.

From the results of Discussion Phase 1, co-occurrence networks with the least relevance were selected for each group (Sect. 3.6). If there were only a few active parts in the discussion, similar co-occurrence networks were drawn. Therefore, the groups in which active parts of discussions were less than 120 s were excluded as co-occurrence network candidates. In addition, to avoid presenting the same co-occurrence network to multiple groups repeatedly, no more than five groups were presented the same co-occurrence network.

5.2   Results of Questionnaire

Table 7 shows the questionnaire results. There were 14 participants in the experimental condition and 21 participants in the control condition. Note that one participant was excluded. As shown in Table 7, the average value of Q2 ("Seeing the co-occurrence network triggered the utterance") is less than those for the other three questions. Here, for each question, the Mann-Whitney U-test was performed on the hypothesis, i.e., the scores in the experimental condition are greater higher than those of the control condition. However, no significant difference was observed for either case.

Table 7. Result of the questionnaire

		Q1	Q2	Q3	Q4
Experimental	Average	3.79	3.36	3.57	3.64
Condition (N = 14)	SD	1.01	1.17	0.82	0.90
Control	Average	3.81	3.62	3.81	4.05
Condition (N = 21)	SD	1.01	0.84	0.79	0.79

As a result, the average evaluation scores were greater than three in all cases. Therefore, we consider that the proposed system with co-occurrence networks has a certain degree of acceptance for the participants.

5.3   Result of the Contents of the Discussion

Based on the criteria listed in Tables 4 and 5, "high: excellent discussion" was considered three points, "medium: standard discussion" was considered two points, and "low: insufficient discussion" was considered one point. Here, 14 participants were included in the experimental condition and 22 participants were included in the control condition. Table 8 shows the average and standard deviation of the results of the spoken text as evaluated by the teacher, and Table 9 shows the average and standard deviation of the results of the worksheets as evaluated by the teacher. Here, the Mann-Whitney U-test was performed on the hypothesis that the scores in the experimental condition are greater than those in the control condition. However, no significant difference was observed in either case. In addition, the spoken text and worksheet in the control condition were evaluated higher than those in the experimental condition.

Table 8. Result of worksheet evaluated by teacher

	Average	SD	Number and percentage of high evaluation	Number and percentage of middle evaluation	Number and percentage of low evaluation
Experimental condition (N = 14)	2.00	0.54	2 (14.3%)	10 (71.4%)	2 (14.3%)
Control condition (N = 22)	2.18	0.83	10 (45.5%)	6 (27.3%)	6 (27.3%)

Table 9. Result of spoken text evaluated by teacher

	Average	SD	Number and percentage of high evaluation	Number and percentage of middle evaluation	Number and percentage of low evaluation
Experimental condition (N = 14)	2.00	0.54	2 (14.3%)	10 (71.4%)	2 (14.3%)
Control condition (N = 22)	2.18	0.65	7 (31.8%)	12 (54.5%)	3 (13.6%)

5.4   Evaluation of the Impression in the Lecture

Several negative opinions were observed in the written comments, e.g., "I did not understand the co-occurrence network for the first time," "There was little explanation of the co-occurrence networks," and "I do not know how the co-occurrence network was drawn." We consider that these comments were given because the introduction of the co-occurrence networks was insufficient to realize effective understanding. It appears that it we must provide additional information so that the participants can become more familiar with co-occurrence networks, e.g., by providing demonstrations using co-occurrence networks. In addition, one participant stated, "I want to look back on our group's co-occurrence network." Thus, we consider that it may be helpful for participants to compare the co-occurrence networks of their own group with those of other groups. It was also suggested that the presentation to the participants who never see the co-occurrence networks is difficult to understand.

In contrast, positive opinions were provided in the written comments, e.g., "That's new for me" and "I get my idea from discussions of the other group." In addition, one participant stated, "it was inconvenient, but I thought deeply by complementing." In other words, we consider that observing the co-occurrence network facilitates further thought.

6   Discussion

In the experiment, the scores in the controled condition is higher than those in the experimental condition in the questionnaire, the worksheet and the spoken text. But there is no significant difference of the results. One of the reason for this is the fact that the range of the discussions appeared in the co-occurrence networks of the experimental condition are narrower than those of the controled condition. This result suggests that the variety of the topics in the co-occurrence networks may stimulate utterance and idea generation of the participants in the discussions more effectively.

Another reason is assumed to be the effect of task setting. In the experiment, we set the theme that "Explain the achievements of this faculty that you belong to. The targets are people who do not know this faculty". However, this theme causes that the range of the discussions varies depending on the number of years of the grade. In addition, the examples of the question items that were expected to be created by the participants were displayed in the classroom as shown in Table 1. As a result, since the participants were affected by the examples, most of the topics of the discussions were classified into the 3 topics of the examples. The co-occurrence networks are drawn based on the co-occurrence of words. Therefore, if the topics is broke up, the co-occurrence networks will have fewer links and will be more easily broke up. In addition, there are many participants who told about their own life experiences. Therefore, the co-occurrence networks may have become difficult to be understood by the other groups.

7   Conclusion for the Future

In this paper, we have proposed a system that presents the outlines of discussions of different groups as co-occurrence networks to reflect the activeness of a discussion. In future, we plan to investigate the detailed relationships among various factors, the presentation of co-occurrence networks and adaptation of low relevance in the discussion. In addition, we plan to examine overlap between the parts of which discussions are active and the parts of which discussions are highly evaluated.

References

1. Fischer, G.: Distances and diversity: sources for social creativity. In: Proceedings of the 5th Conference on Creativity and Cognition, pp. 128–136 (2005)
2. Aronson, E., Patnoe, S.: Cooperation in the Classroom: The Jigsaw Method. Pinter and Martin Limited, London (2011)
3. Nemeth, C.J., Oriston, M.: Creative idea generation: harmony versus stimulation. Eur. J. Soc. Psychol. **37**, 524–535 (2007)
4. Fabo, P., Novotný, M.: Three-level visualization of Internet discussion with extruded word clouds. In: 2012 16th International Conference on Information Visualization, Montpellier, pp. 13–17 (2012)
5. Itou, J., Tanaka, R., Munemori, J., Babaguchi, N.: Tag Chat: a tag-based past topics recollection support system. In: The Ninth International Conference on Collaboration Technologies (CollabTech2017), pp. 29–36 (2017)
6. Wang, H.C., Cosley, D., Fussell, S.R. :Idea expander: supporting group brainstorming with conversationally triggered visual thinking stimuli. In: Proceedings 2010 ACM Conference on Computer Supported Cooperative Work, pp. 103–106 (2010)
7. Sunayama, W., Shibata, Y., Nishihara, Y.: Topic recommendation method related to a present topic for continuing a conversation. Inf. Eng. Expr. Int. Inst. Appl. Inform. **3**(1), 19–28 (2017)
8. Ishikawa, N., Okazawa, T., Egi, H.: DiAna-AD: dialog analysis for adjusting duration during face-to-face collaborative discussion. In: The 25th International Conference on Collaboration Technologies and Social Computing (CollabTech2019), pp. 212–221 (2019)
9. Mikolov, T., Sutskever, I., Chen, K., Corrado, G., Dean, J.: Distributed representations of words and phrases and their compositionality. In: Advances in Neural Information Processing Systems, pp. 3111–3119 (2013)
10. Nishihara, Y., Yoshimatsu, K., Yamanishi, M., Miyake, S.: Topic switching system for unfamiliar couples in face-to-face conversations. In: 2017 6th IIAI International Congress on Advanced Applied Informatics (IIAI-AAI), pp. 319–323 (2017)
11. Kudo, T., Yamamoto, K., Matsumoto, Y.: Applying conditional random fields to japanese morphological analysis. In: Proceedings of the 2004 Conference on Empirical Methods in Natural Language Processing (EMNLP-2004), pp. 230–237 (2004)

User Perception of Wearables in Everyday Learning Contexts: The Impact of Prior Device Experience

Neha Rani$^{(\boxtimes)}$ and Sharon Lynn Chu

University of Florida, Gainesville, FL 32611, USA
{neharani,slchu}@ufl.edu

Abstract. Wearable devices are ubiquitous technology, which is attached to the user itself, allowing it to be available in various everyday life settings. With the growing popularity and increasing affordability of smart wearables devices, their uses are also growing. Traditionally wearables have been used for health and fitness tracking, but now wearable are used for various educational purposes as well. Wearable devices can take the form of daily use accessories like a watch, glasses, clip, necklace, etc. The abundance of form factors brings the question of what preferences people have for these form factors and how prior experience shapes these preferences. In this paper, we explore peoples' attitudes towards different wearable form factors and their preferences of wearable form factors in an everyday learning context. We conducted a survey-based study to find differences between users with and without prior experience with wearable devices. This study will help designers understand why certain wearable devices are preferred and the role of prior experience. In the survey, nine different fictional scenarios of daily life were presented, and participants were asked to imagine themselves using a wearable for learning in those scenarios. Results show a significant relationship between users' prior device experience and which form factor of wearable device they prefer to use for learning. Also, participants with prior experience with fitness trackers rated the social influence of wearable devices significantly lower compared to participants without wearable experience.

Keywords: Smart wearables · Education · Survey · User attitude · Wearable experience

1 Introduction

With technological advancement, smart wearable devices are becoming increasingly embedded in daily lives with more and more features at the same time becoming more affordable. This technological advancement has also made technology compact and smaller in size, which had led to the availability of wearables in a variety of form factors ranging from head-mounted devices to smart

© Springer Nature Switzerland AG 2021
P. Zaphiris and A. Ioannou (Eds.): HCII 2021, LNCS 12784, pp. 361–373, 2021.
https://doi.org/10.1007/978-3-030-77889-7_25

footwear. Health monitoring has been one big area explored for wearable applications. While smart wearables are commonly used for fitness and health tracking [4], they also have untapped potential to support learning processes. Wearables have been explored to support learning in various educational contexts, but mostly in formal settings like in a lab [9], in a classroom [11], etc. Some of the past research work shows that wearables have the potential for informal learning in daily life as well. For example research by Huang et al. explore the use of wearable technology for piano skill learning [6]. Another paper by Shadiev et al. explores smartwatch as a tool for language learning and also coupled language learning with physical activity [15]. However, exploration in that space of wearables for informal or everyday learning has so far been exclusively conducted in research contexts. Hence, our work seeks to advance understanding of the potential of wearable use for learning among general users.

Wearable devices are typically strapped on the body of users and allow the user to have the devices available constantly to assist in a variety of situations in daily life. While in formal education the type of wearable to be used is mostly the decision of the instructor, school administrators, and other school management stakeholders, for informal learning, it is not the case. The choice of wearable type for informal everyday learning is solely dependent on users' preferences. The choice of users depend primarily on their perception and attitude towards technology, wearable cost and their experience [8]. This makes the investigation of people's attitude towards wearable devices and their preferences for wearable form factors to support informal learning in daily life an important question. Exploring differences between users with and without wearable experience will help designers understand why certain wearable devices are more preferred and the role of experience in people's attitudes.

We hypothesize that in the case of informal learning through wearables in daily life the choice of wearable type is heavily impacted by the person's prior experience with existing wearable devices in general. In this paper, we present our survey-based exploration to understand people's attitudes towards wearable for everyday learning in the context of prior experience. We conducted a survey-based study with 70 participants with 38 female and 32 male population. Through our analysis, we found that there is a significant relationship between the choice of wearable type for learning purposes and prior experience.

In the next section i.e. background, we discuss wearable capabilities and form factors. Followed by that, in the related work section, we talk about wearable exploration done in the past for learning purposes. We then state the research question that we are attempting to answer through this study. In the study section, we describe the participants, study procedure, and structure of the survey. Further, we describe the data gathering, filtering and statistical tests used. Finally, we describe the results and discuss the implication of our findings.

2   Background

Wearables that are commonly aimed for a specific task like health tracking and step tracking, now integrating seamlessly into our lives and can be used for more purposes than we can list. For example, wearable devices are now capable of biometric authentication, have virtual and augmented reality, allow for quick payments, have integrated virtual personal assistant, health monitoring through monitoring body vitals, activity tracking, stress tracking, etc. This became possible due to increased computational capacity, advanced sensors, and smaller chips. *Apple SE* watch is one of the latest smartwatches which has built-in sensors like accelerometer, gyroscope, GPS, Siri, etc. [7]. It has multiple functions like calling, texting, voice-based interaction, music, podcast, touchscreen, fall detection, activity tracking, contactless payments, weather forecast, etc. Further, these devices are more affordable than ever and are available in a wide variety of forms. Wearable devices come in multiple form factors, for example, smartwatch, wristband, smart glasses, smart ring, smart clip, smart necklace, smart bracelet, smart shoes, smart clothes, etc. These forms are inspired by the everyday accessory traditionally worn by people, and each form has its own aesthetic, function, and use requirements. Among all these form factors, a wrist-worn wearable device is the most popular and commonly used [1]. A possible reason for this popularity is the early presence in the market and ease of use for fitness purposes. In our study, we consider five major wearable form factors i.e. watch/wristband, glasses, clip, necklace, ring. Table 1 lists all the wearable form factors explored in this study along with a description and an example device.

Table 1. This table describes the five wearable form factors along with examples.

Form factor	Description	Example
Watch/Wristband	A wearable device which is wrapped around wrist of the wearer	Apple watch SE [7]
Glasses	Glasses that are smart and equipped with technology to play sounds or even display screen	Snapchat Spectacles 3 [17]
Clip	A wearable device that is clipped to any part of the clothing like clipped to pocket or to shirt neck	Ditto clip [16]
Necklace	A wearable device that is hanging around neck. It may or may not add to aesthetics	Bellabeat urban leaf [2]
Ring	A wearable device that is shaped like a ring and can be worn on fingers	NFC Ring [13]

3   Related Work

The use of wearables for learning is an emerging area of exploration with a lot of recent research. Wearables have been explored in the past for insitu science reflection in daily life [5]. In another paper, researcher explored smart glasses as a tool for providing a step-wise guide for science experiments in lab settings [11]. Another paper explored the use of smart glasses as an AR tool for everyday informal learning through supporting information gain in meaningful real-life context [14]. In yet another paper, smart glasses were explored for distance learning by facilitating live streaming sessions where the instructor can review students performing the task and provide real-time feedback [18]. Another researcher investigated the use of google glasses in art galleries for facilitating learning through a real-time projection of information related to the art being viewed [10]. Further, Bower and Sturman in his research explored the educational affordances of wearable devices [3]. This brought into light all the main ways of using wearable for learning-based activities as reported by the educators. Through analyzing the perception of educators with a good understanding of wearables, fourteen educational affordances were found. Some of these educational affordances of wearable were, providing insitu contextual information, recording educational events such as class, simulating educational procedures, communication in an educational context, etc. Clearly, we can see that there is an established potential of wearable for learning. Wearable explorations in the past, for understanding users' attitude, are mainly done in the context of fitness, and health care [12,21]. Despite this established potential, there is a lack of understanding of people's attitudes towards wearable for everyday learning. Although many people already have experience of using wearable for the regular purpose of health and fitness tracking, when the purpose transitions to educational use, the preferences of form factor may change. With multiple form factors available, choosing wearable type can be influenced by prior experience. Understanding how prior experience with wearable shapes users current preferences for educational use of wearable will provide researchers insights into prior experience as a factor in general.

4   Research Question

With more and more wearables available in the market, there is a plethora of options to choose from. Understanding how prior experience with wearable devices influence the choice of wearable type will guide wearable designers regarding the form of wearable devices meant for education and exploration purposes.

Our research question was as follows: **Do people's attitudes towards using wearables for learning in everyday life differ if they have actually used a wearable before as opposed to if they have not?**

5   Study

5.1   Study Design and Structure

We conducted a survey-based study to understand people's attitudes towards the use of wearables for everyday learning and to explore the relationship between prior experience and preference of wearable form factor. The survey consisted of 4 Major sections. First section aimed at collecting demographic information of the participants. Then different wearable types were demonstrated through images and example. These wearable devices were demonstrated through images in the survey to familiarize participants with wearable form factors and to understand what is referred to in the later part of the survey. In the study protocol, 5 different major wearable form factors namely, smartwatch/wristband, smart glass, smart ring, smart clip, smart necklace were considered and only these were demonstrated. Considering that there are variations in terms of style, material, and look even within these broader categories, participants were demonstrated at least two variations of each of these form factors. In the next section, participants were asked about their prior experience with wearable devices. They were mainly asked what type of wearable device they owned and for how long. Further, they were asked open-ended questions about how they would imagine using wearable for learning in their daily lives. In the third section, nine different fictional scenarios of daily life were presented, and participants were asked *"Without restricting yourself to current functions and abilities of wearable devices, how can you imagine using the wearable device to support your learning in this scenario?"*; *"What specific kind of wearable device do you think is the most suitable to use for the above scenario?"*. Six options were given for participants to choose from: smartwatch/wristband, smart glasses, smart clip, smart ring, smart necklace, and others; and the participants were asked to imagine themselves using a wearable for learning in those scenarios. "Without restricting yourself to current functions and abilities of wearable devices" was added to enable participants to freely imagine as they have not used wearable in an educational context before. These scenarios were crafted to portray different settings encountered in daily life. These scenarios were designed to vary in terms of formality of nature of scenario setting (i.e. scenario was in a formal setup or informal setup), different social interaction of the user in the setting (i.e. user is alone, with a person or in a group), level of familiarity with other interacting entities in the setting (i.e. user is with friends, family or strangers), and the users' physical mobility in the scenario (i.e. user is moving or is static). Table 3 shows the categories of all nine fictional scenarios in terms of formality of setting, interaction, familiarity, mobility. Some of the scenarios are listed in Table 2

Table 2. This table lists a few sample scenarios from the nine fictional scenarios presented in the survey.

Scenario ID	Scenario description
S3	You are driving home after class or work. Traffic is surprisingly light today. As you drive, you observe that the asphalt of the road ahead appears to shine, as if there is water on the road. But you know that it has not rained recently. You happen to be wearing a wearable device in your vehicle. Without restricting yourself to current functions and abilities of wearable devices, how can you imagine using the wearable device to support your learning in this scenario?
S4	You are at home watching your favorite show on TV. You feel somewhat chilly and decides that hot tea would be nice. You go to the kitchen to make hot tea for yourself while the show is on a commercial break. You want to get back to the living room before the show starts again. As you put the kettle on the stove, you wonder how long you have to stay in the kitchen until water starts to boil. You happen to be wearing a wearable device at home. Without restricting yourself to current functions and abilities of wearable devices, how can you imagine using the wearable device to support your learning in this scenario?
S5	You and your friends are waiting to order food at an authentic Greek restaurant. The restaurant is really busy and loud. This is your first time trying Greek food and you see one item on the menu, Saganaki, that contains shrimp. You love shrimp. But, you are also on a diet currently. You happen to be wearing a wearable device in the restaurant. Without restricting yourself to current functions and abilities of wearable devices, how can you imagine using the wearable device to support your learning in this scenario?

Table 3. Category variations in all nine fictional scenarios.

Scenario ID	Formality	Interaction	Familiarity	Mobility
S1	Not formal	With a person	Friends	On-the-go
S2	Very formal	Self in a group	Stranger	Static
S3	Not formal	Self	None	On-the-go
S4	Not formal	Self	None	Static
S5	Not formal	With person in a group	Friends	Static
S6	Not formal	With person in a group	Family	Static
S7	Somewhat formal	Self in a group	Stranger	Static
S8	Somewhat formal	With a person	Friend	Static
S9	Not formal	Self in a group	Stranger	On-the-go

In the final section, the UTAUT (Unified theory of acceptance and use of technology) scale was used with adapted items from [20] to evaluate attitude towards wearable use for learning in daily life. The questionnaire used a 7 point likert scale. which are explained below in the context of this paper.

- *Performance Expectancy* is defined as the degree to which an individual believes that using the wearable will help him or her to attain gains in learning.
- *Effort Expectancy* is defined as the degree of ease associated with the use of the wearable.
  Attitude Toward Using Technology is defined as an individual's overall affective reaction to using a wearable to support learning.
- *Social Influence* is defined as the degree to which an individual perceives that important others believe he or she should use the wearable.
- *Facilitating Conditions* are defined as the degree to which an individual believes that an organizational and technical infrastructure exists to support the use of the wearable.
- *Self-efficacy* is defined as the judgment of one's ability to use a wearable to support one's learning.
- *Anxiety* is defined as the degree to which a wearable evokes anxious or emotional reaction when it comes to using it to support one's learning.
- *Behavioral Intention* is defined as one's intention to use a wearable for learning in the future.

5.2 Study Participants

The study was approved by our university ethics board and it was conducted through the crowd-sourcing platform called Amazon Mechanical Turk. All participants were compensated through Amazon Mechanical Turk upon completion and a bonus was given for good quality survey responses. Criteria for good quality completion (i) if the duration of survey completion was more than 10 min, (ii) if answers were clearly related to the question, (iii) if the answer is not single worded, if answers were not duplicated and (iv) if the survey is not duplicated and submitted more than once. Consent was collected before starting the survey. Participants were free to withdraw from the study without any consequence. The survey was estimated to take less than an hour for completion. Participants took an average of 29 min to complete the survey.

A total of ninety-three completed survey responses were collected. These collected surveys were further reviewed for quality. Finally, 70 responses were selected after filtering (filtering criteria are described in the data filtration section). These 70 participants consisted of 38 female and 32 male. The average age of the participants was 35.93 years, with a minimum age of 19 years and a maximum age of 67 years. Out of the 70 participants, 58 were employed, while 12 were students. The study population consisted of 39 White/Caucasian, 17 Asian, 5 Black/African American, 4 Hispanic/Latino, 2 American Indian/Alaskan Native, 2 multiple ethnicities, and 1 did not specify.

6 Data Analysis

6.1 Data Filtering

Before proceeding with the analysis, data were filtered to remove low-quality data. All the duplicate survey submissions were removed. Duplication was identified through submission IP, multiple duplicate responses and duplicate submission. Surveys fulfilling the following criteria were removed to improve the quality of response. (i) Surveys that took less than 5 min for completion. (ii) More than 5 repeated responses for open-ended questions. (iii) Multiple duplicated responses. (iv) Multiple unrelated and random responses.

6.2 Quantitative Data Analysis

All the survey responses were organized into a spreadsheet. All UTAUT questionnaire responses were organized by sub-constructs. For each participant average score of each sub-construct was used for representing a single score for that sub-construct. These average scores were used for running the statistical test. Non-parametric tests were used when data were not normally distributed or in case of uneven sample size. Participants' prior wearable experience was determined by their response to the survey question "Have you ever owned wearable devices before?". The "yes" response i.e. participant with prior experience were coded as 1, and the "no" response i.e. participant without any prior wearable experience was coded as 0.

In order to examine if *choice of wearable type* is significantly associated with *prior experience with wearables*, a chi-square test of independence was performed. To further understand how prior experience with a particular wearable type affects people's acceptance of wearable devices, participants with prior wearable experience were grouped by wearable type they previously owned. There were 3 groups formed, one having prior 'experience with smartwatches', another having prior 'experience with fitness tracker', and the third having 'experience with other' wearable types. The third clubbed group was created due to the fewer number of participants with experience with other wearable types like ring, necklace, etc. All these groups were compared with the no prior experience group. UTAUT scores were calculated again for each participant in each group. A non-parametric test called the Mann-Whitney U test was conducted due to the uneven sample size of the groups. This test was conducted to find if participants with prior experience with a particular wearable type rated UTAUT sub-constructs differently than those without prior experience. The significance threshold for all tests was set at .05.

7 Results

Out of the 70 participants, there were 18 without any wearable experience and 52 with wearable experience. These 52 participants had experience with one or multiple wearable types. Among these 52 participants, 8 have owned one type of wearable device, 23 have owned two wearable devices, 9 have owned three wearable devices, and 2 have owned more than three wearable devices. Figure 1 shows the distribution of different type of wearable devices owned by people with prior wearable experience. It was observed that the majority of participants with prior experience owned either a watch (50 participants) or fitness tracker (48 participants), as can be seen in Fig. 1. This was expected as smartwatches and fitness trackers are the most common form factor of a wearable device.

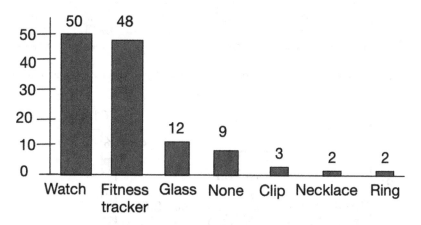

Fig. 1. Tables shows the distribution of different wearable types owned by the participants with wearable experience. There were total of 52 participants with wearable experience

In all the nine fictional scenarios combined, participants chose watch/wristband, the maximum number of times (56.50% of times) followed by glasses (27.50% of the times). Figure 2 shows the percentage of times a particular wearable type was chosen by the participants. *Other* in the wearable type means wearable type other than the five listed wearable form factors. Participants listed *other* wearable type as smart clothing, smart ear buds etc. Further, we compared the choice of each wearable type by participants' experience. Figure 3 shows the distribution of preferences of different wearable types comparing participants with prior wearable experience with participants without wearable experience for all the nine fictional scenarios. The figure can be read for example as follows: 61.1% of the times, participants with prior wearable experience chose watch/wristband to be used for learning in those nine fictional everyday scenarios.

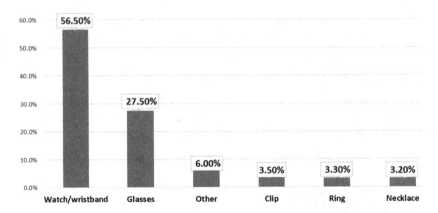

Fig. 2. Tables shows the percentage of each wearable form factor chosen across all the nine scenarios.

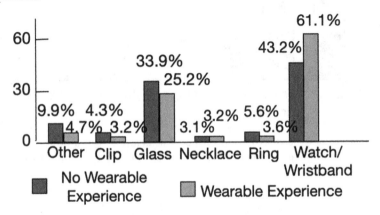

Fig. 3. Cross-tabulation from chi-square test of the presence of prior wearable experience by wearable type

The chi-square test on the combined responses across all the scenarios shows a significant relationship between the choice of wearable type for learning and prior wearable experience, as shown in Fig. 4, $(X2(1, N = 630) = 19.18,$ $p < .005)$. Figure 4 shows the number and percentage of each wearable type chosen, combined across all nine scenarios within participants with experience (Exp) and within participant without experience (No Exp). Results from the Mann-Whitney U test showed that people with prior wearable experience of fitness tracker scored significantly lower (Mean Rank = 27.63, Med. = 4.44, $N = 42$) compared to people with no wearable experience (Mean Rank = 37.19, Med. = 5.44, $N = 18$) on the social influence sub-construct. Social influence is the degree to which an individual perceives that important others believe he/she should use the new system.

Exp	% within	Glasses	Smartwatch /wristband	Clip	Necklace	Ring	Others
No Exp	Count	55	70	7	5	9	16
	%Within No Exp	34.00%	43.20%	4.30%	3.10%	5.60%	9.90%
Exp	Count	118	286	15	15	12	22
	%Within Exp	25.20%	61.10%	3.20%	3.20%	2.60%	4.70%

Fig. 4. Cross-tabulation from chi-square test of the presence of prior wearable experience by wearable type

8   Discussion

Many of the study participants have either owned or experienced wearable devices. As expected majority of participants have experience with smartwatches or wristbands. Results showed a significant relationship between choice of wearable type and prior experience. Experience is one of the primary ways to build the mental model of the use of any technology. With experience, the mental model of users' becomes richer in terms of what actions wearables can afford and possible ways in which they can see themselves using the wearable. Through experience, people also gain insights into what purpose a wearable can be used. Hence, they build a base on which they can further imagine what learning purposes a wearable can be used for. Further, having experienced one type of wearable makes it easier for people to see themselves using it for yet another purpose. Therefore, experience tends to significantly affect the choice of wearable type. Further, looking closely at the cross-tabulation of Chi-square results in Fig. 4, it can be seen that people with prior wearable experience tend to have a higher preference for a smartwatch/wristband 61.1% of the times) to be used to support learning in everyday scenarios followed by smart glasses (25.2% of the times). Interestingly, for people with no wearable experience, the choice of wearable form factor is more diverse, with the distribution being more spread out across the various wearable types. This shows that prior experience influences the choice for wearables even though wearables forms are constantly evolving, and specific wearable types may be more suitable for any one specific learning scenario. Also, the choice of wearable form factor seems to be guided by experience as the majority of the participants have experience with watch/wristband and they chose the same form factor. People with no prior experience, however, tend to be more open in terms of wearable form factors and may choose to go with the wearable type that seems most suitable for the everyday learning scenario. While the people with no wearable experience tend to be open to other wearable types, watch/wristband and glasses still remained the top choice compared to other forms. Possible reason for this could be the obvious popularity of watch/wristband due to early presence and glasses due to the popularity google glass. Another possible reason could be the presence of display on these two form factors is far higher than other forms.

Our results show that people with prior experience with fitness trackers rated social influence as less important than those without experience. In prior literature, a decrease in the importance of social influence was observed as people use technology over time ([19] as cited in [20]). This implies that social influence contribution to people's attitudes towards wearable devices for learning reduces with gain in experience with the devices.

9   Study Limitations

We acknowledge that assessing prior experience with wearable as binary variable is a limitation. Prior experience with a wearable might not mean an equal level of experience for all participants, as one participant might have used a simple version of a fitness band with just step count and activity tracking, whereas the other might have experienced the latest version of a smartwatch with advanced features like GPS, heart rate monitoring, activity tracking. It might not be a significant problem, as the participants were demonstrated various wearable within the same type to help them think more broadly. Moreover, participants were asked to imagine using wearable without limiting themselves to the current functions and capabilities of a wearable device.

Acknowledgement. We thank and acknowledge the contribution of Beth Nam in helping to design and conduct the survey. We thank all the participants of the survey. This project was partially supported by NSF grant #1566469 *Lived Science Narratives: Meaningful Elementary Science through Wearable Technologies.*

References

1. Baldo, T.A., de Lima, L.F., Mendes, L.F., de Araujo, W.R., Paixao, T.R., Coltro, W.K.: Wearable and biodegradable sensors for clinical and environmental applications. ACS Appl. Electron. Mater. (2020)
2. Bellabeat: More than just gorgeous jewelry (2020). https://www.bellabeat.com/products/leaf-urban
3. Bower, M., Sturman, D.: What are the educational affordances of wearable technologies? Comput. Educ. **88**, 343–353 (2015)
4. Custodio, V., Herrera, F.J., López, G., Moreno, J.I.: A review on architectures and communications technologies for wearable health-monitoring systems. Sensors **12**(10), 13907–13946 (2012)
5. Garcia, B., Chu, S.L., Nam, B., Banigan, C.: Wearables for learning: examining the smartwatch as a tool for situated science reflection. In: Proceedings of the 2018 CHI Conference on Human Factors in Computing Systems, pp. 1–13 (2018)
6. Huang, K., Do, E.Y.L., Starner, T.: PianoTouch: a wearable haptic piano instruction system for passive learning of piano skills. In: 2008 12th IEEE International Symposium on Wearable Computers, pp. 41–44. IEEE (2008)
7. Apple Inc.: Apple watch se (2021). https://www.apple.com/apple-watch-se/
8. Kukulska-Hulme, A.: Mobile, wearable, companionable: emerging technological challenges and incentives for learning (2014)

9. Lee, V.R., Drake, J.R., Thayne, J.L.: Appropriating quantified self technologies to support elementary statistical teaching and learning. IEEE Trans. Learn. Technol. 9(4), 354–365 (2016)

10. Leue, M.C., Jung, T., tom Dieck, D.: Google glass augmented reality: generic learning outcomes for art galleries. In: Tussyadiah, I., Inversini, A. (eds.) Information and Communication Technologies in Tourism 2015, pp. 463–476. Springer, Cham (2015). https://doi.org/10.1007/978-3-319-14343-9_34

11. Lukowicz, P., Poxrucker, A., Weppner, J., Bischke, B., Kuhn, J., Hirth, M.: Glassphysics: using google glass to support high school physics experiments. In: Proceedings of the 2015 ACM International Symposium on Wearable Computers, pp. 151–154 (2015)

12. Lunney, A., Cunningham, N.R., Eastin, M.S.: Wearable fitness technology: a structural investigation into acceptance and perceived fitness outcomes. Comput. Hum. Behav. 65, 114–120 (2016)

13. McLear Ltd.: Your world, the way you see it (2019). https://nfcring.com/

14. Rao, N., et al.: Investigating the necessity of meaningful context anchoring in AR smart glasses interaction for everyday learning. In: 2020 IEEE Conference on Virtual Reality and 3D User Interfaces Abstracts and Workshops (VRW), pp. 427–432. IEEE (2020)

15. Shadiev, R., Hwang, W.Y., Liu, T.Y.: A study of the use of wearable devices for healthy and enjoyable English as a foreign language learning in authentic contexts. J. Educ. Technol. Soc. 21(4), 217–231 (2018)

16. Simple Matters LLC: Ditto wearable tech (2021). https://dittowearable.com/

17. Snap Inc.: Your world, the way you see it (2020). https://www.spectacles.com/shop/spectacles-3/

18. Spitzer, M., Nanic, I., Ebner, M.: Distance learning and assistance using smart glasses. Educ. Sci. 8(1), 21 (2018)

19. Venkatesh, V., Davis, F.D.: A theoretical extension of the technology acceptance model: four longitudinal field studies. Manage. Sci. 46(2), 186–204 (2000)

20. Venkatesh, V., Morris, M.G., Davis, G.B., Davis, F.D.: User acceptance of information technology: toward a unified view. MIS Q. 425–478 (2003)

21. Wang, X., White, L., Chen, X., Gao, Y., Li, H., Luo, Y.: An empirical study of wearable technology acceptance in healthcare. Ind. Manage. Data Syst. (2015)

Usability Study of CARTIER-IA: A Platform for Medical Data and Imaging Management

Andrea Vázquez-Ingelmo[1]([✉]) [ID], Julia Alonso[1],
Alicia García-Holgado[1] [ID], Francisco J. García-Peñalvo[1] [ID],
Jesús Sampedro-Gómez[2] [ID], Antonio Sánchez-Puente[2] [ID],
Víctor Vicente-Palacios[3] [ID], P. Ignacio Dorado-Díaz[2] [ID],
and Pedro L. Sánchez[2] [ID]

[1] GRIAL Research Group, Research Institute for Educational Sciences,
University of Salamanca, Salamanca, Spain
{andreavazquez,id00738609,aliciagh,fgarcia}@usal.es
[2] Cardiology Department, Hospital Universitario de Salamanca, SACyL.
IBSAL, Facultad de Medicina, University of Salamanca, and CIBERCV (ISCiii),
Salamanca, Spain
{jmsampedro,asanchezpu}@saludcastillayleon.es,
{acho,plsanchez}@usal.es
[3] Philips Healthcare, Salamanca, Spain
victor.vicente.palacios@philips.com

Abstract. Artificial Intelligence algorithms' application to medical data has gained relevance due to its powerful benefits among different research tasks. Nevertheless, medical data is heterogeneous and diverse, and these algorithms need technological support to tackle these data management challenges. The CARTIER-IA platform enables different roles (including principal researchers, IA developers and data collectors) to unify medical data, both structured data and DICOM images, and to apply Artificial Intelligence algorithms to them in a straightforward way through an online web application. However, given the diversity of roles involved in the platform, it is essential to account for its usability. It is necessary that users feel comfortable using the platform as relevant and complex tasks are carried out through its different services (such as the application of algorithms to the stored data, the manual edition of medical images or the visualization of structured data). This work presents a heuristic evaluation of the CARTIER-IA platform to improve its interaction mechanisms and get the most out of its functionalities.

Keywords: Data management · Structured medical data · Medical imaging · Health platform · Artificial intelligence · Usability · Heuristics

1 Introduction

Artificial intelligence algorithms are turning into a norm in the investigation of clinical information for research purposes, given their usefulness in identifying patterns in data and even images [1]. In fact, the application of deep learning models to medical

© Springer Nature Switzerland AG 2021
P. Zaphiris and A. Ioannou (Eds.): HCII 2021, LNCS 12784, pp. 374–384, 2021.
https://doi.org/10.1007/978-3-030-77889-7_26

imaging has enabled the automation of complex tasks such as disease detection, segmentation of structures, or assessing organ functions [2] with similar performance compared to human skill [3].

However, these advances are generally limited to specific tasks and very specific datasets in which algorithms are trained and validated. That is why applying these technologies in real-world medical contexts is complex, due to the necessity of unifying several sources of image data (cohorts, machine brands, operators, etc.) without losing a reliable performance.

For these reasons, information systems are required to organize and gather all these data from different heterogeneous sources and to apply AI algorithms in a friendly, secure and anonymized manner.

This study presents a usability study of the CARTIER-IA platform. This platform is set to unify both structured data and medical images. Researchers and physicians can inspect data from different projects and also manipulate the images associated with different studies. The image editor also enables users to apply AI algorithms transparently, unburdening unskilled users of having to implement and run complex algorithms through command-line tools.

However, the complexity of the data collection processes, medical imaging edition and the great quantities of data that the platform holds, could make it difficult to use for novice users. That is why a heuristic evaluation of the platform has been carried out; to identify major and minor HCI issues with the goal of solving them and obtaining a friendly platform to get the most out of its features.

The rest of this paper is organized as follows. Section 2 outlines the platform and its main features. Section 3 describes the methodology followed throughout the study. Section 4 presents the results of the heuristic evaluation, which are discussed in Sect. 5. Finally, Sect. 6 concludes the work with a summary of the findings.

2 Platform Architecture

Two main tasks are supported by the platform: structured data and image data management. Different technologies and frameworks have been integrated through a client-server approach to obtain a web service that allows users to explore medical data and medical images without the necessity of installing external tools. Structured data and image data management are accomplished through different features.

The platform is organized into projects, which will have different anonymized patients. Each patient will have associated data, such as structured data, as well as image studies. Studies will be composed of sets of files and can also be characterized by adding more structured data at the study- and file-level.

Inside each projects' page, a data uploader allows users with enough permissions to upload both structured data and medical images. Both types of resources are differentiated, yielding two different uploaders. The structured data uploader accepts CSV and XLSX files containing the data.

Different tables or sheets can be created to further organize the structured data, and there are three levels in which data can be uploaded: patient-level, study-level and resource-level. Data can be explored through a tree-like architecture (Fig. 1) and can be filtered through the different specific variables created for each level (patient, study and file).

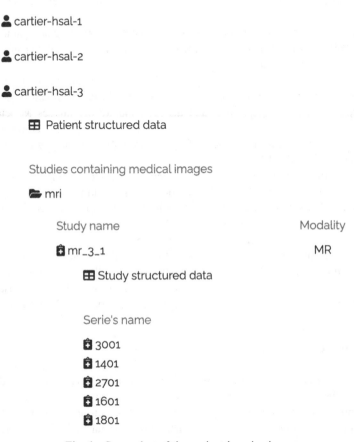

Fig. 1. Screenshot of the projects' navigation

Another main feature is image visualization and edition. The platform relies on an image editor in which users can draw, annotate, segmentize, crop, measure, etc., medical images (Fig. 2). Users can edit the images they are currently viewing. They can make annotations and modifications (such as cropping images). To make these changes permanent, the viewer has a button that sends the modifications to the server, storing all changes in the database.

In this case, annotations, segmentations, measurements, etc. are stores as raw data, so the image itself is never modified. This approach allows the storage of annotations from different users or different dates, thus enabling comparisons or even annotations' version control.

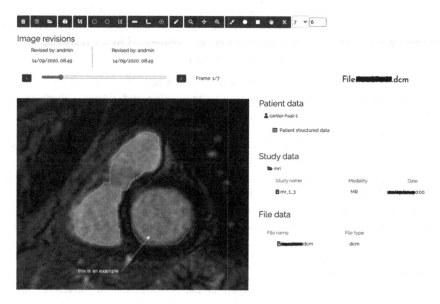

Fig. 2. Screenshot of the image editor

The last main feature of the platform is the integration of Artificial Intelligence (AI) algorithms. This feature allows researchers to upload their AI scripts into the platform and make them available to other users transparently.

Once uploaded, algorithms are available at the viewer component. The application process is straightforward: a button provides information about the available scripts for the current image and the user only needs to select an algorithm and confirm their application.

The algorithm's outcomes can be structured data (which will be saved along with the current patient's structured data) or a new image (for example, a segmented image, which will be displayed along with the original image in the viewer).

3   Methodology

3.1   Participants

According to [4], the optimal number of experts involved in a heuristic evaluation varies among authors. Nielsen [5] considers that three to five evaluators identify 65–75% of the usability problems; meanwhile, other authors used eleven experts to identify 80% of the detectable problems. The review of methods of usability testing in the development of eHealth applications [6] identifies that the studies which only used heuristic methods involve a maximum of five participants.

In this study, we have involved six experts, four single experts and two double experts. These double experts have expertise in user interface issues as well as the domain [7], in particular, they have used the CARTIER-IA platform as users before analyzing it (E2 and E6), the remaining had access for two weeks before completing the analysis (E1, E3, E4, E5). We looked for equitable distribution so that three men and three women participated, with ages ranging between 25 to 45 years old.

The experts were selected according to their profiles:

- E1: Web developer and researcher with eleven years of experience working on developing technological ecosystems for knowledge and learning management. Furthermore, the expert has experience in teaching human-computer interaction in a Computer Science degree.
- E2: A Ph.D. student whose doctoral dissertation deals with customizable dashboards to analyze and visualize any kind of data.
- E3: Student with experience in human-computer interaction and user experience.
- E4: Developer and researcher with more than ten years of experience focused on bioinformatics and information visualization, especially integrating different source data, analysis algorithms and representations for a better understanding of biological problems.
- E5: Researcher with more than ten years of experience in multimodal human-computer interaction.
- E6: Clinical Data Scientist and expert in the development of interfaces for the medical domain.

3.2 Instrumentation

There are numerous heuristics sets, although the most commonly used are the ten heuristics by Nielsen [5]. Despite there are heuristics specific to health care [8], those heuristics are mainly related to the evaluation of Electronic Health Records (EHR) [9]. These EHR heuristics include categories related to patients, collaborative team care or privacy [10]. CARTIER-IA platform is in the health context, but it is mainly focused on diagnosis and research tasks based on medical data, both structured data and DICOM images. Moreover, the medical data upload to the platform is anonymized, so privacy is important but not like in an EHR. Therefore, the selected set of heuristics was Nielsen's heuristics [5]:

- HR1: Visibility of system status.
- HR2: Match between system and the real world.
- HR3: User control and freedom.
- HR4: Consistency and standards.
- HR5: Error prevention.
- HR6: Recognition rather than recall.
- HR7: Flexibility and efficiency of use.
- HR8: Aesthetic and minimalist design.

- HR9: Help users recognize, diagnose, and recover from errors.
- HR10: Help and documentation.

We prepared a simple template and a set of guidelines to support the evaluation process and the reporting. The template was shared with each expert individually, in such a way that individual experts could not have access to the evaluation of the others.

The template has three fields to collect the evaluator's name, the name of the tool evaluated, and the browser used to access the CARTIER-IA platform. Furthermore, the template has a table with three columns - heuristic rule, points from 1 to 10, and problems detected – and one row per problem detected in each heuristic proposed by Nielsen.

3.3   Study Design and Data Collection

The first step was focused on selecting the set of heuristics, as described in the section above, as well as the desired number and characteristics of the experts. We selected the experts among our contact network, searching involving experts from different areas, expertise and non-direct relation with the project. The contact with the experts was made via email, where they were also provided with a brief contextualization of the CARTIER-IA platform.

Each expert applied the following indications:

- Navigate through the interface several times, looking at all screens, options, tasks. It is recommended to navigate at least once through the entire application to get to know the flow of interaction and what the application offers, and then a second review where you focus on specific details of the interface.
- Compare each screen/interface element with the ten usability principles proposed by Nielsen. For each detected problem:
- Give a value from 1 (non-relevant problems) to 10 (serious problems) to each problem detected.
- Brief description of the problem to justify the associated value.
- Indicate which heuristic is affected.
- The score for each heuristic will be an average of the values assigned to the detected problems.
- In addition to Nielsen's heuristics, the evaluator may also consider any additional usability principles or outcomes relevant to a specific interface element.

4   Heuristic Evaluation

Each expert was identified by a number (E1, E2, E3, E4, E5, E6) to show the heuristic evaluation results. The number of problems identified by each expert is small, but the combination of all of them provides an input to improve the CARTIER-IA platform. Table 1 summarizes the quantitative part of the heuristic evaluation providing by each expert. In particular, the table shows the average value assigned to the detected problems in each heuristic. This value is combined with the number of problems detected. Values near 1 indicate that the expert detected non-relevant problems, and values near 10 mean that serious problems were identified. A zero value represents that the expert did not identify problems in that heuristic.

The total average of each heuristic rule was calculated in order to get a final value for each heuristic (Fig. 3). However, not only is the severity of the problems important, but we also wanted to analyze which of the heuristics has the greatest number of problems to solve (Fig. 4).

Most of the experts identified problems associated with all the heuristics, except E1, E3 and E5. In particular, those three experts did not detect any problem related to user control and freedom (HR3); meanwhile the rest of the experts detected few but serious problems such as:

- The deletion processes cannot be stopped (E2).
- Issues associated with the edition and deletion of the user account (E4).
- No support Undo and Redo of the actions available in the platform (E6).
- Moreover, E5 did not detect problems related to aesthetic and minimalist design (HR8). Regarding HR8, highlight the issues described by double experts (E2 and E6):
- On the project's home page, the way of showing information can be messy, as several patients-studies-files are shown using a tree-like architecture (Fig. 1). Also, several data are displayed alongside this structure, which makes the display very cluttered and difficult to read (E2).
- Clarity and simplicity by showing the relevant information of the clinical study (E6).
- Simplify the project creation design (E6).

The heuristic that presents the largest number of usability issues was HR4 (*Consistency and standards*) with 26 different problems (Fig. 4). Regarding the severity rating, the average is 6.84 (Fig. 3), most of them have a value over 5 (19 of 26 problems). The main problems detected are related to the translation of the interface (E1 and E4), the font size and responsive design (E5), the template download and upload data processes inside a project (E4), the different styles applied in links, buttons and icons (E2, E3 and E6), the differences between search or filtering (E3), the project's actions are located in different places inside the interface (E2) and the actions available in the DICOM viewer (E1). It should be noted that only expert E5 has detected problems related to accessibility standards, particularly in terms of the contrast between text and background.

The heuristic with a higher severity rating is help and documentation (HR10). All experts detected different problems mainly related to the lack of tutorials, legends and documentation support. Furthermore, there is no contact information to get technical support when the system breakdown or does not work as the user expects.

The heuristic HR9 (Help users recognize, diagnose, and recover from errors) has the second higher severity rating (Fig. 3). Experts identified problems related to:

- A reset button in the DICOM editor would be useful if the user wants to recover from an error or restart the process (E1).
- Sometimes, the DICOM editor's toolbar is blocked when the user clicks on IA algorithm or crop the image (E1).

- Errors information during the deletion and uploading processes are not displayed (E2, E3, E4, E5, E6).
- Not enough information, no error messages when an action is not permitted (E6).

Table 1. Heuristic evaluation summary by expert. N = number of errors

Heuristic rule	E1		E2		E3		E4		E5		E6	
	avg	N	avg	N	avg	N	avg	N	avg	N	avg	N
HR1: Visibility of system status	5.75	4	5	4	8.5	2	9	1	3	2	9.75	4
HR2: Match between system and the real world	6	1	7.5	4	8	1	8.2	5	5	1	8.5	4
HR3: User control and freedom	0	0	8.5	2	0	0	6.33	6	0	0	9.25	4
HR4: Consistency and standards	7.13	8	4.67	3	7.75	4	7	3	5.25	4	9.25	4
HR5: Error prevention	5	1	7.67	3	6	2	10	2	8	1	9	4
HR6: Recognition rather than recall	4.33	3	8	2	7	4	8.5	2	3	1	9	4
HR7: Flexibility and efficiency of use	4	1	8.5	2	6	1	8.75	4	7	1	9.25	4
HR8: Aesthetic and minimalist design	2.5	4	6	3	7	3	7	3	0	0	9.5	4
HR9: Help users recognize, diagnose, and recover from errors	8.67	3	7.67	3	7	2	10	1	7	1	8.5	4
HR10: Help and documentation	9	2	9	2	8	2	9	2	9.5	2	9.25	4

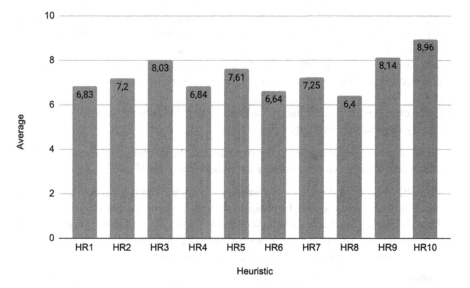

Fig. 3. The final average value for each heuristic rule

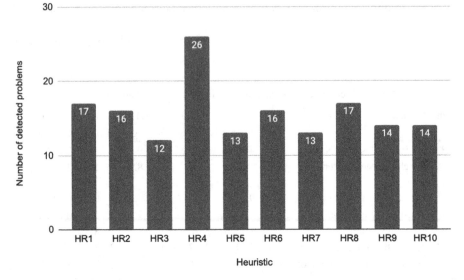

Fig. 4. The total number of detected problems per Nielsen's heuristic

On the other hand, the lowest number of usability problems was detected in HR3, HR5 and HR7. Regarding error prevention, each expert detected few errors; some of them are:

- Not enough information to define the password during the registration process (E1).
- The whole upload process involves different tasks that should be done in a specific order, but all actions are available from the beginning, which can be confusing and introduce errors. Some actions should not be accessible before performing the necessary preliminary steps and the process should be guided (E2, E4, E5).
- When select "download only selected data" and no data are selected, empty files are downloaded and the system does not advise the user he has not selected any data (E3).
- Users can apply erroneous filters when searching for patients in a project (E3).
- Clearly defined user privileges (E6).

Highlight some problems related to the remaining heuristics with high severity ratings. The main problems about the visibility of system status (HR1) are:

- The DICOM viewer does not show inside in which project is the image and you can come back to the project, only navigate through a set of images (E1).
- There is no progress bar indicating the deletion progress, though the process can be time-consuming when you delete several files (E2 and E6).
- No information about the user privileges and role (E4).

The problems related to matching between the system and the real world (HR2) are mainly related to the vocabulary used inside the projects. The language used is very technical, such as table names, code reservation, 'upload' templates, etc. (E1, E2 and E4), and medical acronyms (E3 and E6).

Finally, although experts detected several problems related to recognition rather than recall (HR5), we want to emphasize the patients' section inside a project because it is at the bottom of the page and you have to scroll down to see them. According to E4, a reorganization of this screen will be useful to solve several usability problems.

5   Discussion and Conclusions

The CARTIER-IA platform unifies structure data and medical images, specifically DICOM images, to support researchers and physicians in the analysis associated with different studies, with a particular focus on supporting the application of AI algorithms in images.

The platform has been designed and developed using a user-centered approach, involving researchers and physicians to define the functionality and the different interfaces in an iterative process. Moreover, they were the data providers to test the platform. However, the complexity of the data collection processes, the edition of the DICOM images and the huge amount of data available in each project, whose can also include several studies, difficult the use of the platform for those users that are not directly involved in the design and development of the CARTIER-IA platform.

This study has served to identify the main usability issues to improve the platform with a particular focus on ensuring that novice users would be able to use it without a previous training. The group of experts involved in the study combined users with experience using the platform and users that discover the platform during the heuristic evaluation process. This approach has made it possible to achieve the study's main objective, which was to analyze whether a person joining the system for the first time can use it.

However, a heuristic evaluation does not ensure identifying all the problems that affect a real user of the platform. Some studies reveal whether the problems detected by the usability experts are problems that will affect or be encountered by the actual users of the system. In some areas, evaluators' perception in using this method is not consistent with the users' experience with a system [11]. One of the experts has extensive knowledge of the platform's domain to alleviate this problem, though further research might explore the user experience of the researchers and physicians.

Regarding the results of the evaluation, each expert identified a small number of usability problems. However, the combination of the results provides relevant information to develop a new version of the CARTIER-IA platform to solve the different identified problems. It would be interesting to assess this new version through a user testing and a second heuristic evaluation.

Even though the usability issues detected are related to most of the screens and functionality of the platform, the problems that most affect the use of the platform itself are those related to the information provided in each project and the DICOM viewer and editor. Several heuristics affect both issues. In particular, the DICOM viewer and editor appears in problems detected by three experts (E1, E2 and E6) and associated with seven heuristics (HR1, HR2, HR4, HR6, HR7, HR9 and HR10). Besides, after receiving all the evaluations, we asked the other experts (E3, E4 and E5) about the image editor and all of them confirm that they did not notice the tool; they did not find that part of the platform. A reasonable approach to tackle this issue could be a user experience study with real users only focused on the DICOM viewer and editor.

Acknowledgements. This research work has been supported by the Spanish Ministry of Education and Vocational Training under an FPU fellowship (FPU17/03276). This work was also supported by national (PI14/00695, PIE14/00066, PI17/00145, DTS19/00098, PI19/00658, PI19/00656 Institute of Health Carlos III, Spanish Ministry of Economy and Competitiveness and co-funded by ERDF/ESF, "Investing in your future") and community (GRS 2033/A/19, GRS 2030/A/19, GRS 2031/A/19, GRS 2032/A/19, SACYL, Junta Castilla y León) competitive grants.

References

1. Rajkomar, A., Dean, J., Kohane, I.: Machine learning in medicine. N. Engl. J. Med. **380**, 1347–1358 (2019)
2. Litjens, G., et al.: A survey on deep learning in medical image analysis. Med. Image Anal. **42**, 60–88 (2017)
3. Liu, X., et al.: A comparison of deep learning performance against health-care professionals in detecting diseases from medical imaging: a systematic review and meta-analysis. Lancet Digit. Health **1**, e271–e297 (2019)
4. Ssemugabi, S., De Villiers, M.R.: Effectiveness of heuristic evaluation in usability evaluation of elearning applications in higher education. South Afr. Comput. J. (SACJ) **45** (2010)
5. Nielsen, J.: Heuristic evaluation. In: Nielsen, J., Mack, R.L. (eds.) Usability inspection methods, vol. 17, pp. 25–62. John Wiley & Sons, Inc. (1994)
6. Maramba, I., Chatterjee, A., Newman, C.: Methods of usability testing in the development of eHealth applications: a scoping review. Int. J. Med. Inform. **126**, 95–104 (2019)
7. Nielsen, J.: Finding usability problems through heuristic evaluation. In: CHI 1992: Proceedings of the SIGCHI Conference on Human Factors in Computing Systems, pp. 373–380. ACM, New York, NY, USA (1992)
8. Dobre, J., et al.: Rapid heuristic evaluation: ensuring fast and reliable usability support. Proc. Hum. Factors Ergonomics Soc. Annu. Meeting **61**, 610–614 (2017)
9. Tarrell, A., Grabenbauer, L., McClay, J., Windle, J., Fruhling, A.L.: Toward improved heuristic evaluation of EHRs. Health Syst. **4**, 138–150 (2015)
10. Armijo, D., McDonnell, C., Werner, K.: Electronic health record usability: evaluation and use case framework. AHRQ Publication No. 09(10)-0091-1-EF. Agency for Healthcare Research and Quality, Rockville, MD (2009)
11. Khajouei, R., Ameri, A., Jahani, Y.: Evaluating the agreement of users with usability problems identified by heuristic evaluation. Int. J. Med. Inform. **117**, 13–18 (2018)

On-line vs. in Class Learning in Pandemic Times

Student Response Systems in Remote Teaching

Jean Botev[✉], Christian Grévisse, and Steffen Rothkugel

University of Luxembourg, Av. de la Fonte 6, 4364 Esch-sur-Alzette, Luxembourg
{jean.botev,christian.grevisse,steffen.rothkugel}@uni.lu

Abstract. Student response systems (SRS) are a popular and effective tool to promote active learning on site, improving student engagement and attention, motivation and learning performance. Traditionally, SRS are designed for on-site settings. However, the safety measures in relation to the recent COVID-19 pandemic result in remote teaching at an unprecedented scale, with online courses becoming the rule. In this paper, we discuss the utilization of interactive SRS in such remote settings for which they initially were not designed. Over the last term, we conducted several empirical surveys across different groups of Computer Science students on undergraduate and postgraduate levels, and covering a broad age spectrum. The results indicate that, while common interactive features of videoconferencing tools, such as chat or polls, are well appreciated, there is still a need for dedicated SRS with game-based elements and feature sets beyond standard multiple-choice questions.

Keywords: Student response systems · Active learning · Gamification

1 Motivation and Background

Student response systems (SRS) are a popular and effective tool to promote active learning on site [6], in particular when involving game-based elements [4,5]. Common benefits reported in literature include boosts in student engagement and attention, motivation and learning performance. Traditionally, SRS are designed for on-site settings. As illustrated on the left in Fig. 1, students

Fig. 1. On-site (left) and online (right) application of student response systems.

© Springer Nature Switzerland AG 2021
P. Zaphiris and A. Ioannou (Eds.): HCII 2021, LNCS 12784, pp. 387–400, 2021.
https://doi.org/10.1007/978-3-030-77889-7_27

use mobile devices (e.g., smartphones, tablets or laptops) to respond to questions or other activities, while the teacher can display relevant information such as the aggregated results on the main screen. However, the safety measures in relation to the recent COVID-19 pandemic result in remote teaching at an unprecedented scale, with online courses becoming the rule rather than the exception.

In this paper, we discuss the utilization of interactive SRS in such remote settings for which they initially were not designed. The students and teachers are geographically separated and interconnected only via network from home or elsewhere (Fig. 1, right). Both on teacher and student side, the setups potentially are more heterogeneous and include also desktop machines and other internet-enabled devices, as well as a varying number of screens and formats. Students therefore might not be able to see the teacher's presenter screen, which some SRS use to show the questions in their entirety, leaving their own screen for answer selection only. Teachers might also run into issues managing the different tabs related to an SRS without a dedicated projection screen. Finally, the screen sharing feature of the chosen videoconferencing tool must allow for a fine-grained sharing of specific windows, to prevent inadvertently revealing any information related to the correct answers while playing. We highlight the experiences when employing established tools in different situations and look into how they relate to features available in common videoconferencing software.

Over the last term, we conducted several empirical surveys across different groups of Computer Science students on undergraduate and postgraduate levels, and covering a broad age spectrum. In all courses, the student response framework Yactul [2] was employed alongside other interactive tools in order to explore the following research questions:

* How is the acceptance of SRS in remote/online vs. on-site settings that were initially targeted?
* What are the differences when deploying SRS remotely? Are there any technical issues?
* Do remote options such as companion apps for asynchronous revision gain in popularity?
* How do existing interactive features of videoconferencing systems integrate?
* Which supporting technologies are deemed useful by students and teachers?

The results indicate that, while common interactive features of videoconferencing tools, such as chat or polls, are well appreciated, there is still a need for dedicated SRS with game-based elements and feature sets beyond standard multiple-choice questions. Videoconferencing tools are traditionally developed with business use cases in mind; consequently, they lack a series of important elements offered by game-based SRS, such as playful user interfaces, competition and rewards. We conclude the paper with a series of recommendations and best practices for the successful application of existing SRS and complementary tools in remote teaching scenarios. Finally, we also would like to start a discussion on which features the next generation of game-based SRS necessitates to better accommodate changing requirements and unforeseen circumstances.

2   Yactul

Yactul [2] is a game-based student response system (GSRS), developed at the University of Luxembourg. It enables formative assessment both in the classroom and at home. Based on a modular, decentralized architecture, it allows for an extensible set of activity types, fulfilling the needs of different study domains. Apart from traditional multiple choice questions, where either a single or multiple answers may be correct, Yactul also provides *Focus* activities, in which the different answers are shown consecutively for a given amount of time and the user has to hit the button when the deemed correct alternative is shown. Furthermore, *Point-and-click* activities require the user to pinpoint the location of a given element within an image. This can be particularly interesting in geography or anatomy classes. Finally, *Building pairs* activities are achieved by correctly matching elements from one column with those in a second one. The heterogeneity within quizzes composed of different activity types can provide a certain variation to students to avoid a wearout effect [5]. Activities in Yactul can be annotated with semantic concepts from established knowledge bases, such as *DBpedia*[1], in order to identify the topics addressed in a question which, in turn, facilitates the filtering of the activity set. Further advantages of this semantic annotation are discussed in Sect. 2.2.

2.1   Web Platform

The Yactul web platform has been used primarily in a classroom context, and more recently in remote teaching due to the COVID-19 pandemic. Similar to other GSRS, students can participate in a quiz session by logging in with a PIN code and a nickname. The *projector view*, shown in Fig. 2a, typically presented on the screen of the lecture hall and nowadays shared through a videoconferencing tool, shows the current question, the possible answers and the remaining time. After all students have submitted their answer or the time has expired, this view shows the solutions and overall class performance, as well as the current leaderboard. Unlike, for instance, in the popular GSRS *Kahoot!*[2], the students can see both the question and the answer options on their device, avoiding an unnecessary increase in extraneous cognitive load caused by the *split-attention effect* [1]. Apart from the projector view, teachers mainly interact with the *administration view*. As shown in Fig. 2b, a timeline known from media editing software allows for adding, reordering and setting the duration of the questions to be played in a quiz. Contrary to many popular GSRS, Yactul enables teachers to perform ad-hoc changes of a running quiz, such as to add or skip questions, or to give more time to the currently played activity. As teachers are provided with two different views, a dual screen setup would be ideal, showing the administration view on one screen, and the projector view together with the videoconferencing tool on the other.

---

[1] https://wiki.dbpedia.org.
[2] https://kahoot.com.

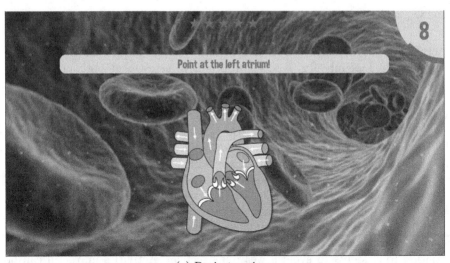

(a) Projector view.

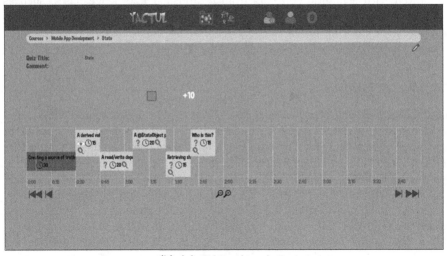

(b) Administration view.

Fig. 2. Yactul web platform.

2.2   Mobile App

The Yactul mobile app, available on both iOS and Android, enables a continuous learning experience, from the classroom to the students' private study environment. It is optimized for offline usage, which is particularly useful when students are abroad without a data plan, or travelling on a plane without in-flight WiFi.

In addition to a *sequential* mode, in which activities are played in the same order as the quizzes in class, the *coaching* mode allows to keep track of the individual player's performance. Based on the record of activities played on the device, a spaced repetition algorithm proposes and repeats questions in a frequency according to the answer performance in the past. As shown in Fig. 3a, a color scheme serves as a visual cue for users to understand how well activities related to a given concept have been answered in the past, and hence which concepts require further attention. In addition, the semantic annotation of Yactul activities enables the retrieval of related learning material (Fig. 3c), which can be helpful when a student is struggling with an activity or the underlying concepts. The Yactul mobile app constitutes a personalized learning assistant, which, along with the Yactul web platform, has been considered useful in a previous study [3].

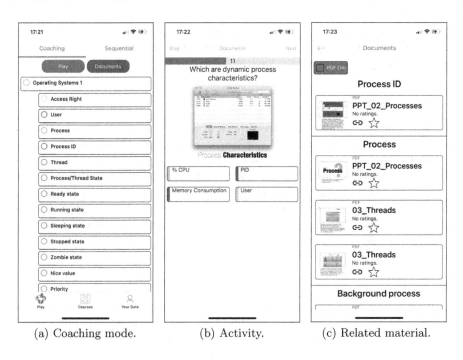

(a) Coaching mode.   (b) Activity.   (c) Related material.

Fig. 3. Yactul mobile app.

3   Evaluation

Over the last term, we conducted several empirical surveys across different groups of Computer Science students on undergraduate and postgraduate levels, including more senior students in a continued professional education program.

Our regular students are usually aged between 18 and 25, while students in continued professional education cover a broader age spectrum anywhere between 25 to 55 years. In all seven courses that were part of the study, the student response framework Yactul [2] was employed alongside other interactive tools. These include the polling and chat functions of the Webex[3] videoconferencing software, as well as digital whiteboard software to integrate and transmit live sketches from tablet devices.

In addition to transmitting their camera audio/video feeds, teachers are generally sharing their screen during the courses to show slides, share sketches and diagrams, or edit and run code examples. When using Yactul, the projector view (Fig. 2a) that would normally be shown using a projector on site is shared with the students, while the teacher also needs to be able to interact with the administration view (Fig. 2b) displayed in another browser tab. As tab-specific sharing is not available in most videoconferencing tools, a dual-screen setup on teacher side is recommendable for this to work seemlessly, sharing the browser window containing the projector view on one screen, while retaining another browser window with the administration view and controls on the other screen.

3.1 Survey Design

To assess the applicability and acceptance of SRS in remote/online versus the initially targeted on-site settings, the survey contains three major sections focusing on (a) live quizzes in online classes, (b) offline quizzes in the dedicated Yactul app, and (c) other interactive tools. For eleven out of the twelve questions in total, the answers follow a 5-point Likert scale to capture agreement respectively frequency. The final question is an open question so as to capture specific feedback regarding the use of other tools in free-form text. Section A of the appendix contains the questionnaire in its entirety.

3.2 Results

This section discusses the aggregated survey results across all seven courses, as well as potential deviations when comparing, e.g., junior with senior student responses, or practical with theoretical courses. Table 1 in the appendix contains the raw data for the different courses and categories.

The first part of the survey focuses on playing live quizzes in online classes and comprises four questions inquiring about their perceived usefulness, entertainment value, trouble-free implementation and desired frequency. As shown in Fig. 4, the results here are overwhelmingly positive, with close to 90% of the students considering playing such quizzes both useful and entertaining (cf. Questions 1 and 2) while two thirds did not find the online mode to be more problematic than playing on site (cf. Question 3). Nearly all students expressed their desire to play live quizzes on a regular basis also remotely (cf. Question 4).

---

[3] https://www.webex.com.

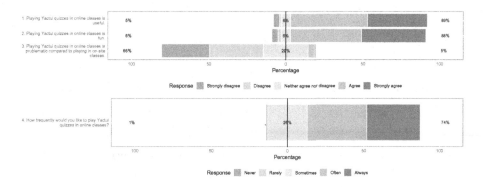

Fig. 4. Aggregated results, questions on live quizzes in online classes.

The results for the second part of the survey, which focuses on the possibility to play offline quizzes in the dedicated companion app, are shown in Fig. 5. Also in this context, the two initial questions inquire about the perceived usefulness and entertainment value, while the third question focuses on the actual frequency of the students playing quizzes within the mobile app. Again, the results are mostly positive (cf. Questions 5 and 6), however, the companion app is used regularly only by slightly more than half of the students (cf. Question 7).

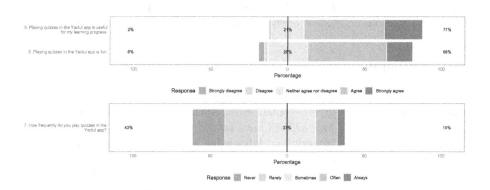

Fig. 5. Aggregated results, questions on offline quizzes in the Yactul app.

Finally, the results related to further interactive tools that are commonly employed alongside dedicated SRS/GSRS in remote teaching are summarized in Fig. 6. The first two questions inquire about chat and polling features which are commonly integrated into videoconferencing software (cf. Questions 8 and 9), while the next question assesses how helpful digital whiteboard software for integrating and transmitting live sketches and diagrams is (cf. Question 10). The final Likert-scale question is specific to Computer Science courses and explores how well the use of code examples is received by the students (cf. Question 11).

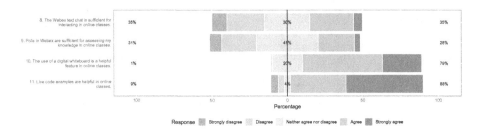

Fig. 6. Aggregated results, questions on other interactive tools.

The added value and helpfulness of both employing live code examples and digital whiteboard software becomes evident in the downright positive response of the vast majority of the students. The response to the standard chat and polling features draws a more diffuse picture, with half of the students deeming them sufficient in online classes while the other half does not. The open question (cf. Question 12) only points to some alternative videoconferencing or whiteboard software. Together with the generally positive assessment in the first part of the survey, this is a clear indicator that there is still a need for dedicated SRS with game-based elements and feature sets beyond standard multiple-choice questions.

As per Mann-Whitney U test, we could not detect a statistically significant difference in opinion between junior and senior students, or between practical and theoretical courses. The results therefore are representative across the entire student body and independent of the practical orientation of the various courses.

4   Conclusion

The safety measures in relation to the recent COVID-19 pandemic result in remote teaching at an unprecedented scale, with online courses becoming the rule. Many useful tools, such as SRS have been designed with on-site settings in mind, and there is little experiential knowledge and data on how well they can be applied in this context.

The empirical study we conducted over the last term across different graduate and postgraduate Computer Science courses fills this gap and provides useful insights on the deployment of such tools. The results indicate that the interactive elements of existing videoconferencing software do not fully cover educational requirements, and that there is still a need for dedicated game-based SRS with extended feature sets. To successfully apply existing SRS/GSRS and complementary tools in remote teaching scenarios, currently the technical equipment remains the most critical element for students and teachers alike. From a teachers' point of view, multiple screens are essential to be able to handle the different software and associated views while presenting only the relevant information to the students. An integration of the necessary controls and administrative tools into the videoconferencing software could significantly reduce the need for screen real estate. Conversely, such integration would also reduce the need for multiple devices or windows/screens on the side of the students; the GSRS would simply come as part of the videoconferencing software.

Some major collaboration and videoconferencing software manufacturers already acknowledge and accommodate this by opening their tools for integration. Microsoft Teams, for instance, allows for custom apps to be integrated in the meeting experience, similar to Office Add-ins[4]. We are therefore in the process of integrating our own GSRS Yactul into available platforms as we believe that there is a long-lasting need for dedicated, yet flexible remote teaching solutions.

Appendix

A. Questionnaire

Live Quizzes in Online Classes

1. **Playing Yactul quizzes in online classes is useful.**

   ○ Strongly disagree
   ○ Disagree
   ○ Neither agree nor disagree
   ○ Agree
   ○ Strongly Agree

2. **Playing Yactul quizzes in online classes is fun.**

   ○ Strongly disagree
   ○ Disagree
   ○ Neither agree nor disagree
   ○ Agree
   ○ Strongly Agree

3. **Playing Yactul quizzes in online classes is problematic compared to playing in on-site classes.**

   ○ Strongly disagree
   ○ Disagree
   ○ Neither agree nor disagree
   ○ Agree
   ○ Strongly Agree

4. **How frequently would you like to play Yactul quizzes in online classes?**

   ○ Never
   ○ Rarely

---

[4] https://docs.microsoft.com/en-us/microsoftteams/platform/apps-in-teams-meetings/create-apps-for-teams-meetings.

○ Sometimes
○ Often
○ Always

Offline Quizzes in the Yactul App

5. **Playing quizzes in the Yactul app is useful for my learning progress.**

○ Strongly disagree
○ Disagree
○ Neither agree nor disagree
○ Agree
○ Strongly Agree

6. **Playing quizzes in the Yactul app is fun.**

○ Strongly disagree
○ Disagree
○ Neither agree nor disagree
○ Agree
○ Strongly Agree

7. **How frequently do you play quizzes in the Yactul app?**

○ Never
○ Rarely
○ Sometimes
○ Often
○ Always

Other Interactive Tools

8. **The Webex text chat is sufficient for interacting in online classes.**

○ Strongly disagree
○ Disagree
○ Neither agree nor disagree
○ Agree
○ Strongly Agree

9. **Polls in Webex are sufficient for assessing my knowledge in online classes**

○ Strongly disagree
○ Disagree
○ Neither agree nor disagree
○ Agree
○ Strongly Agree

10. **The use of a digital whiteboard is a helpful feature in online classes**

○ Strongly disagree
○ Disagree
○ Neither agree nor disagree
○ Agree
○ Strongly Agree

11. **Live code examples are helpful in online classes**

○ Strongly disagree
○ Disagree
○ Neither agree nor disagree
○ Agree
○ Strongly Agree

12. **What additional tools would you like to use in online classes?**
    Open Question.

B. Data

Table 1. Survey results; the different courses are anonymized and numbered C1 through C7, with s indicating senior students attending and p indicating practical orientation of the respective course.

		Courses						
Question	**Answer**	**C1**	**C2**	**C3**	**C4^p**	**C5^p**	**C6^{ps}**	**C7^{ps}**
1	Strongly disagree	3	0	1	0	1	0	0
	Disagree	0	0	0	1	0	0	0
	Neither agree nor disagree	4	1	0	1	0	1	0
	Agree	12	19	3	12	2	6	5
	Strongly Agree	11	10	7	7	4	6	1
	No Answer	1	1	1	8	0	2	0
2	Strongly disagree	3	0	1	1	0	0	0
	Disagree	1	1	0	0	0	0	0
	Neither agree nor disagree	2	2	1	0	1	1	0
	Agree	13	10	3	13	1	9	4

(continued)

Table 1. (*continued*)

Question	Answer	C1	C2	C3	C4^p	C5^p	C6^{ps}	C7^{ps}
				Courses				
	Strongly Agree	10	16	5	7	5	3	2
	No Answer	2	2	2	8	0	2	0
3	Strongly disagree	6	13	6	3	5	0	2
	Disagree	12	8	3	6	2	4	4
	Neither agree nor disagree	9	5	2	10	0	7	0
	Agree	1	2	0	1	0	1	0
	Strongly Agree	0	0	0	1	0	0	0
	No Answer	3	3	1	8	0	3	0
4	Never	0	0	0	1	0	0	0
	Rarely	0	0	0	0	0	0	0
	Sometimes	6	7	1	5	2	5	3
	Often	9	12	6	9	1	4	3
	Always	14	9	4	5	4	3	0
	No Answer	2	3	1	9	0	3	0
5	Strongly disagree	0	0	0	0	0	0	0
	Disagree	2	0	0	0	0	0	0
	Neither agree nor disagree	4	11	2	5	0	1	0
	Agree	16	9	4	12	4	8	5
	Strongly Agree	7	7	4	3	2	4	1
	No Answer	2	4	2	9	1	2	0
6	Strongly disagree	1	1	1	1	0	0	0
	Disagree	2	0	0	0	0	0	0
	Neither agree nor disagree	6	10	3	6	2	2	0
	Agree	14	12	3	10	1	10	6
	Strongly Agree	6	4	2	3	3	1	0
	No Answer	2	4	3	9	1	2	0

(*continued*)

Table 1. (*continued*)

Question	Answer	Courses						
		C1	C2	C3	C4^p	C5^p	C6^{ps}	C7^{ps}
7	Never	7	8	1	4	2	1	1
	Rarely	6	6	3	5	1	3	1
	Sometimes	9	9	3	9	3	6	2
	Often	4	5	3	1	0	2	1
	Always	3	0	0	1	0	1	1
	No Answer	2	3	2	9	1	2	0
8	Strongly disagree	1	7	0	3	0	0	0
	Disagree	0	12	3	5	3	4	1
	Neither agree nor disagree	11	5	1	10	1	4	2
	Agree	14	3	5	2	2	4	2
	Strongly Agree	3	1	1	0	0	1	1
	No Answer	2	3	2	9	1	2	0
9	Strongly disagree	1	6	0	2	0	0	0
	Disagree	5	8	2	6	1	2	2
	Neither agree nor disagree	9	10	5	8	4	8	2
	Agree	13	3	2	4	1	3	1
	Strongly Agree	1	1	1	0	0	0	1
	No Answer	2	3	2	9	1	2	0
10	Strongly disagree	0	0	0	0	0	0	0
	Disagree	0	0	0	1	0	0	0
	Neither agree nor disagree	4	5	2	5	3	2	1
	Agree	10	20	3	12	3	9	2
	Strongly Agree	15	3	5	2	0	1	3
	No Answer	2	3	2	9	1	3	0
11	Strongly disagree	1	1	1	1	1	0	0
	Disagree	4	0	0	0	0	0	0
	Neither agree nor disagree	1	1	0	2	0	0	0

(*continued*)

Table 1. (*continued*)

Question	Answer	Courses						
		C1	C2	C3	C4^p	C5^p	C6^{ps}	C7^{ps}
	Agree	12	8	3	6	0	9	3
	Strongly Agree	11	17	6	11	5	4	3
	No Answer	2	4	2	9	1	2	0
12	Discord	0	5	0	0	0	0	0
	Miro	0	0	0	0	0	1	1
	Invalid	31	26	12	29	7	15	6

References

1. Chandler, P., Sweller, J.: The split-attention effect as a factor in the design of instruction. Br. J. Educ. Psychol. **62**(2), 233–246 (1992). https://doi.org/10.1111/j.2044-8279.1992.tb01017.x
2. Grévisse, C., Botev, J., Rothkugel, S.: Yactul: an extensible game-based student response framework for active learning. In: Proceedings of Virtual Education International Conference (2017)
3. Grévisse, C., Rothkugel, S., Reuter, R.A.P.: Scaffolding support through integration of learning material. Smart Learn. Environ. **6**(28) (2019). https://doi.org/10.1186/s40561-019-0107-0
4. Morillas Barrio, C., Muñoz-Organero, M., Sánchez Soriano, J.: Can gamification improve the benefits of student response systems in learning? an experimental study. IEEE Trans. Emerg. Topics Comput. **4**(3), 429–438 (2016). https://doi.org/10.1109/TETC.2015.2497459
5. Wang, A.I.: The wear out effect of a game-based student response system. Comput. Educ. **82**, 217–227 (2015). https://doi.org/10.1016/j.compedu.2014.11.004
6. Wong, Suet Lai, Yau, Sui Yu.: Impact of student response system on enhancing active learning. In: Li, Kam Cheong, Tsang, Eva Yuen Mei, Wong, Billy Tak Ming (eds.) Innovating Education in Technology-Supported Environments. EIS, pp. 199–213. Springer, Singapore (2020). https://doi.org/10.1007/978-981-15-6591-5_15

E-Learning and M-Learning Technological Intervention in Favor of Mathematics

Omar Cóndor-Herrera[1] and Carlos Ramos-Galarza[1,2(✉)]

[1] Centro de Investigación en Mecatrónica y Sistemas Interactivos MIST/Carrera de Psicología/Maestría en Educación mención Innovación y Liderazgo Educativo, Universidad Tecnológica Indoamérica, Av. Machala y Sabanilla, Quito, Ecuador
`{omarcondor, carlosramos}@uti.edu.ec`
[2] Facultad de Psicología, Pontificia Universidad Católica del Ecuador, Av. 12 de Octubre y Roca, Quito, Ecuador
`caramos@puce.edu.ec`

Abstract. This paper is based on pre-experimental research that assessed the impact of E-Learning and M-Learning technological intervention to promote mathematical skills learning. The sample consisted of 16 students between 11 and 12 years old (Mage = 11.94, SD = .25). They received an educational technology program for 6 sessions. Pre and posttest measurements were performed to assess direct proportionality knowledge and ability to solve problems with 2 artifacts respectively. The results showed statistically significant differences between the pre and posttest (knowledge t (15) = −7.20, p = <. 001, d = .88 and ability to solve problems t (15) = −6.75, p = < .001, d = .87). Consequently, it is highlighted the improvement that the learning process based on E-learning and M-learning has in the learning process of mathematics, as evidenced after the intervention ended. The data is discussed around the need to incorporate this type of technological tools in the learning of calculation skills and previous research.

Keywords: E-learning · M-learning · VLE · ICT

1 Introduction

The technological revolution has changed humanity in all its spheres. Cultural processes have gradually taken turns not only in the forms of production, representation, and diffusion of knowledge but also in how to access it. Each society has had to update its teaching models, although this transition has not developed at the same rate as technological progress [1, 2].

Situations currently experienced in the world have abruptly forced several countries to rethink the approach of their educational systems to move to a pedagogical model of teaching based on information and communication technologies (ICT), developed in virtual learning environments (VLE) and giving way to e-learning and m-learning education, with all the resources, possibilities and tools that technology offers today [3].

The teaching and learning of mathematics have always represented a challenge for the educational community [4] resulting in extensive research in innovative ways of

© Springer Nature Switzerland AG 2021
P. Zaphiris and A. Ioannou (Eds.): HCII 2021, LNCS 12784, pp. 401–408, 2021.
https://doi.org/10.1007/978-3-030-77889-7_28

teaching mathematics with the support of the technology. Borba et al. [1] mapped research focused on digital technology and mathematics education, where the use of mobile technology and virtual environments are considered effective devices to generate significant learning. Also, positive results such as motivation improvement, commitment, and access to technological learning environments have been found when technology is used in virtual learning [5–7].

In this sense, this research shows a longitudinal pre-experimental investigation that developed a technological intervention program based on e-learning and m-learning to improve the learning process of mathematics in primary school students.

2   Benefits of E-Learning and M-Learning in Education

2.1   E-Learning Benefits

E-learning or electronic learning arises as a direct result of the integration of technology into the educational field, including the implementation of a wide range of multimedia tools such as the internet, interactive television and web pages, dynamic platforms and all forms of electronic support, which favors the learning of mathematics, making it flexible and much friendlier for students [8, 9].

As mentioned by Corbett and Spinello, the difference that e-learning offers in relation to conventional education is that the process of construction and assimilation of knowledge takes place in a virtual environment where the advantages offered by web 2.0 allows the creation of online learning communities [10]. Within connectivism, learning occurs when peers are connected and share opinions, points of view, and ideas through a collaborative process [11]. Due to the popularity of this type of teaching, its implementation has improved, more and better resources have appeared to potentiate VLEs reaching not only conventional desktop computers but also mobile devices such as smartphones, tablets, among others, leading to the appearance of m-learning.

2.2   M-Learning Benefits

As mentioned, the application of the web 2.0 to electronic learning allows visualizing new forms of teaching and learning [12]. Part of these possibilities is m-learning, which through the use of mobile devices, allows access to information on different topics and areas of mathematical knowledge, science, language, among others. Additionally, software applications (APPs) allow the teacher to implement different types of activities in innovative ways. Thus, M-learning facilitates the pedagogical process, as students can access a wide range of contents and activities without time, or geographic location limitations [5,13].

The effectiveness of this type of teaching generates great benefits in student learning. For example, in research done by Ramadiani et al. [14], the results showed a positive correlation between the use of smartphones and the quality of learning. Therefore, understanding new academic concepts and improving study habits will be eased by understanding the functioning of VLEs [6, 15].

2.3   The Adaptation of the VLE for an Adequate Virtual Learning Process

Despite the wide range of resources offered by ICT and web 2.0, virtual learning environments, and their platforms, such as Moodle (Modular Object-Oriented Dynamic Learning Environment) and others, in many cases are used as simple documents repositories. This highlights the need of an adequate adaptation and reasonable organization of learning resources within the VLEs, that can allow the generation of a correctly addressed learning route supported by an appropriate teaching methodology for this type of environment, allowing the e-student to meet their learning objective [16–18].

To attain the benefits of the use of technology in education, it is essential that teachers are training in virtual classroom management for those who foray into this teaching methodology, so they can easily coordinate virtual instruction through computers. The successful implementation of e-learning and m-learning depends on the effective preparation of the people in charge of these working environments, otherwise, the learning outcome would not be favorable for students [19, 20].

Therefore, the research question that arises is, what effects are obtained in the teaching and learning process of mathematics, when applying a technological intervention of E-learning and M-learning in the primary educational context.

3   Hypothesis

H1. Students under the e-learning and m-learning technological intervention will show improvements in the learning of concepts on direct proportionality when comparing their performance before and after the intervention.

H2. Students under the e-learning and M-learning technological intervention will show improvements in their mathematical skills to solve problems about direct proportionality before and after the intervention.

4   Methodology

4.1   Participants

The group consisted of 16 participants between 11 and 12 years of age ($M_{age} = 11.94$, $SD = .25$), 6 (37.5%) were women and 10 (62.5%) men. In all cases, the ethical standards for research with humans were complied with, the voluntary participation was respected and the physical and mental integrity of all the participants was safeguarded in each phase of the study.

4.2   Artifacts

Two artifacts were built to perform pre and posttest evaluations. The first artifact assessed the direct proportionality knowledge and the second one the direct proportionality problem-solving.

4.3   Intervention Protocol

An E-Learning and M-Learning intervention program was developed in favor of learning mathematics on direct proportionality, focused on improving the mastery level of knowledge and the ability to solve mathematical problems on the topic raised. The intervention was applied for 6 work sessions, where the E-Learning and M-learning strategies were applied: (a) virtual class, (b) video quiz, (c) serious games, (d) Quizizz questionnaires, and (e) Flashcards (see Fig. 1).

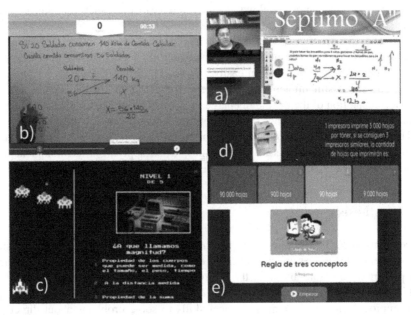

Fig. 1. E-Learning and M-learning program: a) virtual class, b) video quizz, c) serious game, d) QUIZIZZ questionnaires and e) flash cards.

4.4   Procedure

It is important to highlight that this research was approved by the Ethical Committee of Investigation with human beings of the University Indoamerica of Ecuador.

Participant's representatives were asked to sign the informed consent of voluntary participation, the consent was signed and granted by all parents without any exception Throughout this research ethical standards of investigation with human beings were followed, protecting participants' physical and psychological integrity at all times.

Once the respective authorizations were obtained, the procedure was done. Finally, the databases were completed and the respective analyzes were performed.

4.5   Data Analysis Plan

Statistical measures of central tendency and dispersion were used to characterize the sample. To check the hypotheses, the Student's t statistic was applied to make a comparison between the pre and posttest. Also, Cohen's d statistic was applied to calculate the effect size of the comparisons. All analyzes were performed in the SPSS statistical package version 25.

5   Results

5.1   First Hypothesis in Favor of Knowledge Difference

Table 1 shows the descriptive values found in the artifact that quantified the knowledge of direct proportionality in the pre and posttest.

Table 1. Knowledge pre and posttest descriptive measurement

Paired sample statistics

	M	N	SD	SM
Knowledge pretest	1.75	16	1.07	.27
Knowledge posttest	4.50	16	.82	.20

M: median, SD: standard deviation, SM: median standard error.

Subsequently, to analyze the first hypothesis, the Student's t-test was applied, in which a statistically significant difference and a large effect size were found between the pre and posttest measurements, which provided empirical evidence in favor of the first hypothesis (see Table 2).

Table 2. Knowledge pre and posttest median comparison

Paired difference

95% CI

	M	SD	SM	L	H	t	df	P	d
Pretest vs. posttest	−2.5	1.53	.38	−3.56	−1.94	−7.20	15	< .001	.88

M: median, SD: standard deviation, SM: median standard error, CI: confidence interval, L: low, H: high, t: comparison value, df: degrees of freedom, p: p-value, d: effect size.

5.2   Second Hypothesis in Favor of Problem-Solving

Table 3 shows the results found in the assessments performed at the pre and posttest level in the artifact that evaluates problem-solving.

Table 3. Problem solving pre and posttest descriptive measurement.

Paired sample statistics

	M	N	SD	SM
Problem solving pretest	1.88	16	.89	.22
Problem solving posttest	4.25	16	.93	.23

M: median, SD: standard deviation, SM: median standard error.

In the statistical analysis done to analyze compliance with the second research hypothesis, it was found that there are statistically significant differences and a large effect size between the pre and posttest comparisons, which provides empirical evidence in favor of the second research hypothesis. Table 4 shows the comparison made.

Table 4. Problem solving pre and posttest median comparison.

Paired difference

95% CI

	M	SD	SM	L	H	t	df	P	d
Pretest vs. posttest	−2.38	1.41	.35	−3.13	−1.62	−6.75	15	< .001	.87

5.3 Discussion

This research shows the results of a pre-experimental investigation that aimed to analyze the impact of an E-learning and M-learning intervention program in favor of learning mathematical concepts about direct proportionality and the problem-solving ability of this mathematical skill.

To obtain the data, two artifacts were applied in the pre-test, the first measured the understanding of mathematical concepts, and the second the ability to solve problems. Subsequently, the intervention was applied in work sessions with students, using virtual classes, serious games, video quiz, among other E-learning and M-learning activities. Once the intervention was completed, the post-test was performed, where the same skills as the pre-test were measured.

The first hypothesis proposed that the students under the E-learning and M-learning technological intervention will show improvements in learning concepts on direct proportionality when comparing their performance before and after the intervention. When comparing the results obtained between the pre and posttest, a statistically significant difference was found. The initial measurement of the group was 1.75 on average and in the final measurement, it increased to 4.50. This provides evidence that the use of e-learning and M-learning improves mathematical knowledge concepts such as direct proportionality.

The second hypothesis stated that the students under the e-learning and M-learning technological intervention will show improvements in their mathematical skills to solve problems about direct proportionality before and after the intervention. The comparison between the pre and posttest results showed a statistically significant increase. The initial measurement of the group was 1.88 on average and in the posttest, the result rose to 4.25, which allows us to affirm that the use of e-learning and M-learning improves the ability to solve mathematical problems in primary school students.

The results of this research are similar to studies such as those of Malik et al. [21–23]who affirm that the use of technological applications improves the understanding of concepts and enrich student learning. Furthermore, they point out that M-leaning based on smart mobile devices is compatible with the problem-based learning pedagogy the results are obtained beneficial for learning, as supported by the results of this research [24].

The limitations of this study lie in the lack of a control group to contrast the results obtained by the students under the intervention, as this could have enriched the data presented. However, this factor becomes a motivation for future studies with technological applications in favor of learning mathematics, including control groups and also increasing the sample size.

Declaration of Conflict of Interest. On behalf of all authors, the corresponding author states that there is no conflict of interest.

References

1. Borba, M.C., Chiari, A., de Almeida, H.R.F.L.: Interactions in virtual learning environments: new roles for digital technology. Educ. Stud. Math. **98**(3), 269–286 (2018). https://doi.org/10.1007/s10649-018-9812-9
2. Pérez de y, A., Tellera, M.: Las TIC en la educación: nuevos ambientes de aprendizaje para la interacción educativa. In: Revista de Teoría y Didáctica de las Ciencias Sociales, vol. 18, pp. 83–112 (2012). https://www.redalyc.org/articulo.oa?id=65226271002
3. Hardman, J.: Towards a pedagogical model of teaching with ICTs for mathematics attainment in primary school: a review of studies. Heliyon **5**(5), 1–6 (2019). https://doi.org/10.1016/J.HELIYON.2019.E01726
4. Cai, J., Mok, I.A.C., Reddy, V., Stacey, K.: International comparative studies in mathematics: lessons and future directions for improving students' learning. In: Kaiser, G. (ed.) Proceedings of the 13th International Congress on Mathematical Education. IM, pp. 79–99. Springer, Cham (2017). https://doi.org/10.1007/978-3-319-62597-3_6
5. Attard, C., Holmes, K.: "It gives you that sense of hope": an exploration of technology use to mediate student engagement with mathematics. Heliyon **6**(1), 1–11 (2020). https://doi.org/10.1016/j.heliyon.2019.e02945
6. Campos, N., Nogal, M., Caliz, C., Juan, A.A.: Simulation-based education involving online and on-campus models in different European universities. Int. J. Educ. Technol. High. Educ. **17**(1), 1–15 (2020). https://doi.org/10.1186/s41239-020-0181-y
7. Cóndor-Herrera, O., Ramos-Galarza, C.: The impact of a technological intervention program on learning mathematical skills. Educ. Inf. Technol. **26**(2), 1423–1433 (2020). https://doi.org/10.1007/s10639-020-10308-y
8. Al-Fraihat, D., Joy, M., Masa'deh, R.: Sinclair, J.: Evaluating E-learning systems success: an empirical study. Comput. Hum. Behav. **102**, 67–86 (2020.). https://doi.org/10.1016/j.chb.2019.08.004

9. Escobar, F., Muñoz, L., Silva, V.: Motivation and E-learning English as a foreign language: a qualitative study. Heliyon **5**(9), 1–7 (2019). https://doi.org/10.1016/J.HELIYON.2019.E02394

10. Corbett, F., Spinello, E.: Connectivism and leadership: harnessing a learning theory for the digital age to redefine leadership in the twenty-first century. Heliyon **6**(1), 1–9 (2020). https://doi.org/10.1016/J.HELIYON.2020.E03250

11. Dunaway, M.: Web 2.0 and critical information literacy. Public Serv. Q. **7**, 3–4 (2011). https://doi.org/10.1080/15228959.2011.622628

12. El Mhouti, A., Nasseh, A., Erradi, M., Vasquèz, J.M.: Enhancing collaborative learning in Web 2.0-based e-learning systems: a design framework for building collaborative e-learning contents. Educ. Inf. Technol. **22**(5), 2351–2364 (2016). https://doi.org/10.1007/s10639-016-9545-2

13. Al-Emran, M., Mezhuyev, V., Kamaludin, A.: Towards a conceptual model for examining the impact of knowledge management. Technol. Soc. **61**, 1–33 (2020). https://doi.org/10.4067/S0718-50062020000100055

14. Ramadiani, A., Hidayanto, A., Khairina, D., Jundillah, M.: Teacher and student readiness using E-learning and M-learning. Bull. Electr. Eng. Inform. **9**(3), 1176–1182 (2020). https://doi.org/10.11591/eei.v9i3.2006

15. Moreno, J., Álvarez, J.: Mobile videogame as a didactic strategy to facilitate college adjustment. Form. Univ. **13**(1), 55–62 (2020). https://doi.org/10.4067/S0718-50062020000100055

16. Daqian, S., Ting, W., Hao, X., Hao, X.: A learning path recommendation model based on a multidimensional knowledge graph framework for e-learning. Knowl. Based Syst. **195**, 1–28 (2020). https://doi.org/10.1016/j.knosys.2020.105618

17. Jadán, J., Ramos, C.: Learning methodology based on narrative metaphors and gamification: a case study in a blended master's program. Hamut'ay **5**(5), 1–6 (2018). https://doi.org/10.21503/hamu.v5i1.1560

18. Cóndor-Herrera, O., Acosta-Rodas, P., Ramos-Galarza, C.: Gamification teaching for an active learning. In: Russo, D., Ahram, T., Karwowski, W., Di Bucchianico, G., Taiar, R. (eds.) IHSI 2021. AISC, vol. 1322, pp. 247–252. Springer, Cham (2021). https://doi.org/10.1007/978-3-030-68017-6_37

19. Al-araibi, A.A.M., Mahrin, M.N.B., Yusoff, R.C.M.: Technological aspect factors of E-learning readiness in higher education institutions: Delphi technique. Educ. Inf. Technol. **24**(1), 567–590 (2018). https://doi.org/10.1007/s10639-018-9780-9

20. Goos, M., O'Donoghue, J., Ní Ríordáin, M., Faulkner, F., Hall, T., O'Meara, N.: Designing a national blended learning program for "out-of-field" mathematics teacher professional development. ZDM Math. Educ. **52**(5), 893–905 (2020). https://doi.org/10.1007/s11858-020-01136-y

21. Malik, S.I., Mathew, R., Al-Nuaimi, R., Al-Sideiri, A., Coldwell-Neilson, J.: Learning problem solving skills: Comparison of E-learning and M-learning in an introductory programming course. Educ. Inf. Technol. **24**(5), 2779–2796 (2019). https://doi.org/10.1007/s10639-019-09896-1

22. Li, Y., Wang, L.: Using iPad-based mobile learning to teach creative engineering within a problem-based learning pedagogy. Educ. Inf. Technol. **23**(1), 555–568 (2017). https://doi.org/10.1007/s10639-017-9617-y

23. Khan, M.A., Salah, K.: Cloud adoption for e-learning: survey and future challenges. Educ. Inf. Technol. **25**(2), 1417–1438 (2019). https://doi.org/10.1007/s10639-019-10021-5

24. Ramos-Galarza, C., Arias-Flores, H., Cóndor-Herrera, O., Jadán-Guerrero, J.: Literacy toy for enhancement phonological awareness: a longitudinal study. In: Miesenberger, K., Manduchi, R., Covarrubias Rodriguez, M., Peňáz, P. (eds.) ICCHP 2020. LNCS, vol. 12377, pp. 371–377. Springer, Cham (2020). https://doi.org/10.1007/978-3-030-58805-2_44

Teaching Lung Pathology During a Pandemic: Can Further Developments of an Online Quiz Primer Improve the Engagement of Students in a Completely On-Line Delivery?

Mark Dixon[1]($\boxtimes$) and Katherine Syred[2]

[1] School of Engineering, Computing and Mathematics, University of Plymouth, Drake Circus, Plymouth PL4 8AA, UK
mark.dixon@plymouth.ac.uk
[2] Pathology Department, Derriford Hospital, Plymouth PL6 8DH, UK

Abstract. The current pandemic presents additional challenges for undergraduate teaching. This is especially true within the clinical years of a medical school where teaching delivery is provided by transient teaching staff with predominantly clinical commitments.

Previous work considered the use of an on-line quiz primer to support a flipped classroom approach for encouraging active learning amongst third year undergraduate medical students in lung pathology sessions. Student engagement improved in the face-to-face sessions (more students asking questions and the quality of question improving). However, the final session was delivered online (due to the pandemic) and student engagement declined (no student spoke using a microphone, shared screen or used the chat).

The present paper includes details of the final (online) session of 2019–2020 and describes and evaluates both the planned developments for 2020–2021 (additional questions, diagrams within questions and automatic descriptive feedback) and the changes made in response to the continuing pandemic. The aim was to ask: can further developments of the quiz primer improve the engagement of students in a completely on-line delivery?

Data was collected via a student perception questionnaire and participant observation. There was a definite improvement in engagement for this year's online sessions compared to last year's online session, but this is still below that of last year's face-to-face (pre-pandemic) sessions. The issue of a steep technological learning curve for teaching staff is particularly relevant to transient users. Therefore additional functionality and usability enhancements are required within videoconferencing systems to align with specific teaching needs.

Keywords: Pathology education · Flipped classroom · Interface design · User requirements · Zoom videoconferencing

© Springer Nature Switzerland AG 2021
P. Zaphiris and A. Ioannou (Eds.): HCII 2021, LNCS 12784, pp. 409–426, 2021.
https://doi.org/10.1007/978-3-030-77889-7_29

1   Introduction

1.1   COVID-19 Pandemic

In many parts of the world, the COVID-19 pandemic has caused face-to-face teaching to cease and be replaced with exclusively online delivery. Within the academic world this has driven an increase in interest around online delivery. In particular, interest has grown in video conferencing technology (such as Zoom and MS Teams), which is being used to support both remote education and home working (well beyond the original intended application domain that it was designed for).

Zoom video conferencing technology was the most prevalent, mentioned prior to [1, 10] and increasingly since the start of the current COVID-19 pandemic [5, 6, 8, 9, 11]. This technology has been used for both delivery and assessment. The use of various facilities were reported: such as chat, screen-share, and breakout rooms. With several papers describing students working in groups during sessions. One study showed no significant difference in assessment grades delivered face-to-face versus Zoom [11]. The use of pre-recorded primer material is also described [12]. Technical issues are reported, such as participants being disconnection from Zoom, and difficulty allocating desired students to breakout rooms.

Security concerns around the use of video conferencing technology have been reported [7]. In particular, 'Zoom bombing' has been recorded, where uninvited participants join and typically engage in disruptive, abusive and/or offensive behaviour, that often results in the session being abandoned.

Several authors reported a reluctance amongst students to engage online [8, 11], with some describing a 'painful silence' occurring within Zoom sessions [6]. Students seem particularly uncomfortable sharing screens, sharing video, or speaking using their microphone, but more are inclined to post messages using chat [11], instant messaging and forum facilities. The Slack business communication platform was mentioned as providing additional chat functionality compared to that embedded within Zoom [8].

Kay and Pasarica (2019) showed that using low effort (single click) facilities, such as reactions (raised hand and thumbs up) could have a positive impact on students engagement [5].

There has been some interest in the role of student to student interactions in enhancing engagement [3, 5] and the ease with which this can be encourage depending on which technology is used [8]. In particular, the more extensive chat facilities within Slack were found to support small group interactions more effectively than Zoom [8].

The demands of online delivery have been recognised. Several authors have also commented on the increase in workload for educators, with the potential for burnout [6] and some full time teaching staff being advised to reduce content in order to make workloads manageable. The technology learning curve (for both staff and students) is steep in addition to creating/consuming content. Lack of staff familiarity with the facilities provided by the technology can prevent it being used effectively during teaching sessions [9]. For transient staff with only a few hours of teaching per year this is compounded.

1.2   Previous Year's Work (2019–2020)

Previous work [2] considered the use of an on-line quiz primer as a component within a flipped classroom (FC) approach to encourage active learning amongst third year undergraduate medical students and reduce teaching resource requirements. The FC approach seeks to move (usually online) some of the traditional content delivery out of the teaching sessions so that the teaching sessions can be more problem-based and interactive.

In the 2019–2020 academic year the first two sessions occurred pre-pandemic and ran with the planned blend of one week prior access to the online primer quiz, immediately followed by a face-to-face session for each of the two groups. The quiz was intended to constructively align with the Applied Medical Knowledge (AMK) test that is used for summative assessment within the medical school. A paper-based perception questionnaire was administered at the end of the face-to-face session (in order to maximise the response rate). It contained nine questions and occupied a single page of A4 paper (printed on both sides).

The final session of the 2019–2020 academic year occurred during the first UK lockdown and was therefore unexpectedly conducted entirely on-line via the Zoom videoconferencing software (the same one week online primer quiz but followed by an online session). The questionnaire was distributed by email. It was not described in the paper (as it occurred after publication) but was discussed during the conference.

The results from the first two sessions were very encouraging. However, there was an obvious difference between questionnaire response rates from the two sessions that were paper-based (12 and 19 respectively) and the one that was email-based (1).

It was also observed that while the student engagement had improved in the two face-to-face sessions (with more students asking questions and the quality of question having improved), there was a marked decline in student engagement in the final (online) session using Zoom (no student spoke using a microphone, shared screen or used the chat).

1.3   Current Year's Work (2020–2021): Continuing Pandemic

This section considers two aspects: planned changes as a result of the previous study (pre-pandemic), and alterations in response to the continuing pandemic.

Planned Changes (Prior to Pandemic)
As a result of the previous work [2] there were plans to enhance the online quiz so that it would include:

- an increased volume of questions,
- the ability to embed diagrams in questions, and
- automatic descriptive feedback relating to the given response (this was explicitly requested in free-text responses from students).

In particular, it was hoped that the diagrams would give students a greater visual appreciation of the way disease processes interact with anatomy at a time which would normally be their first clinical year, but access to the clinical environments (such as wards and operating theatres) was limited during the pandemic. It was also hoped that the inclusion of feedback specific to responses given during the quiz, would help students appreciate the process of relating prevalence, morbid anatomy, clinical signs, and symptoms to diagnosis and appropriate treatment. This was especially important where the clinical signs were remote from the anatomical site of the pathology.

Response to Pandemic
Unlike the previous year, where the pandemic was unexpected, this year there was considerable opportunity to prepare for a mixed and flexible delivery. It was not possible to predict what restrictions would be in place, so across the University contingency planning aimed to ensure delivery would continue under varying circumstances from complete lockdown (online only delivery) to complete lifting of restrictions (allowing unrestricted face-to-face delivery).

The situation within the medical school was slightly different. Each year's cohort was divided into three groups and the session delivered once per group - three times over the year (in October, January, and April). It was important that the sessions were consistent in content and delivery so that all students had a common learning experience. Also, the online nature of delivery was compounded by the transient nature of the staff-student interaction, where the lecturer was a National Health Service (NHS) employee who delivers a small number of sessions across the year (each with different students). This is in contrast to a more typical situation across Higher Education (HE) where a lecturer interacts with the same students each week.

As a result, the decision was made to deliver the sessions entirely online using Zoom (even though both UK government and university regulations allowed face-to-face teaching at times during the year, social distancing rules drastically reduced the physical room capacity and there was no way to predict when national lockdowns would disrupt this).

A number of options were considered to improve student engagement, such as aligning the session more closely to the quiz and additional visual active content (diagrams or which they would normally observe live but was limited due to the current pandemic). Video of diagnostic procedures was also considered but not implemented due to time and clinical workload constraints.

1.4   Evaluation of Engagement

The aim of the present work is to ask if further developments to the quiz would improve the engagement of students in a completely on-line delivery? It considers the modifications made to the online quiz primer, which was delivered in the same manner as in the previous year (largely unaffected by the pandemic). It also considers the alterations made to the scheduled teaching sessions that the quiz was intended to support, which were entirely on-line this year (replacing last year's face-to-face sessions).

Student engagement with specific online meeting facilities (such as use of a microphone, chat, and screen-share) was also observed (via participant observation). A student perception questionnaire was administered using the Jisc online survey system [4]. It was hoped that this would improve the online survey response rate to be closer to that of the paper-based questionnaire.

2   Method

A mixture of qualitative and quantitative data were collected via an online survey questionnaire and participant observation. As in the previous year:

- the cohort (third year undergraduate medical students) were split into three groups
- three sessions (one per group) were scheduled during the 2020–2021 academic year (two included in the present paper with the third scheduled after submission)
- each session was an hour long
- students were directed (via email including a hyperlink) to engage with the online quiz primer one week prior to each session
- teaching sessions focused on active learning - discussions of a small number of cases related to diagnosis and treatment, with students working in pairs or threes

The following differences were implemented (in response to the ongoing pandemic):

- there were three modifications to the online quiz primer (described in Sect. 2.1)
- all sessions were delivered online via the Zoom videoconferencing software (no face-to-face sessions were conducted) to ensure consistency of experience for all students
- the screen share facility was used in Zoom (instead of physical projection facilities)
- the questionnaire was administered using the Jisc online survey tool, and so was available continuously (instead of at the end of each session)
- a link to the questionnaire was provided at the end of the quiz
- a brief break was included half way through the session, to allow the staff member to respond to chat messages and to display a link to the quiz (for students to repeat or for anyone who had not managed to engage with it prior to the session)

Both the quiz and the questionnaire were available between sessions (across the academic year), but this was not publicised to the students.

2.1   Software

As in the previous year, the quiz begins with an initial page that gives an overview. A total of ten questions are asked (randomly selected from the database). After each question is posed, the student selects a response (from five randomly positioned choices) and automatic feedback is given for some questions (shown in Figs. 1 and 2). Once all ten questions have been completed, a summary page (shown in Fig. 3) is shown indicating how many questions were answered correctly and encouraging them to undertake the quiz again.

The online quiz primer software was modified in three ways, to include:

- Additional questions: an additional ten questions were created and the questions (thirty one) that were developed for the previous year were re-used and (to give a total of forty one questions in the database)

- Diagrams within questions: all ten of the new questions included sketch diagrams of the lung to cover fundamental lung anatomy and some visual aspects of diagnosis (in terms of site of tumour and method of accessing the anatomy for biopsy)
- Automatic feedback: automatic descriptive feedback relating to the given response was provided for some questions

Figure 1 shows a screenshot of the lung pathology primer quiz, where the student has selected an incorrect answer (highlighted in red). An explanation is given of why this answer is not the best fit or not the most likely in terms of the clinical presentation/pathology/epidemiology given in the question text (patient information) above. The correct answer is also identified. The intention was that this feedback would help improve student understanding (potentially encouraging students to look up further information and/or triggering questions directed at staff during the session).

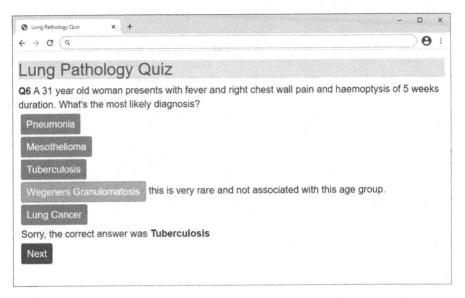

Fig. 1. Screenshot of Lung Pathology Quiz showing the automatic feedback given to an incorrect answer. (Color figure onlne)

Figure 2 shows a screenshot of the lung pathology primer quiz, where the student has selected the correct answer. The correct answer is highlighted and an explanation given regarding how it matches the clinical/patient information included in the question text above. Even though the student has selected the correct answer, it was important to explicitly link the rationale for this with the clinical information provided (to reinforce the student's mental model and in case the answer was selected by guesswork alone).

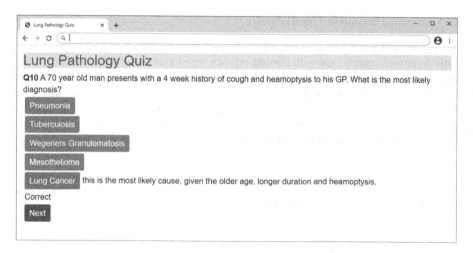

Fig. 2. Screenshot of Lung Pathology Quiz showing the automatic feedback given to a correct answer.

Figure 3 shows the summary page, which appears after 10 questions have been answered. The number of correct responses is given and students are encouraged to attempt the quiz again. There is also a prompt (and hyperlink) for students to participate in the survey questionnaire.

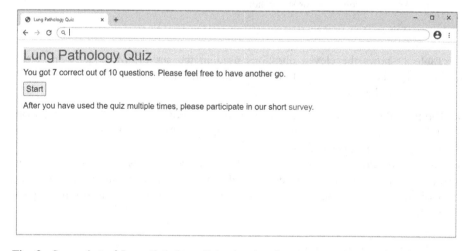

Fig. 3. Screenshot of Lung Pathology Quiz showing the summary page, which includes the number of questions answered correctly out of ten and a hyperlink to the survey questionnaire (the word 'survey' in the last sentence).

2.2 Student Perception Questionnaire

The questionnaire was administered using the Jisc online survey tool. This was chosen partly to ensure compliance with current privacy legislation and partly to improve the response rate. Last year, the paper-based questionnaire was used in the first two sessions, but it was sent to students via email for the third session. This was done as an emergency measure in response to the pandemic preventing the last session running face-to-face. As this was unexpected, it was not possible to consider alternative delivery methods within the time available.

Table 1. Survey questionnaire questions. *Small Cell Carcinoma, Squamous Cell Carcinoma, Mesothelioma, Adenocarcinoma, Lung Cancer

	Text
1	I agree to participate
2	Did you use the online quiz (before or during the session)?
3	What device (phone/computer) did you use to view the quiz website?
4	Did the quiz website work properly on your device?
5	How easy to use (user-friendly) was the quiz website?
6	Before using the quiz, how would you describe your understanding of *
7	After using the quiz, how would you describe your understanding of *
8	Did you look anything up (online or in books) as a result of using the quiz?
9	Did using the quiz help your understanding?
10	Did using the quiz help prepare you for the tutorial?
11	Any other comments or suggestions

Table 1 shows the eleven questions used in the survey. Most questions were retained from the previous year to facilitate comparison. However, two new questions were added (at the start):

- The first additional question asked for participant consent to proceed (good human ethics practice for online surveys - the survey software will only proceed with further questions once consent is given)
- The second additional question asked 'When did you use the quiz?' (the intention was to determine whether students used the quiz before or during the teaching session, and to encourage those who may not have done the quiz to still participate in the survey)

2.3 Participant Observation

A series of debrief discussions were conducted with the pathologist who ran the teaching sessions regarding their perceptions of the process, student engagement, understanding, staff satisfaction and the impact of the pandemic/online delivery.

3   Results

This year there were seven responses to the questionnaire (four after the first teaching session, and three after the second teaching session). This compares to thirty one questionnaire responses in the previous year that were delivered face-to-face (twelve in the first session and nineteen in the second session). The first two sessions of the first year occurred prior to the pandemic and were described in a previous paper [2]. The third session occurred after the start of the pandemic and was discussed during the conference (but not included in the previous paper).

Table 2 shows the number of questionnaire responses received across the 2019–2020 academic years (included for ease of comparison).

Table 2. Summary of the sessions across the 2019–2020 academic year.

Session	Delivery mode	Survey	Responses
Session 1 Oct 2019	*Face to Face*	*Paper-based*	*12*
Session 2 Jan 2020	*Face to Face*	*Paper-based*	*19*
Session 3 Apr 2020	Online via Zoom	Email	1

Table 3 shows the number of questionnaire responses received so far across the 2020–2021 year. The first two sessions have taken place, with the final session yet to be delivered.

Table 3. Summary of the sessions across the 2020–2021 academic year.

Session	Delivery mode	Survey	Responses
Session 1 Oct 2020	Online via Zoom	Jisc online survey	4
Session 2 Jan 2021	Online via Zoom	Jisc online survey	3
Session 3 Apr 2021	*Online via Zoom*	*Jisc online survey*	*Not yet delivered*

3.1   Student Perception Questionnaire

Question 1 related to participant consent and is therefore self-selecting (all seven participants agreed). It is not possible to determine how many students may have clicked on the link and then decided not to participate.

Table 4 shows responses regarding when students used the online quiz primer. This question was partly added to encourage students who did not use the quiz to participate in the survey and yield data regarding any obstacles to quiz use. Unfortunately, (as in the previous year) only students who used the quiz seem to have participated.

Table 4. Q2: Use of the online quiz primer (question 2).

	Count
Before teaching tutorial	4
Before and during tutorial	3
During tutorial	0
Not at all	0

Two of the students who used it before teaching session said that the quiz 'was a good test of knowledge' and 'did the survey [quiz] prior to the session and will repeat following the session tomorrow'. This is supported by usage data on the quiz web server, both sessions had hits before and after, session 2 had more in advance but fewer during the session. It is not possible to tie any of the usage data to questionnaire responses or individual students.

The devices used to access the quiz (question 3) were similar to the previous year (face-to-face sessions), approximately an even split between phones and computers/laptops. All seven participants indicated that the quiz worked properly on their device (question 4), one student said 'worked very well'.

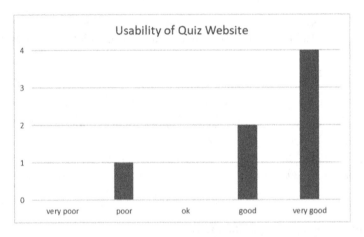

Fig. 4. Student perception of Quiz Website ease of use (question 5).

Figure 4 shows a graph of the students' perception of the quiz websites ease of use, which in general is very good (in line with the previous year). The single poor rating was from a participant using a mobile phone, and included an associated comment that 'the buttons were too small that you'd click on the wrong number [answer]'. This probably reflects the frustration that accidentally clicking the wrong item would cause. This should be further investigated. The only other free-text response was 'great' from another participant.

Table 5 shows mean understanding perception scores for each of the five topics covered by the quiz (and session) from the previous year [2]. It is included for comparison with Table 6 showing the same data for this year (2020–2021). Both tables were constructed using the same method (averages of all student understanding perception scores both before and after using the quiz, with the difference being the before score subtracted from the after score). In both tables, a positive difference indicates that students' perception of their understanding has increased and a negative difference that it has reduced. In both years across all topics, all differences were positive (indicating an increase in understanding in all cases). It also shows that this year's increase (0.69) is slightly smaller than that reported last year (0.93). However, this year's overall before and after scores (2.43 and 3.11) are higher than last year (1.95 and 2.89). As the sample size was smaller this year, this may indicate a bias toward more engaged students (with slightly better understanding). However, a stronger cohort cannot be ruled out.

Table 5. (2019–2020, sessions 1 and 2) Mean student perception scores, using categories from 1 (very poor) to 5 (very good) of self-understanding pre and post quiz. From [2]

	Before	After	Difference
Small Cell Carcinoma	1.94	2.81	0.87
Squamous Cell Carcinoma	1.90	2.81	0.90
Mesothelioma	2.03	3.10	1.06
Adenocarcinoma	1.71	2.77	1.06
Lung Cancer	2.19	2.94	0.74
Overall Average	1.95	2.88	**0.93**

Table 6. (2020–2021, sessions 1 and 2) Mean student perception scores, using categories from 1 (very poor) to 5 (very good) of self-understanding pre and post quiz.

	Before (Q6)	After (Q7)	Difference
Small Cell Carcinoma	2.57	3.00	0.43
Squamous Cell Carcinoma	2.57	3.00	0.43
Mesothelioma	2.14	3.29	1.14
Adenocarcinoma	2.14	3.14	1.00
Lung Cancer	2.71	3.14	0.43
Overall Average	2.43	3.11	**0.69**

Figure 5 shows graph plot of the difference values from Tables 5 and 6 for easier visual comparison. Again all data shows increases in student perception of understanding. It also shows that two topics (Adenocarcinoma and Mesothelioma) yielded a particularly high improvements (relative to the other topics) in both years.

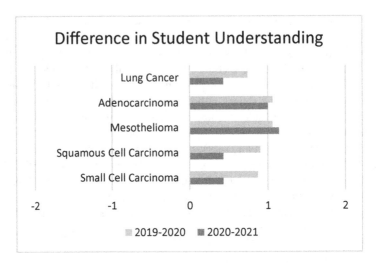

Fig. 5. Graph showing student perception of change in their own understanding after using the Quiz Website, for both 2019–2020 [2] and 2020–2021 (Difference between Questions 6 and 7).

Student perception of change in their own understanding showed improvement across all five topics. Comparison with last year shows that last year's average improvement was slightly higher. This may suggest that a blend of face-to-face with online delivery may be more powerful than online alone. However, this is difficult to compare with such small numbers and the variation in response rates (and is not statistically significant). Alternatively, it is possible that the small numbers this year represent better students so the effect for them was less of an improvement. This is supported by the data (their ratings were higher than last year - both initial and final), but again not statistically significant.

Two students indicated that they looked material up as a result of using the quiz (question 8). Free text comments were '[I] reviewed different types of lung cancers' and 'the quiz was useful to help identity gaps in knowledge but not as a primary learning tool - perhaps a brief explanation of why the chosen answer was right/wrong would be helpful'. This is interesting as some questions did have explanations (a feature introduced this year). It seems that this particular student only received questions without explanations.

Six students (out of seven) indicated that the quiz helped their understanding (question 9). Free text responses were that the quiz 'enthused me to look things up' and 'helped recognise more typical presentations and risk factors'. The student who responded 'no' said 'but [the quiz] did identify gaps in my knowledge to direct my learning'.

All seven students indicated that the quiz helped them prepare for the tutorial (question 10). Free text comments were 'just clarified some of the investigations for me', 'covered the basics', 'baseline knowledge and directed some prior reading of notes', 'Made me think about what I do/don't know', and 'created [a] list of topics to revise'.

There was one response to the question asking for any other comments (question 11), that 'some of the acronyms are unfamiliar so could do with full meaning instead of acronym'.

3.2   Pathologist Educator Participant Observation

The tutor running the teaching session indicated that online engagement during this year's sessions was improved compared to the online session last year, but that engagement was still much better during last year's face-to-face sessions. The tutor said that it is 'better that they get this opportunity than not at all, but I think they are missing out'.

Teaching Process

The tutor commented that the third session last year was 'bit of a shock' as it 'coincided with lockdown', and that they (the tutor) had 'never used the [Zoom] technology before' (but this is likely to apply to the students as well).

The two sessions this year 'felt more comfortable'. They described themselves as 'comfortable with the technology' and in particular more 'familiar with chat now'. Another important change this year was that 'now someone logs on with you and they check that all is working', which referred to administrative staff joining each session as co-hosts to provide support. As a result of these changes the session 'flowed well', 'fitted quite well into the time' and 'I wasn't worried about timing, timeouts and logistics'.

A slight change in the delivery was described that put a short break in the middle of the session. The tutor said that this gave them a 'small breather in middle, mentally I felt a lot better, just the cognitive five minute downtime in the middle makes it feel a lot better from my point of view'. It also provided the tutor with an opportunity to 'respond to chat' and 'display the quiz link', which allowed students to continue to engage.

In previous years the sessions were run in 'a seminar room that was very full', however 'working in pairs worked well'. In face-to-face sessions, the tutor used a 'white board to illustrate complex anatomy relating to pathological processes'. They used the white board to make a 'link to the clinical signs and symptoms and where the pathology is, e.g. being due to a tumour in the chest (e.g. lung cancer can present as hoarseness)'. This was often done by 'draw[ing] a picture and talking it through'. In this way, the tutor would 'adapt delivery to audience response and without seeing the audience delivery is less adaptive'. They commented that it was difficult to 'replicate that in Zoom easily'.

Student Engagement

This year students used the chat facility (which they did not last year). However, no students used their microphone or video. About three to four students per session used the chat facility (from a session size of about twenty students), with 'some directly answering questions and some spontaneously asking new questions'. The tutor remarked that 'that was good' and 'some would only directly chat at me and some directed it to the group (probably more to me)'.

Small Groups

The tutor indicated that breaking students into small groups was challenging, and said delivering via Zoom 'is still very limited, in that you can't go round small groups of people' in the way you would face-to-face.

It was not possible to use breakout rooms during the session due to a 'lack of familiarity'. A brief demonstration at the start of the year included breakout room, but that facility requires more support. The tutor commented 'we use [Microsoft] Teams in work ... different to what we're used to using' and that there was 'difficulty with not being a full time' educator.

Audience Cues

The tutor was not able to 'see the audience', which 'limited interaction'. They missed the visual cues that this provided and said that it wasn't possible to see 'facial expressions', 'if they are smiling' and if students are 'writing anything down'.

Student Understanding

The tutor indicted that due to the lack of audience cues it was 'difficult to gauge' student understanding. The judgement of student understanding was 'difficult' as it had to be based entirely on the questions in the chat, and the proportion of students engaging in the chat was 'slightly less than a quarter of ... [the] group'.

Student Questions

The tutor commented that 'some of them asked good probing questions', 'some of the questions in the chat are better than others, but they are limited' and that 'this would be a lot better in person'.

As a result the tutor 'encouraged the use of the chat facility' and 'cajoled [the students] more' than they normally would. However, the students were 'not answering questions like they would in a group, you always get a few who answer things in a group [face-to-face]' and some students will explicitly say 'I don't understand' but in these sessions 'you're not getting that'.

Staff Satisfaction

The tutor said that they had 'been encouraged that some [students] have obviously answered the quiz' and the 'majority of them have said thank you at the end' (via the chat facility).

Confidentiality

The tutor felt that delivering online changed the delivery, specifically they were more 'careful what I say - especially regarding sensitive information as you don't know if someone is recording it' and that 'you don't really know who's present'.

While the tutor has always been mindful of patient confidentiality, they are now more concerned that the 'bare bones of age and other information can identify people'. They commented that the cohort 'are medical students, so should follow confidentiality', but 'I trust them less because they are not on University or Hospital property and I don't know where this is going'. In general, they indicated that 'I realise I have been a bit more careful about things like that' and as a result the students 'get a little bit less of you'.

Alterations for Next Year

The tutor mentioned several alterations that they were considering for next year's delivery (as a result of this year's experiences):

- Using the quiz more explicitly during the session and 'aligning the content more with the quiz'
- Use of 'polls' during the Zoom session, which 'might help' with engagement
- Use of 'breakout rooms' during Zoom sessions (which would require tutor training) to support student-to-student interaction in groups
- The creation of 'pre-recorded case studies' for students to view as additional primers before the session and then 'discussing [them] during the sessions, with slightly more in-depth questions'.
- Moving away from three duplicated sessions. Possibly toward a common session followed by shorter group sessions. The tutor said that this 'could save tutor time in a period when we are highly pressurised'. Any change in delivery schedule would need to be done at school level to be consistent.

However, the tutor said 'but you've still got to set it up' in terms of preparation time and learning to use those technologies.

4 Conclusions

4.1 Student Engagement

The two 2020–2021 online sessions showed greater engagement than the previous year's (2019–2020) online session (which was necessitated by the first UK National lockdown due to the coronavirus pandemic). However, the two 2019–2020 face-to-face sessions showed significantly higher engagement. There was a definite improvement in engagement for this year's online sessions compared to last year's online session, but this is still below that of last year's face-to-face (pre-pandemic) sessions. The in-session technology and facilities also had an impact and the two are related. The pandemic has acted as confounding factor, making it difficult to link changes in engagement to the quiz separately from the other changes to delivery.

The quiz seemed to function in a similar manner with similar benefits but the following teaching sessions were less effective and more challenging when delivered online (compared with face-to-face). This was still an improvement compared to last year's online session. The use of the quiz during the session was unexpected but beneficial and is likely to increase in future sessions.

This suggests that face-to-face sessions are more effective (in both higher student engagement and student understanding) than online sessions, but that the gap can be closed by appropriate delivery and software functionality within online sessions.

The questionnaire response for this year (2020–2021) was far lower than the previous year, which is in keeping with what is reported in the literature (online surveys have been found to generate lower response rates than face-to-face surveys).

4.2 Technology

More work is being conducted and published, thereby adding to our understanding of what can be done to improve online sessions (in particular the use of videoconferencing systems such as Zoom), which was not available at the start of this academic year.

There is an enormous variety of techniques and technology available. It is impractical for both the educator and students to instantly familiarise themselves with and select the most appropriate for adoption. This is especially true for transient users such as part-time teaching staff whose main role is clinical.

Currently, Zoom restricts student-student interaction. In particular, chat can broadcast to everyone or send to a single participant, but cannot send to two or more participants. This prevents student peer groups forming naturally. The Slack software maybe more effective in this situation. Also, the use of microphones and video is exclusively broadcast to everyone. There is no way for a student to speak, share video, or share screen with a sub-group of participants, or just with the host (lecturer).

The breakout rooms facility allows students to be split into groups. However this facility is limited and complex. It is setup by the host/lecturer, participants cannot chat or speak to people in other breakout rooms, and it is not clear whether sending chat to 'everyone' means all in that room or everyone across rooms. It is difficult for the tutor to chat to others outside the room they are in and difficult for the tutor to move between rooms. This does not match the naturalistic classroom interactions (where a tutor can see all groups in the physical room and move between them quickly).

The tutor was given a short Zoom Training session at the start of the year (which covered chat and breakout rooms). This was successful at allowing them to use the chat facility, but breakout rooms were too complex and would require more time to become familiar with.

4.3 Further Work

Further changes to the online quiz primer and the manner in which the sessions are delivered will be investigated, including:

- An expansion of the question set to provide more balance (as it appeared to be biased toward Mesothelioma and Adenocarcinoma topics)
- Short pre-recorded demonstrations (as additional primers before the sessions), in particular showing how complex anatomy can be affected by pathology
- Increased use of the online quiz during the session (as well as a primer)
- The use of breakout rooms and polls during the teaching sessions

More work needs to be done to determine the prevalence and rationale for students (staff and professionals) being wary of using microphones and video during online sessions (in zoom and/or other online meeting systems). This may link to issues around social anxiety and privacy influencing student engagement. It should ask how teaching methods and technology can be adapted to allow wider participation, while addressing staff difficulties in delivering sessions without seeing all participants.

There is a need for additional functionality and usability enhancements within videoconferencing systems (such as Zoom) to align with specific teaching needs. Additional functionality could include:

- rapid creation, alteration and movement between rooms
- persistent representation of the state of breakout rooms. Currently, the breakout room list disappears when moving between rooms and the main session, which is disorienting for the host (increasing cognitive load). This makes it very difficult to move through groups or individual students in a consistent manner (ensuring all students have an equitable slice of the host's time).
- integration of breakout room status with the participant list, so the user can see who is where and can add/remove rooms quickly and easily and freely move between rooms (without closing interface elements).

These changes would replicate a physical room, where the tutor can see who is where and can easily move between groups and individual students.

References

1. Basko, L., Hartman, J.: Increasing student engagement through paired technologies. J. Instruct. Res. **6**, 24–28 (2017)
2. Dixon, M., Syred, K.: Development of a flipped classroom approach to teaching lung pathology: the evaluation of a formative on-line quiz primer to encourage active learning. In: Zaphiris, P., Ioannou, A. (eds.) HCII 2020. LNCS, vol. 12205, pp. 456–465. Springer, Cham (2020). https://doi.org/10.1007/978-3-030-50513-4_34
3. Gay, G.H.E.: From discussion forums to eMeetings: integrating high touch strategies to increase student engagement, academic performance, and retention in large online courses. Online Learn. J. **24**(1), 92–75 (2020)
4. JISC online survey tool homepage. https://www.onlinesurveys.ac.uk/. Accessed 09 Feb 2021
5. Kay, D., Pasarica, M.: Using technology to increase student (and faculty satisfaction with) engagement in medical education. Adv. Physiol. Educ. **43**(3), 408–413 (2019)
6. Lee, A.Y., Moskowitz-Sweet, G., Pelavin, E., Rivera, O., Hancock, J.T.: "Bringing you into the zoom": the power of authentic engagement in a time of crisis in the USA. J. Child. Media (2020)
7. Mahr, A., Cichon, M., Mateo, S., Grajeda, C., Baggili, I.: Zooming into the pandemic! A forensic analysis of the Zoom Application. Forensic Sci. Int. Digit. Investig. **36**, 1–12 (2021)
8. Nickerson, L.A., Shea, K.M.: First-semester organic chemistry during COVID-19: prioritizing group work, flexibility, and student engagement. J. Chem. Educ. **97**(9), 3201–3205 (2020)
9. Perets, E.A., et al.: Impact of the emergency transition to remote teaching on student engagement in a non-STEM undergraduate chemistry course in the time of COVID-19. J. Chem. Educ. **97**(9), 2439–2447 (2020)
10. Shadat, A., Sayem, M., Taylor, B., Mcclanachan, M., Mumtahina, U.: Effective use of Zoom technology and instructional videos to improve engagement and success of distance students in Engineering. In: 28th Annual Conference of the Australasian Association for Engineering Education, pp. 926–931. Australasian Association for Engineering Education (2017)

11. Singhal, M.K.: Facilitating virtual medicinal chemistry active learning assignments using advanced zoom features during COVID-19 campus closure. J. Chem. Educ. **97**(9), 2711–2714 (2020)
12. Venton, B.J., Pompano, R.R.: Strategies for enhancing remote student engagement through active learning. Anal. Bioanal. Chem. (2021)

How to Asses Empathy During Online Classes

Karim Elia Fraoua[✉]

Equipe Dispositifs d'Information et de Communication à l'Ere Numérique
(DICEN), Conservatoire national des arts et métiers, Université Gustave Eiffel,
77454 Marne-la-Vallée, France
fraoua@u-pem.fr

Abstract. During this work, we will focus on strategies for understanding learning paths in online courses. Indeed, more and more researchers are interested in the attitude of learners in the learning conditions of online courses. We note that the cameras are often turned off, and different reasons are mentioned, such as the fact of feeling obliged to stare at the camera, the question of the privacy of the home although interfaces allow to create a fictitious decor, and finally that it is not necessarily usual

Keywords: eLearning · Emotion · Chatbot

1 Introduction

The idea of e-learning as it was initiated is based on the premise that this form of learning is more student-centered [1, 2]. In addition, the active participation of the student is important for the success of the system. It must involve a process on the part of the learner such as participation in the co-construction of teaching content and knowledge. This is one of the reasons that is often mentioned, the notion of Personal Learning Environment (PLE) [3]. Just like for trainers, there is a Personal Teaching Environment (PTE) [4]. Even if these spaces overlap, PLEs can be richer than PTEs. Indeed, learners can aggregate in their PLE, other applications or tools that the teacher does not have. From this health crisis emerged the use of the webcam as a tool allowing the teacher to do his lesson by imitating the face-to-face lesson. The e-learning course then moved into a distance course, and very little use of e-learning took place. However, for some researchers, the improvement of e-learning environment can be enriched by the co-construction of the course which the use of digital tools [5, 6]. We have previously analyzed the role of forums in setting up an online course [7].

This notion of online or distance learning to which learners naturally subscribed through their personal choice and to which certain teachers had also been formed was imposed on everyone, including the conditions during which the lessons must be provided by teachers and followed by students.

Moreover, with technological developments, online uses tend to want to replace face-to-face lessons with the use of sound and video. Faced with this technological choice, allowing to the system to penetrate everyone's privacy, many choose to turn off their cameras, even the teacher sometimes… We must not lose from our sight the fact that learning is above all a collective adventure, designed as social learning [8]. In terms

P. Zaphiris and A. Ioannou (Eds.): HCII 2021, LNCS 12784, pp. 427–436, 2021.
https://doi.org/10.1007/978-3-030-77889-7_30

of educational construction and by evoking the socio-constructivist school among others, it is undeniable that the central hypothesis of the social construction of knowledge is at the heart of the social psychology of development, which considers in particular social interaction between peers but also between learners and course leaders as one of the key elements of the cognitive development of the individual. Other schools of thought evoke this encounter, such as socioconstructivism and the proximal zone of development [9] and vicarious learning and socio-cognitivism theory [10].

It is therefore necessary to ask the question about the fact of the extinction of the camera in the propensity of its active role in learning seen from a purely communicational angle. We observe, like the vast majority of colleagues with whom we have spoken, that very often the cameras are turned off, which means that the students have only sound as their interface, so how then we can reproduce the face-to-face course and why this question poses a problem in achieving effective teaching?

In this work, we will be interested in this issue to the interaction linked to human-computer interface and how therefore to put in place practices that can promote empathy in particular, which is a fundamental element in learning. Indeed, pedagogy is intimately associated with communication and it is no coincidence that the two disciplines, namely education sciences and information and communication sciences, overlap on this theme of learning.

Long before the discovery of mirror neurons, which play an important role in empathy, H. Wallon underlined the importance of the postural function in communication [11]. This form of communication is essential to denote the role of emotion in the communication process [12].

2 Motivation and Learning Path

Motivation is a key factor in the learning path [13]. In this regard, teachers use several strategies to successfully capture the attention of students. In this regard, it would be useful to recontextualize learning as it is experienced in France. Indeed, with the massification of access to higher education, this tends to educate a larger proportion of young people of a generation, and which is largely open to the middle classes [14]. Unlike the Grandes Ecoles, the University is no longer exclusively the place of training for the social and academic elite, insofar as it also welcomes the largest share of graduates of a generation.

This ipso-facto generates new problems, with the emergence of new teaching methods due to the erosion of the level but also of the cognitive capacities of the students and also of their working methods. This is one of the reasons for the massive failure of the first cycle in France and for which alternative strategies have been put in place, in particular the work-study model [15], where students alternate a time at the university and a time in the enterprise and in which appropriations are of the order of competence rather than knowledge.

We can see that all these "obstacles" that learners encounter during their university course have a major impact on their motivations to continue their studies, and thus we fall into a vicious circle which inevitably leads to failure. For this reason within universities and in particular that of Gustave Eiffel University, tutoring jobs have been multiplied and which allow the learner, due to his interaction with his tutor who is also a student, to be able to put in place the mechanisms mentioned above and which will promote the success of the learner, by playing on confidence, motivation and acceptance of the error, which as we have discussed are key factors of success before any form of knowledge.

The question then is how to succeed in this transmission in digital space and ensure the success of an online course, while accepting the decline in interactions. Indeed, with the health crisis, the establishment of distance or online courses shows all the problems to ensure effective courses in the educational sense of the term. We often find that measuring course success is based simply on metrics, such as did the course work well, were there any malfunctions, does the bimodal system work well, etc. without however worrying about the complex reality of the course and the environment necessary for its success, and which were detailed above, namely the PTEs and PLEs. In addition, the vast majority of trainers confuse online courses and distance learning courses and are satisfied to teach courses on very easy-to-use videoconferencing tools such as Zoom, which has been so successful thanks to its simple functionalities.

2.1 Motivation

On the question of the motivation that arises from the emotions or feelings that one has, there are a plethora of theories [16]. Besides, that's why we carried out this work. Indeed the essential question is to know how to motivate the students to learn, how to generate the emotions or the feelings necessary to carry out this task knowing that we have several handicaps to overcome as it is indicated in the object of this article to know without communication non-verbal. If we consider that "motivation designates the forces which act on a person or within him to push him to behave in a specific way, oriented towards a goal" [17], we can easily deduce that without stimuli motivation cannot be triggered in an individual. Classical theories also present motivation to us as a result of a need [18], of an expectation [18]. McCelland in 1961 developed the theory of belonging, fulfillment, and power needs, thus providing a different reading of Maslow's theory [19].

Classical theories therefore consider the evolution of social relations in an interpersonal register and more specifically in professional and work relations which put the individual in a position of uniqueness, i.e. the "me" is superior to the "us". In summary, the dynamic of motivation at this level is triggered in a logic of individual reflection. This focus on motivation is essential to allow students to be in ideal learning conditions. It is certain today that inequalities also exist in distance mode and that they are more important than in face-to-face mode where inequalities linked to several factors, including socio-psychological ones, were already noted [20], such as anxiety [21], socialization processes [22] and their emotional impacts and on our learning processes and to recall what has already been noted, namely that we never learn alone and finally the usual emotional states which are managed alone and therefore the difficulty of the learner when he is in a state of negative emotion [23].

2.2 Emotion

The notion of emotion has been studied by several authors and in several disciplines. The term "emotion" is a set of affective reactions, regardless of their duration or intensity. In this sense, emotions are distinguished from feelings, which last a long time unlike emotions which sometimes have a short lifespan such as anger or surprise. It is helpful to note that we are always aware of our feelings, which is not always the case with emotion. For Robert Plutchik [24], there are eight basic emotions which are in opposite situation namely Joy and Sadness, Confidence and Disgust, Fear and Anger and Surprise and Anticipation. Each of these emotions has a role, such as the fact that fear allows protection or trust which allows incorporation and finally anticipation which allows exploration. We can clearly see the role of these emotions in the educational function and the role of the communicational space in the transmission or encouragement of these emotions. We all know that emotions are transmitted to others via artefacts, as we will see below about mirror neurons. Other authors have developed an approach based on valence namely positive or negative then on fundamental positive or negative emotions also such as joy and love or anger and sadness and which then break down into sub-emotions.

For Paul Ekman [25], there are so-called primary emotions which are identical to many cultures, including certain animals. They correspond to more specific mental states, characterized in particular by a rapid onset, a limited duration, and an involuntary appearance. We have defined here so-called basic emotions and as it was indicated by Ekman, these emotions are found in all individuals, including in certain animals, in particular chimpanzees. However, our most complex emotions are very dependent on our cultures and sociological factors. For Paul Griffiths, there are two classes of emotions, namely emotions called "affect programs" and emotions known as "higher cognitive emotions". It is for this reason that certain emotions are accompanied by facial reactions and of which Paul Ekman has produced an extremely elaborate catalog. They indeed produce specific facial, vocal or muscle reactions.

The role of these emotions is essential in our decision making and this is what is shown by Plutchik among others. Since the work of Damasio [26] which made it possible to understand how emotions can exert a decisive influence on the decision-making process. Other authors have consolidated this path such as Dan Ariely [27], Alain Berthoz [28] confirm the hypothesis according to which emotions, by influencing our choices and by motivating them, are a determining element in leading to decision-making.. Our analysis of this notion of emotion is very important to the success of a course and even more so of an online course especially when the cameras are off and which is undeniably the case in most courses. To be able to take action, you have to be motivated and this is not only a rational process, but it is accepted that motivation is linked to emotion [29].

3   Social Cognitive Theory

Albert Bandura, who developed the Social Learning Theory, demonstrates that there is an interaction between the mind of the learning person and his environment. Indeed, cognitive social theory shows us that human functioning is complex due to its existence and its environment and the product by its actions. He argues that "human functioning is the product of a dynamic and permanent interaction between cognitions, behaviors and environmental circumstances. This shows us how important our emotions and our interactions are in our reactions with our self but also with others. This is summarized according to this triple approach between interaction of our behavior, our internal personal factors in our environment [30].

We understand well then how the interaction of learners with trainers is important but also between learners which allows to strongly consolidate the theory of socio-constructivism and which results in the success of the learner. Included in these forms of interactions we also find the forms of social persuasion that allow us to act on the beliefs of others by giving them the feeling that they have the capacities required to succeed. This exchange between trainers and learners is essential for success, especially at the time of doubts or questions by authorizing errors, an important step to be taken in order to succeed in learning [31].

By making the link between the need for interaction and learning and interaction and motivation, we see that contact is important for effective learning. This link is then reinforced by the communication function such as it was initiated by Wallon in terms of postural function and emotion [32] and subsequently widely studied by Martin-Juchat on the question of the role of emotion in communication [33]. Through this initiation carried out by Wallon, the link is clearly identified between the postural function of communication and the brain function. We then allow ourselves to create the continuum between the communicational approach and motivation and brain function. The latter through mirror neurons will make it possible to act at the level of this interaction to trigger this continuum. These mirror neurons are the trigger for the transmission of emotion. This transmission of emotion is essential in the learning journey, it allows errors in the student because of the attitude of the teacher but also of other students, and it must be remembered that there is no error-free learning. This transmission of emotions takes place primarily through mirror neurons during interactions that take place in a classroom. What about non-verbal interaction during online lessons and more when the cameras are off? This loss of interaction raises an obvious question, namely how to allow the student to interact and verify his knowledge if it is not through a learning path, certainly structured but without any prior interaction. And it remains a question which is how to check during the learning path that the student is following the course and other aspects necessary for memorizing knowledge.

This emotional function is very important in the learning mechanisms. J. Papez in 1937 notably hypothesized that the thalamus represents the central nucleus of this neural network and that it allows the attribution of emotional meanings to sensory perceptions [34]. This circuit known as the Papez circuit is involved in memory and learning functions [35]. We will see later the role of memory neurons in the transmission of emotions. Adding to this the Flow effect developed by Csíkszentmihályi

[36], we clearly see the role of these interactions in the success of the learning journey. In fact, this author shows that this effect is achieved when the learner is absorbed in his action and is completely satisfied with his results. This author then speaks of an optimal experience and this state can only be achieved if the learner is motivated by the task he is accomplishing, by attaching the emotions necessary to reach this level of motivation and therefore success. Obviously these emotions must be channeled in order to generate the actions required to succeed and its interactions between the different elements or actors and will then be decisive if we integrate the work of Bandura. For example, this Flow effect is achieved by an athlete while performing his exercise [37].

We must not lose sight of the fact that the learner is at a distance and as we have indicated with the camera off. He is then subjected to motivational conflicts, because of the possibility of carrying out other tasks more pleasant than following the course which is often difficult for some students, also because of what we mentioned above like the massification of the university system and the isolation of the student. Indeed our brain has two areas, one called emotional brain represented by the limbic brain and which often seeks immediate gain, and the other so-called rational zone which is more calculating and which defines more or less long-term rewards.. This area of the prefrontal cortex allows the regulation of executive functions, that is, the management of action according to the goals of the individual in relation to his environment [38]. This gap implies a conflict on the individual and which can effectively generate a motivation gap between immediate action and future action.

We clearly understand how this emotion, which we transmit to learners, can be contagious on the limbic zone and therefore will ensure motivational coherence unlike the motivational conflict that can arise from a decline in our verbal and non-verbal interactions. or even an unstructured course, whether online or face-to-face, even if in the latter case, trainers may resort to coercive measures. So this state of flow can be achieved without conflict or stress. Emotional contagion leads the observer to feel the same emotion as that expressed by his interlocutor [39].

4   Non-verbal Communication and Mirror Neurons

The "mirror neurons" activate when an individual perceives, for example, a smile, and this then creates in the receiver a virtual smile in his brain. In fact, mirror neurons are activated when an individual performs or observes this same action in others. This capacity for imitative reproduction of the experiencer's expressions is automatic and unintentional. This is an illustration of the primary visual functioning of mirror neurons. A very detailed documentation on the theory of mirror neurons can be found in an article by Gallese [40]. The discovery was made by chance by Rizolatti's team [41], based on the comparison between primate and human brain function. This discovery led to a better understanding of the mechanisms involved in the perception of the actions of others [40]. These mechanisms of reproduction of the actions of others are based on a set of neurons called mirror neurons. It is thanks to mirror neurons that witnessing an emotional facial expression implicitly activates the same neural circuit that is activated when the observer is subjected to this same emotional reaction [42]. This form of exchange is essential for us as a teacher, as it will influence the course of events in his classroom. Remember that a course is based on means of communication and that communication is any verbal or non-verbal means used by an individual to exchange ideas, knowledge or feelings with others. The total utterance of a message would result from the combination of a verbal part and a non-verbal part.

This form of verbal and non-verbal communication creates the phenomenon of empathy with the observer, and in connection with cognitive social theory, this emotion will generate behavior based on the emotion felt between the two interlocutors. It should be noted that there are three forms of empathy, namely understanding the emotions of others, their intentions and thoughts and finally the ability to put yourself in someone's shoes.

Several possibilities are available to us today to try to remedy this question. The first is the use of emoticons in online exchanges as well as in the chat room or forum. Emoticons were created by S. E. Fahlman [43], they are used in the field of computer mediated communication or CMC. This form of communication by computer (CMC) [44] today constrained by the health crisis in the field of education replaces certain face-to-face interactions; the nature of communication between trainers and learners but also between learners has changed.

With this new form of teaching and despite the fact that the millennial generation is more accustomed to this mediated communication, the communication of emotions is often lost and as we have specified above, it allows in particular the error for the student but also interaction between peers. Therefore, finding ways to enrich the medium is important. The issue with Computer-Mediated Communication is that in the absence of a camera, it cannot realize the role and traditional non-verbal dimensions of human communication such as facial expressions, gestures, body positions, personal distance, vocal variety or prosody and eye contact.

However, given the position of some trainers, the use of emoticons does not seem to be easily implemented. There is opposition to these uses by some teachers, and young people are more accustomed to delivering a form of emotion no longer through the quality of writing but the use of emoticons. This notion has already been approached from the angle of the theory of Generational Determinism of Recipients [44]. This theory makes clear in a fairly formal way that each generation has different values, points of view, and this leads to therefore different means of communication. Finally, we have seen, like many, that the different tools do not offer the same opportunities for discussion. Most have been defined from corporate communication perspective and the presence of emoticons is limited or nonexistent.

Another way to answer this question that we will be interested in in this work is the implementation of an emotional chatbot that can appear regularly in the user interface to maintain the attention of the student, and therefore, at least hopefully his motivation to continue taking the course. This will create a form of empathy through the development of machine learning and especially Deep learning in the implementation of emotional chat-bot. It is also useful to have recourse to formal and informal exchanges on the forum or the Chat space to measure the emotional state of the students and the class and to be able to generate emoticons by the Chatbot and which are more and more adopted by students during lessons.

5   Chatbot and Empathy

Indeed, these empathetic chatbots [45] will modify our relationship with others, They will allow new communicational models to emerge, thus generating new forms of emotions within the framework of human interaction and creating a new paradigm in the context of human-machine interaction with the emergence of a new form of interaction namely, human-robot interaction. Several disciplines are at the congruence of this new application, such as cognitive sciences, neurosciences, sociology, sciences of education, sciences of information and communication and computer science. We have previously worked on the notion of emotional Chatbot [46], and here we find an obvious field of application with the online courses which will become of certain use even after the passage of the health crisis, because of its practical aspect and by what it answers to sociological questions in particular, to answer the question of mobility, handicap,.. Solving this complexity will make it possible to establish the use of the online courses in an efficient way and not only to answer to crises.

In our use, we believe that this chatbot will allow, for example, launching quizzes or surveys, which will maintain the learner's attention during the online course. We adopted these assumptions and found that the students were more caring and more motivated to pass the exercises. By collecting the discussions in the discussion spaces, we were able to analyze the emotional state of the class and could see that the feeling was quite positive. It will also allow us during a chat conversation to define the emotional state of the class thanks to a sentiment analysis and thus provide a chatbot that will take this emotional state into account.

6   Conclusion

In this paper, we want to explain how it can be considered as very difficult both for students and teachers to do an online course without there being the dimension of verbal and non-verbal communication. The latter shows the consistency of the message and for the teacher the absence of a camera can lead to difficulty in the efficiency of online lessons. While most teachers turn on their cameras, it's not generally the case for students for a variety of reasons and therefore the lack of interaction between teacher and student but between students can lead to the "failure" of the elearning process. One of the ways to increase efficiency is to put in place tools that allow the transmission of the emotion felt by the learners and also by the class in order to better carry out the course. We are still making progress on the implementation of the emotional chatbot and further integration of emoticons into online exchanges.

References

1. Nichols, M.: A theory for eLearning. J. Educ. Technol. Soc. 6(2), 1–10 (2003)
2. Downes, S.: E-learning 2.0. ELearn 2005(10), 1 (2005)
3. Van Harmelen, M.: Personal learning environments. In: Sixth International Conference on Advanced Learning Technologies, pp. 815–816. IEEE Computer Society, July 2006

4. Richardson, A.: An ecology of learning and the role of eLearning in the learning environment. Global Summit of Online Knowledge Networks, pp. 47–51 (2002)
5. Jonassen, D.H., Howland, J., Moore, J., Marra, R.: Building technology-supported learning communities on the Internet. Learning to solve problems with technology: a constructivist perspective, pp. 70–120 (2003)
6. Huang, Y.M., Yang, S.J., Tsai, C.C.: Web 2.0 for interactive e-learning (2009)
7. Fraoua, K.E., Leblanc, J.M., Charraire, S., Champalle, O.: Information and communication science challenges for modeling multifaceted online courses. In: Zaphiris, P., Ioannou, A. (eds.) HCII 2019. LNCS, vol. 11590, pp. 142–154. Springer, Cham (2019). https://doi.org/10.1007/978-3-030-21814-0_12
8. Bandura, A., McClelland, D.C.: Social Learning Theory, vol. 1. Prentice Hall, Englewood Cliffs (1977)
9. Vygotsky, L S.: Mind in Society: The Development of Higher Psychological Processes. Harvard University Press, Cambridge (1930). (1978)
10. Nabavi, R.T.: Bandura's social learning theory & social cognitive learning theory. In: Theory of Developmental Psychology, pp. 1–24 (2012)
11. Piaget, J.: The role of imitation in the development of representational thought. Int. J. Ment. Health 1(4), 67–74 (1972)
12. Knapp, M.L., Hall, J.A., Horgan, T.G.: Nonverbal Communication in Human Interaction. Cengage Learning (2013)
13. Gopalan, V., Bakar, J.A.A., Zulkifli, A.N., Alwi, A., Mat, R.C.: A review of the motivation theories in learning. In: AIP Conference Proceedings, vol. 1891, no. 1, p. 020043. AIP Publishing LLC, October 2017
14. Euriat, M., Thélot, C.: Le recrutement social de l'élite scolaire en France: évolution des inégalités de 1950 à 1990. *Revue française de sociologie*, pp. 403–438 (1995)
15. Gagnon, C., Mazalon, É., Rousseau, A.: Fondements et pratique de l'alternance en formation à l'enseignement professionnel: quelques données de recherches autour de l'élaboration et de la mise en œuvre à l'Université de Sherbrooke. Nouveaux cahiers de la recherche en éducation 13(1), 21–41 (2010)
16. Cofer, C.N., Appley, M.H.: Motivation: Theory and Research (1964)
17. Louart, P.: Maslow, Herzberg et les théories du contenu motivationnel. Les cahiers de la recherche, pp. 1–18 (2002)
18. Gawel, J.E.: Herzberg's theory of motivation and Maslow's hierarchy of needs. Pract. Assess. Res. Eval. 5(1), 11 (1996)
19. McClelland, D.C.: Human motivation. CUP Archive (1987)
20. Lassarre, D., Giron, C., Paty, B.: Stress des étudiants et réussite universitaire: les conditions économiques, pédagogiques et psychologiques du succès. L'orientation scolaire et professionnelle (32/4), pp. 669–691 (2003)
21. Fisher, S.: Stress in Academic Life: The Mental Assembly Line. Open University Press, Bristol (1994)
22. Erlich, V.: Les nouveaux étudiants: un groupe social en mutation. A. Colin (1998)
23. Watson, D., Pennebaker, J.W.: Health complaints, stress, and distress: exploring the central role of negative affectivity. Psychol. Rev. 96(2), 234 (1989)
24. Plutchik, R., Kellerman, H. (eds.) Theories of Emotion, vol. 1. Academic Press, New York (2013)
25. Ekman, P.: Expression and the nature of emotion. Appr. Emot. 3(19), 344 (1984)
26. Bechara, A., Damasio, H., Damasio, A.R.: Emotion, decision making and the orbitofrontal cortex. Cereb. Cortex 10(3), 295–307 (2000)
27. Andrade, E.B., Ariely, D.: The enduring impact of transient emotions on decision making. Organ. Behav. Hum. Decis. Process. 109(1), 1–8 (2009)

28. Berthoz, A.: Emotion and reason: the cognitive neuroscience of decision making. OUP Catalogue (2006)
29. Reeve, J.: Understanding Motivation and Emotion. Wiley, Hoboken (2014)
30. Bandura, A.: Organisational applications of social cognitive theory. Aust. J. Manag. **13**(2), 275–302 (1988)
31. Bandura, A., Caprara, G.V., Barbaranelli, C., Gerbino, M., Pastorelli, C.: Role of affective self-regulatory efficacy in diverse spheres of psychosocial functioning. Child Dev. **74**(3), 769–782 (2003)
32. Rosenwein, B.H., Debiès, M.H., Dejois, C.: Histoire de l'émotion: méthodes et approches. Cahiers de civilisation médiévale **49**(193), 33–48 (2006)
33. Martin-Juchat, F.: Le capitalisme affectif: enjeux des pratiques de communication des organisations (2015)
34. Papez, J.W.: A proposed mechanism of emotion. Arch. Neurol. Psychiatry **38**(4), 725–743 (1937)
35. Tyng, C.M., Amin, H.U., Saad, M.N., Malik, A.S.: The influences of emotion on learning and memory. Front. Psychol. **8**, 1454 (2017)
36. Csikszentmihalyi, M.: Flow and education. NAMTA J. **22**(2), 2–35 (1997)
37. Kowal, J., Fortier, M.S.: Motivational determinants of flow: contributions from self-determination theory. J. Soc. Psychol. **139**(3), 355–368 (1999)
38. De Sousa, R.: The Rationality of Emotion. MIT Press, Cambridge (1990)
39. Hatfield, E., Rapson, R.., Le, Y.C.L.: Emotional contagion and empathy. In: The Social Neuroscience of Empathy, p. 19 (2011)
40. Gallese, V., Keysers, C., Rizzolatti, G.: A unifying view of the basis of social cognition. Trends Cogn. Sci. **8**(9), 396–403 (2004)
41. Rizzolatti, G., Craighero, L.: The mirror-neuron system. Annu. Rev. Neurosci. **27**, 169–192 (2004)
42. Mondillon, L., Tcherkassof, A.: La communication émotionnelle: quand les expressions faciales s' en mêlent. Revue électronique de psychologie sociale **4**, 25–31 (2009)
43. Fahlman, S.E.: Original Bboard Thread in which :-) was proposed (1982). http://www.cs.cmu.edu/~sef/Orig-Smiley.htm
44. Krohn, F.B.: A generational approach to using emoticons as nonverbal communication. J. Tech. Writ. Commun. **34**(4), 321–328 (2004)
45. Xu, A., Liu, Z., Guo, Y., Sinha, V., Akkiraju, R.: A new chatbot for customer service on social media. In: Proceedings of the 2017 CHI Conference on Human Factors in Computing Systems, pp. 3506–3510, May 2017
46. Fraoua, K.E., Leblanc, J.M., David, A.: Use of an emotional chatbot for the analysis of a discussion forum for the improvement of an E-learning platform. In: Zaphiris, P., Ioannou, A. (eds.) HCII 2020. LNCS, vol. 12206, pp. 25–35. Springer, Cham (2020). https://doi.org/10.1007/978-3-030-50506-6_3

CodeLab: An Online Laboratory for Learning to Code

Carles Garcia-Lopez$^{(\boxtimes)}$ ⓘ, Enric Mor ⓘ, and Susanna Tesconi ⓘ

Universitat Oberta de Catalunya (UOC), 08018 Barcelona, Spain
{carlesgl,emor,stesconi}@uoc.edu

Abstract. Educational laboratories are flexible environments that allow learners to learn by practice, fostering their creativity, learning awareness, and collaboration with peers. Bringing these laboratory environments to an online setting is both challenging and necessary, particularly nowadays, when a significant part of learning takes place in online settings. Educational laboratories are well-suited places for learning to code, which is stated to require a great effort from learners, especially for non-STEM learners. This paper presents the design, development, and evaluation of CodeLab, a laboratory-based platform for learning to code through practice. A user-centered design approach was carried out, making learners active members of the design process through different design methods. As a result of two design iterations, CodeLab provides an integrated practice environment with a learning path based on a list of challenges and activities. Learners solve these activities and engage with their learning process by being aware of their own progress. The tool conveys a laboratory experience to non-STEM learners, fostering their practice skills, assessment, and autonomy.

Keywords: Design · Interaction design · User-centered design · Learning labs · Learning tools · Technology-enhanced learning · Learning to code

1 Introduction

Educational laboratories are flexible and multidisciplinary spaces where knowledge is built through social interaction and experimentation. In these spaces, students' creativity, self-training, and self-management are fostered, and the learning process is expanded to the educational community, developing and sharing learner's creativity with peers. Thus, a laboratory is an ideal place for testing and experimentation to learn from mistakes and acquire learning by practicing skills and learning by doing [1].

Currently, a relevant part of learning takes place in online settings. Therefore, there is a need to provide the learning community with an online laboratory that brings face-to-face laboratory's strengths to an online learning environment. However, although online learning has multiple advantages, it can sometimes lead to a disconnection between learners and teachers, promoting isolated and individual work. Designing and developing an online laboratory is a significant challenge that requires a deep understanding of users' needs and making them active participants in the design process to

© Springer Nature Switzerland AG 2021
P. Zaphiris and A. Ioannou (Eds.): HCII 2021, LNCS 12784, pp. 437–455, 2021.
https://doi.org/10.1007/978-3-030-77889-7_31

create an environment that provides them with a good user experience and satisfaction to foster learners' engagement.

Learning to code is known to require a lot of practice [2, 3] since learners need to acquire coding and computational thinking skills and not just knowing the syntax of a particular programming language [3, 4]. In response to the requirements of the learning by doing approach [1], students need to monitor their learning process to direct, correct, and think deeply about their coding errors and solutions [6]. In such a challenging learning process, social interaction is also an essential component that allows students to share their knowledge, experiences, and questions with their peers and teachers while they are coding.

Given this major challenge of learning to code, continuous practice appears to be a viable approach to facilitate the learning process. In this respect, a laboratory-based tool becomes an essential tool to support the learning process in online settings.

CodeLab is a project that aims to create an online laboratory, offering students a workspace to practice, promoting the interaction between peers that occurs in a face-to-face laboratory, and fostering the awareness of their learning progress [6]. To do so, these key features were integrated into the same interface, providing students with a laboratory experience where they can easily access (1) learning content and activities, (2) progress and assessment feedback, (3) coding console, (4) execution and visualization and (5) a place to interact with other learners and teachers. From the instructors' perspective, CodeLab is expected to offer teachers an environment to keep track of students' activity and learning process and to provide feedback during the course.

CodeLab project follows a human-centered design (HCD) approach that aims to involve users in all phases of the design process [7] through an iterative process. This design approach is especially useful when designing interactive technologies [8] and technology-enhanced learning (TEL). Involving users in each step of the process, rather than waiting until the product is completed [9], helps to align the final product with users' needs and characteristics, which leads to a good learning experience [10].

This paper is organized as follows; the state of the art of learning to code by practice is presented in Sect. 2. Section 3 presents the approach to design and develop a learning tool to practice. The implementation and the evaluation of this tool are presented in Sect. 4. Finally, in Sect. 5, the conclusions and future work are discussed.

2   The State of the Art

As mentioned above, educational laboratories provide learners with a flexible environment for learning through practice, fostering creativity, learning awareness and interaction with peers and teachers. Recreating this favorable situation in an online setting can be very challenging. Commonly used learning management systems (LMS) provide a set of tools and features to scaffold the learning process, but in general they are mainly oriented to the acquisition of content than to the promotion of practice-based learning [11]. Technology-enhanced learning (TEL) research is trying to address the need for more active and engaging online learning environments by proposing several tools and platforms for autonomous learning through practice [12–14]. Such tools are key elements for the design and implementation of online learning laboratories.

Literature is abundant on how challenging it can be to learn to code and the great effort students have to make during the learning process [15–18]. It can even be more challenging when those who have to learn to code are non-STEM students. Schachman [19] describes these students as "alternative programmers" since they do not identify themselves as programmers, but they need to program to achieve some of their goals.

Programming is widely understood as a creative and collaborative process between programmers and machines [19]. Thus, learning to code is not only about acquiring specific knowledge of the syntax but also about acquiring specific skills [20]. Among these skills, problem-solving is one of the most relevant ones [21], making students understand the context, identify key information, and plan to solve the problem [22, 23], emphasizing the ability to solve it by cooperating with their teachers and peers [24, 25]. Furthermore, time management is also a crucial skill that allows students to plan the use of time and the stages during the learning process [24, 26]. To acquire these programming and general skills, programming courses are generally characterized by providing students with many activities to practice coding intensively [27]. Students' autonomy is crucial during this learning process since students need to learn to decide what is essential to succeed in their learning goals [28, 29].

Considering this need to practice intensively and how challenging it can be to learn to code to non-STEM students, it makes sense that these students might sometimes feel overwhelmed. In this context, student engagement takes on a significant relevance in their learning process. Engagement is understood as how actively students are involved in activities [30, 31], and there is stated to be a close connection between students' engagement and the interactions between learners, teachers, and the learning environment [32, 33]. The learning platform plays a key role in an online course since it becomes the place where these interactions occur [34].

Given the importance of the learning platform in an online course, it makes sense to focus efforts on designing a useful and easy-to-use platform. In this regard, Davis remarks in [35] the connection between the level of perceived usefulness and the user behavior and intention to use it. In other words, the easier it is to use a platform, the less effort it will require from the users, making them more likely to accept and use it [35–37].

A human-centered design approach facilitates users to have a satisfactory first experience with the program and makes them willing to keep using it [9]. Interface and interaction design may also facilitate users to feel comfortable with the platform and its interface [38]. Interface takes on particular relevance on a platform to practice to code since there is a direct link between how programmers work and the design of the platform's interface [19]. In this regard, discrepancies between how users and software designers understand the platform are inevitable [19]. However, being some of these discrepancies seen as the root of usability issues [39], it is important to design a satisfactory user experience, focusing on the interface design and its usability.

According to what has been exposed above, several design goals (DG) are identified to provide non-STEM students with a learning tool to practice coding that allows them:

- **DG1.** to practice autonomously solving provided activities,
- **DG2.** to split the activities into pieces,
- **DG3.** to be aware of their learning process,
- **DG4.** to communicate with their teachers and peers.

Next section details how these design goals were addressed through later stages of a user-centered design process, involving different types of users in the process through different design methods.

3   CodeLab Tool

CodeLab was conceived as a learning tool to promote learning through practice in an online laboratory setting. The tool provides non-STEM students with a platform that allows them to practice coding autonomously and collaboratively with their teachers and peers. The tool allows teachers to follow each student's particular learning progress and provide support. The interface was designed to foster student's exploration and discovery. According to Schachman [19], alternative programmers drive their work by feelings, intuitions, or emotions. Thus, CodeLab provides students with a list of activities for each challenge, where they can find assessment, recommended and complementary activities. These activities are shown with no visual-hierarchy difference.

3.1   Design Process

CodeLab was designed, developed, and evaluated through a user-centered design (UCD) approach, following the principles and phases of the ISO 9241-210 human-centered design process [40]. This is an iterative process divided into four main phases: (1) understand and specify the context of use; (2) specify the user requirements in sufficient detail to drive the design; (3) produce design solutions which meet these requirements and (4) conduct user-centered evaluations of these design solutions and modify the design taking into account the results. As Fig. 1 shows, different design methods and tools were used in each phase of the project during the first two iterations presented in this work.

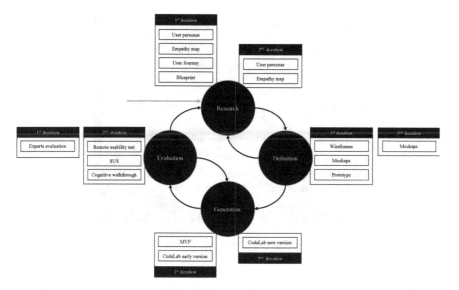

Fig. 1. Design process and methods.

As introduced above, the first phase of the design process focused on understanding the context and gathering information about the users. In this case, the final users are divided into two groups: non-stem students and teachers. This exploratory phase also aims to generate ideas, searching for diverse concepts and alternatives [41]. With this purpose, a collaborative workshop was carried out based on a design thinking process. As a starting point, two user personas were created to emphasize with the final user [42] and to understand these users' needs and goals that had to guide the design process [43–45]. During the two iterations of the UCD process, different methods that were used are described below:

Empathy Map. The empathy map (EM) method is an essential tool of a user-centered design approach [46]. Through an EM, people involved in the design process can understand, emphasize, and internalize a specific person's experience while using the product or service [47]. In this case, the updated version of Gray's initial EM was used, which consists of six areas: (1) See, (2) Say and Do, (3) Think and Feel, (4) Hear, (5) Pain, and (6) Gain [48].

It should be highlighted that most of the pains identified were related to the feeling of loneliness that a student might feel while learning to code in an online learning setting. Furthermore, they might feel that they have to make a great effort to achieve the goals and learn to code. On the other hand, the gains were related to their satisfaction with the results and the desire to share them with others.

User Journey. A User Journey (UJ) is a useful tool when a system is being developed from scratch [49]. A UJ aims to show, step by step, the interaction that users do while using the service or the product, describing emotions and reactions in each touchpoint. UJ usually considers the interaction that occurs before, during, and after using the service [50]. In this project, two UJ were built, focused on students and teachers (Fig. 2).

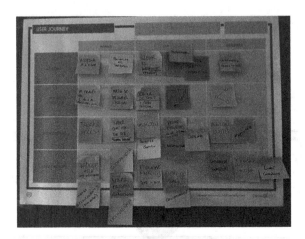

Fig. 2. Students' User Journey created during the co-creation workshop

Each UJ arose some specific opportunities that CodeLab could bring. From the students' perspective, four initial opportunities were identified: (1) a bar to show the learning progress of the student, (2) exercises tagged by type and difficulty, (3) a space to communicate with teachers and peers, and (4) a space to provide feedback. On the other hand, from teachers' perspective: (5) notification widget, (6) import and write new exercises, (7) Statistics to identify the most common errors, (8) provide enriched and contextual feedback.

Blueprint. A UJ can be implemented with a blueprint method. This method adds more detailed information to the user interactions, identifying the artifacts that need to be developed to provide a good user experience [51]. Some artifacts and features were listed to be integrated into the CodeLab tool.

Prototypes and Minimum Viable Product. A Minimum Viable Product (MVP) can be understood as an experimental object that enables designers and developers to empirically test the value hypotheses [52]. That is, a tool to collect users' feedback to improve the product or service [53]. Thus, this MVP must address the needs of the core group of users [54]. Taking into account the outputs of the methods mentioned above, different prototypes were built. Prototypes evolved from wireframe to mockups, and finally, a navigational prototype was designed. This navigational prototype ended as a MVP that was internally evaluated by experts.

The second iteration of the process was based on the results of the first one. First, the user personas defined in the previous iteration were redefined. As a result, two different archetypes of learners were identified and defined (Fig. 3).

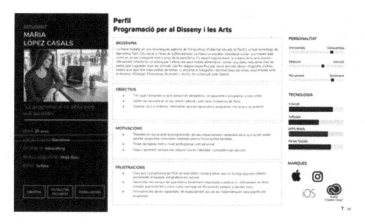

Fig. 3. The second version of the User Persona.

During the first iteration of the design process, the need to provide a broader view of the student experience was identified, from the information gathering phase to the completion of the course. In this regard, a new UJ was built, taking into account the five phases that a UOC student follows. In each phase, different touchpoints were identified (Table 1).

Table 1. Phases and touchpoints of the second UJ.

Phase	Touchpoints
Course registration	Course information, recommendations
Onboarding	Welcome, learning plan, and study guide
Methodology	Syllabus, learning resources, tools and programming environments
Support	Communication, mentoring
Evaluation	Evaluation criteria, feedback

In addition to the specific design opportunities identified, through the two iterations described above, it was also possible to identify a set of findings (F) about the students' main concerns in the whole process that they carry out during the course. These findings are listed below:

- **F1.** Students think the course contents and skills to be acquired are too complicated and sometimes do not know how to get started
- **F2.** Students miss being able to practice in the company of their teachers and peers
- **F3.** Students perceive an excessive workload, and it is often difficult to organize themselves
- **F4.** Students are overwhelmed by the frequency of activities submissions and find it difficult to organize their work
- **F5.** Students perceive an excessive workload, and it is often difficult to organize themselves

- **F6.** Students feel that it is difficult to communicate with their peers and the teacher due to the high number of students
- **F7.** Students believe that the forum of the course is underutilized
- **F8.** Students feel they cannot make enough progress as they do not have direct feedback.

3.2   Conceptualization and Design

During the first phases of the design process exposed in Sect. 3.1 and the literature research presented in Sect. 2, different findings (F) and design goals (DG) were identified. In the generation phase of the project, design features (DF) were set, taking into account the findings and design goals (see Fig. 4).

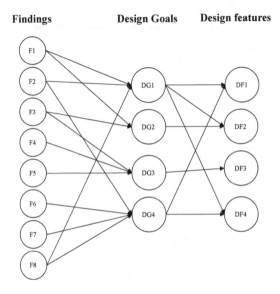

Fig. 4. Relation between findings (F), design goals (DG) and design features (DF).

These design features (DF) are detailed below:

DF1. Laboratory-Based Environment. Providing students with a platform to practice programming follows the idea of providing them with a programming laboratory. However, mirroring the dynamics that occur in a face-to-face laboratory to an online environment can be challenging. The CodeLab experience is designed to give learners a feeling of being in a face-to-face laboratory, where they can practice while interacting with their teachers and peers. Thus, the workspace organization and design are a crucial feature to be addressed. In this regard, CodeLab's interface brings together diverse elements that a student might expect from a practice lab (see Fig. 7): (1) a contextual navigation with information about the exercise, (2) information about the progress, (3) an area to write code, (4) an area to visualize code execution, and (5) an area to share the experience with peers and teachers. Even so, it is important to allow learners to adapt the interface to their needs at any given moment. Thus, CodeLab's programming screen is designed to be adaptable to the students' needs, being able to minimize some of the previously mentioned areas (see Fig. 5).

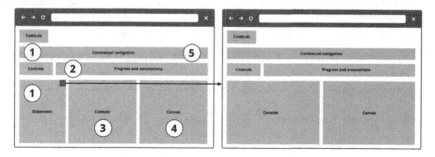

Fig. 5. Lo-fi wireframe of CodeLab's programming screen.

DF2. Challenges and Activities. Learning to code is not just about doing specific activities. The acquisition of programming skills might transcend the fact of solving individual activities and be based on practicing a group of them. In this regard, CodeLab classifies activities into different challenges designed by teachers. These challenges ensure that students will get the knowledge when they finish them. Furthermore, the platform must be sufficiently flexible to allow students to guide their own learning process, allowing them to go into more or less depth on the topics they find necessary. In this sense, it was decided to provide all the activities in each challenge openly and not to block some of them depending on the evolution of the student, fostering their autonomy.

However, in order to facilitate a learning path to students, activities are classified according to two different criteria: difficulty and type of activity. First, teachers indicate difficulty in the three-point Likert scale, one of the easiest and three most difficult ones. Secondly, in order to balance the autonomy and the assessment of their studies, exercises are also tagged to whether they are "recommended", "complimentary", or "assessment" (see Fig. 6).

Activity	Difficulty	Type
1. Name of the activity - Name of the Challenge	● ○ ○	c
2. Name of the activity - Name of the Challenge	● ● ○	e
3. Name of the activity - Name of the Challenge	● ○ ○	c

Fig. 6. Lo-Fi wireframe of the classification of activities according to their difficulty and typology.

DF3. Learning Awareness. A platform focused on practicing should include design elements that allow students to be aware of their position on the learning path. These features were structured hierarchically, from each challenge and activities' progress to the course's general progress. Regarding each exercise's progress, a progress bar was designed to be shown on the screen where they practice (Fig. 7). This progress bar shows the progress of the exercise divided into different steps that have been set by teachers, allowing students to mark their own progress and add personal notes in each step.

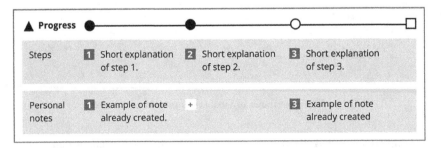

Fig. 7. Lo-Fi wireframes of the progress bar in the activity screen.

On top of that, students can see their general progress from the CodeLab homepage, where they can see at a glance what their overall progress is and access each challenge and activity directly (Fig. 8).

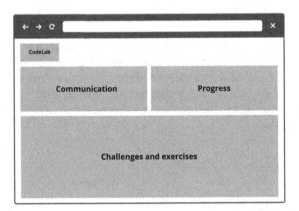

Fig. 8. Lo-Fi wireframes of CodeLab's homepage.

DF4. Scaffolding and Collaboration. During a self-paced practice-based learning process, students are expected to carry out a significant number of editing and compilations before submitting the activity. At this point, it is important to mention the educational settings where CodeLab will be used. During the course, students must submit some assessment activities on specific dates, which are part of the continuous assessment grade. Thus, between these submission dates, students are expected to practice autonomously. In some cases, students might feel that they do not receive feedback until the task is done and submitted, making it challenging to understand the problem [20]. In this regard, taking into account a commonly used feature in Integrated Development Environments (IDEs), it was decided to include feedback to the students when they compile the code, highlighting the line or lines where the error is.

4 Development and Evaluation

CodeLab was designed, developed, and implemented at Universitat Oberta de Catalunya (UOC), an entirely online higher education institution based in Barcelona (Spain).

4.1 Development

CodeLab was conceived as a laboratory-based tool potentially connectable to any learning management system (LMS). To do that, it was developed using the IMS LTI standard [55]. To achieve this laboratory-based environment, wireframes that were designed emphasized the idea of providing learners with a single space where they could find all the resources they would find in a face-to-face laboratory. Once the wireframes were evaluated by experts (interaction designers and programming teachers), they were evolved into mockups that embraced UOC's style guide look and feel (Fig. 9). From a technical point of view, the development of the interface is based on the VueJS framework, the back-end is based on Java SpringBoot, challenges and activities are stored on a MySQL database and learner progress and submitted activities are stored on a GitLab.

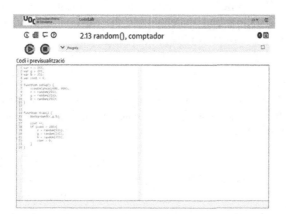

Fig. 9. CodeLab's screen to practice coding.

As explained in Sect. 3.2, one of the key features in this CodeLab version was to show activities classified by challenges to foster learners' exploration. In this sense, it was decided to show the level of difficulty and the activity type. In addition, it was decided to add a progress bar in each activity to facilitate students to be aware of their learning progress. Figure 10 shows how these activities were shown after the visual implementation.

Activity	Difficulty	Type	Progress
1.1 Hello canvas	● ● ●	●	
1.2 Hello World - setup() vs. draw() - Consola	● ○ ○	●	
1.3 Hello World - setup() vs. draw() - Dibuix	● ○ ○	●	
1.4 Coordenades 1	● ○ ○	●	

Fig. 10. List of activities in CodeLab.

Another key aspect of fostering learners' autonomy is the progress bar shown in each activity. This bar is divided into two parts, the first one is where the learner can see each step of the activity and mark it as completed, and the second one is the space where personal annotations can be made (Fig. 11).

Fig. 11. Progress bar into each activity screen.

Due to the project scope, the communication functionality was postponed for the next development iteration, and students used the classical communication channels provided by the UOC's virtual campus.

4.2   Evaluation

The evaluation of this functional version of the tool was based on different design methods with different participants to evaluate the design and development of the platform (see Table 2).

Table 2. Evaluation methods and participants.

Method	Type	Participants
Cognitive walkthrough	Remote test	Teachers and experts
System Usability Scale (SUS)	Remote questionnaire	Students
Usability test	Remote test	Students

Cognitive Walkthrough (CWT). A CWT is a design method to inspect the usability of a platform proven to be useful for identifying problems with navigation and information search into the platform [56]. Through this method, participants are asked to perform different tasks and answer four questions in each task [57]:

- Q1. Will the user try to achieve the right effect?
- Q2. Will the user notice that the correct action is available?
- Q3. Will the user associate the correct action with the effect that the user is trying to achieve?
- Q4. If the correct action is performed, will the user see that progress is being made toward the task's solution?

A total of 6 evaluators performed 10 tasks and sub-tasks on the CodeLab platform and answered these questions. There were three tasks with a rate of success lower than 50% (see Table 3). The feedback that participants provided in each of these tasks arose some usability issues that needed to be addressed:

- **Task 2. Enter a complementary activity of the "Challenge 2'.** Participants who failed in this task indicated that it was challenging to interpret the tag that indicates the type of exercise.
- **Task 2.1. Read the activity. Close the statement and open it again.** All the participants who failed this task agree that it was difficult to understand how to open the exercise again. Some of them suggested that the icon should be more precise.
- **Task 4. Do steps 1 and 2 of activity 1.21. When finished, mark the progress in the progress bar and save the activity.** Some of the participants who failed in this task explained that the steps were not visible enough and how to mark the progress should be improved.
- **Task 4.1. Save the activity. Close it and go back to CodeLab's homepage.** The main problem in this task was related to the closure of the exercises. All the participants expressed that they did not know how to close it. Furthermore, there was a problem when going back to the CodeLab's homepage because some did not know how to do it.

Table 3. Percentage of success of the tasks in the cognitive walkthrough

Task	Q1	Q2	Q3	Q4
1	100	72	75	100
2	69.23	46.15	63.64	77.78
2.1	75	33.33	63.64	90
3	91.67	71.43	81.82	58.33
4	75	40	66.67	72.73
4.1	41.67	50	50	50
5	84.62	91.67	91.67	91.67
5.1	83.33	83.33	83.33	91.67
5.2	75	83.33	75	91.67
5.3	91.67	75	75	81.82

System Usability Scale (SUS). The SUS questionnaire is widely used for evaluating the usability perceived by participants [58, 59], providing a general overview of the usability of the platform [60]. Participants are asked to answer 10 5 Likert-scale questions after having used the platform [61].

The result of SUS was calculated (1) and resulted in an average score of 84.69 (see Fig. 9), which is an acceptable score in terms of usability [62] (Fig. 12).

$$SUS = 2.5(20 + SUM(SUS01, SUS03, SUS05, SUS07, SUS09) - SUM(SUS02, SUS04, SUS06, SUS08, SUS10)) \tag{1}$$

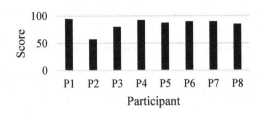

Fig. 12. Results of the system usability scale

However, since the SUS method was designed to be an additional method to complement objective methods [63], remote usability tests were also performed with users.

Remote Usability Tests. A total of 8 students were asked to perform 6 tasks and sub-tasks on the CodeLab platform. During this test, the moderator asked the participant to carry out predefined tasks on the CodeLab platform. This process was captured to be later analyzed quantitatively and qualitatively. Firstly, two of the metrics proposed by Harrati et al. in [59] were used: Completion rate and task duration. Secondly, the moderator took notes about the reactions and comments of the participants while performing the task. The tasks are listed below:

- **Task 1.** Enter the CodeLab tool with your user and password. Take a look at the first page. Open the recommended activity named "Activity 1" and go back to CodeLab's homepage.
- **Task 2.** Enter the complementary activity named "Activity 2 – Automats". How would you close (hyde) the activity statement? Once it is closed, how would you open it again?
- **Task 3.** Solve activity 1.5b. Save it and be sure it has been appropriately saved.
- **Task 4.** Solve steps 1 and 2 of activity 1.21. When finished, mark the progress in the progress bar and save the activity. Go back to the home page.
- **Task 5.** Enter again activity 1.21 and add a comment.
- **Task 6.** Do the two last steps of exercise 1.21 and check that it works. Mark it as completed Do the two last steps of activity 1.21 and check that it works. Mark it as completed and save it.

Results showed that 50% of the tasks were finished by all the participants (see Table 4). Task1, Task 2 and Task 4 did not achieve a 100% completion rate. Task 1 was finished by 50% of participants, and most of the participants had problems when trying to go back to the CodeLab homepage, which made them fail the task. Furthermore, 37.5% reported difficulties understanding the type of the activity. Task 2 was completed by 75% of participants, 25% who failed did not know how to see the statement of the activity when closed. Lastly, Task 4 was completed by % of the participants, 37.5% of them did not pay attention to the exercises' steps and did not see them until the moderator indicated where to find them.

Regarding the average time they spent on doing the tasks, no issue was identified since those tasks that took more time were the ones where participants had to do a real activity.

Table 4. Performance of each task in the test with users.

Task	Completion rate (%)	Average task duration (mm:ss)
1	50	01:53
2	75	01:20
3	100	04:36
4	62.5	07:01
5	100	01:23
6	100	02:16

5 Conclusion and Future Work

This work presents the design process of the CodeLab tool, a laboratory-based platform that allows students to practice during a programming course at the Open University of Catalonia. A key aspect of CodeLab is to convey a similar experience to what students might get in a face-to-face laboratory. The learning tool was designed and evaluated with experts, teachers, and students through a user-centered design approach.

Although some functionalities identified in the early design phases were postponed to future iterations, a fully functional version of CodeLab was designed, developed and evaluated in two different courses.

The results obtained from the design process and the evaluation methods provided important information about the usability and user experience of the platform, pointing to specific design requirements to be addressed. It is worth noting that, although some areas of improvement were uncovered during the internal work process, carrying out evaluation methods through a UCD approach facilitated obtaining detailed information that otherwise would probably not have been possible to obtain.

First, the classification of each learning activity according to its difficulty and typology needs to be more explicit to the user. The results in Task 2 of the CWT arose a problem with the label used to classify each activity, and 37.5% of participants in the usability test pointed to the same issue. Thus, the interface design should organize learning activities in the general list of activities in a more visible way by revising the graphic elements of the interface.

Secondly, an area of improvement was also identified in the progress bar of each activity. Task 4 of the CWT, which involved the progress bar and steps of the learning activities, had the lowest success rate in the CWT. Participants also expressed that the progress bar and the steps were not clear enough on the activity interface. In this sense, 37.5% of participants failed Task 4 on the usability test, where they could not locate activity's steps. Hence, the progress bar must be redesigned in the next iteration of the project.

Finally, in addition to improvements to the functionalities already implemented, it is necessary to address the integration of a direct communication tool through the platform itself to move towards a laboratory-based experience.

In conclusion, the importance of providing tools that facilitate practicing to learners has been highlighted in this work, emphasizing the relevance in a context with non-STEM students who need to learn to code. Designing, developing, and evaluating this laboratory-based platform was a significant challenge that has been addressed and achieved through a user-centered design approach, leading to a practice-based tool that adapts to the learners' needs, resulting in a good user experience and satisfaction.

Since the design goals presented in this work have been successfully addressed, future work should further develop the idea of an online learning laboratory:-based setting: developing analytics features that allow teachers to better support learners, implementing a communication feature in CodeLab to foster collaborative practice between peers and teachers, and improving the interface design of the platform. Since the two first iterations have been centered on evaluating the platform's development, the following iterations must focus on the evaluation of the implementation to understand the impact it might have on learners' engagement and learning outcomes.

References

1. Romero, M., Lepage, A., Lille, B.: Computational thinking development through creative programming in higher education. Int. J. Educ. Technol. High. Educ. **14**(1), 1–15 (2017). https://doi.org/10.1186/s41239-017-0080-z
2. Gomes, A., Mendes, A.J.: Learning to program - difficulties and solutions | Academic Conference Paper, no. May, 2007. https://www.researchgate.net/publication/228328491_Learning_to_program_-_difficulties_and_solutions
3. Lahtinen, E., Ala-Mutka, K., Järvinen, H.-M.: A study of the difficulties of novice programmers. SIGCSE Bull. **37**(3), 14–18 (2005). https://doi.org/10.1145/1151954.1067453
4. García-Peñalvo, F.J., Mendes, A.J.: Exploring the computational thinking effects in pre-university education. Comput. Hum. Behav. **80**, 407–411 (2018). https://doi.org/10.1016/j.chb.2017.12.005
5. Havenga, M., et al.: Metacognitive and problem-solving skills to promote self-directed learning in computer programming : teachers ' experiences. SA-eDUC J. **10**(2), 1–14 (2013)
6. Mor, E., Santanach, F., Tesconi, S., Casado, C.: CodeLab: designing a conversation-based educational tool for learning to code. In: Stephanidis, C. (ed.) HCI 2018. CCIS, vol. 852, pp. 94–101. Springer, Cham (2018). https://doi.org/10.1007/978-3-319-92285-0_14
7. Norman, D.A., Anderson, N.S., Norman, D.A., Draper, S.W.: User centered system design : new perspectives on human-computer interaction to cite this version : HAL Id : hal-00190545. Am. J. Psychol. **101**(1), 148 (1986)

8. Lowdermilk, T., Design, U.-C.: A Developer's Guide to Building User-Friendly Applications. O'Reilly Media, Sebastopol (2013)
9. Leonard, B., Vincenti, G.: Engaging programming students through simpler user interfaces. In: Karwowski, W., Ahram, T., Nazir, S. (eds.) AHFE 2019. AISC, vol. 963, pp. 113–121. Springer, Cham (2020). https://doi.org/10.1007/978-3-030-20135-7_11
10. Garreta Domingo, M., Mor Pera, E.: User Centered Design in E-Learning Environments: from Usability to Learner Experience (2007)
11. Kasim, N.N.M., Khalid, F.: Choosing the right learning management system (LMS) for the higher education institution context: a systematic review. Int. J. Emerg. Technol. Learn. (iJET) 11(06), 55–61 (2016). https://online-journals.org/index.php/i-jet/article/view/5644.
12. Duval, E., Sharples, M., Sutherland, R.: Research themes in technology enhanced learning. In: Duval, E., Sharples, M., Sutherland, R. (eds.) Technology Enhanced Learning, pp. 1–10. Springer, Cham (2017). https://doi.org/10.1007/978-3-319-02600-8_1
13. Goodyear, P., Retalis, S.: Learning, technology and design. Leiden, The Netherlands: Brill | Sense, pp. 1–27
14. Cook, D.A., Ellaway, R.H.: Evaluating technology-enhanced learning: a comprehensive framework. Med. Teach. 37(10), 961–970 (2015). https://doi.org/10.3109/0142159X.2015.1009024
15. Medeiros, R.P., Ramalho, G.L., Falcão, T.P.: A systematic literature review on teaching and learning introductory programming in higher education. IEEE Trans. Educ. 62(2), 77–90 (2019). https://doi.org/10.1109/TE.2018.2864133
16. Robins, A., Rountree, J., Rountree, N.: Learning and teaching programming: a review and discussion. Comput. Sci. Educ. 13(2), 137–172 (2003). https://doi.org/10.1076/csed.13.2.137.14200
17. Pears, A., et al.: A survey of literature on the teaching of introductory programming. SIGCSE Bull. 39(4), 204–223 (2007). https://doi.org/10.1145/1345375.1345441
18. Vihavainen, A., Airaksinen, J., Watson, C.: a systematic review of approaches for teaching introductory programming and their influence on success. In: Proceedings of the Tenth Annual Conference on International Computing Education Research, pp. 19–26 (2014). https://doi.org/10.1145/2632320.2632349
19. Schachman, T.: Alternative programming interfaces for alternative programmers. In: SPLASH 2012: Onward! 2012 - Proceedings of the ACM International Symposium on New Ideas, New Paradigms, and Reflections on Programming and Software, pp. 1–10 (2012). https://doi.org/10.1145/2384592.2384594
20. Lui, A.K., Kwan, R., Poon, M., Cheung, Y.H.Y.: Saving weak programming students: applying constructivism in a first programming course. SIGCSE Bull. (Assoc. Comput. Mach. Spec. Interest Group Comput. Sci. Educ. 36(2), 72–76 (2004). https://doi.org/10.1145/1024338.1024376
21. Medeiros, R.P., Ramalho, G.L., Falcao, T.P.: A systematic literature review on teaching and learning introductory programming in higher education. IEEE Trans. Educ. 62(2), 77–90 (2019). https://doi.org/10.1109/TE.2018.2864133
22. Rusczyk, R.: The art of Problem Solving, volume 1: The basics. AoPS Incorporated, California (2006)
23. García-Peñalvo, F.J.: A brief introduction to TACCLE 3 — coding European project. In: 2016 International Symposium on Computers in Education (SIIE), pp. 1–4 (2016). https://doi.org/10.1109/SIIE.2016.7751876
24. de Lira Tavares, O., de Menezes, C.S., de Nevado, R.A.: Pedagogical architectures to support the process of teaching and learning of computer programming. In: 2012 Frontiers in Education Conference Proceedings, pp. 1–6, October 2012. https://doi.org/10.1109/FIE.2012.6462427

25. Fuller, M.T.: ISTE standards for students, digital learners, and online Learning. In: Handbook of Research on Digital Learning, IGI Global, pp. 284–290 (2020)

26. Bati, T.B., Gelderblom, H., van Biljon, J.: A blended learning approach for teaching computer programming: design for large classes in Sub-Saharan Africa. Comput. Sci. Educ. **24**(1), 71–99 (2014). https://doi.org/10.1080/08993408.2014.897850

27. Lam, M.S.W., Chan, E.Y.K., Lee, V.C.S., Yu, Y.T.: designing an automatic debugging assistant for improving the learning of computer programming. In: Hybrid Learning and Education, pp. 359–370 (2008)

28. Hannafin, M.J., Hill, J.R., Land, S.M., Lee, E.: Student-centered, open learning environments: research, theory, and practice. In: Spector, J.M., Merrill, M.D., Elen, J., Bishop, M. J. (eds.) Handbook of Research on Educational Communications and Technology, pp. 641–651. Springer, New York (2014)

29. Glasgow, N.A.: New curriculum for new times: a guide to student-centered, problem-based learning. ERIC (1997)

30. Appleton, J.J., Christenson, S.L., Kim, D., Reschly, A.L.: Measuring cognitive and psychological engagement: validation of the Student Engagement Instrument. J. Sch. Psychol. **44**(5), 427–445 (2006). https://doi.org/10.1016/j.jsp.2006.04.002

31. Subramanian, K., Budhrani, K.: Influence of course design on student engagement and motivation in an online course. In: Proceedings of the 51st ACM Technical Symposium on Computer Science Education, pp. 303–308 (2020). https://doi.org/10.1145/3328778. 3366828

32. Lear, J., Ansourge, C., Steckelberg, A.: Interactivity/community process model for the online education environment. ... Online Learn. Teach. **6**(1), 71–77 (2010). http://jolt.merlot. org/vol6no1/lear_0310.htm

33. Handelsman, M.M., Briggs, W.L., Sullivan, N., Towler, A.: A measure of college student course engagement. J. Educ. Res. **98**(3), 184–192 (2005). https://doi.org/10.3200/JOER.98. 3.184-192

34. Reese, S.A.: Online learning environments in higher education: connectivism vs. dissociation. Educ. Inf. Technol. **20**(3), 579–588 (2014). https://doi.org/10.1007/s10639-013-9303-7

35. Davis, F.D.: Perceived usefulness, perceived ease of use, and user acceptance of information technology. MIS Q. **13**(3), 319–340 (1989). http://www.jstor.org/stable/249008

36. Lee, M.K.O., Cheung, C.M.K., Chen, Z.: Acceptance of Internet-based learning medium: the role of extrinsic and intrinsic motivation. Inf. Manage. **42**(8), 1095–1104 (2005). https://doi. org/10.1016/j.im.2003.10.007

37. Chen, W.S., Tat Yao, A.Y.: An empirical evaluation of critical factors influencing learner satisfaction in blended learning: a pilot study. Univ. J. Educ. Res. **4**(7), 1667–1671 (2016). https://doi.org/10.13189/ujer.2016.040719

38. Mor, Y., Winters, N.: Design approaches in technology-enhanced learning. Interact. Learn. Environ. **15**(1), 61–75 (2007). https://doi.org/10.1080/10494820601044236

39. Norman, D.: The Design of Everyday Things (2016)

40. I. O. for Standardization, Ergonomics of Human-system Interaction: Part 210: Human-centred Design for Interactive Systems. ISO (2010)

41. Perttula, M.K., Liikkanen, L.A.: Structural tendencies and exposure effects in design idea generation. In: International Design Engineering Technical Conferences and Computers and Information in Engineering Conference, vol. 42584, pp. 199–210 (2006)

42. Acuña, S.T., Castro, J.W., Juristo, N.: A HCI technique for improving requirements elicitation. Inf. Softw. Technol. **54**(12), 1357–1375 (2012). https://doi.org/10.1016/j.infsof. 2012.07.011

43. Adlin, T., Pruitt, J.: The Essential Persona Lifecycle: Your Guide to Building and Using Personas (2010)

44. Castro, J.W., Acuña, S.T., Juristo, N.: Enriching requirements analysis with the personas technique. In: CEUR Workshop Proceedings, vol. 407, no. June 2014 (2008)
45. Miaskiewicz, T., Kozar, K.A.: Personas and user-centered design: how can personas benefit product design processes? Des. Stud. **32**(5), 417–430 (2011). https://doi.org/10.1016/j.destud.2011.03.003
46. Bratsberg, H.M.: Empathy maps of the foursight preferences. In: International Center for Studies in Creativity (2012)
47. Gray, D., Brown, S., Macanufo, J.: Gamestorming: A Playbook for Innovators, Rulebreakers, and Changemakers. O'Reilly Media, Inc., Sebastopol (2010)
48. Gray, D.: Empathy map. In: Osterwalder, A., Pigneur, Y. (eds.) Business Model Generation: A Handbook for Visionaries, Game Changers and Challengers. Wiley, Hoboken (2010)
49. Caddick, R., Cable, S.: Communicating the User Experience: A Practical Guide for Creating Useful UX Documentation. Wiley, Hoboken (2011)
50. Hanington, B., Martin, B.: Universal Methods of Design: 100 Ways to Research Complex Problems, Develop Innovative Ideas, and Design Effective Solutions. Rockport Publishers, Beverly (2012)
51. Patrício, L., Fisk, R.P., Cunha, J.F.: Designing multi-interface service experiences: the service experience blueprint. J. Serv. Res. **10**(4), 318–334 (2008). https://doi.org/10.1177/1094670508314264
52. Münch, J., Fagerholm, F., Johnson, P., Pirttilahti, J., Torkkel, J., Jäarvinen, J.: Creating minimum viable products in industry-academia collaborations. In: Lean Enterprise Software and Systems, pp. 137–151 (2013)
53. Edison, H., Wang, X., Abrahamsson, P.: Lean Startup: Why Large Software Companies Should Care (2015). https://doi.org/10.1145/2764979.2764981
54. York, J.L., Danes, J.E.: Customer development, innovation, and decision-making biases int he lean startup. J. Small Bus. Strategy **24**(2), 21–40 (2014). https://libjournals.mtsu.edu/index.php/jsbs/article/view/191
55. I. M. S. G. L. Consortium and others: Learning Tools Interoperability Core Specification. IMS Final Release Version, vol. 1 (2019)
56. Blackmon, M.H., Kitajima, M., Polson, P.G.: Repairing usability problems identified by the cognitive walkthrough for the web (5), 497 (2003). https://doi.org/10.1145/642696.642698
57. Blackmon, M.H., Polson, P.G., Kitajima, M., Lewis, C.: Cognitive walkthrough for the Web. In: Conference on Human Factors in Computing Systems - Proceedings, vol. 4, no. 1, pp. 463–470 (2002). https://doi.org/10.1145/503457.503459
58. Lewis, J.R.: The system usability scale: past, present, and future. Int. J. Hum. Comput. Interac. **34**(7), 577–590 (2018). https://doi.org/10.1080/10447318.2018.1455307
59. Harrati, N., Bouchrika, I., Tari, A., Ladjailia, A.: Exploring user satisfaction for e-learning systems via usage-based metrics and system usability scale analysis. Comput. Hum. Behav. **61**, 463–471 (2016). https://doi.org/10.1016/j.chb.2016.03.051
60. Kaya, A., Ozturk, R., Altin Gumussoy, C.: Usability measurement of mobile applications with system usability scale (SUS). In: Industrial Engineering in the Big Data Era, pp. 389–400 (2019)
61. Brooke, J.: SUS: a "quick and dirty'usability. Usability evaluation in industry, pp. 189–194 (1996)
62. Bangor, A., Staff, T., Kortum, P., Miller, J., Staff, T.: Determining what individual SUS scores mean: adding an adjective rating scale. J. Usability Stud. **4**(3), 114–123 (2009)
63. Brooke, J.: SUS: a retrospective. J. Usability Stud. **8**(2), 29–40 (2013)

Engaging Students in Online Language Learning During a Pandemic

Angela Kleanthous[✉]

Language Centre, University of Cyprus, Nicosia, Cyprus
angela@ucy.ac.cy

Abstract. Designing a well-rounded, interesting and effective English language curriculum is important in the context of EFL/ESL, but keeping students constantly motivated and engaged in learning during the process is of equally high significance in order for learning to take place. During the Spring 2020 academic semester, schools and universities around the world were forced to close and move to online teaching and learning as a result of the coronavirus pandemic. In effect, instructors were faced with the newfound challenge of transforming their face-to-face lessons into virtual lessons almost overnight. This required the simultaneous utilization of multiple platforms in engaging students both in synchronous and asynchronous learning. This qualitative case study will present my reflections as an English language instructor, as well as my students' reflections following their experience with online learning by discussing different uses of online tools for language tasks that were deemed interesting and motivating for them. A thematic analysis of the data revealed overall positive attitudes towards both the synchronous and asynchronous modes of learning used in their English language course, with particular preference towards collaborative online learning.

Keywords: Online learning · Blogging · ESP · Collaborative learning · Motivation · Engagement

1 Introduction

Motivating and engaging learners is paramount for learning to take place, and the significance of motivation in language learning is highlighted in the literature. As Alizadeh [2] posits, learners feel motivated when they have a goal and direction to follow and in effect, motivation is of primary importance in language learning: "Without desire to learn, it is very difficult for learners to gain effective learning;" [...] "motivated learners can learn language more effectively than unmotivated ones"; [...]" learners with strong desire to learn a language can obtain high level of competence in the target language" [2]. Naturally, different conditions need to exist in order for learners to feel motivated, such as knowing the aim of the activities they are undertaking, participating in interesting activities, feeling responsible for participating in the lesson and being offered opportunities for decision-making [2, 15].

© Springer Nature Switzerland AG 2021
P. Zaphiris and A. Ioannou (Eds.): HCII 2021, LNCS 12784, pp. 456–468, 2021.
https://doi.org/10.1007/978-3-030-77889-7_32

The teacher's role is considered to be instrumental in fostering motivation and in effect student engagement, and instructors often face the challenge of motivating their students to engage and remain active throughout each lesson. More specifically, an instructor should show excitement about the lesson, accept and stimulate students to express their ideas, create a relaxing environment in the classroom where students can enjoy themselves, present the learning tasks clearly in an inviting and motivating way for students, and encourage learners with learning difficulties [6].

Keeping students motivated to learn becomes a bigger challenge when students transition to online learning during a pandemic, since instructors do not have advantage of non-verbal cues and facial expressions to help them communicate with their students [12, 15]. Since March 2020, undergraduate students at the University of Cyprus have been learning English exclusively online, which has involved participating in live online lessons, undertaking online tests and quizzes, engaging in online collaborative work, giving virtual oral presentations and taking their final exams online.

In this paper, I will present different online activities I employed to keep students' interest and motivation to learn both inside as well as outside the virtual classroom. Different activities will be presented that aimed at engaging students in collaborative tasks through peer feedback, discussions, and exchange of opinions. The platform that was used for the synchronous online lessons was Zoom, and the 'Breakout Rooms' feature was often utilized to group students into smaller teams and have them engage in collaborative oral and written tasks. As far as the asynchronous component of the course was concerned, students were required to blog through the Blackboard course management system.

1.1 The Significance of Motivation in Learning

Motivating students to learn is a key factor in student learning and successful academic performance. The literature cites numerous studies pertaining to the significant role of motivation in learning, and language learning in particular. Gilakjani, Leong and Sabouri [10] investigated the impact of motivation in foreign language learning and teaching and highlighted the importance of motivation for successful learning to take place; in particular, they described it as "the essence of language teaching, because of the realities that most of our students face while learning English, such as lack of sufficient language input in their environment, limited opportunities of interacting with English learners, etc." [10]. Ebata [8] also highlights the crucial role motivation plays for learning to take place and for the constant engagement in learning even after a goal is completed. More specifically, he posits that being motivated helps learners stay positive about their learning, which encourages them to acquire the target language, and enjoy the process along the way. Feelings of self-confidence, success and satisfaction, as well as good communication between learners and the instructor are reported as elements that develop motivation.

In their study, Gilakjani et al. [10] presented three levels of motivation: finding learner's passion, changing learner's reality, and connecting to learning activities. Naturally, the instructor's role is acknowledged as highly instrumental in all the stages of the motivational process. First of all, in helping learners find their passion, instructors have to select material that is interesting to their students' profiles, such as age, background, current trends. When learners can relate to the content that is brought into the classroom and they realize that their instructor does not approach them only as language learners but as people as well, then the level of motivation, and in effect of engagement in the lesson will be higher.

Changing the learner's reality is the second stage in the motivational process. English language learners often do not have enough opportunities to practice the language in the classroom, since time restrictions do not allow them to practice sufficiently. In effect, changing this reality can be achieved with the instructor offering more opportunities to learn, practice, and keep contact with the language outside the classroom, and allowing learners to make choices about learning. Some ideas offered by the researchers relate to making different multimedia learning sources available to learners, such as audio and video content, self-access quizzes, games, etc. [10].

Finally, the third level of motivation, which refers to the connection to learning activities, can be achieved by ensuring each learner is engaged in the task; for instance, collaborative learning could be one way to help students be more engaged and active in a task.

As discussed above, collaboration between students is one of the methodologies that are believed to help students stay motivated and engaged in a task [9, 15, 18]. More specifically, McConnell [15] conducted extensive research on the impact of collaboration on learners' enhanced motivation and engagement in learning. According to the researcher, working together enables learners become more active and responsible in their own learning rather than being passive recipients of knowledge, since they put more effort to perform at their best and contribute to the group.

Online collaboration is also claimed to be beneficial in learning as well as in enhancing learners' motivation. Students can engage in online collaboration in different ways both asynchronously through a variety of Web 2.0 tools such as wikis, blogs, etc., and synchronously by working together to either produce a piece of writing on a shared online document, or by engaging in group discussions during the virtual lesson. According to Buchem & Hamelmann [4], university students working with different Web 2.0 tools such as wikis, blogs and microblogs to practise their writing and speaking skills reported feeling more confident about using the tools, and they felt that working with their classmates online was easier.

2   The Current Study

During the Spring 2020 semester, the Covid-19 pandemic forced the entire university community to close and the English courses have been delivered online since then. While an online asynchronous component had already been incorporated in my courses through the *Blackboard Course Management Platform*, which enabled me to communicate with my students and keep them active in learning outside the classroom, the face-to-face meetings with students had to also be replaced by live online sessions. I then started to read and consider new ways to design my online learning tasks, while keeping the students' spirit and motivation alive during these uncertain and stressful times [6].

First, I needed to help my students find their passion by examining their interests and select suitable materials that would make them want to participate stay interested in each lesson by taking advantage of all the media available to me both synchronously, as well as asynchronously [17]. I carefully selected video material, in particular TED talks, which dealt with fun, interesting and relevant topics, pertaining to my students' age and field of study. Language learning tasks such as academic vocabulary drawn from the videos, as well as comprehension and critical thinking questions were extracted from the speeches, in order to help the students delve more deeply into the content of the videos.

In order to change the learners' reality, since they would not have any face to face interactions using the language, I decided that the asynchronous tools I used would need to be further reinforced in order to encourage more student engagement outside the virtual classroom [14]. Kelly, Baxter & Anderson [12] and Vurdien [21] successfully integrated asynchronous online tools in their classes to help students practice their writing skills, which helped them become more motivated by being engaged and active in the learning process through the exchange of online peer feedback. So, I added a blogging link on my Blackboard platform and added more listening and writing tasks for students' further practice outside the lesson, which will be described in more detail in the next section.

Finally, to help students connect to the activities, I set up several opportunities for them to collaborate online, both during the live virtual lessons, as well as asynchronously through the blog, and made sure they receive constant feedback for their work, both from me as the instructor, as well as from their peers [15]. The specific online tasks will be explained in more detail in the next section.

3 Methods

The current study can be described as a qualitative case study [22]. I, as the practitioner, implemented new activities in my teaching through the utilization of online tools with the aim to enhance my learners' motivation and in effect improve their experience during online education. The data used was collected through students' anonymous self-reflections they posted on the blog at the end of the semester as well as from my personal observations and self-reflections recorded in the form of a journal following each group task during the course of each semester. The data was analysed using a thematic analysis of the students' reflections across the two LAN 201 sections, which were posted anonymously through each group's blog at the end of the semester and provided the students' perceptions towards the online nature of the course. Common patterns were identified among the student responses and these were then categorized into different themes based on Braun & Clarke's model [3].

3.1 Participants

The participants of this study were three groups of a total of 59 undergraduate students studying at the University of Cyprus. One group consisted of 22 first-year Cypriot students registered in the LAN 101: Academic English course in the Summer 2020 semester (June-July 2020), 14 female and 8 male students, 18 and 19 years of age.

The remaining two groups consisted of 37 students who were second-year students registered in the LAN 201: Business Communication for Management course in the Fall 2020 semester. The students were young adults of approximately 19 years of age, from Cyprus and Greece, 24 female and 13 male students.

The LAN 101: Academic English course is the second level, academic English course the majority of students from a variety of departments is required to take at the University of Cyprus as a language requirement for their degrees. The specific course aims at further developing students' reading, listening, speaking and writing skills they were introduced to during their first semester, which will help them effectively perform within an academic context. The majority of the students registered in the section I taught during the Summer 2020 semester (June-July 2020), were from the department of Mathematics and Statistics.

The LAN 201: Business Communication for Management course is a third-level English course that the students in the department of Accounting and Finance are required to take as part of their degree's language requirement, as well as students from the Business Administration department, who choose it as an elective course. It is an ESP (English for Specific Purposes) course that focuses more on developing students' reading, listening, writing and speaking skills as well as vocabulary pertaining to the business and finance world [17]. ESP courses differ from general English courses with respect to their focus on the learners' specific professional needs. Therefore, ESP instruction takes both the learner and the learning context into account [5].

3.2 Synchronous Learning Tasks

Synchronous communication refers to the mode of online communication that takes place in real time [11]. During the summer semester, the lessons were held twice a week, for 3 h per session, and the duration was 7 weeks, as it was an intensive summer course. In the Fall semester, the lessons were held twice per week, for 75 min in each session for 13 weeks. The *Zoom* platform was used to meet the students synchronously for both semesters. The 'breakout rooms' feature was used in every lesson for a few minutes, which allowed the students to meet, interact with each other and collaborate. Through this tool students were divided by the instructor into individual rooms, each one consisting of 3–4 students and they were asked to engage in collaborative tasks. This also enabled them to get to know each other more since all their courses were taking place exclusively online by that time; therefore, they had no physical contact with their classmates, but only met through their online sessions.

One activity that students participated in was watching videos, particularly TED talks, and engage in discussions or debates within their groups, delving further into the topics tackled in the talks, in addition to specific vocabulary they encountered in the videos. Some examples of videos chosen for the LAN 201 course pertained to what makes them more employable, what makes a good manager, effective time management, and advertising. Since these topics were specific to their field of study, students had the opportunity to be exposed to experts in their field discussing issues relevant to their interests.

Another example of a collaborative activity the students of the LAN 201 course engaged in through the 'breakout rooms' related to the topic of advertising. In the process of students being exposed to the topic of advertising, they watched videos and engaged in readings relating to the specific topic, learning the different advertising techniques advertisers use to attract customers. As a group task, students were divided into different rooms on Zoom, each consisting of 3–4 students, they were asked to select an online advertisement or commercial and analyse the advertisement by identifying the different advertisement characteristics we had discussed in the lesson (e.g. advertising techniques used, target audience, purpose of the ad, graphics, etc.). Then they put together an impromptu presentation by sharing their advertisements to the rest of the class and analysing them for everyone. During their discussions and preparations I visited each group and monitored their work. I ensured that all the students participated and exchanged ideas and were involved in the task, as each member of the group was required to present one aspect of the advertisement.

3.3 Asynchronous Learning Tasks

In addition to the virtual classroom, students also engaged in blogging asynchronously in order to keep in contact with the course content and with each other and continue practicing outside the lesson. Asynchronous online communication does not require the real time participation of the instructor and learners; tools such as blogs, wikis, forums, and email are tools that facilitate asynchronous communication, which can take place at the participants' own time and place [11, 20]. Through the blogging feature of 'Blackboard,' students worked on different writing tasks where they engaged in peer feedback, watched videos, commented on the content and expressed their opinions, and they also engaged in reflective writing. The blog was private, which means only the registered students in each group and myself had access to the blog and the students' posts.

Students in the LAN 101 group were required to write an opinion essay and share it on the class's blog on Blackboard, and as a follow-up task they were required to choose 2 of their classmates' posts and comment on their essay by following a list of criteria for effective opinion essay writing that I had previously shared with them. By following the specific criteria, students were able to offer more constructive feedback to their peers and at the same time self-reflect on their own writing as well [18] (see Fig. 1 below).

Fig. 1. Peer feedback task on opinion essay writing task on the blog

One of the writing components of the LAN 201 course related to professional email writing. So, in addition to the in-class practice students had in evaluating professional business emails and producing their own, they were also required to write an email on a specific topic given to them and post it on the class blog. As a follow-up task, students were required to choose two of their classmates' emails and evaluate them based on specific criteria (see Fig. 2 below).

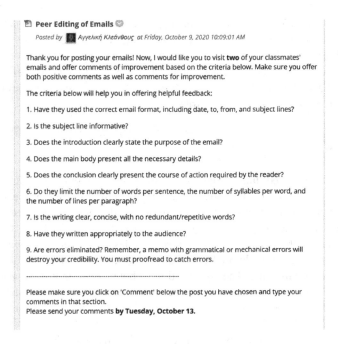

Fig. 2. Peer feedback on email writing on the blog

Another example was a listening task the LAN 101 students engaged in on the blog, where they had to watch two videos on the selfie culture and answer questions related to the topic discussed in the video and also share their own views on the topic in the form of comments below my post (see Fig. 3).

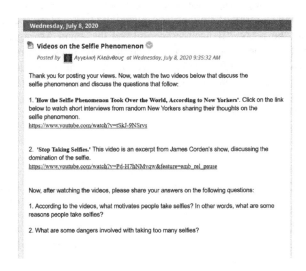

Fig. 3. Listening and discussion task on the blog

These types of activities allowed students to remain active and keep in touch with the language outside of the classroom while at the same time engage in tasks that enhanced their critical thinking skills and offered them opportunities to express their opinions in writing using the target language. By evaluating their peers' work and offering feedback, they also became more responsible and active in the learning process rather than assuming a more passive role in learning [6].

4 Results and Discussion

Overall, it is suggested that online tools offer many possibilities that can assist instructors in keeping students motivated and for learning to take place, even during a pandemic when students feel isolated and are deprived of the social aspect of learning that they enjoy while being in the classroom [13, 14, 16]. Students need to keep constant contact with the language, both during the lesson as well as outside the virtual classroom, since they have limited opportunities to keep in touch with the language, particularly during this time. The combination of both synchronous and asynchronous modes of learning assisted students stay active in learning, as well as stay motivated and interested in the lesson since they felt connected to both the instructor and their classmates [11, 13].

One way that helped students remain active and motivated in learning in the current study was the frequent collaboration with peers and constant interaction with the instructor, as well as the engagement in tasks that afforded them the feeling of responsibility in learning, both synchronously in the virtual classroom, as well as asynchronously [10, 14].

It is worth noting that the tasks students had to complete asynchronously were not part of their overall course assessment, but they were considered as part of their homework and overall class participation, which counted for 5% of their overall grade. Despite the fact that they would not receive a grade for the asynchronous blog and individual tasks, the majority of students completed the tasks. More specifically, 32 out of 37 students in the LAN 201 sections completed the email writing blog tasks (see Table 1) and 15 out of the 22 students completed the opinion essay writing blog task in the LAN 101 course (see Table 2).This may suggest that they had more intrinsic motivation for learning (i.e. to experience joy and satisfaction in doing an activity) rather than extrinsic motivation (e.g. to receive a course grade) in completing the assigned tasks [7].

Table 1. LAN 201 student participation in blog tasks

	Email writing task	Peer editing of email writing task	Reflective writing
LAN 201.1 (n = 19)	15	13	17
LAN 201.5 (n = 18)	17	13	15

Table 2. LAN 101 participation in asynchronous blog tasks

	Discussion task (lead-in to video)	Video blog task	Opinion essay writing task	Peer feedback on opinion essay writing
LAN 101.2 (n = 22)	15	7	15	15

It is also interesting to note that students participated more on the blog tasks that involved collaboration through peer feedback rather than the individual blog tasks (e.g. video blog task), which reinforces their responses that reveal a more positive attitude towards group work, both in synchronous, as well as asynchronous tasks (see Table 2).

At the end of the semester, the LAN 201 students were asked to reflect on the course through the blog and post anonymously their thoughts on the online course, by discussing both what they liked and found interesting, as well as what they disliked about the course. They were asked to post their reflections in the comments' section below my own post. The commenting feature provided the choice for students to decide whether they would post their comments anonymously or not, and this option was offered to them in order to ensure honest feedback on the course. Most students posted their comments anonymously, while a few students chose to have their names revealed. A total of 32 out of the 37 students posted their reflections and 20 of these posts were shared anonymously. The extracts used in this paper were chosen from the anonymous posts.

Students overall showed a positive attitude towards the online version of the course, and even though they stated that they would prefer to have to course face to face, they nonetheless enjoyed it, as they felt they were introduced to useful and interesting topics, and they had the opportunity to collaborate and get to know their classmates. Following a thematic analysis of the student reflections, the following themes emerged from the data:

a. Group work/ expression of ideas
b. Accessibility of course material
c. Use of multimedia
d. Feelings of achievement.

Extracts of some of the comments students posted anonymously are indicated below:

a. Group work/ expression of ideas

"This course was an enjoyable course. We had the chance to cooperate with our fellow students and do assignments together."

"I really liked the breakout rooms and the cooperation that the course demands."
"You helped us adapt easily to these conditions and to get to know each other through teamwork to feel more comfortable with each other."
" In my opinion, the best thing was the breaking rooms, as you had the chance to collaborate with different people every time and have at least an online conversation with them."

"I loved the fact that you divided us into teams and we were able to feel like we were in a classroom by working in teams."

b. Accessibility of Course Material

"Also, it was very helpful that class material was divided into weeks."

"Also, the class materials with the solutions in every lesson was very helpful, because if something was go wrong and you don't write something you can find it then later."
"...and all the information was easily accessible."

c. Use of multimedia

"Also, I really liked the different videos with talks we saw, where people from business talked about their experiences in their field."

"...and the multimedia which has used in the lessons (PowerPoint, videos) was very interesting."
"...the videos were interesting because of their content."

d. Feelings of achievement

"Also I've learned a lot of useful things..."

"I think this course was helpful because we learned new things that we will need in the future."
"I learned a lot of interesting and important things."
"I gained a lot of experience from online lessons and creating content (presentation) only from the internet."

Instructors can take advantage of the different online tools that are available and deliver their language activities in an enjoyable and interesting manner that will keep students' interest alive and more importantly, their motivation to learn. The combination of both synchronous and asynchronous tools for collaboration, according to my findings, can be effective in helping students stay in touch with the language constantly, socialize with their peers and interact with the instructor in real time, while at the same time have the time and space to process their work outside the classroom before they submit their tasks through the blog.

4.1 Limitations

A limitation of the synchronous online collaboration through the breakout rooms was the fact that I could not monitor the groups at the same time and I had to visit the groups one at a time, which meant that I could not effectively oversee their discussions and each member's contribution for every task.

5   Conclusion

Overall, students reported positive attitudes towards the tools incorporated in their online learning experience. Only one student remarked that even though they liked the collaborative tasks through the breakout rooms, they felt that it was not necessary for them to undertake such tasks every lesson. Also, two students in one of the LAN 201 groups stated that they did not enjoy the online team work, as they preferred to work on their own.

Even though the transition to online learning was sudden and not their choice, students stated that they had enjoyed the course and particularly the group tasks they were asked to complete during the synchronous sessions, since they saw that as an opportunity to meet and interact with their classmates, easily communicate with their instructor, use the language in real time, while they also reported that they enjoyed the videos that they had watched and discussions they had engaged in. Instructors can combine different tools in their online classes and offer several opportunities to learners to use the language in a motivating and interesting way to them so that they can remain constantly engaged in the course and ultimately, learn.

References

1. Alawamleh, M., Al-Twait, L.M., Al-Saht, G.R.: The effect of online learning on communication between instructors and students during Covid-19 pandemic. Asian Education and Development Studies (2020)
2. Alizadeh, M.: The impact of motivation on English language learning. Int. J. Res. Eng. Educ. 1(1), 11–15 (2016)
3. Braun, V., Clarke, V.: Using thematic analysis in psychology. Qual. Res. Psychol. 3(2), 77–101 (2006)
4. Buchem, I., Hamelmann, H.: Developing 21st century skills: Web 2.0 in higher education- A case study. eLearning Papers. www.elearningpapers.eu. ISSN 1887-1542. Accessed 19 Feb 2021
5. Chang, K.C.C.: From EAP to ESP: a teacher's identity development. Taiwan J. TESOL 14(2), 71–100 (2017)
6. Dippold, D.: Peer feedback through blogs: student and teacher perceptions in an advanced German class. ReCALL 21(1), 18–36 (2009)
7. Dornyei, Z.: Motivation in second and foreign language learning. Lang. Teach. 31, 117–135 (1998)
8. Ebata, M.: Motivation factors in language learning. Internet TESL J. XIV(4). http://iteslj.org/Articles/Ebata-MotivationFactors.html. Accessed 26 Feb 2021
9. Fernández Dobao, A.: Collaborative writing tasks in the L2 classroom: comparing group, pair, and individual Work. J. Second. Lang. Writ. 21, 40–58 (2012)
10. Gilakjani, A. P., Leong, L.M., Sabouri, N.B.: A study on the role of motivation in foreign language learning and teaching. I.J. Modern Educ. Comput. Sci. 7, 9–16 (2012)
11. Huang, X.S., Hsiao, E.: Synchronous and asynchronous communication in an online environment. Q. Rev. Dist. Learn. 13(1), 15–30 (2012)
12. Kelly, D., Baxter, J.S., Anderson, A.: Engaging first-year students through online collaborative assessments. J. Comput. Assist. Learn. 26, 535–548 (2010)

13. Kohnke, L., Moorhouse, B.L.: Facilitating synchronous online language learning through Zoom. RELC J. 1–6 (2020)
14. Lowenthal, P.R., Borup, J., West, R.E., Archambault, L.: Thinking beyond Zoom: using asynchronous video to maintain connection and engagement during the Covid-19 pandemic. J. Technol. Teach. Educ. **28**(2), 383–391 (2020)
15. McConnell, D.: The experience of collaborative assessment in e-learning. Stud. Contin. Educ. **24**(1), 73–92 (2002)
16. Moorhouse, B.L.: Adaptations to a face-to-face initial teacher education course 'forced' online due to the COVID-19 pandemic. J. Educ. Teach. **46**(4), 609–611 (2020)
17. Pazoki, S.J., Alemi, M.: Engineering students' motivation to learn technical English in ESP courses: investigating Iranian teachers' and students' perceptions. RELC J. **51**(2), 212–226 (2019)
18. Rahman Sidek, E., Yunus, M.Md.: Students experiences on using blog as learning journals. Procedia Soc. Behav. Sci. **67**, 135–143 (2012)
19. Shih, R.: Integrating a blog and face-to-face instruction into an ESP course: English for Hospitality and Tourism. Turk. Online J. Educ. Technol. **11**(4), 204–209 (2012)
20. Terkinarslan, E.: Blogs: a qualitative investigation into an instructor and undergraduate students' experiences. Australas. J. Educ. Technol. **24**(4), 402–412 (2008)
21. Vurdien, R.: Enhancing writing skills through blogging in an Advanced English as a Foreign Language class in Spain. Comput. Assist. Lang. Learn. **26**(2), 126–143 (2013)
22. Yazan, B.: Three approaches to case study methods in education: Yin, Merriam, and Stake. Qual. Rep. **20**(2) (2015)

The Global Challenge of Designing E-learning Tools for Computational Thinking: A Comparison Between East Asia and Scandinavia

Kasper Kristensen[1] , Emanuela Marchetti[2] ,
and Andrea Valente[1]([⊠])

[1] The Maersk Mc-Kinney Moller Institute, SDU Game Development
and Learning Technology, Odense, Denmark
{kakr,anva}@mmmi.sdu.dk
[2] Media, Department for the Study of Culture, University of Southern Denmark,
Odense, Denmark

Abstract. In this paper we investigate status and trends in the pedagogy of Computational Thinking (CT), in Scandinavia and Eastern Asian countries. A more detailed comparison is drawn between two specific countries: Denmark and Taiwan. Combining a literature review on official information about the implementation of this new subject in schools, interviews with experts and practitioners, we identify core aspects in the pedagogy of CT across sociocultural differences, such as: the role and relation between formal and non-formal learning, the relation between CT and other school subjects, coding as an unavoidable part of CT as a subject, the tendency to adopt and adapt globally shared materials originally imported from the North American educational discourse. We also noticed that in Danish primary and secondary schools, current orchestration strategies in CT-related learning activities tend to leverage hands-on tinkering, peer-learning, and collaborative/group-based problem-solving; similar strategies are adopted in Taiwanese clubs. In this respect, we identify a lack of support for group work in existing e-learning tools for coding. Our main contribution is the definition of a scenario and requirements for a new class of e-learning tools, capable of supporting group-based CT learning activities across different culture. We are currently organizing a series of observations of the teaching practices of coding within CT, in cooperation with our network of contacts in Taiwan and Japan. Future work involves the development of a prototype of the new e-learning tool, iteratively, involving experts from Scandinavia and East Asia.

Keywords: Computational thinking · Scandinavia and East Asia · Tools · Programming · Cooperation

© Springer Nature Switzerland AG 2021
P. Zaphiris and A. Ioannou (Eds.): HCII 2021, LNCS 12784, pp. 469–487, 2021.
https://doi.org/10.1007/978-3-030-77889-7_33

1   Introduction

Computational Thinking (CT) [10] has recently seen a nearly universal recognition globally [3] and school systems across the world are at various stages of implementing new curricula including digital literacy, ICT and CT as core subjects. Our study has the double goal of gaining an understanding of the emerging pedagogy of CT as a new school subject from a global perspective, and what are the consequences for the development of e-learning tools that could be applicable across different countries and pedagogical practices.

We start by looking at existing definitions of CT, to appreciate the complexity of finding a common, globally shared, practical definition; this problem stretches from primary schools to higher education. We proceed with a preliminary case study on a comparison between East Asia and Scandinavia, focusing on Denmark and Taiwan, as examples of different pedagogical practices potentially embodying different sociocultural values and needs. The comparison is based on literature reviews [3, 4], interviews [2], and dialogue with local researchers. Our interests for these specific countries emerged from noticing overlapping sociocultural factors, such as: relatively comparable (i.e. small) size of the country, advanced digitization of their society, both committed to implementing CT in their school curricula, and both influenced by North-American advancements in CT and in digital innovation. Our preliminary findings show similarities between the approaches to CT of the two countries, in relation to the importance of the social aspects of learning and the relevance of coding as a central, hands-on activity in CT practices. We are aware of the distinction between coding and programming [9], and we agree that *coding* is the activity of converting instructions from human form to a code runnable by a machine, while *programming* is often taken to include a larger scope and involves also other activities in software development (e.g. planning, debugging, testing, deployment, etc.). Coding is therefore part of programming, and programming is considered an important 21st century skill, providing an advantage in the job market to technical and humanistic graduates [11]; however, programming is not yet a primary school subject, not in Scandinavia nor in East Asia. Furthermore, in the discussion about the nature and definition of CT, it is typically agreed that CT should not be considered simply a programming curriculum for pupils. So we propose to consider coding as a challenging but unavoidable and highly desirable part of CT. We decided, therefore, to analyze existing e-learning tools for coding, targeted at our target group, and look at them through the lens of learning theories such as constructivism, Vygotsky's *Zone of Proximal Development* [22], and peer learning more in general. We found that existing IDE for young beginners are designed with a single user in mind: this might not support adequately current the orchestration strategies for CT that we have found in our case study, which typically leverage forms of peer-learning and collaborative problem-solving. The main contributions of this paper are, therefore, the identification of a lack of support for group work in existing e-learning tools for coding, targeted at primary schools; and the definition of a scenario and requirements for a new class of e-learning tools, capable of supporting group-based CT learning activities across different culture.

The rest of the paper discusses the complexity of finding a definition for CT (Sect. 2) and the theoretical work we used to look at CT in this study; Sect. 3 introduces our case study and our findings, that are further discussed in Sect. 4. Section 5 presents guidelines and specifications for the design of e-learning tools that better fit the emergent needs of the pedagogy of CT. Section 6 concludes the paper.

2   CT – A Concept in Search of a Definition

CT has seen widespread and ongoing adoption both in Europe [5] and East Asia (Kristensen 2020), hence their school systems are in various stages of implementing CT into their school curriculums, focusing more specifically on the cases of Denmark and Taiwan.

Our comparison among countries builds on a conceptual framework, informed by existing complementary views of CT. The term CT was originally coined by Papert in his book *Mindstorms* [2, 30] 30 years ago, but the definition and focus have evolved over the decades. Papert [2, 30] originally envisioned the personal computer as a great facilitator for assimilating knowledge of any kind, as the personal computer's adaptive nature would allow it to be tailored to any individual interest, functioning as a catalyst for intrinsic motivation. Papert laments the fact that computers were yet not powerful enough to create fully engaging activities, but stating than when the technology is sufficiently mature, it will allow CT to be integrated into everyday life [2]. Papert's definition of CT was to be able to use computers for everyday tasks, which could sound already surpassed given the average computer skills of today's pupils and students.

Current CT is clearly not yet mature and each country is trying to figure out how a person becomes a computational thinker, and to cope with the lack of a widely agreed-upon definition of CT, in this paper we follow Wing [10] and define CT as the ability to solve problems *algorithmically* (i.e. in such a way that a computer could be used to solve them). In this sense CT can be seen also as a problem solving method, supported by computers and algorithms. Therefore, CT learners would need to understand how data and information is stored and processed within a computer. A main challenge in the quest for turning CT into a school subject is then to identify which set of skills and knowledge should be possessed by citizens in the 21st century [4, 10, 29], to understand the impact of digital and pervasive systems on society and their individual rights, while being able to use the same systems in their daily jobs, without being IT professionals. As automatic systems become more ubiquitous, the ability to understand and use those systems will be paramount to become an effective agent in the present and future digital world, not unlike reading and writing skills are today, as exemplified by the popularization of the term *digital literacy* [29].

In our comparative study, we coped with this challenge referring to a simple categorization of CT chore elements, designed and widely used for teaching CT notably in the USA, England and Taiwan [5], which gives a general overview of the different elements of CT, such as: decomposition, pattern recognition, abstraction, and algorithms. Decomposition is the first step in the process of dividing a problem into discrete parts. Each part can then be tackled individually, flattening the complexity of the overall problem. Pattern Recognition is the second step, in which commonalities are identified, which could be repeating sequences, generalized categories or other similarities observed in the problem. Abstraction is the third step, in which the solutions are modeled and abstracted. A good CT solution should be general, solving multiple problems of a similar nature and not merely the initial specific problem. The last step is represented by algorithms, in which the problem is expressed as a series of steps necessary to find the solution to the problem.

In conclusion, a universally accepted definition of CT is still missing, and each country is adopting a customized blending of elements CT, referring to different international and national sources [6]. Moreover, the practical implementation of CT in primary school requires to consider more aspects than simply the core elements of CT, such as: classroom orchestration, support for teachers' competences, and development of suitable textbook and online materials in the appropriate language.

2.1   Theoretical Framework

Since we are interested in the learning and pedagogy of CT in different countries, we need to formulate a pedagogical lens to analyze and compare CT approaches. In this sub-section we outline the theories that we adopt in our analysis.

Our study builds mainly on Vygotsky's learning theory [22], which constitutes the basis of constructivism, the approach also adopted by Papert [30]. Instead of focusing on the transmission of knowledge from teacher to student, constructivism is concerned with the process of the learner of gaining knowledge by exploring and applying knowledge in a practical context acting with material toys or tools. As such constructivism sees meaning making as a qualitative, exploratory process [8], in which the learner actively forms new connections with his or her own existing knowledge and understanding, forming new and sharper understanding.

In Vygotsky's theory [22], learning is seen as an inquiry-based process of knowledge acquisition, instead of a one-way street, in which the teacher with eloquent and succinct languages transfers knowledge from himself to his students. Learners are seen in Vygotsky as independently engaging in their learning, participating in social activities with peers and adults, who might provide support when the learners reach their *Zone of Proximal Development*, defined as a natural boundary between what the leaners can accomplish on his or her own, and what which he or she can understand with proper facilitation [22]. The Zone of Proximal Development is delimited by pre-existing knowledge of the learners and by the cognitive developments of young learners, in relation to what they can understand for their age. In this respect, Vygotsky's theory offered already a counterpoint to traditional learning theories, proposing that the student actively builds meaning through a interplay with the teacher, leveraging his or her own preexisting understanding as a foundation.

Vygotsky generally assumes that learners acquire knowledge through a dialectic collaboration with their teachers [22]. However, this dialectic collaboration can be extended to more experienced peers, hence leading to forms of peer learning. This scenario is explored in theories of *apprenticeship learning* [23, 29, 31], which are founded on Vygotsky's theory and build on observations from craftsman apprenticeships. In apprenticeship learners are seen as engaging with peers and adult supervisors in different social activities such as food preparation, which involve a goal not strictly related to learning, that would be the creation of a dish and the social enjoyment of it. These activities involve also a set of material objects and tools, and the adult are in charge in segmenting the activity at hand in smaller tasks with related goals, which could be conducted step by step by the learners under supervision [23, 31]. When encountering difficulties either adults or more expert peers will provide the needed support. As the novice's skills improve the experts will gradually remove themself from the process, gradually enabling the apprentice to complete the activity on his or her own [23, 31]. As such apprenticeship learning includes the principle of *scaffolding* [31], where support from the experts is slowly removed and the overall learning goal is to enable the apprentice to perform the activity independently in future occasions [23]. From the perspective of the Zone of Proximal Development, scaffolding aims to move further the ability of the learners from what they can do with help, to full control on the activity.

Apprenticeship learning highlights the importance of the physical learning environment [23, 31], as resources for meaning making. At its core apprenticeship is learning through practical application of skills and knowledge, in which peer-learning is seen students have an ideal environment for questioning, evaluating and restructuring existing knowledge [23]. This transformation of knowledge can happen as a result of discussion between individuals explaining, or defending their own understanding and viewpoints. In order for peer-learning to be effective, it can be argued that one of the students should act as the expert, being slightly ahead of the other students but both will learn and develop through the process [32].

Forms of peer learning are targeted by *playful learning* and *gamification*, according to which learning can take place through facilitated play. Playful learning is seen as fostering motivation, social engagement, and deeper forms of understanding in the learners [13, 22]. According to Vygotsky, play enables children to develop superior cognitive abilities, enabling them to go beyond their present reality, reflecting on the consequence of hypothetical courses of action. In so doing, children start early to practice forms of conceptual thinking [22]. Gee [13] argues that players create their own *affinity spaces,* seen as imaginary realities defined by the players actions, mutual interests, and the surrounding context.

Similar dynamics take place in the adoption of gamification, in which certain structures from games are applied to learning activities, so to create an engaging motivational reward structure to foster the learners' motivation [14]. Gamification has been applied to learning, but also teambuilding and innovation practice in professional contexts, healthcare, and physical activities. Gamification takes inspiration from reward structures developed from social competitive games, computer games and sports. Therefore, central elements of gamification include social engagement, daily bonuses, and streaks, a typical example would be virtual badges collected through a series of quests while playing a computer game or a public leader-board showing the accomplishment of all participants [14].

According to our preliminary data, forms of playful learning and gamification are being explored to create CT learning activities for primary and secondary schools, and especially in the case of clubs.

3   Case Study: CT Across Countries

This section describes the current status of the discussions and implementations of CT as a primary and secondary school subject, in Scandinavia and East Asia.

3.1   State of CT in Scandinavia and Denmark

In Scandinavia all countries tend to work in close cooperation when global challenges arise, and this is happening such as the global challenge of turning CT into a school subject. In a commissioned report [5] about the implementation of CT in Scandinavia, it is stated that Denmark, Sweden, Norway and Finland are all pursuing this complex task, in similar ways, even if they are at different stages of implementation. More specifically three approaches are identified in Scandinavia to the inclusion of CT in the school curriculum: *"a cross-curriculum strategy, accommodation in subject(s) already being taught, establishment of a new, purposely-designed subject. [...] Finland and Sweden have adopted a blend of cross-curriculum and single subject integration, where the strongest subject link - in terms of coverage and learning outcomes - appears to be with mathematics."*. Instead Denmark and Norway adopted *"pilot initiatives at lower secondary level"* and they appear to *"position CT within an elective subject that has strong links to computer science, leveraging [...] learning contents for developing CT skills."*. Teachers' training is also a central focus in all Scandinavian countries, which have a tradition of defining frameworks for school subjects, but leaving the teachers freedom in the micro-level management of contents in the actual courses.

In Denmark CT has been implemented from the top, it has been pushed from a political institutional level, starting recently in high school with a new course called "Informatik" by the Ministry of Education [17]. Afterwards, CT experiment was moved down to elementary school, where a large trial is currently being conducted since 2019 and will finish in summer 2021. The aim of this trial is to test the inclusion of CT in Danish schools as an independent course or within other courses. The new primary school CT course is named "Teknologiforståelse", which translates to "Technology Understanding" [18]. The core competences of the new course (translated from the official Danish documentation) include:

- *Digital empowerment* - critical investigation and understanding of digital artefacts like apps,
- *Digital Design* - with focus on the design processes,
- *Computational Thinking* - where pupils must analyze, model, and structure data and data processing,
- *Technological skills* - which include mastering computer systems, digital tools, and programming.

So defined, the Danish school system considers programming, and not only coding, as a skill to be included in Computational Thinking.

The implementation of the "Informatik" course is an interesting case: since it is a more mature subject than "Teknologiforståelse", but it represents a close relative and a kind of precursor, a large amount of data is available about the deployment and challenges of "Informatik". Compared to other courses within the Danish school system "Informatik" is unique, as it specifies which pedagogical approaches should be used in teaching its subject matter, not to the exclusion of possible other approaches, but it is worth noting that in Danish education, such decisions are normally left to the teachers' discretion. Similarly, the choice of programming languages, software, or other tools, to be used within the course, are also left to individual teachers, this represents a more typical balance of responsibilities in the Danish school system. Hence, Danish teachers are currently experiencing additional pressure than usual in experimenting with CT, as they are given more rigid instructions from the political level to teach an undefined subject, while not being experts themselves. In this respect, an interesting challenge identified during the ongoing trial with CT is the competence and knowledge gap between teachers and those who are developing the CT curriculum [27]. In Denmark, a curriculum is usually defined in the form of lesson plans and assignments, which teachers and schools can choose from, as a supplement to their own lessons and assignments. However, in the case of "Informatik", the curriculum is reportedly formulated in a specialized IT language, which makes it hard for the teachers to understand how to use and adapt the provided lessons plan to their needs.

Recent lockdowns of schools due to the Covid-19 pandemic has caused additional challenges, as high school students and pupils cannot be followed as closely as usual. Moreover, a reprioritization of subjects has led to focus on core subjects, such as Danish, Mathematics, and foreign languages, with the penalization of lab-based subjects, like sciences, art and design, and CT.

Besides schools, in Denmark CT is being introduced also through various types of computer science *clubs,* where children can experiment with microcontrollers, programming, 3d printers, and digital art after their classes. These clubs are volunteer organizations financed by the municipality, which have become very spread in Denmark over the last couple of years. These clubs offer a variety of informal learning activities in CT related topics, taught by expert volunteers from local education institutions or from within the IT field. Hence, these clubs have often a strong profile and can offer relevant insights for developing a CT curriculum.

Both in Danish schools and clubs, two main pedagogical approaches are used in teaching the subject "Informatik" and in the "Teknologiforståelse" trial such as: *Worked Examples* and *Use-Modify-Create.* In the worked example approach, a solution is to show a solution to a problem, and to show the thought process behind its implementation (as in [19] and [20]). Worked Examples are often produced with multiple modalities in mind such as audio and visual, videos are extensively used as these allow pupils to engage with the example at their own pace. Worked Examples demystify the problem solving process, by showing the process itself in a step-by-step fashion, and considerations of what goes into a design, which is not possible to show in finished code or completed problem solutions, hence Worked Examples are especially useful at early stages of skill acquisition, guiding the pupils step by step showing theory and relevant examples saliently shown in the material [19].

The other pedagogical approach found in "Informatik" is Use-Modify-Create, which was proposed by Lee et al. [21] as a promising pattern for teaching CT. In this pedagogical approach we allow the students to first engage with a given product, for instance a digital game or other interactive media, and afterwards to modify its code.

This process could be informed by improvements the students wish to implement, after having used the product and having noticed small bugs in the code. As the students' understanding of the code increases, they can move from the modification phase to the creation phase: first by implementing new features to the existing product and later to create completely new products (as also suggested in the document from the Danish Ministry of Education [17]).

CT experimentation in Denmark is taking place across educational contexts, moreover, more data are available from high schools and the "Informatik" subject. However, because of fundamental differences among high schools, primary schools and clubs, a pedagogical approach which is highly successful in one setting might still need adapted to another or might need to be discarded entirely. Therefore, it is difficult to directly base a new CT course for elementary schools merely on the pedagogical patterns that has worked for "Informatik" or in the clubs, which are typically informal, participatory, and social. In conclusion, the current Danish and Norwegian trial is providing data and observations that are needed to shed light on these issues. Interestingly we are seeing that hands-on methods like Worked Examples and Use-Modify-Create seem to emerge as widely adopted pedagogical approaches, in Denmark and possibly in other countries attempting the same implementation of CT in schools.

3.2   State of CT in East Asian Countries and Taiwan

In order to gain insight into the development of CT in East Asia, a literature review was conducted. The goal of the literature review was to show the current academic discourse around CT for each country of interest [4]. The focus was on smaller East Asian countries, because they have more similarities with Denmark and the other Scandinavian countries: they are of rather comparable in size, they are striving to implement CT following the North American effort, and they typically have a good level of digitization of the society. As such we assume that they would be frontrunners in the implementation of CT in schools, and that their approaches and contingencies would be more comparable to the Danish context, as opposed to larger countries like China [4].

This review was compiled following a *systematic literature review* method, hence a series of papers was selected and analyzed from prominent conferences within the field of education with a clear focus on CT. We chose conferences held within the Asian region, as these were more likely to include local studies than similar conferences held overseas (a more complete list of criteria is presented in [4]). Table 1 shows a summary of the data found in our review, based on our categorization and thematic analysis of the papers.

The adoption of CT for the East Asian region is developing at a similar pace as in Europe [5]. No government in the East Asian region is completely disregarding the importance of information technology and we see an increasing focus on CT in the area: even if not all country plans to directly teach CT or programming, they are all working towards integrating digital tools in schools.

From our survey, the countries that seem to be of most interest for our study are Hong Kong, South Korea, and Taiwan. In Taiwan CT has been already included into the curriculum for grade 7 through 12; CT is taught for 1 h a week for the first two grades and 2 h for the remaining 3 grades, initially focusing on coding, hence covering control structures, and data structures such as arrays and trees [15]. The official textbook that is going to be used for CT in Taiwanese primary schools suggests the use of MIT's Scratch for the initial courses and AppInventor for more advanced grades. Adopting MIT tools offers many advantages, they are high-quality and well-tested, web-bases and freely accessible, moreover, it is easy to find many books based on the use of such tools for both young adults and children. Hence, following MIT's and North American research appears to be regional as well as global trend.

Table 1. Summary of findings from our literary review.

Country	Status of CT Implementation	Focus/details
China	Implemented	Implemented a new national curriculum in 2017, which included CT
Japan	Working towards	Programming as a compulsory subject for students in primary and secondary schools and should be fully implemented by 2022
Hong Kong	Implemented	ICT and CT has been integrated into the curriculum since 2017, and is currently finalized a supplementary curriculum specifically for CT
Macau	No plans	Focused on computer literacy and the usage of digital tools such as word processing, spreadsheets, and database applications
Mongolia	No plans	Mongolia aims to increase the incorporation of ICT in the classroom and has the general goal to increase the digital literacy of the entire population
North Korea	No plans	
South Korea	Implemented	Started with a nationwide pilot in 2015 and was implemented as a compulsory part of the curriculum for primary and secondary schools in 2018
Taiwan	Implemented	Began in August of 2019 to require every student in secondary school to be fostered with CT competences. This has so far been achieved by integrating CT into the curriculums of other courses

Taiwan has seen, like Denmark, an increased focus on CT and other digital literacy skills from the side of *clubs*. Moreover, many activities are currently conducted in Taiwan, to connect CT teachers with IT experts and learning researchers. We are cooperating with the "Mini Educational Game development group" (NTUST MEG[1]) at the National Taiwan University of Science and Technology in Taipei, to plan further collection of data and observations in-situ in the coming semesters. Thanks to our network, we are currently conducting interviews with teachers from schools and clubs

---

[1] Official web-site: http://www.ntustmeg.net/about.asp.

in Taiwan (mainly in Taipei), to better understand the complementary roles of formal and informal learning settings with respect to CT education. Semi-structured interviews were chosen (and carried out over VoIP) as this allowed salient points to be explored in depth as they occurred, helping us to cope with possible misunderstanding that can easily result from the language barrier or the use of VoIP. Starting with few open-ended questions, the interviews proceeded as a free-flowing dialogue between the interviewees and interviewer. The aim of the interviews is to gather insight from teachers about their motivation, and experiences with CT.

4   Discussion

According to our preliminary findings, despite the sociocultural differences in pedagogical practices in Taiwan and Denmark, the effort of defining and integrating CT as a curricular subject has raised shared questions regarding:

- The relation between formal and non-formal learning practices,
- The relation of CT with other subjects either science or art and design,
- The relevance and necessity of coding as a learning goal.

Given that the term CT originates from North American learning research (e.g. from projects like MIT's lifelong kindergarten, Scratch [9], original and current definition of CT like Wing's), it is perhaps not surprising that we found that many countries are looking at the USA and in particular MIT's tools like Scratch as a de-facto standard starting point for the discussion regarding CT. Therefore, we consider North American research to be an unofficial shared reference for the implementation of CT programs in East Asian and Scandinavian countries alike, as well as in Taiwan and in Denmark.

4.1   Formal and Non-formal Learning Practices in CT

According to our data, the implementation of CT in Scandinavia as well as in East Asia CT has led school teachers to experiment further with non-formal learning practices, integrating forms of playful learning and gamification. In the terms of Vygostky [22], this trend has translated into the orchestration of shared CT learning activities, in which CT have been associated with creative thinking, so that the pupils are asked to create simple games or interactive animations in tools like Scratch or Blockly, under the supervision of teachers or external experts acting as guest lecturers. In this way, the pupils are encouraged to engage with coding in a playful and exploratory way, so that through the design process the pupils engage in conceptual thinking regarding how the choices they make for their code will affect their resulting game [22]. This way of working enables pupils to engage with peer-learning as well as gaining supervision from teachers, in relation to self-motivated development processes, as in a form of apprenticeship [23].

In both Taiwan and Denmark, primary schools are experimenting with short mini-courses in CT, lasting for about a week or two and held by external teachers. These teachers might be researchers from academic institutions or experts from IT companies, who are testing new tools or pedagogical approaches to CT. During a typical mini course the pupils would be required to develop a game in Scratch or would be introduced to programming via Minecraft[2] within a series of 1-day workshops across a few weeks. Among IT experts and academics, PhD students from the University of Southern Denmark were sent to primary schools to hold CT workshops on Minecraft and Scratch. Informal discussion with these PhD students suggests that interacting with a class of pupils and with teachers of varying degree of IT competences may produce inconsistent results in relation to children's learning, as they might be subject to inconsistent and discontinuous forms of training.

Interestingly, coding alone is not the central focus of these workshops, but instead programming is introduced, often via design processes, involving sketching, development, and testing. Similar forms of playful learning are typically adopted in afternoon clubs in both countries, where children are being introduced to CT through workshop-like activities lasting for a semester or a year [6]. Hence in both Danish and Taiwanese clubs, pupils are supposed to develop games, combining coding with design thinking. In this sense, in spite of cultural differences, both countries are exploring a non-formal learning approach to the learning of CT.

Being CT a new subject in formation, it is not clear yet if it might be integrated in other existing subjects and which subjects these might be. CT has been seen in this regard as belonging to Mathematics and Natural Sciences, since the theoretical foundation of CT is rooted in Mathematics and Computer Science. However, CT could also belong with Arts and Design, since the application of CT deals with the design and realization of digital artefacts (often, but not necessarily, of games). On the other hand, it has been proposed that the analytical mindset from CT [10] can be applied to any subject, including for instance text analysis in humanities. This, however, can cause issues regarding the background of teachers formed in the humanities, as they might be less trained in understanding the core elements of CT and algorithmic problem solving than teachers formed within sciences or design related subjects. Moreover, the introduction of CT in existing subjects might lead to redefining the curricula of those subjects, with a risk of compromising the core content of the same subjects, hence, a consensus has not been reached in this regard in neither countries. However, according to our data, it seems that in both countries CT is being increasingly linked to Arts and Design than Mathematics and the Natural Sciences. In fact CT is presented as a collection skills and activities such as: coding, hardware, game design, and 3D printing, and leveraging on design thinking as an interdisciplinary framework providing the backbone of CT learning activities. Moreover, design processes oriented towards interactive media and games are seen as more effective motivational resources for children, than activities related to mathematics, a subject notoriously perceived as challenging.

According to our data, informal and playful learning activities appear as dominant in both schools and clubs, moreover, it is increasingly the case that children have experienced CT before they encounter it in schools participating in clubs informal learning activities. Hence, there might be a need of a dialogue across non-formal and

---

[2] Official web-site for Minecraft: www.minecraft.net/.

formal institutions in both countries. Moreover, the broad use of non-formal learning in CT has also implication for pedagogical alignment (see Biggs [8]) and assessment in schools, hence teachers are experimenting with different ways to test their students' progress, moving towards project-oriented assignments, in which pupils are asked to develop different artefacts, to gather them in portfolios documenting the development process, and to present to the class and the teachers. In Denmark project-oriented assignments are common also in schools and are applied to different curricular subjects. Interestingly, portfolio evaluations (such as those adopted for CT) are graded as written or oral examinations, typically in a qualitative way; however, subjects like Mathematics usually prefer quantitative evaluations. We find that these experiments with assessment are interesting to follow and are necessary, but they emphasize the complexity of placing CT in the curriculum. Central aspects of project-oriented assignments in both countries are group work and peer-learning, which are integrated in the pedagogical approaches of Danish schools as well as clubs. Similarly in East Asia we have found an increasing adoption of gamification approaches, which can be interpreted as an attempt to open up the classroom to forms of apprenticeship-like teaching, where pupils gain points by taking more responsibilities in their own learning (in line with Biggs and active learning [8, 23]). In this sense, the quest of turning CT into a curricular subject is similarly challenging current learning practices and cultures across East Asia and Scandinavia, encouraging an increasing adoption of informal learning approaches, bridging formal and non-formal learning contexts.

Finally, according to our literature review and our dialogue with academics in Taiwan and Japan, we found that both East Asia and Scandinavia are looking at the USA (and the MIT in particular) as leading forces regarding pedagogical approaches and e-learning tools. As a result countries in both regions are adopting books by leading American academics directly or through translations and adaptations, and a tool chain typically based on Scratch, Python and AppInventor. Also the adoption of gamification for technically difficult subjects, the notion of re-conceptualization and re-use of games (e.g. chess for Math, microwords [24] for exploring various domains, etc.) for learning purposes, are inspired by North American research, although reframed within our respective pedagogical traditions. In this respect, in spite of cultural differences, we find that the implementation of CT as a school subject in Denmark and Taiwan is converging towards similar pedagogical models and the adoption of the same digital tools, inspired by the North American context. The emergence of CT as a school subject is challenging local learning cultures, forcing a more global perspective in education than other subjects with a longer didactic tradition like, for instance national languages or History.

4.2 The Role of Coding in CT

Another common challenge we identify from both East-Asian and Scandinavian perspectives regards the importance of programming as a learning goal, and even when focusing only on coding, as a part of programming, it is not easy to re-scale coding to fit the needs of primary school pupils.

Although we tend to agree that CT is not just programming and that coding is a subset of programming, all the approaches we have encountered consider programming (or at least coding) as a desirable but challenging learning goal of CT. In fact, most e-learning tools for CT are de facto aiming in different ways at introducing primary or secondary school pupils to programming [25]. This trend is due to the perception of programming as a precious 21st century skill in the global economy, providing an advantage in the job market to technical as well as humanistic graduates [11]. However, programming itself is not yet a school subject in many countries, not at the high school level, nor in primary schools. Therefore, CT appears as a holistic strategy to enable pupils to get closer to programming through creativity and applied problem-solving, avoiding the challenge of introducing in primary and secondary education Computer Science-related mathematical formalisms, which are found hard by technical students at the university level.

As many studies are simultaneously being conducted in different countries on CT, specifically on the definition of pedagogical approaches and curricula [10] and also on the development of e-learning tools, such as: games, block coding editors, or simplified hardware kits [6]. Hence an increasing number of primary and secondary schools are experimenting with teaching CT through courses or short workshops, led by teachers or external guests. As a result, we find that schools as institutions and individual teachers are experiencing increasing pressure in framing programming within their curricula and in finding proper tools, to enable their pupils to engage with and acquire CT knowledge and skills. In this respect, we find programming as the central challenge across Scandinavia and East Asia, requiring pedagogical framing as well as support from adequate e-learning tools, addressing the needs of pupils and teachers.

We have, therefore, surveyed existing tools for coding in primary schools and found (in line with [16]) that existing IDE for beginners, including the popular Scratch, MU editor, and Blockly-based visual IDEs, are conceptually created with a single user in mind: in general, coding tools assume a lone programmer. In the terms of Vygotsky [22] and Rogoff [23], we see that coding tools embody a perception of coding as an individual activity, therefore, they might not support adequately current orchestration strategies adopted in CT learning activities, which leverage forms of peer-learning and collaborative problem-solving. The computer itself is thought to afford individual use at the keyboard. Perhaps to compensate this lack of support, we find that CT activities are implicitly taking the form of an apprenticeship [23] supported by design thinking and peer-learning in which pupils are given group activities, to be further segmented into individual coding tasks. Game design is often chosen as non-formal, playful activity to encourage pupils to engage with programming and coding, shifting between individual and collaborative tasks.

Typical unsolved problems for the teachers in this area are addressing learners with substantially different skills in the same class, as it can be the case of a class mixing beginners and pupils with prior experience in CT from clubs, or when introductory courses mix students from different educations (as discussed in [12]). In such cases, teachers must be able to provide an activity suitable to pupils with different proficiency levels and avoid the programming version of the "alpha player problem" known in cooperative games, i.e. the tendency of one participant, not necessarily the most expert, to take over an activity and makes cooperation impossible for others. As a result we find that the learners who have the most need to practice will not practice enough to overcome their difficulties, while the stronger programmers in the group are those who practice the most, becoming even more proficient (a problem discussed also in the context of introductory programming courses at university level [12]). The need for planning and structure programming as a social practice is embodied in tools like Trello (trello.com), aimed at planning the activities of Scrum-teams, and platforms like Github provide not only ways to share the codebase, but also networking and management support for developers. However, these tools are typically aimed at advanced and older programmers, and have not been developed with primary school teachers and pupils in mind. Moreover, in professional "peer programming practices", there are well known roles that programmers can take at different stages of development, which are not explicitly supported by coding tools for pupils. Building on these insights, we identify a urgent need for coding tools, accessible to pupils, that regard coding as a social practice and learning to code as an apprenticeship, supporting small teams of learners in their process of crafting code and not just in dividing tasks.

5 Which E-learning Tools to Support CT?

Building on Vygotsky learning theory [22] as well as our preliminary data, our main contribution is the definition of a global-informed scenario (based on [2, 7] and [6]) and requirements for a new class of e-learning tools, capable of supporting emergent strategies in the learning of CT from a global perspective, such as:

- Support for peer-learning in small groups of pupils, leverage on Worked Examples in the form of functioning programs,
- Rely on the Use-Modify-Create approach, for instance by allowing pupils to work together at altering and adding to existing code,
- Support communication among learners and with teachers,
- Involve multiple subjects in the provided programs to allow discussions about technology in society.

As a domain for the provided functioning programs, we consider simple digital games, easy to reprogram, possibly expressed in simplified ways, such as blocks. In fact, building on our data, we find that game design has been adopted as a main domain for the learning of CT in East Asia as well as in Scandinavia, taking inspiration from the North American context, where popular tools like Scratch or Minecraft are specifically designed for supporting children in developing and altering games. Games are seen as fostering pupils' self-motivation, leveraging their interest for games in their everyday life, but also as a concrete domain enabling pupils to envision their final product, to make plans for their code, and the necessary steps to develop such product. In this respect, game development provides an apprenticeship framework, characterized by the goal of creating a game, in parallel to the goal of learning CT, in which kids and adults are mutually engaged [23]. Moreover, in game development as in apprenticeship pupils can learn from each other within their groups and also across other groups, developing similar games, and are allowed to gradually take over responsibility through their process, by planning their design process and distributing tasks with each other. In this way, learning to programming becomes an apprenticeship activity, in which learners are allowed to engage independently with the available coding tools and in making decisions on their process, while at the same time receiving support when reaching concepts and practices on the boundary of their Zone of Proximal Development [22, 23].

The scenario in Fig. 1 is based on [7] and inspired by the "Fabric Robotics" approach described in [6], and follows the Use-Modify-Create paradigm. In Fig. 1 the teacher has divided 5 pupils in 2 groups, and each group starts by using an existing project (possibly a simple game implemented in a block-based language). The group on the left in Fig. 1 is modifying their game and submits a new version to the teacher (or documentation that explains their design and implementation process), the other group (composed of 3 "green" pupils) is instead creating a completely new game, after having played the assigned one.

Scenario

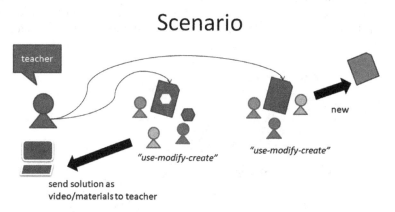

Fig. 1. Visualization of our scenario, with a teacher and learners working in small groups. (Color figure online)

According to these requirements and related learning scenario, the resulting tool would be a system to create and share digital games, easy to reprogram, and providing some form of real-time as well as asynchronous communication capabilities for collaborative learning. This tool should support the scenario in Fig. 1 and could for example be implemented as a generator of Jupyter Notebooks, specific to simple digital games and with block-based code instead of the usual textual commands. In our view, the ideal tool for supporting CT learning should embody the values and relevant functionalities to support an Apprenticeship learning scenario.

Moreover, we can see that in practice both Denmark and Taiwan are adopting a Use-Modify-Create approach, even if only Denmark is explicitly referring to it by name, converging towards constructivism and playful learning. The adoption of this approach might be due to the predominance of constructivist discourse in North American research on CT, which is implicitly informing other countries when they adopt the materials from MIT and similar institutions. In the Use-Modify-Create paradigm, children spontaneously engage in forms of conceptual thinking by playing with an artefact [22], like a computer game in CT activities, and that can enable them to reflect on the hypothetical changes they might perform on the given game and on its code. This approach can be seen as a pedagogical concretization of the concept of proximal development [22], according to which pupils need step by step support, from using to edit software, and finally to become creators of code, the final step in overcoming the challenges faced while reaching the boundary of their CT abilities. This progression also embodies the values from Apprenticeship learning, in which the pupils are supposed to become more in charge of their process, starting with full supervision, in this case translated into use of a given game, to end with independence and the ability to create a new game [22]. Finally this progression can be interpreted as an adaptation of Bloom taxonomy [26] to games-based learning practice for CT, in which the pupils are supposed to gradually reach the ability to use their knowledge to create something new. Based on these insights, we propose that coding tools for learning CT should embody this progression in their design and in the examples provided to the pupils, so to enable them to gradually engage with more complex tasks, in respect on their gradual process of learning to master coding (and possibly also programming).

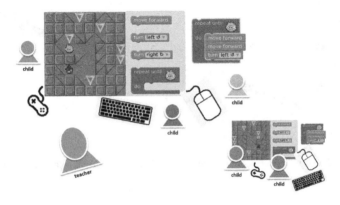

Fig. 2. A possible scenario of use for our new tool. Two groups of pupils work at the same game, with a teacher supervising both groups.

Figure 2 shows a possible situation where 2 groups of pupils are working on the same game, that they received from the CT teacher. Our new tool is used to distribute the game code and for communication among the groups and with the teacher, as well as for delivery of modified or new versions of the game. We propose that each child in Fig. 2 should have a different, explicit role while using the new tool. In the group with 3 "orange" pupils for example the left-most child is play-testing the game using a game controller, while at the same time talking with the child in the middle, who is close to a keyboard and therefore acts as the developer, altering the code to accommodate the feedback of the play-tested child. The third member of the group, on the right, could be using the mouse to take snapshots of interesting moments to document the gameplay as it changes because of the interaction of the tester and the coder.

6 Conclusion

This paper analyzes the emerging pedagogy of Computational Thinking as a new school subject, from an international perspective. Approaches from Scandinavian and East Asian are compared, focusing on Denmark and Taiwan. Preliminary findings from our analysis and initial interviews show that, despite sociocultural differences in pedagogical cultures, both countries are facing similar challenges related to the relationship between formal and non-formal learning practices, the positioning of CT with respect to other school subjects, and the effort to adapt North American discourse to the local educational traditions.

Coding emerges as a highly desirable and necessary activity within CT, as well as a central learning goal. One of the contributions of this paper is the identification of a lack of coding tools for small groups of pupils as a gap in CT e-learning. The other major contribution is the definition of a scenario and requirements for a new class of e-learning coding tools for better supporting emergent strategies in the learning of CT, such as: peer-learning, group-work especially for small groups of pupils, take advantage of pedagogical techniques like Use-Modify-Create and Worked Examples.

Future work involves cooperation with our contacts in Denmark, Taiwan and Japan to observe their practices in teaching programming within CT. We are currently developing, together with our international network, a prototype of a new e-learning tool, that will be tested in primary schools in both Scandinavia and East Asia.

References

1. Huang, C., Lin, H., Wang, S., Hou, H.: Designing a gamified activity with visual representation-based scenario and technology-based scaffoldings for learning electric potential. In: IEEE International Conference on Consumer Electronics - Taiwan (ICCE-TW), Yilan, pp. 1–2 (2019). https://doi.org/10.1109/ICCE-TW46550.2019.8991794.
2. Marchetti, E., Valente, A.: It takes three: re-contextualizing game-based learning among teachers, developers and learners. In: Connolly, T., Boyle, L. (eds.) Proceedings of The 10th European Conference on Games Based Learning, pp. 399–406. Academic Conferences and Publishing International (2016)
3. Kristensen, K.: Towards computational thinking in Scandinavia. In: 27th International Conference on Computers in Education, ICCE 2019, pp. 47–49. Asia-Pacific Society for Computers in Education (2019)
4. Kristensen, K.: Implementation of computational thinking in school curriculums across Asia. In: Stephanidis, C., Antona, M. (eds.) HCII 2020. CCIS, vol. 1225, pp. 269–276. Springer, Cham (2020). https://doi.org/10.1007/978-3-030-50729-9_38
5. Bocconi, S., Chioccariello, A., Earp, J.: The Nordic Approach to introducing Computational Thinking and programming in compulsory education. Report promoted and funded by the Nordic@BETT2018 Steering Group (2018). https://doi.org/10.17471/54007
6. Pedersen, B.K.M.K., Marchetti, E., Valente, A., Nielsen, J.: Fabric robotics - Lessons learned introducing soft robotics in a computational thinking course for children. In: Zaphiris, P., Ioannou, A. (eds.) HCII 2020. LNCS, vol. 12206, pp. 499–519. Springer, Cham (2020). https://doi.org/10.1007/978-3-030-50506-6_34

7. Valente, A., Marchetti, E.: From cards to digital games: closing the loop. In: 2017 6th IIAI International Congress on Advanced Applied Informatics (IIAI-AAI), pp. 507–510. IEEE (2017)
8. Biggs, J.B.: Teaching for Quality Learning at University: What the Student Does. McGraw-Hill Education, New York (2011)
9. Resnick, M.: The next generation of Scratch teaches more than coding (2019). https://www.edsurge.com/news/2019-01-03-mitch-resnick-the-next-generation-of-scratch-teaches-more-than-coding
10. Wing, J.M.: Computational thinking. Commun. ACM 49(3), 33–35 (2006)
11. Marchetti, E.: Bildung and the digital revolution. In: The University of the Future. Academic Conferences and Publishing International (2019)
12. Valente, A., Marchetti, E., Wang, J.: Design of an educational multimedia library to teach Python to non-technical university students. In: LCT: 6th International Conference on Learning and Collaboration Technologies. Springer, New York (2020). https://doi.org/10.1109/IIAI-AAI50415.2020.00041
13. Gee, J.P.: What Video Games Have to Teach us About Learning and Literacy. Palgrave Macmillan, New York (2007)
14. McGonigal, J.: Reality is broken: Why games make us better and how they can change the world. Penguin (2011)
15. Hsu, T.-C.: A study of the readiness of implementing computational thinking in compulsory education in Taiwan. In: Kong, S.-C., Abelson, H. (eds.) Computational Thinking Education, pp. 295–314. Springer, Singapore (2019). https://doi.org/10.1007/978-981-13-6528-7_17
16. Hsu, T.C., Chang, S.C., Hung, Y.T.: How to learn and how to teach computational thinking Suggestions based on a review of the literature. Comput. Educ. 126, 296–310 (2018)
17. UVM. Informatik C, hhx, htx, stx, hf Vejledning (2019). https://www.uvm.dk/gymnasiale-uddannelser/fag-og-laereplaner/laereplaner-2017/hhx-laereplaner-2017. Accessed 25 Feb 2021
18. UVM. Undervisningsvejledning for forsøgsfaget teknologiforståelse (2020). https://www.uvm.dk/-/media/filer/uvm/publikationer/folkeskolen/faghaefter/faelles-maal-2014/200813-teknologiforstaaelse-undervisningsvejledning.pdf. Accessed 25 Feb 2021
19. Atkinson, R.K., Derry, S.J., Renkl, A., Wortham, D.: Learning from examples: instructional principles from the worked examples research. Rev. Educ. Res. 70(2), 181–214 (2000)
20. Caspersen, M.E., Nowack, P.: Computational thinking and practice a generic approach to computing in danish high schools. In: Proceedings of the 15th Australasian Computing Education Conference, ACE 2013, Adelaide, pp. 137–143 (2013)
21. Lee, I., et al.: Computational thinking for youth in practice. ACM Inroads 2(1), 32–37 (2011)
22. Vygotsky, L.S.: Mind in Society. The Development of Higher Psychological Processes. Harvard University Press, Cambridge (1978)
23. Rogoff, B.: Apprenticeship in Thinking: Cognitive Development in Social Context. Oxford University Press, Oxford (1990)
24. Resnick, M., Silverman, B.: Some reflections on designing construction kits for kids. In: Proceedings of the 2005 Conference on Interaction Design and Children, pp. 117–122 (2005)
25. Sorva, J., Karavirta, V., Malmi, L.: A review of generic program visualization systems for introductory programming education. ACM Trans. Comput. Educ. (TOCE). 13(4), 1–64 (2013)
26. Selby, C.C.: "Relationships: computational thinking, pedagogy of programming, and Bloom's Taxonomy. In: Proceedings of the Workshop in Primary and Secondary Computing Education, pp. 80–87 (2015)

27. Børneog: Undervisningsministeriet. Midtvejsevaluering: Forsøg med teknologiforståelse fremmer faglighed og kompetencer (2020). https://xn–tekforsget-6cb.dk/wp-content/uploads/2020/05/Midtvejsevaluering-Maj-2020.pdf. Accessed 25 Feb 2021
28. Johnson, D.W., Johnson, R.T.: Cooperative learning. In: The Encyclopedia of Peace Psychology (2011)
29. van de Oudeweetering, K., Voogt, J.: Teachers' conceptualization and enactment of twenty-first century competences: exploring dimensions for new curricula. The Curriculum J. **29**(1), 116–133 (2018)
30. Tedre, M., Denning, P.J.: The long quest for computational thinking. In: Proceedings of the 16th Koli Calling Conference on Computing Education Research, Koli, pp. 120–129 (2016)
31. Lave, J., Wenger, E.: Situated Learning: Legitimate Peripheral Participation. Cambridge University Press, Cambridge (1991)
32. Smith, P.K., Cowie, H., Blades, M.: Understanding Children's Development. Blackwell Publishing, Hoboken (2003)

The Effects of the Sudden Switch to Remote Learning Due to Covid-19 on HBCU Students and Faculty

Mariele Ponticiello[1]([✉]), Mariah Simmons[2], and Joon-Suk Lee[1]

[1] Virginia State University, Petersburg, VA 23806, USA
mpon3004@students.vsu.edu
[2] Dominion Energy, Richmond, VA, USA

Abstract. The outbreak of the Covid-19 pandemic had wide-reaching effects on the education system. The general response of schools and universities was to shut down non-essential campus operations, as learning and instruction became remote. The switch to remote learning protected against the spread of Covid-19, but it also had secondary effects, like the closure of university labs and libraries. This study seeks to understand if students and faculty had the tools and workspace conditions to continue to teach and learn effectively. The sudden switch to remote learning had the most significant impact on participants whose home environment does not provide for a private workspace. There was a clear trend to engage less. Participants overall find video lectures less engaging. Some participants struggle learning materials. Others changed their approach to academic learning to rely more on self-learning.

Keywords: Remote learning · Covid-19 · HBCU · Technology access · Adequate remote learning environment · Adequate working environment

1 Introduction

1.1 The Switch to Remote Learning Due to the Covid-19 Pandemic

The outbreak of the Covid-19 pandemic had wide-reaching impact on the education system. The general response of schools and universities was to shut down non-essential campus operations, as learning and instruction became remote. Students and faculty had to suddenly change their instruction and learning methods from in-person to remote. Some switched from one day to the next, others had a week or two to prepare. In any case, it was a very sudden and significant change. Universities and schools provided learning and teaching tools so that all students could have access with the necessary to be successful. The switch to remote learning helped reduce the spread of Covid-19, but the decision to close down campus operations and facilities such as university labs and libraries created detrimental impact on education and learning.

On the onset of the pandemic, there were already educational inequalities in place that affect student success [8, 9, 14, 18, 22, 23]. Much previous research clearly documents the correlation between low-socioeconomic status (SES) and low academic performance in children [9, 14, 15]. Students from marginalized racial groups are also

© Springer Nature Switzerland AG 2021
P. Zaphiris and A. Ioannou (Eds.): HCII 2021, LNCS 12784, pp. 488–506, 2021.
https://doi.org/10.1007/978-3-030-77889-7_34

known to have limited access to learning resources [18]. Students with low resources are at a disadvantage to their more affluent peers [9, 14, 15, 22, 23]. Recent research shows such gap has widened after the pandemic [15, 17, 19].

In this research, we document (1) how HBCU students experienced the sudden societal and educational changes, and (2) how Covid-19 affected HBCU students. This research also aims to explore the extent to which the switch to remote learning exacerbated already existing inequalities.

We found that students and faculty were impacted by the pandemic directly, and also by the challenges presented by remote learning. The former was loss of life or health of persons close to participants, reported by some, and the fear and stress of living in a pandemic, more frequent and pronounced in the case of participants with high-risk family members. Remote learning presented participants with challenges and in some cases obstacles that had not been present in the in-person learning environment.

With respect to the remote learning environment, the sudden switch to remote learning had the most significant impact on participants whose home environment does not provide for a private workspace. The participants that faired best in remote learning were those that adapted to the remote situation by managing those distractions or finding new ways of learning. There was a clear trend to engage less in lectures. Participants overall find video lectures less engaging. Some participants struggle learning materials. Others changed their approach to academic learning to rely more on self-learning.

With respect to engagement, there was a clear trend toward less engagement both among peers and between students and their instructors. Exceptions were participants who were able to adapt to new technologies to replace in-person communication in order to create or maintain connection. The remote classroom seems to be a more difficult place for students to participate, because social interaction is less "natural" in an online classroom than in an in-person classroom.

Finally, we address the resourceful ways participants are adapting. Participants are changing the ways and spaces in which they learn. They are adapting new technologies to create and maintain connections.

2   Related Works

2.1   Research on Online Learning

Online learning has provided an alternative mode of education for students who cannot physically be present on the college campus that they are enrolled at. Some students have used online learning as a way to learn if they don't have transportation to their campus or if they have a job that interferes with their class times [5]. Several studies have investigated online learning in regard to student/teacher interaction (e.g., [16]), mental health (e.g. [3, 7, 10, 13]), and student engagement (e.g. [3, 13, 16, 20]).

A research study looked into online learning platforms and the benefits that it provides. In the study, the authors list greater freedom of access, lower education prices, flexibility of education, and the ability to keep up with modern pace of life as the main advantages of online learning [16]. Scholars have also investigated technology issues that students may encounter while taking online classes [6, 10]. Such technology issues may prevent students from completing their assignments on time or even leading them to miss their class sessions. Previous research also reports that some students have limited or no access to internet connection which is a necessity when taking online or remote learning courses [1].

2.2 Research on Remote Learning and Learning Management Systems (LMS)

Remote learning has become the primary source of education for many students since the outbreak of the Covid-19 pandemic [5]. Students experienced the sudden transition from in-person learning to being in their houses and having to figure out how to continue learning from their homes. Being remote also means that students can no longer interact with their professors and classmates in person, which can be an essential part in their learning [16]. Also, social gatherings on college campus may have helped many students de-stress from schoolwork while socially engaging with other students. An article investigating remote learning suggests that college institutions recreate the in-person gathering experiences on the online settings as well as enable social interactions amongst students so that they can still feel a sense of connectivity to their campus and the school body [11].

Many students are now relying on their college's LMS to receive their work and to communicate with their teacher and classmates. Previous research has investigated the use of LMS in education and its disadvantages and advantages [2, 10, 16, 21]. Alokluk [2], for instance, shares a list of online teaching principles that can be considered as best practices. These principles include encouraging active learning, giving student feedback, and encouraging faculty and student interaction.

3 Methodology

3.1 Overview

The analysis in this paper is based on data from an interview-based study and also from a survey study we conducted during the Fall of 2020. To investigate the effects of the sudden switch to remote instruction, we conducted interviews with students and faculty from four different universities in Virginia. We also conducted an online survey with students and faculty whose studies and instruction, respectively, became remote due to the Covid-19 pandemic to understand their experience in the remote learning environment.

3.2 Participants

We recruited participants from a pool of faculty, students and alumni from Virginia State University, a historically black public land-grant university in Petersburg, Virginia. We also used the snowballing method to recruit additional students from NSU

(Norfolk State University), UVA (University of Virginia), and Old Dominion. A total of twenty-four participants were interviewed (13 males, 11 females). The participants' ages ranged from 18 to 40. Twenty-three participants were students or faculty at an HBCU. Twenty-two participants were at Virginia State University, while one participant was from another HBCU, Norfolk State University. Of the twenty-two Virginia State University participants, one participant first experienced the switch to remote learning at VSU during the Spring semester of 2020, and joined University of Virginia, a Predominantly White University (PWI) where he again experienced remote learning in the Fall of 2020. We also had one participant attending Old Dominion University, which is now considered a Minority serving institution (MSI).

Twenty-one participants (88%) identified themselves as African American, one participant as Hispanic/Latino, one as Asian, and one as other. Nine participants (38%) were between 22–25 years old, eight participants (33%) between 18–21, four participants (17%) between 26–29, two participants (8%) between 30–35, and one participant (4%) between the 36–40. Nine participants (38%) were graduate students, nine participants (38%) were seniors, two participants (8%) were faculty, two participants (8%) were juniors, one participant (4%) was a sophomore, and one participant (4%) was a freshman. The participants were also asked if they had taught or taken an online class before. Thirteen participants (52%) stated "yes", and twelve participants (48%) stated "no".

3.3 Interview

Interviews were semi-structured and conducted over a video conferencing platform. The interviewer had both their video display and microphone activated. The participant had their microphone activated and was given an option to turn their video on. Some left their video off and others had it activated. Interviews lasted from 15–45 min. The interviews were audio-recorded and transcribed. We also collected demographic information for each participant prior to the interview through a pre-study questionnaire.

3.4 Survey

Along with conducting interviews with college students and staff, we also conducted a survey that was distributed to current college students. The survey was distributed by the second author to students who then distributed it to their peers. She also distributed survey via college chat groups. No monetary compensation was provided to participants. We received a total of 56 survey responses. The survey covered a range of questions that dealt with Covid-19 and how it may have impacted the life of a college student. To get a clear idea of its impact, we asked questions regarding their educational and personal experience. Questions regarding feelings and emotions, social life, and educational experiences were asked. The participants were asked to rate their responses to the questions by using Likert Scale sliders or button selections to indicate their ratings from 0 to 7 or in some cases, 1 to 7. There were a few yes/no questions that were also asked.

3.5   Interview Data Analysis

The interview data were fully transcribed and read multiple times by the researchers. During the initial analysis, both first and second authors looked at the interview data together and developed an initial coding scheme. The first author went through the interview data in multiple iterations to find recurrent themes in participants' data. After developing the first-round coding scheme, the first and second authors again refined the coding categories and finalized the coding scheme by conducting open and axial coding [4, 24]. The final coding scheme consisted of three top-level categories, eleven second-level categories and fifty third-level categories.

4   Findings

There were three areas of interest in our findings: Health, Life, and Education. The findings in Health revealed that participants have been affected by anxiety and fear of losing family members, caused by the Covid-19 pandemic. Those most affected were participants that had high-risk family members. Participants in general reported mental drain from the remote learning modality, though there were also benefits reported in that remote learning provided participants with the flexibility to work and the access to recorded lectures. In Life, findings reveal that a significant number of participants have had social costs of remote learning. It is more difficult to make connections with peers and have the same level of communication with instructors. However, it's important to note that several participants noted little effect on their social life, and some benefit of not having to interact as much in social and academic spaces. Education findings reveal that in the remote learning environment, it is a significant advantage to have a private study space. Also, participants generally adapted to having campus resources removed, but were not able to fully replace them. This is significant because it creates a significant disadvantage for students unable to access private reliable internet, dedicated study space, appropriate technology tools to replace the campus-wide resources lost in the switch to remote. There was a general trend to engage less in the remote classroom than the in-person classroom, and decreased communication both among peers and between peers and their professors.

4.1   Health

We asked participants how they had been affected on a personal level by Covid-19. Overall, the significant impact that the pandemic has had on the participant has been the death of family members in two cases, the serious infection of family members, and the high-risk status of family members that created anxiety and fear in participants. One participant reported having been infected with Covid-19. Three participants (P1, P17, P13) reported having family members that had been sick with Covid-19. Participant 13 reported having a family member that had to be hospitalized for approximately two months due to Covid-19. Three participants reported having family members that were high-risk. Three of the participants mentioned here described being "scared" or the situation as "scary" when describing their family members being sick with Covid-19 or having a family member that is high-risk. One participant had two family members that were infected.

These are participants for whom living through the pandemic entails living with the fear of losing a family member. These are members of a group of participants living with anxiety and fear directly caused by the pandemic's health risk to people close to them. Participant 9, who lives with a person who is high-risk, explained having to travel to attend a funeral (not Covid-19-related). She stated that traveling made them "*anxious*," and described worry not know "*who was taking it seriously*," referencing their high-risk family members and participant's concern for them. Participant 10 and 22 have family members that are high risk and describe living with some level of fear:

> "*my parents are old and they have health conditions that put them at risk, so I have to be very careful. And it's scary because they still have to work.*" (P10)

> "*No, um because my dad is high uh he's highly like he's high like rate, like he can get it faster than a lot of people, and he's bed bound, so I've been too scared to try to go out, and I don't wanna bring anything in the house that he may not be able to fight off.*" (P22)

The participants with high-risk family members are most directly affected by the health risks of the pandemic. As demonstrated in this section, the risk of infection increased their level of fear, having an effect on their mental state. In the following section we explore the overall affect of the pandemic and remote learning on participants' mental health.

Mental Health

Stress and Mental Drain

We asked participants about how the pandemic and the switch to remote learning had affected their mental health. Although, often participants gave descriptions of their mental state in response to more general questions. For example, when asked about their overall viewpoint of Covid-19, participant 9 used "*scary*" to describe how they were experiencing it. As mentioned in the preceding section, participants who reported having a high-risk family member or member of their household, or who had family members infected with Covid-19 reported feeling "*anxious*," "*worried*," or "*scared*," or a combination of these (P9: "*scary*," "*anxious*," high risk family members; P10: "*scary*," parents high-risk; P17: mom, brother infected with Covid-19, mom's illness "*scary*"). Participant 10 also described their experience of the pandemic as "*scary*," and refers to their parents being high-risk.

Participant 17 reported that they were "*nervous to be outside*" after switching from a job in which they could work from home to one that didn't allow for remote work. They also said they had seen people around them with Covid-19, and "*how scary it is.*" Participants reported some level of mental drain from dealing with the pandemic, citing the risk of doing simple activities, the drain from not being able to see family members, or the burnout from being in front of a screen so repetitively. Participant 7 reported losing their job due to Covid-19 and having to move back in with their parents.

> "*it's scary being around other people because you don't know if you're gonna catch it, and I'm less worried about me catching it and more worried about me giving it to my parents.*" (P7)

Motivation and Morale

One theme that various participants brought up was the morale and motivation level. Often participants mentioned benefits of remote learning—not having to commute, greater flexibility in their schedules that allows them to work, etc.—contrasting this with the drawbacks they've faced. For various participants, one of these drawbacks was the toll on their and others' motivation and morale. Participant 4 said that the difference that they experienced regarding the communication they have with their professors was that *"they're not as excited."* Participant 5 reported that this experience of remote learning made them realize that their routine of getting ready and commuting to class actually played a role in mentally preparing them to study, and that learning from home has presented a challenge in morale. Participant 7 also struggles with motivation attending video lectures:

> *"It's harder to stay motivated and it's easy to get distracted. It's really difficult to pay attention during a Zoom lecture...it's hard to like stay excited and engaged, and that's affecting our professors as well. So you can like, by the way that they're teaching, especially cause they're not getting active feedback anymore."* (P7)

Not all participants experienced increased stress and mental drain as participants in remote learning. Participant 24 has decreased anxiety learning from their remote environment due to the fact that the in-person learning environment is anxiety-producing:

> *"I just never liked being in class. It's not my thing. It gives me high anxiety. So being remote you know I have the option if I want to turn on my camera or not. And I usually don't, I mostly don't. And so that helps me with my anxiety a lot...The workload doesn't affect my anxiety. Like what affects my anxiety is the one day we had to turn on our cameras. And I haven't been turning on my cameras, so I was panicking like oh I haven't had to turn on my camera in months and now look I got to turn on my camera."* (P24)

4.2   Life

Social Impact

One of the patterns emerged in our data analysis was **reduced or changed social routines**. Participant 22 went from seeing friends almost daily to no longer participating in these social activities, explaining that it is because their dad is high-risk, and she is too scared to go out and possibly bringing home infection that their father couldn't fight off. Participant 16 explained that before, they would hang out with their friends at their house. Now, they rely on the connection via online games to interact with some friends, and they have lost connection with other friends who they used to see regularly in person. Participant 15 used to see their friends in person on Saturdays, and since the pandemic, they talk mostly via Snapchat or similar platforms.

Participant 12 realized a lack of support socially, that the situation showed them that not everyone in their social circle is a genuine friend. They are focusing on working on themselves. In the case of participant 7, they ended various relationships, with a partner and with some friends, due to the way those people approached the pandemic without following the safety protocols (e.g., continuing face-to-face meetings in groups).

There were various participants that reported little change due to the fact that they didn't socialize much generally anyway either because they were focused on work/school or because they were just not generally social, *"homebody,"* *"introvert,"* etc. (P1, P3, P5, P17, P24). However, a significant number of participants reported experiencing a change in relationships.

Participant 9 reported a similar situation in not having seen friends since the pandemic began in March 2020 and that a contributing factor to following protocols so strictly was concern for her high-risk family member. Participant 14 also stopped seeing *"multiple people"* completely with no idea as to when he will once again be able to see them. Participant 22's social life had changed in that they can no longer do community outreach which was an important activity for her. Participant 13 is one of various participants that spoke to the fact that social interactions among peers was much more limited in remote learning:

"you meet these people, you know these people, get their numbers, exchange numbers and stuff, like that. Now it's just like it's just a whole bunch of random people in a chat room and we all go our separate ways when class is over." (P13)

On the other hand, participant 8 had a positive social outcome from the pandemic. Because their classes and work switched to remote, they were able to quarantine with their mom and spend more time together.

Economic

A significant number of participants reported economic effect. A small number reported economic benefits from less spending, or a job opportunity offered by the pandemic. More frequent, participants reported income loss and job loss. In one example, participant 22's hours at their job were reduced from approximately 45 h weekly to approximately just five. Several participants lost jobs due to Covid-19.

Benefits

Overall, participants like elements of remote learning that were unavailable in in-person learning. They tended to prefer the access to recorded lectures and the flexibility that remote learning affords them: this allows them to work or saves them resources by not having to commute. Although participants tended to prefer in-person learning overall, there was a distinct tendency to prefer *elements* of remote learning: access to recorded lectures, and the flexibility to learn from a remote location.

Participant 17 highlighted that they usually don't have space in their schedule to both have a job, study, and play sports. But due to current circumstances, they thankfully can work. Participant 3 also cites this benefit: *"I don't mind remote because like I said I work full time and it be kind of hard for me to take off work to make it to class."*

For some of the participants that identified as an introvert or homebody or not socializing much (even prior to the pandemic), it is a benefit to not have to go out continuously, or not having to be around people as one of the benefits of the secondary effects of the pandemic, even noting a decrease in anxiety in one case.

4.3 Education

In this section we examine the effect that remote learning and the sudden switch from in-person to the distance model had on the participants. We present these findings in three subsections. Subsection one, Remote Learning Experience, examines the overall impact on learning and general issues that were caused by the pandemic and the measures put in place in response to the pandemic. The second subsection examines how being remote changed the communication and relationships among peers and between students and their professors, as well as among faculty. Subsection three examines participant's remote environment: did they have access to an adequate working space and technology? Was their remote location the cause of costs or benefits in learning or listed in other sections? Here, we would like to point out two key focus points. The first point is that a significant portion of the difficulties reported by participants seem to be difficulties inherent in remote learning for a student or teacher that is not used to carrying out this learning modality. The second key point is that any additional costs to student beyond these difficulties are costs relating to a lack of resources. An example is internet connection that impedes a student's ability to attend all class times or do coursework, because not all households have access to a high-speed reliable internet connection. Another example are the participants that don't have a workspace dedicated to study or work, because there is no extra space in the home to be converted to an office space. The pandemic caused the closure of some of the resources that previously gave students options. We are concerned to what extent Covid-19 exacerbated already existing inequalities by reducing access to university and public resources that allow for universal access to educational materials that support student success.

Remote Learning Experience. Overall, students reported that learning had become more difficult and more independent. Participants that reported the increased difficulty experienced it in a range of ways: some participants reported that they became better self-teachers, that the experience of studying through the pandemic built their character, that they developed discipline. Some participants reported being a student was harder, and academically things were worse: less learning, issues retaining information, distracted learning. A significant number of participants reported both benefits and costs. As mentioned in previous sections, there was a trend to have benefited from the flexibility provided by remote learning, but costs were reported in terms of difficulty learning the material.

The Transition. Some participants were unable to complete research or coursework because they suddenly lost access to labs and research facilities. One participant reported not being able to access adequate technology to complete a course:

> *"When Covid hit...and they shut everything on campus down I couldn't take my test because they were on lockdown browser and my camera wasn't working at the time. So I ended up failing the class because I couldn't go any place to get my camera fixed and then on top of that my professor was not trying to work with me."* (P11)

The speed at which remote learning was implemented meant that significant parts of participants' lives were changed. Participant 17 was active in university sports and found out the day of that the season was canceled. Her team tried to continue with distance training, but it was too much for the coaching team and various members of coaching staff left during the Spring 2020 transition. Participant 14 was left without housing. His solution was housing with a friend, but this entailed traveling across state lines before social distancing on planes was implemented. He considers himself lucky to have not been infected on this trip.

Discipline, Self-learning, Distracted Learning, Issues Retaining Information

All participants reported less structure and more freedom after the switch to remote learning: they no longer had to be physically present. Most participants interviewed do not have to be visibly present even virtually. Another new freedom is access to course materials. There were interesting results with respect to this less structured learning and in a sense more freedom as a student. One result is the self-learning by students. For example, participants 10 and 14 both reported a new pacing in their learning that was less dependent on the course pace: they took advantage of the availability of the materials to advance at times ahead of the lecture-to-date. Participant 10 said that her professors were *"on it"* in terms of making sure the materials were available for students so that she could take initiative to study ahead. Participant 24 said that in the new learning modality, you *"definitely"* have to self-teach. Participants 10 and 17 explained how they have adapted to distance learning:

> *"I would say depending on the class it was beneficial because um I kind of learned how to uh do things my own way without anyone watching..."* (P10)

> *"so I never ever log into class or do work in my room because my room is not an environment I'm in when I'm focused...Whenever I'm doing homework or I'm in class I literally sit at the same place in my dining room, I prop my laptop up, I get all of my stuff out to get focused for... And now I'm more engaged in my classes, at first, I wasn't. I wasn't comfortable with zoom or getting on the camera and talking like it just wasn't my cup of tea. But now I come to enough of my classes where I'm attentive, I turn my camera on, I'm engaged and that's always been helpful."* (P17)

There was a clear trend of the benefit of having access to the class recording. A significant number of participants cited this as a benefit of distance learning. For example, participant 14 stated that he like being able to work through the material and not necessarily have to wait on the lectures. Participant 17 cited recordings as a positive also:

> *"But some record them and post them so you can go back and watch them and take notes on it. So that's one thing I really do like. So even if you do miss a class you don't miss it because you can watch it later."* (P17)

Harmed Learning, Learning Quality Change, Lack of Explanation, Unconcerned Teachers

Overall, participants reported that there were new challenges in the remote environment. There were participants that reported a negative impact in the quality of their education. There were participants that reported no impact in the quality of their education. One notable finding was the perceived loss of the ability to interact with the professor's explanation in real time: multiple participants said that in the in-person classroom, there was more opportunity to interject if they didn't follow a topic, or more opportunity for professors to see who was struggling to give space for review. Some of these participants had no way to interact with professors during lectures because professors posted pre-recorded lectures (asynchronous classes). Others reported it was more difficult to interject in the online (synchronous) classroom. Participants explained that in a physical environment, professors can *"see"* who is not grasping a topic and make the decision to review or address confusion. Participants explained that in an in-person classroom, they can ask their neighbor to explain a point they didn't understand. Or that multiple people can speak at once in a classroom in a natural way, without obstructing the other conversations, and this allows for greater interaction than in and online space.

Participants 10 and 12 are examples of students that view their education as negatively impacted; participant 10 had some classes that were asynchronous. Some of her professors decided to just "put the work up," citing that they didn't meet (for class). Participant 12 does view her education as being negatively impacted:

> *"I feel like I'm not really learning anything. Because they're just reading PowerPoints… We're not practicing, we're not trying to store the information in our brains."* (P12)

She cited study groups led by her SI leader as an activity that helped her learn prior to remote learning, that hasn't been replaced by a new technology. Participant 17 also identify with this perspective: *"I feel like remote learning now for some bizarre reason I don't understand because it's so backwards"* (P17) Participant 9 cited the added stress in general during the pandemic as a cause of a decrease in education quality:

> *"people are really stressed out about this time of uncertainty so I think a lot of professors aren't necessarily intentionally not doing their job well but you know they have their own families and their own kids they have to worry about."* (P9)

She explained that because of this, their teaching responsibilities come second or third. She also cited that some professors *"throw so much work at you,"* not considering students' other classes or even that some students are parents as well. As to preference, she stated that while she stills does well learning remotely, *"education value-wise, in-person is way better."*

Participant 17 reported that some professors do a great job while others do a very poor job in remote teaching. Referring to one of her professors, participant 17 said that she (professor) is *"the best in regards to communication… she does really well with communicating on blackboard, giving us descriptions to the assignment."* She contrasted this with one professor from a different class she is taking: *"…We are at finals and I still haven't seen a syllabus."* She described the policy of another professor:

> *"…that's one of the professors that has no exceptions at all like he doesn't care that its covid like it's very hard… and when you give him an excuse like hey like I'm doing blah blah blah will you still take the assignment, he's like no sorry there's no exceptions no. Nothing no and I'm just like you can't have a little bit of leeway, like we are literally in a pandemic."* (P17)

Students seem to view the online courses as less responsive especially when students struggle in the class. Students in general stated that asynchronous classes do not allow for students to signal when they need more explanation or when they don't understand (e.g., P14). But participants also stated that it is still more difficult to signal or interject in the remote learning synchronous classroom than in a physical classroom (e.g., P18). One participant (P10) conjectures it may be because students are in an environment where they won't be heard. It is worth examining if this is generally the case, and the implications for students that don't have access to a quiet space, or if there are other reasons why students find professors less accessible during remote class. We found that students do not find it as easy to interrupt a lecture to signal they are not understanding in a remote classroom.

"Compared to in person they can tell you like...'oh yeah you are struggling here' or like 'everyone in the class got these wrong so we are going to work on this'...Compared to remote learning some people don't turn their cameras on some people don't even respond when the professor is talking to say they got it. Or ask questions because they are not in a location where they can be heard...So I think that what I didn't like. And that's why I prefer in person." (P10)

"Instead of watching a recording and you hit a point in the video where you're completely lost, and you're lost from that point on, and you can't really progress until the next time you interact with the professor." (P14)

"At times I feel like I've learned more in person than remote learning again because of the situation where I could walk up to my professor if I had a question in the middle of class or right after class. But other than that I don't think much has really changed." (P18)

One interesting finding was the clear trend in perceived increased workload from Spring to Fall 2020. Sometimes participants conjectured that professors were assigning more work because they were assuming that students were at home and idle. Various participants referenced the increased workload. Some participants said that they were overwhelmed by the increase. One participant described it as professors *"throwing work"* at students.

Communication and Relationships Between Teachers and Students, Among Faculty, and Among Peers

Communication Teacher-Student

Communication has been predictably impacted in a significant way as teacher-student interactions have become remote. One faculty member reported that their freshman students do not all check email regularly or even open Slack, the two methods he uses to communicate: *"So even though I uh communicate multiple times, there are still students who will miss the memo, as they say."* (P1).

In response to how is has been to interact with professors and classmates since the switch to online learning, participant 5 explained: *"Oh...much worse. You know like it's really hard to interact."* Participant 6 actually prefers remote learning in general, but cited the interaction with professors as one of the losses in the move to remote:

"I miss the one-on-one interaction with the um professors. And in person you're still getting that um but a big part of the reason why I um love my program..." (P6)

Participant 13 also cited a lower interaction, saying: *"it's like we really don't interact that much, it's like the professor gets on, or teaches, and then that's it. Like I I personally don't interact too much."* For participant 17 and 15, it is harder to ask questions in the remote classroom and to communicate with instructors and peers. Whereas, participant 22 has had a very positive experience, citing one professor she regularly communicates with when questions come up:

"And I feel like it's kind of harder for me to ask questions on Zoom because one I don't want to take up someone's time and I like to have one on one with my professors after class or go to their office hours." (P17)

"The interaction with like with other students, or uh the um professor, you know, it's you know it's online, it's not like. You can't just talk to 'em, like straight, like any time during the class." (P15)

"They're awesome... Yeah, like Slack has been like I uh Doc—uh I speak to one of my professors all the time, like when I have questions. So Slack is that thing that that's very convenient for these times." (P22)

Participant 9, 10 and 14 had a professor that weren't available, seeming to take advantage of the remote learning to be less responsive. Participant 10 was another student that cited less review of topics compared to in-person learning:

"Compared to in person they can tell you like... "oh yeah you are struggling here" or like "everyone in the class got these wrong so we are going to work on this" That didn't happen anymore like with remote learning." (P10)

Communication Among Faculty

The faculty members interviewed reported that colleagues are responsive in email, and that there are weekly department meetings that allow for communication with other faculty members. One faculty member cited that when staff and faculty worked on campus, it was very convenient to convene or collaborate having everyone in the same place. He also continued to communicate with colleagues remotely but did highlight that it was not as beneficial as working in the same physical space.

Communication Among Peers

As in the case of instructor-student interactions, communication and interactions among peers has overall decreased. Overall, we note a trend to decreased interaction among peers that in general was a difficulty for students. However, there was at least one participant who stated that she benefitted from not having to be in class with peers. There were participants that cited the interaction with peers from in-person learning as something that they missed. Participant 5 described remote learning as having little social interaction among peers. He stated that while in-person learning gives space to talking with colleagues and friends before and after class, there isn't space for this in the virtual classroom. Participant 7 highlighted pros and cons to remote learning. She cited the zero commute (which allows her the time to work) as a pro, but the lack of peer interaction as the main drawback:

"But the negative part is kind of harder to connect with your classmates. I've made a few friendships but they're all like through text or Facetime or something and it's just it's not the same...I think unlike in a real classroom, it's distracting when multiple people are talking, um, like if you're in a room, and there's a group of people who are talking or someone's talking and a professor's talking, it's just it's more natural. But through video, if multiple people are talking, it's confusing." (P7)

Participants 13 and 14 described decreased interaction in the remote learning environment:

"it's like we really don't interact that much, it's like the professor gets on, or teaches, and then that's it. Like I I personally don't interact too much." (P13)

"So what she does on Zoom is make breakout sessions, break out rooms, sorry. So it's randomly assigned, so you don't know what group you're going to be in, so you end up in a room, and say the group is five people. Four people will have their microphone off the camara off, and you now have to do a group assignment." (P14)

Participant 24 also described very little interaction with peers during remote learning; she's part of a group chat, but doesn't talk in the chat, preferring to talk via text with one or two peers only. Interviewer asked participant 24 how this compares to peer interaction during in-person learning, asking how often she interacts with peers or asks questions. Participant said, *"I mean I can't really put a number on it. Just you know when I need help. But I know I talk to them way more in person than I do now."*

Remote Location

Loss of Supplies/Resources

Overall, participants reported some loss of recourses. Commonly, resources that they lost when learning became remote were the library as a quiet place where they could have focused study, and the lab where students had access to software they needed for their courses. At least one participant reported currently needing a printer and not having access to one. Participant 7, among others, cited the library. Participant 13 also said that *"definitely the library"* was a resource that she used as an undergrad (when learning was on campus) *"probably like once a week."* Participant 22 said that she used the library to print. When asked where she prints since the library closure due to the pandemic, she replied that she needed to get a printer (but currently uses apps as a replacement). Participant 11 also cited the library as a resource used prior to the pandemic:

"So most of the time when I used to do that I would go into the library and get my homework done but now that you can't go into the library anymore." (P11)

Inadequate Internet Connection

Participants interviewed had access to in-home internet. There were some participants that reported losing connection periodically. A small number of participants had breaks in connectivity that resulted in missing at least some class time. We also discuss ways in which participants had to adjust to relying on their private internet connection.

Participant 8 moved back to her family's home when things became remote and had to adjust to the inconsistent internet. She had to up the data on her phone to use it as a mobile hotspot. She has since moved to an urban area with better internet, but reported that even here the internet connection drops once a day.

Participant 16 reported that in Spring semester 2020, he got kicked out of his internet about twice per class in that semester, and sometimes got kicked out of his internet at the beginning of Fall 2020 semester. He reported that now his internet is stable. Participant 10 lost Wi-Fi the day her finals were due. She also reported it being "rough" that sometimes due to professors' bad internet kicking them (the professor) out of class.

"Sometimes I would have poor connection so like sometimes if my professors tried to talk to me, I couldn't respond, or it would be choppy, or they couldn't hear me." (P10)

Participant 3 connected to classes via his phone and reported that he lost service *"here or there"* but was able to connect to classes a majority of time. Participant 11 generally connects from her laptop, but sometimes has to log out of the Zoom meeting and join from her phone when the connection is bad.

Inadequate Technology (Device)

The switch to remote learning has exacerbated existing inequalities between students. Prior to Covid-19, students who could afford reliable internet, a good computer and printer had access to these devices. (In this context we define *good* as a reliable device that can run all software required by student's courses.) They likely had their one laptop, and either purchased a printer or used the ones available on campus. Students who could not afford a good computer and printer still had access to a computer on which they could run the necessary software for their classes and also a printer. But now, the latter category might be left simply without access to adequate technology. Two participants did not have computers that could handle the software necessary for their major: one used some savings to buy a new laptop. One uses a Chromebook and codes on repl.it (an online I.D.E). Participant 1 explained that some of his students have to share a family computer and so did not always have access to a computer when needed. A lot of students *"will use their phone to communicate because for whatever reason their computer uh is just too slow to be able to (inaudible) online connection."* Various participants don't have access to printers now. Another area in which we see exacerbation of inequalities is in the working environment, discussed in following sections.

Inadequate Working Environment

We have found in our investigation that generally, students interviewed have a harder time learning from an online classroom than an in-person one. It is pertinent to note that these students had mostly studied in physical classrooms in the past. That is, for most of them, they had little experience studying virtually. But this is nonetheless a cost of the switch to remote learning. We have also found that overall, participants gained benefits from the switch to remote learning. Participants were able to work and attend school, in some cases that wouldn't have been possible without the online learning option. No commute was another general benefit. There were notable exceptions. Not all participants struggled with remote learning. In fact, a participant that never was comfortable in the physical space of academia has benefitted. Nevertheless, prior to the pandemic, these students learned in the same physical space for lectures. That is, their learning environment for lectures was the same for all students. Their studying environment might have varied, but there were some options for students whose home environments didn't foster focus and productivity: university library, labs, possibly the public library. Since the switch to remote learning, participants have been generally confined to their home space. In fact, only one participant detailed studying in a place that was neither his home nor work (in academic labs). This means that students with their own room or a reserved space without distractions have an advantage over students that don't have this access. For example, participant 17 and 7 work from home, as do her family:

"Especially because my mom is right in front of me, and my brother is like a couple feet away from me. So he's in class on the other side and my mom is in front of me talking about work in the other area. So like I just get distracted with that." (P17)

"...our home wasn't really ready for three people to be working from home." (P7)

Participant 10 also had distractions by household members. She related that her parents didn't know when she was in class, so they would look to see what she was doing, or continue to call her, which she says was distracting. Her perspective was that her remote environment harmed more than helped her. Participants 13 and 9 were examples of participants whose home workspace had distractions that interrupted their work:

"when you're home and it's like your family's home, and it's, oh can you do this, or do this, or people are talking to you and you'e in the middle of class, it's pretty distracting...it's I guess every time I have a class, or I'm in classes, always someone coming in my room asking me about something, or some–like every time I have class, I guess I guess there's distraction pretty much, and I have classes twice a week, so." (P13)

"... I have a younger sister and sometimes she will play her music really loud, and I have 2 dogs at my house at my family's house so they will bust in the door. People are in and out the house and then my parents don't know or always realize that I'm in class sometimes and will come in my room talking to me and I'll be in zoom or sometimes taking an exam...they don't really realize um and of course when I tell them they stop but of course they will stop but it's kind of distracting you know because in college you can go to the library or you have your own room where you can just focus." (P9)

Distractions in Remote Workspace

While there was some overlap in the previous and current section, this section is dedicated to looking at elements of participants' remote workspace that presented challenges but without rising to the level of creating what author one interpretated as an inadequate working space. Mainly, these are the distractions inherent to a home workspace generally controlled by participants.

Participant 14 found it quite difficult to study while he only had his bedroom as a study space, as it was very difficult to work *"right next to (his) bed."* Participant 6 does his homework while on break, at work. He has access to a room at work where he can focus. However, he is sometimes interrupted by things that come up. Various other participants reported some distractions from household members. Various participants reported difficulty working from home. For example, participant 8 related that in October of 2020, she felt distressed, and realized it was because she was literally living in her workspace. She took measures to find a solution by dedicating three places in her home where she expressly worked and stopped working in her bedroom. Participant 5 reported it being a challenge to work at home because it's not a conducive environment to working: *"your home is your home; you don't do work here."*

To evaluate whether they have an adequate working environment, we must consider whether the student or faculty member is dealing with added challenges that can be managed, or barriers beyond this. For example, participants that cite the lack of obligation to be visibly present and interact still control this distraction. Does a student whose only study space is a desk next to their bed in their bedroom have an adequate working environment? Do participants whose workspace is "a few feet" away from a younger sibling studying his own classes and a parent working from home have access to an adequate working environment? What is clear is that this is at the least, somewhat of a disadvantage from students who have a distraction-free space in which to study, especially if it is not their bedroom.

In evaluating the workspace of participants during Covid-19, we can divide the challenges and barriers created by the remote workspace (or rather, created by the lack of access to campus study and lecture spaces) into two categories: those that participant controls and those that participant does not control. There were various participants that cite challenges in the workspace belonging to the former category: they can look at their phone, they're at home so they have opportunity for distraction, they are not required to be physically or even sometimes visibly present nor interact, so they have the freedom to pay attention to other things while in class or instead of class. We are more concerned with the challenges and barriers in remote workspaces of the latter category, those that participants don't control. A significant number of participants do not have a space available that they can dedicate to work. Many participants were working from home alongside siblings and parents. All of the participants had access to internet, but several participants had some instability in their internet connection. Once again, this may not disqualify their working space at adequate, but it undoubtedly puts them at a disadvantage to students that don't have to deal with a drop or stoppage of internet connectivity.

5   Conclusion

We found that students and faculty were impacted by the pandemic directly, and also by the challenges presented by remote learning. The former was loss of life or health of persons close to participants, reported by some, and the fear and stress of living in a pandemic, more frequent and pronounced in the case of participants with high-risk family members. Remote learning presented participants with challenges and in some cases obstacles that had not been present in the in-person learning environment.

With respect to the remote learning environment, the sudden switch to remote learning had the most significant impact on participants whose home environment does not provide for a private workspace. For these participants, distractions from household members create a challenge that participants may not be able to control. As to environment distractions that participants do control, it seems that participants that faired best in remote learning were those that adapted to the remote situation by managing those distractions or finding new ways of learning. There was a clear trend to engage less in lectures. Participants overall find video lectures less engaging. Some participants struggle learning materials. Others changed their approach to academic learning to rely more on self-learning.

With respect to engagement, there was a clear trend toward less engagement both among peers and between students and their instructors. The exceptions were participants that had high participation in remote communication like Slack. That is, participants who were able to adapt to new technologies to replace in-person communication in order to create or maintain connection. The remote classroom seems to be a more difficult place for students to participate, because social interaction is less "natural" in an online classroom than in an in-person classroom. As a significant number of participants that reported mental drain or stress or fear due to the pandemic, it's possible that this affected mental state, combined with a more "draining" learning experience and a more challenging communication channel contributed to lower student engagement.

Finally, we address the resourceful ways participants are adapting. Participants that can no longer see each other in person are connecting via Facetime or phone calls. Participants that used to rely on community-based learning on campus are using Reddit communities to read about the course topics they are covering for supplementary information. Now that students cannot have study groups in person, they have created group texts where they discuss courses, remind each other of upcoming deadlines, and help each other with coursework.

References

1. Ali, W.: Online and remote learning in higher education institutes: a necessity in light of COVID pandemic. High. Educ. Stud. **10**(3), 16–25 (2020)
2. Alokluk, J.A.: The effectiveness of blackboard system, uses and limitations in information management. Intell. Inf. Manag. **10**, 133–149 (2018)
3. Corrin, L., de Barba, P.: Exploring students' interpretation of feedback delivered through learning analytics dashboards. In: Rhetoric and Reality: Critical Perspectives on Educational Technology, pp. 629–633 (2014)
4. Corbin, J., Strauss, A.: Basics of Qualitative Research: Techniques and Procedures for Developing Grounded Theory. Sage Publications, Inc. (2008)
5. Daniel, S.J.: Education and the COVID pandemic. Prospects **49**, 91–96 (2020)
6. Dumford, A.D., Miller, A.L.: Online learning in higher education: exploring advantages and disadvantages for engagement. J. Comput. High. Educ. **30**, 452–465 (2018)
7. Fernandez, A.A., Shaw, G.P.: Academic leadership in a time of crisis: the coronavirus and COVID-19. J. Leadersh. Stud. **14**(1), 39–45 (2020)
8. Garcia, E., Weiss, E.: Early Education Gaps by Social Class and Race Start U.S. Children Out on Unequal Footing. Economic Policy Institute. Washington, D.C. (2015)
9. Garcia, E., Weiss, E.: Education inequalities at the school starting gate. Economic Policy Institute. Washington, D.C. (2017)
10. Gillett-Swan, J.K.: The challenges of online learning supporting and engaging the isolated learner. J. Learn. Des. **10**(1), 20–30 (2017)
11. Heitz, C., Laboissiere, M., Sanghvi, S., Sarakatsannis, J.: Getting the next phase of remote learning right in higher education. https://www.mckinsey.com/industries/public-and-social-sector/our-insights/getting-the-next-phase-of-remote-learning-right-in-higher-education. Accessed 12 Feb 2021
12. Koban-Koç, D.: The effects of socio-economic status on prospective English language teachers' academic achievement. Novitas-ROYAL (Res. Youth Lang.) **10**(2), 100–112 (2016)
13. Kreijns, K., Kirschner, P.A., Jochems, W.: Identifying the pitfalls for social interaction in computer-supported collaborative learning environments: a review of the research. Comput. Hum. Behav. **19**(3), 335–353 (2003)

14. Kurtz-Costes, B., Swinton, A.D., Skinner, O.D.: Racial and ethnic gaps in the school performance of Latino, African American, and White students. In: Leong, F.T.L., Comas-Díaz, L., Nagayama Hall, G.C., McLoyd, V.C., Trimble, J.E. (eds.) APA Handbooks in Psychology®. APA Handbook of Multicultural Psychology, vol., pp. 231–246. American Psychological Association (2014)

15. Lewis, C.: Covid Highlights Educational Inequities. In: UNC Charlotte Urban Institute, https://ui.uncc.edu/story/Covid-highlights-educational-inequities. Accessed 10 Feb 2021

16. Liu, Z., Lomovtseva, N., Korobeynikova, E.: Online learning platforms: reconstructing modern higher education. Int. J. Emerg. Technol. Learn. **15**(13), 4–21 (2020)

17. MacGillis, A.: The Students Left Behind by Remote Learning, Pro Publica Inc. https://www.propublica.org/article/the-students-left-behind-by-remote-learning. Accessed 10 Feb 2021

18. Orfield, G., Lee, C.: Racial Transformation and the Changing Nature of Segregation. The Civil Rights Project at Harvard University, Cambridge, MA (2006)

19. Pappas, E. Fighting inequity in the face of COVID. Am. Psychol. Assoc. **51**(4) (2020). https://www.apa.org/monitor/2020/06/covid-fighting-inequity. Accessed 10 Feb 2021

20. Pardo, A., Han, F., Ellis, R.A.: Combining university student self-regulated learning indicators and engagement with online learning events to predict academic performance. IEEE Trans. Learn. Technol. **10**(1), 82–92 (2017)

21. Pishva, D., Nishantha, G., Dang, H.: A survey on how Blackboard is assisting educational institutions around the world and the future trends. In: The 12th International Conference on Advanced Communication Technology (ICACT), vol. 2, pp. 1539–1543 (2010)

22. Rauscher, E.: Education funding and inequality in Kansas, 2009–2015. Kansas J. Law Public Pol. **27**(3), 401–433 (2018)

23. Reardon, S.: The widening income achievement gap. Educ. Leadersh. **70**(8), 10–16 (2013)

24. Saldana, J.: The Coding Manual for Qualitative Researchers. SAGE Publications Ltd., 3rd edn. (2015)

25. Sirin, S.: Socioeconomic status and academic achievement: a meta-analytic review of research. Rev. Educ. Res. **75**(3), 417–453 (2005)

From Studios to Laptops: Challenges in Imparting Design Education Virtually

Surbhi Pratap$^{(\boxtimes)}$, Abhishek Dahiya, and Jyoti Kumar

Department of Design, Indian Institute of Technology Delhi, New Delhi, India

Abstract. This paper investigates the challenges faced by design educators with this new shift in education paradigm, from traditional studio-based learning to online modes of instruction and discussion. The paper reports findings of a study which includes a survey of 150 users of online education and in-depth interviews of ten design educators who are currently taking classes online in India. The findings suggest technical modifications that can be made to designs of online education portals as well as to online design pedagogy so that they can cater to design education in a more efficient manner.

Keywords: E-learning · Design education · Studio based learning · Virtual classrooms · Online teaching challenges

1 Introduction

In the wake of the COVID-19 pandemic situation, most of the countries have observed a long period of lockdown. This has resulted in an unprecedented explosion of online education. Though online classes have existed for a long time, they have taken a newfound relevance with the constant need of virtual connection between students and instructors in present times [1]. Particularly, in the case of studio-based design education, this is a recent phenomenon, and is facing teething issues. This paper reports findings from an investigative study conducted with design students and teachers. The aim of this study was to understand the differences in teaching and learning experience of online studio based design education as compared to conventional methods. The study followed a mixed methods approach to understand issues and pain points faced by the users of online platforms while imparting design education online.

1.1 Background

Studio based education is different from conventional lecture classroom setup and studio spaces are an important part of design education. From a teaching and learning perspective, the primary difference between the two set-ups is that studio based classes allow students to apply theoretical knowledge and skills to create new artefacts. They also promote collaborative learning as well as self-reflection among peers through group activities [2, 3]. Teachers can demonstrate and assess students' performance simultaneously in a studio based setup, resulting in better physical and verbal interactions. With the advent of platforms for online teaching and learning, many studio

P. Zaphiris and A. Ioannou (Eds.): HCII 2021, LNCS 12784, pp. 507–516, 2021.
https://doi.org/10.1007/978-3-030-77889-7_35

based learning activities are now being performed virtually. The authors posit that this shift might change the teaching and learning experience for teachers and students respectively.

Studies which have investigated teaching paradigm shifts of online design education have reported academic stress due to online education [5]; benefits, challenges and strategies of online education [6]; challenges in online education during the COVID-19 pandemic [7]. Literature has also suggested pedagogical changes that can be incorporated in order to overcome its challenges like the reported benefits of combining studio classrooms with online technologies [5, 8], benefits of 'blended learning' that include enhanced learning for students, improved assessments/critiques and decreased faculty workload [9, 10]. It was also noted that a lack of "felt connectedness" affected the teacher satisfaction and learnability of design students [11]. Benefits of using virtual tools alongside physical interaction have also been reported. However, there is limited literature available on the use of online platforms for design education and it may be argued as one of the reasons why online design education is still at a nascent stage [12].

Worldwide lockdowns due to COVID-19 pandemic have not given the opportunity of physical interaction and the teaching and learning mode have been purely virtual. It is argued that design activities such as peer-learning need face to face interaction which is difficult to achieve in full online mode [8, 10, 13]. Further, due to sudden lockdowns in many countries, there was no time to reform educational practices and policies especially for courses involving hands on practices. Online platforms such as Microsoft teams, Zoom, Cisco WebEx etc. became popular among various educational institutions to conduct virtual classes. However, these platforms were not designed specifically for education, particularly in the area of design. Online portals have been constantly updating themselves with features based on user feedback. However, they still have a long way to go in order to improve the teaching and learning experience of their users. This has resulted in a need to identify features for an online education platform that has tools to conduct virtual design classes. This paper reports an investigative study that identifies issues faced by design educators and students while using online platforms for design education.

2 Research Methodology

The study was conducted in three parts: Firstly, an internet-based analysis was done for three popular online platforms used for education in India, to investigate how different features of such portals are being used for education and which of those features are liked and disliked by users. The methodology was content analysis of online reviews posted by users of these popular online portals. The portals which were analyzed were: Zoom, Microsoft Teams and Google Classroom (Fig. 1).

No.		Google Classroom	Microsoft Teams	Zoom Classes
1	Maximum number of users	250	250	1000
2	Accessibility from all devices	☑	☐	☑
3	Compatibility with different OS	☑	☑	☑
4	Easy account management/accessible through all accounts	☐	☐	☑
5	Sharing of documents like lecture notes	☐	☑	☐
6	Quick assignment process	☑	☑	☐
7	paperless assignments	☐	☑	☐
8	Can add comments/Post its to a lecture	☑	☑	☐
9	Scheduling/Calendar	☑	☑	☑
10	Integration with Notes/Docs	☑	☑	☐
11	Automated Quizzes and tests	☑	☑	☐
12	Quality of video and audio	☐	☑	☑
13	Co-visibility of users	☐	☑	☑
14	Learner sharing - with each other	☐	☑	☐

Fig. 1. Sample of internet-based analysis done on three popular online portals used for education in India

Next, based on the findings of the above-discussed analysis, a questionnaire-survey was designed to investigate how users in India are interacting with the popular online education portals. The survey was taken through a google-form and was shared with design students and educators through emails and WhatsApp messages. 150 participants who used online portals for design education participated in the survey. 75.8% of the participants belonged to the age group of 18–25 years and of these, 77 were females and 73 were males. This survey aimed at investigating the most used, liked and problematic features of the popular online education portals presently being used in India. The survey also highlights the pain points of the users while they use these platforms in a country where high internet bandwidth is still a luxury (Fig. 2).

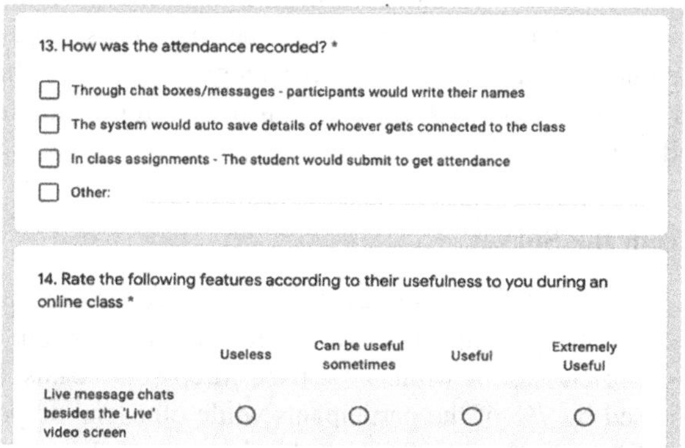
13. How was the attendance recorded? *

☐ Through chat boxes/messages - participants would write their names
☐ The system would auto save details of whoever gets connected to the class
☐ In class assignments - The student would submit to get attendance
☐ Other:

14. Rate the following features according to their usefulness to you during an online class *

	Useless	Can be useful sometimes	Useful	Extremely Useful
Live message chats besides the 'Live' video screen	○	○	○	○

Fig. 2. Sample questions from the survey

Lastly, semi-structured interviews were conducted with ten design educators, 6 males and 4 females, who are currently taking online classes to understand the pain points and desirable impacts of using online portals to impart design education. Purposive quota sampling [14] was used to select the participants for this study. This allowed us to focus on people who would be most likely to experience or have insights into the topic of online design education in India. The interviews were conducted telephonically, and the duration of the interview ranged between 20 min to 35 min. The average duration for all 10 interviews was 28.6 min. The average age of the participants was 33.4 years (st. dev. 5.4 yrs.) and the average experience of working in the design education sector was 4.8 (st. dev. 4.14 yrs.) years. The profiles of the interviewees are summarized in Table 1. Thematic analysis was conducted on the interview data post transcription [15]. From the transcript of interviews of each participant, for both the questions, six 'themes' in responses were identified which are discussed in the subsequent section.

Table 1. Profiles of Design Educators who were interviewed

No.	Gender	Age	Designation	Stream	Exp.
P1	M	36	Associate Professor	Interaction Design	3
P2	M	30	Assistant Professor	Architecture	5
P3	M	34	Associate Professor	Fashion Design	10
P4	M	44	Dean	Fashion Design	15
P5	F	29	Assistant Professor	Interaction Design	3
P6	F	25	Teaching Assistant	Architecture	1
P7	F	40	Teaching Assistant	Design	2
P8	F	36	Teaching Assistant	Interaction Design	4
P9	M	29	Educator	Fine Arts	3
P10	M	31	Teaching Assistant	Design	2

3 Findings

While the findings of the survey revealed the most used, liked and problematic features of online design portals, the observations from the interviews gave insights on the possible modifications towards online design pedagogy as well as technical challenges that can be taken up to redesign online education portals for a more efficient impartment of design education.

3.1 Findings from the Survey

150 participants participated in the survey, who had used online portals for design education. Of these 68% participants reported mostly using zoom classes, 45.8% reported using Google classroom while 19% used Microsoft Teams. Blackboard and Google meet was used by 7% of the participants while other online portals were used by less than 2%. So the findings reflect on the features of the portals used by the majority of the participants.

Listed below are key findings from the survey on the usage of the design portals:

1. The duration of an online design class was reported to be longer than 1 h by most (86.2%) participants.
2. 93.5% reported that most of the lectures were live and not recorded and the majority (70.6%) also preferred it this way.
3. It was also reported that the participants (64.1%) would keep their videos on for most of the time, and when they could not, it was due to either low internet (48.4%) or privacy issues (37.9%).
4. A majority (71.2%) of participants used their laptops to attend the class and 64.7% could access it on their own without the need for any external authorization (for example the institute authorities).
5. The main problems faced due to internet connectivity issues were loss of live instructions (68.6%) and freezing of screens (67.3%).

Listed below are key findings from the survey on the design features of the portals and participant awareness about those features:

1. The online portals had provisions to create separate teams/chat rooms during a session (to aid group work). However, only 24.8% of the users were aware of it and 68.6% reported that they did not know of any such feature in their education portal.
2. The feature Screen sharing was used mainly to give presentations on powerpoint (66%) or to demonstrate the working of a design software (43.8%).
3. The grid view, which allowed to see the peers was a feature that was important to 52.9% of the users while 41.8% reported that it didn't really matter whether they were able to see their peers or not.
4. Although the softwares had features to assign and submit assignments, 72.5% of the users were unaware of those and would use emails or Whatsapp to share their work with the faculty.
5. 52.9% users would take snapshots of the lists of participants and 34.6% would check the chat boxes and messages to record the session attendance.

Table 2 lists the most used, least used features and the most critical problems faced by the users while Table 3 enumerates the pros and cons of the experiential and technical aspects of the portals while attending their online design education classes as reported in the survey.

Table 2. Most used and least used features of the online education portal

No.	Most used features	Least used features	Most critical problems
1	Screen sharing	Renaming participants	Echoes and lags in audio
2	Session recording	Virtual backgrounds	Freezing of screens
3	Feature to mute participants by the host	Sticky notes with offline lectures	Simultaneous audio from multiple sources
4	Scheduling/Calendar	Inbuilt assignments	Pop-ups during lectures
5	Chatbox besides live video		Privacy issues

Table 3. Pros and Cons of experiential and technical aspects of online design education portals

	Experiential Aspects	Technical Aspects
Cons	Restricted interaction/Lack of connect	Problem in scanning and uploading
	Less feedbacks from class	Unsupported file extensions
	Less Peer learning	No uploading confirmation feedback
	Slow lecture delivery	No option to edit the uploaded file
	Difficulty in concentrating	Internet bandwidth dependency resulting in Audio/Video Lags, Screen Pixelations etc.
Pros	Time and space flexibility	
	Flexibility to share/present	Flexibility to watch recorded sessions anytime
	Slow learning in terms of skill development	

3.2 Findings from the Interviews

Ten design educators, 6 men and 4 women, who are currently taking online courses were interviewed to consider the pain points and desirable impacts of using online portals to provide design education. The interview recordings were examined by identifying the following six recurrent themes from participant responses:

1. **Types of users:** A key finding of the study was that an instructor and a student are not the only key users of an online design education portal. Moderators (from the instructor's end) and attendee (who technically helps the student while he/she attends the class) are also key users of such a portal.

   It was found that moderators play an active role in organising classes, managing assignments and acting as a communication link between students and teachers. In order to have a smooth online class session, it is essential that moderators have a fair technical knowledge about the software/online platform used to conduct classes. This becomes more important with faculty who are not very technically updated, for example for any emeritus professor, learning a new software to conduct class is extra load to which they might not be very comfortable. In the interview, moderators pointed out a few problems that they are facing in currently available platforms. These problems were related to coordination between faculty and students. For example, P8 reported that, " *The professor who I was helping would continue the lecture, while I as a moderator had to look at student queries through the chat box. This was not very efficient because there were always interruptions from students while reporting the query and that led to a lot of confusion.* "

   It was observed that most online platforms have not categorised their functions recognising moderators as a distinct user. Hence, while creating such platforms for online design studios, it will be helpful to attend the needs of diverse user groups.

2. **Attendance:** Marking and keeping a track of attendance was a common pain point observed in this study. It was reported that attendees keep logging in/out multiple times in a single session. This could be due to technical reasons like low internet network connectivity. While the portals generally show/record a list of active participants attending a session, the instructor is unable to keep a track of attendees who joined in the middle of the session. It was reported in the interview that users are using conventional methods for managing attendance in online classes. For example, P7: *"Earlier I used to write the names on a piece of a paper, later I used to take snapshot of the screen to take a note of who all are attending the class session"*; P2: *"The number of attendees shown in the status bar keeps on fluctuating because students can go offline in between and then come back again. However, when I take attendance at the start of my lecture, I ask students to raise their hands as I say their name."*

3. **Live Demonstration**: For a design educator, a live demonstration of the design process - 'how' he/she works on a project is as, if not more important as the theory and the 'steps' behind it. This has suffered a setback in terms of the natural flow, because the instructors have to keep in mind various other things like the camera angle, lighting, poor video quality, audio lags etc. and are not able to really demonstrate the process naturally. For example, P9: *"While sketching, it's hard to keep the sketch in the range of the camera. I can't keep the sketching surface still as I need to rotate the paper time and again."*; P7: *"Apart from audio/video lags, it is hard to keep a track of the camera angle/focus and perform at the same time. We took help from another person for holding a camera during these classes."*

   Even in cases of recording and uploading the process, the entire thing becomes extremely tedious and time-consuming.

4. **Group Work:** One of the features of studio based learning is doing projects in groups. Conventionally, the students would be divided into small individual groups to work on a project in the class. This process involved students getting up from their seats to interact, share, discuss, ideate, and create with their peers. Classroom group works have suffered the most in online education as not all portals allow breaking into teams while a session is going on. Even for the ones that do, the formation of teams is random unless a moderator manually selects them. In the next session, however, the teams are to be manually selected again if the same group has to present the work. As design education thrives on group interactions with peers, such limitations are detrimental to the way studio classes function. It was also interesting to note that most users were unaware of these features in the portals that provided them due to inefficient user experience designs. For example P2: *"I didn't know if such a feature exists in any online classroom tool. Honestly, I have never explored it."*

5. **Assignments and assessments:** There are a lot of hand on assignments in design education, which require the critique of a teacher during the process of creation. For example, P9: *"I need to look while the students work many times while teaching… students are not able to sketch and share simultaneously. Even if there are no network issues, problems like lighting conditions or camera resolutions are demotivating for students to show their work"*. Further, design assessments are interactive, so that the student can learn how the teacher observes and then rectifies a mistake. Virtually this does not happen, where both the student as well as the teacher only share the final outcome. Moreover, most of the 'hand-done' assignments which are not directly shared through a common software need to be uploaded and then assessed, which is a very tedious process. For example, P2: *"Architecture students submit A0 size sheets in pdfs through mail. One problem is that the files are heavy, another issue is that assessing the sheet with those dimensions on a desktop/laptop screen is very tedious"*

6. **Student presentations:** One of the important learning outcomes of a design program has been imparting soft-skills, where the students are taught the art of presenting their designs to a client, learn the value of getting critiques and experience the growth in their thought process through peer review and interaction. To conduct such presentations in the natural state are presently very difficult in an online class. For example P6: *"I have seen a drop in the level of class participation in design presentation sessions in online classrooms. Most of the time I have to repeat the same thing to every individual again and again."*

4 Discussion and Conclusion

A face to face interaction between a teacher and a student is irreplaceable. However, this study finds relevance amidst the leap towards a global design community, where design education can be imparted irrespective of the geographical location of the teacher as well as the student, besides dealing with rare situations like the Covid-19 pandemic.

The contribution of this study is towards the manner in which design research leads to shifting pedagogy of design education as well as to the design updates and features needed for technological resources and facilities that have become an integral part of the design curriculum. Technical and pedagogical suggestions from the findings of this study are listed in Table 4.

Table 4. Technical and pedagogical suggestions from the findings of this study

Technical suggestions	Pedagogical suggestions
UX features which are upfront so that users can identify them easily in the portal	E-learning protocols should be made in design institutes which specify the roles of instructors and moderators in an online studio
Automatic tracking and recording of attendance based on the duration for which a student is logged in. Cumulative records of the attendance report for the course duration	There should be a limit to the maximum number of students for an interactive/practical design session online
Embedded Plug-ins of popular design and presentation software in the portal	A protocol to schedule queries within a session should be made to avoid audio lags and confusion
Provision of a moderator/attendee) during the class with specific controls like mute/formation of teams etc	Different modes need to be developed for online presentation as well as for peer reviews
Recording of short timed sessions which are shared directly	Ways need to be identified to ensure efficient virtual demonstration of the design process to students
Formation of non-random teams within the class which can continue through multiple sessions	
In-portal assignment submission and assessment with privacy controls	

5 Limitations and Future Work

The aim of this study was to understand the differences in teaching and learning experiences of design studio education using online platforms. The study was more of an investigative exploration on the topic hence the authors would like to point a few limitations to this study which can be attended to while extending further research in this area. Firstly, the entire study was conducted digitally using online survey forms, feedback, and telephonic interviews. The data collected is based only on the experiences that were recalled by the participants at the time of reporting and not based on direct observations of online design classes. Future studies can be planned to observe teaching and learning experiences while users are attending an online design studio class. Also, in-depth analysis of user interviews with more participants can be done to gain further insights into the online learning and teaching experience. Moreover, future studies can look into other fields of design education like jewellery design, vehicle design, graphic design etc. to suggest more elaborate modifications to the online design education.

References

1. Fleischmann, K.: Online design education: searching for a middle ground. Arts Humanities High. Educ. **19**(1), 36–57 (2020). https://doi.org/10.1177/1474022218758231
2. Schon, D.A.: Educating the Reflective Practitioner. Toward a New Design for Teaching and Learning in the Professions. The Jossey-Bass Higher Education Series (1987)
3. Park, J.Y.: Design education online: learning delivery and evaluation. Int. J. Art Des. Educ. **30**(2), 176–187 (2011)
4. Chandra, Y.: Online education during COVID-19: perception of academic stress and emotional intelligence coping strategies among college students. Asian Education and Development Studies (2020)
5. Bender, D.M., Vredevoogd, J.D.: Using online education technologies to support studio instruction. Educ. Technol. Soc. **9**(4), 114–122 (2006)
6. Paudel, P.: Online education: benefits, challenges and strategies during and after COVID-19 in higher education. Int. J. Stud. Educ. **3**(2), 70–85 (2021)
7. Khati, K., Bhatta, K.: Challenges of online education during COVID-19 pandemic in Nepal. Int. J. Entrepreneurship Econ. **4**(1), 45–49 (2020)
8. Bender, D.M.: Developing a collaborative multidisciplinary online design course. J. Educators Online **2**(2), 1–12 (2005). https://doi.org/10.9743/jeo.2005.2.5
9. Hastie, M., Hung, I.-C., Chen, N.-S., Kinshuk, C.-Y.: A blended synchronous learning model for educational international collaboration. Innov. Educ. Teach. Int. **47**(1), 9–24 (2010)
10. Saghafi, M., Franz, J., Crowther, P.: Perceptions of physical versus virtual design studio education. Archnet-IJAR **6**(1), 6–22 (2012)
11. Gogu C., Kumar J.: Social connectedness in online versus face to face design education: a comparative study in India. In: Chakrabarti, A., Poovaiah, R., Kant, V. (eds.) Design for Tomorrow-Volume 2. Smart Innovation, Systems and Technologies, vol. 222. Springer, Singapore (2021, in press). https://doi.org/10.1007/978-981-16-0119-4_33
12. Kumar, P., Kumar, A., Palvia, S., Verma, S.: Online business educational research system analysis and a conceptual model. Int. J. Manag. Educ. **17**, 26–35 (2019)
13. Silva, N., Lima, E.: Distance learning in architectural design studio: two comparative studies with one onsite teaching. In: Iskander, M. (ed.) Innovative Techniques in Instruction Technology, E-Learning, E-Assessment, and Education, pp. 381–386. Springer, Dordrecht (2008). https://doi.org/10.1007/978-1-4020-8739-4_66
14. Oliver, C.: Robinson, sampling in interview-based qualitative research: a theoretical and practical guide. Qual. Res. Psychol. **11**(1), 25–41 (2014). https://doi.org/10.1080/14780887.2013.801543
15. Kaufman, L., Rousseeuw, P.J.: Finding Groups in Data: An Introduction to Cluster Analysis. Wiley, New York (2009)

Teaching-Learning in the Industrial Engineering Career in Times of COVID-19

Fernando Saá[1] , Lorena Caceres[1] , Esteban M. Fuentes[1,2] ,
and José Varela-Aldás[1,3](✉)

[1] SISAu Research Group, Facultad de Ingeniería y Tecnologías de la
Información y la Comunicación, Universidad Tecnológica Indoamérica,
Ambato, Ecuador
{fernandosaa,lorenacaceres,josevarela}@uti.edu.ec
[2] Facultad de Ciencia e Ingeniería en Alimentos y Biotecnología (FCIAB),
Universidad Técnica de Ambato (UTA), Ambato, Ecuador
e.fuentesp@uta.edu.ec
[3] Department of Electronic Engineering and Communications,
University of Zaragoza, Zaragoza, Spain

Abstract. Since cancellation of face-to-face education during the health emergency caused by COVID-19, higher education institutions, have had to guarantee the right to education through virtualization. Therefore, this work analyzes the teaching-learning process adapted to the virtual mode in the students of technical subjects of the professionalizing axis in the industrial engineering career a private university of Ecuador. Quantitative research is performed for this using surveys, performance index collection, and historical data. The method has a comparative scope between two academic periods, contrasting the data before and after the pandemic, the indicators are taken from students and teachers. The analysis of surveys is carried out in 3 components of teaching, in students are obtained: planning and methodology, with 81.1% considered as satisfied; teacher-assisted activities, with 79.1% content with the activities; and in practical activities, with 74.9% according to the tools used. Comparisons of indicators in different academic periods show minimal variations in performance, teachers improve the average performance score by 4.1%, and students drop academic performance by 2.6%. Finally, the correlation demonstrates a similar perception between students and teacher in the learning practice component.

Keywords: Teaching-learning · Higher education · Virtual education · Teacher performance index · COVID-19

1 Introduction

In December 2019, an outbreak of viral pneumonia began in the city of Wuhan, associated with a new coronavirus, which was initially a local outbreak; it has become a global pandemic with catastrophic consequences. In February 2020, an official taxonomic name was established for the new SARS-CoV-2 virus, and the disease it causes, Coronavirus Disease 2019 (COVID-19) [1]. The virus has now infected more than five

P. Zaphiris and A. Ioannou (Eds.): HCII 2021, LNCS 12784, pp. 517–530, 2021.
https://doi.org/10.1007/978-3-030-77889-7_36

million people and caused the deaths of 350000 worldwide, so most countries stop their face-to-face activities to work remotely or online [2], forcing deep rethinking of the way of life.

The Covid-19 pandemic is a major disaster experienced by almost every country in the world, impacting on all the lifelines of each country; one of the sectors that have been affected is education, aside from governments' efforts to solve the consequences of COVID- 19, they must continue keep the stability and sustainability of the learning process that is the right of all citizens [3]. Because of the pandemic, the entire education system has switched from traditional teaching methods to online learning systems around the world. COVID-19 reinforces the need to explore new learning opportunities [4].

In the field of higher education, the transformation from conventional classes to a virtual format was immediate [5] which has forced the "traditional" education system to migrate to a more dynamic and connected system where the training process is carried out in an assisted and/or remote way [6]. Digital technology becomes an integral part of life, and also essential for connectivity and communication at all levels [7]. Based on the "new reality" facing the world, educational institutions, through online platforms, offered a solution to continue teaching and learning activities by trying to ensure an effective flow of communication between teachers and students; sessions tend to run slower because breaks are required to allow time for people to speak and others to understand, posing an increased risk that students will be easily distracted, that is why the teacher plays a fundamental role because in order to keep students engaged longer, they require preparing more resources [8] which led to a real challenge since they have found the need to "learn by doing", to imitate face-to-face teaching [9]. In this scenario, they continue their academic activities adapting to non-face-to-face formats through different digital platforms [10] that involve the use of virtual classrooms, applications, devices and software that, despite social distancing, communicate us interactively with the world [11].

In Latin American countries, the difficulties of this challenge are increased by socio-economic inequalities, with the consequent digital gaps of both students and teachers [12] as specific resources, skills and competencies are required that are not necessarily owned by each party. Teacher's activity is linked to the pedagogical use of digital technologies, as well as creativity to solve different challenges of the context that allow to develop creative and autonomous learning by the student [13].

According to [14], online education has great advantages as any videoconference must be recorded and socialized for later use, as a source of consultation and support for students. However, there are also disadvantages, one of them the fact that not all students have handy electronic devices and/or internet, which makes it difficult to attend classes and, therefore, their level of learning is reduced.

In [15], it is clear that there are basically three gaps affecting the quality of learning and teaching processes in COVID-19 times due to factors that affect both learning and professional performance through online education. The first gap relates to access to technological means or devices, the second to the efficient use of technology, and the third relates to school capacity, i.e., teacher skills, the availability of online resources to support teaching at all levels.

As [12] points out, the diversity of realities in which the virtual teaching-learning process takes place makes it difficult to propose a standardized communication strategy. The selection of communication channels depends on the technological resources that students have in their homes (devices and internet connectivity), the educational stage and the digital skills of teachers and students.

Undoubtedly, one of the concerns of educational institutions is to find the appropriate method for teaching subjects that require face-to-face practicums to strengthen knowledge. The experimental component presents major challenges for its implementation [16]. One of the branches related to practical education is engineering; due to this global emergency, teachers have found the need to look for tools that allow students to solve problems without carrying out practical face-to-face activities, through case studies, applications, use of simulators, necessary to understand the different processes and further develop their capacity for autonomous and critical thinking [17].

This article sets out the perspective of both teachers and students regarding the teaching-learning process of the subjects in the area of management of productive systems, of the face-to-face mode of the Industrial Engineering career, in order to analyze the level of acceptance of virtual learning during the first partial, of the first half of 2020 (academic period A20), with regard to the face-to-face teaching of the first part, of the second half of 2019 (academic period B19); in this way conclusions can be drawn on the impact of virtual classes in the area of management of productive systems. This article is divided into several sections: introduction, where the problem is contextualized and justified; the method used to obtain the relevant data for research; the results obtained, as well as the conclusions.

2 Methodology

2.1 Research Design

This study is a quantitative research, and its scope is comparative, as an analysis of the results obtained from 187 surveys applied to students who have classes of the subjects of the professionalizing axis in the industrial engineering career is carried out. The surveys were also applied to 21 teachers who teach subjects in this area. In addition, teacher and student performance rates are used to compare them in two different academic periods, before and after the onset of COVID-19. Teaching performance is evaluated from the perspective of the student, who complete a comprehensive assessment to the teacher that measures the level of conformity of students with teaching performance, this quantification is performed in all academic periods to feedback the performance of the teachers. Student performance is obtained from grades generated during the study period, obviously assigned by teachers. These scores are also attained from an earlier academic period, when still working in face-to-face mode.

Figure 1 presents the methodology used for teaching-learning analysis, the data to be collected in different ways; the questionnaire is completed using a Likert scale that allows to measure the perception of teachers and students in three academic components. A teacher evaluation is also applied by measuring student satisfaction with teaching in 6 technical subjects. Regarding learning, students are assessed. In addition, historical pre-pandemic data are used in relation to teacher evaluation and student assessment, with the aim of comparing the data in different circumstances. In addition, a correlation analysis is carried out between the responses of teachers and students to the developed questionnaire, with the purpose of contrasting these different perspectives.

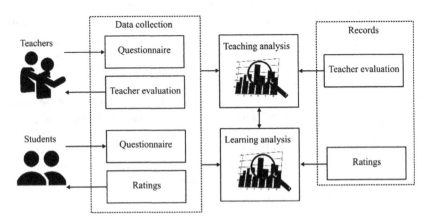

Fig. 1. Methodology for the analysis of teaching-learning in the industrial engineering career.

2.2   Surveys

A survey of 7 questions is prepared in Google Forms, using closed questions divided into three components: 1. Planning and methodology (3 questions); 2. Teacher-assisted activities (2 questions); 3. Practical activities (2 questions), to obtain accurate information about each of them. Each of the questions has four options (never – on occasion – almost always – always). In order to give validity and reliability to the questions posed, they are subject to expert judgement in order to verify their correct approach. The analysis uses the data visualization technique for which graphs are made to detect behaviors and make comparisons with respect to the data obtained, using Excel. Table 1 presents the questions applied to the 187 students and the 21 teachers of the Industrial Engineering career, of the professionalizing axis.

Table 1. Survey questions by components (C).

C	Question
Planning and methodology	-Do you consider that the methodology and planning of the formative projects of the professionalizing axis taught in virtual mode are appropriate to meet the objectives and contents?
	-Do you consider that the contents of the formative projects of the professionalizing axis have been adapted according to the training needs in the virtual mode of education?
	- Do you consider that during classes in the virtual mode of the formative projects of the professionalizing axis, additional teaching resources such as videos, glossaries, presentations that allow to strengthen learning have been used?
Teacher-assisted activities	- Do you consider that the exercises and/or case studies developed during the classes in the virtual mode have been adequate and sufficient for a better understanding of the contents of the formative projects of the professionalizing axis?
	- Do you consider that both individual and collaborative learning has been encouraged during classes in the virtual modality of the training projects of the professionalizing axis?
Practical activities	- Do you consider that the practical implementation and experimentation activities (PAE) developed during classes in the virtual mode have been adequate and sufficient for a better understanding of the contents of the formative projects of the professionalizing axis area?
	- Have simulators been used to carry out practical application and experimentation activities (PAE) during classes in the virtual mode of the formative projects of the professionalizing axis area?

2.3 Assessments and Historical Data

Each academic period (comprises 5 months) an evaluation is carried out to each teacher which is performed by students and authorities of the Industrial Engineering career, in which a percentage of compliance is assigned to the different activities that must be carried out independently or together; for this case, the evaluations of academic periods will be analyzed: B19 (September 2019 to February 2020, which was face-to-face) and the A20 (April–August 2020, which was virtual). Considering that information will be collected only from teachers who teach the subjects corresponding to the profession-alizing axis, with the aim of analyzing the information to see if there is an impact within face-to-face education vs. virtual. Table 2 shows the percentage out of 100% of the outcome of evaluations to teachers in the B19 and A20 periods.

Table 2. Summary of teaching evaluation.

Teacher code	B19	A20	Teacher code	B19	A20
DCII – ACMI	96,4%	100,0%	DCII – ORER	96,6%	96,0%
DCII – CMLE	97,4%	98,8%	DCII – PGDJ	90,4%	90,5%
DCII – CVJS	90,6%	95,2%	DCII – RMMB	96,2%	92,0%
DCII – CNLG	92,2%	98,0%	DCII – STFD	97,2%	97,2%
DCII – CAME	92,2%	65,2%	DCII – SAEL	88,0%	92,0%
DCII – EPCA	96,6%	97,2%	DCII – SDPE	93,8%	98,4%
DCII – FPEM	91,0%	97,4%	DCII – TIME	88,4%	98,6%
DCII – LCAR	97,4%	96,4%	DCII – VAJL	96,0%	99,2%
DCII – MMVH	93,2%	95,4%	DCII – VCCS	88,6%	90,0%
DCII – MVSP	94,4%	90,8%	DCII – VPDA	83,6%	94,8%
DCII – NMOM	90,2%	95,2%			

Then, a history of the average of grades obtained by students in the subjects belonging to the professionalizing axis was made, whose average is out of 5 points (Table 3). These grades correspond to the academic periods B19, which was developed in person, and A20, that was executed virtually due to the "new reality".

Table 3. Average student grades.

Subject	Period B19	Period A20
Programming	4,2	3,6
Work Design and Measurement	3,4	4,6
Method Engineering	4,1	4,3
Operational Research	4,3	4,0
Production Planning and Control	3,7	4,1
Operations Management	4,1	3,9
Production Management	4,1	4,1
Plant Design and New Products	3,5	3,7
Operations Management	4,1	4,5

2.4 Participants

Surveys are conducted to students who are enrolled in the subjects of the area of management of productive systems and to the teachers who teach them. In reference to teachers, it is important to clarify that of the 21 teachers surveyed 3 are hired part-time (TP) 12 hours per week, and 18 are hired full-time (TC) 40 hours per week (8 hours per day). With regard to the ethical standards of this research for data collection, it is important to note that the respective authorization is available by the career authorities to be able to conduct the surveys of both teachers and students with their informed consent. The number of respondents, as well as the evaluated subjects can be observed in Table 4.

Table 4. Participants' Demography - Male (M) and Female (F).

Subjects	Level	Teachers			Students		
		M	F	Age Average	M	F	Age Average
Programming	3	2	1	36	25	1	20
Work Design and Measurement	4	2	0	42	19	5	20
Method Engineering	5	2	0	40	27	1	21
Operational Research	5	2	1	40	27	1	22
Production Planning and Control	6	1	1	42	13	1	22
Operations Management	7	2	1	42	9	3	23
Production Management	8	1	1	40	11	2	23
Plant Design and New Products	9	1	1	37	19	2	24
Operations Management	9	1	1	36	19	2	24
Total		**14**	**7**		**169**	**18**	

3 Results

3.1 Student and Teacher Surveys

Table 5 shows an overall average of the results obtained in the surveys applied to students, within the planning and methodology component where the planning used to teach is analyzed, if the contents are according to the needs of the environment and if the teaching resources such as videos, infographics, glossaries allow to strengthen the learning. There is a 46.5% for almost always. The other component is teacher-assisted activities, which examine the different case studies applied in the classes, autonomous and collaborative work, resulting in 40.9% for almost always. Finally, the practical activities component, whose study corresponds to the tasks where simulators are used, with 42.8% for almost always.

Table 5. Student survey results.

	Planning and methodology component	Teacher-assisted activities component	Practical activities component
Never	2.9%	2.1%	4.3%
On occasion	16.0%	18.7%	20.9%
Almost always	46.5%	40.9%	42.8%
Always	34.6%	38.2%	32.1%

Table 6 indicates the average percentage of surveys applied to teachers in the Industrial Engineering career who teach in the subjects of the professionalization axis. As for the planning and methodology component, 58.7% believe that they always allow learning objectives to be achieved. Regarding assisted activities, 66.7% state that they always help to understand the contents. And 50.0% believe that practical activities almost always contribute to virtual learning.

Table 6. Teacher survey results.

	Planning and methodology component	Teacher-assisted activities component	Practical activities component
Never	.0%	.0%	.0%
On occasion	4.8%	.0%	9.5%
Almost always	36.5%	33.3%	50.0%
Always	58.7%	66.7%	40.5%

3.2   Assessments of Students and Teachers

Figure 2 shows the percentage comparison of the teacher evaluation carried out before and after the "new reality".

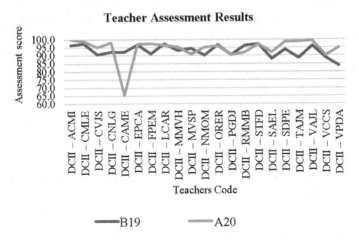

Fig. 2. Result of teacher evaluations in periods B19 and A20.

Figure 3 presents the averages of students' grades in face-to-face mode. Figure a shows the comparison between the periods detailed in the method, contrasting the grades before and after the "new reality". Minimal differences are visible, which are backed up by an average error of 2.6% between both data.

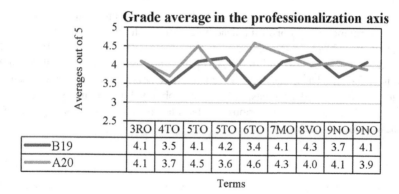

Fig. 3. Average number of student grades in the subjects of the teaching axis.

3.3 Comparison of Scores for Students and Teachers

Box and whiskers plots are used to compare performance and performance results in students and teachers, analyzing the central trend and the distribution of values. Figure 4 presents the graph of student grades in academic analysis periods with the aim of analyzing learning data; period B19 has an average of 4.1/5 and a standard deviation of 0.32, and the A20 period has an average of 4.1/5 and a standard deviation of 0.34. Although the mean remains for both data groups, and the deviation varies minimally, the quartiles of the period in virtual mode are shifted upwards, showing symmetrical quartiles and a small improvement in grades in some cases.

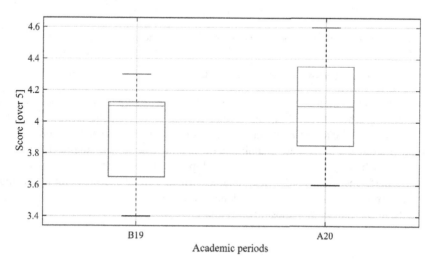

Fig. 4. Box and whiskers plots for students' grades in 2 academic periods.

Regarding the teaching analysis, Fig. 5 shows the box and whiskers plots of the teacher performance indicator in the academic periods studied (discarding the case of score lower than 70%). In the period B19 there is an average mark of 93.2% with a standard deviation of 3.84% and in the A20 period an average of 96% with a standard deviation of 3.01%. These results show an improvement in teachers' assessments for the period in virtual mode, increasing the scores obtained and reducing the dispersion of the values. In general, it is notorious that both teachers and students improve scores in the new mode of study.

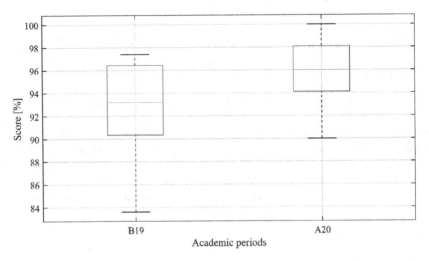

Fig. 5. Box and whiskers plots for the performance of teachers in 2 academic periods.

3.4   Correlation of Student and Teacher Surveys

Figure 6 shows the differences in the criteria with respect to the methodological field of the learning teaching process in the virtual mode, so that teachers show a mostly positive current in the assessment ranges, while students present a small percentage that considers that methodology and planning is not adequate or has not migrated optimally to virtuality, when the analysis of the relationship that the two variables have with each other was performed, a r = 0.811 was obtained which for our interpretation means that both the responses of teachers and students maintain a relationship with each other, especially in the ranges of almost always and always.

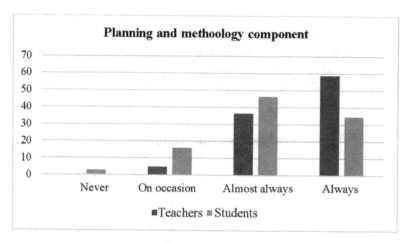

Fig. 6. Relationship of the planning and methodology component.

With regard to the component of teacher-assisted activities, presented in Fig. 7, it can be commented that students, in a percentage of approximately 20%, consider the activities carried out with the teacher have been inadequate or insufficient, although a large majority, approximately 40%, consider that almost always the activities are adequate, however the correlation of these does not exceed an r = 0.811 which indicates that the variables are related but not in a linear way. It is worth highlighting, above all, the perception of teachers regarding this component especially in what corresponds to always.

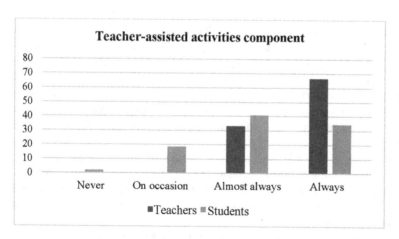

Fig. 7. Relationship of the component teacher-assisted activities.

The component of the practical activities presented in Fig. 8 shows the best correlation with the variables used, with a r = 0.958 based mainly on responses by students in which 96% of students consider that the virtual applications, simulators, and tools used for the development of the practical component, is relevant and provides knowledge and skills that contribute to vocational training.

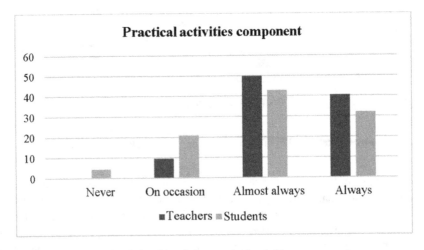

Fig. 8. Relationship of the practical activities component.

4   Conclusions

This research performs the learning analysis in university students who take subjects linked to the area of management of productive systems in the Industrial Engineering career, for this, surveys were applied to students and teachers, investigating the components of planning and methodology, assisted and practical activities. The results indicate that 43.4% of students almost always achieve learning outcomes in the new mode of study. For teachers, 55.3% indicates that learning results are always achieved. In addition, grades are compared before and after adopting the virtual mode to carry out the learning-teaching process, showing slight changes because of the new study scenarios.

In the process of bibliographic review carried out for the preparation of this document, the small number of studies related to the scope of development of this research is evident; this directly related to the atypical situation that the world is going through and therefore, mandatory migration to virtual environments caused by the confinement of the pandemic by COVID 19.

Depending on the results generated in this job, the following relationships can be established. There is no total satisfaction on part of students with the tools and resources used for the development of the learning teaching process used in the new mode of study, while, on the other hand, teachers consider that the methodology used is adequate to develop the critical and cognitive skills of the student. With regard to the differences in grades, they are typical of the process of adapting to a new study environment so they are not considered as representative data to define a sudden and entirely negative effect for the virtual mode and the new reality.

References

1. Carod-Artal, F.J.: Neurological complications of coronavirus and COVID-19. Rev. Neurol. **70**, 311–322 (2020). https://doi.org/10.33588/RN.7009.2020179
2. Al-taweel, D., Al-haqan, A., Bajis, D., Al-taweel, J.A.A.M., Al-awadhi, A.A.F.: Multidisciplinary academic perspectives during the COVID-19 pandemic, pp. 1–7 (2020). https://doi.org/10.1002/hpm.3032
3. Murad, D.F., Hassan, R., Heryadi, Y., Wijanarko, B.D., Titan: the impact of the COVID-19 pandemic in Indonesia (Face to face versus online learning). In: Proceeding - 2020 3rd International Conference Vocational Educational Electrical Engineering Strength Framework Socio 5.0 through Innovation Education Electrical Engineering Informatics Engineering ICVEE 2020, pp. 4–7 (2020). https://doi.org/10.1109/ICVEE50212.2020.9243202
4. Sabri, N., Musa, N.H., Mangshor, N.N.A., Ibrahim, S., Hamzah, H.H.M.: Student emotion estimation based on facial application in E-learning during COVID-19 pandemic. Int. J. Adv. Trends Comput. Sci. Eng. **9**, 576–582 (2020). https://doi.org/10.30534/ijatcse/2020/8091.42020
5. Ripoll, V., Godino-Ojer, M., Calzada, J.: Teaching chemical engineering to biotechnology students in the time of COVID-19: assessment of the adaptation to digitalization. Educ. Chem. Eng. **34**, 21–32 (2021). https://doi.org/10.1016/j.ece.2020.11.001
6. Mendoza-Lizcano, S.M., Palacios Alvarado, W., Medina Delgado, B.: Influence of COVID-19 confinement on physics learning in engineering and science students. J. Phys. Conf. Ser. **1671**, 012018 (2020). https://doi.org/10.1088/1742-6596/1671/1/012018
7. Code, J., Ralph, R., Forde, K.: Pandemic designs for the future : perspectives of technology education teachers during (2020). https://doi.org/10.1108/ILS-04-2020-0112
8. Coiado, O.C., Yodh, J., Galvez, R., Ahmad, K.: How COVID-19 transformed problem-based learning at carle illinois college of medicine. Med. Sci. Educator **30**(4), 1353–1354 (2020). https://doi.org/10.1007/s40670-020-01063-3
9. Radu, M.C., Schnakovszky, C., Herghelegiu, E., Ciubotariu, V.A., Cristea, I.: The impact of the COVID-19 pandemic on the quality of educational process: a student survey. Int. J. Environ. Res. Public Health. **17**, 1–15 (2020). https://doi.org/10.3390/ijerph17217770
10. Kahraman, C., Cevik Onar, S., Oztaysi, B., Sari, I.U., Cebi, S., Tolga, A.C. (eds.): INFUS 2020. AISC, vol. 1197. Springer, Cham (2021). https://doi.org/10.1007/978-3-030-51156-2
11. Arce-peralta, F.J.: La transición del paradigma educativo hacia nuevos escenarios : COVID-19, vol. 9 (2020)
12. De Montevideo, O.: Enseñar en tiempos del Covid-19 Una guía teórico-práctica para docentes (2020)
13. García-Peñalvo, F.J., Corell, A., Abella-García, V., Grande, M.: La evaluación online en la educación superior en tiempos de la COVID-19. Educ. Knowl. Soc. **21**, 26 (2020). https://doi.org/10.14201/eks.23086
14. Carrera, N., De Central, U.: Educación virtual : creando espacios afectivos de convivencia y aprendizaje en tiempos de COVID-19, vol. 9 (2020)
15. Pérez- Narváez, M.V., Tufiño, A.: Teleeducación y COVID-19. CienciAmérica **9**, 58 (2020). https://doi.org/10.33210/ca.v9i2.296

16. Stavroulia, K.-E., Lanitis, A.: Addressing the cultivation of teachers' reflection skills via virtual reality based methodology. In: Auer, M.E., Tsiatsos, T. (eds.) ICL 2018. AISC, vol. 916, pp. 285–296. Springer, Cham (2020). https://doi.org/10.1007/978-3-030-11932-4_28
17. Granjo, J.F.O., Rasteiro, M.G.: Enhancing the autonomy of students in chemical engineering education with LABVIRTUAL platform. Educ. Chem. Eng. **31**, 21–28 (2020). https://doi.org/10.1016/j.ece.2020.03.002

Designing Learning Environments in a Digital Time – Experiences in Two Different Subjects at NTNU, Norway Autumn 2020

Tord Talmo(✉), Øystein Marøy, and Helene Røli Karlsen

Norwegian University of Science and Technology, Trondheim, Norway
{tord.m.talmo, oystein.maroy, helene.r.karlsen}@ntnu.no

Abstract. This paper focuses on digital learning environments. More specifically, the paper studies two research questions, namely "comparing with in-class lectures; what are the difficulties with lecturing digitally, and how can these be best mended?" and "when designing digital lecture materials: how can lecturers facilitate so that students are able to achieve the subjects' learning aims?". To answer these questions, different approaches were tested in two different subjects, namely in physics and communication and language. Moreover, previous literature and especially Salmon's e-tivities theory are relevant, and the results are obtained through a questionnaire as well as interviews with the student representatives. The results entail that students participate less from home than on campus, and that the students' perceived learning outcome is higher when it comes to activities done on campus. Furthermore, although the learning designs were created for collaboration and social interaction, many students avoid engaging in groups. The authors suggest that lecturers need to be aware of students' insecurities when designing digital learning environments as well as consider providing solution guides. Nevertheless, more research is needed to conclude.

Keywords: Blended learning · Active learning · Digital collaboration

1 Introduction

Spring 2020 became quite a special ending to a year of study in Norway. Due to the Covid19-virus, all higher education institutions (HEI) closed their campuses for almost all students, and instead focused on providing online solutions for education. Although the institutions received good feedback and many honorary comments from the society abroad, the students still demanded better lectures for the autumn semester [1]. The criticism from the students is mostly directed towards lecturers lack of digital competence, and the fact that most lectures were made digital in its original form, instead of using the tools available and rethinking the design and format of the traditional lecture.

This was the background the staff at the Preparatory Course for Engineering Studies at the Norwegian University of Science and Technology (NTNU) used to prepare the semester. The course consists of four subjects: mathematics, technology and science (TekSam), physics, and communication and language (KomNorsk). This article focuses on the methodology and format introduced in the two latter subjects. The study took

P. Zaphiris and A. Ioannou (Eds.): HCII 2021, LNCS 12784, pp. 531–546, 2021.
https://doi.org/10.1007/978-3-030-77889-7_37

place during the first two months of the semester, August until October 2020. The paper will show the blended learning approach introduced, and explain why this was conducted.

One of the main reasons for implementing different blended learning approaches at the course was to research which learning environments aided the students the most when doing online learning. The purpose of this paper is to report on these learning environments and the results collected. Moreover, the paper aims to answer the research questions 1) comparing with in-class-lectures; what are the difficulties with lecturing digitally, and how can these be best mended?, and 2) when designing digital lecture materials; how can lecturers facilitate so that students are able to achieve the subjects' learning aims?

2   Background

The course consists of five groups with 60–65 students each, and the groups have their own classrooms equipped with state-of-the-art educational technology. Physics has eight hours of lectures every week, whereas KomNorsk has nine, and the final exam in both subjects is a written exam of five hours.

Before the semester began, the capacity in the classrooms was almost halved. The focus group in this article consisted of 65 students in the KomNorsk-group and approximately 100 students in the physics group. The classroom for the KomNorsk-group only had capacity for 41, and for the physics group only 62 students were allowed at the same time. This meant that we had to divide the group in two. Furthermore, we decided to divide the groups into smaller clusters, so-called cohorts, of five students, in case even more severe restrictions would be implemented later in the semester. In addition, the cohorts could work physically together, as well as spending time with each other during their spare time.

During the study period, different blended learning approaches were introduced in the two subjects researched in this article. Firstly, some lectures were fully digital, i.e. all students attended live lectures online. Some lectures were streamed, i. e. some of the students attended lectures physically, while others stayed at home and watched the live lecture online. Thirdly, some lectures were designed as practical exercises at campus, where a limited amount of students attended each exercise. Additionally, to provide sufficient learning outcomes for the students forced to stay at home, there were designed digital home activities. These were intended to be done either individually or in small groups of approximately five students. These groups were the same throughout the period.

The physics students had four sessions of 90 min each week, where each session consisted of a different activity. Moreover, there were two exercise sessions, one with written problems and one session with practical exercises [2]. In the final two sessions only half of the students had access to the auditorium due to the Covid-19 restrictions. Consequently, the class was split in two groups of equal size where each group had one lecture every week, and one session where they did different activities from home. These activities included watching a stream of the lecture given to the other group, watching learning videos from Campus Inkrement [3], working individually with written problems, and working in fixed digital groups using a video lecture system implemented in NTNUs preferred Learning Management System (LMS) Blackboard; Blackboard Collaborate [4]. In the digital groups, three different activities were used: 1) multiple choice questions, most of them conceptual; 2) activities and problem-solving using simulations from PhET [5]; and 3) creating summaries of a previously reviewed part of the subject by expanding on given learning goals. In all these home-based activities, apart from watching a stream of the lecture, it was not possible to communicate with the lecturer as he was giving a lecture to the other half of the class.

When it comes to KomNorsk, the students were divided in two separate groups, C1/C2. Each group attended classes at campus every other week where they had seven lectures. Additionally, there was one common digital lecture for the class every Tuesday. During the Tuesday-lecture, all the theoretical background from the curriculum was taught, mainly in a traditional lecture format. The lecturer had prepared either a PowerPoint or tasks to exemplify, and the students attended digitally through Blackboard Collaborate. The students were provided the opportunity to chat and to ask questions orally. Mainly it was the chat functions that were preferred in these lectures. A few times the lecturer aimed at creating some interaction, through either break-out rooms for collaborative work or the response tool iLike [6]. Thus, the theoretical elements for the week were common for the whole group. During the rest of the week the two groups worked in different ways with the curriculum. At campus there was an extended amount of guided writing, discussions and group works, based on assignments provided by the lecturer. In addition, there were some small lectures to explain curricular phrases and/or other difficult passages in the curriculum. The group working at home was provided different materials, like video clips, additional writing tasks and assignments to work with throughout the week, which were intended to be used at campus the following week. They were also urged to collaborate in fixed groups of five students.

3 Theoretical Framework

There is always much to consider when designing learning environments at higher education institutions. You must contemplate resources, infrastructures, class sizes, the students' background and the student group's previous knowledge [7]. No matter what you consider, and what your aims are, aiding the student group in achieving their goals will always be the most important aspect. The design might be even more important when doing online learning, due to the lack of direct communication between teacher and students, peer learning and micro-communication. In this project we based our approach to the digitalization of the curriculum mainly on theories retrieved from development of MOOCs and e-tivities-design.

For the first part of the study, which is described in a previous article [8], the design was mainly based on MOOC theory. When the pandemic COVID19 hit in March 2020, closing campus lectures, the staff members at NTNU mainly had access to the preferred LMS Blackboard. This put some restraints and limitations on the opportunities, but during summer and early autumn 2020, there was time to investigate successful approaches of delivering an adequate design also for online learning. For the focus group in the present study it was necessary to create interaction and communication also online, and it was therefore interesting to look into the research and solutions provided through the development of MOOCS, starting back in 2008 with Siemens and Downes in Canada [9]. In this study, Blackboard was used as the platform, and the system Collaborate as a video conferencing system.

When considering the pedagogy in MOOCs, there are different formats and approaches that could be implemented. For instance, a c-MOOC would focus on establishing networks between learners and led by faculty members, something that is already present in our focus group [10]. However, a typical c-MOOC would also base its learning resources on different open source learning platforms, thus pedagogically relying heavily on connectivism, autonomy, peer-to-peer learning, social networking diversity, openness, emergent knowledge and interactivity [11]. A different approach is found in the xMOOCs, which is more concerned with learning by doing, and their structure is more similar to teacher-led university courses, built on lectures and assessment [12]. This includes a higher number of small video lectures, collaborative tasks, Q and As and even streamed live-lectures to some extent. The MOOC pedagogy is based on an innovative learning approach, something that is necessary in a time like 2020. However, due to limited time and the framework for the course, it was impossible to design a whole MOOC-course for our pilot group [8].

In order to have a successful implementation of online learning environments it is necessary to encourage students to actively participate and create a sense of belonging to a community of learning. "In the new culture of learning, people learn through their interaction and participation with one another in fluid relationships that are the result of shared interests and opportunity" [13: p. 50]. In the first study [8], we realized that creating communities for online learning is difficult when students have to watch lectures online. The students were reluctant to participate actively in discussions, they avoided discussing with peers online, and rarely used the video and/or chat functionalities to ask questions in plenary. It was therefore difficult to create a collaborative learning environment with a high degree of information exchange. Hence, it was needed to look beyond the MOOCs pedagogy in order to design better and more fluent learning environments.

Following the implementation of the streamed activities spring 2020, we identified five problematic areas that needed to be mended during the design of online learning lectures:

1. Active participation
   a. Students attended lectures, and followed classes, but they turned off their cameras, did not use the microphone and in general participated less than they would have done in an ordinary lecture at campus. This included fewer questions for the lecturer, and less interaction between peers. Some did, however, use the chat function available in BB Collaborate, which allowed the lecturer to address some questions. Active participation is essential for learning amongst new students, especially when introducing technological tools and systems [14], entailing that the learning designs need to include ways of activating the students.
2. Collaborative work
   a. One of the reasons why gamification has been increasingly popular in the latter years might be because it allows students to participate and interact through

educational technologies [15: p. 20]. It is important to allow students to collaborate when doing online learning. This has been the subject in many papers discussing both online learning in general and MOOCs [10], and needs to be addressed. Active learning and gamification have been a well-known source for learning and increase the learning effect for new students. One of the key elements for collaborative learning is face-to-face-interaction [16], which is removed when implementing online learning environments. When designing online learning activities, one needs to keep in mind the difficulties concerning the lack of face-to-face-interaction, and look for possible solutions for replicating the effects of this in a new way.

3. Self-regulated learning
   a. An essential argument for students' learning and development as students throughout their study life, is their ability to self-regulate and understand their own learning process: "Self-regulated learning strategies refer to action and processes, directed at acquisition of information or skills that involve agency, purpose, and instrumentality perceptions by learners." [17: p. 5]. This includes the ability to access curricular elements, treat curriculum in an adequate way and learn how to study in an effective way.

4. Access to curricular elements
   a. In an ordinary lecture, the teacher will always provide the curriculum and subjects relevant for the students and their final exam. This is one of the essentials missing when doing online learning without close moderation from the teacher. According to Salmon (2013), information exchange is step three in a successful deliverance of online courses, and highly necessary for knowledge construction [18]. The absence of the moderating lecturer needs to be mended and/or replaced, mainly through intelligent and effective ways of peer-to-peer collaboration. In an online environment collaboration can be defined as "To interact, communicate and collaborate through digital technologies while being aware of cultural and generational diversity" [19]. This includes interacting, sharing, engaging socially and culturally, using digital tools for collaborative processes, netiquette and even managing your own digital identity, meaning that it is difficult to achieve for new students without thorough training and practice.

5. Learning design (mainly for the teacher)
   a. The alteration from ordinary, physical lectures on campus to an online environment includes a change in the learning design provided by the lecturer. It is problematic, if not impossible, to replicate physical learning environments online, something that is often being tried. One needs to consider the available tools, without letting the tools and technology define the pedagogy: "Pedagogy and technology are intertwined in a dance: the technology sets the beat and creates the music, while the pedagogy defines the move" [20]. One must consider teaching styles, especially ways of structuring the content and one must acknowledge the lack of direct communication. Hence, the teaching design needs to not replicate or copy ordinary lectures, but instead use the inherent opportunities already found in the technology and environment. In many aspects this is the most difficult point to achieve and needs extra attention in the course design.

The aim of this study was to see if these problematic areas could be improved through blended learning approaches. According to Gilly Salmon (2013) there are five stages of development that a learner in an online community needs to go through, and that the lecturer must consider [18]:

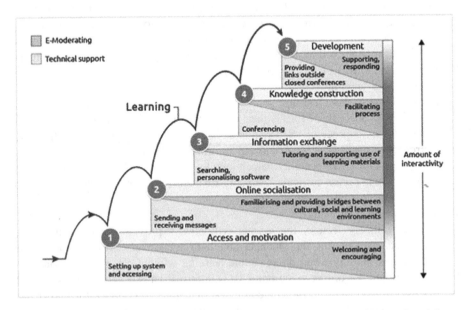

Fig. 1. G. Salmons five stages of successful online learning implementation (retrieved from: https://www.gillysalmon.com/five-stage-model.html)

As shown in Fig. 1, Gilly Salmon (2013) claims that there must be close interaction between lecturer, technical support and the learners themselves to succeed with online implementation of learning activities. In an environment as the one at the Preparatory Course for Engineering Studies at NTNU, some of the infrastructure is already defined, such as class-size, designated teachers, choice of LMS and workload for students throughout the week. NTNU, as most HEIs, is pre-set with ICT support, and therefore Salmon's technical support is a factor that this study did not consider when designing the courses. Still, considering that online learning was quite unknown for the students, and the fact that they are first-year students, accessing new systems takes some time. This is also commented on by some of the students in the reference group (for reference groups, see methodology). When asked an open-question about what they think of the lectures and design so far, one of the students finishes the answer as follows (all translations made by the authors)[1]: "[…] In general I believe it works very well, but people lack training and experience with some of the tools. That shows. There are some

---

[1] All interviews, transcriptions and use of these are approved by Norwegian Centre for Research Data. The transcriptions can be accessed by contacting the authors of this paper.

measures that should be introduced, such as with Blackboard, to make it more suited for streaming." This emphasizes the need Salmon introduces for technical support, or at least training in using the systems and tools. The students are still very clear in the interviews that the subject should be prioritized, something that was the main aim also for the learning designs created for this study. For future studies the technical support phase should be even more integrated also in the objectives and present in the research question.

This study primarily considers the implemented *activities* that should aid the five problematic areas for the student group not allowed or able to attend physical lectures on campus. The key area is to be able to create interactivity and aid the students to actually collaborate and be able to access the third level in Salmon's model: information exchange in order to gain more insight to curricular information.

4   Methodology

Seeing that one research question for this study being 'When designing digital lecture materials; how can lecturers facilitate so that students are able to achieve the subjects' learning aims?', it was especially important to implement the first three stages of Salmon's five stage model. It seemed, considering the research period (mid-august until mid-October 2020), difficult to train and equip a whole group for stage four and five, but still possible for some of the students to reach these levels through the activities delivered.

At level one, there is a question of granting students access and encouraging them to engage in the online environment. The encouragement seems a bit given, since the students are positive and attend the study by choice. Nonetheless, it is important to motivate, and especially explain the reasoning behind implementing this type of learning environment. Previous research done at NTNU shows the importance of introducing new technology and the methodological reasoning to the students as this helps build expectations and motivation [21]. Salmon states her motivational purposes in the expectancy theory, which says "[…] that the learning activity must have value to the learner and that the learner must expect to succeed." [18: p. 21]. This was important also in our learning design, especially considering the aspect of self-regulated learning. This was stressed by the teachers, and the students were explained the importance of active participation and collaboration with peers.

Additionally, the formal rules were introduced, the number of students allowed in the classroom was limited, and the message from the board was clear that all students should be provided some physical lecturing during the semester. The lecturer explained thoroughly the reasoning behind the blended learning approaches, and especially focused on the extraordinary opportunity these first-year students were granted to self-regulate their learning and become more independent throughout the year. One of the most important measures that was taken, which needed extra explanation and motivation, was the meaning of the cohorts. With online socialization, it is vital to create smaller groups that can work together and learn from one another [18: pp. 22–25].

The most problematic area when creating the design was how to make an environment for exchanging information, both from lecturer to students but also among peers. One important factor is that students often are reluctant to turn on their cameras and ask questions orally during digital lectures with the whole group: "(Student D) [...] students only participate via chat [...] I think that many do not bother to write a question because it takes too much time. The teacher might just move on, and then you lose what has been going on." Even worse is the fact that they have the same behavior also when collaborating in smaller groups:

> (Student D) And then it is a bit like people, I should not say it too certainly, but I have a feeling that people do not engage when they are on stream. We see it in these group tasks where I end up on a group with one. The mic is muted, camera off. Been sitting there for ten minutes...

The fact that students do not actively participate, discuss, and exchange information with each other needs attention when designing online learning environments. The lecturer needs to create activities and safe environments that enhance and/or force the students to collaborate.

The methodology and design of the first survey can be found in Talmo & Karlsen 2021 [8]. This study consisted of one quantitative survey with nine questions, and two thematic interviews with a total of four students involved. During the latter, we asked questions to gain more insight to interesting results from the quantitative data. This approach gave useful information and was copied and refined in the second survey.

In the second group of informants (consisting of approximately 100 students) the survey consisted of a questionnaire on Blackboard open to all students in the class as well as an interview with the group of student representatives. These are students elected by their peers to represent the student group in meetings with the subject teacher, in order to improve the quality of the curricular lectures [22]. The questions focused on the students' motivation for the different activities used, and their perceived learning outcome. In the questionnaire the students were asked to evaluate their motivation and their learning outcome from eight different learning activities that had been used in the first two months of the semester. The questionnaire used a five-point Likert-scale ranging from very unmotivated to very motivated and from very low learning outcome to very high learning outcome. There was also one open-ended question for each learning activity where the students were asked for suggestions to improve this activity. The students had time to answer the questionnaire during a student-active learning session. Moreover, those not attending this session were encouraged, by announcements on Blackboard, e-mail, and in a streamed lecture, to answer the questionnaire. In total 83 out of 102 enrolled students answered the questionnaire. The interview with student representatives focused on the same questions, using the answers from the questionnaire as background information. Also, the representatives had collected some information from the students concerning the activities and brought this to the meeting.

In the following we present the results from the survey done in the second study. The results are compared and underlined with previous results reported in the article Talmo & Karlsen (2021) [8], as well as qualitative results from the interviews with the reference group (Fig. 2).

5   Results

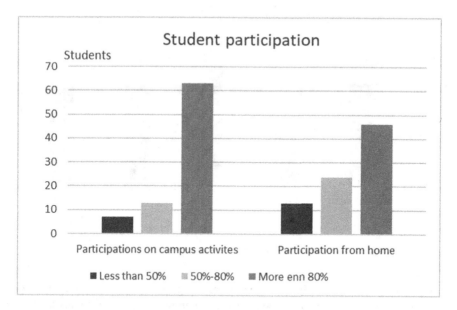

Fig. 2. Student participation in lecture.

In the previous survey we asked the students whether they preferred in-class-lectures or digital lectures. 78,4% of the students answered that they favored classroom lectures, and only 32,4% chose digital tasks [8]. In the physics group, almost 80% of the students attend ordinary lectures, something that is also emphasized as the most ben-efitting in the interviews. Fewer students, 55%, participate from home. Although the former study focused on the preferences and the latter on the actual participation, these two might correlate, especially since the interviewees commented on which type they favoured. Consequently, the results can entail that physical lectures and physical presence are the formats that feel most beneficial for the students considering their learning outcome. On the other hand, it might indicate that these students prefer lec-tures above all other activities. Considering streamed lectures, student H claims: "(Student H) In my opinion, lectures are the type of teaching I think is easiest to do at home, […] group tasks and stuff, I feel it is better to do with people, and then lec-ture…" The students prefer to attend lectures, at campus or streamed, regardless of subjects, activities and lecturer (Fig. 3).

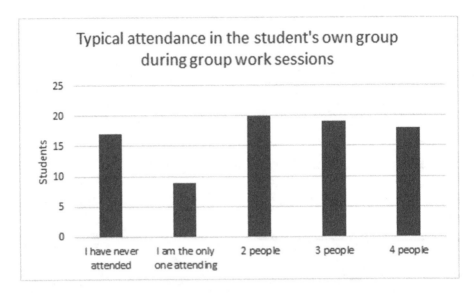

Fig. 3. Number of students (max. 5) showing up for group work.

Since many of the learning activities were designed for collaboration and social interaction, including interactive tasks, videos, and group tasks, it was interesting to see if there was sufficient attendance in the cohorts. The results show that the attendance is low and there are few groups where everyone participates. Consequently, it is difficult to achieve the goals of active participation and collaboration. However, when asked in the interview how the groups had worked together, the students claim that when group members participate, the cohorts are helpful, which entails that some students benefit from student collaboration. Still, the interviews also show that there have been problems in some of the groups due to lack of participation:

(Student F) Ehm, I think it has varied a lot from group to group if the tasks have been done or not. [...]
(Student H) Yes, we have not talked and so, then we have not received any feedback there, but maybe it shows in the questionnaire? [...] But I anticipate...
(Student F) I do not believe most groups actually meet in the morning. [...]
(Student E) Everything I have done with my group has been excellent. Those who meet, of course.

According to Salmon (2012), at stage three in her model, participants "have learned how to find, contribute and exchange information productively and successfully through e-tivities..." [18: p. 29], but this is difficult to achieve if the members of the cohorts do not attend group meetings and work sessions. The focus group of this survey indicates that the insecurity and lack of social interaction affect their ability and willingness to participate actively:

(student H): Maybe if we had, if everybody used the discussion forum a bit more, because it might be that peers also do the equations and then are able to explain, because then one can use the thing that you get it explained, either that they send pictures of what they have done and then write, because that is like a solution guide, and then you read and understand their way of thinking.

(Student G) I think somebody just needs to dare to write in it, because if one begins it is ok, in a way. It is just that someone needs to dare start writing, if not, nobody will dare.

These statements might indicate that students are unsure of their own abilities and afraid of asking questions in discussion forums. It might seem as if the insecurity of showing skills or possible lack of these is raised when participating in a digital learning environment (Fig. 4).

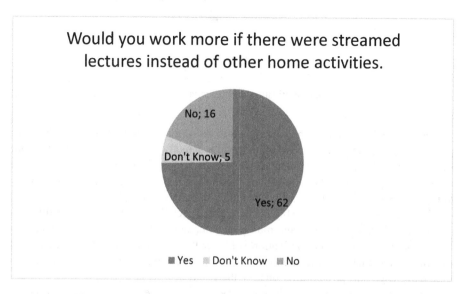

Fig. 4. Would students work more if every lecture was streamed?

Question 3: "Would you work more if there were streamed lectures instead of other home activities?" is interesting when comparing the results with the previous study. The learning design was different in the study involving physics, and more aware of the difficulties with blended learning approaches. The results show that fewer students in the second group are interested in working more with the subject if everything was streamed. In the first study only 21,62 of the students answered that they would work more with the subjects if everything was streamed [8]. In the second study only 62% claim that they would prefer streamed lectures. These factors indicate that learning design affects the students' sense of learning effects.

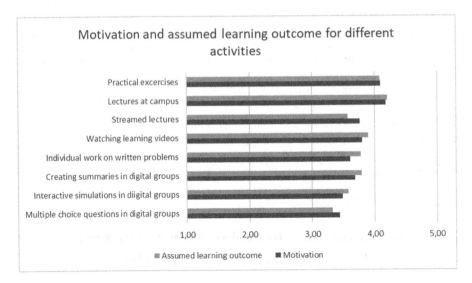

Fig. 5. Student motivation and perceived learning outcome.

The essential question of the survey was to see if the learning effect was sufficient, and to measure if the students were motivated for actually working collaboratively with peers in a digital learning environment. This was measured through question four in the survey, asking the students to rate their motivation and expected learning outcomes from different learning activities. In general, it seems as the students' motivation and perceived learning outcome are high. There are especially two activities that differ in the answers: Streamed lectures and multiple choice questions in digital group work. In both of these categories, the motivation is higher than the students' expected learning outcome. When analyzing the open-ended questions of these two activities, one can see some tendencies and possible reasons for the results.

Firstly, considering streamed lectures, the students have a tendency to lose attention, spend time on other distractions, and there is a lack of interaction in this format, i.e. students believe that the chat should be used in a way that benefits learning more: "(student A) [...] sometimes I feel that sort of the students attending on chat, sometimes the teacher do not pay attention, which means you do not get the answer straight away. And sometimes also, yes, sometimes you are ignored in a way [...]".

Secondly, there are two main issues when considering digital group work; 1) Students do not attend lessons, and 2) the lack of physical presence and a common area of focus, for example a shared screen or whiteboard.

In the interviews the students suggest possibilities for improvements. One example is how to increase interaction through the short videos:

(Student G) Yes, or rather maybe separate it in two sessions in a way. If there are four videos, and then see two on Tuesday and two on Thursday for example, like that. Because there are many students commenting that it is a bit too much to watch in one go. [...]
(Student E) Could also divide lectures and examples [...] Yes, you see, here is a five minute lecture, or ten minutes or however long it takes. And then you have: here is example one,

example two, example three. And then, if you understand it already after example one you can jump directly to the next round.

One way of overcoming difficulties in information exchange phases of a learning design is to provide more information from the moderator, or in this case the lecturer. Students in the physics group emphasize the need for solution guides to the task done outside campus, something that was also a concern for the students in the first focus group. One of the main objectives when creating learning designs in an online community is to facilitate so that students achieve the courses' competence aims before the exam. In the first group, the students showed uncertainty, something that could have been mended through clearer instructions and a solution guide:

(Student A): [...] doing tasks on their own. I feel that can work as a challenge as well, that you test yourself, but as mentioned, a solution guide if you are confused or something."

This is a severe flaw in the learning design from the lecturer and enhances students' uncertainty considering the learning effect in an online learning environment.

6   Discussion

Although this study entails that students prefer to attend lectures on campus, and also believe that the learning effect is higher when attending and participating in a physical learning environment, there are several aspects of the results that are interesting to elaborate further.

Considering the five problematic areas of online teaching identified in this study, some measures were taken to mend these. As stated in Sect. 2, to ensure active participation and collaboration, small groups were designed to make students more comfortable among their peers. This seemed to be a good move, and the students would prefer to stay in the same groups throughout the whole semester:

(Student G) At least those who have chosen to do it in a way. But when we changed groups now it can become in a way that people are more shy and that the focus is not the same as before, because I got a message saying there was a couple wondering why we had changed groups [...] because of the pandemic and in a way because they feel that they work better together when they have known the group members a bit longer, that you get more focused on the work instead of everything else and in a way know how to work well together and stuff [...] and then you dare to say: hey, come on, lets meet, even if it is eight o'clock, you wouldn't say that to a stranger.

Even if the students also emphasize the pandemic in this quote, several quotes indicate the same; in order to discuss, engage and participate in an online environment, you need to feel safe, know your peers and get the impression that your opinions and knowledge matter to the others. This is easier to obtain in small groups than in plenary sessions.

It is also obvious that uncertainty is a vital factor in the students' perception of learning effects. The same student G claims: "We are young people, so it is easy to slack if you are less motivated. Then, it is important to state that you at least have to do this [...] and you can do this, extra tasks and such...". This was also something the first group of students was concerned about. In Talmo & Karlsen (2021) the main conclusion is that "It is clear from this study that the students feel that they learn more when participating in-class. This might be because they are inexperienced students and have not learned sufficiently to regulate their own learning" [8].

It is difficult to create solid collaborative learning environments online, and the students, when asked, emphasize the opportunities delivered with physical presence, and would mainly try to replicate these in online learning environments. Considering the results from Q4 in the survey (Fig. 5), we see that the main difference in motivation and assumed learning outcomes is between activities done at campus (alternatives 1 and 2) and activities done at home (alternatives 3–8). The difference between home activities done individually and in groups are, even if not significantly, leaning towards a preference for learning individually (alternatives 3–5). The motivation and assumed learning outcome from group activities (alternatives 6–8) are lower. The exception is writing summaries, a task that does not require a lot of interaction and peer-to-peer learning. We suggest three possible reasons for why the students prefer individual tasks instead of collaborative work in this study: 1) technical difficulties (sharing screen, collaborative writing, unwillingness to use microphone and discussion forums), 2) lack of facilitation and aid from the lecturer to get started (including the need for solution guide), and 3) lack of presence from group members. The students are inexperienced at this stage, something that could have been addressed better in the learning design. At the same time lecturers involved in the study are more accustomed to designing face-to-face collaborations, and the tasks might not have been adjusted sufficiently for online learning environments.

At the same time the students see the effect of practicing individually, something that is more known to them as former pupils:

(Student F) It is probably very, very different from person to person [...] you kind of know, after attending school for a long time, what you learn the most from [...] and you have to do the tasks to prepare for the exams, but if you do not learn the most from that, then it is no point in cramming, sort of, just, just learn, yes.

The quote from Student F shows some of the difficulties when moving from one (well-known) learning environment, to new ways and environments of delivering learning objectives, both for the lecturer and the students.

Learning designs need to consider activities and tasks which students find interesting since that can improve students' motivation for working with the curriculum. This is something that modern pedagogical approaches should be aware of and try to replicate in collaborative online environments. Active learning and collaboration have proven to be good ways of learning. Some would even say that the implementation of new technologies are transforming education from "a contrived performance, on a stage, to a shared experience of a contingent reality that no-one, lecturer or student, has experienced before" [23: p.14–15], but these factors are not useful if the students are not engaged and actively participating. In other words, engagement and participation is a necessity for creating high level collaboration environments [23].

There are several difficulties still remaining when designing online learning environments for new students in HEIs. We clearly see uncertainty in the student group; fear of missing out on important curriculum for the exams and the importance of micro-communication in class, which was highly emphasized in the previous study [8]. This might be connected to lack of active participation, maybe due to lack of digital competence or just general uncertainty towards unfamiliar settings and people. This leads to less collaboration, making it difficult to achieve the information exchange stages in Salmon's model. Some useful implementations might be to include solution guides designed by the lecturer, and encourage students to trust the design provided by the lecturer.

The study has revealed areas of improvement, as well as providing insight to activities that increase the learning effects of a student group in online environments. More research is needed in order to conclude, especially towards what makes collaboration in an online environment easier. It is also necessary to include technical support -issues in the following studies, to see to what extent the software influences the learning process.

References

1. Opheim, A.: Nå forventer vi at alle NTNU-foreleserne har brukt sommeren til å lage god digital undervisning. In: adressa.no (2020). https://www.adressa.no/pluss/nyheter/2020/08/08/N%C3%A5-forventer-vi-at-alle-NTNU-foreleserne-har-brukt-sommeren-til-%C3%A5-lage-god-digital-undervisning-22418184.ece
2. Andersen, T.H., Korpås, G.S., Hansen, G., Kahrs, M.S.: The interactive whiteboard supports joint focus in collaborative learning. In: Proceedings of the 46th SEFI Annual Conference. Brussel, Belgium: SEFI Brussels, Belgium 2018. ISBN 978-2-87352-016-8. pp. 549–556 (2018)
3. https://campus.inkrement.no/
4. Blackboard. Blackboard Collaborate: Distance Learning System (2021). https://www.blackboard.com/teaching-learning/collaboration-web-conferencing/blackboard-collaborate
5. https://phet.colorado.edu/
6. One2Act. Tools – iLike (2021). https://www.one2act.no/?page_id=50
7. Allan, C.N., Campbell, C., Crough, J.: Blended Learning Designs in STEM Higher Education: Putting Learning First. Springer, Singapore (2019). ISBN 978-981-13-6981-0
8. Talmo, T., Karlsen, H.R.: Experiences on using different digital environments and tools for enhancing learning experiences. In: Inted2021 Proceedings (2021). https://doi.org/10.21125/inted.2021 (unpublished)
9. Morrison, D.: The Ultimate Student Guide to xMOOCs and cMOOCs" (2013). http://moocnewsandreviews.com/ultimate-guide-to-xmoocs-and-cmoocso
10. Athabasca & Manitoba Universities.: The Maturing of the MOOC - literature review of massive open online courses and other forms of online distance Learning (2013). https://www.gov.uk/government/uploads/system/uploads/attachment_data/file/240193/13-1173-maturing-of-the-mooc.pdf
11. Mackness, J., Mak, S., Williams, R.: The ideals and reality of participating in a MOOC. In: Paper presented at the Seventh International Conference on Networked Learning, Aalborg, Denmark (2010). http://www.lancs.ac.uk/fss/organisations/netlc/past/nlc2010/abstracts/PDFs/Mackness.pdf
12. Yousef, A.M.F, Chatti, M.A., Schroeder, U., Wosnitza, M., Jakobs, H.: MOOCs, A Review of the State-of-the-Art. In: 6th International Conference on Computer Supported Education (2014). https://www.researchgate.net/publication/275823066_MOOCs_a_review_of_the_state-of-the-art

13. Thomas, D., Seely Brown, J.: A new culture of learning: cultivating the imagination for a world of constant change. CreateSpace Independent Publishing Platform (2011)
14. Abidin, Z., Mathrani, A., Hunter, R.: Gender-related differences in the use of technology in mathematics classrooms: student participation, learning strategies and attitudes. Int. J. Inf. Learn. Technol. **35**(4), 266–284 (2018). https://doi.org/10.1108/IJILT-11-2017-0109
15. Johnson, L., Adams, S., Cummins, M.: The NMC horizon report: 2008 Australia-New Zealand Edition. Austin, TX: The New Media Consortium (2012). https://files.eric.ed.gov/fulltext/ED532397.pdf
16. Talmo, T., Sivertsen-Korpås, G., Mellingsæter, M., Einum, E.: Experiences with use of new digital learning environments to increase academic and social competence. In: Proceedings from the 5th International Conference of Education, Research and Innovation (iCERi2012), 19.-21.11.2012, Madrid, Spain, pp. 4540–4545 (2012). ISBN: 978-84-616-0763-1 ISSN: 2340–1095
17. Zimmermann, B.: Self-regulated learning and academic achievement: an overview. Educ. Psychol. **25**(1), 3–17 (1990). https://doi.org/10.1207/s15326985ep2501_2
18. Salmon, G.: E-tivities, 2nd ed. Routledge, New York (2013). ISBN: 978-0-203-07464-0 (ebk)
19. EU SCIENCE HUB. The European Commission's science and knowledge service (09/01/2019). DigiComp. Digital competence Framework for citizens. https://ec.europa.eu/jrc/en/digcomp/digital-competence-framework
20. Anderson, T., Dron, J.: Three generations of distance education pedagogy. Int. Rev. Res. Open Distrib. Learning **12**(3), 80–97 (2011). https://doi.org/10.19173/irrodl.v12i3.890
21. Nielsen, K.L., Stav, JB., Hansen-Nygård, G., Thorseth, T.M.: Designing and developing a student response system for mobile internet devices. In: Lu, Z. (Ed.), Learning with Mobile Technologies, Handheld Devices, and Smart Phones: Innovative Methods, pp. 56–68 (2012). IGI Global. https://doi.org/10.4018/978-1-4666-0936-5.ch004
22. NTNU.no (2020). "Reference groups – quality assurance of education.". https://innsida.ntnu.no/wiki/-/wiki/English/Reference+groups+-+quality+assurance+of+education
23. Traxler, J.: The 'learner experience' of mobiles, mobility and connectedness. In: Background paper to presentation ELESIG Symposium: Digital Futures. UK: University of Reading (2010). https://www.researchgate.net/publication/265043104_The_%27Learner_Experience%27_of_Mobiles_Mobility_and_Connectedness
24. Titova, S., Talmo, T.: Mobile voting systems for creating collaboration environment and getting immediate feedback: a new curriculum model of a university lecture. In: Parsons, David (ed.) (2014) International Journal of Mobile and Blended Learning (IJMBL), vol 6/3 (2014), pp 18–34 (2014). ISSN: 1941-8647. EISSN: 1941-8655. https://doi.org/10.4018/IJMBL

Rapid Response to the Needs of ESL Students of a Technical University in the Time of Emergency Covid-19 Transfer to Online Classes: ITMO University Case Study

Evgenia Windstein[1] and Marina Kogan[2]

[1] St. Petersburg University of Information Technologies Mechanics and Optics (ITMO), St. Petersburg, Russia
evwindstein@itmo.ru
[2] Higher School of Language Teaching and Translation, Peter the Great St. Petersburg Polytechnic University, St. Petersburg, Russia
kogan_ms@spbstu.ru

Abstract. The disruption caused by the 2020 COVID-19 pandemic entailing a transfer to the fully online emergency remote teaching (ERT) put many teachers in Russia and across the globe in the role of facilitators, course designers, technical support specialists and psychologists. To address the new challenge, a group of instructors of St. Petersburg University of Information Technologies Mechanics and Optics (ITMO), Russia, attempted to adopt a blended ESL methodology piloted in 2017–2018 and calibrated in the intermittent period to build a Zoom- and LMS-based mostly synchronous upper-intermediate emergency remote General English course for 99 first and second year bachelor's of science students (7 groups). To increase student satisfaction with the design and content of the course, learners' needs were monitored during the fall 2020 semester through a series of surveys. To measure student satisfaction with the emergency ESL course, a summative cross-sectional survey, a series of semi-structured interviews and fall 2020 course completion rate were analyzed.

Keywords: ESL students' needs · ESL students' satisfaction · ESL for STEM students · Technical university ESL program · Emergency Remote Teaching (ERT) · Course completion rate · Dornyei's motivational strategies

1 Introduction

The 2019–2020 outbreak of COVID-19 and subsequent imposition of social distancing, self-isolation and lockdown policies across the globe dealt a serious blow to the educational process. To bridge the gap, schools and universities made an unprecedented effort to transform face-to-face classes to their online equivalents.

On March 16, 2020, Russian institutions of HE including ITMO launched an expeditious transition to fully online teaching in accordance with the provisions of the decree of the Ministry of Education and Science of the Russian Federation.

© Springer Nature Switzerland AG 2021
P. Zaphiris and A. Ioannou (Eds.): HCII 2021, LNCS 12784, pp. 547–567, 2021.
https://doi.org/10.1007/978-3-030-77889-7_38

Though the period of the emergency transfer to online education was testing, Russian universities stayed afloat owing to the experience gained while integrating high tech learning methodologies, approaches and models in their curricular in the pre-pandemic period. ITMO alone shared about 225 MOOCs on such platforms, as ITMO courses, the Russian National Open Education and edX[1].

Though the prospects of online education had been analyzed extensively by the teacher-scholar community in view of the ever rising costs of education in the developed countries, inadequate educational infrastructure in the developing countries and low population density in some rural areas of large countries, like Russia, it was not until spring 2020 that online education transformed from a model with high potential described in numerous research papers, including meta-analysis studies (e.g., [1, 2]) and studies focusing on Language MOOCs [3], to a model with no alternative, a scenario, which could not have been foreseen even by the international and national leaders in the field of online education (e.g., [4, 5]).

Of course, there was no comparison between the development of a MOOC, SPOC, LMOOC, a blended or distant course in a regular setting and in an emergency. To differentiate the two, a new term "emergency remote learning" (ERT) was coined [6].

Efficiency comes with experience, and educational institutions whose staff experimented with digital technologies in the pre-pandemic period had a better chance of designing robust clear-cut emergency remote courses [7, 8].

Though each Russian university elaborated its own scenario of transfer to ERT, the range of technological tools was rather similar and included a platform serving as a content storage and students' knowledge assessment hub, a video conferencing service for online lectures and consultations, a social networking site and an instant messenger or email for student-teacher communication [9].

In this research paper, we will present a case where a group of ITMO ESL instructors undertook to adapt a blended ESL learning methodology to the ERT conditions while rapidly responding to STEM students' needs [10].

2   Background

2.1   ITMO ESL for Bachelors Teaching Process Prior to 2020 ERT

At ITMO, bachelor's students study ESL for three years, which is one year longer than at any typical non-linguistic Russian university. ITMO ESL instructors build their curricular on the principles of communicative approach. Students are encouraged to speak English only in the classrooms. An academic year is broken down into two semesters and four modules. Prior to the COVID-19 outbreak, students studied on campus only. General English classes were taught in a traditional way with whiteboards, markers, handouts and occasional PC/laptop demonstrations of presentations/videos, sometimes with the use of an overhead projector (OHP).

---

[1] For details see ITMO.education portal, https://edu.itmo.ru/ru/edu_online.

The blended learning model was first tested in ITMO in spring 2018. At that time, third year ITMO students were offered a blended Moodle-backed ESP course and three experimental second year proficiency STEM groups – a tripartite General English blended course with elements of flipped classroom and bring your own device (BYOD) methodologies [10]. The Spring 2018 blended General English learning methodology pursuant to which proficiency students were taught (further GEM0) was further verified and calibrated in 2018–2019. Later, at the time of emergency transfer to ERT in spring 2020, it was used as a foundation for the development of the Spring 2020 emergency remote General English course (GEC1) and Fall 2020 emergency remote General English course (GEC2).

2.2 Preliminary Stage of the Spring-Fall 2020 ERT Experiment

Phase I. Our first experiment on the designing and field-testing of a blended tripartite General English course (GEC0) was conducted in the spring 2017–2018 semester, when we built a course for three groups of 47 proficiency STEM students pursuant to Ausubel's significant learning approach. The course comprised a General English Class (2 ac. h./wk), a Video Class designed with the use of Open Educational Resources (OER) (2 ac. h./wk) and a Research Class based on the *Developing Your Research Project* MOOC by University of Southampton streamed on FutureLearn platform (2 ac. h./wk) [11]. Students studied in the classroom using their own devices (BYOD) in line with the flipped classroom methodology. The course consisted of the tasks either created on Schoology LMS platform, or digitized (automated tests, polls, presentations, etc.) or created with the use of OER materials (videos, graphical materials, quizzes, surveys, etc.). A final survey demonstrated that 2/3 of students were satisfied with C0 to one degree or another [10]. We took it as a signal that some aspects of the Spring 2018 blended General English learning methodology (GEM0) needed to be further fine-tuned. For example, students complained about Schoology's insufficient operation (later it was discovered that the problem was in the unstable internet connection on campus), not very convenient mobile version, an intricate system of files and folders and intermediate relevance and overly generalized nature of the Research Class MOOC.

There was an option to swap the freemium version of Schoology for Moodle, as, according to the findings of our review of various LMSs, they both were free of charge and functioned not only as a cloud storage, but also as a hub for task creation and sharing. Both platforms allowed for student-teacher/student-student communication through the system of chats/blogs and administering formative/summative assessments fostering collaboration and real-time feedback.

To decide on the fate of Schoology, we collected feedback from one of our spring 2018 target groups (12 students) after they completed a Moodle-based ESP course the following year. Students' feedback showing Schoology approval rate of 75%

persuaded us to keep it. Students noted that Schoology was easier to navigate, more intuitive and better organized. Changes made to (GEM0) are described in Table 8 (Appendix 1).

Phase II. It is important to note that ITMO teachers might get groups of 1st, 2nd or 3rd year with different English proficiency levels in different academic years. In 2018–2019 and in the fall semester of 2019–2020, we continued using Spring 2018 blended General English learning methodology (GEM0) to teach first, second and third year STEM students with different levels of proficiency, while keeping to ESL teaching process. The flipped classroom methodology was abandoned due to the presence of Cambridge LMS (for General English groups) and Moodle (for ESP students) with pre-programmed homework tasks.

In the fall/spring of 2018–2019 and in the fall of 2019, we further improved (GEM0) by revamping the system of files and folders. The description of the updated version of GEM0 (the Intermittent blended General English learning methodology (GEM_int) is presented in Table 8 (Appendix 1).

Phase III. In March 2020, after ITMO along with other Russian universities took a sharp turn towards ERT, the Spring Emergency remote General English course (GEC1) based on the Intermittent blended General English learning methodology GEM_int was created for 12 groups of STEM students with English proficiency levels ranging from intermediate to advanced. After the completion of GEC1, we collected feedback from 2 intermediate third year computer science and biotechnology groups studying exclusively pursuant to the Spring 2020 ERT methodology (GEM1) (groups co-taught by two teachers were excluded from the experiment due to a difference in teaching approaches). Since the number of contact hours was cut from 4 to 2 per week in spring 2020, students were assigned extra tasks for self-study. At this point, we reintroduced the original flipped classroom concept, but substituted BYOD with Zoom communication (hybrid methodology). Details of GEM1 and GEC1 are highlighted in Table 8 (Appendix 1).

At the end of the spring 2020 semester, after the completion of GEC1, the groups (34 students) were administered a two-part cross-sectional online survey to assess their satisfaction with online English classes, course design, the flipped classroom element, core technology tools (Schoology and Zoom) and to identify their preferred mode of study (face-to-face or online) (Table 1).

We asked students to respond to three types of questions in the 14-question survey: nine 5-point Likert scale questions, one open-ended and five close-ended questions. A total of 22 usable responses were collected. Among 22 third year intermediate English proficiency respondents there were 9 females and 13 males.

Table 1. Spring Emergency remote General English course (GEC1) student feedback.

	Question	N	Mean	St. dev.
1	How would you rate your overall online English study experience?	22	3.96	0.79
2	How would you rate your satisfaction with the course materials (articles, quizzes, video/audio tasks, etc.)?	22	4.64	0.68
3	How would you rate your satisfaction with the technological infrastructure used in the course (Zoom, Schoology, email)?	22	4.09	0.81
4	How would you rate teaching methods used in this online course?	22	4.72	0.55
5	How would you rate your Zoom experience?	22	3.96	0.90
6	How would you rate your Schoology experience?	22	4.18	1.06
7	In this online course, you were asked to study grammar topics on your own by watching videos, reading explanations, practicing (flipped classroom). How would you rate this experience?	22	4	0.95
8	Rate your level of satisfaction with the balance between the online and offline (homework) parts of the course	22	3.82	0.91
9	Each online lesson you have had in this course consisted of three basic parts: discussions, practical work and quizzes. Were you satisfied with this structure?	22	4.59	0.59

Analysis of students' feedback showed that students were overall satisfied with GEC1 course and its design, except that 2 students were not particularly happy with the balance of the offline/online workload and 3 students explicitly said they didn't like the flipped classroom element. When asked which mode of study – online or offline – they liked more, 8 students demonstrated an inclination towards offline classes, 8 had no preferences and 6 showed an affinity for the online communication. Responding to a close-ended question of how their online ESL experience could be improved, 8 students said they were happy with the class, 8 students suggested adding more discussions, 4 opted for more grammar practices, 2 – for more quizzes. Answers to a similar open-ended question "If you had a chance to improve the online/offline balance of the course, what would it be like?" were consistent with the distribution of choices in the close-ended question. In addition, when answering the open-ended question, one student said that they would like to have four not two online classes per week. Another student suggested using Discord instead of Zoom.

The Cronbach's Alpha measured at 0.75 indicating sufficient reliability of the test results.

Students' feedback on their satisfaction with GEC1 prompted us to focus on the course design issues in the next phase of the experiment.

2.3   Fall 2020 Emergency Remote General English Course (GEC2)

At the beginning of the fall 2020 semester, we used the Spring 2020 ERT methodology (GEM1) to put together the Fall 2020 emergency remote General English course (GEC2) for seven first and second year upper-intermediate groups (99 students) studying at ITMO's School of Computer Technologies and Control, School of Photonics, School of Translational Information Technologies, School of Biotechnology and Cryogenic Systems and Faculty of Technological Management and Innovations.

2.4   Design

In general, ITMO has been encouraging teachers to move instruction to Moodle, but because we already had a good scope of readily available proofread tasks, especially grammar quizzes, and remembering the results of the "Moodle vs. Schoology" survey where 75% of students voted for Schoology, we decided to keep it as the classroom LMS platform. Since an online communication channel could be chosen at the teacher's discretion, we decided to continue using Zoom in the implementation of GEC2.

Availability of an LMS with preprogrammed homework tasks (Cambridge LMS) and a sufficient number of study hours (4 per week) meant we did not have to rely on the flipped classroom element as we did in the Spring 2020 ERT methodology (GEM1).

To account for the above said, to observe the ERT limitations and to keep to the upper-intermediate General English curriculum, we opted for the following technological and pedagogical tools in the implementation of GEC2:

1. Zoom for synchronous online classes/consultations covered by the license purchased by ITMO.
2. Schoology LMS to create, share and store materials, to facilitate online communication, provide real time feedback to students in the virtual classroom, conduct formative assessment and administer asynchronous compensation classes.
3. Google Drive to create and store writings and track students' progress.
4. Cambridge LMS to conduct formative assessment and assign homework.
5. Email and VKontakte social networking site for communication.
6. Pan-university platform tracking students' academic standing.

The following materials were used in the development of GEC2:

- Empower Upper-intermediate Students' Book – a major source of classroom materials, including grammar and vocabulary instruction, listening, video, reading and writing tasks. Materials were digitized, stored and shared on Schoology.
- E-handouts, e.g., PowerPoint presentations, .doc/.pdf handouts.
- OER resources (videos, cartoons, memes, pictures, surveys, quizzes).
- Instructions (general course, communication, writing guides).
- Surveys (4 Google Form surveys).

Our spring ERT teaching experience and the range of problems we encountered immediately upon the inception of online classes in fall 2020 challenged us to further refine the Spring 2020 ERT methodology (GEM1).

To continue working in line with the communicative approach principles and remembering that the number of tasks completed in a virtual classroom is usually somewhat lower than in offline classes, we offered mostly speaking, listening/video and creative tasks involving communication between students working in small groups. While working in breakout rooms, students were required to make comments on Schoology. Not only did this approach allow students to practice writing and reading (students were encouraged to read each other's comments, upvote the best ideas, peer check fellow students' entries and read teacher's comments), but also it proved to be a valid classroom management tool for supervision of students left unattended in breakout rooms.

Students and the teacher were expected to have cameras on at all times according to ITMO policy. This policy, however, turned into a real nightmare for some students. If the students living in dorms had issues with privacy, students whose families moved to summerhouses to minimize chances of contracting COVID-19 experienced Internet connection problems. While some students were truly shy by nature and showed signs of psychological strain having a close-up of their face observed by a group of people, others had an attitude problem where they took online classes as an opportunity to get attendance marks while engaging in unrelated tasks. Yet another group of students connecting from mobile devices reported that it was daunting to hold the iPhone, type and have the camera on simultaneously.

3   Research Questions

A broad scope of students' interests reported at the introductory lesson, a varying perception of the essence of online classes and netiquette, suboptimal motivation and gaps in attitude demonstrated by some first year students, discontent with the "web camera on" policy, a noticeable difference in English proficiency among students and absenteeism due to illness or technical issues set the following research questions for us to answer:

1. What aspects of the Spring 2020 ERT methodology (GEM1) should be modified for the Fall 2020 emergency remote General English course (GEC2) to fully satisfy the existing ERT conditions while complying with the curriculum?
2. How to improve student satisfaction with the emergency remote course?
3. How to cater to students with high absenteeism due to illness, technical or personal issues?

To answer the questions, we developed a system of teacher-student communication encouraging students to share their opinion about the course and inviting them to take on the role of course co-creators. Students' feedback was reinforced with interviews and analysis of student retention. Results of our efforts are discussed in "Results and Discussion" section.

4   Methodology

To diagnose ongoing problems and improve student experience and attitude towards GEC2 and online ESL in general, a system of feedback collection was designed in the Google Forms environment. Three web-based panel surveys (S_int1, S_int2, S_int3) designed to tap into student satisfaction with GEC2 course design and content and to collect students' suggestions on the improvement of subsequent lessons were administered at the end of Unit 1, Unit 2 and Unit 3 (according to Cambridge Upper-intermediate Empower Student's Book[2] syllabus) [12: 393–395]. Each survey focused on a different aspect of the course. Out of 99 students studying in accordance with the Fall 2020 ERT methodology (GEM2) (Table 8, Appendix 1), 63 participated in S_int1, 60 in S_int2 and 67 in S_int3, rate or return being 60%–65%.

S_int1 was designed to analyze the relevance of cognitive load provided in GEC2 and assess which tasks students enjoyed/disliked doing. The questionnaire consisted of 4 questions, two of which were open-ended and two – close-ended.

In S_int2 that consisted of one close-ended question and one 5-point (1-absolutely positive – 5-absolutely negative) Likert scale question [13], we asked students to answer more general questions, express their attitude towards GEC2 and indicate the degree of their satisfaction with online classes.

In S_int3 that consisted of 3 questions (two open-ended and one 5-point Likert scale question), students were asked to reflect on whether there were any novel, unexpected facts they came across in GEC2 and share ideas on further GEC2 improvement.

A web-based follow-up panel survey (S_fin) was conducted at the end of the fall 2020 semester to collect students' feedback on their satisfaction with GEC2 adjustments and measure the change in their attitude towards online education in general [12: 394–395]. The rate of survey return amounted to 87%. The survey comprised 22 questions (16 5-point Likert scale, 5 close-ended and 1 open-ended questions). It was broken down into 4 sections. The first focused on the measurement of changes in student motivation and attitude towards GEC2 and online education. The second section aimed to assess student satisfaction with the changes implemented in the design. The third section solicited feedback on their satisfaction with the gamification elements. The final block asked students to provide their personal information.

To gain a better insight into the student satisfaction with GEC2, we conducted a semi-structured interview with 4 volunteer students. In addition, we analyzed the course completion rate by comparing an average completion rate of 7 experimental groups against an average completion rate of 7 randomly chosen first and second year control groups of the same English proficiency level.

---

[2] Adrian Doff, Craig Thaine, Herbert Puchta, Jeff Stranks, Peter Lewis-Jones: Cambridge Upper-intermediate Empower Student's Book, Cambridge University Press, Cambridge (2015), https://www.cambridge.org/gb/cambridgeenglish/catalog/adult-courses/cambridge-english-empower/cambridge-english-empower-upper-intermediate-students-book.

5 Results and Discussion

5.1 Survey S_int1 Results

Data collected from two open-ended questions in the first Intermittent survey (S_int1) were categorized and arranged into groups. Answers to the first question "Type all the new words you've learnt in Unit 1" showed that a vast majority of new words that students had learned came from extra tasks (89%). Only 11% were from the textbook, which was an indicator that, on the one hand, the first unit of the textbook focusing on refreshing intermediate vocabulary was relevant for the majority of students, on the other, to keep students' interest high, we needed to enhance tasks from the textbook with OER. The open-ended question concerning grammar tasks "Type the new grammar points that you have learned in Unit 1" revealed the fact that 42% of students learned new grammar, 14% learned new grammar and revised old rules and 47% revised the grammar they had already known. Only 10% explicitly stated that all grammar topics were familiar to them. Since Unit 1 contained tasks mostly intended to refresh students' intermediate grammar and vocabulary, it was evident that a little more than half of all students had solid knowledge of the intermediate English grammar, which meant that we needed to offer some grammar review tasks on an as-needed basis.

Other two questions were designed as close-ended questions. There we asked students about their satisfaction with the pedagogical element of the course. Feedback received from students is outlined in Table 2 below.

Table 2. Answers to S_int1's close-ended questions.

	Question	%
	What classroom activities did you like?	
1	Explanation of grammar material	60%
2	Explanation of new vocabulary	64%
3	Whole class discussions	57%
4	Breakout room (small group) discussions	57%
5	Listening tasks	37%
6	Video tasks	43%
7	Extracurricular (additional) tasks	32%
8	Other	3%
	What classroom activities did you not like?	
1	Explanation of grammar material	0%
2	Explanation of new vocabulary	5%
3	Whole class discussions	5%
4	Breakout room (small group) discussions	9%
5	Listening tasks	27%
6	Video tasks	13%
7	Extracurricular (additional) tasks	5%
8	Other	5%

Feedback collected on the appeal of tasks demonstrated that there was some problem with the listening and video tasks (extracurricular tasks were, mostly, video and listening assignments). Upon its discussion with the students, we decided to change the way the listening and video tasks were done by allowing each student to listen/watch videos individually or in breakout rooms to minimize the background noise.

5.2   Survey S_int2 Results

The first question in this survey asked students to share their attitude towards their online English class. The distribution of answers was as follows: absolutely positive – 71%, somewhat positive – 20%, neutral 9%.

The second question measured the degree to which student attitude towards online education improved to compare to the beginning of the fall semester. Half of the students said that is was positive from the beginning, 2% of students said that there was no positive change, 8% of students noted that their attitude improved by 25%, 18% of the students reported that their attitude improved by 50%, 13% – by 75% and 9% of students indicated that their attitude towards online education improved by 100%.

Though we did not ask students the same question about course design in the second survey, we continued working on the improvement of the aspects that students deemed important. We noticed, for example, that stronger students were bored with grammar tasks. To increase their satisfaction and add some novelty, we introduced more OER and self- or student-developed grammar games [13].

5.3   Survey S_int3 Results

Our third survey was intended to identify what topics students found to be most unexpected and to see whether students perceived GEC2 as a source of some novel information. The survey consisted of 2 open-ended questions. Answers to the open-ended questions were categorized and coded [12: 393–395].

Responses to the question "What was the most unexpected piece of information about the English-speaking world or Russia you learned in Module I (Units 1–3)?" were distributed into 7 categories: "Invalid answer" – 23 students (34%), "Nothing" – 4 (6%), "Cultural differences" – 19 (28%), "Grammar" – 11 (16%), "Nature" – 5 (8%), "Natural disasters" – 2 (3%), "Other" – 2 (2%). Judging by the answers and classroom observations, topics connected with cultural differences and, especially, teacher's experience living in the United States was perceived as one of the most exciting discussion themes. Many students noted that they were not aware of the degree of English indirectness and politeness and that American English and British English were so different.

The second open-ended question asked students to share their ideas on how we could further improve GEC2. Responding to this question, 29 students (43%) said that they were happy with the lessons and did not think they could be improved, 9 students (20%) set unrealistic goals, for example, to move lessons to a later time or have offline lessons, 7 students (10%) noted that they would love having more speaking practices, 3 students (5%) said they needed more time with the teacher, 6 students (8%) said they enjoyed group talk, but it would be nice to see the end time for their discussion, 3 students (5%) asked to reconsider the "web camera on" policy, as, in their opinion, it was not always convenient or necessary to have cameras on, one student (1%) asked for more interactivity, 1 (1%) – for more pictures, 1 (1%) – to improve the quality of the sound and video, 1 (1%) – more cultural classes; 13% of the answers were classified as "invalid". At this point, we decided to implement some of the suggestions having checked them against Dornyei motivational strategies [13]. A full list of course innovations compliant with Dornyei's strategies are highlighted in Table 3.

Table 3. Alignment of the changes made to GEC2 with Dornyei's motivational strategies.

Dornyei's motivation strategy	Innovation	Implemented after
1 Language level		
- Include a sociocultural component in the L2 syllabus	Enhancing GEC2 with extracurricular materials	S_int1
2 Learner level		
- Decrease student anxiety	Relaxing the "web camera on" policy	S_int3
- Increase the attractiveness of the course content	Incorporating topical authentic OER, improving course design	S_int3
- Arouse and sustain curiosity and attention (not allowing lessons to settle into too regular a routine)	Offering different modes of student interaction ("rotating lesson styles in different lessons", "according to each student's choice", "whole class only", "in small groups only", "diversified" (a mix of all modes)	S_int3
- Increase student interest and involvement in the tasks (including game-like features, such as puzzles, problem solving)	Offering more creative tasks, including trivia, puzzles, surveys, grammar games, crosswords, etc.	S_int2
3 Teacher-specific motivational components		
- Try to be empathic, congruent, and accepting	Relaxing the "webcam on" policy; allowing students to choose the preferred study mode; giving students who missed classes due to COVID-19 or technical problems to compensate by doings the same class tasks in asynchronous mode	S_int3
- Adopt the role of a facilitator	Letting students choose the preferred mode of study ("with the teacher", "in a small group", "individually", mixed), while standing by and providing necessary support to students in small groups or working individually	S_int3

We also introduced a more democratic way of choosing the preferred mode of classroom interaction, where students could select to study "according to each student's choice", "whole class only", "in small groups only", "diversified" (a mix of all mode). At the end of the lesson, we allowed about 20 min to recap and discuss any challenges students had working in small groups. Besides, we started indicating the time limit for each task posted on Schoology, made the "web camera on" policy more relaxed and increased lessons' interactivity by adding more links to OERs, including pictures, memes, games boosting aesthetic appeal and cognitive load of lesson materials.

At the end of the fall semester, after the implementation of the aforementioned suggestions, we conducted a 22-item follow-up survey S_fin.

5.4 Survey S_fin Results

The rate of return for S_fin amounted to 86% (86 students out of 99 responded to S(fin) questions). There were fifteen 5-point Likert scale questions, one open-ended and five close-ended questions in the survey.

Out of 86 participants, 62 students (72%) were males, 24 (28%) – females. The distribution of the first and second year students was 48 (56%) and 38 (44%), respectively. The number of students with a positive online study experience at the beginning of the fall 2020 semester amounted to 64 (74%) against 15 (17%) of students with a negative experience. The number of students who enjoyed studying ESL online at the beginning of fall 2020 came to 68 (79%) against 6 (7%) of those who identified their experience as unsatisfactory. Out of 86 respondents, 6 (7%) reported that they had never studied online and 12 (14%) of students said that they had never studied ESL online prior to fall 2020.

The survey was developed to measure student satisfaction with GEC2 and the design of GEC2 lessons. Students were also asked to assess their online learning experience. The distribution of responses is presented in Table 4. Internal validity of the test was verified by calculating Cronbach's Alpha (0.81) that confirmed good internal consistency.

Table 4. Student Fall 2020 emergency remote General English course (GEC2) feedback.

	Question	N	Mean	St. dev.
1	Please rate your satisfaction with English classes at the beginning of the fall 2020–2021 semester	86	4.34	0.78
2	Please rate your satisfaction with English classes at the end of the fall 2020–2021 semester	86	4.49	0.59
3	I have become more satisfied with online education in general during the fall semester	86	4.16	0.91
4	My motivation to study English has improved during the fall semester	86	4.13	0.97
5	The organization of online English lessons (clarity of instructions, quality and speed of communication, etc.) has improved during the fall semester	86	4.33	0.83

(continued)

Table 4. (*continued*)

	Question	N	Mean	St. dev.
6	The technical aspect of online English lessons (ease of navigation, quality of online communication, etc.) has improved during the fall semester	86	4.13	0.89
7	The content of online English lessons (topics, culture points, range of tasks, etc.) has improved during the fall semester	86	4.09	0.88
8	The structure of online English lessons (the balance of speaking, listening, reading, writing tasks) has improved during the fall semester	86	4.12	0.94
9	The design of teaching materials has improved during the fall semester	86	4.23	0.85
10	The set time limit for each task (written in red at the top of each task) was a useful innovation	86	3.70	1.25
11	Revision of some grammar and vocabulary topics covered earlier in the course was adequate	86	4.40	0.72
12	Grammar games (Present Perfect Simple/Present Perfect Continuous, Used to/Would board games with e-dice) were useful	86	4.21	1.05
13	PowerPoint grammar presentations for individual/small group learning were useful	86	4.27	1.01
14	I found memes, cartoons and pictures among lesson materials useful	86	4.42	1.07
15	The hyperlinks to the Merriam-Webster dictionary helped me to improve the pronunciation of complex/awkward English words such as "arduous", "grueling"	86	3.85	1.10

A mean of 4 or above and a standard deviation of less than 1 on the majority of questions demonstrated that students were overall satisfied with GEC2 and that the responses were consistent. However, there were two adjustments that some students viewed as excessive, namely "the time limit message included in each Schoology task" and links to dictionaries. Perhaps, the problem was that students had expected to see a built-in timer, not a written message. The problem with links to dictionary articles might have arisen because students could easily find such links themselves.

Students were also asked to express their opinion about the preferred mode of online ESL study: "rotating lesson styles in different lessons", "according to each student's choice", "whole class only", "in small groups only", "diversified" (a mix of all modes). Table 5 demonstrates the distribution of students' responses.

560   E. Windstein and M. Kogan

Table 5. Preferred mode of online ESL study.

Rotating lesson styles in different lessons	According to student's choice	Diversified (a mix of all three modes)	Whole class only	In small groups only	Other
25 students (29%)	20 students (23%)	15 students (17%)	12 students (14%)	11 students (13%)	3 students (6%)

The data reflected in Table 5 shows that over a quarter of students appreciated our experiment on providing a more "democratic" way of choosing the learning mode. Those three students who chose "Other" highlighted their special satisfaction with the "choose it yourself" approach. However, the majority (25 students) expressed an opinion that rotation of different lesson styles would be the best choice.

The open-ended S_fin question was intended to solicit students' suggestions on further improvement of the course and to see if the complaints shared in S_int3 were alleviated. Answers were categorized. The results of S_int3 and S_fin are demonstrated side-by-side. S(int3) data were adjusted for the number of S_fin respondents.

Table 6. Comparison of students' suggestions proposed in S_int3 and in S_fin.

	Suggestions	N of responders S_int3	Adjusted N of S_int3 resp *	In %	N of respondents S_fin	In %	Difference, %
1	Unrealistic expectations	6	7	8%	6	7%	−1%
2	Invalid/no answer	9	11	13%	9	10%	−3%
3	Happy	21	26	30%	29	34%	+3%
4	Content						
	More speaking	7	9	10%	8	9%	−1%
	More reading	1	1	1%	1	1%	0
	More grammar	2	2	2.5%	3	3%	+0.5%
	More listening	0	0	0%	0	0%	0%
	Review of previous topics	1	1	1%	0	0%	−1%
	Culture						
	More movies and songs	0	0	0%	8	9%	+9%
	More cultural differences	2	2	2%	2	2%	0%

Table 6. (*continued*)

	Suggestions	N of responders S_int3	Adjusted N of S_int3 resp *	In %	N of respondents S_fin	In %	Difference, %
5	Organization						
	More individual tasks	0	0%	0%	1	1%	+1%
	More group work	5	6	7%	1	1%	−6%
	More whole class work	3	4	5%	3	3.5%	−1.5%
6	Design						
	More gamification	3	4	5%	5	6%	+1%
	See the time limit for the task	1	1	1%	0	0%	−1%
	Technology						
	Relaxed "web camera" policy	3	4	5%	0	0%	−5%
	Low sound quality	1	1	1%	0	0%	−1%

*The number of S_int3 participants was adjusted to align with the number of S_fin participants

Table 6 shows that overall students embraced the majority of changes to GEC2 with enthusiasm. Apparently, they were happy with a more flexible "web camera" policy, as no more complaints were registered. They did not have any complaints about the quality of sound either, most probably, because listening and video tasks were being done individually and not in groups after S_int1. Those who wanted to see the time limit identified for each task, did not bring this issue up in S_fin. There were no students who asked for more group work, though their share before S_fin was 7%. Those who mentioned group work in S_fin, suggested to change the way in which it was done (rotate students more often, have fewer group work tasks). Apparently, students were happy with the share of listening and reading tasks.

The only area students thought would benefit from fine-tuning was the share of authentic movies and songs.

5.5   Course Completion Rate

To get a broader picture, we compared an average number of students who successfully passed the fall semester final GEC2 tests (experimental groups) and an average number of students who successfully completed fall 2020 upper-intermediate General English course (control groups). Control groups were chosen randomly. The pool of students was similar to the pool of students taught in GEC2: three 1st year and four 2nd year groups of the same English proficiency from the same ITMO Schools. Our calculation showed that the number of students who passed final GEC2 tests (95%) was 9% higher than in the control groups (86%).

5.6   Semi-structured Interviews with Students

We followed the convenient sampling protocol when selecting four students for the semi-structured interview. Students answered two questions: "How did your expectations of the fall 2020 semester online English course compared to reality?" and "What would be your preferred study format for spring 2021?" Since in the spring semester of the 2020–2021 academic year majority of Russian technical universities transferred back to the offline study mode, the four volunteer students, all of whom identified themselves as "online dissidents at the beginning of 2020–2021 academic year", were interviewed on campus between February 10 and 12, 2021. The interviews were held face-to-face in English. Each interview took an average of 10 min. The data transcribed during the interview were analyzed immediately. We coded students "1", "2", "3", "4" to protect their identity. When analyzing the transcripts, we followed the "focused coding" protocol [14] and identified two major themes: "Was unhappy with online English classes at the beginning; would like to continue studying in the online only format"; "Was unhappy with online English classes; would like to continue studying in the hybrid format". Excerpts from the interviews and preferred study modes are presented in Table 7.

Table 7. Interview results.

Participant's code	Interview excerpts	Preferred mode of study in spring 2021
1	At the start, I thought that these online classes would be a bit boring (because at school, at the end of the year, they were), but my expectations were not justified, and our online classes were interesting and useful	Hybrid learning
2	I was very upset about studying English online in fall. I thought that we had to continue in this mode until the end of spring. At the end of 2020, I liked online English. Now I expect to have hybrid learning, but seeing everyone in the classroom is great	Hybrid learning
3	Well, I knew that English would be online, so it went exactly how I expected it to be. English was probably one of my favorite subjects in the fall semester	Online only
4	Talking about expectations of the fall 2020 online English classes, they were low, because I thought it would be easier and less interesting. The actual situation was exactly the opposite and this fact pleased me	Hybrid learning

Results of the semi-structured interviews demonstrate that before fall 2020 English classes started, majority of students had low expectations and negative feelings towards them (students 1, 2, 4), partially due to unsatisfying experience at school, as noted by student 1. One student (student 3) had high expectations, which were met. Three out of the four interviewees said that they would want to study in the hybrid mode in spring and only one opted for online classes.

6 Conclusion, Future Work

As the results of our research demonstrate, our experiment on building an emergency remote course (GEC2) on an existing blended learning methodology (GEM1) proved to be overall successful. In the course of adaptation of GEM1, we attempted to answer two research questions of what aspects of GEM1 should be changed to fully satisfy the ERT conditions and comply with the curriculum and how to improve student satisfaction with GEC2. To accomplish these goals, we collected students' feedback through a series of surveys (S_int1, S_int2, S_int3). Students' suggestions and our interpretation of the results of three surveys verified against Dornyei's motivational strategies informed our decision on the introduction of new tasks/procedures.

After S_int1 we integrated grammar review tasks on as-needed basis, introduced extra vocabulary in addition to that offered in Cambridge Empower Upper-intermediate textbooks and changed the listening/video tasks arrangement allowing students to listen/watch videos individually or in small groups in Zoom breakout rooms to reduce the background noise.

Results of S_int2 and classroom observation of students with higher level of English proficiency convinced us to garnish textbook materials with more interactive grammar tasks, including OER, self- or student-developed games.

After S_int3 we decided to liberate the classroom interaction by giving students an opportunity to choose the mode of in-class interaction. Students could work in small groups (teacher standing by to guide and assist), students could choose to work with the teacher or could choose to have a mixed-mode lesson. At the same time, and pursuant to students' request, we provided time limit notes for each task, relaxed the camera-on policy for students with technical/psychological problems and expanded the range of interactive tasks with more games, presentations, hyperlinks, memes, cartoons, OER videos, songs. To answer our last research question of how to cater to students with high absenteeism due to COVID-19, technical or personal issues, we designed lessons in such a way that students were able to access class materials on Schoology in asynchronous mode and do the same tasks as students in the virtual classroom did. Absentees' progress was assessed during Zoom individual consultation sessions. Necessary instructions were provided.

At the end of our experiment, we conducted a final survey (S_fin) to see how satisfied students were with GEC2, in general, and with major changes introduced throughout the fall semester. The overall satisfaction with online English classes to compare to the beginning of the fall 2020 semester grew insignificantly (only by 4%), but standard deviation of 0.59 indicates, that at the end of the fall 2020 semester there was more unanimity among students as to the satisfaction with the fall General English emergency remote course. In addition, if we had two students (2%) who were mostly dissatisfied with their English class at the beginning of the fall semester and 10 students (12%) whose perception of online English did not change, there were no dissatisfied students at the end of the fall semester and the number of students whose attitude did not change dropped to 4 (5%). At the same time, 23 students (27%) reported that their attitude to online education in general did not change, 26% and 47% of students reported that their attitude towards online education in general improved and significantly improved. The majority of students reported that their motivation to study English increased significantly (45%), increased (29%), remained the same (20%), decreased (5%) and dropped significantly (1%). Therefore, we can conclude that there is a clear positive trend in the attitude towards the online English class, online education in general and student motivation to study English.

Judging by the students' feedback, they appreciated the improvements made to the organization, technical aspect, content, structure and design of the English course. Students also thought that the amount of revision materials was adequate. As for the innovative element of the course, students found grammar games, PowerPoint grammar presentations and interactive materials to be highly appealing, while time limit indicators and links to dictionaries not so useful (Table 4). Students appreciated a more democratic way of choosing the in-class study mode –"according to each student's choice", "whole class only", "in small groups only", "diversified" (a mix of all modes) and noted that we should continue implementing this arrangement in the future online classes.

To triangulate the results of our study, we verified GEC2 completion rate against the completion rate in similar groups of the same English proficiency level. Our assessment showed that the completion rate among students who took GEC2 (95%) was 9% higher than among the control groups (86%).

We also conducted four semi-structured interviews with volunteer students who reported that their expectations of GEC2 were either met or exceeded, and that if they could choose the mode of study for the spring 2021 semester, they would go either with a hybrid course (3 students) or an online only course (1 student).

We believe that though our experiment on the adaptation of an existing blended learning methodology (GEM0) was overall successful and demonstrated GEM0's versatility where the three core GEM0' elements – the LMS platform (Schoology), the flipped classroom and bring your own device methodologies – could be easily "mixed, matched and replaced" in the emergency COVID-19 situation, we still have room for further research and improvement. For example, right now ITMO along with other Russian universities is transferring to offline teaching. Considering that the pandemic is still raging and PPE and social distancing policies are still being enforced, it is of vital importance to find a way to maintain a safe study and work environment while giving the students a full-fledged classroom experience and building up their English competencies. Therefore, we are intending to continue our experiment with "GEM0 turned GEM2" to see how blended methodology and BYOD approach combined with Zoom in-class streaming can facilitate the implementation of this goal.

Appendix 1

Table 8. Evolution of the Spring 2018 blended GE learning methodology (GEM0).

Categories	Blended methodology (GEM0, GEC0)	Blended methodology (GEM_int), GEC_int)	Hybrid methodology (GEM1, GEC1)	Hybrid methodology (GEM2, GEC2)
I. Time period	Spring 2018	Fall'18–Fall'19	Spring 2020	Fall 2020
II. Motivation for creation	Automation/improved course management and design/increased motivation	Supplement to General English course	Nationwide emergency transfer to remote teaching due to the COVID-19 outbreak	Nationwide emergency transfer to remote teaching due to the COVID-19
III. Pedagogical objectives	Improvement of communicative, linguistic, interactional competencies; cult. awareness; soft skills	Improvement of interactional competency; development of soft skills	Improvement of communicative, linguistic, interactional competencies; cult. awareness; soft skills	Improvement of communicative, linguistic, interactional competencies; cult. awareness; soft skills
IV. Pedagogical tools				
Theory	Significant learning, Connectivism	Connectivism	Connectivism	Connectivism
Methodology, approaches, models	Communicative, blended learning, flipped classroom, BYOD, MOOC	Communicative approach, hybrid learning, BYOD, OER	Communicative approach, hybrid learning, flipped classroom, BYOD	Communicative approach, hybrid learning, BYOD
Pedagogy	Learner-centered, project work, gamification	Learner-centered, self-directed learning	Learner-centered, self-directed learning, ERT	Learner-centered, self-directed learning, ERT
ESL pedagogy	CALL	CALL	CALL	CALL
V. Technological tools				
LMS	Schoology	Schoology/Cambridge LMS	Schoology/Cambridge LMS	Schoology/Cambridge LMS
File storage and progress tracking	Google Drive	Google Drive	Google Drive	Google Drive
Mode of study	Face-to-face	Face-to-face/online	Online	Online
Communication type	Synchronous/asynchronous	Synchronous/asynchronous	Synchronous/asynchronous	Synchronous/asynchronous
Communication channel	Schoology/emails/Google Drive/VK chat	Schoology/emails/Google Drive/VK chat	Schoology/emails/Google Drive/VK chat	Schoology/emails/Google Drive/VK chat
Video	–	–	Zoom	Zoom
Zoom mode	–	–	Conference/breakout rooms	Conference/breakout rooms
VI. Course organization				
Course elements	MOOC-based Research Class, Gen. English and Video Class	Cambridge-based General English Class	Cambridge-based General English Class	Cambridge-based General English Class
Lessons/ac.hrs/wk	3/6	2/4	2/4	2/4
Contact hours/wk	6	4	2	4
Schoology lessons arrangement	By week->by class type (Gen. English, etc.->by work type (classwork/homework)	By unit->by unit	By lesson->by work type (classwork/homework)	By unit->by lesson
Schoology lessons (classwork, homework)	72	20+ (varied by group)	18	29
VII. Assessment				
Formative	Randomized, timed automated Schoology quizzes/writings/peer review/presentations	Cambridge LMS/automated Schoology quizzes/writings/peer review/presentations	Cambridge LMS tests/randomized, timed automated Schoology quizzes/peer review/writings	Cambridge LMS tests/randomized, timed automated Schoology quizzes/peer review/writings

(continued)

Table 8. (*continued*)

Categories	Blended methodology (GEM0, GEC0)	Blended methodology (GEM_int), GEC_int)	Hybrid methodology (GEM1, GEC1)	Hybrid methodology (GEM2, GEC2)
Summative				
1. Mid-module	–	–	–	Use of English
2. End-of-module	Use of English/speaking test	Use of English/speaking test	Use of English/speaking test	Use of English
3. End-of-semester (tests, exams)	Use of English/speaking test/thesis prospectus	Use of English/speaking test	Use of English/speaking test	Writing/speaking test
VIII. Compensation of classes missed in excess of 30%	Asynchronous completion of Schoology lessons/face-to-face compensation classes	Face-to-face compensation classes	Asynchronous completion of Schoology lessons/online compensation classes	Asynchronous completion of Schoology lessons/online compensation classes

References

1. Grgurović, M., Chapelle, C., Shelley, M.: A meta-analysis of effectiveness studies on computer technology-supported language learning. ReCALL **25**(2), 165–198 (2013). https://doi.org/10.1017/S0958344013000013

2. Saad Mohamed, A.F.: Feedback in Computer-Assisted Language Learning: A Meta-Analysis. TESL-EJ **24**(2) (2020). http://www.tesl-ej.org/wordpress/issues/volume24/ej94/. Accessed 21 Jan 2021

3. Monje, E.M., Bárcena, E. (eds.): Language MOOCs: Providing Learning, Transcending Boundaries. De Gruyter, Warsaw/Berlin (2014). https://doi.org/10.2478/9783110420067

4. Polat, E.S. (ed.): Teorija i praktika distancionnogo obuchenija [Theory and Practice of Distance Learning]. Publishing house "Akademija", Mocsow (2004). (in Russian)

5. Vaindorf-Sysoeva, M.E., Grjaznova, T.S., Shitova, V.A.: Metodika distancionnogo obuchenija: uchebnoe posobie dlja vuzov [Methodology of Distance Teaching: A Textbook for Institutions of HE]. Urait, Moscow (2019). (in Russian). https://urait.ru/bcode/433436

6. Hodges, Ch.B., Moore, S., Lockee, B.B., Trust, T., Bond, M.A.: The difference between emergency remote teaching and online learning. Educ. Rev. https://er.educause.edu/articles/2020/3/the-difference-between-emergency-remote-teaching-and-online-learning. Accessed 02 Feb 2021

7. Bailey, D.R., Lee, A.R.: Learning from experience in the midst of COVID-19: benefits, challenges, and strategies in online teaching. CALL-EJ **21**(2), 178–198 (2020). http://callej.org/journal/21-2.html. Accessed 21 Jan 2021

8. Almazova, N., Krylova, E., Rubtsova, A., Odinokaya, M.: Challenges and opportunities for Russian higher education amid COVID-19: teachers' perspective. Educ. Sci. **10**, 1–11 (2020). https://doi.org/10.3390/educsci10120368

9. Pevneva, I., Edmunds, P.: Online learning vs. extreme learning in mining higher education under COVID. In: VTH International Innovative Mining Symposium, E3S Web of Conferences vol. 174, p. 04001, 6 p. (2020). https://doi.org/10.1051/e3sconf/202017404001

10. Windstein, E.V., Taylor, J.: Programming an English course: technology and interdisciplinary learning at a technical university. In: Nikulina, E.A., Belyaeva, E.E., Blokh, M.Ya., Fryedina, E.L., Kharitonova, I.V. (eds.) Proceedings of International Conference to 70-th Anniversary of Foreign Language Institute of Moscow State Teacher Training University. Part 3, pp. 91–99. Publishing house of MPGU, Moscow (2019). https://elibrary.ru/item.asp?id=37822472. Accessed 21 Jan 2021

11. Ausubel, D.P.: The Psychology of Meaningful Verbal Learning. Grune & Stratton, New York (1963)

12. Fraenkel, J., Wallen, N., Hyung, H.: How to Design and Evaluate Research in Education, 8th edn. McGraw-Hill, New York (2012)
13. Dörnyei, Z.: Motivational Strategies in the Language Classroom. Cambridge University Press, Cambridge (2001). https://doi.org/10.1017/CBO9780511667343
14. Thornberg, R., Charmaz, K.: Grounded theory and theoretical coding. In: Flick, U. (ed.) The SAGE Handbook of Qualitative Data Analysis, pp. 153–169. SAGE Publications Ltd., London (2014). https://doi.org/10.4135/9781446282243

Author Index

Printed in the United States
by Baker & Taylor Publisher Services